LIGHT AT THE END OF THE TUNNEL

A Vietnam War Anthology

Third Edition

Edited by
Andrew J. Rotter

ROWMAN & LITTLEFIELD PUBLISHERS, INC.

Lanham • Boulder • New York • Toronto • Plymouth, UK

To my students (again)

Published by Rowman & Littlefield Publishers, Inc.
A wholly owned subsidiary of The Rowman & Littlefield Publishing Group, Inc.
4501 Forbes Boulevard, Suite 200, Lanham, Maryland 20706
http://www.rowmanlittlefield.com

Estover Road, Plymouth PL6 7PY, United Kingdom

British Library Cataloguing in Publication Information Available

Library of Congress Cataloging-in-Publication Data

Light at the end of the tunnel : a Vietnam War anthology / edited by Andrew J. Rotter. — 3rd ed.
p. cm.
Includes bibliographical references.
ISBN 978-0-7425-6133-5 (cloth : alk. paper) — ISBN 978-0-7425-6134-2 (pbk. : alk. paper)
1. Vietnam War, 1961–1975—United States. 2. Vietnam—Politics and government—1945–1975. I. Rotter, Andrew Jon.
DS558.L54 2010
959.704'3373—dc22

2009052939

∞™ The paper used in this publication meets the minimum requirements of American National Standard for Information Sciences—Permanence of Paper for Printed Library Materials, ANSI/NISO Z39.48-1992.

Printed in the United States of America

Contents

Preface

THIS IS THE THIRD EDITION OF A BOOK OF READINGS on a conflict that ended over a generation ago. After the first edition came out in 1991, I never imagined doing another one, much less a *second* other one, but it has come to this, and I must say I am delighted. That there remains a good deal of interest in the Vietnam War is due, I think, to several factors. First, students want to know how or why the United States lost the war. Losing a war is something the United States had not done until it was forced to leave Southeast Asia by treaty in 1973, its objectives unachieved and within two years defeated. Some students find this upsetting. Others simply want to understand how it happened, with the hope that it never happens again. Second, and connected to this, are the comparisons many commentators make between the United States' war in Vietnam and U.S. conflicts in Iraq and Afghanistan that continue at this writing. Many students think that the lessons of Vietnam, insofar as they understand them (and in truth my own charges are modest on the first day of the semester, having rarely had much exposure to the Vietnam War in high school history courses), should have prevented the United States from going to war in Iraq, at least. Others, more skeptical of the comparison between the two wars, still wonder whether U.S. policymakers and military officers were sufficiently attentive to the consequences of Vietnam before embarking on the efforts to remove Saddam Hussein from power and to create a stable and democratic Iraq.

Most of all, though it takes some gentle prodding to get the stories, this generation of American college students has older relatives—parents, aunts and uncles, now sometimes even grandparents—who were part of the Vietnam War generation. Some of their relatives, the students report, never talk about the war, either because they managed to stay aloof from it or because the memories are too painful to discuss. Others opposed the war, to greater or lesser degree; some of these remain proud of their antiwar activities, while others, the students note with surprise, hint at what they say were shameful deeds done in the interest of bringing the war to a close. Nearly every American man born during the early 1950s still remembers his draft lottery number. And each spring in which I teach History 217: The United States in Vietnam, 1945–1975, I have students whose fathers, aunts, or high school social studies teachers served in Vietnam. "My father was an artillery officer." "My aunt was a nurse at a field hospital." "My teacher was there, but I don't know what he did because he refuses to talk about it." It is more and more the need to find out about their parents' generation's war, that awful, divisive war, that brings today's college students to a class on the subject, and that makes necessary yet another revision of this volume.

The scholarship and writing on the Vietnam War has become considerably richer and often more sophisticated since I put together the second edition of *Light at the End of the Tunnel* in the late 1990s. I have thus made a number of changes in the readings offered here, and I have tweaked the organization of the book to reflect in particular the growing interest in understanding the war as an international event, not just a bilateral or trilateral conflict. The book is divided into twelve chapters, the first four of which provide a chronological survey of the U.S. war in Vietnam. Each of these chapters contains two or three scholarly accounts of the war and, with the exception of chapter one, a passage or two from the personal accounts of participants. Chapters 5 and 6 concern the war itself, examining, in turn, the Vietnamese who fought with and against the Americans and the Vietnam battlefield. The remaining chapters treat the consequences of the war for Southeast Asia, the United States, and the world. They cover, respectively, the global Cold War context of the conflict, the overflow of the Vietnam War into neighboring Laos and Cambodia, the scholarly controversy that has emerged over the sources and results of the war, the antiwar movement and some of its impact on American society, and the legacy of the war for the two countries and peoples most directly involved in it.

Chapter 12, an afterword, is an excerpt from a book by Le Ly Hayslip, a Vietnamese woman. I include it not only because it is a moving piece of writing but also in order to leave the reader with the testimony of someone who lived in Vietnam while the war was going on. Most American students who take courses on the Vietnam War are by their own admission chiefly interested in the American side of the conflict; if, for example, you ask how many died in the Vietnam War, most will unthinkingly give their estimate of the number of Americans who died there. But it is important to remind students, and all readers, that the war engulfed Vietnam to a far greater degree than it involved the United States—indeed, Vietnamese today see the American War as just one more in a long and bloody sequence of conflicts undertaken, in their view, to dominate them. Le Ly Hayslip's tale conveys some of the pain and pathos of the Vietnamese experience of the war, and it thus seems to me an appropriate place to end the anthology.

I have tried to choose readings that are diverse in their coverage and orientation, interesting, provocative, and, as ever, intellectually responsible. Teachers may, of course, edit the collection by assigning only certain of its sections or reorganizing the book to suit their needs. While I have previously suggested that the book be used with a published collection of primary source documents on the war, such volumes are hard to find today; some enterprising scholar should produce such a book. In the meantime, the presence of documents available online, including those at the presidential libraries, the State Department series *Foreign Relations of the United States*, and the Texas Tech University Virtual Vietnam Archive, makes it possible to assign selected ones that support the readings here . I hope above all that this book will be of use to students, mine and others, who, a generation removed from the Vietnam War, nevertheless continue to look for answers to their questions about the conflict.

Acknowledgments

MY THANKS TO NIELS AABOE AT ROWMAN & LITTLEFIELD, who encouraged me to do a third edition of *Light.* Michelle Cassidy at the press kept the balls in the air; I hope it was not this project that drove her to graduate school. Jehanne Schweitzer saw the project through. Many scholars made valuable suggestions for improving this edition; Seth Jacobs was particularly helpful and supportive. Julia Meyerson drew the map that appears on page xxii, and Noam Chomsky, Tom Wells, and William Shawcross generously allowed me to reprint their words without charge. Judith Oliver, chair of the Colgate Faculty Research Council, and Lyle Roelofs, Colgate's Provost and Dean of Faculty, provided a significant publication subvention and thus made this book happen. Padma Kaimal once more bailed me out again and again. Over the years, Vietnam veterans Pappy Patchin and Nellie and Tom Coakley have enriched my thinking about the war. I am most grateful to my students at Colgate University, who amaze me, year after year, with their dedication to History 217: The United States and Vietnam. This one, like the last one, is for them.

Introduction

FOR YEARS, MOST WESTERNERS WHO STUDIED Vietnam depicted it as a geopolitical empty space into which periodically came migrants or invaders from bigger places. The Vietnamese, scholars claimed, got their religion, their notions about statecraft and economics, their system of agriculture, and their art and architecture from China and India, whose peoples "diffused" into Southeast Asia or imposed their culture through conquest. The Vietnamese thus created nothing; they simply absorbed the ideas their neighbors brought.

Recent investigations by historians and anthropologists have pointed to different conclusions. Although there is no question that traditional Vietnamese culture was syncretic—that is, blended from various forms, some of them external to Vietnam—the country was not simply a cultural sponge, indiscriminately soaking up every idea with which it came in contact. For example, sometime in the first century A.D., a kingdom called Funan was established in southern Vietnam, near the delta of the Mekong River. It was a strong and prosperous place; two hundred years after Funan's founding, a Chinese visitor noted the kingdom's walled cities and grand palaces and, according to G. C. Bentley, observed that Funan's people "paid their taxes in pearls, gold, and perfumes." Scholars have determined that Funan's political and religious institutions were indigenous, not the products of other people's cultures. Religious rituals and political practices elsewhere in Vietnam were also based on internally created forms.

Historically, most Vietnamese lived in small villages and grew rice. Because they rely on the land for sustenance, farmers are powerfully bonded to the soil, to a particular place. These peasants define themselves according to their position in their families, presenting themselves not as "I" but as "my parents' second son" or "your father's sister," a participant in a kinship network. Respect for one's elders and one's social betters is the source of stability for the family, the village, and the state. At the same time, however, respect is a reciprocal obligation. Those who are socially and politically powerful must demonstrate qualities of leadership; they must live virtuously, worship the gods properly, and protect their villages and families from harm. In other words, they must be effective and behave themselves. Inability or unwillingness to abide by these obligations is ground for popular dissatisfaction.

Comfortable with their culture and their place in the cosmos, the Vietnamese have never suffered invasion gladly. The Chinese were the first to discover their resistance. They came to northern Vietnam late in the third century B.C., and ultimately the Han dynasty (106 B.C.–A.D. 222) extended its control into what is now central Vietnam. For centuries the Vietnamese gave their conquerors little peace. Vietnam gained its independence in 967 and fought off repeated Chinese efforts to repossess it, only to be reabsorbed once more late in the fourteenth century, when it was weakened by its own bullying of its smaller neighbors. The end of Chinese rule finally came in 1428, after Emperor Le Loi decisively defeated Chinese forces near Hanoi. The Chinese went home; the Vietnamese, seeking safety against future invasions, agreed to pay a yearly tribute to China.

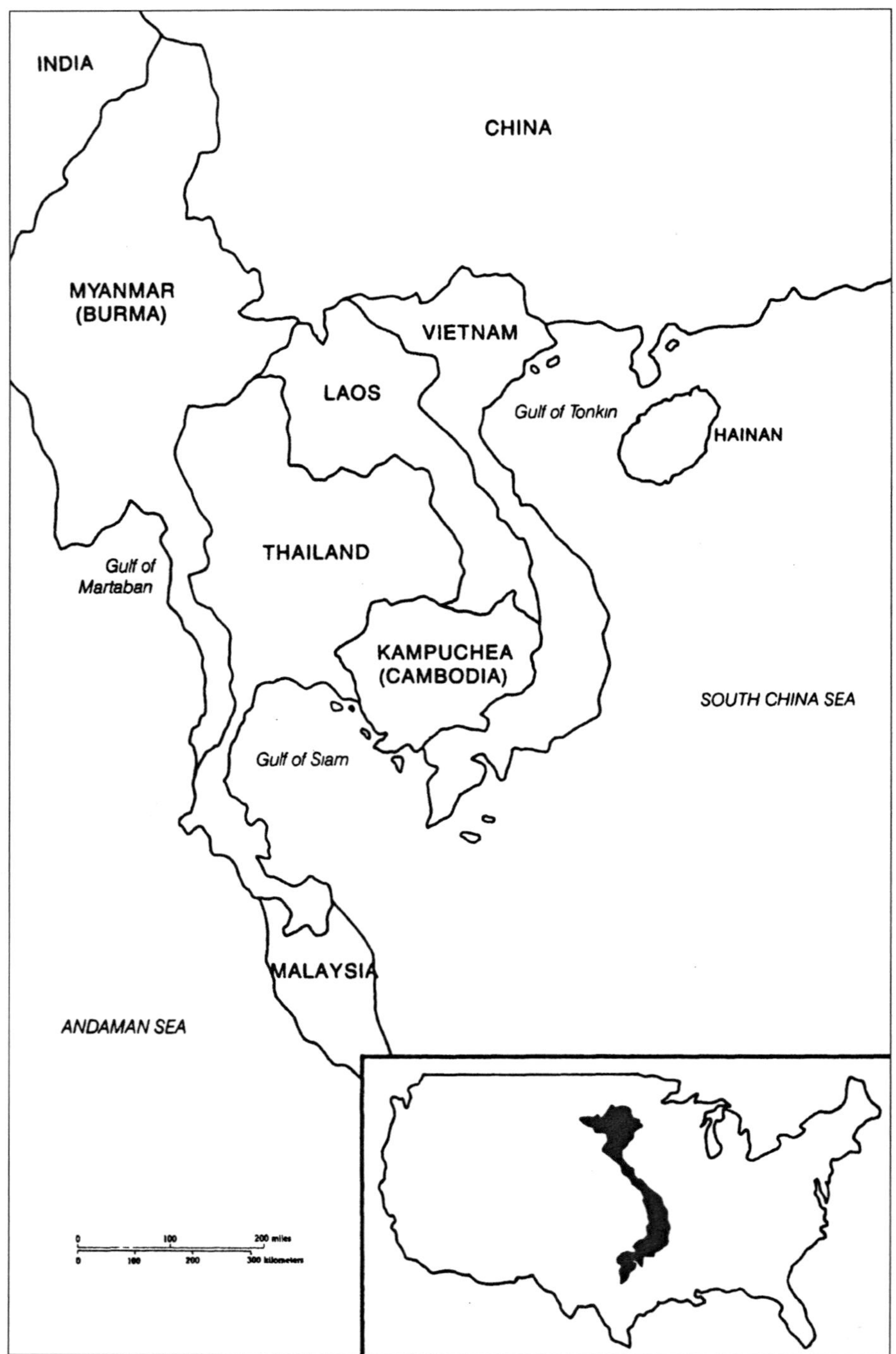

Map 1. Southeast Asia; (insert) Vietnam in scale with the United States

The independence of Vietnam was not threatened again for four hundred years. By the nineteenth century, weakened by internal warfare, the country again fell prey to outsiders. The interlopers this time were the French. They came because they had a *mission civilisatrice*—to lift the shroud of heathenism that covered the Vietnamese and replace it with the gilded robe of Christianity. They hoped to protect their position in the emerging China market to the north  and to secure Vietnamese resources. And, in the last half of the nineteenth century, the prestige of a nation was measured by the number of dependencies it held. The French divided Vietnam into three states: Tonkin, in the north; Annam, in the narrow central waist of the country; and Cochin China, encompassing the Mekong River delta in the south. The last state they made a colony in 1867; in 1884 they established a protectorate over Tonkin and Annam. The French improved sanitation and started new schools. They also institutionalized the production and consumption of opium (despite the *mission civilisatrice* this was good money), insulted the Vietnamese with their arrogance, threw the social structure into chaos, and badly mistreated the Vietnamese who worked for them on their rubber plantations, in their factories, and in their mines. The French frequently disrupted time-honored patterns of authority in the villages and created an educated urban elite, many of whom would come to oppose the control of their country by another. As the old order came unstuck, the people were left angry and frustrated, and the way was opened to resistance. By the early twentieth century, sporadic tax revolts indicated an incipient Vietnamese nationalism.

The man who would finally give direction to the anti-French sentiment in the country was Ho Chi Minh. A man of many pseudonyms and nearly as many identities, Ho traveled widely, to the United States, Great Britain, and France. In post–World War I Paris, he experienced a political epiphany. Rejected by the Allies when he pleaded that President Woodrow Wilson's idea of self-determination should apply to the Vietnamese, Ho (then known as Nguyen Ai Quoc—Nguyen the Patriot) moved quickly through the halfway house of European socialism and became a Communist. The reason for this affiliation was simple: the Communists were unequivocally anticolonialist, and they alone, with their base in Moscow, might help him remove the French from his country. (Years later, U.S. foreign policymakers would sneer at the claim made by American liberals that Ho was a nationalist first and a Communist second. The claim was true.) Ho went to the Soviet Union and China. In 1929 he founded the Indochinese Communist Party.

In Vietnam, resistance to the French had intensified. A variety of organizations sought in their own ways to mobilize the people. The Vietnam Nationalist Party, or the Viet Nam Quoc Dan Dang (VNQDD), staged an abortive revolt in 1930. There were persistent rebellions by dislocated farmers and strikes by unhappy workers. A quasireligious sect, the Cao Dai, gained the support of thousands of poor peasants and became a powerful force in the south, but it was politically unpredictable. By the late 1930s the Communists were in the best position to rally the nationalists. Early in 1941, Ho Chi Minh returned to Vietnam and announced the formation of the Vietnam Independence League, or Vietminh. All nationalists were to join, the Communists would lead it, and Ho was its General Secretary.

At this point, Japan forcefully entered Southeast Asian political affairs. Intent on creating an Asian empire euphemistically called the Greater East Asia Co-Prosperity sphere, the Japanese had seized Manchuria in 1931 and six years later expanded the conflict to China proper. By late 1939, when the war in Europe broke out, the Japanese were bombing targets in south China and coveting the raw materials of Southeast Asia, including tungsten, tin, rubber, and, above all, oil. French Indochina—Laos and Cambodia as well as Vietnam—was a repository of and a gateway to these natural riches. When France surrendered to Germany in June 1940, the Japanese asked the French collaborationist, or Vichy, government for permission to place military observers in Hanoi; in July they demanded the right to build military bases throughout Indochina. The French were not in a position to refuse.

The Japanese threat to Southeast Asia caught the attention of the United States. In 1940 few Americans even knew where Vietnam was, and few felt any motivation to find out. The level of sophistication in government circles was scarcely higher: some years later, when a State Department officer wrote a profile of "Ho Chi Mink," the error went undetected. The Americans, however, came to see the connection between the colonial economies of Southeast Asian nations and the fighting capabilities of the colonies' European owners. Specifically, they understood that the British, who faced Nazi Germany virtually alone after the summer of 1940, would be in deep trouble if Japan cut off their supply of Malayan rubber and tin and their oil from the Dutch East Indies. The United States decided to draw the line against Japanese expansion at Indochina. When the Japanese moved to construct military installations in Indochina in July 1940, the State Department embargoed exports of aviation fuel and high-quality scrap iron and steel to Japan. Negotiations between the two powers over the next year proved fruitless, and the Japanese, running out of fuel for their war machine, demanded in July 1940 that the Vichy regime permit their troops to occupy southern Indochina. This decision apparently resulted from Japan's misapprehension of American concern for Southeast Asia, and it cost Tokyo dearly. The Americans now embargoed all exports to Japan, save those of food and cotton, and froze Japan's assets in the United States, a move immediately imitated by Great Britain and the Dutch East Indies. These steps persuaded Japanese militants that their country was trapped and that the only way out was military action. On December 7 the Japanese attacked the U.S. base at Pearl Harbor. On that same day they moved against the Philippines, Hong Kong, and Malaya.

The Japanese quickly conquered most of Southeast Asia. In Vietnam they decided to leave the Vichy French government in place, while retaining nominal powers of control. Thus, the Vietminh had two different colonial powers to battle. Ho Chi Minh directed what military efforts he could against the Japanese with frequent skirmishes until 1945. The Vietnamese leader also planned for the eventual independence of his nation. He drafted a platform calling for representative government, a balanced economy, the eight-hour day, and a minimum wage. In March 1945, in retreat throughout Asia and witnessing the liberation of France, the Japanese overthrew the Vietnamese Vichy government and took charge. When they themselves surrendered in August, the way seemed open at last for the Vietminh. On September 2, 1945, Ho Chi Minh, speaking to a cheering crowd in Hanoi, declared Vietnam independent. "We hold these truths to be self-evident: that all men are created equal," he began, quoting a document well known to Americans. He believed this to be true. He also knew that France would want his country back and that only the United States could prevent Vietnam from being reclaimed.

Ho had some reason to hope that Washington would support him. In August 1941, President Franklin D. Roosevelt had endorsed (with a reluctant Winston Churchill, the British prime minister) the Atlantic Charter, a statement that declared, among other things, that people had the right to determine their own form of government. Even though Roosevelt died in April 1945, the Vietnamese continued to take this declaration seriously. In the last days of the war, operatives of the U.S. Office of Strategic Services (OSS) had worked with Ho in the Tonkin jungle. In return for help in finding downed American pilots, some of the OSS officers proffered advice and support. The Americans on the scene believed that Ho was sincerely interested in their assistance and thus could be influenced by the United States. "We had Ho Chi Minh on a silver platter," one of them said later.

Roosevelt's views on colonialism are worth considering, largely because both the OSS men and the Vietminh turned out to be naive about the president's intentions. In an ideal world, FDR thought, all nations would be democracies and would trade with each other freely and openly. But the postwar world would be a troubled place, not instantly susceptible to utopian solutions.

Although it was good to have the Atlantic Charter on the books, defining as it did the ideal world, it would be necessary to compromise its philosophy temporarily to achieve peace and stability. This conclusion had particular implications for colonialism. Not all nations were ready for independence. Places such as Algeria, Palestine, and Vietnam might require tutelage by a Great Power—instruction in the practices of liberalism and capitalism—for some time. FDR imagined a world divided into four blocs, each one overseen by a powerful "policeman": the United States, Great Britain, the Soviet Union, and China. Gradually, the president hoped, these blocs would dissolve and a world system based on the principle of self-determination would emerge, but until that time nationalist aspirations threatened order and so must be put on hold.

Roosevelt concluded that Vietnam, Laos, and Cambodia were not ready for self-rule. At the same time, France did not figure prominently in the president's plans for the postwar system. The French, FDR told British officials, were "hopeless." They were bad colonialists, cruel and shortsighted. They had capitulated to Germany with shocking speed and then had collaborated much too easily with the Nazis and the Japanese to be considered trustworthy. FDR was suspicious of even the courageous resistance movement, for it was led by Charles de Gaulle, whom he regarded as an arrogant opportunist. Instead of reverting to French control, then, Indochina should be given in trust to China, under the leadership of Generalissimo Chiang Kaishek (Jiang Jieshi).

Those who consider Franklin Roosevelt a realist might ponder the practicality of this plan. Certainly there were many at the time who believed that it was unworkable. The British feared that FDR's hostility toward French colonialism might soon come to rest upon them. (The British ambassador to Washington worried that "one of these days" FDR "might have the bright idea that the Netherlands East Indies or British Malaya would go under international trusteeships.") Officials in London were also skeptical that China would become a Great Power—and a worthy policeman—after the war. The Vietnamese would object, to put it mildly. Most compelling, however, was the opposition to the Chinese trusteeship scheme by officials in the Roosevelt administration. By 1944 most State Department experts anticipated trouble with the Soviet Union in Europe. Because defeated Germany would not provide a bulwark against Soviet expansion into Western Europe, it was essential that France be made strong enough at least to forestall a Soviet invasion. To strip France of its Indochina colony would shatter French pride, weaken the nation's economy, and destroy the French will to resist Soviet incursions or homegrown communists. State Department officials, joined by military leaders, pressured Roosevelt to give up the scheme altogether.

Early in 1945, FDR changed his mind. The first indication of this shift came at Yalta at the Big Three Conference (Roosevelt, Churchill, and Joseph Stalin) in February, when the president reluctantly agreed that nations need not place their colonies under trusteeships unless they wanted to. Even more revealing was a conversation that FDR had with an adviser in mid-March, when he expressed concern for "the brown people in the East" and stated that the U.S. "goal must be to help them achieve independence." When the adviser asked specifically about Indochina, FDR "hesitated a moment and then said—'well, if we can get the proper pledge from France to assume for herself the obligations of a trustee, then I would agree to France retaining these colonies with the proviso that independence was the ultimate goal.'" By the time of Roosevelt's death on April 12, hopes for self-determination had not quite disappeared from U.S. policy toward Indochina, but they had been overmatched by sympathy for the return of French control.

This policy was left to Harry S. Truman, a former senator from Missouri who had been vice president for only two and one-half months when the death of FDR elevated him to the presidency. Truman's experience with foreign affairs was limited, and, like most Americans, he did not know who Ho Chi Minh was. Relations with French Indochina were handled largely by Truman's secretaries of state—James F. Byrnes (1945–1947), George C. Marshall (1947–1949), and Dean Acheson (1949–1953)—and their staffs in the State Department, with assistance from civilian and military officials in other departments. The president, however, provided the fundamental principles of U.S. foreign policy and set its tone. Truman came to believe that the Soviet Union was determined to spread communism across the globe through military and political means. Only the United States, acting in concert with other free nations, could prevent Russian expansion. Truman likened the Soviets to the Nazis: "There isn't any difference in totalitarian states. I don't care what you call them, Nazi, Communist or Fascist." The administration implemented the containment strategy in an effort to stop the Russians. With the Truman Doctrine speech in March 1947, the president divided the world into two armed camps, one for the Communists and the other for everyone else, and offered economic and military assistance to Turkey and Greece, two anti-Communist governments with little claim to democracy. Less than three months later, Secretary of State Marshall announced the plan that would bear his name: a massive grant of economic aid to the war-devastated countries of Western Europe in order to provide the United States with trade partners and diminish the appeal of communism. Then came the signing of the North Atlantic Treaty in April 1949, which created a military alliance between the United States, Canada, and various Atlantic and Western European nations. These policies left no room for accommodation with Communists such as Ho Chi Minh.

In Vietnam, meanwhile, matters had taken a serious turn. The Great Powers ignored Ho's declaration of independence and instead fabricated a stunted version of Roosevelt's trusteeship plan. Vietnam was divided at the sixteenth parallel, with China occupying the north and Great Britain the south. All the outside parties acknowledged that this scheme would soon give way to French repossession of both sectors, and indeed that is what happened. In September 1945 the British military commander in Saigon obediently armed fourteen hundred French troops who had been imprisoned by the Japanese. The soldiers, acting with appalling brutality, forced the Vietminh government to flee and recaptured Saigon. In the north, on March 6, 1946, Ho Chi Minh managed to get the marauding Chinese out by accepting, under duress, an agreement to make Vietnam a free state within the French Union—not an independent nation—and the return of French troops to Vietnamese soil.

The French quickly demonstrated their determination to keep all of Vietnam in the fold. In negotiations they dithered or threatened; outside the conference room they gathered their forces. The March 6 agreement was never implemented. Political instability in France had something to do with this; so did poor communication between politicians in Paris and military officials in Vietnam. During the summer of 1946, Ho went to Paris, seeking greater French flexibility. He came away with the Fontainebleau agreement of September, which offered, again, almost nothing. In the meantime, the French separated Cochin China from the rest of Vietnam and placed it by fiat under the French Union. Ho, under rising pressure to act from more radical members of the Vietminh, begged the French to make concessions that would give him "a weapon against the extremists." They were unyielding.

Ho and the Vietminh were not dewy-eyed pacifists. They were quite capable of brutality and shrank not at all from the use of force to gain their objectives. By the fall of 1946 there was open warfare in the south, and tensions ran high in the northern cities of Hanoi, where the Vietnamese Assembly convened in late October, and especially in Haiphong, where there were armed clashes in early November. The French bore primary responsibility for starting the violence. On November 23 their artillery opened up on the Vietnamese quarter of Haiphong, killing some six thousand people. Ho pleaded for calm, but it was no good. On the night of December 19, 1946, the Vietnamese in Hanoi, probably acting without Ho's orders, attacked the French with a full array of weapons. Fighting erupted throughout the countryside; by the dawn of the Western New Year, there was no turning back. "Before all, order must be reestablished," said the French premier, Léon Blum. "The war will be long and difficult," said Ho Chi Minh.

The French soldiers who fought the Vietminh soon came to appreciate Ho's words. Confident of quick victory, French authorities discovered instead that the Vietnamese desire for independence would not be easily denied. They decided, therefore, to fabricate a new government that would prove more cooperative; for its leader they selected the former emperor and erstwhile collaborator with the Japanese, Bao Dai. It took some doing to persuade Bao Dai to take the job. The former emperor was not without sympathy for the nationalists' position, and in 1947 he was leading a safe and comfortable life, dividing his time between Hong Kong and the French Riviera. The French cajoled him with various promises of self-government, and Bao Dai ultimately found the attractions of partial power irresistible. In April 1949 he returned to Vietnam as head of state "within the French Union."

The Bao Dai government held no interest for the Vietminh or for the majority of Vietnamese, who regarded the new regime as a sham. The war intensified. The French, for their part, introduced their protégé around, in particular to the Americans, who alone had the wherewithal to bankroll the former emperor. When Bao Dai returned to Vietnam, the French formally asked the Truman administration to offer diplomatic recognition and financial and military assistance to the new government.

The Americans hesitated. They had many questions about Bao Dai. Did he have popular support? Assuming that he did not, could he get it if the United States helped him? Was he essentially a playboy, involved in politics only for prestige or financial gain? What was his relationship with the French? Was he merely their stooge, a useful way for the French to maintain colonial control? Or was he another Chiang Kaishek, the Chinese leader whose government at that moment was crumbling before the Communists? The evident answers to these questions were not reassuring to policymakers. Many of the Asian experts within the Truman administration counseled caution. At least, these experts warned, the French should promise that they were moving toward independence for Vietnam.

However, 1949 and 1950 were years of crisis in U.S. foreign policy, and patience became increasingly difficult to summon in Washington. America's allies were still struggling to recover from the war. Japan and Germany—really the Allied occupation zone in the western part of Germany—had moved quickly from being wartime enemies to peacetime friends, but both nations depended heavily on U.S. economic aid, and West Germany seemed an imperiled frontline state in the Cold War between Western and Eastern Europe. The economy of Great Britain had shown signs of life in 1948, the first year of the Marshall Plan, but, by the summer of 1949, British exports and dollar reserves dropped dramatically, and officials in London pleaded for help. France's economy was staggering too. Production and wages remained depressed, thereby burdening workers especially, and many turned to communism. The French government claimed that it could do little to help labor because of the country's costly obligations in Vietnam. To make matters worse, the Other Side, the Communist world that most Americans believed was monolithic, seemed by the end of 1949 to be enjoying remarkable success. Communist parties had political clout in Italy and France, and Ho Chi Minh had the French on the run in Vietnam. Late in the summer the Soviet Union detonated its first atomic bomb, years before most Western experts believed that Moscow would have such capability. In October the Chinese Communist leader Mao Tse-tung (Mao Zedong) announced the formation of the People's Republic of China, and soon after Chiang Kaishek retreated to Taiwan.

The Truman administration tried to regain the initiative both militarily and diplomatically. It pressed forward with efforts to ensure the recovery of its Allies in Europe and the Pacific. In January 1950 the president authorized a program to build a hydrogen bomb and asked for a reassessment of U.S. "objectives in peace and war" and "the effect of these objectives on our strategic plans." The result was the National Security Council (NSC) document number 68, which called for an enormous increase in defense spending. Policymakers talked of arming West Germany. Of lesser magnitude but with equally profound implications, in the spring Truman decided to give $10 million in military aid and a small quantity of economic assistance to the French-backed Indochina governments. The administration hoped that the limited commitment represented by the aid would strengthen the anti-Communist forces in Southeast Asia, secure regional markets for the Japanese, protect key British investments in Malayan raw materials, and offer some relief to the French who had domestic problems (and now German rearmament) to worry about. It was far too much to expect of $10 million. Outside of a small group of statesmen and area specialists, few noticed that the outlay had been made at all.

On June 25, Communist North Korea attacked non-Communist South Korea, its peninsular neighbor south of the thirty-eighth parallel. Although North Korea was a Soviet client and had Stalin's permission to launch the assault, the timing and nature of the invasion had as much to do with Korean politics as Cold War conditions. The Truman administration was nevertheless convinced that the North Korean attack represented a Soviet thrust by proxy, and in the week following the invasion sent American forces (under United Nations auspices) to defend the besieged ally. Ultimately, the Americans stemmed the tide, pushed the North Koreans back across the thirty-eighth parallel, and then joined South Korean troops in a drive to liberate North Korea. This move came to a halt in the late fall of 1950, when the Chinese intervened and forced the Americans to retreat south. By mid-1951 the Americans had rallied and stabilized their lines near the thirty-eighth parallel. On the battlefield a bloody stalemate ensued, while acrimonious negotiations between the two sides dragged on fruitlessly.

The Korean War had important implications for U.S. policy in Southeast Asia. For one thing, it became for policymakers a model of how Asian conflicts broke out during the Cold War: small Communist states, acting on behalf of the Soviet Union or the People's Republic of China, invaded their weak, non-Communist neighbors. Regarding Indochina this was a misplaced analogy, for it assumed that the two states in question were equally legitimate, which was not the case in Vietnam. Immediately following the North Korean attack, the Americans, who along with the French expected the next major Communist thrust to come in Vietnam, significantly increased their aid for Indochina; by 1952 they were covering nearly one-third of the cost of the conflict. This support partly bolstered French confidence, but it also made the French wary of displacement in the region by the United States. To show their mettle, the French now decided to take the offensive against the Vietminh. In late 1953 the French commander, General Henri Navarre, decided to try to lure the enemy into a set-piece battle in the northwest part of Vietnam, at a place called Dienbienphu. The Vietminh general, Vo Nguyen Giap, accepted the challenge. By early 1954 the French garrison, ensconced in a valley, found itself surrounded by Vietnamese soldiers and artillery, along with a number of Chinese military advisers. Disaster loomed for the French, who now urgently requested U.S. military intervention to rescue Dienbienphu.

There was a new administration in Washington: the Republican Dwight D. Eisenhower had been elected president in 1952. Eisenhower certainly allowed himself to be represented as a tough-minded realist on the Cold War, a president who would not shrink from confronting the Russians and the Chinese. His secretary of state, John Foster Dulles, a gimlet-eyed lawyer from upstate New York, rejected the containment strategy as "futile and immoral" and proposed instead the "liberation" of Communist countries by any means. Dulles also endorsed a policy of "massive retaliation" against perceived aggressors, a term with patently awful implications.

Because Eisenhower never publicly repudiated Dulles's pronouncements, most people assumed that he shared them. But recent scholarship on the Eisenhower period has demonstrated that the president's thinking about foreign policy was not nearly as virulent as Dulles's statements might suggest. The president was not the passive, rather slow-witted bungler that liberals labeled him, but rather a shrewd man who managed the foreign policy bureaucracy with care and took responsibility for making the key decisions. (Some have suggested that the hopelessly tangled sentences that Eisenhower offered up during press conferences were deliberately designed to confuse or mislead the American public.) Eisenhower used Dulles's public posture to ensure for the administration the support of the Republican right wing and to sow doubt among America's enemies. Massive retaliation, which effectively replaced expensive conventional weapons with efficient nuclear missiles, was a cost-cutting measure. Ike's broad grin and awkward golf swing concealed a mind of energy and subtlety.

Unlike his immediate predecessors, President Eisenhower had been a career military man. As commander of the Allied forces in Europe during World War II, he understood both war's horrors and its limitations. He believed that the stalemate in Korea was a disaster, so he had brought the conflict to a speedy conclusion in 1953—in part by threatening privately to drop atomic bombs on China. When the French approached the administration seeking military help at Dienbienphu, Eisenhower was dubious. He allowed the proposal a serious hearing by the Joint Chiefs of Staff and mused out loud about the possibility of a U.S. air strike against Vietminh positions, as long as the planes were disguised as French ones. In the long run, however, because the president believed that U.S. military intervention would serve no useful purpose, he made it conditional on congressional acquiescence, the cooperation of the British, and French willingness to accept the eventual independence of Vietnam. It was unlikely that even one of these conditions would be met; that all three would be met was impossible, as Eisenhower surely knew. Despite some embarrassing public blustering by Dulles and Vice President Richard Nixon, Eisenhower kept his "hidden hand" firmly on the decision-making process. Thus, when Dienbienphu fell on May 7, 1954, it did not take American prestige with it.

Even before the debacle, the French sensed that their time in Vietnam was growing short. They had already asked for discussion of the Indochina problem at a conference on Far Eastern issues that opened in Geneva in late April. If the French had any leverage when the conference began, their influence disappeared with the collapse of Dienbienphu. On June 17 a new government in Paris, led by Socialist Premier Pierre Mendès-France, promised to resign unless it could reach a negotiated solution to the war within thirty days.

At last, Ho Chi Minh must have thought, the years of struggle would be rewarded by a diplomatic victory over France. It was not to be, for the Great Powers had their own interests to pursue in Vietnam. Stalin's death the previous year had caused tumult in the Russian political elite but had removed a major obstacle to change in Soviet foreign policy. The British worried that persistent instability in Indochina, or a Communist triumph there, would jeopardize their position in the economically valuable and unstable colony of Malaya. The Chinese, for whom the Vietnamese had no love, hoped that the annoying upheaval on their southern frontier would not bring U.S. intervention—the truce in Korea was not yet a year old—and therefore sought a political solution in Vietnam that would not humiliate the West. Just offstage the Americans glowered, as if daring the Vietminh to appear intractable.

The result was a remarkable arm-twisting session in the last hours before Mendès-France's self-imposed deadline, in which V. M. Molotov, the Soviet foreign minister, and the Chinese premier, Chou Enlai (Zhou Enlai), forced the Vietminh to accept a series of proposals that seemed to disregard the latter's superior military position on the ground. A cease-fire was proclaimed for Vietnam, Laos, and Cambodia. (Communist forces enjoyed a military advantage in the latter two states as well.) Vietnam was partitioned at the seventeenth parallel. The northern part of the country, the Democratic Republic of Vietnam, would be governed by the Vietminh, and the south, called the State of Vietnam, would remain under the nominal control of Bao Dai, backed by the French, who would remain in place. The two zones were not to be permanent: elections were to be held throughout the country in 1956 to choose a single government. These elections would be overseen by an international commission that would guarantee their fairness.

The Vietminh had hoped for more territory and quicker elections, but Ho Chi Minh was willing to wait for the 1956 referendum, certain that he and his political allies would win. Thousands of southern Vietminh fighters were summoned north of the seventeenth parallel to await reunification. Ho, meanwhile, tried to whip the northern economy into shape—no easy task, given that most of Vietnam's food was grown in the south—and carried out a draconian land-reform policy in which thousand of landlords were killed. In the south, Bao Dai found himself outmaneuvered politically by Ngo Dinh Diem, whom Bao Dai had appointed prime minister in June 1954. Diem was a Catholic mandarin who was, in his own mind, a patriot and a would-be despot. Westerners who met him found Diem a fascinating bundle of contradictions—alternately puzzling, magnetic, and infuriating as he talked compulsively about Vietnamese philosophy and statecraft. Whatever Diem may have been, he had more backbone than Bao Dai. With the help of Col. Edward G. Lansdale, head of the U.S. military advisory mission in Saigon, Diem asserted himself against the powerful Vietnamese sects and his other political rivals. By early 1955 he had established himself in American circles as a Vietnamese George Washington. The French could not abide him, nor stomach their steady usurpation by the United States. In one of modern history's great anticlimaxes, by early 1956 they had largely pulled out of Indochina.

That withdrawal left the United States as Vietnam's sole outside support. The Eisenhower administration was hostile to the agreements reached at Geneva, believing that the French had conceded too much by allowing the Vietminh to control the area north of the seventeenth parallel. U.S. representatives had difficulty understanding the complexities of Vietnamese politics—at Geneva, Undersecretary of State Walter Bedell Smith had said that "one-third of the Vietnamese people supported Bao Dai, one-third supported Ho Chi Minh, and two-thirds were on the fence"—but the Americans were resolved to prevent the Vietminh from taking control of the whole country. The administration decided to support Diem as head of government in a South Vietnam that was not just an artificial construct created as an expedient at Geneva but a nation with an independent future. Dulles found a way to tie South Vietnam to a regional defense association, the Southeast Asia Treaty Organization (SEATO), although this arrangement was specifically prohibited by the Geneva accords. Washington backed Diem when he refused to hold the 1956 elections, and by 1961 it had subsidized his regime to the tune of $1 billion. Under the foreboding rubric "black psywar," U.S. intelligence agents and their Vietnamese trainees conducted subversive operations against the Vietminh in the north. Typical activities included gun running, distributing phony leaflets, and contaminating the gas tanks of North Vietnamese vehicles. Occasionally, matters got out of hand: the *Pentagon Papers*, a secret Defense Department study of the war written in the late 1960s, disclosed that an alleged Communist prisoner was "interrogated by being handcuffed to a leper, both [men were] beaten with the same stick to draw blood, [the prisoner was] told he would now have leprosy, and both [were] locked up in a tiny cell together."

Although these policies enraged Ho and the government in Hanoi, they mostly resisted making a response to Diem's actions. Not so the Communist Party members who had remained in the south, in their home villages, after 1954. They and their families were the victims of intimidation, arrest, torture, and murder by the Saigon government. Restrained by Hanoi's policy of patience, the Southern Party, according to historian Gabriel Kolko, lost at least two-thirds of its membership to arrest or execution during 1957–58. The survivors struck back. The chief tactic of the southern Vietminh was to assassinate Diem's officials along with uncooperative village leaders. Finally, in January 1959 the North Vietnamese government acceded to its southern allies; by midyear, arms and advisers had begun to flow south. The National Liberation Front (NLF), a collection of Communists, angry peasants, and disgruntled former sectarians, was formed in late 1960 to carry out the armed struggle in the south. The NLF was called by Diem the Viet Cong, or Vietnamese "Commies."

In the United States, President Eisenhower was succeeded by the Democrat John F. Kennedy, who defeated Richard Nixon in 1960 after a hard-fought campaign. As a senator from Massachusetts, JFK had been a champion of Diem, and during the presidential campaign he had attacked the Eisenhower administration for letting the Communists push the United States around, especially in Cuba and on two islands off the coast of China, Quemoy and Matsu. Kennedy charged that the Republican strategy of massive retaliation—the threat of nuclear attack—had paralyzed American foreign policy, robbing it of the flexibility it needed to respond to small conflicts in the developing world. It was not always credible to threaten a country with nuclear annihilation because nuclear weapons were inefficient in rural areas, unable to discriminate between soldiers and civilians, and provocative, to say the least, and assassination or removal of unfriendly leaders did no good in the presence of genuine nationalism, always capable of producing a new leader to replace the one departed. JFK's solution to this strategic conundrum was "flexible response," which promised to fashion for policymakers an instrument that was somewhere between the penknife of CIA subversion and the battle axe of atomic weaponry.

Everything about Kennedy suggested motion. Eisenhower played golf; Kennedy and his brothers played touch football, with undisguised brio (though off camera Kennedy stopped playing, to rest his chronically ailing back). During the campaign, JFK had said, "It's time to get the country moving again." Where the country was to move and why movement was important were not so clear. As a Kennedy staffer put it: "The United States needs a *Grand Objective.* We behave as if . . . our real objective is to sit by our pools contemplating the spare tires round our middles. . . . The key consideration is not that the *Grand Objective* be exactly right, it is that we *have* one and that we start moving toward it." In fairness, it must be said that JFK pointed toward "a new frontier," one with a variety of dimensions. One of them was Southeast Asia.

Kennedy was determined to "oppose any foes," as he put it in his inaugural address, and very quickly he found an opportunity to do that. Cuba had a Communist government led by Fidel Castro. From the Eisenhower administration, JFK had inherited a plan mandating an invasion of Cuba by a group of anti-Castro exiles, trained in Guatemala by the CIA. Kennedy gave the scheme the go-ahead, and on April 16, 1961, the attack began. The invaders never had a chance: they were vastly outnumbered, American air support was inadequate, and the people of Cuba, either frightened or reasonably content with their lot, failed to rise against the government when the exiles splashed ashore at the Bay of Pigs. Everyone knew, or soon found out, that the CIA had been involved in the scheme. Kennedy blamed "the experts" for giving him bad advice, and he fired Allen Dulles, head of the CIA and brother of the late John Foster. But it was the president who suffered the humiliation of failure.

Laos offered a chance for redemption. When Eisenhower briefed Kennedy on Southeast Asian problems in January 1961, he warned the incoming president that serious trouble was brewing in Laos, where an insurgency threatened to topple the royalist government of Phoumi Nosavan. It might be necessary, Ike suggested, to intervene unilaterally to salvage the situation. (About Vietnam, Eisenhower said little, although it must have been clear that prospects were not encouraging.) Phoumi's regime was in good part the creature of the CIA, which was one of the largest employers in the country, and was financed by a vigorous opium trade. It was besieged by a coalition of parties that ran the gamut from moderate (a group led by Prince Souvanna Phouma) to Communist (the Pathet Lao). The coalitionists seemed close to victory by early 1961.

Before the Bay of Pigs fiasco, Kennedy's inclination was to use military force to protect the royalist government in Laos. Robert McNamara, the new secretary of defense, suggested air strikes. The Joint Chiefs of Staff went further, calling for an invasion of Laos by 250,000 American and Thai troops, with tactical nuclear strikes held in reserve. It seemed likely that the United States would intervene. Then, in late April, the administration's "roving ambassador," W. Averell Harriman, weighed in strongly for a negotiated solution to the conflict. At the eleventh hour Harriman and others, especially John Kenneth Galbraith, the U.S. ambassador in India, achieved a cease-fire in Laos and an agreement by both sides to reconvene the Geneva Conference to discuss a joint Laotian government. It was a victory for diplomacy, some would argue, but on one level the president was disappointed. Negotiations with Communists were neither vigorous nor "manly," both important values in Kennedy's Camelot.

Another opportunity to oppose foes with determination came in Vietnam. When JFK took office, the United States was committed to Diem. Most of the $1 billion that South Vietnam had received from Washington had gone to the military. There were over fifteen hundred American military advisers in Vietnam, and the CIA was still conducting its "psywar" north of the seventeenth parallel. In the late spring, following the Bay of Pigs and the decision to negotiate in Laos, Kennedy took several small but symbolically meaningful steps toward greater involvement in the war. He sent in one hundred more advisers. He recalled his ambassador, Elbridge Durbrow, who had urged the administration to make further aid to Diem conditional on genuine social reform; Durbrow was replaced by Frederick Nolting. Most critically, the president secretly sent four hundred Special Forces troops to teach the South Vietnamese how to fight guerrilla warfare. The Special Forces, the best known of whom were the Green Berets, were avatars of flexible response and great favorites of JFK. The Special Forces were not combat troops in the technical sense, but they often found themselves on the front lines anyway because of the realities of counterinsurgency warfare and the inexperience (or cowardice) of their South Vietnamese hosts.

Kennedy did not do as much as some officials in the administration would have liked. He was not sure how many soldiers it would take to defeat the Communists, and he was aware that if he sent thousands of troops to Vietnam, as adviser Walt W. Rostow urged, they would surely take casualties and involve the United States further in the war. But retreat was unthinkable. The perception of defeat in Cuba and Laos drove Kennedy to seek victory in Vietnam. The president was also convinced that Nikita Khrushchev, the Soviet premier who had emerged from the power struggles following Stalin's death, respected only toughness: Khrushchev baited JFK mercilessly during their first summit conference, at Vienna in June 1961. And there was the commitment itself. Kennedy believed that American credibility was at stake in Vietnam. If the United States abandoned its charge, no one, friend or enemy, would ever again respect America's word. Kennedy thus sought a middle path in Vietnam, something short of full-scale military intervention, but a military presence that would signal the communists that he was resolved to tough it out.

Kennedy's decision to deepen his administration's commitment collided with the increasing popularity of the NLF in the countryside, the willingness of the North Vietnamese to fight indefinitely for the unification of the country on their terms, the persistence of Soviet and Chinese support for the Communists, and, most of all, the alarming degradation of the Diem government. Diem had a mind of his own; he was no puppet. But he was a poor administrator, incapable of incisiveness and grudging on the matter of delegating authority, except to members of his immediate family. He felt himself unsuited for leadership, and as his self-doubts increased, he more and more allowed himself to come under the influence of his authoritarian brother, Ngo Dinh Nhu, and Nhu's peculiar wife, Madame Nhu. The main reason for Diem's failure was his lack of a political base beyond certain neighborhoods in Washington. He was not a man of the people. When the South Vietnamese voted for him in a desultory referendum in 1955, it was because there was no choice, or he seemed no worse than anyone else, or he hated communism, or they were afraid not to vote for him. Frances FitzGerald called Diem "the sovereign of discord" and observed that peasants defined his government by the behavior of its representatives, the "arrogant officials who took bribes" and the soldiers who "drank too much, stole food, and raped the village girls." Diem hoped he had secured the Confucian "mandate of Heaven." It was his only hope, for he ruled without the true consent of the governed.

A crisis involving South Vietnam's Buddhists led to Diem's downfall. Buddhist leaders believed that Diem, a Catholic with a quasi-Confucian ideology, did not respect their religion, a view apparently confirmed on May 8, 1963, when government soldiers fired on a Buddhist gathering in Hué. The following month, in protest, a Buddhist monk named Thich Quang Duc sat down at an intersection in Saigon and allowed himself to be burned to death. The world was shocked, but the Diem government responded coldly. Madame Nhu spoke sadistically of "bronze barbecues," and in August Ngo Dinh Nhu's Special Forces, trained by Americans, raided Buddhist pagodas throughout the country and carted protesting citizens off to jail. There were many injuries and some deaths.

Some members of the Kennedy administration now decided that Diem must go. With the latest ambassador in Saigon, the strong-minded Henry Cabot Lodge, leading the effort, the administration fitfully encouraged a group of Diem's' disgruntled generals who were known to be planning a coup. The generals, led by Duong Van ("Big") Minh, were a skittish bunch who sought guarantees of American support for their efforts. The administration responded inconsistently, sometimes seeming to back away from a coup, but also tightening ever so slightly the aid conduit to Diem. This proved signal enough. The coup took place on November 1, 1963. Diem and Nhu, left friendless, escaped to a Catholic church. They surrendered early the following morning, having been promised safe passage, but Big Minh had them both killed. (He later claimed that the brothers had committed suicide, although he could not explain the multiple entry wounds, some of them made with a knife.) Kennedy was appalled by the murders and may have experienced a flicker of doubt about his Vietnam policy. We will never know. Just three weeks later, ironically and tragically, he himself was assassinated in Dallas.

In later years, many of the slain president's advisers and a number of historians did indeed claim that Kennedy was contemplating a withdrawal from Vietnam before the killings of Diem and Nhu. They pointed to a White House policy statement of October 2, 1963, that described the planned withdrawal of 1,000 men by December and implied that the rest would be home by the end of 1965. Read closely, however, the statement explained that withdrawal would be contingent on victory, which the authors of the statement assumed would be at hand within two years. It is also true that most of Kennedy's key advisers on Vietnam—Robert McNamara, Walt Rostow, Secretary of State Dean Rusk, and national security adviser McGeorge Bundy—stayed on with the next administration, which *increased* the U.S. commitment. We know only that in November 1963 there were roughly 16,000 U.S. troops in Vietnam, and that seventy Americans had died there.

Kennedy's successor, Lyndon Baines Johnson, was a shrewd politician from Texas. There is evidence that Johnson was insecure in his new office. He hated to be alone or understimulated,

Map 2. Indochina, circa 1965

so he surrounded himself with television sets, spent hours on the telephone cajoling members of Congress to support one bill or another, and even briefed aides while he sat on the toilet. Added to this apparent insecurity was the burden of his predecessor's legacy. Kennedy's luster shone brighter with his death, and LBJ never escaped the feeling that he was a usurper, an awkward Southerner who had rudely stumbled into the sanctum of the Harvard Club (or the dining room at Camelot) and who would not be forgiven for having done so.

Vietnam—"that bitch of a war," in LBJ's colorful, mournful phrase—would come to obsess the new president. As vice president, Johnson had been to Vietnam, and he had concluded upon his return that the United States must fight communism in Southeast Asia or face a threat to its own security. Like his predecessors, and like most Americans in the 1960s, LBJ feared and loathed communism. He also believed in the importance of the U.S. commitment to South Vietnam. Beyond that, Johnson came to regard Vietnam as a personal test of manhood. He likened the war to a hunt—a rite of passage for southern men. With victory in Vietnam, he said he would "nail the coonskin to the wall," a step a man takes at the end of a successful hunt. Defeating the enemy would stop communism, reassure the allies, and establish LBJ's reputation as president.

Johnson had the misfortune to take office as the military situation was worsening. Following the overthrow of Diem, Vietnam "went on an emotional binge," in Douglas Pike's phrase. Big Minh and his generals proved incompetent; the government virtually ceased to govern. The NLF took the offensive in the countryside; and when North Vietnamese regulars joined their comrades in the south in ever-increasing numbers, the killing escalated. In January 1964 there was another coup in Saigon, this one led by General Nguyen Khanh and a group of young officers. Khanh tried to walk the line between U.S. demands for stability and pacification of the countryside and the expectations of his people for peace and justice, but he ended up pleasing no one. Khanh was an anti-Communist general, not a national leader. By the end of 1964, the Americans deduced, the NLF controlled 40 percent of the territory and 50 percent of the population in South Vietnam, estimates that were probably conservative. Khanh had temporarily resigned, to be replaced by a months-long power struggle.

From Lyndon Johnson's viewpoint, this turmoil simply would not do. Frustrated below the seventeenth parallel, the president contemplated carrying the war to what he believed was its source. Early in the summer of 1964, his advisers drew up plans for U.S. bombing attacks on targets in North Vietnam. To implement these plans would require a good deal of discretionary power for the president, who had no desire to consult Congress each time a bombing sortie seemed necessary. Johnson got his opportunity in August, when a series of dubious incidents in the Tonkin Gulf brought from an obedient Congress a resolution authorizing the president to take "all the necessary measures to repel any armed attacks against the forces of the United States and to prevent further aggression" in Southeast Asia. It was not a declaration of war, but for years it was the functional equivalent. It also gave Johnson a chance to show toughness as he faced a presidential campaign that fall against the conservative Republican Barry Goldwater. Johnson won in a landslide victory that November.

Apart from a bombing raid on North Vietnamese patrol boat bases, the administration stayed its hand in the immediate aftermath of the Tonkin Gulf Resolution. But not for long. On February 6, 1965, the NLF attacked the American barracks at Pleiku, in the central highlands, killing nine men. That evening, Johnson ordered retaliation bombings north of the seventeenth parallel. Four days later, he decided reprisals were not enough, and Operation Rolling Thunder, a systematic program of bombing was begun. (Actually, it joined a program of bombing in Laos, Operation Barrel Roll, already in progress.) The bombing was the brainchild of the U.S.

Air Force, and particularly of General Curtis LeMay, who was known for the ruthless effectiveness of American strategic bombing late in World War II. LeMay promised "to bomb them back to the Stone Age."

The rejoinder was that the Vietnamese were still in the Stone Age, a culturally arrogant reply, but one that contained a germ of truth. The bombings, although terribly destructive, failed to demoralize the North Vietnamese. Indeed, the closed system in which bombing times and targets were selected leaked badly. "It was uncanny," wrote General Bruce Palmer, Jr., "how the Viet Cong and the North Vietnamese were able to defeat our security precautions." The North Vietnamese also responded with alacrity to the bombing. As quickly as bridges or roads were destroyed, mass labor reconstructed them. And the North Vietnamese economy was readily decentralized, denying the Americans large, tempting targets. Within a couple of years, pilots in their powerful aircraft, some of them massive B-52s, were reduced to targeting bicycle repair shacks in the Vietnamese jungle.

Johnson made another fateful decision later in February 1965. Responding to a request from General William Westmoreland, commander of U.S. forces in Vietnam since the middle of 1964, the president sent two Marine battalions—about 3,500 men—to defend the U.S. air base at Danang. They arrived on March 8. These were neither advisers nor "support troops," as their predecessors were called, but plain combat troops whose job description called for them to kill the Vietcong. As some people predicted, the presence of the Marines in Vietnam made it easy to justify the military's requests for more, if only to protect those who were already there. LBJ authorized 40,000 additional troops in April. By December there were 185,000 American soldiers in Vietnam; two years later the total was 500,000, and the generals were asking for 200,000 more. But growing U.S. troop strength failed to bring stability to the government of South Vietnam. From the power struggle of early 1965 emerged an exaggeratedly stylish air marshal named Nguyen Cao Ky. Like his predecessors, Ky tried to live up to the image that his American backers had fashioned for him and, like them, he failed. Ky was involved in the lucrative Vietnamese heroin trade, and association with him was embarrassing for the Americans. He was eased aside in September 1967 in favor of Nguyen Van Thieu, who won a rigged election with Ky as his running mate.

The decisions to bomb and send combat troops in early 1965—decisions to "choose war," as historian Fredrik Logevall has it—brought indignation and anger from many Americans, especially college students. There were rallies, marches, and "teach-ins," in which faculty members and students discussed the history of the war and its implications. Disturbed, if not yet alarmed, by the unrest on campus, LBJ dispatched administration "truth squads" to many universities, hoping to set the record straight. Confrontations occurred. Some protestors saw Vietnam as the latest and most brutal exercise in American imperialism, and they demanded fundamental changes in the political and economic system so as to make imperialism impossible. Many who opposed the war were veterans of the black civil rights movement who instinctively mistrusted the liberal administration's commitment to social change and in some cases felt racial solidarity with the Vietcong. Some simply feared being drafted to fight in Vietnam. The leading radical organization for white college students was the Students for a Democratic Society, or SDS. At its national convention in June 1965 the SDS decided to take up the antiwar cause. From that point onward, the movement grew: 100,000 people marched on the Pentagon (and a few tried to levitate it) in October 1967; in November 1969 more than 500,000 protestors came to Washington, thus constituting the largest demonstration to that point in the capital.

Despite what many on the left said of him, Lyndon Johnson did not revel in the expanded war. Between 1965 and 1968 he flirted occasionally with the possibility of negotiations. LBJ continued to insist, however, on attaining goals in Vietnam that were incompatible with the aspirations of the North Vietnamese and the NLF. Johnson viewed the war as a case of aggression by the North Vietnamese against a legally constituted state in the south. Thus, before there could be peace, the North Vietnamese would have to withdraw their own and NLF troops from South Vietnam and recognize the legitimacy of the South Vietnamese government. The Communists and their allies countered that the Americans, not the Vietnamese, were the aggressors, that it was absurd to talk of removing indigenous forces (the NLF) from South Vietnam, and that the government of South Vietnam was a fabrication of the United States and had no popular support. Potential talks were further complicated by Thieu, the South Vietnamese president, who gambled that his hawkish sponsors in Washington would support him even if he objected to sitting down with the Communists. For a time, he was not wrong.

Then came Tet 1968. Beginning on the night of January 30, 1968—the night of the lunar New Year, or Tet—thousands of NLF and North Vietnamese troops attacked U.S. strongholds throughout South Vietnam. The provincial capital of Hué was taken, followed by the horrific slaughter of civilians by the Vietcong. Just outside Saigon, the Tan Son Nhut air base, then the world's busiest airport, came under intense fire. Most shocking to the Americans, a handful of Vietcong entered the compound of the U.S. embassy in Saigon. They killed two guards and held the grounds for over six hours.

In the ensuing days, every Communist thrust was parried. Hué was retaken in bloody, house-to-house fighting. Tan Son Nhut did not fall. Every Vietcong who entered the embassy compound was slain; the building was secured in time for business the morning after its siege. The North Vietnamese command confessed to making serious mistakes in planning and executing the Tet offensive, and the NLF, whose soldiers served as shock troops in the attacks, was badly damaged. But Tet did not seem like a victory to politicians, opinion makers, and ordinary people in the United States. It is possible, as Peter Braestrup has argued, that the media unfairly represented Tet as a military defeat for the United States and South Vietnam. More to the point, however, the administration had raised hopes that the enemy was on its last legs and presumably incapable of launching such a powerful assault as the Tet offensive. Victory "lies within our grasp—the enemy's hopes are bankrupt," Westmoreland had said on a visit back home the previous November. The offensive also seemed to exhibit, and exacerbate, the special ugliness of the war. Americans witnessed the summary execution of a suspected Vietcong terrorist by the chief of South Vietnam's national police. The officer, America's ally, placed his pistol to the prisoner's head and squeezed the trigger; a photographer caught the spray of blood and the man's death grimace. Walter Cronkite, anchor of the CBS Evening News and to many the most trusted man in America, was visibly shaken by the events of Tet and soon became a doubter.

Johnson's Vietnam policy had been tottering near the abyss, and the Tet offensive pushed it over the edge. Defense Secretary McNamara, disillusioned by his own failures, had already announced his intention to resign (with the president's blessing) and actually left within a month of the Tet offensive. His replacement was Clark Clifford, a political veteran and a Johnson loyalist. Within days, however, Clifford had reached the same conclusions as McNamara: despite its insatiable appetite for more soldiers, the military could not promise that increased force would bring success in Vietnam. Clifford thus refused to endorse a request for 200,000 more troops, a position consistent with that of the apostate McNamara. On March 12 the president, bidding for reelection, suffered a stunning blow in the New Hampshire Democratic primary, when antiwar Senator Eugene McCarthy came within a few hundred votes of defeating him. Johnson had had enough. On March 31 he told the American people that he unilaterally had stopped the bombing of most of North Vietnam and that he sought negotiations toward a peace settlement. He closed with a surprise: he would not seek another term as president.

The Democratic Party split wide open. The antiwar Senator Robert Kennedy, JFK's attorney general and brother of the slain president, joined the contest. But Robert was assassinated in June, on the night of his victory in the California primary. George McGovern tried to take up his mantle. During a tumultuous convention in Chicago, in which demonstrators were confronted by Mayor Richard Daley's ill-tempered police, who clubbed and tear gassed them lavishly, Vice President Hubert Humphrey secured the nomination. He had shown touching loyalty to LBJ by refusing to criticize the administration's Vietnam policy, but Humphrey's discretion was not the best politics. Although he did become more dovish as the campaign went along, it proved too late to save the Democrats. The Republican Richard Nixon, unsuccessful in previous campaigns for president and for governor of California and now rising like the phoenix from the political ash heap, narrowly defeated Humphrey and inherited the war.

What all this meant for those actually fighting in Vietnam was unclear. The North Vietnamese put a brave face on the Tet offensive and were pleased by the dramatic shift in American public opinion, but they admitted that their strategy had "many deficiencies and weak points" that "limit our successes." The death of Ho Chi Minh in September 1969 was also sobering. The troops of South Vietnam—the Army of the Republic of Vietnam, or ARVN—had frequently fought well during the Tet engagement. Nevertheless, the ranks continued to suffer high rates of corruption and desertion. The strain was beginning to show on the Americans, too. Eager volunteers such as future author Philip Caputo, who went ashore at Danang in March 1965, increasingly were replaced by draftees. These men, who were disproportionately poor and undereducated, were sent to the "front"—on patrols into the jungle and rice paddies. Derided by other military units and often treated as cannon fodder by their officers, these "grunts" turned sullen and dangerous. By 1969 the troops routinely dulled their fears by using drugs, and the incidence of "fragging," or killing one's own officers, climbed steeply.

Nixon promised to end the suffering. The new president was a suspicious man, given to secrecy and duplicity, yet he had some advantages his predecessors had not enjoyed. Nixon's credentials as an anti-communist were impeccable. He had cut his political teeth on the sensational Alger Hiss case in the late 1940s, in which Hiss, a former high-ranking official in the State Department, had been found guilty of lying about his past associations with the Communist Party. Nixon hated bureaucracy and had no compunction about circumventing it, openly or with stealth, and he was not constrained by any scruples about morality in international affairs. Following his national security adviser, Henry Kissinger, the president professed himself a realist. It did no good to pursue a moralistic foreign policy, he argued, because morals were relative: one nation's morality was another nation's high crime. Above all, Kissinger and Nixon agreed that stability among the Great Powers was essential for the maintenance of world peace. Different ideologies, presumably based on different perceptions of morality, should not stand in the way of dialogue between nations. Thus, the Nixon administration would open serious talks with the Soviets and make an astonishing overture to the Chinese Communists in 1971-72. Because it prevented détente, a measure of understanding between the Great Powers, the war in Vietnam must be liquidated, one way or another.

What followed was an exercise in foreign policy schizophrenia. On the one hand Nixon and Kissinger moved to reduce American troop commitments. Without waiting for any change in Hanoi's position, the president began to order withdrawals: 65,000 in 1969, 140,000 in 1970, and 160,000 in 1971. This move was consistent with the Nixon Doctrine, announced in July 1969, which implied that Asians should fight Asians, albeit with help from their Great Power patrons. The administration also moved to revitalize negotiations with the other side. Initiated by the Johnson administration, the Paris peace talks had been unproductive. In February 1970, Kissinger began secret negotiations with North Vietnamese representatives. At first as fruitless as the Paris discussions, these "back channel" negotiations ultimately achieved some success: by the spring of 1971, Kissinger and Hanoi's negotiator, Le Duc Tho, were moving despite considerable strain toward a kind of accommodation.

On the other hand, the Nixon-Kissinger policy demanded the intensification of the war. Vietnamization, as it was called, meant arming the ARVN to the teeth to protect the retreating Americans and to hold up the Thieu government once the Americans were gone. South Vietnam's troops were augmented by over 15 percent, and its air force was made the fourth largest in the world. The Nixon administration also expanded the war to Cambodia and Laos. Both nations provided sanctuaries, albeit without enthusiasm, to the NLF and North Vietnamese. The leaders of both countries, Prince Norodom Sihanouk in Cambodia and Prince Souvanna Phouma in Laos, desperately hoped to avoid a wider war. But they could not. Early in 1969, during the first months of his administration, Nixon authorized the bombing of enemy sanctuaries in Cambodia. These attacks, which continued for over a year, were concealed from most of Congress and the American people—although they were, of course, no secret to the Cambodian peasant families whom they decimated and displaced. In April 1970, U.S. and South Vietnamese troops invaded Cambodia. Laos had been bombed for years; its turn for invasion came in February 1971, when the ARVN crossed the border in the first serious test of the Nixon Doctrine. The invasion was a disaster, with some ARVN units taking casualties at a rate of 50 percent. All the while, American pilots continued bombing North and South Vietnam.

Nixon's dual policy of negotiation and deadly force—"fighting while talking," said the North Vietnamese, who did it too—failed to placate the antiwar movement at home. Some, it should be said, were mollified by the troop withdrawals. On the whole, however, the left mistrusted Nixon and Kissinger, and protestors correctly pointed out that the killing in Vietnam had not diminished under the Nixon Doctrine. The antiwar demonstrations grew larger and angrier. News of the invasion of Cambodia in the spring of 1970 sent thousands into the streets. On college campuses across the country, students denounced the invasion and the institutional complicity of their universities in the war. At Kent State University the Ohio National Guard killed four young people on May 4; later that month, two students were slain by police at Jackson State College, in Mississippi. The ranks of the demonstrators were by then swelled by housewives who had been touched by the war, African-Americans angered by the conflict's racism, disgruntled veterans, even high-school and grade-school students. Public opinion polls indicated widespread disenchantment with Nixon's policy. The president called the protestors "bums" and instructed his subordinates to spy on his critics, a decision that led to the Watergate scandal and to Nixon's eventual downfall.

In Vietnam the North Vietnamese had been rather subdued since the failures of the Tet offensive; they were content, it seemed, to harass the departing Americans and blunt any ARVN initiatives. In the spring of 1972, however, the Communists launched a massive offensive, including the use of Soviet-supplied armor. If the Communists hoped that the attacks would end U.S. support for the Thieu regime, they were disappointed. But the Eastertide offensive achieved several other objectives. It exposed once more the folly of Vietnamization. The ARVN, writes James William Gibson, "went into immediate shock," taking 140,000 casualties and surrendering hundreds of allegedly secure villages. Again, as in the Tet offensive, an American-inspired counterattack rolled back the northern forces. A furious Nixon warned the Soviet Union that détente would be jeopardized unless the Russians could make their clients behave, and then he escalated the war. Again, B-52 bombers were unleashed to pound the enemy in the north and south. The president authorized the mining of Haiphong harbor.

The new bloodshed seemed to have had a briefly sobering effect on both sides, and in May there were at last signs of movement in the talks. Speaking for Hanoi, Le Duc Tho proposed a tripartite coalition government for the south, to include representatives of North Vietnam, the NLF, and the existing Saigon regime, although Thieu himself was unacceptable. Kissinger rejected the idea of coalition, but he sensed flexibility on the Communist side and bore down. By September the North Vietnamese had dropped their demand that Thieu be replaced and transformed the coalition scheme into an all-parties council that would administer free elections in the south. Both sides squabbled and fine-tuned a bit; then, on October 1, they achieved substantial agreement on the text of the peace agreement. Kissinger was triumphant and flew off to Saigon to get Thieu's approval.

No one should have been surprised when Thieu balked at the agreement. He had previously objected to a number of the provisions to which Kissinger had just agreed, and he argued that the language of the treaty was sufficiently vague to permit the Communists dangerously wide latitude in interpreting it. Kissinger raged at Thieu, threatening to halt aid for his government and even hinting that the United States might make peace without him. Kissinger was seeking at minimum a "decent interval" between full U.S. withdrawal and the fall of Thieu's government. He returned home and, despite the remaining disagreements, announced: "We believe that peace is at hand."

Nixon was not as willing as his national security adviser to abandon Thieu just yet. A week after he was overwhelmingly reelected to the presidency—his opponent, the dove George McGovern, won only seventeen electoral votes—Nixon reassured Thieu of his full support and told Kissinger to take Thieu's objections to the North Vietnamese. Reluctantly, Kissinger did so. Le Duc Tho was indignant, and after a month of pointless bickering between the sides, he broke off the talks and went home. This was Nixon's signal to renew the air war over North Vietnam. Thirty-six thousand tons of bombs were dropped there during the 1972 Christmas season, more than had been dropped in the period from 1969 to 1971. The pilots did not try to hit civilians, but with all the ordnance, precision was impossible: a bomb fell on Hanoi's Bach Mai Hospital, killing eighteen people and wounding dozens more. The well-equipped North Vietnamese air defense took its toll on the Americans, who lost twenty-six planes and had ninety-three fliers killed or captured. The administration's critics reacted with anger. It was a bleak and ghastly time for everyone. It did, however, usher in the final phase of the war. An apparently chastened Nixon now decided to press Thieu to go along with the Paris accords, essentially as presented in October. Without the president's backing, Thieu believed that he had no choice, and so at last he acquiesced. Smiling tightly, Kissinger and Le Duc Tho signed the Paris peace agreement on January 27.

There followed what Gareth Porter has called "the cease-fire war" as both sides jostled for advantage. The Nixon administration claimed that the Communists were responsible for most of the violations, but it did not look that way to outsiders, who recorded numerous ARVN transgressions and pointed out that the Communists seemed more aggressive because their moves were more successful. Nixon tried hard, within the constraints placed on him by the Paris agreement and an impatient Congress, to bolster Thieu by providing extensive aid, moral support, and threats directed at the North Vietnamese. He had assumed that, in a pinch, he could resume bombing. Ultimately, none of it worked. Congress cut off funds for U.S. military activity in or over Indochina as of August 15, 1973. By that time, Nixon had been implicated in the Watergate affair, and his power to pursue an unpopular foreign policy dropped dramatically as he fought to keep his office. Kissinger, now secretary of state, moved into the breach, reviving the argument that the allies would be demoralized if the United States let South Vietnam go. Congress refused to accept this claim. The North Vietnamese sensed that their time had come, and early in 1975 they began a massive offensive, which they hoped would bring victory by the following year. It would not take that long.

South Vietnam fell during the brief presidency of Gerald Ford, who had succeeded Nixon upon the latter's resignation in August 1974. Ford was widely regarded as a decent man, but there was not much he could do about the situation in Southeast Asia. Alarmed at the collapse of ARVN forces during the spring of 1975, the president asked Congress for more military aid for Thieu, perhaps hoping that his own obvious integrity would change some minds on Capitol Hill. The efforts were unavailing. Thieu resigned on April 21 and left the country four days later. By the 29th the Communists had reached the outskirts of Saigon and were making plans to share their rice with starving Saigonese, if necessary. Amid the panic of those South Vietnamese who had worked closely with the United States and who feared what was to come, the last Americans departed the U.S. embassy and a building nearby by helicopter. The next day the Communists captured the presidential palace. For the Americans, the war was over.

The end of the war did not instantly have a profound effect on the United States. There was a vigorous debate about what came to be called by conservatives "The Vietnam Syndrome," the alleged reluctance of the U.S. government to assert itself in foreign policy for fear of public criticism. The controversies over Americans still alleged to be missing in action in Southeast Asia, the treatment of veterans, the construction of the Vietnam Veterans' Memorial in Washington, and the meaning of the war for American culture would emerge in the 1980s. Ultimately, passions would cool enough to allow the administrations of George Bush (1989–1993) and Bill Clinton (1993–2001) to move toward normalizing relations with Vietnam. The United States extended diplomatic recognition to Vietnam in 1995, by which time several American corporations and investors were champing at the bit to get at the Vietnamese market. A bilateral trade agreement that took effect in late 2001 inspired a rapid expansion of trade between the United States and Vietnam. By 2007, U.S. exports to Vietnam had a value of nearly $2 billion. Vietnam's sales to the United States were worth over five times that total, making the United States Vietnam's largest export market. Veterans, aging baby boomers, and their children now have the common experience of wearing shirts and pants sewn in Vietnam.

In Vietnam, postwar problems were greater and more immediate. At least a million and perhaps as many as three million people had been killed, millions bore wounds, and millions more were refugees. The land was devastated and the economy was wrecked. Relations with neighboring nations quickly soured: Vietnam invaded Cambodia in 1978, overthrowing its atrocious and truculent Communist government; early the following year, Vietnam itself was attacked by China, which had supported the Cambodian regime. Domestically, Hanoi's rigid policies prevented immediate reconciliation between north and south. Industry was nationalized, agriculture collectivized, and southerners who had opposed the revolution were subjected to rigorous political "reeducation." Millions of southerners, many of them ethnic Chinese and others the Amerasian children of Vietnamese women and U.S. soldiers, fled Vietnam; many settled in the United States. On the other hand, there was no bloodbath in Vietnam, and with the advent of *doi moi* economic reforms beginning in the mid-1980s, life gradually improved. Today, the revolutionary generation has grown old. Like the People's Republic of China (a comparison the Vietnamese dislike), Vietnam has achieved a dynamic economy under authoritarian political control. In an age of recession and the barrier-breaching internet. the country's economic and political future is unclear, but one can say that, once more, Vietnam has been restored to itself. It is no longer a cockpit of empires.

PART I

A CHRONOLOGY OF U.S. INTERVENTION

Chapter 1

Getting In, 1945–1952

Although American interest in Vietnam began before 1945, President Franklin D. Roosevelt's grudging decision early in that year to permit the return of French colonialism to Indochina provides a convenient starting point for this account. The readings in this chapter describe relations between the United States, Great Britain, France (and its Vietnamese clients), and the communist-nationalist Viet Minh, led by Ho Chi Minh, during the administration of Roosevelt's successor, Harry S. Truman. Robert Shaplen, a journalist who covered Vietnam for the *New Yorker* for many years, details Ho's efforts to cultivate American representatives of the Office of Strategic Services (OSS) during the mid-1940s. Historian Mark Atwood Lawrence offers a close look at French, American, and British sparring over what to do to counter Ho's influence in Vietnam, including whether (or how) to support the creation of a French-backed government in the south led by the former emperor Bao Dai. At the root of these readings, and much other work on U.S. policy toward French Indochina during this period, is the classic question: Was Ho Chi Minh a nationalist or a communist first? Would it have been possible for the United States to work with Ho, even despite his communism, rather than isolate him or drive him into the arms of the communist powers? Was it thus a mistake to underwrite the French-supported Bao Dai regime in 1950?

❮ 1 ❯

Ho Chi Minh: The Untried Gamble

Robert Shaplen

IF THE RELATIONSHIP BETWEEN the Americans and the Vietminh in Cochin China was never more than a tentative one, it was much closer in the north, both in the months preceding the end of the war and in the period immediately afterward. There are moments in history when certain events, however obscure and fragmentary they may seem in retrospect, nevertheless serve as an endless source of speculation: *if* they had been approached in another way, *if* they had been allowed to run their course, would the whole chain of events that followed have perhaps been different? There is certainly some reason to believe that this might have been true about the relations between Ho Chi Minh and a number of Americans in 1945 and 1946, and, more significantly, about Ho's relations with a small group of French politicians and diplomats. It is easy now to dismiss these events and their meaning as unimportant if one assumes that the Communists, and Ho in particular, never had any other intention than to create a Communist state in Vietnam. However, in the opinion of those who, with varying degrees of political sophistication, lived through this early postwar period and helped form part of its history, such broad assumptions are over-simplifications of what was a highly tenuous and complicated set of political circumstances.

I have always shared the belief of many, if not most, observers who were in Indochina at the time that a serious mistake was made by both the French and the Americans, especially by the dominant French policymakers in Paris, in not dealing more realistically with Ho in 1945 and 1946, when there was a strong possibility that he might have been "Titofied" before Tito and Titoism were ever heard of; that the whole course of events might thereby have been altered and a great deal of bloodshed averted; and that today a unified Vietnam, even under some form of left-wing leadership, might have been the bulwark of a neutral bloc of Southeast Asian states seeking, above all, to avoid Chinese Communist domination. Some of the highest American officials have privately told me, in recent years, that they now believe the gamble with Ho should have been taken; in fact, a considerable number of them are again talking about Vietnam becoming a Southeast Asian Yugoslavia, a possibility that seems to me now rather remote. History, contrary to the popular belief, seldom does repeat itself, and second chances are seldom offered. It is one of the particular tragedies of American postwar policy that so many first chances have been missed.

There are many facets to the story of Ho's relations with the West during and after the Second World War. Let us start with the somewhat naïve but at the same time revealing account of a former young lieutenant in the United States Army—I shall have to refer to him only as John—who in May, 1945, parachuted into Ho's jungle headquarters near the village of Kim Lung in northern Tonkin on a mission to establish an underground that would help Allied personnel escape to freedom. Kim Lung lies on the edge of a heavy rain forest, thickly underlaid by brush. Amid sugar-loaf formations of mountains lie tiny valleys, and it was in one of these, near a small stream halfway up a tall hill, that Ho Chi Minh's camp, consisting of four huts, lay sequestered. Each of the huts was twelve feet square, set four feet off the ground on bamboo stakes, and Ho's was as bare as the others.

In this crude revolutionary cradle, deep in Japanese territory, John had the unique experience of living and working with Ho for several months. He found Ho completely co-operative in lending the support of his guerrillas for scouting and raiding parties, including one to rescue some French internees near the China border. John used his portable radio to put Ho in preliminary touch with French negotiators who were in Kunming, China, and who would soon be debating Indochina's postwar future with Ho in Hanoi, but John himself played a more immediate role in Vietnamese affairs by informally helping Ho frame a Declaration of Independence.

"He kept asking me if I could remember the language of our Declaration," John says. "I was a normal American, I couldn't. I could have wired up to Kunming and had a copy dropped to me, of course, but all he really wanted was the flavor of the thing. The more we discussed it, the more he actually seemed to know about it than I did. As a matter of fact, he knew more about almost everything than I did, but when I thought his demands were too stiff, I told him anyway. Strange thing was he listened. He was an awfully sweet guy. If I had to pick out one quality about that little old man sitting on his hill in the jungle, it was his gentleness."

He and John exchanged toasts and shared stewed tiger livers. John now admits his naïveté in being ready to believe that Ho was not a Communist. But even if he was, John felt certain that Ho was sincere in wanting to co-operate with the West, especially with France and the United States. Some of Ho's men impressed John less. "They go charging around with great fervor shouting 'independence,' but seventy-five per cent of them don't know the meaning of the word," he wrote in his diary. John still has two letters in English Ho sent him in the jungle. One of them, written soon after the Japanese surrender, when the Vietminh was about to seize control of the nationalist movement, reads as follows:

> Dear Lt. [John],
>
> I feel weaker since you left. Maybe I'd have to follow your advice—moving to some other place where food is easy to get, to improve my health. . . .
>
> I'm sending you a bottle of wine, hope you like it.
>
> Be so kind as to give me foreign news you got.
>
> . . . Please be good enuf to send to your H.Q. the following wires.
>
> 1. Daiviet [an anti-Vietminh nationalist group] plans to exercise large terror against French and to push it upon shoulder of VML [Vietminh League]. VML ordered 2 millions members and all its population be watchful and stop Daiviet criminal plan when & if possible. VML declares before the world its aim is national independence. It fights with political & if necessary military means. But never resorts to criminal & dishonest act.
>
> Signed—NATIONAL LIBERATION COMMITTEE OF VML
>
> 2. National Liberation Committee of VML begs U.S. authorities to inform United Nations the following. We were fighting Japs on the side of the United Nations. Now Japs surrendered. We beg United Nations to realize their solemn promise that all nationalities will be given democracy and independence. If United Nations forget their solemn promise & don't grant Indochina full independence, we will keep fighting until we get it.
>
> Signed—LIBERATION COMMITTEE OF VML
>
> Thank you for all the troubles I give you. . . . Best greetings!
>
> Yours sincerely Hoo [*sic*]

What spells the difference between 1945 and 1965, between John's jungle love feast with Ho Chi Minh—the vast prestige America then enjoyed in Asia—and the complex tragedy of the war in Vietnam today, in which Americans are engaged in bombing Ho's country? Those who insist that we should have tried to win Ho to our side maintain this even though they were aware of the fact that he had never wavered from a straight Marxist-Leninist course. Despite his orthodox ideological convictions (or perhaps because they were so orthodox), and because Indochina was a long way from Stalin's Moscow, Ho had already written his own unique revolutionary case history. He was, at this time, less a potential apostate than a kind of old Bolshevik maverick, a last Marxist Mohican in the anti-colonial wilderness of Southeast Asia. If it appears that he simply bewitched a handful of Americans in an atmosphere of dangerous and rollicking camaraderie late in the war and the months afterward, there is considerable more evidence than John's alone to substantiate the theory that Ho meant what he said, that he very much wanted the friendship of liberal Americans and liberal Frenchmen, with whose help he hoped to steer a moderate course to Vietnamese freedom. Was it only a game he was playing, as a superb actor, and did he just use this small group of foreign friends to further his own burning cause in Moscow's image? There is enough proof of his sincerity to doubt this over-simplified conclusion. Not only was Moscow far off, with a record of having done little to help Ho concretely in the difficult years gone by, but, significantly, Communist China did not yet exist. Who, then, more than the Americans, professing themselves to be ardently against colonialism in the projected postwar world, were in a position to help him win liberty from France and simultaneously ward off Chinese penetration?

Official wartime American policy had been alternately positive and vague about Indochina. President Roosevelt had obtained the tentative approval of Stalin and Chiang Kai-shek for a postwar Indochina trusteeship, though both had expressed themselves as favoring ultimate independence for the Vietnamese. Churchill's reaction to the trusteeship proposal had been negative, and Roosevelt had chided him as an old imperialist. Roosevelt had been somewhat ambivalent himself, however, when it came to doing anything to pave the way for Vietnam's independence. In October, 1944, he had told Secretary of State Cordell Hull that "we should do nothing in regard to resistance groups in Indochina," and when a Free French mission to Kandy, Ceylon, sought help from the Allied Southeast Asia Command, Roosevelt gave orders that "no American representatives in the Far East, whether civilian or military, are authorized to make any decisions on political questions with the French or anyone else."

The "anyone else" presumably included Ho Chi Minh, although Roosevelt may never even have heard of him. Ho had long been a man of mystery and many names. For the moment, one need only go back to 1939, when Ho was still known as Nguyen Ai Quoc (Nguyen, the Patriot). In that year, following the fall of the Popular Front in France, the Indochina Communist Party Ho had welded together was disbanded and went underground. When the Japanese swept into Tonkin in September, 1940, the Communists and the non-Communist nationalists launched uprisings against both the French and the Japanese, but they were quickly crushed. In May, 1941, after the Japanese had established their puppet regime of Vichy Frenchmen, Ho and other Vietnamese Communists met with other nationalists at Tsin-li, just across the Tonkinese border in China. They reorganized their scattered ranks into the Vietnam Doc Lap Dong Minh—Vietminh for short—and the guiding spirit, the man selected as General Secretary, was bearded little Nguyen Ai Quoc, who had unexpectedly shown up at the meeting, though many had thought he had died of tuberculosis years before in the jungle. Without any flexing of Communist muscles, Ho and his friends concentrated on creating a common nationalist front to continue the fight against both Japan and France and to gain Vietnamese freedom.

At the end of 1941, Nguyen Ai Quoc was arrested by the Kuomintang secret police. They knew he was a Communist but chose to describe him as "a French spy" and threw him into jail at Liuchow. Eying Tonkin, as the Chinese had for many years, the Kuomintang had its own plans to build an anti-French "independence" movement around picked pro-Chinese Vietnamese. They soon discovered, however, that it was Nguyen Ai Quoc's Communist guerrillas of the Vietminh front who had the only real experience in Indochina. No one else, with one exception, had a network of agents there. The exception, oddly enough, was a civilian group headed by a dozen Allied businessmen, each of whom had his private organization of French, Chinese, and Vietnamese operatives; their original purpose had been to do what could be done to protect Allied assets and property in the Far East, and after Pearl Harbor this unique group had started working with Ho's guerrillas to gather intelligence for Allied air forces based in China and in India.

Early in 1943, Nguyen Ai Quoc sent a message from his prison cell to the southern Chinese warlord, Chang Fa Kwei, who, while an important leader of the Kuomintang, had frequently fought for power with Chiang Kai-shek and had his own ideas about Indochina. Nguyen Ai Quoc told Chang Fa Kwei that if he were set free, he would regather his intelligence network in Indochina and, presumably, work on Chang's behalf. Chang thereupon ordered his release from the Liuchow jail, and did so without telling Chiang Kai-shek. It was at this point that Nguyen Ai Quoc adopted the name Ho Chi Minh (He Who Shines), primarily to hide his identity from Chiang Kai-shek's secret-police chief, Tai Li. As Ho, he became the directing head of the umbrella organization of Vietnamese revolutionary groups called the Dong Ming Hoi, which the Kuomintang was sponsoring and of which the Communist-dominated Vietminh was at first simply a part.

Ho received and disbursed a hundred thousand Chinese Nationalist dollars a month to carry on espionage and sabotage in Indochina. During 1943 and 1944, the Vietminh built up its own political strength at the expense of the other Dong Minh Hoi organizations, and by the end of 1944 it had an independent army of ten thousand rebels under the command of the young lawyer and teacher, Vo Nguyen Giap, who had already begun to demonstrate a remarkable military talent. Inevitably, as a result of the Vietminh's growing independence, relations between Ho and the Kuomintang in Chungking and Kunming became strained; under the circumstances, there was little his guardian angel, Chang Fa Kwei, could do about it. Equally unhappy about Ho were both the Vichy and the Free French, who buried their differences long enough to exchange secret information about him.

In the second half of 1944, Ho began to look to the Americans; what took place over the next two years, including the strange jungle romance between Ho and young soldiers like John, had overtones of comic opera, although the story had a sad ending. Ho, on four separate occasions, came secretly to the office of Strategic Services in Kunming, late in 1944 and early in 1945, seeking arms and ammunition in return for intelligence, sabotage against the Japanese, and continued aid in rescuing shot-down Allied pilots. He was rejected each time. According to Paul E. Helliwell, who was O.S.S. intelligence chief in China at the time and who has since denied that O.S.S. in any way "managed" Ho, "O.S.S. China was at all times consistent in its policy of giving no help to individuals such as Ho, who were known Communists and therefore obvious postwar sources of trouble." At the same time, however, and despite President Roosevelt's expressed policy of hands off the Indochina resistance movement—Helliwell says he was personally unaware of any direct orders—the decision not to help Ho was principally based, he adds, on Ho's refusal to pledge that any arms he received would be used only against the Japanese and not against the French.

Ho kept on trying. Helliwell finally gave him six .38-caliber revolvers and twenty thousand rounds of ammunition, but this was simply a token of appreciation for Vietminh assistance in bringing out three American pilots. Later, Ho wrote to Richard Heppner, who was chief of O.S.S. in China late in the war, requesting the help of the United States, which had already pledged the Philippines their freedom, in pressuring the French to grant Indochina independence. The fact is Ho did get some assistance from O.S.S. and from other American and Allied agencies over and above Helliwell's six pistols, although the material aid he received was not as great as the inspirational encouragement he was unofficially accorded. As a subsequent American intelligence chief in the Far East put it, "Ho offered to be our man, and we never grabbed his hand because we couldn't bankroll him."

Ho tried several Allied sources. Major General Claire Chennault, head of the 14th Air Force, who was warned by his Kuomintang friends to steer clear of him, at one point unwittingly had Ho introduced to him as "an old Vietnamese guide." Nothing came of that, but the British were somewhat more helpful and dropped some supplies to Free French and Vietminh guerrillas in November, 1944, after Ho had secretly moved back into Tonkin with about two hundred of his Vietminh followers. With him came a representative of the civilian group of former American businessmen in Indochina, who had for some time been co-operating with Ho's men. This hush-hush group had been under the wing of the O.S.S. at first but was now unofficially attached to another American Army group, the Air Ground Aid Service (AGAS). The arms that Ho and his handful of Vietnamese carried with them into Tonkin at this point are known to have come partly from O.S.S. supplies, although they had not been initially distributed for that purpose, and partly from some other American arsenals.

In the northern Tonkin jungle, in a mixed-up area where Chinese bandits, Free French and American paratroopers, and various groups of nationalists were all active, Ho Chi Minh set up his revolutionary headquarters. Vietminh troops, under young Giap, successfully harassed the Japanese, proselytized in behalf of Vietnamese freedom, and helped rescue additional Allied pilots. An American who was with Ho at his forest headquarters during this period remembers above all "his strength of character and his single-mindedness." His appraisal of Ho was as follows: "You've got to judge someone on the basis of what he wants. Ho couldn't be French, and he knew he could fight the French on his terms. He was afraid of the Chinese, and he couldn't deal with them because they'd always demand their pound of flesh. Moscow, so far away, was good at blowing up bridges, but not much good at building them again. If it weren't for the war, of course, Ho wouldn't have had a chance against the long background of French colonialism. But now he was in the saddle, although it wasn't clear what horse he was riding. For the moment, surely, he was helping us, on the ground. We and the French were in a position to help him in the future. I think he was ready to remain pro-West."

Ho Dickers with France

In the light of the above summary of Ho's career as a long-time trusted worker in Communist vineyards, let us return to the jungle and to the months, just before the end of the war in 1945, when he sounded out the French in Kunming over the radio of the young American lieutenant, John.

The messages John sent out for Ho reached Léon Pignon, a political career man of the French who was later to be High Commissioner of Indochina, and Major Jean Sainteny, a Free French Army officer who became the chief French representative in North Vietnam. After reading Ho's demands for guaranteed independence from France in five to ten years, Pignon and Sainteny replied that they were willing to negotiate, but no time or place was set. The Americans by this time were posing a new problem for the French. When Roosevelt's orders against helping the underground in Indochina were lifted, early in April, the Office of Strategic Services had begun to retrain and equip some two thousand French soldiers who had made their way to Kunming after the Japanese takeover. The plan was to drop Franco-American teams back into Indochina, with supplies to follow if guerrilla resistance bands could be organized. In point of fact, while willingly taking any material help they could get, the French wanted to avoid any direct American involvement. Helliwell, the former O.S.S. intelligence head, later said: "It was perfectly obvious by June of 1945 that the French were infinitely more concerned with keeping the Americans out of Indochina than they were in defeating the Japanese or in doing anything to bring the war to a successful conclusion in that area."

Not too many Americans did get into Tonkin, but several O.S.S. teams were dropped into the jungle, and with their help Ho's forces managed to augment their supplies with a small number of tommy guns and carbines. At the war's end, replenishing their arsenal with captured or surrendered Japanese equipment, Vietminh troops moved swiftly to carry out Ho's orders of a general insurrection. All over Indochina, there was rising support for the independence movement. Under Giap, now a self-styled General, the Vietminh troops moved into Hanoi on August 17, 1945. A week later, Major Sainteny parachuted into the city from a Free French bomber, with Major Archimedes Patti, of the O.S.S. Patti's mission was to liberate war prisoners, for which he had to obtain the co-operation of the Japanese, since the Chinese occupation forces had not yet arrived. Sainteny found himself immediately hamstrung by the Vietminh and by the Japanese, who, with Patti's apparent blessing, completely restricted his movement, on the grounds of his personal safety, and kept several hundred French citizens virtually locked up in the Hotel Metropole. Sainteny was incensed, and five days after his arrival he telegraphed Calcutta: "We are before a collusive Allied maneuver with the purpose of throwing the French out of Indochina." He had a point, but it was far more accidental than collusive.

Within a period of weeks, other American officers arrived in Hanoi, among them some top officers of the China Combat Command. At the same time came a number of American correspondents. Their open sympathies, in typical American fashion of supporting the underdog, were clearly with the Vietminh, and especially with Ho. Major Patti made no bones about favoring Vietnamese independence; French sources say he even offered to help Ho get arms, and that an American general on the scene indicated he had some business connections back home that would sell the new regime heavy equipment for rebuilding the country. That Ho needed help was obvious. My *Newsweek* associate, Harold Isaacs, saw Ho in November, and Ho expressed his readiness to permit the French to maintain their economic position in Vietnam if they recognized Vietnamese independence. "Why not?" Ho asked. "We've been paying out our life's blood for decades. Suppose it costs us a few hundred million more piastres to buy our freedom?"

Recalling his long struggles, his years in Chinese and British prisons, Ho was full of humility and neither looked nor played the part of a head of government. He wore a faded khaki jacket and trousers, a white shirt, and old slippers. "They call me 'Excellency.' Funny, eh?" he remarked.

The sympathy Americans had for Ho late in 1945 and early in 1946 found expression in the formation of the Vietnam-American Friendship Association. Its first meeting in Hanoi was attended by an American general and his officers. After listening to Vietnamese professions of esteem and fondness for America, the general returned the compliments and looked forward to such things as student exchanges. Major Sainteny, who had suffered the further indignity of being arrested by the Japanese while riding in his jeep, which carried a French flag, and having an American colonel obtain his release, later referred to the Americans' "infantile anticolonialism, which blinded almost all of them." Despite his dismay, it was Sainteny who, more than any other Frenchmen, was to sympathize with Ho Chi Minh and try to promote a real policy of co-operation with him.

After two meetings with Ho, late in September and early in October, Sainteny felt that he was "a strong and honorable personality." Subsequently, in his book, *The Story of a Lost Peace, 1945–1947*, Sainteny wrote that "this ascetic man, whose face revealed at once intelligence, energy, cleverness, and fineness, was a personality of the highest order who would not be long in placing himself in the foreground of the Asian scene." Pignon, who was more interested in building up other nationalists than in adopting Ho, was also impressed but was less sure of his sincerity. From the outset, Pignon had no illusions about "Ho's Communist face" and considered him "a great actor." Nevertheless, both Frenchmen regarded Ho as "a man of peace," and Pignon's reservations about Ho's honesty did not include skepticism about Ho's preference for moderation and for compromise over killing. The two French negotiators differed most strongly perhaps on their assessment of Ho's humility and pride: Sainteny was always impressed with the first; Pignon flashed warning signals about the second.

Sainteny did most of the negotiation with Ho that led to the agreement of March 6, 1946, whereby the Republic of Vietnam was recognized as an independent part of the French Union, with French troops permitted to return to Tonkin. During the period of the negotiations, Sainteny has written, Ho "aspired to become the Gandhi of Indochina." Ho is quoted as saying: "While we want to govern ourselves. . . . I need your professional men, your engineers, and your capital to build a strong and independent Vietnam." Ho, says Sainteny, wanted the French Union to be constructed with "a Vietnamese cornerstone. . . . He wanted independence for his country, but it was to France herself that he wanted to owe it. . . . It is certainly regrettable that France minimized this man and was unable to understand his value and the power he disposed of." Sainteny points out that China was Vietnam's age-old enemy, that Ho's overtures to the Americans had already proved "rather disappointing," and that, "against the wishes of an important faction of his party," Ho was not inclined to look for aid in Moscow, "which he knew too well." Sainteny, nevertheless, was realistic enough to admit that Ho's preference for French backing was partly predicated on the expectations of a Communist victory in France.

When the Communists in France lost out, Sainteny says, Ho felt he needed the support of French liberals and moderates more than ever if he was successfully to "muzzle his opposition" in Vietnam, which had begun to cause him some trouble. This particularly included some of the old Chinese Dong Minh Hoi groups, which Ho had subjugated in the late-war jungle days, when the Vietminh had become the dominant part of the underground front. The Chinese in Hanoi sought to reactivate these organizations, notably the Dong Minh Hoi and the more important Vietnam Quoc Dan Dang (VNQDD), the leading Vietnamese national party; they specifically wanted Ho to include representatives of these groups in his government.

The Chinese in the northern part of Vietnam had several objectives. In the first place, they were there for profit, if not for outright loot, and they succeeded—by inflating the Chinese dollar at the expense of the Indochina piastre; by making off with huge amounts of opium, which they seized both in Laos and in Vietnam; and by engaging in heavy black-market operations in Hanoi and Haiphong, where there was a large Chinese mercantile population. In the second place, the Chinese had no use for the French or the Vietnamese, and they did not hesitate to terrorize the local French and Vietnamese citizens. The fact that many of their occupation troops were more ragtail than professional encouraged this, and in the winter of 1945 things became so bad that Sainteny cabled Paris to ask for a United Nations investigation of the conduct of the Chinese forces; both the British and the American representatives in Hanoi supported him. As events turned out, this was not necessary, since the French finally managed to get the Chinese out of the north by renouncing their extraterritorial and other rights in China and by granting numerous concessions to the Chinese in Vietnam, including a free zone for Chinese goods at Haiphong and certain customs exemptions for goods shipped in over the railroad from Kunming.

Though the Chinese agreed to leave by mid-March, 1946, they actually didn't pull out the bulk of their troops until the summer. In the meantime, they kept up their political offensive, and they obtained some advantage from the fact that initially the Vietminh's strength was largely concentrated in Hanoi itself and in a few other cities but not yet in the countryside, where both the Dong Minh Hoi and the VNQDD had previously built up considerable support, especially in the areas near the Chinese border. Much of the Vietminh's support, despite its Communist leadership, came from non-Communist Vietnamese, whose passionate desire for independence was a powerful factor in enabling Ho Chi Minh to form his original broad front in his own dynamic image. In order to stress his nationalist feelings more than his Communist background and doctrine, and also as a result of the orders that had come from the French Communist Party, Ho, in mid-November, 1945, dissolved the Indochina Communist Party in the north. (A small group of Communist extremists, including Giap and Dang Xuan Khu—better known today as Truong Chinh, the strongest pro-Peking man among the Hanoi Communists—formed what they called Marxist Study Groups, which later became the nucleus of the Laodang, or Workers, Party, the successor of the old Communist Party in Indochina.)

To obtain the support of as many groups as possible for the agreement he was about to sign with Sainteny, Ho selected the chief of the Dong Ming Hoi to be his Vice-president, and he gave three top Cabinet jobs to VNQDD men, including the Ministry of Foreign Affairs. At the same time, to pacify the Chinese further, he dropped Giap and one other leading Communist from the Cabinet. As the Vietminh began organizing People's Committees to replace the old Councils of Notables in the villages, it made further temporary concessions to the Chinese parties, promising the VNQDD fifty seats and the Dong Minh Hoi twenty out of a total of three hundred and fifty in the assembly elections that were to be held in January, 1946. The vote took place on a limited basis only, in some parts of the country, and about half of those elected, as it turned out, were nonpolitical-party people, though the Vietminh did well by controlling the vote in many villages, and in Hanoi Ho received an alleged ninety-eight percent of the ballots. Ho had other reasons for wanting to go slow politically. He had an extremely difficult economic situation on his hands. There had been a famine early in 1945, followed by floods that had swept over the broken dikes of the Red River Delta. Then came a severe drought. The breakdown of the Vietnamese transportation system had made it impossible to ship rice from the south, which was having its own troubles. In 1945 and through the early part of 1946, it was estimated that a million Vietnamese died of starvation in the north.

Modus Vivendi Is Signed

In the face of all these difficulties, Ho's eagerness in wanting to conclude the March, 1946, agreement with Sainteny can better be understood. When he signed it, he made a direct and dramatic appeal to the Vietnamese people at a big outdoor meeting in Hanoi. "Fellow countrymen, who have followed me up to now," he asked, "follow me once more. I would prefer death a hundred times to betraying my country."

Two months later, as the French were doing their best to sabotage Ho by holding the separatist conference at Dalat, in the south, and by getting ready to set up their independent puppet regime in Cochin China, Ho left for France with a small delegation to negotiate what he hoped would be a full implementation of the March contract he had made with Major Sainteny. During the summer, while he was away, and with both Sainteny and Pignon out of Hanoi, too, the extremist group among the Communists, led by Giap and Dang Xuan Khu, rode roughshod over the non-Communist nationalists. As in the south, terror also struck the country, and many pro-French Vietnamese as well as Frenchmen were assassinated. There are those who say that this was all part of the game, that Ho went to France and remained there as the pretender of peace, tortuously seeking an agreement, while the extremists were given a free hand back in Vietnam. Sainteny, among others, vehemently denies that this was the case.

In Biarritz, where he first rested, in Paris and then at the conference in Fontainebleau, Ho enjoyed huge personal success. He charmed everyone, especially the press. He distributed roses to women reporters, signed his name in blood for an American male correspondent. He was widely compared to Confucius, to the Buddha, to St. John the Baptist, to anyone's doting grandfather, and it was noted that he was an ascetic, since, among other things, he refused to take a drink. Everywhere he went, whether to the opera, to a fancy reception, to a picnic, or to a press conference, he appeared in his simple, high-buttoned linen work suit. "As soon as one approaches this frail man, one shares the admiration of all men around him, over whom he towers with his serenity acquired from wide experience," wrote one reporter. Noting his "tormented face and his eyes of blue which burn with an inner light," another declared that he "hides a soul of steel behind a fragile body." His wit, his Oriental courtesy, his *savoir-faire*, his mixed profundity and playfulness in social intercourse, his open love for children, above all his seeming sincerity and simplicity, captured one and all.

Unfortunately, in point of accomplishment Ho's trip was far less successful. The fault, now generally admitted, was chiefly that of the French, who, while the conference went on, continued to violate its spirit by further fostering the idea of the separate south and central federation in Indochina. In Paris, the shakiness of the national government delayed the start of the sessions with Ho. He stayed at Biarritz to wait and go fishing. "The conference was fishy from the start," one of his delegates remarked. Sainteny later wrote that Ho was "reticent and nervous," but after playing pelota, roaming the countryside, and visiting Lourdes, he "found his smile again" and was "as affable and simple as before." When three leading Communists, including the Minister of Air, paid him a visit and commented, for propaganda purposes, about the "indescribable conditions" in which Ho was quartered at Biarritz, Ho announced that, on the contrary, he was "enchanted" by his stay on the Basque coast.

When he and Sainteny finally flew up to Paris for the start of the talks, Sainteny described him as "pale, eyes brilliant, and tight-throated," and he quoted Ho as saying, when the plane was settling down, "Above all, don't leave me, whatever you do." As the conference dawdled in the shadow of defeat, by now the result of the activities of the Vietminh extremists in Hanoi as well as of the French maneuvers in Cochin China, Ho grew more and more restless. Sainteny agreed he ought to return to Hanoi as soon as possible. "What would I be able to do if I went home empty-handed?" Ho asked. "Don't let me leave this way," he begged Sainteny and Marius Moutet, the Socialist Minister of Overseas Territories. "Arm me against those who would seek to displace me. You will not regret it." It was a sign)ficant plea, as significant as what Ho said on another evening to Sainteny and Moutet, "If we have to fight, we will fight. You will kill ten of our men and we will kill one of yours, and in the end it will be you who will tire of it."

At midnight on September 14, 1946, the frail figure of Ho Chi Minh, in its military tunic, walked out of the Hotel Royal-Monceau in Paris (the Fontainebleau sessions had ended) and strolled to Moutet's house nearby. There Ho and Moutet signed a *modus vivendi*, which, while it underlined Vietnamese (and some French) concessions for safeguarding French rights in Indochina, only postponed agreement on basic political questions; it at least placed upon the French the responsibility for restoring order in Cochin China. This was nothing more than had been agreed to in the spring and been vitiated since, but Ho publicly called the *modus vivendi* "better than nothing." He murmured to a security officer who accompanied him back to the hotel early in the morning, however, "I have just signed my death warrant."

Despite the failure of his mission, Ho, in his true cosmopolitan fashion, had enjoyed his stay in Paris, a city he had always loved. Years before, standing on a bridge across the Seine, he had remarked to a Communist comrade, "What a wonderful city, what a wonderful scene!" When his friend had replied that Moscow was also beautiful, Ho had said, "Moscow is heroic, Paris is the joy of living." During the 1946 conference, Ho had revisited some of his former haunts and, mixing socially with several foreign correspondents, had talked freely about himself and his politics. "Everyone has the right to his own doctrine," he had said. "I studied and chose Marx. Jesus said two thousand years ago that one should love one's enemies. That dogma has not been realized. When will Marxism be realized? I cannot answer. . . . To achieve a Communist society, big industrial and agricultural production is necessary. . . . I do not know when that will be realized in Vietnam, where production is low. We are not yet in a position to meet the conditions."

Ho's self-analysis, in relation to Indochina's development, is a markedly honest one, in Marxist terms. From the outset, Marxism was far more than a blueprint for him. It was a *logique*, and as one of the keenest Indochina scholars, Paul Mus, has pointed out, it was acquired by Ho as a vital Western weapon, an arsenal in fact, with which, as an Asian, he could combat his French masters. Ho, as a Marxist, was quick to appreciate how his country was being robbed, kept in economic penury by a purposefully unimaginative colonial power. While the French took out rubber or rice or whatever else they wanted and sold it in the world market at a high profit, the Vietnamese lived under a system in which only human labor and not money, in any international sense, counted; goods were in effect bartered for subsistence. Such an economic condition became the fulcrum of Ho's anger and drove him way back, almost inevitably, to Marxism and thence to Communism. "Ho had to build on what every Asian must build *per se*," Mus says, "a Western logic to deal with us Europeans. Whether it be a profession such as the law or medicine or what have you, an Asian must find this *logique* or be lost. Ho found it first in Marxism and he became a Leninist, since Lenin was faced in Russia with the same problem of the vacuum at the village level. Ho was successful because he remained true to Leninism and Marxism. In this sense, straightforward according to *his* view, he belongs to a proper fraternity."

Along with Sainteny, Mus is one of those Frenchmen who admit that France and the Western world missed a proper opportunity with Ho in 1946. Mus himself, as a French negotiator, met Ho a year later, and he has the same queer fondness for him most men who knew him have retained. "I have no reason, as a Frenchman, to like Ho for what he has done," Mus told me long afterward, "but still I like him. I am not afraid to say so. I like him for his strong mind. Although he is a great actor—one cannot afford to be naive with him—he does not go back on his word. He believes in the truth as he sees it. But he is a Marxist, and that is where we part company." He quotes Ho as telling him, in 1947, "My only weapon is anger. . . . I won't disarm my people until I trust you." Ho's willingness to deal with the French, Mus believes, was largely predicated on his need for French advice, above all for financial advisers. "Marxist doctrine calls for the proletarian state to use, at least temporarily, the accountancy of the bourgeois-capitalist countries," Mus says. Because of the inbred economy imposed by the Bank of Indochina, Ho knew that Vietnam could not stand on its own feet, either in terms of money or trade. He also knew he could not rely on the colonial French. His political approach was through metropolitan France. He wasn't convinced that this was his only chance, but he was determined to play the possibilities. He wavered between his affection and regard for France, which had given him his self in the Marxist image, and his new disillusion of 1946. "If we had supported him more strongly then," Mus added, "we might have won. . . . We thought we could crush him if it came to war. We did not appreciate how hard he could fight. But we must not forget that he really wanted an agreement with France at the time of Fontainebleau because it would have served him. That part of his motivation afterward died, of course, but we should understand that it existed at the time and that he was truly disappointed."

When Ho returned to Vietnam from France at the end of that sad 1946 summer, he was confronted with a difficult internal political situation. While the conflict between himself and the extremists was perhaps exaggerated, there is no doubt that the younger men around Ho, especially Giap and Dang Xuan Khu, had disapproved of his moderation and patience at Fontainebleau. They almost certainly wanted to move on to violence at once. Considerable conjecture about Ho's troubles with this group soon arose, and then shifted to speculation that ranged from rumors of Ho's retirement into mere figurehead status to the increasingly heard report, of which the French sporadically claimed proof, that he was dead. It is a fact that for many months he was not seen and was hardly mentioned, but what seems to have happened was this:

Ho became quite ill when he arrived back in Hanoi. He stayed in bed for several weeks. During this period, he may have been under some protective form of house arrest (British sources insist this was so); apparently he was surreptitiously moved in and out of a nearby jungle headquarters. Various elements within the Vietminh and out—among them the old pro-Chinese groups, for their own obvious purposes—openly accused Ho of having sold out to France with the *modus vivendi*, and tracts distributed in the Hanoi area bitterly attacked him. "When a man remains in foreign countries for a long while, he becomes their slave," one of them read. These were probably nothing more than the dying gasp of the pro-Chinese Vietnamese leaders, some of whom had already fled to China when Giap, with the departure of Chinese troops, unrestrainedly cracked down on them.

If Ho was temporarily and perhaps deliberately kept in the background, his eclipse did not last long. His policy of moderation was surely in evidence once more in the fall of 1946, when a constitution of surprising temperance, by Communist terms, was adopted. Two months later, in December, following the incident over customs control in Haiphong harbor and the outbreak of Vietminh terror and French Army reprisals in Hanoi, the war between the French and the Vietminh began. Both sides by then seemed not only ready but anxious to fight. Ho and his government fled into the jungle. However, by April, 1947, Ho's position as the commanding figure in the Vietminh was again supreme. It was in that month that Paul Mus traveled through the forest as a French emissary to meet Ho and offer him what amounted to terms of unconditional surrender. When Ho asked Mus if he—were he in Ho's place—would accept them, Mus admitted he wouldn't. "In the French Union there is no place for cowards," Ho then declared. "If I accepted those conditions, I should be one." Mus says it was completely obvious to him that Ho was running his own show, and that he had the power to reject the French offer without even having to consult the Tong Bo, the five-man Vietminh "politburo."

Even if Ho had had trouble with the extremists, if he had still at that time been a moderate hoping for a *rapprochement* with France, this would not have meant that he was not also, as he always has been in the final analysis, Moscow's man; the two Ho's were not incompatible, and much of what has since happened in the postwar world would seem to corroborate this. Moscow, as a matter of fact, may very well have intervened secretly to restore fully Ho's power and prestige; in substantiation of this theory is the belief that some of the other Vietminh leaders, notably Dang Xuan Khu, have always been under the influence of the Chinese Communists rather than Moscow-orientated. If Ho was torn, within himself and with relation to his followers, a little Moscow glue may have put him together again.

An interesting comment on Ho came at this time from none other than Bao Dai, whose brief tenure as Ho's adviser ended when he fled to Hong Kong, from which place the French would soon resurrect him to head an opposition government in the south. "During the few months I was in Hanoi as Supreme Counselor," Bao Dai said, "I saw Ho Chi Minh suffer. He was fighting a battle within himself. Ho had his own struggle. He realized Communism was not best for our country, but it was too late. Ultimately, he could not overcome his allegiance to Communism."

After Paul Mus's 1947 visit, no non-Communist Westerner is believed to have seen Ho in the jungle until late in 1954. On several occasions, however, he replied telegraphically to questions sent him by Western correspondents. What gradually evolved was a somewhat altered version of him. While he became more cynical and coy, he also became more folksy. "Uncle Ho," the patriarch, emerged. And as he increasingly became more anti-American, he hewed closer than ever to the Communist line, as handed down by Moscow and later by Peking as well. He continued, however, to speak the truth about himself, in his own peculiar lights. "When I was young, I studied Buddhism, Confucianism, Christianity, as well as Marxism," he once told a United Press questioner. "There is something good in each doctrine." Asked his opinion of American intentions in Asia, Ho snapped back, "Marshallization of the world." The Russians, he said, were "against Marshallization of the world." In the next breath, with sad truth, he declared that American aid "is a good thing if it goes directly to the people," thereby touching a sore spot inasmuch as the United States aid to the Vietnamese became a sensitive issue with the French in the south. Ho denied vehemently that Vietnam was or could become Russia's or anyone else's "satellite." He kept insisting he could remain neutral, "like Switzerland," in the world power struggle. "If the Chinese Communists offer you artillery and heavy mortars, would you accept them?" he was subsequently asked. Ho fell back on coyness. "What friendly advice would you give us in that case?" he wired back to his questioner. To a Siamese journalist who inquired, "Is there any truth in the rumors that Mao Tse-tung and you have set up a close relationship and that you favor Communism of the Moscow kind?" Ho replied—with an odd quality of dishonesty vis-à-vis his Asian questioner—"What is astonishing is that many intelligent foreigners believe these French slanders."

Events themselves belied Ho's last answer. There was no doubt that after 1950 he moved swiftly and snugly into the Moscow-Peking ideological camp.

As it evolved, the Vietminh emphasized the dominant role of the working class, in accordance with the decisions of the Asian and Australian Trade Union Conference held at Peking in November and December, 1949. Ho and Mao exchanged cables at that time, and soon thereafter eight hundred Vietnamese labor leaders met in rebel Indochina territory and, among panoplied pictures of Stalin, Mao, and Ho, demonstrated their total allegiance to Communism. Titoism was attacked, although when Yugoslavia quickly recognized Ho's regime, along with Soviet Russia and China, Ho had some embarrassing moments; he solved them typically, by pointing out that he had announced his readiness to establish relations with "any government" while at the same time continuing to blast Tito on the Vietminh jungle radio.

Early in 1951, when the Communists resumed their open leadership of the Vietminh movement, Ho lapsed into another period of silence. It was then that rumors of his death in the jungle again were heard. From time to time, Dang Xuan Khu, who became General Secretary of the new party, or someone else in the hierarchy, would publicly extol him. The tone grew reverential; a Ho myth in the milder image of a Stalin myth was reared, and a much tougher, more rigid Ho than he had ever made himself out to be slowly emerged. In 1953, Joseph Starobin, correspondent of the *Daily Worker* in New York, met Ho in the Tonkin jungle. He was not unexpectedly charmed by "the legendary president" who wore such simple peasant clothes and who knew so much about the world. Starobin rhapsodized: "As we sat there that first evening, these facets of the president's personality emerged. He was the world traveler, in whom each recollection of a crowded past was still vivid. He was the old-timer, the Communist leader of an older generation, for whom the lamps of memory needed only the reburnishing of conversation to become shiny and bright. There was also the Uncle Ho who works his own garden, types his own messages, teaches the four virtues—industriousness, frugality, justice and integrity—to the youth." Starobin was with Ho when Stalin died. He described the rapt jungle scene: "Crude benches illumined by candles set in a makeshift candelabra made out of bamboo; at the front was a portrait of Stalin wreathed in flowers . . . two violins played softly."

This touching bit of pastoral Stalinoidism was real enough in the context of the time, or real enough, at least, for so stalwart a Stalinist as Starobin; but it seems somehow doubtful that Ho took it quite so seriously or regarded it so poignantly. He was far too clever for that, and he had seen far too many of his old comrades purged by Stalin to render such an unqualifiedly touching response to the old tyrant's death. Nevertheless, it was certainly true that by this time the die had been cast, and that Ho, rejected by the West, no longer had any option—if one may assume that he had one earlier—but to attach himself firmly to the Communist camp. The wandering minstrel of Southeast Asia was home again, but there were to be many moments in the future when his relationship to the Communists, especially after the Sino-Soviet split, would once again be tenuous and difficult to define. Perhaps no one anywhere in the world would be called upon to perform such a unique balancing act between Moscow and Peking as the adroit old guerrilla, Nguyen Ai Quoc. For the moment, however, it is sufficient to reemphasize "what might have been" in that crucial year between August, 1945, when the big war ended, and July–September, 1946, when the abortive conference at Fontainebleau preceded by a few months the start of the Indochina war. This was the first important turning point in the unfortunate history of Indochina, and this, perhaps more than any other time, was when "the lost revolution" was actually lost.

2

The United States, Its Allies, and the Bao Dai Experiment

Mark Atwood Lawrence

WASHINGTON'S CAUTIOUS EMBRACE of Bao Dai in June 1949 reflected the Truman administration's growing conviction that Southeast Asia represented a new front in the struggle against communist expansion. A lengthy State Department study prepared for the National Security Council in July directly linked the Kremlin to the surge of unrest in Southeast Asia. "It is now clear," the report stated, "that SEA as a region has become the target of a coordinated offensive plainly directed by the Kremlin." There could be "little doubt," it added, "that the Kremlin seeks ultimate control over SEA as a pawn in the struggle between the Soviet World and the Free World." The paper asserted that Soviet leadership was willing to rely largely on the Chinese Communist Party to promote its agenda in Southeast Asia. Geographical proximity meant that that it was simply more feasible for the Chinese to take the lead, while the presence of eight million ethnic Chinese in Southeast Asia and greater Chinese experience with the two most salient issues underlying Southeast Asian unrest—nationalism and agrarian revolt—seemed to give them more influence in the area. The report insisted, however, that the Soviet government was determined to increase its own role in the region, not least because Moscow feared Chinese "hegemony" there.[1]

While specific evidence of Soviet ambitions remained scarce, the paper left no doubt that communist takeover of the region would be disastrous. It acknowledged that Southeast Asian nations had little "power potential" of their own and were unlikely to be a significant battleground in any U.S.-Soviet war. But economically, the report argued, Southeast Asia had a key role to play in sustaining successful worldwide resistance against communist expansion. "SEA is important to the free world as a source of raw materials, including rubber, tin and petroleum and as a crossroads in east-west and north-south global communications," the paper asserted. "It is therefore in our interest," it added, "to prevent these resources and passageways from falling under a control hostile to us." It was not that the United States itself depended heavily on Southeast Asian materials or shipping lanes. Rather, it was the destiny of three other parts of the world—Western Europe, Japan, and India—that seemed to hang in the balance. At the moment, the paper pointed out, military commitments in Southeast Asia made the region a net drain on the French and Dutch economies. The study left open the possibility, however, that a stable Southeast Asia could be an important economic advantage for Europe. Similarly, it asserted that a stable, Western-oriented Southeast Asia would help ease worries about looming food shortages in India and, most important of all, provide the markets and resources necessary to Japan's economic revival.[2]

Political and strategic considerations also pointed toward resisting communist takeovers in Southeast Asia. Mao's nearly completed victory in China represented a "grievous defeat" for the United States, asserted the State Department study. "If SEA also is swept by communism," it said, "we shall have suffered a major political rout the repercussions of which will be felt throughout the rest of the world, especially in the Middle East and in a then critically exposed Australia." The West therefore needed to stand its ground along China's southern periphery. "With China being overwhelmed by communism," the paper stated, "SEA represents a vital segment on the line of containment, stretching from Japan southward around to the Indian peninsula." The study predicted utter catastrophe if the line were not held, arguing:

> The security of the three major non-communist base areas in this quarter of the world—Japan, India, and Australia—depends in a large measure on the denial of SEA to the Kremlin. If SEA, particularly the Philippines and Indonesia, is lost, these three base areas will tend to be isolated from one another. If SEA is held, the links will exist for the development of an interdependent and integrated counter-force to Stalinism in this quarter of the world.[3]

All of these considerations led to the conclusion that the Viet Minh, with its avowedly communist leadership, represented a threat to U.S. interests. They did not, however, point to the conclusion that the United States should immediately throw its economic and military power behind the French war in Indochina. Indeed, the State Department report roundly condemned French decision making and expressed caution about deeper U.S. involvement on the French side. Old liberal concerns continued to weigh heavily in U.S. policymaking, especially the notion that French colonialism was responsible for generating the very threat of radicalism that Washington wished to oppose. Deploying the medical metaphor common in the early days of the Cold War, the paper argued that suppression of nationalist grievances was "no antidote to communism." On the contrary, a policy of force, by stirring up old anticolonial hatreds, was "an ideal culture for the breeding of the communist virus." Satisfying "militant nationalism," rather than quashing it, was "the first essential requirement for resistance to Stalinism," the State Department paper insisted. So far, it argued, the French government had failed to follow this path. After an "initial show of conciliation" in 1946, Paris had opted for a policy of naked force. When that failed, the paper continued, the French government opted for a political solution. But to date the French had shown more interest in establishing a "puppet regime" that would "allow France to retain its paramountcy" than in a solution that would realistically siphon support from the communists. "A constructive solution of the Indochina impasse depends on the French yielding their claims of sovereignty to a native regime," the study asserted.[4]

The report's expression of discouragement about French policy extended even to the suggestion that a French withdrawal in favor of Viet Minh rule might be preferable to the current state of affairs. Gratification of nationalist demands might, after all, lead to a future in many ways preferable to the "Stalinist blind alley down which French policy is now blundering." Clearly, however, the paper's authors preferred to see the Bao Dai solution succeed. To achieve this result, they proposed renewed U.S. pressure on the French government to implement the Bao Dai solution more fully and to offer additional concessions aimed at giving the former emperor a realistic chance of rivaling Ho Chi Minh for the mantle of leadership. The United States must, as the paper put it, "induce" the French "to adapt their policies to the realities of the current situation in Southeast Asia." Only with a truly independent nationalist government in power could a genuine commitment to resist communism sink "deep and extensive roots in the Indochinese scene," the report contended. Conditions would then be ripe for the United States to throw its weight behind the Vietnamese state. "It would then be necessary for us, working through a screen of anti-communist Asiatic, to ensure, however long it takes, the triumph of Indochinese nationalism over Red imperialism." At the same time, the paper urged that the United States carefully embed its policy in the region within a multilateral framework involving the British Commonwealth as well as independent Asian states, notably India and the Philippines. Washington, in other words, should avoid taking the lead in a way that might give rise to charges of U.S. imperialism or U.S. support for European domination.[5]

The State Department thus specified two conditions that had to be met before the United States would go further toward supporting French policy in Vietnam. The French government had to give further indications of its dedication to meaningful Vietnamese independence, and other Asian states had to pledge their support for the Bao Dai state. Without these prerequisites American officials doubted that U.S. material backing would help. "The overriding preoccupation of Vietnamese intellectuals and common people alike is the issue of independence," as another State Department study put it in September 1949. In the absence of propitious political circumstances, no amount of material aid, it seemed, would do much good. American insistence on further elaboration of the Bao Dai solution centered on the need for the National Assembly to approve the Elysée agreements. The legislature had approved Vietnamese unity—an important precondition for implementation of the Bao Dai policy—in May, but the fate of the Bao Dai agreements themselves remained uncertain. Sometimes U.S. ambitions ranged further, with officials expressing hope that the Elysée accords would be merely a starting point for further negotiations leading to full independence. Indeed, Secretary of State Acheson instructed George Abbott, the U.S. consul in Saigon, to make that view clear to the French high commissioner at the end of June. As an opening bid, the State Department pressed the French government to transfer responsibility for Indochina from the Ministry of Overseas France to the Foreign Ministry—a step that would highlight the Bao Dai regime's status as a sovereign government.[6]

For the most part, however, U.S. pressure focused on the more limited goal of Assembly ratification of the existing agreements—a move that became litmus test of the sincerity of French intentions in Vietnam. U.S. officials acknowledged that they could not press Paris too hard. Given the fragility of the French political scene, Washington had to avoid "riding rough-shod" over French "sensibilities" by demanding too much, as State Department officials put it. Antagonizing the French government, they warned, would risk hardening its attitude, provoking an internal political crisis damaging to the parties most cooperative with the United States, and even disrupting the cohesion of the nascent "Atlantic community." Still, Americans repeatedly hammered away on the need for Assembly ratification. Ambassador [David] Bruce insisted to Foreign Minister Robert Schuman at the end of June, for example, that the cabinet seek an early vote on the agreements and then dedicate itself to a "liberal and enlightened" interpretation of its provisions. In Saigon Abbott made a similar appeal, complaining to [Léon] Pignon's senior political adviser that on their face the Elysée agreements did not seem to contain "a single right accorded to the Vietnamese which was not limited in some way to [the] requirement for approval or consultation with [the] French." If Paris continued to drag its heels or refused to embrace a liberal interpretation of the agreements, Abbott and other Americans insisted, Vietnamese nationalists would never rally to Bao Dai.[7]

The second U.S. demand—that Asian nations must indicate their backing for Bao Dai—was still more ambitious. The Truman administration hoped to achieve this goal, partly through its own diplomatic pressure. It worked throughout 1949 and early 1950 not only to persuade the Indian, Philippine, Thai, and other governments to endorse the Vietnamese regime as a genuinely nationalist government but also to head off any actions that would call attention to its dependence on the Western powers. For example, the State Department worked strenuously in June to prevent the Dutch government from publicly endorsing Bao Dai, a move that Acting Secretary of State James Webb believed would fuel Soviet propaganda portraying Bao Dai as the "puppet of imperialists." U.S. officials believed, however, that they could do only so much to enhance Bao Dai's standing in Asia. For the most part, as Bruce insisted to Schuman, his success or failure in the eyes of Asian nationalists depended on French willingness to concede meaningful autonomy.[8]

The British government backed Washington in its two conditions. As usual, the Foreign Office was torn between conflicting objectives. With persistent disorder throughout Southeast Asia and the Chinese threat pressing against Tonkin, British policymakers believed more than ever that the French presence in Vietnam was critical to their country's economic and strategic interests in the Far East. Anxious to see the French military restore stability in Vietnam, some British officials were inclined to accept the Elysée accords as sufficiently liberal and to call for diplomatic recognition of the new state. In the view of Esler Dening, head of the Foreign Office's Southeast Asia division, the establishment of the new regime represented "a genuine effort on the part of the French to meet the nationalist aspirations of the Vietnamese" and, as such, deserved British support. In Saigon consul [Frank] Gibbs was especially anxious to extend British backing for French policy by officially recognizing Bao Dai, proposing as early as April 1949 that the Foreign Office begin exploring the possibility. When Bao Dai formally requested recognition by several Western and Asian nations in late August, Gibbs and several other British diplomats in the Far East advocated "de facto" recognition pending ratification of the Elysée accords by the National Assembly. After that, they urged, British recognition should become "de jure."[9]

Familiar considerations deterred the British government from taking any bold, unilateral step. For one thing, British policymakers feared that overzealous support for French policy would damage British relations with Commonwealth governments that remained skeptical of Bao Dai. Indian and Burmese objections to the Bao Dai solution were longstanding, while the Australian and New Zealand governments remained to be convinced that the policy would help to resolve, rather than to inflame, a Southeast Asian situation that seemed increasingly to menace their security. But it was the attitude of the United States that weighed most heavily in British calculations with regard to Bao Dai. Foreign Office policymakers believed that Britain's best hope of achieving its long-held aim of gaining U.S. support for British objectives in Indochina and elsewhere in the region depended on satisfying Washington's insistence that Paris quickly advance the Bao Dai policy and that Asian nations take the lead in forming an anticommunist coalition. The second condition seemed especially important in view of the possibility that Britain might use its considerable influence in Asia to promote the American objective. "Only if we show our willingness and ability to bring about greater Asian solidarity," a Foreign Office memorandum asserted in August 1949, "will the Americans be prepared to assist or come into any regional arrangements."[10]

In the second half of 1949, British officials saw mixed prospects of success in their bid to attract U.S. involvement. On the positive side, they recognized the rapid evolution of American attitudes toward Southeast Asia. Both public and official opinion in the United States seemed to be moving steadily in the direction of accepting a commitment to fight communism in Asia. Eventual American membership in a "Pacific Pact" or some other kind of organization involving both Asian and Western nations seemed to be possible. Above all, the Washington embassy reported, the Chinese Communists' looming victory was generating a strong sense within the Truman administration that the United States needed to "do something" about the spread of communism in Asia. Most promising of all, the Republican-controlled U.S. Congress was beginning to press the administration to spend $75 million previously allocated for the Chinese Nationalists on assistance for other Asian nations threatened by communism. In September the State Department issued a public declaration supporting the principle of Asian independence while warning against the dangers of communism and promising American aid for countries attempting to resist outside aggression. At last, a consensus seemed to be forming behind U.S. aid for Southeast Asia.[11]

The impact of Mao's victory on U.S. policy was not altogether clear, however, and some British officials, like their French colleagues, worried that it would render Washington more reluctant, rather than more eager, to take an active role elsewhere on the Asian continent. One Foreign Office report noted in August that the State Department, stung by the China debacle, was "holding aloof" from Southeast Asia because of reluctance to make any new commitments in a part of the world where the political tide seemed to be running against the West. The apparent American preference for a "perimeter defense" of island bases only encouraged British fears that the United States would choose to leave Southeast Asia as a problem for the Europeans to solve on their own.[12] Even if Washington did come forward with aid, Dening worried that it would be too little, too late. "We must not run away with the idea," Dening wrote,

> that because the Americans are now taking an increased interest in the state of South East Asia they are in a position to furnish large quantities of dollars to meet the needs of that area. Our studies show that the bill is virtually unlimited, but even when we have narrowed it down to those projects which really merit support, it is doubtful whether United States aid will be forthcoming in sufficient volume to meet what is required.

Chances of gaining American support in Vietnam seemed especially slim. The new British ambassador in Washington, Oliver Franks, reported in November 1949 that the State Department, anxious to avoid another China imbroglio and uncertain how to balance its conflicting interests, had "thrown up its hands in despair over Indochina." Under the circumstances, mounting evidence of French military inadequacies seemed more likely to dissuade Washington from deeper involvement than to encourage it. R. H. Scott, chief of the Foreign Office's Southeast Asia division, anxiously reported in November that American diplomats were convinced that French forces in Vietnam would soon be forced to withdraw into the main cities.[13]

British officials complained bitterly about the slow evolution of U.S. policy. Commissioner-General [Malcolm] MacDonald, perhaps the British official most eager for a major U.S. commitment in Southeast Asia, charged at the end of 1949 that Washington showed "inadequate appreciation" of the urgency of the situation in Indochina. U.S. policy, he complained, was "developing much too slowly."[14] Most, however, held out hope that Washington, even if a major disappointment so far, would soon provide what was needed. Skillful diplomacy, they believed, might bring results. "The present is probably a favorable opportunity for influencing the State Department in the way in which the United Kingdom would like them to go," wrote J. F. Ford, a senior adviser at the embassy in Washington. In London the government considered its ultimate goal—a combination of British ideas and U.S. resources—to be within reach. "It should not be impractical to maintain the political influence of the United Kingdom in South East Asia while arranging for the United States to provide much of the capital investment that was required," the cabinet concluded at a late October meeting.[15]

The key to winning active American support for Bao Dai clearly lay in convincing Washington that its final conditions for doing so were being met. For that reason British diplomats supported American efforts to apply pressure on the French government to ratify the Elysée accords and to implement them liberally. British officials left no doubt of their fundamental support for France. The Foreign Office readily approved MacDonald's proposal in September that he visit Saigon later in the year as a sign of British support for French policy.[16] In private, too, British policymakers expressed sympathetic understanding for the political constraints on the French government and worried that granting too much autonomy to Bao Dai would only compound Paris's problems. Yet British diplomats also recognized the need to do whatever it took to win American involvement and repeatedly stressed to French counterparts the necessity of submitting the accords for speedy ratification and interpreting the agreements liberally. In talks with Foreign Minister Schuman and Secretary of State Acheson in November 1949, [Foreign Secretary Ernest] Bevin asserted that the "immediate obstacle" to British recognition of Bao Dai was the French failure to ratify the Elysée agreements. Once the Assembly had acted, Bevin asserted, London would "take the necessary steps."[17]

British officials were even more fully committed to satisfying American insistence that Asians, rather than Westerners, be the first to throw their support behind Bao Dai—a stipulation that meshed neatly with London's longstanding determination to cater to Asian nationalist opinion. "If the countries of South East Asia, such as India, Siam or the Philippines, could be persuaded to take the initiative, we and the United States could follow suit without fear of giving the impression of too much ganging up of the Western powers in this part of the world," wrote Donald Hopson, an aide in the British consulate in Saigon. Efforts to generate regional collaboration moved ahead on two tracks. First, the Foreign Office sought to use Commonwealth mechanisms to create embryonic forms of international cooperation that non-Commonwealth nations could join later. At a conference in Singapore in November 1949, British colonial administrators and diplomats agreed that the Commonwealth should move urgently to build economic cooperation as a near-term method of countering communist expansion. Over the longer term, the meeting concluded, Britain should aim to form a "regional pact" grouping Commonwealth nations, especially Australia and New Zealand, with the North Atlantic powers and independent Asian governments such as Thailand, the Philippines, and Vietnam.[18]

The second strand of Britain's regional policy consisted of diplomatic efforts to persuade Asian governments to take a positive view of Bao Dai. Unsurprisingly, the Foreign Office focused its efforts on New Delhi, the biggest potential prize among Asian regimes. British observers expected that, if [Indian Prime Minister Jawaharlal] Nehru embraced Bao Dai as a genuine nationalist alternative in Vietnam, other Asian regimes would follow suit. Following Bao Dai's return to Vietnam and his inauguration on June 14, the British high commissioner in India detected some softening of Nehru's attitude toward French policy. The U.S. statement of support for Bao Dai rekindled Indian hostility, however, and Nehru lodged new complaints about Western interference in Indochina. Nehru persisted in his view that the Viet Minh was essentially a nationalist movement. "One of the main difficulties" in Anglo-Indian relations, reported one British diplomat passing through Delhi at the beginning of August, "was the reluctance of the Indians in high places, and particularly of Pandit Nehru himself, to believe that Ho Chi Minh was really a Communist." Stymied by Indian firmness, British diplomats resigned themselves to a long campaign to change Nehru's mind.[19]

By fall 1949 U.S. diplomats were working along the same lines. Just like Foreign Office personnel, U.S. representatives pressured Nehru to throw his support behind Bao Dai, repeatedly pointing to Moscow's pro-Viet Minh statements as evidence of Ho Chi Minh's affinity for Stalin. When Nehru insisted that the Vietnamese people must be allowed to choose Ho's leadership if they liked, Dean Acheson contended that no free people had ever chosen communism; all communist regimes, he asserted, were imposed by conspiratorial cliques. Such blandishments brought no results. Indian foreign secretary Sir Girja Bajpai told a British diplomat in December that New Delhi had no intention of using its influence on Bao Dai's behalf. So far, Bajpai complained, the French government's only objective in Vietnam seemed to be "to hold onto the imperialist position they had before the war."[20] Elsewhere in Asia, things went little better.

By the end of the year, only Ceylon had responded favorably, sending Bao Dai a message of "good wishes." Elsewhere the boldest step toward regional cooperation against communism was hardly what London and Washington had in mind. In July Chiang Kai-shek, newly established in Taiwan, South Korean strongman Syngman Rhee, and Philippine president Elpidio Quirino proposed formation of a "Pacific Pact" centered on their triumvirate. Washington immediately dismissed the idea, not only because Chiang's role would alienate other Asian nations but also because the proposal was an obvious scheme to extract aid from the United States. Not even the Thai government, despite its eagerness for U.S. aid, showed signs of interest in backing Bao Dai. The former emperor was proving to be merely a "French puppet," the Thai ambassador in Washington told State Department officials in December.[21]

French supporters of the war grew increasingly anxious as these time-consuming diplomatic initiatives unfolded. To be sure, the French government was gratified by small alterations in U.S. policy. Despite persistent reservations, the State Department acquiesced to French pressure in the late summer by permitting Paris to transfer U.S.-manufactured equipment to Southeast Asia without explicit permission.[22] From the vantage point of French generals in Indochina, however, far more was required. The French command insisted that the arrival of some twenty thousand Chinese Communist troops at the Tonkin border during the fall made it vital to achieve a diplomatic breakthrough before long. In fact, the command in Saigon calculated that without significant international help, French forces would be unable to hold their positions in Tonkin. French hawks also worried about plummeting morale among French troops, a trend they attributed to low pay and lack of equipment. As usual, the situation promised only to worsen. In November the Minister of Overseas France, Jean Letourneau, ordered Pignon to cut French spending in Indochina, asserting that "all economies [and] all reorganizations must be studied." Faced with these circumstances, the military and the High Commission urged the ministries in Paris to do all they could to close ranks with the United States and Britain. Hoping for the best, the French command continued drafting lists of equipment that it hoped to obtain from the United States. Around the same time, it handed British officers in Singapore a similar wish list, including ammunition of various kinds, several varieties of vehicles, landing craft, and radios.[23]

Rigid limits remained, however, on how far the French government could go to satisfy U.S. and British demands. The cabinet clearly wanted the Assembly to ratify the Elysée accords as much as Washington or London. The Bao Dai solution was, after all, the linchpin of the whole effort by the French hawks to keep the war going. But the political situation in Paris remained extraordinarily fragile in 1949. And Assembly endorsement remained problematic. The Socialists once again demonstrated their unreliability during a party conference in July, when the rank and file endorsed a proposal calling for an UN-brokered armistice and, in a clear bid to reopen the possibility of dealing with Ho Chi Minh, for negotiations with "all elements of Viet Nam, without excluding anyone."[24] With the Gaullists and Communists stridently opposed to government policy, the cabinet remained cautious about bringing the matter to a vote. But there were deeper reasons for the government's resistance to U.S. and British demands. Those who supported Bao Dai and wished to see the Elysée accords approved did not, after all, share the American view that those agreements should be liberally implemented, much less that they should be the starting point for further concessions to bao Dai. The MRP [Mouvement Républicain Populaire]-dominated ministries that presided over the Bao Dai solution accepted the longstanding assumptions underpinning French exertions in the Far East; their country's standing as a global power depended on its position in Southeast Asia, and any climb down there would inevitably call into question French rule in North Africa and other parts of the

French empire. Full independence for the Indochinese states was simply incompatible with fundamental French geostrategic objectives.

Accordingly, French concessions to U.S. and British pressure during 1949 were modest at best. Most were targeted at easing criticism alleging that France was denying the Bao Dai state the right to conduct an independent foreign policy. In August French authorities arranged for Bao Dai to send letters notifying other Asian governments of the formation of the new Vietnamese state and its readiness to "participate in international life." Similar letters were sent to Washington and several European capitals shortly thereafter. The new government followed this gesture by dispatching "goodwill missions" to India and Thailand. In October the Bao Dai government, thanks to strong French support, won associate membership in ECAFE, the UN economic development organization for the Far East. Even if French advisers retained a prominent place in any future Vietnamese delegation to the organization, Vietnamese membership suggested at least a semblance of independence.[25] Beyond that, though, French leaders would not go. They dismissed the possibility of supporting Vietnamese membership in the United Nations. The French government refused in August even to allow Bao Dai to send a note to the United Nations secretariat notifying the organization of his government's establishment. Similarly, the French cabinet barred Vietnamese representatives from taking part as an independent delegation in regional conferences of international bodies such as the International Monetary Fund, the World Bank, the International Labor Organization, and the World Health Organization. In internal correspondence, French authorities left no doubt of their fear that Bao Dai would use any autonomy he was given to escape French control. When the new government sought to take advantage of its new latitude in the fall by sending an unofficial delegation to meet with State Department officials in Washington, French officials in Saigon insisted that the mission be carefully monitored in case it sought to obtain U.S. political support against France or to arrange U.S. aid in a way that bypassed the French government.[26]

The challenge for French officials lay in convincing Washington and London that Paris had gone far enough to merit substantial foreign backing. As so often in the past, French diplomats strongly accentuated the positive in hopes of tipping the balance in foreign capitals. In Saigon Pignon urged new efforts around the world to highlight the degree of independence enjoyed by the Bao Dai regime. "It seems to me," he urged, "that we should underscore that the [autonomy] offered by the French government on the diplomatic matter will always be very significant." If France had denied Vietnam certain privileges, Pignon suggested, it was only to "avoid wide divergences" between French policy and the policy of a small state with limited international experience. For his own part, Pignon announced to the Foreign Ministry his intention, "in order to deprive our adversaries in America and India of easy arguments to use against us, to give as much publicity as possible to the transfer of authority that has been or will soon be carried out by the High Commission." French officials also sought to downplay restrictive aspects of the Elysée accords by suggesting that some of them were necessary in order to win political support for the agreements in Paris and were not intended to be permanent. In response to U.S. pressure for ratification, meanwhile, Foreign Minister Schuman promised in summer 1949 to submit the accords to the Assembly before its term ended in October. When that date passed without action, Schuman promised ratification no later than mid-January 1950. Meanwhile, he gave favorable, if vague, responses in late 1949 to U.S. insistence on expanding Bao Dai's diplomatic powers and shifting responsibility for Indochinese affairs to the Foreign Ministry.[27]

At a ministerial meeting in Paris in November 1949, Schuman deployed these and other arguments in an effort to meet U.S. and British pressure with some counter pressure of his own. France had acted "with determination" to defend against communist expansion but was now,

Schuman told Acheson and Bevin, running into "great administrative, military and financial difficulties" because of the enormity of the task at hand. At present, the military situation was "relatively good," but he could not predict, Schuman added ominously, "what would happen if two to three hundred thousand Communist troops were just across the frontier and if they were co-operating with Ho Chi Minh in his subversive activities." The foreign minister added that Bao Dai was prepared to "proceed on his own initiative" to build a state capable of resisting communist expansion. But, Schuman asserted, Bao Dai was "given over to much reflexion and required a lot of assurances." The former emperor also "worried about whether French policy with respect to him was supported and approved by the Governments of Great Britain and the United States." These circumstances, said Schuman, led him to pose a question: would the U.S. and British governments inform Bao Dai that they "approved of him and French policy toward him?" Schuman said he understood that Washington and London would not extend diplomatic recognition until after the assembly had approved the Elysée accords. But Schuman, according to Bevin's record of the meeting, "urged once more upon us the importance which he attached to an expression of good will from our governments."[28]

Recognition

In the final weeks of 1949, then, the French government and its key Western partners reached a new deadlock over Vietnam. Paris demanded that Washington and London offer a gesture of support for Bao Dai and insisted that he could not succeed without it. In the French view, American insistence on additional concessions was meaningless since without some sort of immediate Western endorsement, the Bao Dai experiment would not survive long enough to make the ultimate degree of self-government enjoyed by the new state a relevant topic. U.S. officials, generally backed by their British counterparts, viewed matters differently. Only if the French government clearly laid out a plan for full Vietnamese autonomy could Bao Dai succeed in winning the support of his people. And only when he had succeeded in doing that would other nations embrace him as a legitimate ruler deserving international support. In this view any quick move by Washington or London to endorse Bao Dai would inevitably seem to be merely part of a Western bid to establish a puppet regime and to deny the Vietnamese, once again, control over their own destiny. Indisputably, the three Western governments had greatly narrowed their differences over the previous two years. All three spoke of the need for recognition of Bao Dai and the need for an international partnership in Southeast Asia that would bring material assistance for political movements fighting communism. But the conditions under which these steps would be taken remained a source of sharp disagreement.

To French disappointment, the diplomatic letters that Bao Dai sent to various Asian and Western capitals in August yielded meager results. In Asia the governments in New Delhi, Colombo, Bangkok, and Manila continued to express grave reservations about Bao Dai's prospects and resentment against French methods, both military and diplomatic. Even in Thailand, the nation most amenable to the idea of endorsing Bao Dai, French efforts failed. Indeed, they were counterproductive, producing a minor diplomatic clash. Following receipt of Bao Dai's letter, the Thai foreign ministry accused the French embassy in Bangkok of attempting to trick the government into publicly endorsing Bao Dai by claiming that other Southeast Asian nations had already done so.[29] In Europe and North America the situation was hardly more promising. By the end of the fall, only the Vatican had responded favorably to Bao Dai's initiative by replying with its own letter vowing support for the new Vietnamese state. Meanwhile, the

British government, apparently determined to avoid moving ahead of the Americans, decided against replying to Bao Dai's letter on the grounds that it did not yet recognize the Vietnamese regime and therefore should not correspond directly. Instead, the London government offered informal assurances through the British embassy in Paris of general backing for French policy. The Truman administration similarly decided against replying to the letter, reasoning that Bao Dai's Vietnam was not yet an independent state.

For French advocates of the *politique de force*, such a feeble response came as a grave disappointment. "The reestablishment of confidence [in French policy] in the West is the basis of success for our entire policy," Pignon wrote in late December. With Chinese Communist forces now ensconced across the Tonkin border, U.S. and British material support was more critical than ever to French plans to keep the war going. Although the Chinese showed no signs of overt intervention in Vietnam, the prospect of Chinese–Viet Minh cooperation nevertheless loomed. With military problems mounting, the French government focused above all on Western recognition for Bao Dai's government—a step that French officials saw as a stepping stone to the broader objective of military partnership. Still more important, Western recognition seemed certain to bolster the French government's chances of winning Assembly ratification of the Elysée agreements. Support from French allies thus remained the key to avoiding political defeat domestically—a situation that was hardly lost on astute observers of the French policymaking scene. In London Foreign Secretary Bevin concluded that the French government hoped to use Western recognition of Bao Dai as a "lever" in the Assembly. The French, Bevin suggested, wanted U.S. and British recognition "so they could present a 'fait accompli' to the Assembly and the Assembly would have to ratify the Elysée agreements."[30]

To accomplish these objectives, French diplomats insisted to U.S. and British counterparts that the best way to strengthen Bao Dai in the eyes of other Asian governments was to lend him their recognition first—a reversal of the timetable preferred by many U.S. officials who insisted that any indications of U.S. support must follow gestures of support by Asians. Asian governments, insisted French officials, would regard Bao Dai as capable of surviving in power, and therefore worthy of their support, only if he had Western backing. At the moment, as Pignon put it, the whole matter was caught in a "vicious cycle." Western governments demanded evidence that Bao Dai would be accepted as a legitimate nationalist leader by Asian opinion before they would embrace him, but Asian nations as well as ordinary Vietnamese nationalists would regard him as a good bet only if he had Western support. French officials appealed to U.S. and British counterparts to break the cycle. "Genuine nationalists would be encouraged to join in with Bao Dai and the Western powers in opposition to Chinese communism if they had the impression that the Western powers were really serious about it all," Pignon's senior political adviser told British embassy aides in Paris.[31]

French officials accompanied this line of argument with assurances that any constraints on Bao Dai's autonomy were probably temporary and would be reconsidered once the military crisis had subsided. The indefinite postponement of further concessions enabled the French government to avoid specific commitments while offering foreign opinion some hope that demands for further reforms would be accommodated. In this way, French officials sought to turn the severe problems confronting the French military to their advantage. Premature concessions, they insisted, would harm the Western cause in Vietnam by weakening the military effort at precisely the moment when strength and cohesion were most urgent. Pignon suggested to Paris that the government inform U.S. representatives that "we would be ready, *once the crisis is passed,* to give the Vietnamese a more complete political, diplomatic and administrative independence than they now have."[32] Through the fall, diplomats stressed that greater autonomy could not be transferred quickly because of the danger of contributing to the chaos in Vietnam. During a trip to Paris, for example, Pignon told U.S. ambassador Bruce that Asian leaders had "neither the strength of character, nor the necessary cohesion," to resist communism "without a minimum of Western guidance." The terms of the Elysée accords could not therefore "be considered a subject for revision as long as the current international crisis in the Far East persists," Pignon argued. His political adviser, Robert du Gardier, struck much the same theme in Saigon, telling British diplomats that the Elysée accords were "only a temporary measure while the civil war continued."[33]

If France seemed stingy, diplomats emphasized, it was only in order to serve the broader Western interest in putting up effective resistance against communist encroachment. "The situation has gone well beyond the defense of French interests," Foreign Minister Schuman told Acheson during a meeting in September. "We are blamed and even penalized instead of supported," he complained. Two months later Schuman returned to the same theme, telling Acheson and Foreign Secretary Bevin that France was "erecting a barrier against the advance of Communism" and required the assistance of its allies. Indeed, the French government began in November to press Washington and London for public declarations stating that they not only backed Bao Dai but would also come to the aid of France in the event of a Chinese attack on Indochina. Pignon turned up the rhetorical heat further in January 1950. In a meeting with U.S. special ambassador Philip Jessup, the high commissioner insisted that while France was actively working to counter the "constant dynamism of the Soviet bloc," the "great democratic states" were conspicuously failing to show the same will by coming to the aid of a loyal ally.[34]

Under the circumstances, French diplomats insisted that the Western powers must not demand perfection. There had been plenty of occasions in the past, Pignon noted in internal correspondence, when Washington and London had recognized new quasi-independent governments "for reasons of opportunity." In the Vietnam case, they must be led to do so again. The High Commission in Saigon and the French embassy in London were especially hopeful that the British government might recognize Bao Dai without its conditions being met in advance. Du Gardier appealed to Ashley-Clarke in late October "not to be too legalistic in the matter of recognition," arguing that Britain had often experimented with in-between forms of independence in its own empire. "At its inception," du Gardier argued, "the British Commonwealth was full of features which were not easily capable of logical explanation." France, he continued, was "trying to work out something analogous and there were bound to be anomalies and imperfections, especially since the experiment was being made in an area which was in a state amounting to civil war."[35] To accentuate progress to date, French authorities in Saigon planned an elaborate ceremony to mark the formal handover of administrative authority to Bao Dai on December 31. The occasion carried little real significance, but it bore the trappings of a landmark event. More than fifty thousand people gathered in front of the Saigon city hall to hear self-congratulatory speeches by Bao Dai and Léon Pignon. As usual, of course, the most important audiences sat thousands of miles away in London and Washington.

By the turn of the year, French officials sometimes sprinkled their efforts at persuasion with threats. If the United States failed to act in Vietnam, they made clear, Paris might be left with no choice but to pull out of the country altogether—an eventuality that, it went without saying, would result in either an immediate communist victory or the transfer of the entire mess into American hands. Such threats reflected awareness among French officials that their military effort in Vietnam, no matter how fraught with problems, gave them leverage over Washington. By December 1949 they were willing to use it. In talks with U.S. consul Abbott in Saigon, Pignon warned of mounting "lassitude" among French public opinion as losses mounted in Vietnam—

a warning that France would not be willing to shoulder the burden in Vietnam for much longer by itself. The high commissioner's aide was more explicit: "Du Gardier claims to be much worried over [the] growing number of influential French whose reaction to this situation is 'to hell with it, let's pull out of Indochina, lock, stock and barrel,'" Abbott reported. Ambassador Bruce warned in January that French officials were "occasionally" raising this specter in Paris as well, while in London French embassy personnel asserted ominously that 1950 would be the "last chance" for the Western powers to bolster the French war effort.[36]

It is difficult to establish whether French decision makers seriously contemplated withdrawal. Unquestionably, though, U.S and British policymakers saw good reason to take seriously the risk of a French pullout. The possibility of French withdrawal from Tonkin had long ago come to the attention of foreign officials. In addition, U.S. and British officials perceived in 1950 that the Indochina war, now three years old was beginning to generate fierce opposition within France. In 1947 and 1948 the French left, consumed with economic and political crises closer to home, remained relatively inattentive to Vietnam policy. In the second half of 1949, however, surging antiwar dissent inside France began to attract attention internationally. British and American wire services reported a steady diet of stories about acts of defiance against government policy. In August Dunkerque dockworkers voted to stop work for two hours each day on a French cargo ship bound for Indochina and called on their colleagues elsewhere to do the same. At the end of October, Marseilles longshoremen belonging to the Communist-led Confédération Générale du Travail declared that they would no longer load arms and munitions on ships bound for Indochina. The following weeks produced new reports of unrest in Marseilles as well as evidence of growing dissent among French intellectuals. On December 27 the *New York Times* reported that a group of prominent leftists, including the writer André Gide, had written a letter to President Auriol protesting French policy and urging a UN-supervised plebiscite to resolve outstanding problems.[37]

By the turn of the year, key British policymakers concluded that the time had come for London to make a final push to overcome remaining obstacles to an Anglo-French-U.S. partnership in Indochina. While most still insisted on ratification of the Elysée accords—an event that seemed probable once a new French legislative session opened in January—the British government backed away from its support of Washington's other demands, including insistence that Asian recognition of Bao Dai had to precede any such step by Western nations. French insistence, along with the consolidation of Communist control in southeastern China, emboldened British officials to take this step. London was also motivated by its new determination to grant full diplomatic recognition for the new Communist regime in China. Concerned about protecting British rights in Hong Kong and keeping channels of communication open with Mao's regime, the Attlee government decided to set aside its distaste for the new Chinese leadership and take that step as soon as possible. The issue quickly became intertwined with the Vietnam problem. The Foreign Office calculated that Western recognition of Mao's regime without recognition for Bao Dai might amount to a stinging affront to the French government while undercutting the new Vietnamese state in the eyes of both the Vietnamese people and Asian opinion more broadly. The cabinet concluded that the best course was to grant recognition to both governments at the same time.

Another factor also contributed to changing British calculations at the end of 1949: a burst of enthusiasm for Bao Dai from Malcolm MacDonald, the British commissioner-general in Singapore. Previously skeptical of Bao Dai, MacDonald came away from a visit to Saigon in late November proclaiming to both London and foreign diplomats that Bao Dai was no mere puppet. It is impossible to know whether MacDonald, a fierce anti-communist, was sincerely impressed or simply believed that Britain must adopt a more active policy in Vietnam. In any case, he claimed in a cable to the Foreign Office that Bao Dai had a better than 50 percent chance of success in his bid to draw support away from Ho Chi Minh and create a viable Vietnamese state. MacDonald wrote that Bao Dai was not the "dull dog" that he was commonly believed to be. Rather, he was, as MacDonald put it, a "talkative, intelligent and charming" man, full of "physical courage and patriotism." The Foreign Office, in turn, passed along MacDonald's appraisal to the U.S. embassy. R. H. Scott, chief of the Foreign Office's Southeast Asia department, told an American diplomat that MacDonald had been "very much impressed with Bao Dai whom he considers a person of integrity and charm and altogether worthy of the support of the British government." Although Bao Dai was "not brilliant," Scott continued, "he was nobody's fool."[38] MacDonald's appraisal hardly amounted to a ringing endorsement, but with London teetering on the brink of moving ahead with a more assertive policy in Indochina, it helped create a more upbeat atmosphere.

For all these reasons, the British government took bold steps toward supporting Bao Dai in the closing days of 1949. First, Bevin promised Paris that Britain would grant "de facto" recognition for the new government immediately after a meeting of Commonwealth prime ministers at the end of January. To announce the British decision ahead of that meeting, Foreign Office officials agreed, would diminish the chance of convincing other Commonwealth nations to follow suit. Although French officials worried that British recognition of Mao Zedong's government would distract attention from Vietnam, they nevertheless expressed satisfaction that at last they had achieved one of their major diplomatic objectives.[39] They may have taken particular pleasure in the fact that the British government made its intentions public. Western media reported during December 1949 that London would move toward recognition of Bao Dai on roughly the same schedule as it proceeded toward recognition of Mao Zedong.[40]

Those promises raised the prospect of other types of British assistance. In the second half of December, the British government showed new willingness to begin close military cooperation with France in Southeast Asia. Although the cabinet ruled out sending British troops to Vietnam, commanders in Singapore agreed to hold staff talks with French counterparts in Saigon with a view to coordinating French and British defense policy and even establishing a combined staff to plan for the possibility of Chinese aggression.[41] Old reservations about close Anglo-French cooperation lingered in the background. The British Far Eastern Command stipulated that the staff talks must focus on determining what assistance the French would need to resist external aggression and insisted that Britain would not involve itself in maintaining internal security. Moreover, the Foreign Office insisted that the talks not commit Britain beyond what its resources would allow or sacrifice the principal objective it had sought for more than five years—partnership with the United States. On the latter point, Scott insisted that the staff talks must under no circumstances alienate Washington by, for example, committing British and French forces, without American knowledge, to a potentially major undertaking that would inevitably rely on U.S. equipment. Furthermore, Scott insisted that London and Paris must do everything they could to involve the United States in the talks. "Without American participation," he wrote, "the defense of Indochina cannot be guaranteed."[42]

Despite these reservations, the British government had taken a dramatic step away from its earlier support for the conditions imposed by the United States for backing Bao Dai. London was rapidly closing ranks with the French government. Instead of insisting that Asian governments take the lead in recognizing the new state, the Attlee government was now ready to act unconditionally. "In view of the urgency of the situation Western nations cannot afford to await prior sponsorship of Bao Dai by the Asiatic nations" before taking action themselves, British diplomats agreed at a meeting in Singapore in mid-November.[43] In conversations with French counterparts, British officials sometimes pressed for additional concessions such as a declaration of future French intentions in Vietnam. But internally, the assumption increasingly took hold that, once the French National Assembly had acted, Britain would move quickly toward recognition. That shift, effectively abandoning insistence that France offer additional concessions, left the Truman administration alone in requiring conditions.

In Washington, however, the tide was also changing. To be sure, American officials continued to express anxiety about the inadequacy of French policy. Secretary of State Acheson insisted publicly throughout the fall that Bao Dai could succeed only if he were assured genuine autonomy.[44] As late as November the State Department's Southeast Asia division still weighed the possibility of involving the United Nations. Distrustful of French intentions, division head Charles Reed suggested that a UN commission might be appointed to oversee the transfer of powers to the Bao Dai government according to a timetable established through new negotiations between the French government and the former emperor.[45] Such schemes became increasingly fanciful, however, as French and British pressure mounted for a firm American commitment of support for the Bao Dai experiment as currently conceived.

French and British arguments in favor of Western partnership in Vietnam increasingly found favor among U.S. decision makers desperate by December to do something about worsening conditions in Southeast Asia. From Paris Ambassador Bruce insisted that the tumultuous state of French politics meant certain doom for any French government that promised full independence for Vietnam. At the moment, the Bao Dai solution was the best a moderate, Western-oriented government would be able to offer, Bruce asserted. Contributing to U.S. worries about moves that might inadvertently strengthen the French Communist Party, American diplomats in France reported at the end of the year that party propaganda was increasingly concentrated on exploiting popular discontent over the war in Vietnam. Meanwhile, the mounting threat from Communist China lent credibility to the French position that it was impossible to concede more autonomy to Bao Dai as long as a grave state of emergency persisted in Vietnam. Limitations on Vietnamese sovereignty established in the Elysée agreements could be "gradually removed when peaceful conditions [are] restored," asserted Bruce. Under wartime conditions, he added, there was no chance that the French government could accede to U.S. pressure for a timetable leading to full independence.[46]

At the same time, American officials eager to reorient U.S. policy followed MacDonald in offering unprecedented upbeat appraisals of Bao Dai. Despite the lack of evidence that Bao Dai was in fact gaining ground, [W.]Walton Butterworth, chief of the State Department's Far East office, asserted in late November that "under certain circumstances," Bao Dai might be successful and that he deserved American support. "Because the odds are heavily against a horse entered in a given race," Butterworth added, "is no reason to withdraw that horse from the race, although I agree that there is likewise no reason in these circumstances to back that horse heavily." Here Butterworth came close to validating the logic so strenuously advanced by French officials: Bao Dai would have some chance with immediate international assistance but no chance without it. Acheson wrote a month later that Bao Dai, although "far from being a success at the present moment," was nonetheless "stronger today than was anticipated six months ago."[47]

Reappraising Bao Dai was only half the battle as U.S. officials searched for ways to justify decisions to throw U.S. support behind him. They also needed to overcome the nagging sense that ordinary Vietnamese would never back a leader who had been installed by a foreign power. Americans thus accompanied their reappraisal of Bao Dai with a reappraisal of the Vietnamese people. The innate qualities and capabilities of the Vietnamese had been discussed for years in American debates over Southeast Asia. During the Pacific war and in its aftermath, liberal policymakers had, as part of their push for an American policy that would back self-determination, described the Vietnamese as capable, energetic people. Other officials who supported restoration of French colonial power in Southeast Asia had generally written them off as badly unprepared for self-rule. As U.S. policy shifted gradually in favor of France, the question lingered: what was the appropriate solution for the people of Vietnam? By the start of 1950, Washington tottered on the edge of decisions that seemed to serve U.S. interests. But what about the Vietnamese? For American officials, who perceived their country as the purveyor of progress and democracy, it was a question that demanded an answer. A handful of diplomats eager for decisions in favor of supporting the French war provided one: the Vietnamese had few real political convictions and would willingly throw their support behind Bao Dai if they were confident that he would win.

In the last weeks of 1949 and the first part of 1950, U.S. officials, in an abrupt flurry of commentary aimed at clearing away old reservations about adopting a pro-French policy, recast the Vietnamese as inherently apolitical and ignorant of political ideologies except insofar as they affected their ability to subsist on the land. Some of this Orientalist commentary followed French opinion in suggesting that the Elysée accords should be accepted as the basis of Western policy in Vietnam because the Vietnamese were incapable of handling any greater degree of self-rule. But U.S. appraisals went far beyond French reporting, indulging in virulent depictions of the Vietnamese as wholly lacking in political sophistication—a kind of rhetorical overkill that suggests the difficulty American policymakers faced in embracing a political arrangement that ran roughshod over democratic principles. After touring Tonkin in fall 1949, William M. Gibson, the U.S. consul in Hanoi, reported to Washington that the typical Vietnamese peasant was "more interested in being able to tend his rice patch and pursue his village's trade in peace than in the relative merits of the Viet Minh and the Bao Dai government. If he must make a choice," Gibson added, "he will choose that which disturbs his own personal life least with little concern for political theories." The State Department's Policy Planning Staff warned U.S. officials in mid-1950 against taking "a folksy approach to foreign peoples," apparently alluding to the earlier tendency among liberal policymakers to describe Southeast Asians as well prepared for democratic government. "We sometimes tend to forget," the report continued, "that the majority of Asians is a peasant steeped in medieval ignorance, poverty and localism. Preoccupied with extracting a meager livelihood his horizon barely extends beyond the next village."[48]

This supposed lack of sophistication carried clear advantages: it would not take much to convince the Vietnamese that they should throw their support to Bao Dai, and once they did, other countries would follow. Consul Abbott wrote in January 1950 that Bao Dai might be the beneficiary of "the normal Oriental tendency to climb on the bandwagon of the winning side." But the same characteristics could also lead to disastrous consequences. If the West failed to back Bao Dai, the Vietnamese might just as easily fall prey to communist manipulation. This view reflected an increasingly prevalent belief among the American political elite by 1950 that communism found most support within inferior social groups. George Kennan, head of the Policy Planning Staff and one of the most influential architects of U.S. foreign policy in the early Cold War, expressed this view succinctly in 1949 when he wrote that communism appealed most to "maladjusted groups in our country—Jews, Negroes, immigrants—all those who feel handicapped in the framework of national society." The same generalization seemed to apply in Southeast Asia. Robert S. Folsom, the new U.S. consul in Hanoi, worried in late 1949 that the communists might succeed in Vietnam because the local people were "generally apathetic to all politics" and might be duped by communist promises of independence and prosperity. Communism, Folsom wrote, had succeeded elsewhere by appealing to "malcontents, opportunists, those in political disfavor, misguided idealists and reformers, and ignorant lower class elements" and was doing so again in Vietnam, where such people existed in abundance.[49]

Americans who backed the French government also asserted familiar concerns about security and stability in Europe as they sought to win their case in early 1950. The economic and military drain in Vietnam constituted "a major obstacle in the path of French financial stabilization and economic progress, with all that implies for the European Recovery Program as a whole," wrote Ambassador Bruce. Heavy French spending on Vietnam in 1949 imposed "such a burden on the French public finances as to constitute an important obstacle to the success of the whole French recovery and stabilization effort," Bruce argued. He acknowledged that France faced many other intractable problems, but, he asserted, the "Indochinese problem is one the United States can do something about." In the meantime, Bruce embraced French claims that the United States was unfairly letting down its ally. It was "small wonder," he contended, that the French government would consider withdrawing entirely from Indochina, since it was expending "so much money and blood" and receiving so little support.[50]

This view received powerful reinforcement from a series of high-level studies completed around the turn of the year assessing U.S. policy in light of Mao's victory in China. The most important of these studies, NSC-48/1, approved by the president on December 30, concluded that Washington must lend its support to regional anticommunist groupings and generally must meet communist threats in Asia "by providing political, economic and military assistance and advice where clearly needed to supplement the resistance of other governments in and out of the area which are more directly concerned." In places the paper stressed old themes about the dangers of seeming to prop up European colonialism. In Indochina, it stated, "action should be taken to bring home to the French the urgency of removing the barriers to the obtaining by Bao Dai or other non-Communist nationalist leaders of the support of a substantial proportion of the Vietnamese." Yet this compunction would no longer stand in the way of a more active U.S. role in the region. "The United States," insisted NSC-48/1, "should exploit every opportunity to increase the present Western orientation of the area and to assist, within our capabilities, its governments in their efforts to meet the minimum aspirations of their people and to maintain internal security." As a starting point, the paper committed the Truman administration to distribute "as a matter of urgency" the $75 million set aside by Congress in 1949 for military aid to Southeast Asia.[51]

In public, Truman administration officials held back from any bold statement of the new drift of American policy. In a widely reported speech at the National Press Club in Washington on January 12, Secretary of State Acheson stressed that American interests were concentrated on the periphery of Asia, the offshore island chain that included Japan, Taiwan, and the Philippines. On the Southeast Asian mainland, he insisted, the United States was only "one of many nations" interested in checking communist encroachment and would help only when U.S. aid was the "missing component" for success. In conversations with French officials, too, American officials made no promises and sometimes even renewed their demands for further liberalization of French policy. Internal correspondence makes clear, however, that officials had little doubt that the United States was nearing a decision to support Bao Dai. In Saigon Abbott, closely attentive to developments in Washington, wrote on December 27, 1949, that he "assume[d]" that the administration would extend diplomatic recognition to Bao Dai following ratification of the Elysée accords, now expected in January. No longer, it was clear, would Washington insist on Asian acceptance of Bao Dai as a condition for U.S. action. Like the Attlee government, the Truman administration, despite continued lip service to the principle that Asians would lead and Western nations merely support, effectively dropped any insistence on the point.[52]

This shift became abundantly clear when the French National Assembly at last voted on January 29, 1950, to ratify the Elysée agreements. In the end, the Socialists supported the government's policy, making possible a lopsided, 401–193 vote. During the frequently heated debate, Socialist deputies repeatedly voiced their unease about the Bao Dai policy, insisting that France keep its promises to establish a truly democratic state. But such subtleties dropped away as the government proclaimed its triumph to the world. Empowered by the Assembly's vote, the minister of Overseas France, Letourneau, declared Bao Dai's Vietnam, along with Laos and Cambodia, to be "Associated States" of the French Union, enjoying "unity, independence and sovereignty." There was "no incompatibility," he added, "between independence and membership in the French Union."[53]

To demonstrate the point, the Foreign Ministry quietly prevailed on the Ministry of Overseas France to permit Washington and London to exchange diplomatic missions with Vietnam—a provision that exceeded the letter of the Elysée accords but, in the words of one Foreign Ministry report, would show "the liberality of our intentions and would have a very favorable effect for our policy." With the long-awaited Assembly vote finally in hand, however, the French government made clear that it would offer little more. Schuman told U.S. ambassador Bruce on January 25 that it would be politically impossible for the government to gratify Washington and London by making a declaration of intentions to permit further liberalization in Vietnam. Similarly, Schuman refused any commitment to transfer authority over Indochinese affairs to the Foreign Ministry.[54]

French leaders correctly judged that they could now forthrightly resist U.S. and British pressure. Washington and London had, after all, gotten what they had demanded most adamantly—Assembly ratification. The road was open to diplomatic recognition and material support. Foreign Ministry officials understood that the State Department had already been studying the modalities of extending recognition since mid-January. And then on January 27, two days before the Assembly's ratification of the Elysée accords, Philip Jessup, the U.S. special ambassador touring Southeast Asia, handed Bao Dai a note informing the former emperor of the secretary of state's "best wishes for the future of the State of Vietnam" and promising "a closer relationship." U.S. recognition was clearly, as British consul Frank Gibbs put it, "only a matter of time."[55]

The Soviet decision to recognize Ho Chi Minh's Democratic Republic of Vietnam on January 30 provided the final impetus for Western decisions to open relations with Bao Dai. Mao's People's Republic of China had already become the first nation to recognize Ho's government on January 18—a move that had been under consideration among the Beijing leadership for nearly a month.[56] From the Western standpoint, Chinese recognition of the Democratic Republic of Vietnam had become inevitable following Mao's victory in the fall of 1949. Soviet recognition on January 30 marked the far more significant moment for Washington and London—an unambiguous indication of Moscow's links to Ho Chi Minh's movement. We now know that Stalin delayed the move because of his desire to avoid provoking the French government at a moment when Paris was steadfastly opposing U.S. plans to rearm Germany. But Western officials detected little subtlety in Stalin's approach. The Foreign Office quickly scrapped the idea of granting Bao Dai merely "de facto" recognition and embraced the full "de jure" variety. Britain became the first nation to recognize Bao Dai's government on February 7, followed quickly by Australia and New Zealand. In the United States, meanwhile, Acheson told the press on February 1 that Moscow's new relationship with Ho Chi Minh should remove any doubts about the latter's communist affiliation and the need for a strong U.S. stand. Two days later Truman and his cabinet approved Acheson's recommendation to recognize Bao Dai. Washington extended formal recognition on February 7, a few hours after London.[57]

Chapter 2

Fighting Shy, 1953–1961

PRESIDENT TRUMAN'S MODEST COMMITMENT of aid to the French-backed government in Vietnam in 1950 proved a snare from which the United States never extricated itself. The readings in this chapter suggest why. Truman's successor, Dwight D. Eisenhower, was unwilling to commit American power and prestige to salvage the dismal French military position in Vietnam, but he was equally unwilling to allow the subjugation of the country to communism. Thus, as David Anderson demonstrates, Eisenhower ultimately intensified the American commitment to a non-communist state in Vietnam. The Americans were dismayed when the French, in the aftermath of their defeat by the Viet Minh at Dienbienphu in 1954, agreed to partition Vietnam. Ellen Hammer shows why, describing in some detail the diplomatic maneuvering that occurred at the Geneva Conference during that spring and summer.

Colonel Edward Lansdale picks up the story in 1955, when he was formally assigned to the U.S. Military Assistance Advisory Group (MAAG) in Saigon. Lansdale, who had managed to elevate counterinsurgency warfare to the level of art form in the Philippines, now worked to help South Vietnamese leader Ngo Dinh Diem gain control of the southern part of Vietnam. In part through Lansdale, the Eisenhower administration hoped to build a nation from what was to be a temporary ceasefire zone in the south, subverting the purpose of the Geneva accords. Although Eisenhower for the most part kept the United States out of a shooting war in Vietnam, one may reasonably ask whether his administration's opposition to the Geneva agreements and its support for Diem set the stage for deeper U.S. involvement in the future.

« 3 »

Dwight D. Eisenhower and Wholehearted Support of Ngo Dinh Diem

David L. Anderson

"THE LOSS OF SOUTH VIETNAM WOULD set in motion a crumbling process that could, as it progressed, have grave consequences for us and for freedom," President Dwight D. Eisenhower declared in an April 1959 speech.[1] This statement reaffirmed the famous "falling domino" analogy that he had used five years earlier to explain the strategic importance of Indochina. If the states of Southeast Asia fell under "the Communist dictatorship," he asserted in April 1954, the result would be a "disintegration" with the "most profound influence" for "millions and millions and millions of people."[2] Throughout his eight years as president, Eisenhower never wavered in his conviction that the survival of an independent, noncommunist government in southern Vietnam was a vital strategic imperative for the United States. This objective, which Eisenhower's successors in the White House would also support, was the cornerstone of his policies in Southeast Asia, but it left open the question of the means of achieving that goal.

Eisenhower and his foreign policy advisers went through two stages in attempting to devise a successful method of securing U.S. interests in Vietnam. The first approach, which lasted through 1954 and into 1955, was to continue the Truman tactic of working with and through the French and other Western allies to contain communism in Southeast Asia. During this early phase, Eisenhower showed remarkable restraint considering the administration's Cold War rhetoric about the global danger of communist expansionism. He managed to avoid involving the United States militarily in Indochina as France suffered a humiliating defeat at Dienbienphu at the hands of the communist-led Vietminh army. After the French surrender at Dienbienphu, an international conference at Geneva, Switzerland, arranged a Franco-Vietminh cease-fire in July 1954. In the following months, the Eisenhower administration tried to maintain an allied strategy in Indochina. It established the Southeast Asia Treaty Organization (SEATO) and sent a special mission to Vietnam headed by General J. Lawton Collins to attempt, among other things, to continue a joint U.S.-French program in the region.

By the spring of 1955, however, the administration had begun a second, essentially unilateral approach in which the United States sought to protect its strategic interests in Southeast Asia by building a new Vietnamese nation around a reclusive autocrat named Ngo Dinh Diem. For the remainder of the Eisenhower presidency, the United States pegged its Vietnam policy on the questionable ability of Diem. In contrast to the cautious good judgment of the first phase that limited U.S. risks in Southeast Asia, the second phase exhibited a tragic irresponsibility by enmeshing the United States in the tangled web of Vietnamese politics and exposing Americans and American interests to considerable danger.

Eisenhower brought with him to the White House the conviction that the areas of the world "in which freedom flourishes" were under assault from a "Communist-regimented unity."[3] In his first State of the Union address in February 1953, he described France's struggle against the Vietminh as holding "the line of freedom" against "Communist aggression throughout the world."[4] As he prepared to leave office eight years later, his bipolar perception of the world divided between freedom and tyranny—with Southeast Asia at the center of that conflict—had not altered. Eisenhower's farewell address to the nation is remembered primarily for its warning against the dangerous influence of the military-industrial complex in America, but the speech opened with the stern reminder that the nation had faced and would continue to confront "a hostile ideology—global in scope, atheistic in character, ruthless in purpose, and insidious in method."[5] The next day, on January 19, 1961, he warned president-elect John Kennedy that the civil war then raging in Laos threatened to spread communism throughout the entire region.

Besides his commitment to no compromise with world communism, the other hallmark of Eisenhower's policies in Indochina and elsewhere was cost reduction. In a strategy labeled the New Look, his administration sought the most economical ways to protect U.S. security. Commonly associated with the threat to use nuclear force for "massive retaliation," the New Look also called for a greater reliance on military alliances and covert operations.[6]

The New Look was apparent during the initial phase of the administration's Indochina policies in the effort to work with France to defeat the Vietnamese communists. Although they shared the Truman administration's displeasure at the French intent to recolonize Indochina, the Republicans decided that the Cold War required them to stand with their North Atlantic Treaty Organization (NATO) ally. Secretary of State John Foster Dulles candidly admitted to the Senate Foreign Relations Committee that U.S. choices in this situation were distasteful, but in "the divided spirit" of the world today, the United States would have to tolerate the colonialists a bit longer to help block Soviet and Chinese infiltration of Southeast Asia.[7] Dulles also felt compelled to cooperate with France in Indochina because he wanted French officials to accept a rearmed West Germany (a frightening prospect for many in France) as part of a U.S.-backed plan for NATO called the European Defense Community. To bolster French resolve in both Indochina and Europe, the Eisenhower administration increased U.S. aid to the point that it accounted for almost 80 percent of France's military expenditures in Southeast Asia by January 1954.[8]

As the Eisenhower administration observed its first anniversary in office, however, Paris's perseverance was waning. The French public and politicians were tiring of the seven-year burden of the Indochina war. The resilient Vietminh, under the charismatic leadership of Ho Chi Minh, continued to exact a heavy price in blood and treasure from their would-be masters. To the regret of Washington, French leaders accepted a Soviet proposal for a multinational conference at Geneva, set to begin in April, that would attempt to structure a diplomatic settlement in Indochina. Then, in March, the Vietminh assaulted an entrenched French garrison at Dienbienphu with such overwhelming force that a French military disaster appeared possible on the eve of the truce talks. The French might decide at Geneva to capitulate to their communist foes.

The prospect of a socialist ally of the Soviet Union and the People's Republic of China (PRC) emerging triumphant over a member of NATO that had been openly aided by the United States deeply troubled U.S. leaders, who began serious consideration of the New Look's trump card—massive retaliation. Although this option implied the possibility of using nuclear weapons, few U.S. planners believed that the atomic bomb was necessary to balance the military scales at Dienbienphu. In this case, the proposal involved a staggering conventional bombardment of the attacking force using as many as 350 planes from U.S. aircraft carriers and from bases in Okinawa and the Philippines.[9]

Throughout March and April, Eisenhower, Dulles, and other top administration officials weighed the air strike idea but never used it. In early May, the French garrison surrendered after sustaining heavy losses, and this outcome set the stage for the signing of a cease-fire agreement between France and the Vietminh at Geneva. This turn of events has long fascinated observers of Eisenhower's foreign policies. The president and his secretary of state encouraged the image that their hands were tied by congressional and allied reluctance to countenance a risky and perhaps unwarranted rescue of France's failed ambitions. Although this characterization made the White House appear passive, it paid excellent political dividends. It helped shield Eisenhower from personal attacks that he had "lost" something in Vietnam, as Truman had been excoriated for allegedly losing China.

While in office, Eisenhower was beloved by many Americans who admired his leadership of the Allied forces that defeated Nazi tyranny during World War II and who appreciated his humble demeanor and engaging grin. At the same time, however, he seemed to be a rather lackadaisical chief executive who presided over but did not propel his administration. The later declassification of confidential White House files reversed this picture dramatically. The record revealed Eisenhower to be directly and often decisively involved in key decisions such as those on Indochina in 1954. His management of the Dienbienphu crisis has become something of a centerpiece of the rehabilitation of his presidential image in recent years. He utilized the skills of talented subordinates such as Dulles and let them absorb some of the public pressure produced by controversial actions, but the president kept a firm, if hidden, hand on the administration's helm.[10]

The origin of Eisenhower's leadership ability is clear. His rise to the pinnacle of the nation's military structure as a five-star general provided him with a wealth of experience that prepared him to be president. The military had been his leadership laboratory, and his advancement up the ranks in competition with other extremely able officers revealed that he was an adept student of management theory. His method of handling subordinates, for example, was carefully considered. During World War II, he delegated extensive responsibility to such forceful commanders as George Patton and Omar Bradley, but he retained the authority to call them to account when necessary. Similarly, his approach to public relations, contingency planning, and other areas of executive responsibility demonstrated active leadership and effective management style.[11]

The details of the Dienbienphu decision have especially enhanced Eisenhower's reputation. Confronted with a military-diplomatic problem that corresponded to his personal experience, he confidently shaped the policy deliberations. Neither Dulles nor Vice-President Richard M. Nixon, both of whom often spoke out publicly and stridently on foreign policy, fashioned the administration's actions. The president made the decisions that kept U.S. ground and air forces out of combat. "It would be a great mistake for the United States to enter the fray in partnership only with France," Eisenhower believed; "united action by the free world was necessary, and in such action the U.S. role would not require use of its ground troops."[12] The prudence of his course appears statesmanlike in contrast to the steps of later presidents who plunged U.S. forces into hostile action in Southeast Asia.[13]

Yet praise for the decision can easily be overdrawn. Eisenhower's restraint had more to do with the immediate predicament of the French and the perception that Paris had lost the will to fight than with any careful reassessment of U.S. purposes in Vietnam. He was willing to accept a tactical setback in the Cold War at Dienbienphu but was not prepared to question the proclaimed importance of Indochina in the global balance of power. Also, it is a mistake to conclude that Eisenhower was an energetic leader just because the career soldier chose to involve himself personally in a national security issue. A few days after the French garrison surrendered, for example, the U.S. Supreme Court issued its momentous school desegregation decision, *Brown v. the Board of Education of Topeka*. On the matter of racial injustice, which burdened millions of American citizens every day, the president chose to stay uninvolved, declaring that he would express neither "approbation nor disapproval" of the Court's action.[14]

When the Court ruled on the *Brown* case, U.S. delegates were sitting at the Geneva Conference deliberating the fate of Vietnam. The Vietminh victory at Dienbienphu made it likely that the French would accept a compromise with the communists. The Eisenhower administration took a largely passive role in the proceedings to avoid any responsibility for the outcome, but the United States maintained a presence there because the president and his advisers were not willing to embark on a separate, solitary course in the region. With Britain, the USSR, and the PRC mediating, the French and Vietminh reached a cease-fire agreement that temporarily partitioned the country at the 17th parallel. The communist-led Democratic Republic of Vietnam (DRV) would control the North, and France would regroup its military forces in the South. An all-Vietnam election was to be held in two years to determine the future political structure of the nation. The U.S. delegation publicly acknowledged these terms but did not sign or verbally endorse any of them.[15]

Determined to salvage the southern part of Vietnam from communist domination and to do so by collective defense if possible, the Eisenhower administration championed the creation of SEATO in September 1954. Comprising the United States, France, Britain, Australia, New Zealand, the Philippines, Thailand, and Pakistan, this alliance was not a binding security pact like NATO, but it did provide a mechanism for possible joint action in future crises like Dienbienphu and especially in the event of overt aggression by the DRV or PRC. Under the terms of the Geneva Accords, Vietnam and neighboring Laos and Cambodia could not enter into military agreements, but the SEATO pact extended a vague commitment to their security in an attached protocol. Despite the treaty's weaknesses, Dulles hailed it as a "no trespassing" sign to warn away potential communist aggressors, and Eisenhower and his successors in the White House cited SEATO as the authority for U.S. intervention in the region's affairs.[16]

Eisenhower's handling of Dienbienphu, Geneva, and SEATO, taken together, highlighted the strengths and weaknesses of his leadership style. He was managing the Vietnam issue politically but not solving it substantively. Using Dulles as his primary spokesman, Eisenhower had urged "united action" during the siege of Dienbienphu to counter the communist threat in Southeast Asia. With the formation of SEATO, such allied unity seemed possible. Opinion polls indicated that the American public favored this kind of multilateral approach over unilateral action. Similarly, Eisenhower's decision to maintain a discreet distance from the negotiations and final settlement at Geneva avoided a charge that he had accepted a compromise with communists—an allegation that critics had made against Franklin Roosevelt after the Yalta Conference of 1945. The American people wanted toughness in U.S. policy without the risk of war, and the administration's coolness toward the Geneva Accords and its creation of SEATO suited this public mood. In terms of policy, however, toughness alone was not a solution. The true alternatives were either to use force to break DRV power or to accept DRV success. The administration would do neither and hence only deepened the U.S. commitment in Southeast Asia with no realistic prospect for resolving the dilemma of how to protect U.S. interests without war.[17]

Although France entered SEATO, U.S.-French cooperation in Southeast Asia after the Geneva Conference was strained almost to the breaking point. Eisenhower and many of his aides believed that Paris had essentially forfeited its influence on Western policies in Indochina with its weak performance against the Vietminh. The president complained that he was "weary" of the French and their "seemingly hysterical desire to be thought such a 'great power.'"[18] Still, many of the French had strong economic and personal ties with Indochina and were loath to surrender what remained of their position.

In an effort to reestablish a working relationship with French officials in South Vietnam, Eisenhower sent General J. Lawton Collins, a trusted World War II colleague and former army chief of staff, to Saigon in November 1954 as his personal representative. "Lightning Joe" Collins was also to formulate "a crash program to sustain the Diem government and establish security in Free Vietnam." The president thought that French officials in Saigon would cooperate, but, if not, "we ought to lay down the law to the French," he told the National Security Council. "It is true that we have to cajole the French with regard to the European area," Eisenhower added, "but we certainly didn't have to in Indochina."[19]

Collins had some success with military training programs and bureaucratic changes, but eventually his mission and U.S. policy in general reached an impasse with the French over the internal political structure of the South. At issue was the leadership of Ngo Dinh Diem. While the Geneva Conference was under way, Emperor Bao Dai had made Diem prime minister of the State of Vietnam, the vacuous regime that French officials had created as a Vietnamese nationalist alternative to the Vietminh and their alien Marxist ideology. It was this government, currently under the protection of the French in their regroupment zone south of the 17th parallel, that would face the DRV and its president Ho Chi Minh in the Geneva-mandated elections. Not all Vietnamese approved of the Vietminh, who had often ruthlessly silenced their political rivals, but the leaders of the DRV enjoyed the advantage of having forced the capitulation of the colonialists. Diem's regime would have to prove its ability and its patriotism if it was going to shake the appearance of dependence on the Westerners. Some Americans thought Diem might be able to meet this challenge, but only if the French allowed him the true independence to do so.

Diem himself was a complex individual. He was personally honest and courageous and had a well-established record of resistance to French domination of his homeland. These qualities were assets for a Vietnamese politician. He had genuine liabilities, though, that the French were quick to emphasize. He had no political base except his own large family, which had a well-earned reputation for clannish self-interest. His Catholic religion may have pleased the French but only served to isolate him from his predominantly Buddhist countrymen. His personality was aloof, even monkish—the opposite of the modern politician. In addition, he had lived briefly in the United States and knew some influential American politicians and church leaders, such as Senator Mike Mansfield (D-Mont.) and Francis Cardinal Spellman. In fact, it may have been Diem's ties to the United States that prompted Bao Dai to name him prime minister, in a move to court official U.S. support as French power waned in Vietnam.[20]

How Bao Dai came to appoint Diem, a man whom he disliked immensely, is not known with certainty. Some accounts have speculated that the CIA or some other secret U.S. influence was behind the selection. There is no particular evidence available for this scenario, however, and Bao Dai may well have had his own reasons. Clandestine American contact with Diem after he became prime minister has become well known. Covert initiatives were an explicit element of the New Look, and CIA Director Allen W. Dulles (the secretary of state's brother) sent a special agent to Saigon at the same time that Diem assumed office. Allen Dulles's choice was Air Force Colonel Edward G. Lansdale, an unconventional warfare officer who had aided the Philippine government's successful resistance of a communist rebellion. Lansdale quickly became Diem's confidant and an ardent advocate for firm U.S. support of the prime minister.[21]

Despite endorsement of Diem from Lansdale and others, Eisenhower had given explicit instructions to Collins to evaluate Diem's leadership qualities.[22] After five months of close observation, Collins reported that he judged Diem incapable of providing South Vietnam with the dynamic leadership it needed. Diem and his brothers were running a "practically one-man government," the general informed Washington, and they were stubbornly resistant to helpful advice. Collins recommended other Vietnamese officials whom he thought could better organize a broad-based coalition to compete with the communists. Collins's report shocked Secretary of State Dulles. Although initially dubious of Diem's prospects, the secretary had come to accept the argument of Diem's American friends that the prime minister was the best hope for a nationalist alternative to Ho and that all Diem needed was the confidence that he had the "*wholehearted* backing" of the United States.[23]

Unlike the Dienbienphu discussions of the previous year, debate on the Diem issue in the spring of 1955 did not directly engage the president; Eisenhower chose to stand aside and let Secretary Dulles and General Collins reach a conclusion. The president was preoccupied with the Taiwan Straits crisis and the approach of his first summit conference with Soviet leaders. Meeting with Dulles and other State Department officials in Washington on April 25, Collins maintained his position that Diem was not indispensable, and the secretary reluctantly agreed. Literally at the moment these decisions were being made, street fighting erupted in Saigon. Probably instigated by Diem himself in a desperate demonstration to Washington, the violence enabled the prime minister to obtain enough backing from the fledgling South Vietnamese armed forces to quell the unrest. As Collins rushed back to Saigon to oversee U.S. interests in the unstable situation, Dulles's Asian advisers convinced him to reverse himself and to make wholehearted support of Diem the basis of U.S. policy. The aides argued that the violent outbreak proved that it was an inopportune time to tamper with Saigon's internal politics.[24]

Once the Eisenhower administration had determined that it would stick with Diem, the task remained to convince the French to accept this course. In early May, exactly a year after the surrender of Dienbienphu, Dulles met several times with French premier Edgar Faure. The sessions were stormy, but Faure finally acquiesced to Dulles's insistence on Diem.[25] It was clear that Paris no longer wished to contest Washington over the direction of Western policy in Vietnam. Through the rest of 1955, the French rapidly withdrew the remainder of their forces in South Vietnam and left the fate of the would-be nation to the Americans and their client Diem.

In the long-term history of U.S. involvement in Southeast Asia, Washington had turned an important corner. SEATO had provided a semblance of collective sanction to the U.S. intent to bolster South Vietnam, but the departure of the French demonstrated that the effort actually would be a unilateral U.S. program. The feasibility of the plan hinged on the questionable judgment that Diem could make it work. The administration entered a new and perilous policy phase.

With the basic decision having been made to build a nation around Diem, the implementation now fell to the foreign policy bureaucracy with little additional input from the president or Dulles. After Eisenhower suffered a heart attack in September 1955, many issues that his staff deemed routine, such as Vietnam, were kept from his schedule. The following year, Dulles developed abdominal cancer, and although he remained in office almost until his death in 1959, his personal agenda too became more restricted.[26] Yet the course that Eisenhower and Dulles had set in Vietnam remained the administration's policy until the end of Eisenhower's presidency, and occasionally the two men would publicly reaffirm the concept of wholehearted support for Diem.

The task of nation building loomed large before the administration. The legitimacy of Diem's regime rested only on his appointment by the heir of Vietnam's last royal dynasty, and Sa Majesté Bao Dai had taken up permanent residence on the French Riviera. The State of Vietnam had a small army of 150,000 led by an inexperienced officer corps that, under the French, had never been allowed to have any command or staff authority. The civil bureaucracy consisted only of *fonctionnaires* trained to take orders, not to solve problems. Industry was virtually nonexistent in South Vietnam, and the agricultural base of rice and rubber, although potentially valuable, had been wrecked by exploitative landlords who had impoverished much of the peasantry. Diem himself had no political following that could compete with the regimented and motivated cadre in the DRV.[27]

Diem's political weakness seemed especially important because of the national reunification elections that were supposed to occur in 1956. Although many observers of all ideological perspectives believed that Ho Chi Minh would win any truly free countrywide election, the chances of a referendum occurring were slim from the beginning. The Geneva conferees had drafted a vague proposal for elections because they could not fashion any workable political formula themselves. How the Vietnamese were to vote and on what was never specified. No official in North or South Vietnam had ever organized or conducted a free election, and there was no reason to expect that the Vietnamese would do so now under these strained circumstances. In the months following the Geneva Conference, it was clear that Diem and his American patrons had no enthusiasm for an election, but there was also no pressure for a vote from China, the Soviet Union, Britain, or France. None of these governments was inclined to assume any risk to itself to champion elections in Vietnam for the benefit of the DRV. The Eisenhower administration can be given little credit or blame for the failure of the election provisions of the Geneva agreements.[28]

Even without the serious possibility of a reunification vote, Diem's specious political legitimacy posed grave difficulties for U.S. objectives. Kenneth T. Young, the State Department officer in charge of Southeast Asian affairs, saw the problem as a paradox. He believed that if South Vietnam did not become a republic the anachronistic State of Vietnam would be easy prey for the revolutionary line of the DRV. At the same time, though, he feared that voting for a representative assembly in the South might open the door to political anarchy.[29] While Young and other Americans worried, Diem acted. He staged a lopsided referendum in October 1955 to depose Bao Dai and to make himself president of a newly created Republic of Vietnam (RVN). In March 1956, Diem organized an election of a constituent assembly, heavily stacked in his favor, to draft a constitution. The voting was not an exercise in democracy, but it was impressive evidence of the ability of the Ngo family, especially Diem's brothers Ngo Dinh Nhu and Ngo Dinh Can, to manipulate ballots. The RVN provided a facade of popular government for an ambitious family aspiring to centralized authority.[30]

Evidence of the emerging Ngo family dictatorship mounted. Nhu and Can operated a secret organization, the Can Lao, that used bribery and intimidation to garner personal support for Diem from key members of the military and bureaucracy. Vietminh "suspects," that is, persons thought disloyal to the regime, were arrested and sent to "reeducation camps." An RVN ordinance abolished elected village councils and substituted government appointees to run local affairs. Some U.S. officials, including Secretary Dulles, excused this authoritarianism as typical of Asia and even saw it as prudent because it provided a measure of stability in a nation still developing its institutional structure. Among his criticisms of Diem, Collins had warned that the Ngos' penchant for self-protection would only isolate Diem from the people and weaken the regime. That caution had been rejected, however, in favor of wholehearted support for Diem. As Collins had predicted, the Ngos increasingly behaved as if they could take U.S. aid for granted regardless of how they acted.[31]

The level of U.S. assistance to South Vietnam was high, almost $250 million annually through the end of the Eisenhower years. Some of these funds were designated for economic development. Very little aid went to the agricultural sector, but after U.S. urging, the Diem government announced some rent controls and land transfer plans, which went largely unimplemented. In the urban areas, a U.S.-designed Commercial Import Program made U.S. dollars available to subsidize imports. Rather than stimulate economic activity, however, the plan produced an influx of consumer goods, such as refrigerators and motorbikes, that created an appearance of prosperity but masked the lack of real economic growth.[32]

The bulk of U.S. aid, about 80 percent of it, went directly to the South Vietnamese armed forces. During the Eisenhower presidency, the number of U.S. military personnel in the RVN never exceeded 700, but the large percentage of U.S. aid that went for military purposes revealed the high priority placed on the military security of the new nation. Eighty-five percent of the funds for paying, equipping, and training the RVN's 150,000-man force came from the U.S. Treasury.[33]

Eisenhower and his advisers chose to declare Diem's leadership of South Vietnam a grand success, despite the repressive nature of the Saigon regime and its heavy dependency on aid. On May 8, 1957, the president himself stood on the hot parking apron at Washington National Airport to greet Diem as the RVN leader arrived for a highly publicized state visit. During the next four days, among lavish receptions and private meetings, Diem conferred with Eisenhower, Dulles, and other officials and addressed a joint session of Congress. This pageantry was part of a series of such events hosted by the administration for a number of Asian and African dignitaries. The purpose was to improve U.S. relations with the Third World, which, as Washington had learned during the Suez Canal crisis of 1956, could be vitally important. Diem was a beneficiary of this administration initiative in personal diplomacy.[34]

Eisenhower and other American speakers hailed Diem as a "tough miracle man" and the "savior" of South Vietnam.[35] The administration congratulated Diem and itself on his survival since 1954 and characterized the RVN as a stalwart ally in the struggle against world communism. Behind closed doors the rhetoric was friendly but somewhat more restrained. When Diem asked for an increase in U.S. aid, for example, Eisenhower rebuffed him with the explanation that U.S. global aid commitments prevented greater assistance. The Eisenhower-Diem summit reconfirmed the administration's earlier decisions to treat South Vietnam as strategically important and to give wholehearted endorsement to Diem's regime. It also showed that, even in a region of vital interest, the New Look principle of fiscal restraint still applied.[36]

In the late 1950s, Congress too was determined both to contain foreign aid budgets and to continue assistance to the Diem regime. Only once during the decade did congressional committees hold hearings specifically on Indochina, and that occasion was an investigation of alleged corruption in the management of the aid program in Saigon. Although both Democratic and Republican members questioned the amounts and uses of some funds, the probe uncovered no serious misconduct. At no time during the Eisenhower presidency did Congress as a body challenge the goals of the administration's policies in Vietnam. During the Dienbienphu crisis, some congressional leaders, including Senator Lyndon B. Johnson (D-Tex.), urged the White House to avoid a unilateral U.S. intervention in the French war, but that position was already preferred by the president. Later, as the U.S. commitment to Diem grew, a bipartisan alignment of lawmakers—many of them in an interest group called the American Friends of Vietnam that included Senator John F. Kennedy (D-Mass.)—staunchly defended U.S. involvement in the region.[37]

During Eisenhower's second term, two pressures largely shaped the conduct of U.S. policy in Southeast Asia: (1) the proclaimed value of South Vietnam to U.S. security and (2) the need to manage economically the United States' global obligations. These twin concerns often exasperated the diplomats and military officers charged with devising and implementing appropriate actions. The problem was how to do more with less. With his attention on Sputnik, Cuba, and elsewhere, the president provided no additional direction to U.S. policymakers as conditions within Vietnam worsened.

By 1957 and 1958, terrorism and armed insurrection were on the rise in South Vietnam. This violence often represented retaliation and resistance to Diem's increasingly repressive regime. Most of these incidents occurred without the instigation of Hanoi. The DRV had not given up its objective of reuniting Vietnam under its rule, but its leaders had ordered their southern cadres to be patient. Hanoi preferred to try propaganda and other destabilizing techniques first rather than to plunge into an armed conflict that could prompt a U.S. military attack on the North. Southern resistance leaders, who faced being jailed and even executed, refused to wait, however, and began acting on their own with assassinations, firebombings, and small attacks on RVN military units and outposts.[38]

Both Vietnamese and American officials in Saigon shared a mounting feeling of crisis, but the instructions from Washington remained clear that the nation-building program would have to make do with what it was already receiving, or likely even less, as the total foreign aid budget shrank.[39] The result was a bitter and debilitating battle between American diplomats and the Ngo family and among the Americans themselves over how to utilize the available resources. The issue was whether to increase the already high percentage of U.S. funds that went to military use or to place more emphasis on economic development and political reform.

U.S. Ambassador in Saigon Elbridge Durbrow took the lead in arguing that the RVN government would remain under attack from within as a neocolonialist dependent as long as it failed to take genuine steps toward improving the economic and social welfare of its citizens. He even went so far as to suggest to Washington that helicopters and other military items that Diem desired be withheld until the RVN president demonstrated progress on land reform, civil rights, and other abuses—urgent problems that were fueling the hostility toward his regime. Meanwhile, Diem and Nhu vehemently demanded more military aid of all types with which to increase the size and armament of their forces.[40]

Lieutenant General Samuel T. Williams, the chief of the U.S. Military Assistance Advisory Group in Vietnam, took sharp exception to Durbrow's views and sided with the Ngos. He argued that economic and political reforms remained impossible until the partisan violence had been crushed militarily. He also considered it deplorable that Durbrow would propose threatening to deny matériel to Diem at a time when the RVN government was under attack by armed and ruthless opponents. The general complained privately that the ambassador was better suited to be a salesman in a ladies' shoe store than a diplomat in Asia. Williams got support from Lansdale, now a brigadier general in the Pentagon, who advised his Defense Department superiors that Durbrow was "insulting, misinformed, and unfriendly" toward Diem.[41]

Lansdale's and Williams's personal attacks on the ambassador demonstrated that there was more to the policy debate than just the merits of military versus economic aid. In question was the long-standing Eisenhower administration commitment to wholehearted support of Diem. The generals contended that rather than criticism and pressure, Diem needed Washington's acceptance and reassurance. With the backing of the State Department's Southeast Asia specialists, Durbrow maintained that no one, including Diem, was indispensable. In a pointed comment to his diplomatic colleagues, the ambassador recalled his Pentagon critic's past association with Diem: "We have to recognize that we are dealing with a somewhat more complicated situation in the case of the GVN [Government of Vietnam]," Durbrow declared, "and that we have left the 'Lansdale days' behind."[42] The intensity with which both sides argued revealed how important these officials considered Vietnam to be to the United States. The debate also gave no indication that any of these policymakers thought of doing nothing and simply leaving the outcome in Vietnam up to the Vietnamese.

In January 1961, a few days before John Kennedy took the oath of office as Eisenhower's successor, Lansdale returned from an inspection visit to South Vietnam with a dire report. The RVN was in "critical condition," he declared, and the Vietcong (Washington's new term for Vietnamese communists) "have started to steal the country and expect to be done in 1961."[43] His urgent tone may have derived in part from his ongoing debate over tactics with State Department officers, but it also revealed that the time had come for either reaffirmation or reassessment of the United States' wholehearted support of Diem and the RVN.

As Lansdale delivered his evaluation to the Pentagon, Eisenhower was briefing the president-elect on current world conditions. With a civil war under way in Laos in which the United States and the Soviet Union were supplying weapons to the contending sides, their discussion turned to Southeast Asia. The retiring chief executive claimed that the SEATO treaty obligated the United States to defend the region from communist encroachment. The United States should protect the area's security in cooperation with the SEATO allies if possible, but if not, Eisenhower advised, "then we must go it alone."[44] The next day, January 20, Eisenhower's constitutional authority over the direction of U.S. foreign policy expired, but the course that he had charted in Vietnam would continue.

A review of the long-term significance of the two phases of Eisenhower's Vietnam policies reveals that the second or post-1955 stage with its unilateral and assertive commitment to South Vietnam prevailed over the original multilateral and cautious approach. The goal during both periods was the same: to deny Vietnam or as much of it as possible to the Vietnamese communists. Phase one was a setback to this objective because it ended with de facto acceptance of communist control of the northern half of the country. Eisenhower's negative decision—to avoid taking overt action to resist this outcome—appears as a wise, statesmanlike acceptance of the reality of the Vietminh's success in resisting French colonialism. It was a caution dictated by the immediate circumstances, however. The second phase was also based upon a negative decision—to avoid acceptance of an internal Vietnamese resolution of political authority in the country.[45] This decision was far from statesmanlike. It failed to acknowledge Diem's neocolonial dependence on U.S. support. It placed U.S. actions in conflict with the manifest Vietnamese desire for national independence. Yet Washington's wholehearted support of Diem continued. By the time Eisenhower left office in 1961, the goal of a noncommunist South Vietnam and the means of obtaining that objective—nation building premised on the survival of the Diem regime—were so deeply embedded in U.S. global strategy as to be virtually unassailable.

Eisenhower's personal strengths served him well during the first phase. His knowledge of military affairs and the politics of war enabled him to perceive clearly the military and political costs inherent in U.S. intervention in the French war. His talent for utilizing a good staff organization also enhanced his analysis of policy options and enabled him to present the outcome as a bureaucratic decision. This maneuvering mitigated potential criticism about being pusillanimous in Vietnam.[46] During the second phase, these same strengths failed him. Once the Geneva cease-fire took effect, the issue in Vietnam was not one of military strategy but of the internal political and economic development of a new nation. Although his experience on General Douglas MacArthur's staff in the Philippines in the 1930s made Eisenhower sensitive to the aspirations of Asian nationalists and familiar with the frustrations of dealing with them, he had no personal acquaintance with any Vietnamese leaders and little grasp of the complex sociopolitical realities of the Asian communism that Diem faced.[47] His one meeting with Diem was largely ceremonial. Similarly, his system of having his staff sift through options did not help alleviate this problem of comprehending complexity. Indeed, the key staff member upon whom he relied for foreign policy advice, Secretary Dulles, generally accepted the single-minded fixation on Diem. It could be argued that Eisenhower's 1955 heart attack made him excessively dependent on his staff, but even after his recovery and return to a rather heavy work load, he gave little personal attention to the details of Vietnam, which his staff presented to him as an issue that was being managed well.[48] He accepted their optimistic assessments and, during Diem's 1957 visit, lent his voice to the chorus of praise for the RVN's achievements. Beneath the miracle facade, however, were serious problems: Diem's narrow political base, his regime's weak military structure, South Vietnam's weak economy, and the growing insurgency. When Eisenhower yielded the White House to Kennedy, the policy of wholehearted support of Diem remained in place not because it was achieving U.S. objectives but because to waver even slightly could risk collapse of the administration's eight-year effort to keep the dominoes from falling. Eisenhower's accomplishments in Vietnam were negative: no war, but no peace. It was a record of nonsolution and ever-narrowing options.

« 4 »

Geneva, 1954: The Precarious Peace

Ellen J. Hammer

IN 1954 A PRECARIOUS PEACE CAME to Indochina. It came because Frenchmen had lost any desire to continue a fight which they could not possibly win against the Viet Minh; because the United States was not prepared to take over the war alone; because for the Soviet Union an Indochinese cease-fire seemed consistent with Communist international strategy; because the Chinese, finally, courting public opinion in neutral Asia and the free world, urged concessions on the Viet Minh. Even so, peace came only with difficulty.

Making peace was such a complex task because it had been so long neglected. More than ten years before, Franklin D. Roosevelt, who was concerned about the future of Indochina, had expressed the belief that the Vietnamese people merited a regime under which they could achieve their freedom, and that it was the responsibility of the United States and its allies to establish such a regime. In the years that followed, the American people and the leaders of both parties, Democrats and Republicans alike, often forgot the meaning of these objectives even though they sometimes paid lip service to them. It was only in 1954 that an American delegation arrived in Geneva to consider how to stop a war which should never have been allowed to start; and then the bargaining power of the United States' friends in Indochina was so slight that American officials were not at all sure that the timing or the circumstances were right for negotiations.

This was an awkward time for American policymakers; they were forced to recognize the unpalatable fact that practically all of the assumptions underlying United States policy in Indochina were simply not true.

First, there was the assumption that the American Government had been helping the French and the peoples of Indochina not only to fight Communism but also to win freedom for Viet Nam, Laos, and Cambodia. In Viet Nam, this would have made sense if the people knew something of the nature of political freedom and understood the oppressive nature of international Communism; some American officials seemed to have confused the Vietnamese peasant masses with the sophisticated German workers who rose in open revolt against Communism in East Berlin. The only freedom that most Vietnamese wanted was not from Communism, about which they knew little and understood less, but from France; and Communist-dominated though it was, the Viet Minh was the only force in the country fighting for an independence which the French were persistently unwilling to grant. This was the reason why so many Vietnamese supported the Viet Minh and why the neutralist nations of Asia, with their aversion for colonialism, no matter how anti-Communist their own internal policies, would not take an open stand against the Viet Minh. Only in Laos and Cambodia was the independence issue fairly clear-cut; and the people of both those countries, although determined to oppose any Viet Minh encroachments on their territory, were primarily interested in achieving their independence from France—which they did by means of diplomacy, exploiting in their own interests French difficulties with the Viet Minh.

Second, there was the assumption that the Bao Dai regime, put into power by the French and recognized by the United States, had substantial popular support. This corrupt, ineffectual government had been instituted by French officials in 1949 not to oppose Communism, for the Vietnamese were not alone in making the Communism of the Viet Minh a secondary issue (the French have never felt so intensely as the United States about the Communist menace in Asia), but to enable France to divide and win control over the Vietnamese independence movement. There was never any secret that this was French strategy and the Vietnamese did not have to be particularly intelligent to realize it. It is true that there were honest Nationalists anxious to set up a truly independent and representative regime which could compete effectively with the Viet Minh for popular support but they received little help from the United States and, not unnaturally, none at all from France. As a result, most Vietnamese withheld their active support from Bao Dai, with grave political and military consequences for American policy.

It is not surprising that American officials did not wish to probe too deeply into the validity of their assumptions; it was naturally painful to have to recognize that by choosing to oppose Vietnamese Communism almost entirely by military means, the United States had failed to win the friendship of the Vietnamese people. This does not mean that the Vietnamese wanted to be Communists and that the Americans tried in vain to stop them. What it does mean is that they wanted to be independent under their own leaders, with American aid, and that the United States refused them. Even when the American Government started pouring money into the military effort against the Viet Minh, the United States refused to give meaning to that military effort by helping the men around Bao Dai to stand on their own feet and make an honest bid for popular support.

American policy was based on still a third and equally erroneous assumption. This was that the French military position in Indochina was strong and growing stronger. For seven and a half years France and the United States had been fed on illusions and half-truths about the Vietnamese situation; they regarded Indochina through a thick fog of unreality. The American Government continued to give the French Union forces substantial aid but failed to give the Vietnamese who supported the Viet Minh, or were asked to go to war against it, a reason for fighting alongside the French; and by 1954 the most important single fact in Indochina was the grave deterioration of the French military position in the north. If French officials were reluctant to admit this fact before French public opinion, they were even more reluctant to admit it before their American allies. The result was a widening gap between the two countries. As the French spoke of the need for negotiations, the Americans called for a war to the end; when the French talked of necessary concessions to the Communists, the Americans warned against appeasement and capitulation.

Foreign Minister Georges Bidault carried home a diplomatic success from the four-power conference in Berlin, in February 1954, when Secretary of State John Foster Dulles and Soviet Foreign Minister Molotov, as well as British Foreign Secretary Anthony Eden, agreed to the holding of a conference in Geneva not only to discuss Korean problems but also to try to reach a peace settlement in Indochina. But that was not to meet until April 26 and in the meantime the war went on, on the political front as well as the military one.

The problem for the West was that it had little with which to bargain at Geneva. The obvious method of trying to moderate the demands of the Communist powers by promising American recognition of Communist China or its admission to the United Nations would have been rejected by the American Senate under the leadership of Senator [William] Knowland; the Senate would not accept at any price even the appearance of conciliation of the Chinese, nor would most of the American public at that time. There remained the bargaining strength of military force, but this, it was soon clear, would have to be American force; the French were hardly in a position to bargain. The first official intimation that the United States received of French military weakness came when General Paul Ely arrived in Washington in March and described the difficult situation of the French forces in the strong terms which French generals had used privately for years. French sources, in fact, reported General Ely's mission to be a request by the French Government, hitherto firmly opposed to more open American intervention in the war, for such intervention, although it does not appear to have been treated as such by the United States.

Highlighting General Ely's gloomy report was the military situation itself. General Vo Nguyen Giap had opened an all-out offensive after the announcement of the forthcoming Geneva Conference, and on March 13 he launched an attack on Dien Bien Phu. This was no guerrilla maneuver, as so many previous Viet Minh actions had been; backed by substantially increased Chinese aid, it was a major action that speedily developed into a nutcracker movement as the Viet Minh slowly and mercilessly closed in on the highly vulnerable French positions.

Under other circumstances this could have been just one battle among many, with a Viet Minh victory or defeat at Dien Bien Phu of no determining importance for the outcome of the war; although some attempt was made by Frenchmen to explain the action as defending Laos, it had no overriding strategic importance. But it rapidly assumed enormous political meaning as the imminence of the Geneva Conference turned a high-powered lens upon each event of these March and April weeks.

For the Viet Minh, Dien Bien Phu had a crucial significance. This was the last opportunity before the Geneva Conference for the Viet Minh to show its military strength, its determination to fight until victory. And there were those who thought that General Giap was resolved on victory, no matter the cost, not only to impress the enemy but also to convince his Communist allies that the Viet Minh by its own efforts had earned a seat at the conference table and the right to a voice in its own future.

For the French people, who watched the siege of Dien Bien Phu with a strained attention they had not shown any previous event of the war, it became a symbol of their will to fight. Upon the outcome of the battle depended much of the spirit in which they would send their representatives to Geneva.

Dien Bien Phu was a poorly chosen place in which to make a stand, a valley exposed on all sides to the enemy artillery in the hills and impossible to supply except by air. And having chosen it, General Navarre was later accused by well-informed critics of failing to give the embattled garrison the total support it needed. Certainly French Intelligence underestimated the effectiveness of the heavy artillery supplied by the Chinese which the Viet Minh was able to bring against Dien Bien Phu.

For fifty-six days Viet Minh troops pounded at the beleaguered fortress. In desperation, the Laniel-Bidault government, taking literally Washington's frequent affirmations of the importance of the American stake in Indochina, appealed for American air intervention. They made one appeal early in April and another more urgent one later that month.

At one point in these tense days high American military authorities considered seriously dropping some atomic bombs on the Viet Minh but decided against it. The United States did not only decide against using atomic bombs; it also announced that it was not prepared to undertake any military intervention of its own in Indochina. An astonishing attempt was made at one point by State Department spokesmen to place the responsibility on the refusal of the British to join in any military action on the eve of Geneva, but in fact the decision not to intervene was an American one. Put to the test, the American Government, with Congress lacking support from a public disillusioned over the Korean war, was not prepared to give the all-out help that the belligerent declarations of American officials had led the French Government to expect.

Secretary Dulles tried to create a position of strength through diplomacy. Even before the April 3rd request of the French for aid, he had issued a call for "united action" against the Communists in Southeast Asia, and he hurried off to London and Paris in an effort to bring his allies into a formal Southeast Asian alliance of ten anti-Communist nations which would have had the effect of including Viet Nam, Laos, and Cambodia in a Southeast Asian defense system guaranteed by the Western powers. But this maneuver did not work. Even when Mr. Dulles said that the Chinese were "awful close" to intervention, he could not persuade the British and the French to join him in a move which seemed to them inevitably to give the impression that the United States had no intention of taking the Geneva Conference seriously. Eventually the British and the French were prepared to consider a Southeast Asian alliance but, having committed themselves to the principle of negotiation, they were determined first to give that a fair trial, and they pointedly noted that the Americans had done the same in Korea after a much shorter war.

The weeks leading up to the Geneva Conference were thus a record of failure for the West. The American diplomatic barrage of threats and warnings directed against increasing Chinese aid to the Viet Minh proved to signify nothing more than Washington's quite understandable dissatisfaction with the state of affairs in Southeast Asia, and contrasted sharply with its evident reluctance to undertake any concrete action. From the viewpoint of Western solidarity and American prestige, it was unfortunate that the French Government had been allowed to get to the point of asking for an intervention which the United States had no intention of undertaking, and that "united action" had been proclaimed only to spotlight disunity and inaction in the West.

From some of the neutralist Asian governments came proposals for a cease-fire in Indochina. Prime Minister Nehru took the lead in this peace drive and India was followed by its fellow members of the Colombo bloc, Indonesia, Burma, Pakistan, and Ceylon. The importance of these well-intentioned gestures was underscored by the course of the military struggle. On May 8, the anniversary of the end of the Second World War in Europe, France mourned the fall of Dien Bien Phu. It was a poor omen for the outcome of the conference already in session in Geneva. Frenchmen saw it as a symbol of the tragedy and mismanagement of the eight-year struggle and in France there was despair and final disillusionment.

In Geneva, the fall of Dien Bien Phu came as a body blow to the West.

Few international conferences have begun in an atmosphere of greater uncertainty than the Far Eastern Conference which opened in Geneva on April 26, 1954. Its discussions on Korea will not be dealt with here; it is enough to state that, to no one's surprise, they proved fruitless. The Korean situation remained unchanged. For a while it seemed that the Indochinese conversations might also be deadlocked, there was so little initial agreement among the great powers. But as the weeks passed it became evident that the Geneva Conference was going to be a tremendous victory for China, Russia, and the Viet Minh.

The conference marked wide international acceptance, outside the United States, of Communist China as one of the five great powers, although American officials made a great point of avoiding even the most casual contacts with the Chinese during the time they spent at Geneva.

The Chinese and Russians insisted on the presence of the Viet Minh at the conference table, and out of the jungles and mountains of northern Viet Nam came the delegation of the Viet Minh or, more accurately, "the Democratic Republic of Viet Nam."[1] Three of the four delegates were no strangers to negotiations with France; in 1946, when they found that they were getting nowhere with their demands, they had broken off their talks with the French at Fontainebleau. Now they came to Geneva determined to force far more drastic terms on France and this time with the strength to back them up. Heading the delegation, as he had formerly headed the delegation at Fontainebleau, was Pham Van Dong, Vice President and Acting Foreign Minister, and with him were two other Fontainebleau veterans, Phan Anh, Minister of Economy, and Ta Quang Buu, Vice Minister of National Defense. The fourth delegate was the Viet Minh ambassador to Peking, Hoang Van Hoan.

The French Government had not demonstrated much interest in consulting the Associated States but at the last moment delegations from Laos, Cambodia, and Viet Nam also arrived in Switzerland. It was part of the tragic irony of the Vietnamese war that the key figures in the Vietnamese Nationalist delegation, Nguyen Quoc Dinh and Nguyen Dac Khe, had last seen members of the Viet Minh delegation when acting as legal advisors to them during the Fontainebleau Conference.

Behind the scenes were certain prominent figures on the Nationalist side, like former Prime Minister Tran Van Huu, who also came to Geneva to investigate the intentions of the Viet Minh and to advocate a united Viet Nam, neutralized politically and strategically, and independent of China. Even the Cao Dai pope, Pham Cong Tac, went there to try to evaluate Viet Minh intentions.

Foreign Minister Bidault, who attacked the problem from a different angle, had long been counting on opening negotiations with Communist China to strike a bargain under which the Chinese would have ended their considerable aid to the Viet Minh, leaving it an easy prey to the French Union forces. Bidault had never sought or even believed in the usefulness of direct negotiations with the Viet Minh, but his exaggerated expectations of American military aid backfired and for the first time he had to try to reach a compromise with the enemy.

In this effort he found himself quite alone. The American delegates, divided among themselves and highly sensitive to domestic political pressures against any concessions to the Communists, having nothing to offer either to their allies or to their enemies in the direction of conciliating their opposing positions, could hardly take over leadership at Geneva. It was left to Foreign Secretary Anthony Eden, who attempted to link the Colombo Powers to the Geneva Conference, to act as mediator between the Communists and the French. The Indian Government, which was well intentioned if not always well informed on Indochina, although not officially a member of the conference, also played a certain role, directly through Krishna Menon, Nehru's personal representative in Geneva, and indirectly by means of the influence which India as a key member of the Commonwealth exerted on the British.

Unlike the United States, the British came to Geneva with a plan for peaceful settlement; and their plan, which called for a partition of Viet Nam, was in the end accepted by the conference. But what kind of partition? A division of the country by which at least a part of Viet Nam could be saved from the Communists? Or just a face-saving device for giving the entire country to the Viet Minh?

The Russians had come to Geneva because they were ready to negotiate on Indochina. And if Chou En-lai was there, it was obviously because he was prepared to make some concessions, or at least to make the Viet Minh consent to them. This was particularly the case after Chou, during a recess in the conference, made flying visits to Nehru in New Delhi and U Nu in Rangoon, and then conferred with Ho Chi Minh in northern Viet Nam, reportedly to convince him of the opposition of non-Communist Asia to Viet Minh insistence on French capitulation.

The French, for their part, were in Geneva because they had to negotiate; they had no other choice since they now knew finally that the United States was not willing to intervene in the war. Evidently the French would have to give up something, and it was soon clear that this would be northern Viet Nam, where the Communists were most firmly entrenched.

None of the Western governments liked this. The "State of Viet Nam" (the Nationalist government), which was most directly affected, was very unhappy about it, but did not help the situation when it insisted at all costs on unifying Viet Nam under Bao Dai. This was a preposterous demand at a time when the intrinsic failure of his regime was more obvious than ever. And the insistence on a unified Viet Nam was a dangerous one. If military and political necessity dictated partition, an intelligent diplomacy should have recognized this, however unpleasant it was, and fought to safeguard whatever region was granted to the Nationalists. Above all, it was essential to construct a juridical wall at the northern limits of the Nationalist zone which the Communists could not penetrate under any pretext; but that would have required a political realism which was absent from Geneva. Instead, the Nationalist delegates, supported by the United States, insisted righteously and unrealistically on unity, which led inevitably to their acceptance of the principle of national elections to determine the future even of their own zone. And any elections, in view of the political chaos in the non-Communist areas of Viet Nam, threatened to open the entire country to the highly organized Communists.

Cambodia, though a small state, demonstrated that it was possible to make an independent policy even at a great power conference like Geneva. With Laos, it received Western help in successfully opposing Viet Minh claims on behalf of the Laotian and Cambodian dissident movements and in rejecting Viet Minh demands on the territories of the two states. But at the eleventh hour, with all the powers against it, Cambodia stood alone. It declared that it would not be neutralized and insisted on its right to self-defense. And the great powers gave way.

The Cambodian delegates followed the spirited precedent laid down by their King Norodom Sihanouk, standing up for their own rights when these were challenged. But the Vietnamese Nationalists had only Bao Dai, who had long since given up any hope of independent action, relying on foreigners to save himself.

Bidault, struggling to salvage something for France, tried to separate the arrangements for a cease-fire in Viet Nam from those for a political settlement, reasoning soundly enough that he could get better terms once the fighting had ceased. He tried to avoid even a temporary partition, which would come about if the opposing military forces were regrouped in separate zones, suggesting instead that the cease-fire be imposed on pockets of French and Viet Minh troops scattered throughout the country. But the obvious advantages to France of such proposals made them naturally unacceptable to the Communists.

To all the weaknesses of the French position was now added the instability of the French Government itself. Within the period of a month the Cabinet of Premier Laniel had twice had to ask the French Assembly for votes of confidence on its Indochina policy. It had won them but not easily, and by June Bidault was under bitter attack in the Assembly. Having continually to fight on two fronts, in Paris as well as Geneva, while the military situation deteriorated daily in Viet Nam, he was badly placed to carry on effective negotiations.

The Laniel government finally fell after a smashing attack on the Indochina issue led by Pierre Mendès-France, who on June 17 succeeded Laniel as Premier. He carried the Assembly by an impressive majority when he promised that in thirty days (by July 20) he would either achieve peace terms ending the Indochina war or resign.

As his own Foreign Minister, Mendès-France hurried off to Geneva to take up where Bidault had left off. The bitter personal enmity between the two men and the widespread personal antagonisms which afflicted French internal politics had the effect of obscuring many of the realities of the Indochinese situation. It is little wonder that foreign governments and the French public experienced such difficulty in arriving at a correct estimate of the French position. If his predecessors had painted the French military position in too rosy a light, Mendès-France now had his own reasons for darkening it.

Whereas Bidault had long since been identified with a "tough" policy toward the Viet Minh grounded on internationalizing the peace and the war, Mendès-France had consistently favored a negotiated peace, achieved by direct talks with the Viet Minh; and soon after he assumed office he proceeded to initiate conversations with Pham Van Dong. American suspicions of this policy were highlighted rather overdramatically when Mr. Dulles decided to withdraw the official American representation at Geneva, thereby undercutting the Western position by underlining the general impression that the United States had washed its hands of the conference.

Bowing to urgent French and British requests, however, Dulles dashed over to Paris and, after consultations with Mendès-France and Eden, announced that he did after all have confidence in the intentions of the French Premier to conclude an honorable peace. Under Secretary of State Walter Bedell Smith, who for a time had replaced Dulles at the conference, was sent back to Geneva.

But this byplay did not really alter the situation. The United States had in fact washed its hands of the conference, thereby facilitating the task of the Communists at Geneva. It would seem that the Communists, suspecting premeditated organization against them even when it did not exist, had placed an unwarranted faith in the unity of the Western powers and had believed, at first, that they might be called upon to make substantial concessions. There is some evidence that at a time when they were insisting publicly on Vietnamese unity, they would actually have been prepared to accept a Korean-type settlement, namely, partition of the country for an indefinite period.[2] However, as the conference proceeded, they saw that the unified Western front which they dreaded did not exist; and so the negotiations revolved around, not the maximum concessions which the Communists would make, but their maximum demands which, with some modifications, were finally accepted. By failing to take a leading role in the discussions once it became clear that the West had no choice but to surrender at least a part of Viet Nam to the Communists, the American delegation withheld from Mendès-France the only real bargaining strength he had left, that of diplomacy, making it impossible for him to salvage intact even southern Viet Nam from the Geneva debacle. Instead, he had to agree that national elections be held in Viet Nam in the near future, even though there was good reason to fear that such elections would give the entire country to the Communists.

If the conference moved faster after Mendès-France replaced Bidault, it was partly because of the thirty-day limit he had set for himself, which, given the willingness of the Communists to make peace terms, undoubtedly speeded up the proceedings considerably. Also the Communists were aware that Mendès-France would give them the best terms they could expect from France; if he failed it was fairly certain that the conference would break dawn and that he would be replaced by a government determined to continue the war, doubtless with increased American military backing.

To these political advantages, Mendès-France tried to add a third when he announced that if the conference failed, French conscripts would be sent for the first time to Indochina to reinforce the expeditionary corps. This was a move so unpopular among the French public that hitherto no French politician had dared to advocate it. But even this announcement did not counteract the devastating news of the sudden withdrawal of French Union forces from the southern part of the Tonkinese Delta, where they were under strong Viet Minh pressure, in order to strengthen what remained of the French military position in the rest of the country. The evacuation left the French in control of a small area around Hanoi (which almost certainly would fall to the Communists anyway in a partition agreement), but abandoned to the Viet Minh important non-Communist areas, notably the Catholic bishoprics of Phat Diem and Bui Chu.

On the diplomatic front, once Mendès-France had accepted the basic Communist demands—not only that the Viet Minh be given immediate control over northern Viet Nam, but also that national elections be held fairly soon—final agreement could hardly be in doubt. It was then only a question of deciding where the partition line would be drawn (the Communists had asked for the thirteenth parallel but finally agreed on the seventeenth[3]); when the Vietnamese elections were to be held to re-establish national unity (the Viet Minh had asked for six months but finally accepted two years); and what international controls were to be set up.

In the meantime, discussions between the military authorities of both sides on a cease-fire agreement began in Geneva, then were transferred to Trung Gia in Viet Minh territory in North Viet Nam. In Geneva, the nine delegations, making no genuine attempt to negotiate real political problems, worked out a series of face-saving devices, avoiding the basic issues involved. The result was the Geneva accord (finished just in time to meet the deadline set by Mendès-France) which divided Viet Nam at the seventeenth parallel.[4] All of north Viet Nam and part of central Viet Nam—from the Chinese frontier almost down to the old imperial capital of Hué, and including the important cities of Hanoi and Haiphong—were recognized as under the control, no longer of "rebels," as they had been described for years by the French, but of the Democratic Republic of Viet Nam. The south was left under the control of the State of Viet Nam.

Other provisions of the agreement called for the grouping of the military forces of one side which remained in the territory of the other into specified areas, which were to be evacuated in stages aver a period of three hundred days; a broad political amnesty throughout the country and a ban on reprisals against citizens for their wartime activities; the safeguarding of democratic liberties; and a free option for all Vietnamese to choose in which zone they wished to live.

Neither zone was permitted to receive reinforcements of foreign troops, arms, or military supplies, or to establish new military bases. Nor could either government have foreign bases in its territory nor enter military alliances. The French Union forces in southern Viet Nam were the exception to this rule; they were to remain, to be withdrawn only at the request of the southern Vietnamese government.

Responsibility for the carrying out of these terms was, in the first instance, recognized as that of the French and the Viet Minh. They in turn were made subject to the surveillance of an international commission (composed of Canadian, Indian, and Polish representatives, under Indian chairmanship) which was generally to vote by majority although on certain important questions unanimity was required.

The independence of Viet Nam, as of Laos and Cambodia, and also the principle of Vietnamese unity, were formally recognized by the conference.[5] In July 1956 the future of Viet Nam was to be decided by free and secret elections under the control of the international commission constituted by Canada, India, and Poland. And consultations between the Democratic Republic of Viet Nam and the State of Viet Nam about the elections were scheduled to begin a year in advance, on July 20, 1955.

For Laos and Cambodia, the peace arrangements, although on paper not unlike the Vietnamese settlement, were in practice very different. They also were to have national elections—the Cambodians in 1955, the Laotians in September 1956—and the carrying out of the accords was to be under the surveillance of the same three nations as in Viet Nam. But while elections in Viet Nam looked like a convenient way of giving the entire country to the Communists, in Cambodia and Laos they seemed certain to constitute popular endorsement of the royal governments which were recognized by the Communist powers as well as by the West as the only legitimate authorities in both countries.

The agreement on Laos, which recognized the right of the Laotians to keep two French military bases and French military instructors, as the Laotians had requested, offered a general amnesty to the Viet Minh-controlled Laotian dissidents known as Pathet Lao. However, this did not finally settle the Communist problem in Laos. Alien military troops were to be evacuated within four months, but the Laotian rebels who did not choose to be reintegrated into the Laotian community were given two northern provinces of Laos, Phang Saly and Sam Neua, where they were to have special representation under the royal administration. This arrangement was supposed to last only until the elections.

The agreement on Cambodia made no provision for setting up regrouping areas. Within three months all French and other foreign troops were to have evacuated Cambodia. Although until the last hours of the conference it had been accepted that Laos and Cambodia would be neutralized, thanks to Tep Phan, Cambodian Foreign Minister, both countries won recognition of their right to ask for foreign aid in men and matériel if it became necessary to do so to defend themselves, to allow foreign military bases on their territory if their security was menaced, and to enter into alliances which were not contrary to the United Nations Charter.

On July 21 the official documents were signed, which brought peace to Indochina. The United States maintained its strong reservations on the accord and, like the State of Viet Nam, which protested hopelessly against the agreement, did not join the other seven countries in accepting the final declaration of the conference. General Bedell Smith, who thanked Eden and Molotov, the two presidents of the conference, for their good will and tireless efforts in reaching an agreement, issued a separate American declaration. It declared that the United States would abstain from any threat to modify the accords, and that it would regard any resumption of aggression in violation of the accords with grave concern and as a serious menace to international peace and security.

The Viet Minh may not have won all that it wanted at Geneva but it had every reason to be pleased. Its Communist dictatorship was reinforced by international recognition. And not only was its control recognized over the northern and more populous half of Viet Nam, but excellent opportunities were opened to the Viet Minh to take over the south as well, by infiltration. In large part at least, this was the inevitable result of the disastrous political and military policy pursued over the years by the French Government in Indochina, supported by the United States.

In any case, peace, however controversial its form and dubious its content, had come to Viet Nam. On August 11, after nearly eight years of war, the cease-fire was operating throughout all Indochina.

5

The CIA Comes to Vietnam

Edward Geary Lansdale

After months of doing business out of my hip pocket in Vietnam, I was delighted to be assigned a formal office of my own in January 1955. Perhaps "formal" is too elegant a term. It actually was a little shed in the yard of MAAG headquarters in Cholon. Duckboards covered the dirt floor. Two bare lightbulbs, dangling from their cords, lit the interior. Folding chairs and field tables, and some open crates to hold files, completed the furnishings. The shed was one of several clustered around the main building of the headquarters, which was an old French colonial schoolhouse of cement and stucco noted principally in the neighborhood for having once been a whorehouse set up by the Japanese for the convenience of their troops. The French had assigned this place to the Americans as one of their many "in" jokes. I never did find out the genesis of my own particular shed.

My move to a daily stint in this shed at MAAG came after I volunteered for the Franco-American organization that had been agreed upon in December as the instrument for training the Vietnamese Army. While details of just how the French and the Americans were to work together were being thrashed out, General [John] O'Daniel gathered together the Americans selected to staff the new organization and put us in the only available space at his headquarters, the sheds in the yard, to do some advance planning for the work ahead. There were four staff divisions: army, navy, air force, and pacification. I headed pacification, which was to guide the Vietnamese Army in its moves to reoccupy former Vietminh zones as well as to oversee any security operations in areas where guerrillas were still terrorizing the population.

The next couple of weeks saw most of our basic planning done, including suggested directives for the Vietnamese whenever they were ready to start the program. Although my own planning drew heavily upon the lessons I had learned in the Philippines and from my travels around the Vietnamese countryside, it also was tailored and shaped by the Vietnamese. I discussed each step with the prime minister, the minister of national defense, and the leaders of the Vietnamese Army, whom I was continuing to see almost daily. This Vietnamese input was the most important element in the planning. We Americans and French would be guiding the Vietnamese into taking control of their own affairs. If they were to succeed, the proposed operations would have to be wholly understood and accepted by the Vietnamese.

The first change they made was in the name of our program. They objected to the word *pacification*, saying that it denoted a French colonial practice devised by General Lyautey in North Africa and applied to Vietnam by GAMOs (Mobile Administrative Groups) which had set up local governments and home guards in areas cleared by French Union forces. (I had seen the work of the GAMOs and thought that much of it was excellent.) The Vietnamese leaders did agree with the concept of using the Vietnamese Army to help and to protect the people, so I insisted that if they didn't like *pacification*, they pick a name themselves. After much head-scratching, the leaders chose a Vietnamese term for the work, which translated into English as *national security action*. We adopted this name promptly. Amusingly enough, the Vietnamese themselves (along with the French and Americans) continued to speak of the work as *pacification*. Years later, despite other official changes of name, it still is spoken of as *pacification*. Habit dies hard.

Toward the end of January, the new Franco-American training organization, TRIM, became a reality. The French command made the Cité Lorgeril, a walled compound in Cholon, consisting of a collection of pleasant villas around a courtyard, available as headquarters. Its organization was balanced, with scientific precision, between the Americans and the French. General O'Daniel was the chief of TRIM but acted under the authority of the top French commander, General Ely. TRIM's chief of staff (and my immediate boss) was [the] French briefing officer, Colonel Jean Carbonel. . . . His deputy was an American, Lieutenant Colonel Bill Rosson. Under them were the chiefs of the four staff divisions (army, navy, air, and national security), two of whom were French and two American, each with a deputy of the other nationality. I was chief of the national security division. My deputy was a French paratrooper, Lieutenant Colonel Jacques Romain-Defosses. Our staff division had equal numbers of French and American officers.

There was too little amity in TRIM for me. The French chief of staff who was my immediate boss seemed perpetually piqued at me and showed his feelings by refusing to speak to me directly. Instead, he would position his adjutant, a French officer, next to him and, while looking at me, would ask the adjutant to relay such and such a message to me. When the adjutant had finished, I would reply directly to the chief of staff, who promptly would ask the adjutant, "What did he say?" My reply would be repeated. It was lugubrious, since we all were being stiffly correct in military fashion and were speaking English face-to-face. He carried this practice into our official social life. At receptions he would stamp his feet and turn his back when I approached. I hardly endeared myself to him by my own behavior. I would put an arm across his shoulders familiarly and announce to those standing nearby in a grating American manner, "This guy is my buddy. You treat him right, you hear?" This made him explode, angrily shaking my arm off his shoulders.

Most of the French officers in my staff division let me know openly that they were from various intelligence services. Once in a while, they would have the grace to blush when I came upon them as they were busy writing reports of my daily activities, presumably for a parent service. On the other hand, all of them had served in Vietnam for periods of six years or more and were exceptionally well-informed about Vietnamese life and geography. Thus, my problem was to divert them from an unduly psychotic suspicion of everything I did and toward genuine help in the Vietnamese preparation for the serious and complex national security operations then underway. I was only partially successful.

For example, one of the French officers was from a clandestine service. He sat at a desk facing me, busied himself with paper work for a time, and then just sat there, staring. I noticed that his stare became more and more fixed on a telephone near me which was designated for English-language use. Even the telephones at TRIM were evenly divided between the two nationalities, although the execrable service was impartial. Both the French- and English-speaking phones were subject to sound effects apparently from outer space, additional voices picked up in midsentence or in shouts of "Allo, allo!" and dead silences. Nearly every incoming call would begin with blasphemous complaints about the long delays and frustrations involved in getting the call through to us. Then the caller would hurriedly shout his message before he was cut off. Knowing the performance record of the telephone, I assumed that the French officer staring at it was simply giving it a silent hate treatment.

But one morning, this English-language telephone rang. The French officer, who had been scribbling on a piece of paper and referring frequently to his French-English dictionary, jumped to his feet, snatched up the piece of paper, and rushed over to the ringing telephone before an American could reach it. Holding up the paper and reading from it, he spoke carefully into the mouthpiece, "I do not speak English, goodbye." Then he hung up. He looked at me to see if I had noticed his zany prank. I laughed aloud. He looked a bit surprised at my reaction and then grinned himself.

I went back to his desk with him. The French officer at the next desk was fluent in English and I asked if he would mind interpreting for the two of us. It was time that we all became better acquainted. We embarked upon a session of mutual talk. The prankster admitted that he had only three months longer to stay in Vietnam and frankly was sitting out the time until departure. I confessed that I didn't have all the answers on how to help the Vietnamese at the present moment. Since he had served many years among them, surely there must be at least one thing that he had long wanted to do for the Vietnamese that the war had prevented him from doing? If he named it, and if it could be fitted into our work, he could spend all of his remaining time at such a self-chosen task and have all the support I could muster.

He replied thoughtfully that he had long waited to assist Vietnamese children and would like to draft an explicit proposal for a youth program to fit in with the national security concept. This sounded good, I said, worthy of backing, and his eyes lighted up. With such work to do, he told me that he would put in for further service in Vietnam, although he did want some brief home leave first because he had been away from his family for years. We parted on this agreeable note. The next day, at TRIM, he stood at attention before my desk, saluted, and informed me in formal tones that he had been ordered rotated back to France. His departure was set for the next day. Did he ask for an extension of duty in Vietnam, as we had discussed? He answered brusquely, "Yes, sir," his eyes showing a silent inner hurt. He told me that he would have to go. We said farewell.

Other French officers in my division also had deep feelings about ways in which they would really like to help the Vietnamese. I dug patiently for their ideas and put them to work on self-projects whenever I could. Abrupt departures continued. The staff division gradually settled into an atmosphere of surface civility, marred occasionally by outbursts pinned up on the bulletin board anonymously by both nationalities. We tackled a heavy workload of operational and logistical planning with the Vietnamese. Two large-scale national security campaigns and scores of other activities were enough to keep us all busy for a time.

The preoccupation of the French establishment in Vietnam with my presence led to a confrontation in this period. Apparently the various stories about my doings had been collected by the French clandestine service, whose officers made complaints about me to the CIA, their normal liaison. They claimed they had a long list of charges against my conduct. I learned of this from the ambassador, who said that the French wanted to confront me, make the charges one by one, and record my answers. Although he warned me that he objected to such a confrontation, because of the star-chamber aspect of the proceeding, I was eager to accept. I had had my fill of attempts at character assassination by so many of the French, and it was time to meet them head-on.

When this was being discussed in the ambassador's office, the CIA chief, a smug smile on his face, offered to host the meeting with the French at a luncheon at his home, saying that this would be acceptable to the French. He seemed to be relishing the meeting, apparently expecting me to get a severe verbal mauling or worse from his French associates. The French, he added, would let him sit in as an observer of the interrogation, and he promised to give the ambassador a complete report for forwarding to Washington. I said quickly that I would submit a report also, which could be forwarded concurrently. I felt like Daniel about to enter the lion's den.

So, one noon soon afterward, I met with the French at the home of the CIA chief in Saigon. The local director of the French clandestine service, a colonel with whom I had had a most friendly association in my work with the O'Daniel mission to Indochina in 1953, sat at a card table, papers spread out before him, face stern, back rigidly erect, and started the meeting by formally requesting that I respond as I wished to any of the charges which were listed in the papers before him. Since the list was very long, it was doubtful that all the items could be taken up before luncheon. We could break the meeting long enough to dine and then return to the inquisition. There were several of his officers present who were thoroughly knowledgeable about the incidents on his list, and did I mind their presence, since they would be advising him on the correctness of any answers I gave? I assured him that I was pleased to have them present.

The first item charged me with supplying arms to Ba Cut, the Hoa Hao rebel, by an airdrop on a specific date. I could hardly believe my ears. I broke out laughing. The French officers glared. My laughter offended them. When I caught my breath again, I explained to them that on the specific date they had named, an airdrop indeed had been made to Ba Cut (who had been made a colonel in the Vietnamese Army by General Hinh just before his departure for Paris, although Ba Cut remained antagonistic toward the Saigon government). However, the operation demonstrably wasn't mine.

The Vietnamese Army, I informed them, had observed this airdrop and had investigated it. The Vietnamese Army had recovered three of the parachutes and traced them by their markings to a French military unit. French officers had been present with Ba Cut when he received the airdrop. The tail markings of the delivery aircraft had been noted, and a check with flight operations records and personnel at Tan Son Nhut airport had revealed the names of the French pilots and crew who had been aboard the aircraft at the time the delivery was made to Ba Cut. The Diem government had lodged a formal complaint to the French command about this incident, thoroughly documented. Whatever made them feel that, by some magic, I had had a hand in this purely French operation?

My inquisitors were shaken. The colonel turned aside and whispered urgently to the panel of "informed experts" who were sitting in. Then he gamely read off the second item. I was charged with supplying arms to Trinh Minh Thé, thus assisting him in his fight against the French who, after all, were allies of the Americans. I answered this assertion in as quiet a tone as I could. Trinh Minh Thé and his Lien-Minh troops were on their way to Saigon to be integrated into the regular Vietnamese Army and were certainly not about to fight the French unless the French tried to stop this move and thus interfere with the best interests of the Vietnamese Army—which they had asserted formally that they would aid. The fighting had ended *after* I had visited Trinh Minh Thé in Tay Nihn, and I trusted that the significance of this fact, along with the safe return of three French prisoners whom the Lien-Minh had held, wasn't lost on them.

However, I continued, speaking of weapons, I had noticed several U.S. machine guns which the Lien-Minh had captured from French forces sent against them, and I had copied down the serial numbers of these guns to have them checked against U.S. lists in Saigon. They had been supplied originally by the U.S. to the French in Hanoi in 1951, to support French actions against the Communists. I had some sharp questions in my mind about how these weapons had been switched from use against the Communists to use by French forces against a Vietnamese officer who was known to be fighting the Communists, since he had captured the weapons in question from the French.

At this point in the proceedings, luncheon was announced. The French officers told our host that they couldn't stay for lunch. As a matter of fact, they couldn't continue the meeting any longer because they had urgent business to attend to elsewhere. They rose, gathered up their papers, and prepared to depart. Their faces were flushed with embarrassment. The first two items had blown up against them like exploding cigars, and they didn't want to sit there and be exposed to further humiliation. I insisted that they stay and finish the inquisition, whether they ate lunch or not, since the whole business was their idea, not mine. Reluctantly, they sat down again and we worked our way through the whole list. It was clear that the French officers thoroughly regretted having to go through with the farce they had begun.

All but one of the charges were patently inventions, easily destroyed fictions. The exception was the charge that my team in Haiphong was planning "to blow up the harbor of Haiphong." I admitted that they had talked about this subject and then explained the background. The French admiral commanding in Haiphong was an older man who lived next door to the house where my team and other Americans lived. The Americans had noticed that the French admiral's water closet was only a few feet from their house and that he spent an unusually long time seated on the toilet every morning; and whimsy had seized them. How could they give the old gentleman a thrill while he sat there of a morning? Should they throw firecrackers through the window? No, his heart might not stand the strain. They had hit instead upon the idea of talking loudly about blowing up the whole harbor, water and all, before it had to be turned over to the Vietminh. The admiral, overhearing this, bolted out of the bathroom to send an urgent message to General Ely. I had been informed of the incident promptly and had told these American officers to stop scaring French admirals. They had promised to behave. However, if the French Navy officers were still frightened, I would take further measures. The French officers told me curtly that that wouldn't be necessary.

The meeting ended. Presumably, the French command received a report of these proceedings. I gave my own summary report to our ambassador, to forward to Washington with whatever information the local CIA chief was reporting. The whole business should have ended there. Of course it didn't, the perversity of human nature being what it is. French attempts at character assassination continued, reaching their peak some weeks later in the spring of 1955. The fictions invented by French circles in Saigon found their way into the French press and eventually into the lurid journalism of weekend supplements in newspapers of other European countries. Well-meaning people would clip these stories and send them to me. They added a Mad Hatter touch to the events I was living through.

The whistle could have been blown on me for other activities in early 1955, though. For example, I passed along some psywar ideas to a group of Vietnamese nationalists who were getting ready to leave North Vietnam for the South. They described the long barrage of Communist propaganda which they had suffered for years. They were burning to strike a final blow in return before they departed from their northern homes. Did I have any suggestions? Indeed I did. I gave them two, which they promptly adopted.

The first idea was used just before the French quit the city of Hanoi and turned over control to the Vietminh. At the time, the Communist apparatus inside the city was busy with secret plans to ready the population to welcome the entry of Vietminh troops. I suggested that my nationalist friends issue a fake Communist manifesto, ordering everyone in the city except essential hospital employees to be out on the streets not just for a few hours of welcome but for a week-long celebration. In actuality this would mean a seven-day work stoppage. Transportation, electric power, and communication services would be suspended. This simple enlargement of plans already afoot should give the Communists an unexpectedly vexing problem as they started their rule.

An authentic-looking manifesto was printed and distributed during the hours of darkness on the second night before the scheduled entry of the Vietminh. The nationalists had assured me that they could distribute it safely because the chief of police in Hanoi was a close friend of theirs and would rescue any of them who might be caught and arrested. The next day the inhabitants of Hanoi read the fake manifesto and arranged to be away from homes and jobs for a one-week spree in the streets. The manifesto looked so authentic that the Communist cadre within the city bossily made sure, block by block, that the turnout would be 100 percent. A last-minute radio message from the Communists outside the city, ordering the Communists inside to disregard this manifesto, was taken to be a French attempt at counterpropaganda and was patriotically ignored. When the Vietminh forces finally arrived in Hanoi, their leaders began the touchy business of ordering people back to work. It took them three days to restore public services. A three-day work stoppage was a substantial achievement for a piece of paper.

When the nationalists saw me later in Saigon, however, they were woebegone. One arrest had been made when the manifesto was distributed. Their friend, the chief of police, became so imbued with the spirit of the affair that he had taken a stack of the manifestoes out in his car to help directly in the distribution. The French caught him in the act and, with the evidence of the copies of the manifesto in his possession, were convinced that he was a Communist agent. They had arrested him and put him in his own prison. He begged to be taken south as a prisoner. The French had done so and had turned him over to the Vietnamese government in Saigon. Nobody believed his story that the manifesto was a fake. He was being held in jail. Would I help? I explained what had happened to Prime Minister Diem. It took me until January to overcome his skepticism and obtain the release.

The second idea utilized Vietnamese superstitions in an American form. I had noted that there were many soothsayers in Vietnam doing a thriving business, but I had never seen any of their predictions published. Why not print an almanac for 1955 containing the predictions of the most famous astrologers and other arcane notables, especially those who foresaw a dark future for the Communists? Modestly priced—gratis copies would smack too much of propaganda—it could be sold in the North before the last areas there were evacuated. If it were well done, copies would probably pass from hand to hand and be spread all over the Communist-controlled regions.

The result was a hastily printed almanac filled with predictions about forthcoming events in 1955, including troubled times for the people in Communist areas and fights among the Communist leadership. To my own amazement, it foretold some things that actually happened (such as the bloody suppression of farmers who opposed the poorly-executed land reforms and the splits in the Politburo). The almanac became a best seller in Haiphong, the major refugee port. Even a large reprint order was sold out as soon as it hit the stands. My nationalist friends told me that it was the first such almanac seen in Vietnam in modern times. They were embarrassed to discover that a handsome profit had been made from what they had intended as a patriotic contribution to the nationalist cause. Unobtrusively, they donated this money to the funds helping the refugees from the North.

Chapter 3

Digging In, 1961–1968

THE U.S. PRESENCE IN VIETNAM ESCALATED during the administrations of two Democratic presidents, John F. Kennedy and Lyndon B. Johnson. In 1961, Americans barely thought about the conflict in Vietnam; by 1968 it had become the Vietnam War, in which thousands of Americans were fighting and dying. Scholars have wondered about the seeming rashness of decisions made by these bright and sophisticated men. Perhaps Kennedy's most momentous decision was to send thousands of American advisers to train and support the Army of the Republic of Vietnam (ARVN). The selection from Herbert Parmet's book on the Kennedy presidency offers a possible explanation for this step. Though many historians disagree, Parmet sees little evidence that Kennedy expected to be able to withdraw U.S. forces from the war by a near-term and certain date. In August 1964, President Johnson used an alleged North Vietnamese attack on U.S. ships in the Gulf of Tonkin to win from Congress a resolution giving him enough latitude to intensify the war. Robert McNamara, who was secretary of defense at the time, looks back at the Gulf of Tonkin incident in this excerpt from his 1995 memoir.

Historian Fredrik Logevall picks up the story in the immediate aftermath of Johnson's easy victory over Barry Goldwater in the election of 1964. Logevall argues that there was no real imperative to escalate the war at this time: Johnson's domestic flank was protected against conservative criticism, other nations had no enthusiasm for the conflict, and some in the administration expressed doubt about the wisdom of carrying on. The president, nevertheless, chose war. By early 1968, there were over 500,000 American soldiers in Vietnam. The Tet Offensive, launched by the North Vietnamese and southern-based National Liberation Front (NLF) in late January, failed to topple the American-backed Saigon government, but it proved psychologically devastating to Americans who had previously been confident of victory in Vietnam and led Johnson to withdraw from the presidential race, as George Herring demonstrates here. Finally, George Ball, undersecretary of state in the Johnson administration, offers the perspective of an in-house dissenter from July 1965 to early 1968. In light of what happened in Vietnam, Ball's views are startling in their prescience.

6

No "Non-Essential Areas": Kennedy and Vietnam

Herbert S. Parmet

The presidential summer retreat that year [1963] was not at Hyannis Port but at the nearby Squaw Island cottage that [President Kennedy] rented from his father's friend Morton Downey, the tenor. There, just a few miles to the west of the family compound, was the possibility of more seclusion for himself, Jackie, and the children.

While Jackie was there, she had to be rushed to the nearby Otis Air Force Base Hospital for an emergency cesarean operation. The President heard the news while meeting with his Citizens Committee for a Nuclear Test Ban. By the time his plane landed at Otis at 1:30 that afternoon, their baby had already arrived. Five weeks premature and weighing just four pounds, ten and a half ounces, he had to struggle against a burden not uncommon among infants born so early, hyaline membrane disease. A coating of the air sacs was making breathing so difficult that although he seemed to be doing well at first, emergency assistance soon became necessary. He was rushed from Otis to the Children's Hospital Medical Center in Boston and placed in a chamber where oxygen was administered under pressure. But the infant, who was baptized as Patrick Bouvier Kennedy before leaving Otis, still couldn't overcome the condition. At 4:04 A.M. on August 9, just thirty-nine hours after his birth, his heart gave out under the strain.

The President was with his wife almost constantly during those hours. After the death he stayed at Squaw Island with Caroline and little John until their mother returned from the hospital. Patrick was originally buried near the President's birthplace, at Holyhood Cemetery in Brookline. [Kenneth] O'Donnell and [David] Powers have written that "The loss of Patrick affected the President and Jackie more deeply than anybody except their closest friends realized."[1]

By the late afternoon of Monday, August 12, the President was back in the Oval Office for a meeting on the situation in the Far East. With the ratification of the test ban treaty at the center of his attention, and with Cuba remaining as a potentially vulnerable spot politically, there were new dangers to his position emanating from deteriorating conditions in South Vietnam. After a long period of relative stability, one in which Kennedy had been able to maneuver between those advocating stronger American commitments to the government in Saigon and others, such as Averell Harriman and Chester Bowles, who had opposed any major involvement, the "limited partnership" with [Ngo Dinh] Diem was becoming less tenable. North Vietnamese support for the Vietcong had been stepping up. By the end of 1962 there was a tenfold increase in the number of Americans killed and wounded over the previous year. In December, Mike Mansfield had gone there at the President's request and in effect confirmed what such American correspondents as David Halberstam and Neil Sheehan were filing from the war zone. Just as had the French, Mansfield warned, the United States was in danger of being sucked into a futile conflict. "It wasn't a pleasant picture I depicted for him," said the senator afterward.[2] Diem had resisted having American combat troops. He did not want the U.S. to take over his war and his country. Moreover, he continued to defy the Kennedy administration's insistence that he make internal reforms.

Kennedy's "limited partnership," as General [Maxwell] Taylor called the enterprise, was characteristic of his approach. He increased the level of American "advisers," and the numbers of helicopters and other equipment. The CIA, under Station Chief John Richardson, worked actively to provide intelligence support. Diem meanwhile adopted the strategic-hamlet program of Sir Robert Thompson. Thompson, a British counterinsurgency expert, had experimented with the plan in Malaya and the Philippines. In South Vietnam, it was hoped, the guerrillas could in effect be starved out by preventing peasant villages from becoming sanctuaries, and that meant regrouping the villages into hamlets under the protection of the army with such barriers as moats and stake fences. At the same time, the number of Americans there under the Military Assistance and Advisory Group headed by General Paul Harkins escalated to some eleven thousand by the end of 1962.[3]

Later on it would become almost inconceivable to realize that the Vietnamese situation did not capture major attention from the American press until after the start of 1963. Only then did stories from that part of Southeast Asia command steady front-page coverage. Nor was it at the center of the President's own interest. Such matters as the Congo, Berlin, and Cuba had taken far more of his time.

In December, in addition to the Mansfield trip and the gloomy dispatches about the Diem government's inability to make much progress, further discouragement came from a State Department intelligence report. There was, in short, little room for optimism. Instead of giving more emphasis to nonmilitary means of counterinsurgency, reorganizing his government, and sharing some of his authority, Diem was moving too slowly in that direction and relying too much on the strategic-hamlet program and military measures. The adjustments he had been tentatively making in response to Washington's pressures had slowed down the Vietcong somewhat, but neither had their forces weakened nor the "national liberation war" abated. The guerrilla force was estimated at about twenty-three thousand elite fighting personnel, in addition to another 100,000 irregulars and sympathizers. The enemy still controlled about one fifth of the villages, had varying degrees of influence among an additional forty-seven percent, and was thought to be dominant over some nine percent of the population. Furthermore, "Viet Cong influence has almost certainly improved in urban areas not only through subversion and terrorism but also because of its propaganda appeal to the increasingly frustrated non-Communist anti-Diem elements," reported Roger Hilsman in an intelligence memorandum to Dean Rusk.[4]

There was increasing internal discontent among important military and civilian officials, who were participating in plots to overthrow Diem. If the fight against the Communists should deteriorate much further, Hilsman also warned, a "coup could come at any time."[5] Diem himself had been responding by turning inward and relying more on his brother, Nhu. "The two men," George Herring has written, "personally controlled military operations in the field and directed the strategic hamlet program, and they brooked no interference from their American advisers."[6] Nhu's wife had become the government's chief spokesman. Her insensitivity to the Buddhist critics of the Catholic family oligarchy ruling the government gradually brought increasing unpopularity to the regime.

Kennedy meanwhile feared the consequences of negotiating an American way out. His position had not altered from the off-the-record press briefing he gave on August 30, 1961, in which he said, "It is probably true in hindsight that it was not wise to become involved in Laos, but how do we withdraw from South Korea, from Viet-Nam. I don't know where the non-essential areas are. I can't see how we can withdraw from South Korea, Turkey, Iran, Pakistan. Over-extended commitments is a phrase with a lot of appeal, including to some at Harvard."[7] Holding fast in each area had long since become a test of American credibility. To yield in one would mean signaling susceptibility to withdrawal everywhere. As late as September 9, 1963, he was asked by David Brinkley on an NBC television program whether he subscribed to the domino theory. "I believe it," he replied. "I think that the struggle is close enough. China is so large, looms so high just beyond the frontiers, that if South Viet-Nam went, it would not only give them an improved geographic position for a guerrilla assault on Malaya, but would also give the impression that the wave of the future in southeast Asia was China and the Communists. So I believe it."[8]

At the start of the year Roger Hilsman and Michael Forrestal went to Saigon for the President. Kennedy wanted still another view. This time he knew it would come from two critics of Diem. Considering their outlook, a glowing report would have relaxed him.

Forrestal and Hilsman had separate sessions with Diem and his brother. From Diem, Forrestal heard about the importance of strength rather than reforms for maintaining loyalty from the peasants. The long conversation left the American visitor convinced that the South Vietnamese president was not only immovable but had rationalized the rule exerted by his own family as one that was consistent with the family structure of the society itself. Forrestal left without many doubts that Diem was a serious obstruction to any kind of settlement. Hilsman himself was an experienced guerrilla fighter. During World War II he had served with the famed Merrill's Marauders in Asia and with the Office of Strategic Services. When he met with Diem's brother, he thought that Nhu had been on drugs. He seemed devious, unattractive, harsh, and very explicit about his own ambitions. He also boasted about his connections with the northerners and some of their leaders. His attitude toward the problem of relocating the peasants in the delta was far more brutal than Diem's. Nhu also supported the use of chemical warfare and defoliants. Both Americans, Hilsman explained afterward, discovered that the war was "a fraud, a sham. The American military are still chasing Viet Cong and advising the Vietnamese to chase Viet Cong. They're not adopting the program the President has recommended, our own military are not. Diem has turned the strategic-hamlet program over to Nhu, who's taken the title, the name of it, and nothing else. And in fact, what Diem signed, what we persuaded him to, had not been adopted."[9]

Their report was less critical than Mansfield's, but still disturbing. Conceding that some progress had been made over the past year, it pointed out that the negatives were still "awesome." Even the officially supplied figures were disturbing. Despite U.S. urgings, it said, "there is still no single country-wide plan worthy of the name but only a variety of regional and provincial plans," and they seemed to be "both inconsistent and competitive." The strategic-hamlet program was mostly a sham, "inadequately equipped and defended," or "built prematurely in exposed areas." But the real question Forrestal and Hilsman raised was "whether the concentration of power in the hands of Diem and his family, especially Brother Nhu and his wife, and Diem's reluctance to delegate is alienating the middle and higher level officials on whom the government must depend to carry out its policies." The government had to be pushed harder for an overall plan.[10]

Meanwhile the Joint Chiefs of Staff came up with a plan for the possible withdrawal of American advisers starting in late 1963 and ending in 1965.[11] It was, however, one plan among many, and Kennedy's own reevaluation of the situation offered little evidence for believing that he was ready to negotiate and begin pulling out. He knew that falling back would leave him wide open to American conservatives. "If I tried to pull out completely now from Vietnam," he explained to Mansfield, "we would have another Joe McCarthy red scare on our hands, but I can do it after I'm reelected. So we had better make damned sure that I am reelected."[12]

Then came a sharp setback, an entirely new phase, and the upgrading of the war on the President's list of priorities. On May 8 a crowd gathered in Hué to celebrate the anniversary of

Buddha's birth was fired into by government troops. Protesting against religious persecution and demanding a reversal of such policies, Buddhist priests went on hunger strikes. Far more startling to the world was the subsequent photograph of a monk seated in the middle of a downtown Saigon street totally enveloped in flames. That picture of his self-immolation in protest against the government became the most graphic evidence of the dissension. It was only the first in a series of such suicides and helped raise new questions about the entire American commitment.[13]

The division within Kennedy's administration was centered around whether or not support for Diem should be withdrawn. Those who argued against undermining the regime held that there was no adequate replacement in sight. Meanwhile, Kennedy had sent several emissaries to Saigon to try to get Diem and the Buddhists together, but each side was immovable. When Ambassador Frederick Nolting's tour of duty expired that summer, the President replaced him by sending Henry Cabot Lodge, Jr., to Saigon.

Why Lodge? He spoke French, he had had experience in international affairs as Eisenhower's representative to the United Nations, but most of all, as Dean Rusk's biographer explains, Kennedy was persuaded by his secretary of state that "Lodge was to the Republican Party of 1963 what Dulles had been in 1950: the personification of its liberal internationalist wing. . . . Rusk sought to coopt part of the Republican Party, to outmaneuver . . . Goldwater. . . ."[14]

Actually the Lodge appointment was entirely consistent with Kennedy's placement of people like John McCloy and John McCone in positions of potential partisan conflict. In his 1964 interview Bob Kennedy explained that "Lodge was interested in going someplace where there was a difficult problem, they needed somebody who would work with the military, spoke French, had some diplomatic experiences. So he fitted into it."[15]

The most intriguing possibility eventually raised is that Lodge was sent to effectuate the overthrow of Diem by working with the generals who hoped to bring about a coup.[16] Lodge has explained that Kennedy was very much disturbed by the picture of the monk on fire. He talked about the overall reportage of what was going on in Saigon and said that the Diem government was entering a terminal phase. The American embassy had also had poor press relations. "I suppose that there are worse press relations to be found in the world today," Lodge remembered that the President told him, "and I wish you would take charge of press relations." As far as helping to overthrow Diem, Kennedy said that the "Vietnamese are doing that for themselves and don't need any outside help."[17]

Almost immediately after that, Diem helped to speed his own downfall. Just before Lodge's arrival, in complete contradiction of a promise made to Ambassador Nolting, Nhu's American-trained Special Forces went on a rampage against Buddhist pagodas in Hué, Saigon, and other cities. More than fourteen hundred Buddhists were arrested. Right after that American intelligence also reported that Diem was actively engaged in trying to work out a deal with the Hanoi regime of North Vietnam.[18]

If Lodge had been sent with an understanding that he might have to support the generals wanting to get rid of Diem, his actions appeared to confirm that purpose. He showed as little outward support toward the South Vietnamese president as possible, disassociating himself almost completely.[19] On August 24, with Kennedy at Hyannis Port and, "by a strange coincidence, most of the other senior members of the administration" out of town for the weekend, word arrived that South Vietnamese generals knew that Ngo Dinh Nhu was negotiating with the Communists. The information was relayed to Washington via long-distance telephone by Admiral Harry Felt.[20]

Quickly on that Saturday, after a series of consultations and telephone calls—including to the President, Forrestal, and Hilsman—Harriman sent a cable to Lodge in the name of the State

Department. Its message was clear: The U.S. could no longer tolerate a situation where power remained in Nhu's hands. "We wish to give Diem reasonable opportunity to remove Nhu, but if he remains obdurate, then we are prepared to accept the obvious implication that we can no longer support Diem. You may also tell appropriate military commanders we will give them direct support in any interim period of breakdown central government mechanism." Lodge cabled back that it was most unlikely that Diem would get rid of both his brother and sister-in-law and that Nhu was in control of the combat forces in Saigon. "Therefore," he replied, "propose we go straight to Generals with our demands, without informing Diem. Would tell them we prepared to have Diem without Nhu but it is in effect up to them whether to keep him."[21]

For a time it almost seemed that it was the American State Department, in the absence of Dean Rusk, Robert McNamara, John McCone, or McGeorge Bundy, that had undertaken its own coup against those who continued to believe that there was little choice but to back Diem. General Maxwell Taylor first heard about the cable when Ros Gilpatric called him that evening at Fort Myer with the information that clearance from the President had already been obtained and that, in Rusk's absence, George Ball had consented while playing golf. Gilpatric has since observed that "I frankly thought it was an end run. I didn't see why it had to be done Saturday night with the President away, with Rusk away, with McNamara away, Bundy away. I was suspicious of the circumstances in which it was being done. . . . In other words the Defense and military were brought in sort of after the fact."[22] To General Taylor it seemed somewhat of a *fait accompli*. Even if Diem wanted to comply, the telegram to Lodge was obviously an open encouragement "to plotters to move against him at any time."[23]

Mike Forrestal agrees that the circumstances indeed were suspicious. Harriman had originated the cable. The senior diplomat, by then undersecretary of state for political affairs, wanted to take advantage of the weekend conditions because he knew how much trouble he would have getting support if everybody were present.[24] Still, the most important—and often the least noticed element—was the endorsement that came from the President himself, not at the center of action in the Oval Office, but at the other end of a wire in Hyannis Port.

But there was no immediate result. The cable had advised the Voice of America radio people to publicize only that part of the message that would prevent the Vietnamese army from being associated with any plot. Hilsman tried to work that out by briefing a news correspondent so the information could be fed to the Voice, thereby maintaining the usual procedure according to which the propaganda network operated. But the people who actually made the broadcast failed to check their instructions with a telegram sent to guide them. The entire story then went out on the airwaves, "not only," as Hilsman wrote, "that the United States had proof that the Vietnamese Army was innocent of the assault on the pagodas and that Nhu's secret police and Special Forces were to blame," but about the threatened sharp American reduction of aid to Diem.[25]

At a meeting in the embassy in Saigon, Lodge was furious. "Jack Kennedy would never approve of doing things this way," he shouted. "This certainly isn't his way of running a government."[26]

When the President returned from the Cape and met with his staff that Monday, he found more opposition to the Harriman cable than he had evidently expected. "And so the government split in two," the attorney general later said. "It was the only time really, in three years, the government was broken in two in a very disturbing way."[27] In Saigon the generals were unable to get the backing of key army units and remained uncertain, despite CIA assurances, of what American intelligence would do, and withheld any actions.[28]

When the coup came, it resulted from the appropriate opening, which was a combination of the muffled hand from Washington and changed circumstances in Saigon. In the interim Kennedy's customary indecision made the entire process seem more diabolical than it was. First of all the failed move of August provided an opportunity to reassess the situation. At the end of the month Lodge cabled that there was "no turning back" from the overthrow. American prestige was already too committed.[29] Kennedy sent him a personal and private message that pledged his full support to enable his ambassador to "conclude this operation successfully," and, with the clear memory of what happened at the Bay of Pigs, added, "I know from experience that failure is more destructive than an appearance of indecision."[30] On September 2, after [French President Charles] De Gaulle had criticized the American involvement in Vietnam, Kennedy was interviewed by Walter Cronkite on a CBS television news program. At that point, in response to a question about Diem changing his pattern, the President answered in a matter that has too often been quoted incompletely. What he said at that point was: "We hope that he comes to see that, but in the final analysis it is the people and the government itself who have to win or lose this struggle. All we can do is help, and we are making it very clear, but I don't agree with those who say we should withdraw. That would be a great mistake."[31] It was not immediately evident that, in reality, he was talking just as much about the Vietnamese choice of a leader as about the American commitment. On the same day that he talked to Cronkite, Kennedy called Hilsman and asked whether his undersecretary of state had done any thinking about "selective cuts in aid that would not hurt the war effort but still make Diem and Nhu understand that we mean business."[32] Encouragement was also given to Senator [Frank] Church's threat to introduce a resolution calling for the suspension of aid to South Vietnam unless it ended its repressive policies.[33] During this period, however, the President had no way of knowing that things in Saigon would be better without Diem. But his hand was being pushed. An Alsop story in *The Washington Post* on September 18, evidently based on interviews with Diem and Nhu, gave further information about their dealings with Hanoi.[34] Reacting to such stories, Kennedy sent McNamara and General Taylor to Saigon. Once again Diem was immovable, contending that the war was going well, pointing with pride to favorable results from just completed rigged elections, and, as McNamara wrote, offering "absolutely no assurances that he would take any steps in response to the representations made to American visitors. . . . His manner was one of at least outward serenity and of a man who had patiently explained a great deal and who hoped he had thus corrected a number of misapprehensions." The McNamara-Taylor report, however, cautioned that it was not the time to take the initiative in trying to change the government. "Our policy should be to seek urgently to identify and build contacts with an alternative leadership if and when it appears." Mainly the suggestion of the mission was to apply selective pressures on the regime.[35]

On October 2 the White House announced that a thousand men would be withdrawn by the end of the year. Gilpatric later stated that McNamara did indicate to him that the withdrawal was part of the President's plan to wind down the war, but that was too far in the future. They were still, at that moment, deeply divided about what to do about the internal situation in Saigon.[36] At just that point the recall of John Richardson, the CIA station chief who was close to the regime, seemed to be another signal, although it may not have been intended for that purpose.[37] Still, it is hard to believe that the move, along with the talk about reductions of American aid to the government, lacked the purpose of giving further encouragement to the anti-Diem generals.

During a series of meetings that were held from August 23 through October 23 between Lodge, General Harkins, and the anti-Diem plotters, including Duong Van Minh (Big Minh), there was agreement on what had to be done: The U.S. agreed that Nhu had to go and that the disposition of Diem ought to be left to the generals. There could be no American help to initiate the action, but support would come during the interim period in case of a breakdown of the central government's mechanism. What was also clear was that if they did not get rid of the

Nhus and the Buddhist situation were not redressed, the United States would end economic and military support.[38]

Lodge later reported that he had advised the President "not to thwart" a coup. That act, rather than initiating one, would have constituted interference.[39] Yet even at that point Kennedy wavered, suffering a recurrence of earlier doubts. He told Bundy that the U.S. should be in a position to blow the whistle if it looked as though the coup was failing.[40] Bundy cabled Lodge that there should be no American action that would reveal any knowledge that a coup was even possible. The "burden of proof" must be on the plotters "to show a substantial possibility of quick success; otherwise we should discourage them from proceeding since a miscalculation could result in jeopardizing U.S. position in Southeast Asia."[41] Indeed, the Americans in Saigon behaved as though things were normal.

On the morning of November 1 Admiral Felt paid a courtesy call on Diem at the presidential palace. In the afternoon Diem called Lodge to ask about the American attitude toward the coup. Lodge was evasive, but admitted he was worried about Diem's personal safety. That night, the president and Nhu escaped from the palace to a hideout in the Chinese quarter of Saigon. From there Diem contacted the generals and asked for safe conduct back so he could make a graceful exit from power. On his return, however, according to a prearranged plan, he and his brother were shot and killed by Big Minh's personal bodyguard.[42]

The news of Diem's death outraged Kennedy. General Taylor wrote that he "leaped to his feet and rushed from the room with a look of shock and dismay on his face which I had never seen before."[43] George Smathers remembered that Jack Kennedy blamed the CIA, saying "I've got to do something about those bastards"; they should be stripped of their exorbitant power.[44] Mike Forrestal called Kennedy's reaction "both personal and religious," and especially troubled by the implication that a Catholic President had participated in a plot to assassinate a coreligionist.[45] Every account of Kennedy's response is in complete agreement. Until the very end he had hoped Diem's life could be spared.

It has now become clear that however futile his efforts Kennedy tried to prevent the murder. He told Francis Cardinal Spellman that he had known in advance that the Vietnamese leader would probably be killed, but in the end he could not control the situation.[46] At least one attempt, and possibly three, came from a direct attempt to communicate with Diem by using a personal emissary, someone completely loyal to Jack Kennedy, someone totally without any other obligation, his intimate friend, Torby Macdonald, the Massachusetts congressman.

As far as is known, there are no written records. It was completely secret. Mike Forrestal remembers briefing Macdonald for the trip.[47] Torbert Macdonald, Jr., recalls that his father told him about it.[48] The congressman's widow is certain that he made at least three trips to Saigon for the President.[49] Torby's closest friend during his final years, who desires to remain anonymous, has a photograph of him posing before the ancient temple at Angkor Wat in Cambodia, indicating that he went through that country while traveling to South Vietnam as a private citizen.[50]

Macdonald himself explained why Kennedy sent him. The President had begun to develop personal sources of information from FBI men who were bypassing J. Edgar Hoover and going directly to him. Some CIA people were following a similar route and avoiding the Agency. By that time the President was learning. When he first came into office, he had been intimidated by the Pentagon and the CIA, but he had begun to find out how to get around them. When he heard that Big Minh and his group were planning to assassinate Diem, he wanted to make a direct contact. He was hesitant about using the embassy in Saigon because he could not trust his own people there. Nor did he have enough confidence in Lodge, who had maintained a distant relationship with Diem. Finally, there was no South Vietnamese he could trust. So he called on

Torby, who then carried the President's personal plea, which was to get rid of his brother and take refuge in the American embassy. As Macdonald later explained it, he told Diem: "They're going to kill you. You've got to get out of there temporarily to seek sanctuary in the American embassy and you must get rid of your sister-in-law and your brother." But Diem refused. "He just won't do it," Macdonald reported to the President. "He's too stubborn; just refuses to."[51]

Diem's death preceded Jack Kennedy's by just three weeks. What JFK would have done about American involvement in South Vietnam can never be known for certain. It is probable that not even he was sure.

Ken O'Donnell has been the most vigorous advocate of the argument that the President was planning to liquidate the American stake right after the completion of the 1964 elections would have made it politically possible. The withdrawal of those thousand advisers, he said, was but a first step in that process.[52] At the time the Joint Chiefs asked for an increase of American strength to seventeen thousand, Kennedy told his military aide, Ted Clifton, that he would go along with the request but had warned that he would approve no more.[53]

At that moment Kennedy could not have anticipated the shape of either the domestic political climate or the situation in Southeast Asia. Still, for him to have withdrawn at any point short of a clear-cut settlement would have been most unlikely. As Sorensen has said in an oral-history interview, Kennedy "did feel strongly that for better or worse, enthusiastic or unenthusiastic, we had to stay there until we left on terms other than a retreat or abandonment of our commitment."[54] The remarks he had planned to deliver at the trade Mart in Dallas on the afternoon of November 22 contained the following statement of purpose: "Our assistance to these nations can be painful, risky and costly, as is true in Southeast Asia today. But we dare not weary of the test."[55] "I talked with him hundreds of times about Vietnam," said Dean Rusk, "and on no single occasion did he ever whisper any such thing to his own secretary of state." In addition, and what was more important, Rusk pointed out, was that a decision in 1963 to take troops out in 1965 following the election of 1964 "would have been a decision to have Americans in uniform in combat for domestic political reasons. No President can do that and live with it."[56] When Ken O'Donnell was pressed about whether the President's decision to withdraw meant that he would [not] have undertaken the escalation that followed in 1965, the position became qualified. Kennedy, said O'Donnell, had not faced the same level of North Vietnamese infiltration as did President Johnson, thereby implying that he, too, would have responded in a similar way under those conditions.[57] As Bobby Kennedy later said, his brother had reached the point where he felt that South Vietnam was worth keeping for psychological and political reasons "more than anything else."[58]

« 7 »

The Tonkin Gulf Resolution

Robert S. McNamara

THE CLOSEST THE UNITED STATES CAME to a declaration of war in Vietnam was the Tonkin Gulf Resolution of August 1964. The events surrounding the resolution generated intense controversy that continues to this day.

Before August 1964, the American people had followed developments in Vietnam sporadically and with limited concern. The war seemed far off. Tonkin Gulf changed that. In the short run, attacks on U.S. warships in the gulf and the congressional resolution that followed brought home the possibility of U.S. involvement in the war as never before. More important, in the long run, the Johnson administration invoked the resolution to justify the constitutionality of the military actions it took in Vietnam from 1965 on.

Congress recognized the vast power the resolution granted to President Johnson, but it did not conceive of it as a declaration of war and did not intend it to be used, as it was, as authorization for an enormous expansion of U.S. forces in Vietnam—from 16,000 military advisers to 550,000 combat troops. Securing a declaration of war and specific authorization for the introduction of combat forces in subsequent years might well have been impossible; not seeking it was certainly wrong.

Many people look upon the nine days from July 30 to August 7, 1964, as the most controversial period of the "Twenty-five-year War." No wonder. For three decades, intense debate has swirled around what happened in the gulf; how we reported what happened to the Congress and the public; the authority we sought from Congress in reaction to events; and how the executive branch under two presidents used that authority over the years that followed.

The key questions and my answers are these:

- Attacks by North Vietnamese patrol boats against U.S. destroyers reportedly occurred on two separate occasions—August 2 and August 4, 1964. Did the attacks actually occur?
  Answer: The evidence of the first attack is indisputable. The second attack appears probable but not certain.
- At the time—and still more so in later years—some elements of Congress and the public believed the Johnson administration deliberately provoked the attacks in order to justify an escalation of the war and to obtain, under a subterfuge, congressional authority for that escalation. Does this view have any merit?
  Answer: None at all.
- In response to the attacks, the president ordered a strike by U.S. naval aircraft against four North Vietnamese patrol boat bases and an oil depot. Was the strike justified?
  Answer: Probably.

- Would the congressional resolution have been submitted if the action in the Tonkin Gulf had not occurred and, without that action, would it have passed?
  Answer: Almost certainly a resolution would have been submitted to Congress within a matter of weeks, and very likely it would have passed. But the resolution would have faced far more extensive debate, and there would have been attempts to limit the president's authority.
- Was the Johnson administration justified in basing its subsequent military actions in Vietnam—including an enormous expansion of force levels—on the Tonkin Gulf Resolution?
  Answer: Absolutely not. Although the resolution granted sufficiently broad authority to support the escalation that followed, as I have said, Congress never intended it to be used as a basis for such action, and still less did the country see it so.

The events in the Tonkin Gulf involved two separate U.S. operations: the Plan 34A activities and what were known as DESOTO patrols.

As I have said, in January 1964 the National Security Council had approved CIA support for South Vietnamese covert operations against North Vietnam, code-named Plan 34A. Plan 34A comprised two types of operations: in one, boats and aircraft dropped South Vietnamese agents equipped with radios into North Vietnam to conduct sabotage and to gather intelligence; in the other, high-speed patrol boats manned by South Vietnamese or foreign mercenary crews launched hit-and-run attacks against North Vietnamese shore and island installations. The CIA supported the South Vietnamese 34A operations, and MACV maintained close contact with them, as did General [Victor] Krulak of the Joint Staff in Washington.

The 303 Committee—so named because it originally met in Room 303 of the Old Executive Office Building—reviewed the schedules of the clandestine operations. All of the CIA's covert operations worldwide required clearance by the 303 Committee. The president's national security adviser (Mac [McGeorge] Bundy) chaired the group, whose other members at that time included the undersecretary of state (George Ball), the deputy secretary of defense (Cyrus R. Vance, who had succeeded Ros Gilpatric in early 1964), and the CIA's deputy director for plans (Richard Helms).

The CIA has often been called a "rogue elephant" by its critics, but I consider that a mischaracterization. During my seven years in the Defense Department (and I believe throughout the preceding and following administrations), all CIA "covert operations" (excluding spying operations) were subject to approval by the president and the secretaries of state and defense, or their representatives. The CIA had no authority to act without that approval. So far as I know, it never did.

DESOTO patrols differed substantially in purpose and procedure from 34A operations. They were part of a system of global electronic reconnaissance carried out by specially equipped U.S. naval vessels. Operating in international waters, these vessels collected radio and radar signals emanating from shore-based stations on the periphery of Communist countries such as the Soviet Union, China, North Korea, and, more to the point here, North Vietnam.[*][1] These patrols resembled those of Soviet trawlers off our coasts. The information collected could be used in the event U.S. military operations ever became necessary against these countries. Fleet naval com-

[*] The closest approach to North Vietnam was set at eight miles to the mainland and four miles to the offshore islands. Because the United States had no record of a North Vietnamese assertion regarding its territorial waters, Washington concluded that international waters extended to three miles offshore—the limit established by France when it controlled Indochina. Only *after* the Tonkin Gulf incidents did Hanoi claim a twelve-mile limit. At no time during August 1964 did U.S. ships approach closer than five miles to the offshore islands.

manders—in this case, Pacific Fleet Commander Adm. Thomas Moorer—determined the frequency and course of DESOTO patrols and reviewed them with the Joint Staff in Washington.

Although some individuals knew of both 34A operations and DESOTO patrols, the approval process for each was compartmentalized, and few, if any, senior officials either planned or followed in detail the operational schedules of both. We should have.

Long before the August events in the Tonkin Gulf, many of us who knew about the 34A operations had concluded they were essentially worthless. Most of the South Vietnamese agents sent into North Vietnam were either captured or killed, and the seaborne attacks amounted to little more than pinpricks. One might well ask, "If so, then why were the operations continued?" The answer is that the South Vietnamese government saw them as a relatively low-cost means of harassing North Vietnam in retaliation for Hanoi's support of the Vietcong.

On the night of July 30, 1964, a 34A mission carried out by South Vietnamese patrol boats attacked two North Vietnamese islands in the Tonkin Gulf thought to support infiltration operations against the South. The next morning, the U.S. destroyer *Maddox* on a DESOTO patrol steamed into the gulf well away from the islands. Two and a half days later, at 3:40 P.M. (3:40 A.M. Washington time) on August 2, the *Maddox* reported it was being approached by high-speed boats. Within a few minutes it was attacked by torpedoes and automatic weapons fire. The *Maddox* reported no injuries or damage. No doubt existed that the vessel had been fired upon: crew members retrieved a North Vietnamese shell fragment from the deck, which I insisted be sent to my office to verify the attack; furthermore, North Vietnam, in its official history of the war, confirmed that it ordered the *Maddox* attacked. At the time of the incident, the *Maddox* lay in international waters, more than twenty-five miles off the North Vietnamese coast.[2]

At 11:30 A.M. on August 2, the president met with his senior advisers to study the latest reports and consider a U.S. response. Cy Vance represented my office. The group believed it was possible that a local North Vietnamese commander—rather than a senior official—had taken the initiative, and the president therefore decided not to retaliate. He agreed instead to send a stiff protest note to Hanoi and to continue the patrol, adding another destroyer, the *C. Turner Joy*.[3]

Max [Maxwell] Taylor, by then ambassador in South Vietnam, opposed the decision not to retaliate. In a cable to the State Department late in the night of August 2, he said that our failure to respond to an unprovoked attack on a U.S. destroyer in international waters would be construed as an "indication that the U.S. flinches from direct confrontation with the North Vietnamese."[4]

At 3:00 P.M. the next day, Dean Rusk and I briefed members of the Senate Foreign Relations and Armed Services committees in closed session on the events of July 30 and August 2. We described the 34A operations, the attack on the DESOTO patrol, and why the president had decided not to retaliate. Although I have been unable to locate any record of the meeting, I believe we also stressed that we had no intention of provoking a North Vietnamese attack on the DESOTO patrol. We informed the senators that the DESOTO patrols, as well as the 34A operations, would continue, and in fact another 34A raid occurred about this time against the coast of North Vietnam (it was then early morning August 4 Saigon time).

At 7:40 A.M. Washington time (7:40 P.M. Saigon time) on August 4, the *Maddox* radioed that an attack from unidentified vessels appeared imminent. *Maddox*'s information came from highly classified reports from the National Security Agency, which had intercepted North Vietnamese instructions. An hour later the *Maddox* radioed that it had established radar contact with three unidentified vessels. A nearby U.S. aircraft carrier, the *Ticonderoga*, launched fighter aircraft to the *Maddox*'s and the *Turner Joy*'s assistance.

Low clouds and thunderstorms on this moonless night made visibility extremely difficult. During the next several hours, confusion reigned in the gulf. The *Maddox* and the *Turner Joy* reported more than twenty torpedo attacks, sighting of torpedo wakes, enemy cockpit lights, searchlight illumination, automatic weapons fire, and radar and sonar contacts.

As the situation intensified, Cy and I met with members of the Joint Staff to consider how to react. We agreed that, assuming the reports were correct, a response to this second unprovoked attack was absolutely necessary. While we had not accepted Max Taylor's view that the August 2 attack required retaliation, a second, and in our minds, unprovoked attack against U.S. vessels operating in international waters surely did. Therefore, we quickly developed a plan for carrier aircraft to strike four North Vietnamese patrol boat bases and two oil depots that supplied them.

At 11:40 A.M., I met with Dean, Mac, and the chiefs to review our options. We continued our discussion at an NSC meeting, and then at lunch with the president, Cy, and John McCone.

North Vietnamese attacks on U.S. destroyers on the high seas appeared to be so irrational (in that they were bound to escalate the conflict) that we speculated about Hanoi's motives. Some believed the 34A operations had played a role in triggering North Vietnam's actions against the DESOTO patrols, but others, pointing at 34A's ineffectiveness, found that explanation hard to accept. In any event, the president agreed that a second attack, if confirmed, required a swift and firm retaliatory strike.

The question then became: Did a second attack actually occur?

As I have said, visibility in the area at the time of the alleged attack was very limited. Because of that and because sonar soundings—which are often unreliable—accounted for most reports of the second attack, uncertainty remained about whether it had occurred. I therefore made strenuous efforts to determine what, indeed, had happened. At my request, Air Force Lt. Gen. David A. Burchinal, director of the Joint Staff, called Admiral [U.S. Grant] Sharp in Honolulu several times to obtain details of the incident.

At 1:27 P.M. Washington time, Capt. John J. Herrick, DESOTO patrol commander aboard the *Maddox*, sent this "flash" message to Honolulu and Washington:

> Review of action makes many reported contacts and torpedoes fired appear doubtful. Freak weather effects on radar and overeager sonar men may have accounted for many reports. No actual visual sightings by *Maddox*. Suggest complete evaluation before any further action taken.[5]

Forty-one minutes later, Sharp telephoned Burchinal and told him that, despite Herrick's message, there was "no doubt" in his mind a second attack had occurred. Captain Herrick sent another message at 2:48 P.M. Washington time, which read: "Certain that original ambush was bona-fide."[6]

I placed several calls myself to obtain as much information as possible. Because the facts remain in dispute even now, thirty years later, I wish to relate some of my conversations (recorded at the time) in detail. At 4:08 P.M., I called Admiral Sharp by secure phone and said, "What's the latest information on the action?"

"The latest dope we have, sir," replied Sharp, "indicates a little doubt on just exactly what went on . . . apparently the thing started by a sort of ambush attempt by the PTs." He added, "The initial ambush attempt was definite." However, he mentioned "freak radar echoes" and "young fellows" manning the sonars, who "are apt to say any noise is a torpedo, so that, undoubtedly, there were not as many torpedoes" as earlier reported. Sharp said the *Turner Joy* claimed three PT boats hit and one sunk, while the *Maddox* claimed one or two sunk.

"There isn't any possibility there was no attack, is there?" I asked Sharp. He replied, "Yes, I would say that there is a slight possibility."

I said, "We obviously don't want to do it [launch the retaliatory strike] until we are damn sure what happened."

Sharp agreed and said he thought he could have more information in a couple of hours.[7]

At 4:47 P.M., Cy and I met with the chiefs to review the evidence relating to the alleged second attack. Five factors in particular persuaded us it had occurred: the *Turner Joy* had been illuminated when fired on by automatic weapons; one of the destroyers had observed PT boat cockpit lights; antiaircraft batteries had fired on two U.S. aircraft overflying the area; we had intercepted and decoded a North Vietnamese message apparently indicating two of its boats had been sunk; and Admiral Sharp had determined there had probably been an attack. At 5:23 P.M., Sharp called Burchinal and said no doubt now existed that an attack on the destroyers had been carried out.[8]

At 6:15 P.M., the National Security Council met at the White House. I outlined the evidence supporting our conclusion and presented our proposed response. All NSC members concurred in the action, and the president authorized the launch of our naval aircraft.[9]

At 6:45 P.M., the president, Dean Rusk, the new Joint Chiefs chairman, Gen. Earle G. "Bus" Wheeler, and I met with congressional leaders to brief them on the day's events and our planned response. Explaining the basis for our retaliation, Dean told the leaders that North Vietnam had made a serious decision to attack our vessels on the high seas, that we should not interpret their action as accidental, that we must demonstrate U.S. resolve in Southeast Asia, and that our limited response would show we did not want a war with the North. The president informed the group that he planned to submit a resolution requesting Congress's support for U.S. combat operations in Southeast Asia should they prove necessary. Several of the senators and representatives said they would support this request.[10]

At 7:22 P.M., the *Ticonderoga* received the president's strike authorization message, as did a second carrier, the *Constellation*, a few minutes later. The first planes took off from the carriers at 10:43 P.M., Washington time. In all, U.S. naval aircraft flew sixty-four sorties against the patrol boat bases and a supporting oil complex. It was considered a successful mission—a limited, but we thought appropriate, reply to at least one and very probably two attacks on U.S. vessels.

It did not take long for controversy to attach itself to the incident. On August 6, several senators disputed our report of what had occurred. The dispute was not resolved, and several years later (in February 1968), a Senate hearing was convened to reexamine the evidence. It also challenged the administration's reporting. In 1972, Louis Tordella, then deputy director of the National Security Agency, concluded that the intercepted North Vietnamese message, which had been interpreted as ordering the August 4 attack, had in fact referred to the August 2 action. Ray S. Cline, the CIA's deputy director for intelligence in 1964, echoed this judgment in a 1984 interview. And James B. Stockdale—a *Ticonderoga* pilot in 1964, who later spent eight years in a Hanoi prison and subsequently received the Congressional Medal of Honor—stated in his memoirs that he had seen no North Vietnamese boats while flying over the two destroyers on August 4, and he believed no attack had occurred.[11] The controversy has persisted until this day.

At 9:00 A.M. on August 6, 1964, Dean, Bus, and I entered the Senate Caucus Room and took our seats before a joint executive session of the Senate Foreign Relations and Armed Services committees to testify on the August 2 and 4 events in the Tonkin Gulf and in support of the joint congressional resolution then before both houses.

Dean began his prepared statement by stressing that "the immediate occasion for this resolution is, of course, the North Vietnamese attacks on our naval vessels, operating in international waters in the Gulf of Tonkin, on August 2nd and August 4th." He continued: "The present attacks . . . are no isolated event. They are part and parcel of a continuing Communist drive to conquer South Vietnam . . . and eventually dominate and conquer other free nations of Southeast Asia." I then described the two attacks in detail, and Bus stated the Joint Chiefs' unanimous endorsement of the U.S. retaliatory action, which they considered appropriate under the circumstances.

The committees' questioning centered on two separate issues: What had happened in the gulf? And was the resolution a proper delegation of power to the president to apply military force in the area?

Senator Wayne Morse vehemently challenged our description of events in the gulf, our military response, and the resolution itself:

> I am unalterably opposed to this course of action which, in my judgment, is an aggressive course of action on the part of the United States. I think we are kidding the world if you try to give the impression that when the South Vietnamese naval boats bombarded two islands a short distance off the coast of North Vietnam we were not implicated.
>
> I think our whole course of action of aid to South Vietnam satisfies the world that those boats didn't act in a vacuum as far as the United States was concerned. We knew those boats were going up there, and that naval action was a clear act of aggression against the territory of North Vietnam, and our ships were in Tonkin Bay, in international waters, but nevertheless they were in Tonkin Bay to be interpreted as standing as a cover for naval operations of South Vietnam.
>
> I think what happened is that [Nguyen] Khanh got us to backstop him in open aggression against the territorial integrity of North Vietnam. I have listened to briefing after briefing and there isn't a scintilla of evidence in any briefing yet that North Vietnam engaged in any military aggression against South Vietnam either with its ground troops or its navy.

This last comment went contrary to voluminous, and ever-growing, evidence of North Vietnam's support for the Vietcong—by land and sea, with men and military equipment. The senator concluded his statement by asserting, "American naval vessels [were] conveniently standing by as a backstop" for South Vietnamese 34A operations.

In reply I said, "Our Navy played absolutely no part in, was not associated with, [and] was not aware of any South Vietnamese actions." As I have explained, the U.S. Navy did not administer 34A operations, and the DESOTO patrols had neither been a "cover" for nor stood by as a "backstop" for 34A vessels. Senator Morse knew these facts, for he had been present on August 3 when Dean, Bus, and I briefed senators on 34A and the DESOTO patrols. That portion of my reply was correct. However, I went on to say the *Maddox* "was not informed of, was not aware [of], had no evidence of, and so far as I know today had no knowledge of any possible South Vietnamese actions in connection with the two islands that Senator Morse referred to." That portion of my reply, I later learned, was totally incorrect; DESOTO patrol commander Captain Herrick had indeed known of 34A. My statement was honest but wrong.

The hearing then turned to a discussion of the resolution. Its key passages stated:

> Whereas naval units of [North Vietnam] . . . in violation of . . . international law, have deliberately and repeatedly attacked United States naval vessels lawfully present in international waters . . . and Whereas these attacks are part of a deliberate and systematic campaign of aggression . . . against its neighbors, . . . the United States is, therefore, prepared, as the President determines, to take all necessary steps, including the use of armed force, to assist any member or protocol state of the Southeast Asia Collective Defense Treaty requesting assistance in defense of its freedom.

Discussing the proposed language, Dean stressed it granted authority similar to that approved by Congress in the 1955 Formosa Resolution, the 1947 Middle East Resolution, and the 1962 Cuba Resolution. His prepared statement noted that "we cannot tell what steps may in the future be required," and he added: "As the Southeast Asia situation develops, and *if it develops in ways we cannot now anticipate, of course there will be close and continuous consultation between the President and the Congress* [emphasis added]."

Senate Foreign Relations committee Chairman William Fulbright—who presided over the hearing, managed the resolution on the Senate floor, and later severely criticized the Johnson administration's handling of the Tonkin Gulf events—offered complimentary remarks that day: "The promptness and decision . . . which all of you exhibited on this occasion was commendable," he said.

Others present endorsed the resolution's extensive delegation of power to the president. Sen. Clifford P. Case (R-N.J.), for example, asked if three resolutions previously referred to contained the broad language "as the President determines." "They have had language equivalent to that," responded Senator Fulbright. Senator Case declared his hearty support. The two committees favorably reported the resolution to the full Senate by a vote of 31–1, with Morse dissenting.[12]

During floor debate that afternoon, Sen. John Sherman Cooper (R-Ky.) had the following exchange with Senator Fulbright:

> COOPER: Are we now giving the President advance authority to take whatever action he may deem necessary respecting South Vietnam and its defense, or with respect to the defense of any other country included in the [SEATO] treaty?
>
> FULBRIGHT: I think that is correct.
>
> COOPER: Then, looking ahead, if the President decided that it was necessary to use such force as could lead into war, we will give that authority by this resolution?
>
> FULBRIGHT: That is the way I would interpret it.[13]

There is no doubt in my mind that Congress understood the resolution's vast grant of power to the president. But there is also no doubt in my mind that Congress understood the president would not use the vast grant without consulting it carefully and completely.

The Senate and House voted on the resolution the next day, August 7. The Senate passed it by a vote of 88–2, Morse and Ernest W. Gruening (D-Alaska) voting nay; the House approved it unanimously, 416–0.

Critics have long asserted that a cloak of deception surrounded the entire Tonkin Gulf affair. They charge that the administration coveted congressional support for war in Indochina, drafted a resolution authorizing it, provoked an incident to justify support for it, and presented false statements to enlist such support. The charges are unfounded.

The resolution grew out of the president's belief that should circumstances ever necessitate the introduction of U.S. combat forces into Indochina—as some of the Joint Chiefs had been suggesting since January 1964—such deployments should be preceded by congressional endorsement. For that purpose, the State Department had drafted a resolution in late May. However, because Max Taylor, as chairman of the Joint Chiefs, had recommended against initiating U.S. military operations at least until the fall—a recommendation that the president, Dean, Mac, and I concurred in—it had been decided to defer presenting the resolution to Congress until after the Civil Rights Bill cleared the Senate in September.

We had this schedule in mind until the North Vietnamese attacks on U.S. vessels led us to believe the war was heating up and to wonder what might happen next. This, in turn, led to our belief that a resolution might well be needed earlier than we had previously anticipated. The president may also have been influenced by what he saw as an opportunity to tie the resolution to a hostile action by Hanoi, and to do so in a way that made him appear firm but moderate, in contrast to Republican presidential candidate Barry Goldwater's hawkish rhetoric.

The charge of deliberate provocation has endured, in part, because some former government officials endorsed it. George Ball, in a 1977 BBC radio interview stated: "Many of the people who were associated with the war . . . were looking for any excuse to initiate bombing. . . . The DESOTO patrol was primarily for provocation. . . . There was a feeling that if the destroyer got into some trouble, that would provide the provocation we needed."[14]

In contrast, Bill [William] Bundy told the same radio audience that the United States did not intend to create a crisis and had not "engineered" the incidents as an excuse for military action. In fact, he said, "it didn't fit in with our plans at all, to be perfectly blunt about it. We didn't think the situation had deteriorated to the point where we had to consider stronger action on the way things lay in South Vietnam." Elsewhere he wrote, "The case on any Administration intent to provoke the incidents is not simply weak, it is nonexistent."[15]

He went on to make a different but no less crucial point:

> Miscalculation by both the U.S. and North Vietnam is, in the end, at the root of the best hindsight hypothesis of Hanoi's behavior. In simple terms, it was a mistake for an Administration sincerely resolved to keep its risks low, to have the 34A operations and the destroyer patrol take place even in the same time period. Rational minds could not readily have foreseen that Hanoi might confuse them . . . but rational calculations should have taken account of the irrational. . . . Washington did not want an incident, and it seems doubtful that Hanoi did either. Yet each misread the other, and the incidents happened.[16]

I agree with both of these comments. And I believe Dean, Mac, and Max would agree as well.

Of course, if the Tonkin Gulf Resolution had not led to much more serious military involvement in Vietnam, it likely would not remain so controversial. But it did serve to open the floodgates. Nevertheless, the idea that the Johnson administration deliberately deceived Congress is false. The problem was not that Congress did not grasp the resolution's potential but that it did not grasp the war's potential and how the administration would respond in the face of it. As a 1967 Senate Foreign Relations Committee report concluded, in adopting a resolution with such sweeping language, "Congress committed the error of making a *personal* judgment as to how President Johnson would implement the resolution when it had a responsibility to make an *institutional* judgment, first, as to what *any* President would do with so great an acknowledgement of power, and, second, as to whether, under the Constitution, Congress had the right to grant or concede the authority in question [emphases in original]." I agree with both points.[17]

Senator Fulbright, in time, came to feel that he had been misled—and indeed he had. He had received definite assurances from Dean at the August 6, 1964, hearing (and I believe privately from LBJ as well) that the president would not use the vast power granted him without full congressional consultation. But at the February 20, 1968, hearing called to reexamine the affair, Senator Fulbright graciously absolved me of the charge of intentionally misleading Congress. "I never meant to leave the impression that I thought you were deliberating trying to deceive us," he said. Senators Mike Mansfield, Claiborne Pell, and Stuart Symington made similar statements.[18]

The fundamental issue of Tonkin Gulf involved not deception but, rather, misuse of power bestowed by the resolution. The language of the resolution plainly granted the powers the president subsequently used, and Congress understood the breadth of those powers when it overwhelmingly approved the resolution on August 7, 1964. But no doubt exists that Congress did *not* intend to authorize without further, full consultation the expansion of U.S. forces in Vietnam from 16,000 to 550,000 men, initiating large-scale combat operations with the risk of an expanded war with China and the Soviet Union, and extending U.S. involvement in Vietnam for many years to come.

The question of congressional versus presidential authority over the conduct of U.S. military operations remains hotly contested to this day. The root of this struggle lies in the ambiguous language of the Constitution, which established the president as commander in chief but gave Congress the power to declare war.

In December 1990, just before the Persian Gulf War, I testified before the Senate Foreign Relations Committee on the possible use of U.S. forces there. A few days earlier, Secretary of Defense Richard B. Cheney had asserted that President Bush possessed the power to commit large-scale U.S. forces to combat in the gulf (ultimately we had 500,000 men and women there) under his authority as commander in chief. Senator Paul S. Sarbanes (D-Md.) asked my opinion of Cheney's assertion. I replied that I was not a constitutional lawyer and therefore declined to answer. Certain that I would repudiate Cheney's statement, Senator Sarbanes pressed me very hard for a reply.

Finally, I told the senator that he had asked the wrong question. The issue did not come down to legalities. It involved at its most basic level a question of politics: should a president take our nation to war (other than immediately to repel an attack on our shores) without popular consent as voiced by Congress? I said no president should, and I believed President Bush would not. He did not. Before President Bush began combat operations against Iraq, he sought—and obtained—Congress's support (as well as that of the U.N. Security Council).

President Bush was right. President Johnson, and those of us who served with him, were wrong.

⋘ 8 ⋙

Lyndon Johnson Chooses War

Fredrik Logevall

IN TERMS OF HIS DOMESTIC FLANK, [President] Johnson had considerable freedom of action on Vietnam after the election [of 1964]. The political context he faced with respect to the war was a much more fluid one than is often suggested, with little or no national "consensus" about which way to proceed. The pressure for escalation was minimal. The fact that [Richard] Nixon and [Strom] Thurmond preached the need for victory is much less significant than that hardly anyone else in the GOP joined them. The same is true of the press, where the few newspapers advocating a stepped-up American involvement were vastly outnumbered by those that explicitly ruled out such a course. The latter group included not only those papers . . . that urged a negotiated settlement but others that said that all options were equally bad—this group included the *Christian Science Monitor*, the *Baltimore Sun*, the *Philadelphia Inquirer*, the *San Francisco Chronicle*, the *Wall Street Journal*, and the Portland *Oregonian*.[1] In Middle America, ignorance and disengagement were the rule—it is doubtful that more than 20 percent of Americans could have placed Vietnam on a map, or provided concrete details about the ally on whose behalf the United States had intervened. Of those who paid attention, most were confused, not wanting to see a humiliating defeat for their country but seeing little sense in a land war on behalf of a weak government in a small country in a remote corner of the globe. In such instances, the natural inclination for people is to trust government to make the decision.

All of which suggests that William Bundy, one of the architects of the escalation, was correct when he later conceded that LBJ could have carried American public opinion with him "on whatever course he chose."[2] No doubt the president would have taken political heat had he opted for withdrawal, with Goldwater Republicans accusing him of "losing" Vietnam like Truman had "lost" China, but it would not have been debilitating heat. Vietnam was not a deeply partisan issue at the end of 1964, and the Goldwater faction was but one wing of a Republican Party that lacked a singular vision of what should happen in Southeast Asia. His Democratic Party might have suffered in the 1966 midterm elections (though quite possibly not), but the in-party almost always loses seats in any nonpresidential election, especially following a landslide such as occurred in 1964.

For Bundy and most other Vietnam advisers, the domestic context mattered much less than the international one, and the next question to be considered is whether global considerations compelled Johnson to stay the course in Vietnam. Here again, the evidence suggests not. Among its friends in the world, America in late 1964 was largely isolated on Vietnam. Johnson's early-December demand that allied nations step up their assistance had by the end of the month yielded virtually nothing, despite the fact that special letters over Johnson's signature went out to targeted governments and despite the fact that the NSC joined what had up to this point been purely a State Department effort. The NSC's James Thomson and Chester Cooper succinctly summarized the situation at year's end: despite a "whirlwind of activity and a mass of cable traffic" on "third country assistance," they informed McGeorge Bundy on New Year's Eve, "very little has yet come out of the funnel."[3]

In later years, after America's isolation on the war had become plainly evident, Dean Rusk liked to argue that, even though friendly governments might be unwilling to contribute materially to the war effort, they nevertheless desperately wanted Washington to persevere in the fight. A decision to withdraw prematurely (in other words, before an independent, noncommunist South Vietnam had been ensured) would be taken by these countries as a sign that the United States could not be trusted to live up to its commitments. Even France? Especially France. "If we were to get out, de Gaulle would be the first to say, 'See, I told you one cannot depend on the United States under a security treaty,'" Rusk declared time and again during the height of the war.[4]

It was a tortuous line of reasoning. George Ball, Rusk's top deputy, was surely on the mark in making exactly the opposite argument in his October memo: American credibility vis-à-vis its allies, he declared, did not depend on adhering to prior commitments regardless of the odds but on showing intelligence and good judgment. Far from harming U.S. credibility, an early political settlement would actually enhance it, because the majority of allies would "applaud a move on our part to cut our losses." The *New York Times,* in an end-of-the-year assessment, accurately summarized European allied thinking on Vietnam as a mixture of "sympathy and bafflement": sympathy toward Washington's predicament, bafflement at its dogged perseverance against long odds in a place of little import. Asian allies were perhaps less perplexed, given their proximity to the fighting, and some of them hoped that the United States would stick it out. But few if any viewed the outcome in Vietnam as vital to their own security, and there is little evidence that they would have questioned an American decision to withdraw support from what all saw as a hopeless Saigon government. Even a "good doctor" cannot forever help a patient who has given up fighting for life. As for de Gaulle, did Rusk really believe that the French leader would invite certain ridicule by suddenly condemning the Americans for taking the very action he had publicly advocated for so long?[5]

The more difficult aspect of the international context of Johnson's dilemma pertains to the views and intentions of the Soviet Union and, especially, China. In October, Nikita Khrushchev had been ousted as the USSR's leader in a Kremlin power struggle. The new leadership under Leonid Brezhnev and Alexei Kosygin continued the basic two-part policy on Southeast Asia followed by Khrushchev in his final months. On the one hand, they sought to increase Soviet influence in the region, partly to counter growing Chinese influence and partly because they smelled a communist victory in Vietnam and wanted to claim part of the credit. On the other hand, they feared a larger war that might force them to become more directly involved, or might bring the Chinese into the DRV in large numbers, and so they hoped to restrain both Washington and Hanoi from initiating a major escalation. Moreover, there is little reason to believe that Soviet leaders thought that American credibility was on the line in Vietnam or that they would have viewed a negotiated American withdrawal as a sign of Washington's impotence and proof that the United States would no longer challenge communist expansion elsewhere. On 9 December, Foreign Minister Andrei Gromyko, sounding much like de Gaulle, told Rusk that America had no important stake in the Vietnam conflict and that none of the U.S.-sponsored governments in Saigon had been worthy of the name. He told Rusk that all outstanding questions on the war could be solved at a great-power conference. (Rusk's response: If Hanoi and Beijing would "leave their neighbors alone," peace would come.)[6]

Senior American officials were well aware of the depth of the Sino-Soviet split and of Moscow's desire to discourage an expansion of the war in Vietnam. In the November-December policy deliberations both the split and the Soviet opposition to a wider war were taken as givens by most analysts. At the beginning of January 1965, William Bundy told Australian officials that in the American estimation the increased Russian interest in the war stemmed largely from the desire on the part of Kremlin leaders to redress the Sino-Soviet balance in Hanoi. Brezhnev and Kosygin wanted to keep the Chinese from expanding their influence in North Vietnam, Bundy said, and were sympathetic to any course—including negotiations—that would accomplish this aim.[7]

As for China, there can be no doubt that its outlook and ambitions weighed on the minds of a majority of American officials. But not as much as one might think—in the many hundreds of pages of memoranda produced in the Working Group policy discussions, it is startling how seldom analyses of China's posture and aims appear. This relative lacuna is graphic proof of how fundamentally uninterested leading U.S. officials were in reopening basic questions about America's involvement in the war; their overriding concern was what to do next. On the rare occasion when Beijing's intentions did come up for discussion, little consensus emerged. Michael Forrestal of the Far East desk at the State Department, remarking on the lack of attention in the early Working Group papers to China's role, stated one view: "If China did not exist, the effect of our withdrawal from a situation in which the people we were trying to help seemed unable to help themselves might not be politically so pervasive in Asia." Much like the USSR after World War II, China possessed an "internal political necessity for ideological expansion," and a communist victory in Vietnam would encourage Beijing to pursue further successes. The U.S. aim, Forrestal argued, should therefore be to "contain" China for as long as possible, and the place to start was in Vietnam. James Thomson, the NSC's China expert, rejected this view of a Chinese expansionist imperative driven by internal need and countered the claim that containing the Chinese required the United States to remain in Vietnam. George Ball, though no China specialist, made the same argument as Thomson. With respect to both Moscow and Beijing, Ball maintained, U.S. credibility would in the long run suffer much less from a settlement than from getting drawn into a deep, perhaps bottomless, morass.[8]

More important, the two leading members of the Working Group appear to have possessed strong doubts about Forrestal's formulation. Near the end of the deliberations, John McNaughton and William Bundy, while arguing against the do-nothing Option A, conceded that its adoption might not bring disastrous results, especially given the deep Sino-Soviet split. Should the administration opt for Option A and against the new military measures, the two men wrote, "the most likely result would be a Vietnamese-negotiated deal, under which an eventually unified Communist Vietnam would reassert its traditional hostility to Communist China and limit its own ambitions to Laos and Cambodia." A prescient remark if ever there was one, this assertion suggests that senior American officials could see the logic of what critics were saying, that containing China did not necessarily depend on standing firm in South Vietnam.[9]

For each of the important audiences, both foreign and domestic, identified in the foregoing discussion, the actual situation on the ground in South Vietnam was of critical importance in their judgment of the American stake in the struggle. This brings us to the biggest reason why Lyndon Johnson had considerable freedom to maneuver in the months following his election: the continuing inability or unwillingness of the South Vietnamese leaders to live up to their end of the bargain. Since Dwight Eisenhower had first laid down aid stipulations a decade earlier, American officials had consistently maintained that continued U.S. support depended on the Saigon government performing effectively and doing its part in the struggle against the Vietcong. In December 1964, it was clearer than ever that it was doing neither. The situation that [Maxwell] Taylor encountered upon his return from Washington was utterly dismal. He carried with him instructions to demand greater governmental stability and political cohesion from the South Vietnamese leaders, in return for which the United States would assume a major role in the war and pay for the increase of Saigon's armed forces by one hundred thousand men, bringing their total strength to 660,000.[10]

The effort failed, and South Vietnam in the final weeks of 1964 descended deeper into chaos. While Taylor was absent, Buddhist leaders initiated a campaign of nonviolent noncooperation with the [Tran Van] Huong government, on the grounds that it was just another American creation that was pro-Catholic and anti-Buddhist. After his return, they stepped up their agitation, demanding that the United States withdraw its support from the regime and blaming Washington for selling out Vietnam to the anticommunist right wing. Taylor was at a loss about how to proceed. He assured LBJ on 16 December that "the Mission is giving this entire matter of the Buddhist opposition its priority attention," but in a follow-up cable the same day, he conceded that the monks "will not be greatly swayed by efforts at direct persuasion by us." Nor did the ambassador have much influence over the faction-ridden South Vietnamese military. He briefed [Nguyen] Khanh and the other senior officers on Washington's new inducements for political unity and improved military performance, but the internecine warfare among the officer corps continued to rage.[11]

On 20 December, in a bid to enhance their own power, Khanh and a group of younger officers known as the "Young Turks" staged a bloodless coup d'état by arresting some three dozen high officers and civilian officials. In addition, they abolished the largely powerless civilian legislative body, the High National Council, and created an "Armed Forces Council" (AFC) to "oversee" (in other words, control) the actions of the Huong government. The AFC, the group declared, would act as a "mediator to achieve national unity." It was a transparent power grab, but the Huong regime, crippled by Buddhist opposition, was too weak to resist.[12]

Taylor was outraged. He cabled Washington that Khanh and his friends had "felt no reluctance in acting without consulting with U.S. representatives and in disregarding our advice on important matters.... Perhaps most serious of all is the deliberate disregard of the message which I brought from Washington and personally transmitted to most of these generals that continued and increased U.S. aid for S.V.N. depended upon governmental stability and evidence of national unity." That, of course, was untrue, and the generals knew it. They felt certain that continued and increased aid did *not* depend on their meeting this demand, that the Johnson administration felt too deeply committed to withdraw its support. When Taylor hauled four of them into the embassy and began making threats ("Now you have made a real mess," he barked. "We cannot carry you forever if you do things like this"), they were not unduly worried. Taylor's lecturing as if they were schoolboys offended them, however, and they responded by closing ranks behind Khanh, who in turn seized on the latent anti-Americanism that the episode brought to the surface to bolster his own position. Khanh accused Taylor of interfering in South Vietnam's internal affairs and publicly vowed independence from "foreign manipulation." American aid was no longer needed, he proclaimed, especially given that the United States had imposed a new colonialism on South Vietnam.[13]

It was an altogether bizarre state of affairs, with the de facto leader of South Vietnam, a man who early in the year Washington had hailed as a savior of his country, trading insults with Taylor and calling for anti-American demonstrations in Saigon. The Buddhists, meanwhile, continued their agitation against the rickety Huong government and its "American masters." Neutralist rumors were rampant, as were reports that former government leader Duong Van Minh might be orchestrating a coup to oust Khanh and place himself in power. ARVN operations in the field virtually ceased. So chaotic was the situation that when the Vietcong attacked the Brinks U.S. officers' billet in Saigon on Christmas Eve, killing two and injuring fifty, it took several days for the embassy to verify that the attack had been Vietcong-orchestrated and not the result of the intramural squabbling among South Vietnamese officials. That delay, coupled with Johnson's desire not to disrupt Americans' Christmas celebrations, led the White House to reject Taylor's recommendation for a reprisal strike against the North. "Under present conditions the American public might even doubt VC responsibility," Washington officials told Taylor in explaining the president's decision.[14]

Prominent outside observers saw the new developments as ample justification for an American extrication from the war. The *New York Times* put the matter bluntly: "The necessary, inevitable, inescapable consequence of not being wanted would be withdrawal." The *Washington Post* spoke in similar tones, as did a broad range of West European newspapers, among them pro-Social Democratic *Neue Rhein-Ruhr Zeitung* of Essen, centrist *Messaggero* of Rome, moderate-left *Frankfurter Rundschau* of Frankfurt, and conservative *Het Laatste Nieuws* of Brussels and *Muenchner Merkur* of Munich. Of special interest to officials at the United States Information Agency, who monitored press trends closely, the leading press organs in France and Britain now forcefully urged an American withdrawal. Said the Manchester *Guardian*, "Perhaps the least damaging decision for America and for those nations which now look to her primarily for their protection would be a withdrawal based on a clear and detailed statement explaining the impossibility of assisting a sovereign country to defend itself when it refuses to concentrate its own efforts for its own defense, or to abandon its internal factional struggles." *Le Monde* and the London *Times* made the same point and speculated that Washington was now actively considering extrication. The latter noted that the Buddhists in South Vietnam, who were an "approximation of public opinion," wanted an end to the war, and it further claimed that U.S. officials in Washington and Saigon were privately admitting defeat. The only question, the paper said, was whether a withdrawal would be possible in American domestic political terms. Leading American columnist James Reston said it would be. He noted that Johnson had most often explained American Vietnam policy in terms of the United States intervening to help a legal government defend its freedom. In view of the current in-fighting among South Vietnamese officials, and the rising anti-Americanism, such a defense was neither necessary nor warranted, Reston argued, and thus the president could justifiably withdraw.[15]

Reston was correct. A large window of opportunity on Vietnam existed for Lyndon Johnson in the wake of his 1964 election triumph. It is undeniable that he wanted to avoid a major American war in the jungles of Southeast Asia; it should be equally clear that he could have avoided one, and that a broad range of important observers saw this at the time . . . neither the domestic nor the international political context demanded a steadfast American commitment in Vietnam, especially given the almost surreal quality of the South Vietnamese political context in the final weeks of the year. No less a figure than General William Westmoreland, commander of the Military Assistance Command, Vietnam (MACV), later put it this way: "So obvious was the bickering, the machination, the inefficiency, the divisiveness among the Vietnamese that I suspect few in the world would have faulted us at that point had we thrown up our hands in despair [and withdrawn]."[16]

That was Westmoreland several years later. In late 1964, however, neither he nor any of his fellow senior American officials would consider withdrawal. It is this fact, this unwillingness to even explore in a meaningful way the disengagement option, that would have puzzled so many outside observers had they known about it. Almost everyone outside the administration could agree that escalation was legitimately one of the options before Lyndon Johnson; they would have been flabbergasted, however, had they known that it was the only one under serious consideration. American policymakers from mid 1963 onward were not merely skeptical of the possibility of finding an early political solution to the war but acutely fearful of such a prospect and strongly determined to prevent one. Both the fear and the determination had increased by the close of 1964. Nothing—not pessimistic intelligence reporting, not allied opposition, and not pervasive South Vietnamese war-weariness and burgeoning anti-Americanism—could dissuade these men from continuing their pursuit of a military solution. Talk of a "fall-back" option had faded early in the November deliberations, never to be resurrected. Option A, which contained no military escalation (but which also, significantly, ruled out early negotiations), likewise found little support. A negotiations option never emerged, even after important elements within South Vietnam expressed support for it. On New Year's Eve, Maxwell Taylor suggested that the administration could consider withdrawing the bulk of American personnel from Vietnam and focusing exclusively on air and maritime defense of the South, thereby forcing the GVN "to walk on its own legs and be responsible for its own stumbles." The idea received no consideration, because of what Taylor himself saw as a likely—and wholly unacceptable—result of such a move: Saigon leaders "compet[ing] with each other in making a deal with the National Liberation Front."

As for the option of pursuing bilateral talks with Hanoi, which now enjoyed sizable support on the nation's editorial pages, it was no more palatable to policymakers than it had ever been. In September UN Secretary General U Thant had won assurance from the DRV that it would enter talks but had been rebuffed by the United States. In November, with Johnson safely reelected, Thant tried again, telling the American ambassador to the UN, Adlai Stevenson, that the Burmese government of Ne Win had agreed to serve as host for the talks. Stevenson was sympathetic and passed on the information to Dean Rusk. Now was not the time for talks with Hanoi, Rusk told him, and therefore the secretary general should be told to put the idea on the shelf. Thant had been rejected again.[17]

Also in late November, Canadian officials asked Washington for a substantive message that J. Blair Seaborn could deliver to North Vietnamese officials during his upcoming visit to Hanoi. Much to their dismay, the administration showed scant interest in the issue and gave Seaborn no real message to convey, beyond one affirming America's continued commitment to the GVN. The Johnson administration, Ottawa officials concluded among themselves, no longer had much use for the diplomatic track, preferring instead to pursue a military solution.[18]

Were the North Vietnamese sincere in professing a desire for talks aimed at finding a political solution to the war? There can be little doubt that they were. In the final weeks of 1964 they continued confident in their ability to prevail in South Vietnam. They were not keen on compromising their fundamental objectives in the struggle and saw little reason to do so, given the growing chaos in the South. At the same time, Hanoi's leaders still sought to avert an Americanization of the conflict and likely were prepared to compromise on nonfundamentals to achieve that objective—on the speed of the American withdrawal, for example, or the timing of reunification of the country. In October, the prospect of Americanization was a subject of discussion when Pham Van Dong met Mao Zedong in Beijing. The two leaders agreed that Washington did not want to fight a major war. "The United States is facing many difficulties, and it is not easy for it to expand the war," Pham Van Dong said, no doubt referring both to the weak GVN base upon which such an escalation would be launched and the lack of enthusiasm for such a move among many in the United States and in western capitals. "We must adopt a very skillful strategy, and should not provoke [the United States]," he said. This meant keeping the level of fighting at about its current level. "If the United States dares to start a [larger] war, we will fight it," Pham Van Dong assured Mao, "and we will win it," But it would be better if it did not come to that.[19]

Accordingly, in the aftermath of the American election Hanoi also sent subtle signals that it was open to peace talks. William Bundy acknowledged as much when he told Canadian officials in Washington on 3 December that Hanoi had been putting out hints in many quarters in November that it was interested in pursuing a settlement to the war, though only on its previously stated terms. What did Bundy think those terms to be? The record does not indicate.[20] Likely he believed them to involve (1) a coalition government in Saigon, with prominent NLF representation; (2) American withdrawal; and (3) eventual reunification of the country under Hanoi's control. But within these terms there were gray areas that could be the subject of discussion during bilateral talks or at a Geneva-type conference. For the past six months, since Pham Van Dong had met Blair Seaborn in June, Hanoi officials had emphasized that they were flexible on the question of diplomacy.[21] There was but one way to probe them on this. That was to meet with them.

A year later, in the late fall of 1965, U Thant's efforts in 1964 became public knowledge. When the story broke, senior officials in the Johnson administration instantly knew they faced a sticky problem. The disclosures, they realized, made them appear to have been not merely skeptical of a diplomatic settlement in Vietnam in late 1964, but actively opposed to such a solution. Critics were bound to pose one question above all, they knew, a question for which they had no ready answer. People were certain to ask, George Ball said to a colleague, "Why didn't you find out [what Hanoi had in mind]?" A satisfactory reply had to be found. Ball could not think of one.[22]

Looming over the policy process, as always, was Lyndon Johnson. He complained to [Walter] Lippmann and others in late 1964 that he was trapped in a commitment he had inherited, a commitment he did not like but could not abandon. The question Lippmann might have asked him was why he made no attempt to break out of the trap. If Johnson felt that he had no options on Vietnam, why did he not deliberately externalize the conflict rather than internalize it? Why did he not encourage a national debate on the war, right now, when his political power was at its zenith and the Saigon political situation was at its nadir? If, as is likely, the American people wanted it both ways, wanted to win in Vietnam but did not want to fight for it, why did Johnson not put the burden on them to decide, after laying out the likely costs? Which did they want more?[23]

Johnson could have encouraged a congressional debate between hawks and doves, a debate wrangling over the pros and cons of maintaining the U.S. commitment. Given his mastery of the workings of Capitol Hill, he could have orchestrated such a debate to provide himself both with cover and with alternatives not to be found within his small and cloistered team of policy advisers. The three most influential Democratic foreign-policy thinkers on Capitol Hill—Mike Mansfield, Richard Russell, and William Fulbright—would have relished taking part in that debate, provided Johnson wanted it. Lippmann and [Joseph] Alsop, whose respective syndicated columns appeared in some two hundred American newspapers, could have duked it out before the public. At the very least, a debate would have made Vietnam a shared responsibility, not "Johnson's War." If things went badly, as he feared they would, the entire country would have to accept blame. But Johnson rejected a debate; indeed, he worked hard to avoid one. Why he did so is one of the great mysteries of the war.

Or maybe not. Maybe it is no mystery at all. Maybe Johnson failed to externalize the Vietnam problem because he was incapable of such a thing. "The role of public debate in securing popular assent to policies and, ultimately, national unity, was a concept he could not grasp," his former aide George Reedy has written. Talk, to Johnson, had true meaning "only when it was directed at getting something done." Other Johnson observers have argued likewise. But there was also something else, something deeper. Johnson's profound personal insecurity and his egomania led him not only to personalize the goals he aspired to but also to personalize all forms of dissent. Hence his vow not to be the president who lost Vietnam; hence his conviction that critics of the war were critics of him personally. In late 1964, Johnson's dislike of conflict, his need to create consensus and to avoid confrontation, remained unshaken, as did his insistence that Americans must support a president in foreign policy and unite behind a policy of anti-communism.[24] To reverse course in Vietnam would be to admit defeat, and that was something Johnson was loath to contemplate. Robert Thompson was more accurate than he ever could have realized when he referred to escalation in Vietnam as the "bad-loser" option.

At the end of December, while the turmoil in Saigon raged, Johnson held a meeting at the LBJ Ranch in Austin with McGeorge Bundy and Dean Rusk. Prior to its start, the president had told Bundy that the war in Vietnam was a civil war, that it had to be won in the South, and that the United States had to persevere. Now the three men discussed the next step. They probably discussed Taylor's growing estrangement from the South Vietnamese leadership and the need to get him to alter his approach. They almost certainly reached agreement that bombing the North would be insufficient to turn things around and that dispatching American ground forces would likely be necessary, though only after dependents had been removed. (It is surely significant that Robert McNamara, the fourth member of the "Awesome Foursome" and the only one strongly opposed to using U.S. ground troops, was not in attendance.) A postmeeting presidential memo to Taylor, drafted in Austin and dated 30 December, revealed a president determined in the new year to press on to victory in Vietnam, through escalation if necessary. In the memo, Johnson criticized Taylor for his handling of the Saigon political crisis and declared his belief that dependents should be removed in anticipation of expanded military action. "We are facing war in South Vietnam," Johnson wrote. "I have never felt that this war will be won from the air, and it seems to me that what is much more needed and would be much more effective is a larger and stronger use of Rangers and Special Forces and Marines, or other appropriate military strength on the ground and on the scene." Such a deployment would involve the acceptance of larger American sacrifice, the president acknowledged, but it was worth it. He vowed, "I myself am ready to substantially increase the number of Americans fighting in Vietnam."[25]

Nineteen-sixty-four, so often depicted as an "off year" in Vietnam but in reality the most crucial year of all, still had a few hours left in it. Already, it was becoming an American war.

« 9 »

The Tet Offensive, 1968

George C. Herring

AT 2:45 A.M. ON JANUARY 30, 1968, A TEAM of National Liberation Front (NLF) sappers blasted a large hole in the wall surrounding the U.S. embassy in Saigon and dashed into the courtyard of the compound. For the next six hours, the most important symbol of the American presence in Vietnam was the scene of one of the most dramatic episodes of the war. Unable to get through the heavy door at the main entrance of the embassy building, the attackers retreated to the courtyard and took cover behind large concrete flower pots, pounding the building with rockets and exchanging gunfire with a small detachment of military police. They held their positions until 9:15 A.M., when they were finally overpowered. All nineteen were killed or severely wounded.

The attack on the embassy was but a small part of the Tet Offensive, a massive, coordinated assault against the major urban areas of South Vietnam. In most other locales, the result was the same: the attackers were repulsed and incurred heavy losses. Later that morning, standing in the embassy courtyard amid the debris and fallen bodies in a scene one reporter described as a "butcher shop in Eden," [General William] Westmoreland rendered his initial assessment of Tet. The "well-laid plans" of the North Vietnamese and NLF had failed, he observed. "The enemy exposed himself by virtue of his strategy and he suffered heavy casualties." Although his comments brought moans of disbelief from. the assembled journalists, from a short-term tactical standpoint Westmoreland was correct: Tet represented a defeat for the enemy.[1] As Bernard Brodie has observed, however, the Tet Offensive was "probably unique in that the side that lost completely in the tactical sense came away with an overwhelming psychological and hence political victory."[2] Tet had a tremendous impact in the United States and ushered in a new phase of a seemingly endless war.

General Offensive, General Uprising

During the summer of 1967, the North Vietnamese and NLF decided on a change in strategy, a "general offensive, general uprising" to achieve decisive victory. Some Americans have depicted the Tet Offensive as a last-gasp, desperation move, comparable to World War II's Battle of the Bulge, in which a beleaguered enemy attempted to snatch victory from the jaws of defeat. This description seems quite doubtful, although the decision to take the offensive probably did reflect growing concern with the heavy casualties in the south, the damage done by the U.S. bombing of North Vietnam, and the possible costs of a prolonged war of attrition with the United States. It may have been born of excessive optimism, a growing perception that the urban areas of South Vietnam were ripe for revolution and the United States was vulnerable.[3] It came after weeks of soul-searching and agonizing on the part of the politburo in Hanoi and heated debate between northerners and southerners on the aggressiveness with which to pursue the war in the south.

During the second half of 1967, the politburo began developing plans to implement the new strategy. To lure U.S. troops away from the major population centers and maintain heavy casualties, a number of large-scale diversionary attacks would be launched in remote areas. These attacks would be followed by coordinated guerrilla assaults against the major cities and towns of South Vietnam designed to rock the Saigon government to its foundations, ignite a "general uprising" among the population, and shake the will of the United States. Seeking maximum shock effect, the politburo even planned an attack on the U.S. embassy. "Let us say to the world that we can attack anywhere, in a place the United States could never expect," a southern leader proclaimed.[4] Simultaneously, new efforts would be made to open negotiations with the United States. The maximum aim was probably to force the collapse of South Vietnam and a U.S. withdrawal. At the very least, the politburo hoped through these coordinated actions to initiate a new phase of "fighting while negotiating" that would stop the bombing, bring about negotiations, weaken the Saigon regime, and exacerbate differences between the United States and South Vietnam. The politburo's ultimate objective would be a negotiated settlement providing for an American withdrawal and a coalition government controlled by the NLF.

Hanoi began executing its plan in late 1967. In October and November, North Vietnamese regulars attacked the Marine base at Con Thien, across the Laotian border, and the towns of Loc Ninh and Song Be near Saigon and Dak To in the Central Highlands. Shortly after, two North Vietnamese divisions laid siege to the Marine garrison at Khe Sanh near the Laotian border. In the meantime, crack NLF units moved into the cities and towns, accumulating supplies and laying final plans. To undermine the Saigon government, the insurgents encouraged the formation of a "popular front" of neutralists and attempted to entice government officials and troops to defect by offering generous pardons and positions in a coalition government. To spread dissension between the United States and Thieu, the front opened secret contacts with the U.S. embassy in Saigon and disseminated rumors of peace talks. Hanoi followed in December 1967 by stating categorically that it would negotiate if the United States stopped the bombing.

The first phase of the plan worked to perfection. Westmoreland quickly dispatched reinforcements to Con Thien, Loc Ninh, Song Be, and Dak To, in each case driving back the North Vietnamese and inflicting heavy losses but dispersing U.S. forces and leaving the cities vulnerable. By the end of 1967, moreover, the attention of Westmoreland, the president, and indeed much of the nation was riveted on Khe Sanh, which many Americans assumed was General [Vo Nguyen] Giap's play for a repetition of Dien Bien Phu. The press and television carried daily reports of the action. Insisting that the fortress be held at all costs, Johnson kept close watch on the battle with a terrain map in the White House war room. Westmoreland sent 6,000 soldiers to defend the garrison, and B-52s carried out the heaviest air raids in the history of warfare, eventually dropping more than 100,000 tons of explosives on a five-square-mile battlefield.

While the United States was preoccupied with Khe Sanh, the North Vietnamese and NLF prepared for the second phase of the operation. The offensive against the cities was timed to coincide with the beginning of Tet, the lunar new year and the most festive of Vietnamese holidays. Traditionally, at Tet, people returned to their native villages and engaged in a week of celebrations, renewing ties with family, honoring ancestors, indulging in meals, and shooting firecrackers. Throughout the war, both sides had observed a cease-fire during Tet, and Hanoi correctly assumed that South Vietnam would be relaxing and celebrating, with soldiers visiting their families and government officials away from their offices. While the Americans and South Vietnamese prepared for the holidays, NLF units readied themselves for the bloodiest battles of the war. Mingling with the heavy holiday traffic, guerrillas disguised as Army of the Republic of Vietnam (ARVN) soldiers or civilians moved into the cities and towns, some audaciously hitching rides on American vehicles. Weapons were smuggled in on vegetable carts and even in mock funeral processions. At Cu Chi in the Iron Triangle, recruits practiced getting inside a replica of the U.S. embassy grounds.

Within twenty-four hours after the beginning of Tet, January 30, 1968, the NLF launched a series of attacks extending from the demilitarized zone to the Ca Mau Peninsula on the southern tip of Vietnam. In all, they struck thirty-six of forty-four provincial capitals, five of the six major cities, sixty-four district capitals, and fifty hamlets. In addition to the daring raid on the embassy, NLF units assaulted Saigon's Tan Son Nhut Airport, the presidential palace, and the headquarters of South Vietnam's general staff. In Hué, 7,500 NLF and North Vietnamese troops stormed and eventually took control of the ancient Citadel, the interior town that had been the seat of the emperors of the Kingdom of Annam.

U.S.-South Vietnamese Response

The offensive caught the United States and South Vietnam off guard. American intelligence had picked up signs of intensive enemy activity in and around the cities and had even translated captured documents that, without giving dates, outlined the plan in some detail. The U.S. command was so preoccupied with Khe Sanh, however, that it viewed evidence pointing to the cities as a diversion to distract it from the main battlefield. As had happened so often before, the United States underestimated the capability of the enemy. The North Vietnamese appeared so bloodied by the campaigns of 1967 that the Americans could not conceive they could bounce back and deliver a blow of the magnitude of Tet. "Even had I known exactly what was to take place," Westmoreland's intelligence officer later conceded, "it was so preposterous that I probably would have been unable to seil it to anybody."[5]

Although taken by surprise, the United States and South Vietnam recovered quickly. The timing of the offensive was poorly coordinated, and premature attacks in some towns sounded a warning that enabled Westmoreland to get reinforcements to vulnerable areas. In addition, the NLF was slow to capitalize on its initial successes, giving the United States time to mount a strong defense. In Saigon, American and ARVN forces held off the initial attacks and within several days cleared the city, inflicting huge casualties, taking large numbers of prisoners, and forcing the remnants to melt into the countryside. Elsewhere the result was much the same. The ARVN fought better under pressure than any American would have dared predict, and the United States and South Vietnam used superior mobility and firepower to devastating advantage. The NLF launched a second round of attacks on February 18, but these were confined largely to rocket and mortar barrages against U.S. and South Vietnamese military installations and steadily diminished in intensity.

Hué was the only exception to the general pattern. The liberation of that city took nearly three weeks, required heavy bombing and intensive artillery fire, and ranks among the bloodiest and most destructive battles of the war. The United States and South Vietnam lost an estimated 500 killed, while enemy killed in action have been estimated at as high as 5,000. The savage fighting caused huge numbers of civilian casualties and created an estimated 100,000 refugees. The bodies of 2,800 South Vietnamese were found in mass graves in and around Hué, the product of NLF and North Vietnamese executions, and another 2,000 citizens were unaccounted for and presumed murdered.

It remains difficult to assess the impact of the battles of Tet. The North Vietnamese and NLF did not force the collapse of South Vietnam. They were unable to establish any firm positions in the urban areas, and the South Vietnamese people did not welcome them as "liberators." Their battle deaths have been estimated at as high as 40,000, and although this figure may be inflated, the losses were huge. The NLF bore the brunt of the fighting; its regular units were hurt badly and would take months to recover, and its political infrastructure suffered crippling losses.

If, in these terms, Tet represented a "defeat" for the enemy, it was still a costly "victory" for the United States and South Vietnam. ARVN forces had to withdraw from the countryside to defend the cities, and pacification incurred another major setback. The destruction within the cities heaped formidable new problems on a government that had shown limited capacity to deal with the routine. American and South Vietnamese losses did not approach those of the enemy, but they were still high: in the first two weeks of the Tet campaigns, the United States lost 1,100 killed in action and South Vietnam 2,300. An estimated 12,500 civilians were killed, and Tet created as many as one million new refugees. As with much of the war up to then, there was a great deal of destruction and suffering, but no clear-cut winner or loser.

Confusion and Uncertainty

To the extent that the North Vietnamese designed the Tet Offensive to influence the United States, they sueeeeded, for it sent instant shock waves across the nation. Early wire service reports exaggerated the success of the raid on the embassy, some even indicating that the guerrillas had oecupied several floors of the building. Although these initial reports were in time corrected, the reaction was still one of disbelief. "What the hell is going on?" the venerable newscaster Walter Cronkite is said to have snapped. "I thought we were winning the war!"[6] Televised accounts of the bloody fighting in Saigon and Hué made a mockery of Johnson's and Westmoreland's optimistic year-end reports, widening the credibility gap; cynical journalists openly ridiculed Westmoreland's claims of victory. The humorist Art Buchwald parodied the general's statements in terms of Custer at the Little Bighorn. "We have the Sioux on the run," Buchwald had Custer saying. "Of course we still have some cleaning up to do, but the Redskins are hurting badly and it will only be a matter of time before they give in."[7] The battles of Tet raised to a new level of public consciousness basic questions about the war that had long lurked just beneath the surface. The offhand remark of a U.S. Army officer who had participated in the liberation of the Mekong delta village of Ben Tre—"We had to destroy the town to save it"—seemed to epitomize the purposeless destruction of the war. Candid photographs and television footage of the police chief of Saigon holding a pistol to the head of an NLF captive—and then firing—starkly symbolized the way in which violence had triumphed over law.

The Tet Offensive left Washington in a state of "troubled confusion and uncertainty."[8] Westmoreland insisted that the attacks had been repulsed and that there was no need to fear a major setback, and administration officials publicly echoed his statements. Johnson and his advisers were shocked by the suddenness and magnitude of the offensive, however, and intelligence estimates were much more pessimistic than Westmoreland was. Many officials feared that Tet was only the opening phase of a larger Communist offensive. Some felt that Khe Sanh was still the primary objective, a fear that seemed borne out when the besieging forces renewed their attack in early February. Others feared a major offensive in the northern provinces or a second wave of attacks on the cities. An "air of gloom" hung over White House discussions, [Maxwell] Taylor later observed, and General [Earle] Wheeler likened the mood to that following the first Battle of Bull Run.[9]

The president responded with a stubborn determination to hold the line at any cost. He insisted that Khe Sanh be held and advised Westmoreland that he would send whatever reinforcements were needed to defend the fortress or meet any other threat. "The United States is not prepared to accept a defeat in South Vietnam," Wheeler advised Saigon, "... if you need more troops, ask for them." When Westmoreland indicated that he would appreciate any help he could get, Johnson immediately ordered an additional 10,500 men to Vietnam. In the first few weeks after Tet, the president's main concern seemed to be to "get on with the war as quickly as possible," not only by sending reinforcements but also by stepping up air attacks against North Vietnam.[10]

Proposals for Escalation

From the standpoint of the military, the new mood of urgency in Washington provided a timely opportunity to force decisions that had been deferred for too long. Wheeler and the Joint Chiefs had been pressing for mobilization of the reserves since 1965, and by February 1968 they were certain this step must be taken at once. The Tet Offensive raised the distinct possibility that significant reinforcements would have to be sent to Vietnam. North Korea's seizure of the American warship *Pueblo* in January and a new flare-up in Berlin aroused fears that additional troops might have to be dispatched to these perennial Cold War trouble spots. Available forces were nearly exhausted, and Wheeler worried that unless the United States mobilized the reserves, it could not meet its global commitments.

Confident that he could exploit the enemy's defeat at Tet and buoyed by the president's apparent willingness to send substantial reinforcements, Westmoreland revived his 1967 proposals to expand the war. The enemy's decision to throw in "all his military chips and go for broke," the general advised Washington, provided the United States with a "great opportunity." The North Vietnamese and NLF could not afford the heavy losses sustained in the Tet Offensive, and with large numbers of additional troops, Westmoreland was certain he could gain the upper hand. His "twofisted" strategy envisioned an "amphibious hook" against North Vietnamese bases and staging areas across the demilitarized zone, attacks on the sanctuaries in Laos and Cambodia, and an intensified bombing campaign against North Vietnam. By taking the offensive at a time when the enemy was overextended, the general was confident he could shorten the war.[11]

Wheeler and Westmoreland conferred in Saigon in late February and devised an approach to force the president's hand. Wheeler appears to have been considerably less optimistic about the immediate prospects in Vietnam than Westmoreland was, but he agreed that whether Tet provided new opportunities or posed increased dangers, it justified a call for major reinforcements. The two men settled on the figure of 206,000 soldiers, a number large enough to meet any contingency in Vietnam and force mobilization of the reserves. Roughly half of the troops would be deployed in Vietnam by the end of the year; the rest would constitute a strategic reserve. Wheeler raised no objections to Westmoreland's proposed changes in strategy, but he persuaded the field commander that it would be best to defer such recommendations until the president had approved the new troop level. He was keenly aware of Johnson's opposition to widening the war, and he apparently feared that if he presented the case for additional troops on the basis of an optimistic assessment and an offensive strategy, he would be turned down again. Troops, not strategy, offered the "stronger talking point."[12]

Wheeler's report to Washington was deeply pessimistic. Describing the Tet Offensive as a "very near thing," he warned that the initial enemy attacks had almost succeeded in numerous places and had been turned back only by the "timely reaction" of U.S. forces. The North Vietnamese and NLF had suffered heavily, but they had repeatedly demonstrated a capacity for quick recovery, and they would probably attempt to sustain the offensive with renewed attacks. Without additional troops, he concluded, the United States must be "prepared to accept some reverses," a line calculated to sway a president who had already made clear he was not willing to accept defeat. Wheeler insisted that large-scale reinforcements were necessary to protect the cities, drive the enemy from the northern provinces, and pacify the countryside. His pessimism may have been sincere; he had never been as confident as Westmoreland was. It seems clear, however, that by presenting a gloomy assessment he hoped to stampede the administration into providing the troops to rebuild a depleted strategic reserve and meet any contingency in Vietnam. His proposal reopened in even more vigorous fashion the debate that had raged in Washington throughout 1967.[13]

Wheeler's report shocked a government already in a state of deep alarm. In terms of policy choices, it posed a hard dilemma. The general suggested that denial of the request for 206,000 troops could result in a military defeat, or at least in an indefinite continuation of the war. Acceptance of his recommendations, on the other hand, would force a major escalation of the war and impose heavy new demands on the American people in an election year and at a time when public anxiety about Vietnam was already pronounced. Not inclined to make a hasty decision on a matter fraught with such grave implications, Johnson turned the problem over to his new secretary of defense, Clark Clifford, with this grim instruction: "Give me the lesser of evils."[14]

The Clifford Task Force

Clifford seized the opportunity to initiate a full reevaluation of Vietnam policy. The magnitude of the request was such that it demanded careful study. Clifford had consistently defended the president's policies in Vietnam, but his newness to the job and his need to clarify many fundamental issues also led him toward a füll reassessment. He was encouraged in this regard by the senior civilians in the Pentagon, men such as Paul Warnke, Townsend Hoopes, and Paul Nitze, who had long been disenchanted with American strategy and had been partially responsible for [Robert] McNamara's conversion. Thus, Clifford immediately began raising at the highest levels questions that had been avoided for years. He demanded of Wheeler and Westmoreland precise information on how the additional troops might be deployed and what results could be expected. He instructed his civilian advisers to study all the implications of the request and to review possible alternatives.

The Pentagon civilians responded with a sharp indictment of prevailing policy. Alain Enthoven of Systems Analysis attacked the request for more troops as another "payment on an open-ended commitment" and questioned whether it would shorten the war.[15] North Vietnam had already demonstrated that it could match American increases and that it could limit its losses if it chose. Even with 206,000 additional troops, Enthoven and others concluded, the current strategy could "promise no early end to the conflict, nor any success in attriting the enemy or eroding Hanoi's will to fight." The costs would be heavy, moreover. The provision of substantial additional troops could lead to "total Americanization of the war," encouraging the ARVN's tendency to do nothing and reinforcing the belief of South Vietnam's "ruling elite that the U.S. will continue to fight while it engages in backroom politics and permits widespread corruption." Expansion of the war would bring increased American casualties and require new taxes, risking a "domestic crisis of unprecedented proportions." Clifford's advisers thus agreed that the administration should maintain existing limits on the war and give Westmoreland no more than a token increase in troops.[16]

The Pentagon civilians went further, however. In their final report, they urged a shift from search and destroy, with its goal of "attriting" the enemy, to a strategy of "population security." The bulk of American forces would be deployed along the "demographic frontier," an imaginary line just north of the major population centers, where they could defend against a major

North Vietnamese thrust and, by engaging in limited offensive operations, keep the enemy's main forces off balance. At the same time, the United States would force the ARVN to assume greater responsibility for the war and compel the Saigon government to "end its internal bickering, purge corrupt officers and officials and move to develop efficient and effective forces." The goal of the new approach would be a negotiated settlement rather than military victory, and in this regard the civilians urged the scaling down of American objectives to a "peace which will leave the people of SVN [South Vietnam] free to fashion their own political institutions." The plan closely resembled McNamara's proposals of 1967, but it was stated more emphatically and went further in outlining specific alternatives.[17]

The military bitterly opposed the Defense Department recommendations. Recognizing the threat to his request for additional troops—indeed, to his entire strategy—Westmoreland, with the support of Wheeler, warned that rejection of his proposals would deny the United States a splendid opportunity to take advantage of an altered strategic situation. Wheeler found "fatal flaws" in the population security strategy, admonishing that it would lead to increased fighting near the population centers, and hence to more civilian casualties, and that it would leave the initiative with the enemy.[18] The United States was at a "cross-road," warned Admiral U.S. Grant Sharp, commander in chief of the Pacific forces. It must choose between using its power without restriction to achieve victory, accepting a "campaign of gradualism" and a "long drawn-out contest," or retreating "in defeat from Southeast Asia," leaving its "allies to face the Communists alone." Along with Westmoreland, the Joint Chiefs continued to urge that the military be permitted to pursue enemy forces into Laos and Cambodia, "beat up" North Vietnam from the sea and air, and after an Inchon-type landing, take and occupy parts of North Vietnam as far as thirty miles north of the demilitarized zone.[19]

As had happened so often before, Clifford recommended against the military's proposals without resolving the debate on strategy. The secretary seems to have leaned toward the population security strategy and a scaling down of American objectives. "I see more and more fighting with more and more casualties on the U.S. side and no end in sight to the action," he complained on March 4.[20] He seems to have felt, however, that the proposed change, with its implicit assumption that U.S. policy had failed, would be more than the president could accept, and he may have wished to prepare Johnson gradually for change rather than confront him immediately. Clifford's formal report kept the strategie issue alive by calling for continued study of possible alternatives, but it did not address the issues raised by the civilians in the Pentagon. The secretary of defense merely recommended the immediate deployment to Vietnam of 22,000 troops, a reserve call-up of unspecified magnitude, and a highly forceful approach" to [Nguyen Vanh] Thieu and [Nguyen Cao] Ky to get the South Vietnamese to assume greater responsibility for the war.[21]

The President's Decisions

The administration accepted Clifford's recommendations without serious debate. The president and his top civilian advisers had long opposed expansion of the war, and they seem to have agreed as early as November 1967 that American forces should not be enlarged above prevailing levels. In the immediate aftermath of the Tet attacks, Johnson had been ready to send additional troops if necessary to hold the line, but by the time he received Clifford's report, the military situation in South Vietnam seemed well in hand. Westmoreland and Ambassador Ellsworth Bunker reported that U.S. and South Vietnamese forces had fully recovered from the initial shock of the enemy offensive and were ready to mount a major counteroffensive. Under these circumstances, there seemed no need for immediate large-scale reinforcements, and although Johnson did not formally approve Clifford's recommendations at this time, he agreed with them and was prepared to act on them.

The administration also accepted the principle that South Vietnam should do more to defend itself. Johnson's advisers agreed that from a long-range standpoint the key to achieving American objectives was South Vietnam's ability to stand on its own, and they had concluded in late 1967 that more should be done to promote self-sufficiency. The ARVN's quick recovery from the initial panic of Tet and its surprising effectiveness in the subsequent battles reinforced this notion by suggesting that "Vietnamization" might work. Indeed, in the discussions of late February and early March 1968, some of the strongest arguments against sending massive reinforcements were that it would encourage the South Vietnamese to do less at a time when they should be doing more and that it would take equipment that might better be used by the ARVN. The administration thus agreed in early March that Thieu and Ky should be bluntly informed that the United States was willing to send limited reinforcements and substantial quantities of equipment but that continued American assistance would depend on South Vietnam's ability to put its house in order and assume a greater burden of the fighting.[22] The decision represented a significant shift in American policy—a return, at least in part, to the principle that had governed U.S. involvement before 1965 and adoption, at least in a rudimentary fashion, of the concept of Vietnamization, which would be introduced with much fanfare by the Nixon administration a year later.

While agreeing in principle to Clifford's recommendations, the administration also began serious consideration of a cutback in the bombing and a new peace initiative. The secretary of defense had recommended against further peace moves in his report and, perhaps as a sop to the military, had even urged intensification of the bombing. The initiative came from Secretary of State Rusk. Rusk had felt for some time that the bombing had produced only marginal gains at a heavy cost, and he proposed that the administration restrict it, without condition, to those areas "integrally related to the battlefield," namely, the supply routes and staging areas just north of the demilitarized zone. Such a move would cost the United States nothing, he argued, since inclement weather in the next few months would severely restrict raids over the northern part of North Vietnam. Bunker had speculated that Hanoi's purpose in launching the Tet Offensive may have been to establish a favorable position for negotiations, and in late February neutral intermediaries had brought several peace feelers to the State Department. Rusk believed that the chances for productive negotiations remained "bleak," but relaxation of the ambiguous San Antonio formula might entice Hanoi to the conference table and at least would test its intentions. Even if North Vietnam did not respond positively, domestic critics would be persuaded that the administration was trying to get negotiations under way. The United States could resume air attacks on Hanoi and Haiphong later, if necessary, the secretary pointed out, probably with increased public support.[23]

Johnson had steadfastly opposed any reduction of the bombing, but he was attracted to Rusk's proposal. The president was certain that North Vietnam had suffered heavily in the Tet Offensive, and he appears to have concluded that the United States could undertake negotiations from a vastly strengthened position. He recognized the need to do something to still the growing outcry against the war at home. And he was responsive to the idea because it came from Rusk, a man whose loyalty, caution, and measured judgment he had come to cherish.[24] Johnson later claimed to have accepted the idea of a reduction of the bombing and a new peace initiative as early as March 7, but he was not inclined to move hastily, and he remained outwardly noncommittal for several weeks. He urged his advisers to study the matter carefully and develop specific proposals for inclusion in a major speech he was to deliver at the end of the month.

Public Opinion and Politics

The administration's inclination to move in new directions was strengthened by mounting evidence of public dissatisfaction with the war. Discussion of Vietnam during February and March 1968 took place in an atmosphere of gloom and futility. The media continued to depict events in highly unfavorable and sometimes distorted terms. Early reports of a smashing enemy victory went largely uncorrected. The fact that the United States and South Vietnam had hurled back the attacks and quickly stabilized their position was lost in the image of chaos and defeat.[25] For those television and newspaper commentators who had long opposed the conflict, Tet provided compelling evidence of its folly. "The war in Vietnam is unwinnable," the columnist Joseph Kraft reported, "and the longer it goes on the more the Americans will be subjected to losses and humiliation." Many opinion makers who had supported the president or had been only mildly critical now came out forcefully against the war. Tet made clear, *Newsweek* commented, that "a strategy of more of the same is intolerable." In a much-publicized broadcast on February 27, Cronkite eloquently summed up the prevailing mood: "To say that we are closer to victory today is to believe, in the face of the evidence, the optimists who have been wrong in the past. To suggest that we are on the edge of defeat is to yield to unreasonable pessimism. To say that we are mired in stalemate seems the only reasonable, yet unsatisfactory conclusion."[26]

A *New York Times* story of March 10, reporting that the administration was considering sending another 206,000 soldiers to Vietnam, added to the furor. By this time, Johnson had decided to turn down Westmoreland's request, but he had not revealed his intentions publicly, and the story set off a barrage of protest.[27] Critics asked why so many troops were needed and whether more would follow. Skeptics questioned the results of further escalation, warning that the North Vietnamese would be able to match any American increase. The only thing that would change, NBC's Frank McGee observed, would be the "capacity for destruction." The time had come, he concluded, "when we must decide whether it is futile to destroy Vietnam in the effort to save it."[28]

The possibility of another major troop increase provoked a stormy reaction in Congress. Democrats and Republicans, hawks and doves, demanded an explanation and insisted that Congress share in any decision to expand the war. On March 11 and 12, the Senate Foreign Relations Committee grilled Rusk for eleven hours, dramatically revealing a growing discontent with the administration's policies and a determination to exercise some voice in future decisions. A week later, 139 members of the House of Representatives sponsored a resolution calling for a full review of American policy in Vietnam. The congressional outcry reinforced the administration's conviction that it could not escalate the war without setting off a long and bitter debate, and persuaded some officials, Clifford included, that major steps must be taken to scale down American involvement.[29]

Indexes of public opinion also revealed a sharp rise in disillusionment. Support for the war itself remained remarkably steady between November 1967 and March 1968, hovering around 45 percent.[30] But approval of Johnson's conduct of it, which had risen to 40 percent as a result of the 1967 public relations campaign, plummeted to an all-time low of 26 percent during Tet. By March, moreover, an overwhelming majority of Americans (78 percent) were certain that the United States was not making any progress in Vietnam. The polls indicated no consensus for either escalation or withdrawal, only a firm conviction that the United States was hopelessly bogged down and a growing doubt that Johnson could break the stalemate.[31]

By mid-March, public discontent had assumed ominous polirical overtones. Senator Eugene McCarthy of Minnesota, an outspoken dove, had audaciously challenged Johnson's renomination, and his surprisingly strong showing in the New Hampshire primary on March 12 suddenly transformed what had seemed a quixotic crusade into a major political challenge. Johnson's name had not been on the ballot, but the party organization had mounted a vigorous write-in campaign for him, and when McCarthy won 42 percent of the vote, it was widely interpreted as a defeat for the president. Subsequent analysis revealed that hawks outnumbered doves by a wide majority among McCarthy supporters in New Hampshire. Early appraisals, however, emphasized that the vote reflected a growing sentiment for peace, and within several days a more formidable peace candidate had entered the field. After weeks of hesitation and soul-searching, Senator Robert F. Kennedy of New York announced that he, too, would run against the president on a platform of opposition to the war. With his name, his glamour, and his connections in the party, Kennedy appeared to be a serious threat to Johnson's renomination. Worried party regulars urged the president to do "something exciting and dramatic to recapture the peace issue" and to shift the emphasis of his rhetoric from winning the war to securing "peace with honor."[32]

The impact of public opinion on the decision-making process in March 1968 is difficult to measure. Westmoreland and others have charged that hostile and all-too-powerful members of the media, especially the television networks, seized defeat from the jaws of victory by turning the public against the war and limiting the government's freedom of action just when the United States had a battered enemy on the ropes.[33] Vietnam was the first television war, to be sure, and it is possible, over a long period of time, that nightly exposure to violence did contribute to public war-weariness. Up until the Tet Offensive, however, television coverage of the war had been overwhelmingly neutral or favorable to the government and, because of the isolated and remote nature of combat in Vietnam, had shown little of the actual horrors of war.[34] The intense and up-close action in the cities at Tet did expose the public more directly to the war, and the coverage was more critical. After the distorted accounts of the embassy battle, coverage was also for the most part more accurate and thus could not help but show the enemy's toughness and tenacity, increase already strong doubts about the South Vietnamese government and army, raise questions about the administration's claims of progress, and widen the president's already yawning credibility gap. It is difficult to measure the impact of television coverage on public attitudes, but it seems probable, as historian Chester Pach has concluded, that coverage of the battles at Tet intensified the "sense of shock, anguish, and uncertainty" felt by Americans and by top government officials.[35]

The Johnson administration itself was at least partially responsible for media and public disillusionment during Tet. Its unduly optimistic pronouncements of 1967 made the shock of Tet greater than it might otherwise have been and widened an already large credibility gap. The president and his advisers might have challenged the reporting of the media, but their public response to Tet was itself halting and confused, in part because they were uncertain what was happening and how to respond.

The idea that a hypercritical media undercut the [administration] just at that point when the war could have been won is suspect on more basic grounds. That victory was within grasp, even had Westmoreland been given all the troops he requested, remains highly doubtful, and despite their later claims many top military officials knew this at the time. They perceived quite clearly the enormous damage the enemy offensive had done to the war effort, and they recognized that success was not forthcoming. By making requests they knew would not be approved, in fact, some military leaders may have been trying to put the onus for failure on the backs of the civilians.[36] The influence of public opinion does not appear to have been as great as Westmoreland alleges. None of Johnson's civilian advisers favored expansion of the war and another large troop increase, and the president had rejected Westmoreland's proposals even before the public protest reached significant proportions. Evidence of growing popular discontent merely confirmed that it would be disastrous to escalate the war. Public anxiety persuaded some officials that the United States must move toward withdrawal from Vietnam, but the president did not go this far. He eventually concluded that he must make additional conciliatory gestures, but he did not alter his policy in any fundamental way or abandon his goals.

The Gold Crisis

An economic crisis in mid-March, itself in part provoked by the war, also significantly affected post-Tet policy deliberations. Johnson had attempted to finance the war as he had dealt with public opinion—by deceit and trickery—and for the same reason. From the outset, he had a reasonably clear idea what the war would cost, but in dealing with the public and Congress he repeatedly minimized the price tag and he refused to ask for new taxes for fear such a request would force cuts in Great Society programs. Until 1967, he financed the war through budgetary sleight of hand. His tax request of that year was too little and came too late, and in any event, as he had feared, an increasingly restive Congress refused to pass it without domestic spending cuts he refused to make.

Thus by March 1968, the United States faced an economic crisis some harried officials compared to the Great Crash of 1929. The war imposed a burden of as much as $3.6 billion a year on a U.S. economy already strained by Great Society spending. Military expenditures stoked inflation and contributed to a spiraling balance-of-payments deficit that weakened the dollar in international money markets and threatened the world monetary structure. A late-1967 financial crisis in Britain, leading to devaluation of the pound, caused further problems, including huge losses from the gold pool. In March 1968, pressure on the dollar mounted again, and gold purchases reached new highs. On March 14, the United States lost $372 million in gold trading. At Washington's urging, the London gold market was closed. The economic crisis in the spring of 1968 marked the beginning of the end of the post-World War II economic boom. It shattered the postwar myth of American invincibility and raised severe doubts among business and government leaders that the nation could do it all and have it all in terms of domestic reform and national defense.[37]

As a result of the gold crisis of March 1968, Westmoreland's request for additional troops was increasingly linked to the nation's mounting economic woes. Secretary of the Treasury Henry Fowler warned that adoption of Westmoreland's proposals would cost $2.5 billion in 1968 and $10 billion in 1969, adding $500 million to the balance-of-payments deficit and requiring a major tax increase and cuts in domestic programs. Leading organs of business opinion began to question the nation's ability to finance the war at higher or even existing levels. "The gold crisis has dampened expansionist ideas," former Secretary of State Dean Acheson wrote a friend. "The town is in an atmosphere of crisis."[38]

In this context, some leading "establishment" figures, including the architects of America's major Cold War policies, concluded that the war was doing irreparable damage to the nation's overall national security position and began to press for disengagement. Acheson, W. Averell Harriman, and Paul Nitze, all of whom had served in the Truman administration and had helped formulate the original containment policy, agreed, as Acheson put it, that Vietnam was a dangerous diversion from Europe and that "our leader ought to be concerned with areas that count."[39] Fearing that the nation was hopelessly overextended and that Vietnam was eroding popular support for an internationalist foreign policy, they pressed for a review of Vietnam policy in the larger context of America's global national security concerns. In a long letter on March 26, Acheson warned the president that the gold crisis and concern with America's "broader interests in Europe" required a "decision now to disengage within a limited time."[40] The old Cold Warriors labored tirelessly behind the scenes to influence the president's decision, and they converted Clifford to their position.

On March 22, Johnson formally rejected Westmoreland's proposals to seek victory through an expanded war. He was undoubtedly influenced by public opinion and the economic crisis, and the steadily improving situation in South Vietnam seems to have been decisive. The Saigon government was responding to American pressures. Stability and order had been restored to the cities, and in late March, Thieu announced a massive increase in draft calls that would raise the ARVN's strength by 135,000. The intensity of enemy rocket attacks was steadily diminishing. Enemy forces were withdrawing from the positions established before Tet and splitting into small groups to avoid destruction or capture. In mid-March, Westmoreland informed Johnson of plans for a major offensive in the northern provinces, the central objective of which was to relieve the siege of Khe Sanh.

Under these circumstances, Johnson saw no need for a major increase in American forces. Indeed, he did not even authorize the 22,000 soldiers recommended by Clifford, agreeing merely to deploy 13,500 support troops to augment the emergency reinforcements sent in February. At the same time, he decided to bring Westmoreland back to Washington to be chief of staff of the army. The general had come under heavy fire for his prophecies of victory and his failure to anticipate the Tet Offensive, and Johnson wanted to spare him becoming a scapegoat. The president may also have wished to remove him from the untenable position of fighting a war under conditions he did not approve. Whatever the precise purpose, the recall of Westmoreland signified the administration's determination to maintain the limits it had placed on the war and, tacitly at least, to check its further escalation.

The March 31 Speech

During the last week of March, the internal debate reached a decisive stage and became increasingly sharp and emotional. Some of the president's advisers still insisted that the United States must "hang in there." At one time during the Tet crisis, [Walt W.] Rostow had proposed sending to Congress a new Southeast Asia Resolution to rally the nation behind the war, and he continued to urge the President to stand firm at what could be a critical turning point. Rusk persisted in working for the partial bombing halt he had outlined in early March. He was concerned by the domestic protest, but he had not despaired of success in Vietnam, nor was he disposed to capitulate to the administration's critics. He seems to have been certain that the North Vietnamese would reject his proposal, but a conciliatory gesture would show the American people that the administration was doing everything possible to bring about negotiations, thus buying time to stabilize the home front and shore up South Vietnam.

By this time, Clifford had moved significantly beyond his position of late February. He was concerned by the apparent damage Vietnam was doing to the nation's international financial position. He was alarmed by the growing domestic unrest, particularly the "tremendous erosion of support" among the nation's business and legal elite. These executives felt the United States was in a "hopeless bog," he reported, and the idea of "going deeper into the bog" struck them as "mad." Although unclear about precisely how to proceed, he had set his mind on a "winching down" strategy that would put the United States irreversibly on a course of step-by-step de-escalation. U.S. forces should not be expanded above existing levels and should be used primarily to protect the South Vietnamese population from another enemy offensive. Thieu should be pressed to clean up and broaden his government. Clifford seems also to have been prepared to make major concessions to secure a negotiated settlement. He frankly conceded that the United States might have to settle for the best it could obtain. "Nothing required us to remain until the North had been ejected from the South and the Saigon government had established complete control of all South Vietnam, " he later wrote. At a meeting on March 28, he delivered an impassioned plea to initiate the process of de-escalation. Working behind the scenes with Acheson and White House aide Harry McPherson, he waged an unrelenting battle for the president's mind.[41]

While the debate raged about him, Johnson remained noncommittal. Instinctively, he leaned toward the Rusk position. He was infuriated by the desertion of Clifford, on whose support he had counted, and he was deeply opposed to abandoning a policy in which he had invested so much, particularly in view of the improved situation in South Vietnam. Publicly, he continued to take a hard line, proclaiming that "we must meet our commitments in Vietnam and the world. We shall and we are going to win!"[42]

On the other hand, he could not ignore the protest that was building around him, inside and outside the government, and he concluded, gradually and with great reluctance, that some additional conciliatory steps must be taken. In a highly emotional March 26 meeting with Generals Wheeler and Creighton Abrams, Westmoreland's successor, an obviously embattled commander in chief sought to head off military criticism of his peace moves. In tones that verged on despondency, he lamented an "abominable" fiscal situation, panic and demoralization in the country, near universal opposition in the press, and his own "overwhelming disapproval" in the polls. "I will go down the drain," he gloomily concluded.

Trusted advisers from outside the government seem to have clinched it for Johnson. To move the president from his indecision, Acheson suggested that he call his senior advisory group, the Wise Men, back to Washington for another session on Vietnam. After a series of briefings by diplomatic and military officials on March 26, the group, in a mood of obvious gloom, reported its findings. A minority advocated holding the line militarily and even escalating if necessary, but the majority favored immediate steps toward de-escalation. After its last meeting in November, McGeorge Bundy reported, the group had expected slow and steady progress. This had not happened, however, and the majority view, as summed up by Acheson, was that the United States could "no longer do the job we set out to do in the time we have left and we must begin to take steps to disengage." The Wise Men disagreed among themselves on what to do, some proposing a total and unconditional bombing halt, others a shift in the ground strategy. Most agreed, however, that the goal of an independent, non-Communist South Vietnam was probably unattainable and that moves should be made toward eventual disengagement. "Unless we do something quick, the mood in this country may lead us to withdrawal," Cyrus Vance warned.[43] "The establishment bastards have bailed out," an angry and dispirited Johnson is said to have remarked after the meeting.[44]

Keeping his intentions under wraps until the very end, the President in a televised address on March 31 dramatically revealed a series of major decisions. Accepting Rusk's proposal, he announced that the bombing of North Vietnam would henceforth be limited to the area just north of the demilitarized zone. Responding to the entreaties of Clifford and the Wise Men, however, he went further. "Even this limited bombing of the North could come to an early end," he stressed, "if our restraint is matched by restraint in Hanoi." He named the veteran diplomat W. Averell Harriman his personal representative should peace talks materialize, and he made clear that the United States was ready to discuss peace, any time, any place. In a bombshell announcement that caught the nation by surprise, Johnson concluded by stating firmly: "I shall not seek, and I will not accept, the nomination of my party for another term as your president." He later revealed that for some time he had considered not running for reelection. He was exhausted physically and emotionally from the strains of office. He realized that he had spent most of his political capital and that another term would be conflict-ridden and barren of accomplishment. By removing himself from candidacy, he could emphasize the sincerity of his desire for negotiations and contribute to the restoration of national unity and domestic harmony.[45]

Johnson's speech is usually cited as a major turning point in American involvement in Vietnam, and in some ways it was. No ceiling was placed on American ground forces, and the president did not obligate himself to maintain the restrictions on the bombing. Indeed, in explaining the partial bombing halt to the embassy in Saigon, the State Department indicated that Hanoi would probably "denounce" it and "thus free our hand after a short period."[46] Nevertheless, the circumstances in which the March decisions were made and the conciliatory tone of Johnson's speech made it difficult, if not impossible, for him to change course. March 31, 1968, brought an inglorious end to the policy of gradual escalation.

The president did not change his goals, however. The apparent American success in the battles of Tet reinforced the conviction of Johnson, Rusk, and Rostow that they could yet secure an independent, non-Communist South Vietnam. "My biggest worry was not Vietnam itself," the president later conceded, "it was the divisiveness and pessimism at home. . . . I looked on my approaching speech as an opportunity to help right the balance and provide better perspective. For the collapse of the home front, I knew well, was just what Hanoi was counting on."[47] By rejecting major troop reinforcements, reducing the bombing, shifting some military responsibility to the Vietnamese, and withdrawing from the presidential race, Johnson hoped to salvage his policy at least to the end of his term, and he felt certain that history would vindicate him for standing firm. The March 31 speech did not represent a change of policy, therefore, but a shift of tactics to salvage a policy that had come under bitter attack.

The new tactics were even more vaguely defined and contradictory than the old, however. Johnson's decisions marked a shift from the idea of graduated pressure to the pre-1965 concept of saving South Vietnam by denying the enemy victory. Precisely how this goal was to be achieved was not spelled out. The debate over ground strategy was not resolved, and General Abrams was given no strategie guidance. Administration officials generally agreed that ground operations should be scaled down to reduce casualties, but it was not clear how they would contribute to the achievement of American goals. The bombing was to be concentrated against North Vietnamese staging areas and supply lines, but that tactic had not reduced infiltration significantly in the past, and there was no reason to assume it would be more effective in the future. The exigencies of domestic politics required acceptance of the concept of Vietnamization, and the surprising response of the ARVN during Tet raised hopes that it would work. There was little in the past record of various South Vietnamese governments to suggest, however, that Thieu and his cohorts could conciliate their non-Communist opponents and pacify the countryside while effectively waging war against a weakened but still formidable enerny. Negotiations were also desirable from a domestic political standpoint, but in the absence of concessions the administration was not prepared to make, diplomacy could accomplish nothing, and its failure might intensify the pressures the talks were designed to ease. In short, the tactics of 1968 perpetuated the ambiguities and inconsistencies that had marked American policy from the start.

10

A Dissenter in the Administration

George W. Ball

The Critical Decision

THE WAR CONTINUED TO GO BADLY. When my colleagues and I assembled at the White House on the morning of July 21,1965, we were given a memorandum from the Joint Chiefs of Staff. Only the prompt deployment of large bodies of American troops could, it argued, save the situation. That meant committing thousands of our young men not merely to passive defense missions but to aggressive combat roles. The war would then become unequivocally our own. There would be no turning back for months, perhaps years—not until we had suffered horrible casualties, killed thousands of Vietnamese, and raised the level of national anxiety and frustration above the threshold of hysteria.

Because of the importance of the July 21 meeting it may be useful to outline the colloquy which suggests the substance and flavor of our many long discussions.[1] It also provides some sense of the President's agonizing reluctance to go forward, his desire to explore every possible alternative, and, finally, his inability to reconcile his vaunted Texas "can-do" spirit with the shocking reality that America had painted itself into a corner with no way out except at substantial costs in terms of pride and prestige.

The President began with searching questions. Could we get more soldiers from our allies? What had altered the situation to the present point of urgency? McNamara produced a map. The Viet Cong, it showed, controlled about 25 percent of the South. United States forces would not be committed in those areas; they would be deployed "with their backs to the sea, for protection." They would conduct search and destroy operations against large-scale units.

"Why," I asked, "does anyone think that the Viet Cong will be so considerate as to confront us directly? They certainly didn't do that for the French." General Wheeler, the chairman of the Joint Chiefs of Staff, replied, "We can force them to fight by harassment."

After the others had expressed support for the proposed new escalation, the President asked whether any of us opposed it, looking directly at me. I made my usual speech, pointing out that we would be embarking on "a perilous voyage" and could not win. But, he asked, what other courses were available? We must, I replied, stop deceiving ourselves, face reality, and cut our losses. "If we get bogged down, the costs will be far greater than a planned withdrawal, while the pressures to create a larger war could become irresistible. We must stop propping up that absurd travesty of a government in Saigon. Let's let it fall apart and negotiate a withdrawal, recognizing that the country will face a probable take-over by the Communists."

The President replied, "You've pointed out the dangers but you've not really proposed an alternative."

After others had expressed similar sentiments, the President once more turned to me. "George," he asked, "do you think we have another course?" I answered, "I certainly don't agree with the course Bob McNamara's recommending." "All right," said the President, "we'll hear you out; then I can determine if any of your suggestions are sound and can be followed. I'm prepared to do that if convinced."

I could, I said, present to him only "the least bad of two courses." The course I could recommend was costly, but we could a least limit the cost to the short-term. At that point—just as I was beginning to speak—the President interrupted. "We'll have another meeting this afternoon where you can express your views in detail." Meanwhile, he wanted a further justification for the introduction of one-hundred-thousand more troops. In response to the President's concern about increased losses, General Taylor directly contradicted a view expressed earlier by Secretary McNamara that our losses in Vietnam would be proportional to the number of our men in that country. "The more men we have," the General now declared, "the greater the likelihood of smaller losses."

When we reconvened at 2:30 that afternoon, the President asked me to explain my position. I outlined why, in my view, we could not win. Even after a protracted conflict the most we could hope to achieve was "a messy conclusion" with a serious danger of intervention by the Chinese.[2] In a long war, I said, the President would lose the support of the country. I showed him a chart I had prepared showing the correlation between Korean casualties and public opinion. As our casualties during the Korean War had increased from 11,000 to 40,000, the percentage of those Americans who thought that we had been right to intervene had diminished from 56 percent in 1950 to a little more than 30 percent in 1952. Moreover, as our losses mounted, many frustrated Americans would demand that we strike at the "very jugular of North Vietnam" with all the dangers that entailed. Were it possible for us to win decisively in a year's time, friendly nations might continue to support us. But that was not in the cards.

"No great captain in history ever hesitated to make a tactical withdrawal if conditions were unfavorable to him," I argued. "We can't even find the enemy in Vietnam. We can't see him and we can't find him. He's indigenous to the country, and he always has access to much better intelligence. He knows what we're going to do but we haven't the vaguest clue as to his intentions. I have grave doubts that any Western army can successfully fight Orientals in an Asian jungle."

"That's the key question," the President remarked. "Can Westerners, deprived of accurate intelligence, successfully fight Asians in the jungles and rice paddies?"

We had, I continued, underestimated the critical conditions in South Vietnam. "What we are doing is giving cobalt treatment to a terminal cancer case. A long, protracted war will disclose our weakness, not our strength."

Since our main concern was to avoid undermining our credibility, we should shift the burden to the South Vietnamese government. We should insist on reforms that it would never undertake, which would impel it to move toward a neutralist position and ask us to leave. "I have no illusions," I said, "that after we were asked to leave South Vietnam, that country would soon come under Hanoi's control. That's implicit in our predicament." I then discussed the effect on other nations in the area.

The President then asked the question most troubling him, "Wouldn't we lose all credibility by breaking the word of three Presidents?" I replied, "We'll suffer the worst blow to our credibility when it is shown that the mightiest power on earth can't defeat a handful of miserable guerrillas."

Then, asked the President, "aren't you basically troubled by what the world would say about our pulling out?"

"If we were helping a country with a stable, viable government, it would be a vastly different story. But we're dealing with a revolving junta. How much support," I asked rhetorically, "do we really have in South Vietnam? "

The President then mentioned two of my points that particularly troubled him. One was that Westerners could never win a war in Asia; the other was that we could not successfully support a people whose government changed every month. He then asked, "What about the reaction of the Europeans? Wouldn't they be shaken in their reliance on us if we pulled out of Vietnam?"

"That idea's based on a complete misunderstanding of the way the Europeans are thinking," I said. "They don't regard what we are doing in Vietnam as in any way comparable to our involvement in Europe. Since the French pulled out of Vietnam, they can hardly blame us for doing the same thing; they cut their losses, and de Gaulle is urging us to follow suit. Having retired from their empire, the British recognize an established fact when they see one. They're not going to blame us for doing the same thing, although they might get a little mischievous pleasure from it—what the Germans call *schadenfreude*. But basically they only care about one thing. They're concerned about their own security. Troops in Berlin have real meaning; troops in Vietnam have none."

I then summarized the alternatives. "We can continue a dragged out, bitterly costly, and increasingly dangerous war, with the North Vietnamese digging in for a long term since that's their life and driving force." Or "we can face the short-term losses of pulling out. It's distasteful either way; but life's full of hard choices."

McGeorge Bundy then intervened to suggest that, while I had raised truly important questions, the course I recommended would be a "radical switch in policy without visible evidence that it should be done." "George's analysis," he said, "gives no weight to losses suffered by the other side. The world, the country, and the Vietnamese people would have alarming reactions if we got out." Dean Rusk then stated that, if the Communist world found out that we would not pursue our commitment to the end, there was no telling where they would stop their expansionism. He rejected my assessment of the situation. The Viet Cong had not established much of a position among the Vietnamese people, and he did not foresee large casualties unless the Chinese should come in. Ambassador Lodge agreed. There would, he said, be a greater threat of starting World War III if we did not go in with our forces. There were great seaports in Vietnam, and we did not have to fight on the roads.

After more talk along the same lines the meeting was adjourned.

Support from an Unexpected Quarter

The next day we met once more to hear the President's report of what the generals had told him. That meeting stands out in my memory not for anything I said—I had, after all, exhausted my persuasive arsenal—but rather because, for the first time, I found support from an unexpected quarter.

The President had asked his old friend Clark Clifford to attend and called on him to express his views. Presenting his argument with elegant precision and structure as though arguing a case before the Supreme Court, Clifford voiced strong opposition to the commitment of combat forces. He put forward the same arguments I had made the day before; in addition, he gave the President a more authoritative assessment of the probable domestic consequences. Whether or not President Johnson knew in advance of the position Clifford would take I cannot say; sometimes I suspected that he staged meetings for the benefit of the rest of us. But, whatever the answer to that question, Clifford emerged as a formidable comrade on my side of the barricades.

When the meeting was over, I asked Clifford to join me in the Fish Room. I told him that ever since the fall of 1961 I had been making the same arguments he now made so eloquently, and I gave him copies of the memoranda I had submitted to the President. The next day Clifford told me that he had spent the previous evening until two in the morning carefully studying my memoranda. They were, he said, "impressive and persuasive." Throughout the last year he had come more and more to my opinion as he continued to receive reports of our deteriorating situation.

I told Clark that judging from the meeting we had just had that day with the President, his intervention had had a salutary effect. Clifford replied that he had been told through "another source" that there would have to be a great effort made if we were to block this critical escalatory step that would change the character of the war. Though he hoped that through our combined exertions we could make progress, he was not optimistic. Unfortunately, "individuals sometimes become so bound up in a certain course it is difficult to know where objectivity stops and personal involvement begins." In any event, he had tried to impress on the President that we should down-play the talk that "this was the Armageddon between Communism and the Free World."

Clark Clifford had been close to the President for many years. Perhaps his opposition might turn the balance. We had one other powerful supporter, Senate Majority Leader Mike Mansfield, who, at the President's meeting with the Congressional leadership, had weighed in along the same line we were taking. There was, he had argued, no legitimate government in South Vietnam and we owed nothing to the current cabal. We were being pushed progressively deeper into the war, and even total victory would be enormously costly. Our best hope was for a quick stalemate and negotiation; the American people would never support a war that might last three to five years. We were about to get into an anti-Communist crusade. "Remember," he had concluded prophetically, "escalation begets escalation." Finally. there was my friend Senator J. William Fulbright, who had arrived at a position similar to mine, but the President had already written him off and rejected his view of the war.

As the whole world now knows, we did not carry the day—neither Mansfield, Clifford, Fulbright, nor I—and the balloon went up farther and farther.

As the war became progressively larger and bloodier, some of my colleagues talked with increasing wistfulness of a negotiated solution, which, in their vocabulary, meant Hanoi's capitulation. That was, I thought, quite unrealistic; the North Vietnamese would never stop fighting until they had obtained terms that would assure their takeover of the entire country. I had, therefore, only a marginal interest in efforts to open channels: they were not the answer. I did not see us achieving peace by the two techniques then being strongly urged: bombing pauses and the establishment of a multiplicity of diplomatic contacts. The battle-hardened leaders in Hanoi had no interest in mechanisms that would facilitate their crying "Uncle" in a low voice and with minimal loss of face: their interest was in forcing us to go home.

Bombing Pauses

A bombing pause, unaccompanied by significant concessions, was merely pulling up a plant to see how well its roots were growing. From the middle of 1964 until the end of September 1966, when I left the State Department, there were two pauses. I supported both, not because I expected anything to come of them, but because I hoped they would break the rhythm of escalation. The first pause, which began on May 13,1965, and lasted only until May 18, was, as I pointed out to my staff, not so much a pause as a hiccup. We told the Soviets in advance and tried to pass word to Hanoi (which rejected the receipt of our message) but we neglected to tell the American people or even the American military. The foreign minister of Hanoi denounced the pause as a "deceitful maneuver to pave the way for American escalation"—which I thought a perceptive appraisal. Peking called it a "fraud."

In spite of the failure of the first pause, Secretary McNamara continued to advocate "low-key diplomacy" to lay the groundwork for a settlement, stating that "We could, as part of a diplomatic initiative, consider introducing a 6-8 week pause in the program of bombing the North."[3] He repeated that recommendation in a memorandum to the President on November 3. On November 30, 1965, he sought to justify it as primarily a ritual gesture "before we either greatly increase our troop deployments to Vietnam or intensify our strikes against the North." It would, he argued, "lay a foundation in the mind of the American public and in world opinion for such an enlarged phase of the war, and"—he added, I thought, with no conviction—"it should give North Vietnam a face-saving chance to stop the aggression."[4] Secretary Rusk was not convinced; a pause was a serious diplomatic instrument; it could be used only once, and this was not the time to use it. President Johnson had a different concern; a pause that evoked no response would, he feared, provoke a demand for much stronger action from the American right wing—and they, he warned me, were "the Great Beast to be feared."

For several weeks the debate continued. On December 23, I left to spend Christmas at our family house in Florida. On the evening of Monday, December 28, the President telephoned me to say, "George, you wanted a pause and I'm giving you one. Now I need you to get it going. I'm sending a plane for you in the morning."

The President called me home to help plan a diplomatic extravaganza. He would send Administration personalities flying all over the world; they would tell heads of state and chiefs of government about the pause and enlist their help to bring Hanoi to the negotiating table. Averell Harriman would visit Poland and Yugoslavia, McGeorge Bundy Canada, Ambassador Foy Kohler would speak with Soviet officials, while Arthur Goldberg would call on General de Gaulle, Prime Minister Wilson, the Pope, and the Italian gavernment.[5] My own travel assignments were modest. I was to fly to Puerto Rico to meet Senator Fulbright fresh off the eighteenth green and then to Florida to see Senators Dirksen and Mansfield.

Although President Johnson obviously enjoyed this frenetic to-ing and fro-ing (he delighted in his ability to send well-known people flying all over the world), I thought the spectacle futile and unbecoming. Still, as I was to reflect later, better a Christmas peace extravaganza than the Christmas bombing Nixon ordered in 1974 [1972]. If that was part of the price we paid for a bombing pause, so be it; we at least broke the momentum of escalation, even though we would be under grave pressure to increase the pace of the war once the pause was completed.

Negotiating Gestures

The Administration constantly scanned the sky for smoke signals from Hanoi. It used disavowable envoys to try to provoke indications of willingness to talk and carried on probing operations with Iron Curtain diplomats.[6] Meanwhile, more and more of our young men were being sent to South Vietnam and casualties were rising. To borrow a phrase I had once heard Walter Lippmann use to describe his own frustrations, I felt I was "trying to swim up Niagara Falls." Not that I was idle; the President constantly pressed me for new negotiating ideas—though he really meant merely new channels and procedures. We were, as I told my colleagues, "following the traditional pattern for negotiating with a mule: just keep hitting him on the head with a two-by-four until he does what you want him to do." But that was useless with Hanoi; the mule's head was harder than the two-by-four.

On January 5, 1966, I sent the President two memoranda. One called for him to approach the heads of governments of the United Kingdom, Soviet Union, China, North Vietnam, and South Vietnam to request a secret meeting of the foreign ministers of those five countries with the United States to be held in Vienna beginning January 17, for preliminary discussions of the problem of Vietnam. The timing seemed propitious since a key member of the Soviet politburo, Alexander Shelepin, would shortly be visiting Hanoi, and we might thus arm him with specific proposals to press on the North Vietnamese. The second memorandum discussed possible ways and means of involving the United Nations in a peace effort, using either the Security Council or a special session of the General Assembly. Though I had little faith the United Nations could be useful, I still included a draft Security Council resolution.

As expected, the bombing pause evoked no response: by January, pressures were mounting to resume bombing and escalate the war. On January 20, I sent a memorandum to the President arguing that "the resumption of bombing may well frustrate the very political objectives we have in mind. There is no evidence that bombing has so far had any appreciable effect in weakening the determination of Ho Chi Minh and his colleagues. Whatever evidence there is points in the opposite direction." I recalled my experience on the Strategic Bombing Survey, pointing out that in both Europe and Japan the Survey found that "one does not break the will of the population of a police state by heavy bombing."

I followed my memorandum against bombing with a long analytical memorandum to the President. Prepared with the advice of recognized China experts Professors Allen Whiting and Fred Green, it pointed out why and how our bombing posed grave dangers of war with China. Today— with the wisdom of hindsight—it is clear that I overestimated the prospect of Chinese intervention. But President Johnson was deeply preoccupied with the China menace and the more I emphasized it, the stronger was my case for cutting our losses.

McNamara's Views

I had a distaste for ex parte Presidential approaches and whenever I wrote a memorandum to the President calling for our extrication, I showed it first to Rusk, McNamara, and Mac Bundy. Secretary McNamara and John McNaughton almost always responded by a prompt and courteous visit. Two or three times they showed me memoranda prepared by McNaughton commenting on what I had written, sometimes expressing views along the same general line while avoiding my hard conclusions. Though momentarily exhilarated by this prospect of support, I found McNamara unwilling to express those same realistic, if discouraging, views in meetings called by the President to discuss my various memoranda. Whether he privately discussed them with the President I do not know.

By May 1967, seven months after I had left the government, a draft memorandum by John McNaughton finally accepted the analysis I had been urging for the three previous years: "it now appears that no combination of actions against the North short of destruction of the regime or occupation of North Vietnamese territory will physically reduce the flow of men and materiel below the relatively small amount needed by enemy forces to continue the war in the South."[7]

First Meeting of "The Usual Suspects"

Even after my resignation in September 1966, I could not free myself from the oppressive burden of the war. It was a blight on all America—the continued killing, the dark apprehensions as we ventured more and more onto bottomless quicksand, and the hysteria in the universities that was taking an increasingly nasty turn. On November 1, 1967, at President Johnson's request, I attended a meeting at the State Department as a member of the so-called Senior Advisory Group—or, as the press called us, "the wise old men," the "elder statesmen" or, more derisively, "the usual suspects." We had dinner with Secretary Rusk and then met the following morning with the President. I made my usual plea for extrication to the usual deaf ears; the war, said the other members of the group, must be vigorously pursued. The major problem, they superciliously asserted, was how to educate American opinion. As I came out of the Cabinet Room, I said to Dean Acheson, John J. McCloy, and—if I recall properly—John Cowles of Minneapolis, "I've been watching across the table. You're like a flock of old buzzards sitting on a fence, sending the young men off to be killed. You ought to be ashamed of yourselves." I was as surprised as they—and a little embarrassed—by the intensity of my outburst.

The year 1968 caught Washington off guard with the shattering Tet offensive, which lasted for twenty-five days, from dawn on January 31 until February 24. In February, the President commissioned Dean Acheson to make an independent study of the war. Much to the President's dismay, Acheson concluded that we could not win without an unlimited commitment of forces—and that even then it might take five years. The country, Acheson told Johnson, was no longer behind the Administration, nor did Americans any longer believe what the President was telling them. Then, during the next few months, Clark Clifford, the newly appointed Secretary of Defense, accumulated mounting evidence that the war could not be won.[8] Outnumbered eight to one within the circle of advisers closest to the President, and now faced with a request from General Westmoreland for the deployment of 206,000 additional men, Clifford looked about, as I had done earlier, for outside help. The President should, he proposed, meet once again with members of the Senior Advisory Group, who would be briefed on the war and asked to express their views.

Second "Senior Advisory Group" Meeting

At 7:30 P.M. on Monday, March 25, 1968, five months after our earlier meeting, we met in the office of Secretary of State Dean Rusk: Dean Acheson, Omar Bradley, McGeorge Bundy, Arthur Dean, Douglas Dillon, Abe Fortas, Robert Murphy, General Matthew Ridgway, Cyrus Vance, and I. After dinner we heard briefings from three government officials: Deputy Assistant Secretary of State Philip Habib, who reviewed the political situation, Major General William DePuy, who spoke of our military posture, and George Carver of the CIA, who talked about pacification and the condition of the enemy. If the North Vietnamese were to be expelled from the South and the country pacified, it would—so our briefers estimated—take at least five to ten more years. The following morning, we talked with the senior officials of the government: Dean Rusk, Clark Clifford, and others. Secretary Clifford spoke bluntly about the choices our country faced. We could either expand the war and muddle along or pursue a "reduced strategy"— cutting back on the bombing and using American troops only to defend certain populated areas.

Dean Acheson was the first of our group to acknowledge that he had changed his mind; we could not, he said, achieve our objective through military means.[9] Views were expressed around the table, and I thought to myself, "there's been a mistake in the invitation list; these can't be the same men I saw here last November." Toward noon, we went to the White House to lunch with the President in the family dining room. During lunch, General Creighton Abrams, just back from Vietnam, told us how he was training the South Vietnamese army with the object of "Vietnamizing" the war.

The President then dismissed all members of the government so as to meet alone with our group of outsiders. When we had gathered in the Cabinet Room, he asked McGeorge Bundy to summarize our collective views. Bundy mentioned particularly Dean Acheson's current opinion that we could not achieve our objectives within the limits of time and resources available. We would therefore have to change our policy drastically. Though that reflected the general view of the group he noted that Abe Fortas and Bob Murphy had dissented. Bundy then made a remark that deeply impressed me not merely for its import but its generosity: "I must tell you what I thought I would never say—that I now agree with George Ball." Bombing in the North, which Bundy had earlier favored as the way of raising the price of insurgencies around the world, staving off defeat in the South, and providing an ultimate bargaining chip was, he had now decided, doing more to erode the support of the war on the homefront than harming the North Vietnamese.

Dean Acheson announced his position in his clear, lawyerlike way. We could not stop the "belligerency" in Vietnam by any acceptable means within the time allowed to us. In view of our other problems and interests, including the dollar crisis, we should seek to disengage by midsummer. There was little support for the war in South Vietnam or in the United States. Acheson did not think the American people would permit the war to go on for more than another year. Douglas Dillon spoke against sending additional troops and advocated stopping the bombing in an effort to move toward a negotiated settlement. He had been deeply impressed by the comments he had heard the night before that it would take five to ten years to conclude the war. General Ridgway, who had, from the first, opposed our intervention, also recommended the withdrawal of American forces, while Cyrus Vance, who, when Deputy Secretary of Defense, had always appeared to support our Vietnamese efforts, now insisted that since the war was bitterly dividing the country, it was time to seek a negotiated settlement.

I made my usual speech against the war. We could not hope to negotiate a sensible withdrawal until we stopped bombing North Vietnam. I emphasized, as I had done many times before, that the war was demoralizing our country and creating grave political divisions and that we had to get out.

There is no doubt that the unexpected negative conclusions of the "elder statesmen" profoundly shook the President. Later he grumbled to me, "Your whole group must have been brainwashed and I'm going to find out what Habib and the others told you."

No one will ever know the extent to which our advice contributed to President Johnson's decision—announced to the American people in a television speech six days after our meeting—that he would not run for President in 1968. He had, he announced, "unilaterally" ordered a halt to the air and naval bombardment of most of North Vietnam. Even that "very limited bombing of the North could come to an early end if our restraint is matched by restraint in Hanoi." Only at the end of his address did he announce his decision to withdraw from the Presidential race.

Though I knew President Johnson desperately wanted to get us out of Vietnam, he was incapable of it. His Administration had accumulated too much baggage of past statements and actions, too many fixed ideas, and too many positions it could not easily reverse. But by taking himself out of the Presidential race, Lyndon Johnson had paved the way for America's extrication, and I hoped our Vietnamese nightmare might soon be over. In spite of Hubert Humphrey's loyal and excessively exuberant support for President Johnson, I knew that he was personally revolted by the war. Once a Humphrey Administration were in place, we might then move promptly toward extrication. . . .

Chapter 4

Getting Out, 1968–1975

FOLLOWING THE TET OFFENSIVE, MANY Americans sickened of the war and responded favorably to politicians who promised a way out of Vietnam. During the 1968 presidential campaign the Democratic candidate, Vice President Hubert H. Humphrey, was until late in the game reluctant to challenge publicly Johnson's policies, whereas the Republican candidate, Richard M. Nixon, made himself credible as a man with a plan to end the suffering. Nixon was narrowly elected. As Nixon began his presidency, he and his national security adviser, Henry A. Kissinger, weighed their options. Despite their stated determination to withdraw U.S. troops from Vietnam, Nixon and Kissinger soon found themselves facing many of the same difficulties that plagued their predecessors, as Jeffrey Kimball suggests here. The administration struggled in particular to balance its felt need to win an honorable settlement in Vietnam with its desire to ease tensions with the Soviet Union and the People's Republic of China, a policy known as *détente.* The historian Stephen Ambrose explores that dilemma in an excerpt from his biography of Nixon.

The author of the last selection in the chapter is William Colby, a longtime master spy who joined the OSS during the Second World War and came to Vietnam in 1969 as deputy chief of the CIA station in Saigon. By 1971, the year in which this account opens, Colby was head of pacification for all of Vietnam. He was most strongly associated with the Phoenix program, which was designed to "neutralize" NLF agents operating in southern villages. In its own terms the program was successful, but it was denounced by antiwar Americans as indiscriminate and immoral, and Colby's picture appeared on "Wanted" posters on college campuses everywhere. In this excerpt from his biography, Colby hits back at his critics.

11

Nixon, Kissinger, and a Pax Americana

Jeffrey Kimball

> But any settlement. . . . must provide for the territorial and political integrity of South Vietnam.
>
> —Richard Nixon[1]

Policy Goals

DESPITE HIS APPARENT DISDAIN FOR Americans' foreign policy idealism, Nixon publicly spoke and wrote of his goals in Vietnam as if they were generous in spirit and noble in purpose. Thus, he began his term on January 20, 1969, with an inaugural address reminiscent of Woodrow Wilson's, in which he pledged to open an era of negotiation in search of a peace of compassion and understanding, of opportunity for all, and without victory over others.[2] Explaining ten years later in his memoir, *RN*, why he did not take advantage of the moment, blame the war on the Democrats, and then withdraw from Vietnam—a step recommended by at least one friend in Congress and most of the antiwar movement—Nixon associated the well-being of the South Vietnamese people and their right to self-determination with the survival of President Nguyen Van Thieu's government. "A precipitate withdrawal would abandon 17 million South Vietnamese, many of whom had worked for us and supported us, to Communist atrocities and domination. . . . Almost everything involving a Vietnam settlement was negotiable except . . . I would not agree to any terms that required or amounted to our overthrow of President Thieu."[3]

Nixon's commitments to the people of South Vietnam and President Thieu's government were conditional, however, for they had been made and would be kept not because of their sentimental or idealistic content but because of their relationship to Nixon's own reelection and the global interests of the United States—as he and other policy makers perceived them. Although believing that the American people had "to be appealed to on idealistic terms," he was convinced that in reality nations should and did "go into war for pragmatic reasons."[4] Linking his presidency with previous administrations, Nixon faithfully enumerated these long-standing reasons in his postwar history, *No More Vietnams:*

> Truman, Eisenhower, Kennedy, and Johnson . . . were in total agreement on three fundamental points: A Communist victory would be a human tragedy for the people of Vietnam. It would imperil the survival of other free nations in Southeast Asia and would strike a damaging blow to the strategic interests of the United States. It would lead to further Communist aggression, not only in Southeast Asia but in other parts of the free world as well. I strongly agreed with those conclusions.[5]

The new American president's concern about the fate of the Saigon regime and the South Vietnamese people was probably no greater in degree or quality than that of President Johnson's assistant secretary of defense, John T. McNaughton. In an internal policy memorandum in 1965, McNaughton had made it clear that "to help a friend" for its own sake was "NOT" a reason for America to be fighting in Vietnam. He gave top priority to the aim of avoiding "a humiliating U.S. defeat (to our reputation as a guarantor)," weighting its decisive relative importance with the mathematical value of 70 percent. Specifically, what needed protection was the U.S. reputation as a "counter-subversion"—aka counterrevolution—guarantor. Preventing Southeast Asian dominoes from falling into "Chinese hands" was worth 20 percent. The third and final goal of permitting "the people of SVN to enjoy a better, freer way of life" received a negligible valuation of 10 percent.[6]

McNaughton had been part of an NSC working group in 1964 and 1965 that had considered U.S. interests, objectives, and options in Vietnam. The group had determined that the "initial" national objective was to prevent South Vietnam from coming "under Communist control 'in any form,'" for this would constitute a "major blow to . . . U.S. prestige." Yet it realized that the costs and risks of maintaining South Vietnam's independence might be too great, and that South Vietnam "might still come apart." Thus, America's "fallback" goal was "to hold the situation together as long as possible so that we have time to strengthen other areas of Asia."[7]

Nixon had made and expressed similar conclusions at least as early as 1967, and he continued to hold these views through his presidential tenure. In a briefing paper about American aims in Vietnam he circulated to White House staffers, the president argued that the United States could not survive should it abandon "a continent where 60 percent of humanity will live in the year 2000." If the United States pulled back so fast "as to cause an Asian collapse . . . , a great vital arc of free nations . . . would lose their independence"; "the hard-liners in Peking would be encouraged"; Japan would "go neutral"; and Germany, Japan, and India would "go nuclear" to protect themselves. The United States must therefore "withdraw in [a] way Asians can take over their defense, not withdraw in [a] way Asians will collapse. The mistakes this generation makes will be paid for by the next generation."[8]

In 1969 the survival of the Saigon regime was crucial to Nixon mainly in relation to the goal of creating and maintaining a Pax Americana. "I was not personally attached to Thieu," Nixon wrote in *RN*, "but I looked at the situation in practical terms." Thieu was not the most "enlightened or tolerant or democratic" anti-Communist leader in South Vietnam, but he was the strongest. "My determination to honor our commitment to Thieu was a commitment to stability. . . . To abandon South Vietnam to the Communists now would cost us inestimably in our search for a stable, structured, and lasting peace."[9] The re-creation of an American-centered world order, however, was contingent on the reestablishment of American global hegemony: "[The] power of the United States must be used more effectively, at home and abroad, or we go down the drain as a great power," Nixon told Kissinger, [John] Ehrlichman, and [H. R.] Haldeman in July 1969. "[We] have already lost the leadership position we held at [the] end of WWII, but [we] can regain it, if [we move] fast!"[10]

Kissinger, too, spoke and wrote publicly in idealistic terms about the administration's aims: redeeming the sacrifices of those who had struggled before in good causes; maintaining dignity; keeping faith in the future; pursuing the goal of peace. He most probably believed in these and the other responsibilities and high principles to which he often appealed, but, like Nixon, he put them in the service of a fundamentally pragmatic and self-interested goal: an American-led global system, which itself was portrayed as a high-minded, principled objective. Kissinger recalled in *White House Years*, for example, that he could not allow himself "to succumb to the fashionable debunking of 'prestige' or 'honor' or 'credibility.'" To have abandoned South Vietnam to "tyranny" would have been "profoundly immoral and destructive of our efforts to build a new and ultimately more peaceful pattern of international relations."[11] This attitude matched his perception of Nixon's aims: "Nixon was eager," Kissinger wrote in *Diplomacy,* "to negotiate an honorable extrication, which he defined as almost anything except turning over to the North Vietnamese communists the millions of people who had been led by his predecessors to rely on America. He took credibility and honor seriously because they defined America's capacity to shape a peaceful international order."[12]

Neither Nixon nor Kissinger was personally attached to Thieu in a sentimental sense, but because Thieu had helped Nixon win the election, Nixon may have felt compromised, concerned that Thieu would leak the real story of their November surprise. Convinced that he had contributed to Nixon's election, and knowing that Nixon had encouraged him to withhold "support [for]...Johnson's peace initiative," the South Vietnamese president believed that the new American president "owed him a political debt."[13] On this Anna Chennault agreed with Thieu. When she learned after the election that Nixon now wanted Thieu to participate in the Paris negotiations, she, like Thieu, felt betrayed, the victim of "politics," but the kind of politics, she told the Nixon camp, she did not play. Her irritation was such that Nixon became concerned she would reveal their preelection "arrangement with Thieu" to the press. One emissary after another visited or telephoned her—Attorney General Mitchell, Director of Communications Klein, Senators Everett Dirksen, John Tower, and George Murphy, and other Nixon lieutenants—all asking her to persuade Thieu to cooperate and also to remain quiet about past intrigues. "The ultimate handshake came months later, at a White House function," she remembered, "when Nixon took me aside and, with intense gratitude, began thanking me for my help in the election. I've certainly paid dearly for it," she told him. "Yes, I appreciate that," Nixon murmured uncomfortably, "I know you are a good soldier."[14]

Nixon's nascent strategy for the Vietnam War did not yet embrace the so-called decent-interval solution, that is, withdrawing from the struggle without having achieved a clear-cut victory but having created conditions in South Vietnam that would avoid or postpone some future downfall of the Saigon regime—in essence, protecting America's credibility as a counterrevolutionary guarantor, an effective repeller of outside aggression, and a trustworthy ally. Kissinger had seemed to advocate this solution in his *Foreign Affairs* article of late 1968, and some pundits have suggested this was *the* Nixinger strategy from the beginning of the administration: "As for the United States," Kissinger wrote, "if it brings about a removal of external forces and pressures, and if it gains a reasonable time for political consolidation, it will have done the maximum possible for an ally—short of permanent occupation."[15] But this policy was hardly different from that of the Johnson administration at the time of Nixon's election. The operative phrases—the "removal of external forces and pressures" and "political consolidation"—suggested that "victory" was the goal. Kissinger's intention was to consolidate Thieu's government while the United States made an honorable exit. It required not only the expulsion or the negotiated withdrawal of the People's Army of Vietnam (PAVN) from South Vietnam but the strengthening of the RVNAF's [Republic of Viet Nam Armed Forces] military power and the crushing of insurgent resistance before and after a ceasefire. The year 1969 was too early in the Nixinger "game plan" to settle for a solution that would merely bring about a mutual North Vietnamese-American withdrawal, only to be followed by a sufficiently long interval to paper over the collapse of the RVN and the ignominy of policy defeat.[16]

Not sentimentally attached to Thieu, Nixon nonetheless felt personally responsible for his survival. He, like Johnson before him, did not want to be the first president to lose a war. In one private, angry moment, Kissinger, who did not want to be the first national security assistant to lose a war, put the issue this way: we "can't preside over [the] destruction of [the] Saigon government."[17] This was their definition of "defeat" in South Vietnam. Like previous stewards of American foreign policy, Nixon and Kissinger took seriously the necessity of avoiding defeat, with its personal and global humiliations and consequences. If the collapse of the Saigon government meant defeat, the obverse, its continuance, meant victory, which, however, required not only the survival of Thieu's government but also the expansion of its sovereignty over the non-Communist RVN.

Strategic Options

During the postelection, preinauguration transition period, Kissinger commissioned a RAND Corporation study of National Security Agency views on the current "realities" of the war and the "future prospects" for victory in South Vietnam. Daniel Ellsberg and Fred Ikle, who led the RAND team, met with Kissinger at the Pierre Hotel after Christmas Day to deliver their findings. In their written report, which was framed as an options paper delineating the alternative strategies proposed by agency heads and staff, they defined the conditions of victory as: "The destruction or withdrawal of all NVA units in South Vietnam, the destruction, withdrawal, or dissolution of all (or most) VC forces and apparatus, the permanent cessation of infiltration, and the virtually unchallenged sovereignty of a stable, non-Communist regime. . . , with no significant Communist political role except on an individual, 'reconciled' basis."[18]

Although government agencies agreed on the meaning of victory, Ellsberg and Ikle reported finding a "systematic, . . . distinct cleavage in opinion" between two groups about the current status of the Saigon regime, the military balance on the field of battle, and the prospects for victory. Designated "Group A" and "Group B" in the RAND report, each included subsets of officials who recommended variant military and diplomatic strategies. In Group A these strategies were aimed at "Communist 'fade-away' or negotiated victory"; in Group B they were intended to produce a "compromise settlement" with the other side. Ellsberg and Ikle noted a third strategy, "C," which called for the "unilateral withdrawal of all U.S. forces within one to two years," even without a settlement. Alternative C, whose goal was to extricate the United States from South Vietnam, had, however, "no advocates within the U.S. Government, but might become necessary if some of the other alternatives failed."[19]

Group A comprised officers and officials at highest levels in the JCS, MACV, the State Department, and the American embassy in Saigon, as well as some CIA analysts. They believed that enemy forces were in strategic retreat and the Saigon regime was growing stronger, with more hamlets than ever under its control. The enemy was in Paris to negotiate "from a sense of weakness and failure,"[20] and hence the United States should insist on the withdrawal of all Communist forces from South Vietnam, Laos, and Cambodia. Although the RVN was stronger than before, Group A recommended that the United States maintain a large military presence and avoid putting destabilizing pressures on the Saigon government until victory was assured: sizable American troop withdrawals should not be made for twelve to eighteen months, and U.S. demands upon the RVN to make political reforms should be restrained.

Meanwhile, if U.S. and RVN armed forces resumed military operations at pre-Tet levels, Group A argued, the war could be concluded in twelve to twenty-four months. Escalation beyond pre-Tet levels, however, would ensure a swifter and more complete victory. There were several escalation options: air and ground operations in Cambodia and Laos; unrestricted bombing and mining of North Vietnam; limited invasion of North Vietnam and Laos; full-scale invasion of North Vietnam; or any combination of these. Depending on the option chosen, U.S. force levels would have to be increased and the reserves mobilized; there would be higher casualties and greater dollar expenditures; and the Soviets and Chinese might take countermeasures. But Group A argued that the American public would accept the costs, while there would be a small risk of a strong Soviet or Chinese response. In any event, it was likely that none of the options mentioned would be necessary, because—they claimed in a recommendation that resembled the madman theory—"the credible threat, explicit or tacit, of unrestricted bombing or limited invasion of North Vietnam might well cause the DRV to accept our conditions for victory immediately."[21] To enhance threat credibility, compromises should not be offered in negotiations.

Dissidents in Group A doubted that the old American military methods of big-unit operations and bombing would succeed. They recommended an alternative that went beyond the "one war" strategy of General Creighton Abrams, who had replaced Westmoreland as commander of MACV in July 1968: a radical restructuring of U.S. and RVN forces into small units deployed in populated areas to carry out counterinsurgency activities. American troops could be withdrawn more rapidly with this strategy, they maintained, but victory would probably not be achieved for a period of four to five years.

Group B, which included the secretary of defense and most of his staff, a minority at high levels in the State Department, and some CIA analysts, believed that a return to pre-Tet operations or a resort to one or more kinds of escalation would lead to military failure and unacceptable risks and costs, while triggering even greater domestic opposition to American policy in Vietnam. Expanded counterinsurgency would also fail. Hanoi would be encouraged to hold out, and the United States would eventually have to withdraw without winning concessions.

Members of Group B disagreed with those in Group A not because they were ready to surrender—or "cop out,"[22] as Nixon and Kissinger would later phrase it—but because they had become convinced Group A's bankrupt strategy would result in crisis or defeat. Although uncertain of Hanoi's motives, they did not believe that Hanoi was in Paris from weakness or desperation. Group B was less sanguine about the length of time required to reach an agreement or terminate U.S. intervention—two to three years, compared with Group A's one to two. Persuaded that victory through military escalation was unlikely or impossible, they recommended instead that the United States seek a formal or tacit diplomatic compromise—namely, "a coalition government . . . [and] mutual withdrawal [of U.S. and North Vietnamese forces] or ceasefire . . . as part of an agreed overall settlement."[23] A formal settlement was preferable to a tacit one, for "there would be a clear expression, politically useful both for the GVN [Government of Vietnam] and the United States, that the main purpose of the U.S. involvement had been accomplished—hence U.S. withdrawal was appropriate."[24] This, of course, was one of the meanings of "honorable exit." Although compromise fell short of victory, it averted defeat and salvaged credibility.

Agreeing on the wisdom of diplomatic compromise, Group B nevertheless gave diverse specific recommendations: the continuation of current military operations and the negotiation of both a mutual withdrawal from and a coalition government for South Vietnam; a tacit or explicit mutual de-escalation and the negotiation of mutual withdrawal only, while the United States encouraged the South Vietnamese to assume a larger burden of the war; a substantial initial withdrawal of American troops combined with the building up of the RVNAF while seeking a compromise settlement; and variants of the last two. Whether in favor of mutual withdrawal only or a more comprehensive settlement that included a political compromise in South Vietnam, Group B's members were more willing than those in Group A to pressure the Saigon regime into making an accommodation with non-Communist political elements in

South Vietnam, refraining from obstructing bilateral talks between Hanoi and Washington, and negotiating in good faith with the NLF.

Those in Group B who favored an agreement on the sole issue of the mutual withdrawal of U.S. and DRV armed forces pointed out that a negotiating strategy that concentrated only on that issue freed the United States from the troublesome task of working out a political settlement for South Vietnam. Following the mutual withdrawal of North Vietnamese and American forces, the Saigon regime, they believed, would have a fair chance of gradually overcoming the NLF's insurgency. "Afterwards, it might survive, like South Korea, with an acceptable level of U.S. support." Yet, willing to accept the eventual defeat of the Saigon government and its army by the VC, their position would later be known as the "decent-interval solution": "The United States could accept such a Communist take-over in SVN, since it would have resulted from a primarily indigenous conflict [during the interval after U.S. withdrawal]. The principal U.S. objective of repelling external aggression would have been met." Besides maintaining credibility, this approach had two additional benefits: a settlement on the military issue of mutual withdrawal alone could more likely be concluded in less than three years than one that included a political component, and mutual withdrawal "would be the one objective for which domestic support in the United States is least divided."[25]

The RAND report confirmed the existence of deep divisions within and between government agencies, leading Ellsberg to suggest to Kissinger that he carry out a more comprehensive survey once the new administration took power, but he proposed that the questions be put to each agency separately, so that Kissinger could compare discrepancies between their responses agency by agency. Kissinger liked the idea of a new survey because it would provide him with more information about agency thinking on the war, while at the same time burdening the bureaucracy with paperwork, thus giving him and Nixon more room to maneuver. He told one aide, "I'm tying up the bureaucracy for a year and buying time for the new president."[26] The procedure of requiring separate responses also appealed to him because it prevented agencies from compromising their differences and colluding against the executive branch, which he considered the bureaucratic bane of presidential leadership.

NSSM 1

On January 21, the day after Nixon's inauguration, Kissinger issued a "study directive," ordering key national security agencies and their heads to respond by February 10 to twenty-nine major and over fifty subsidiary questions.[27] Many of the agency heads and staff were holdovers from the previous administration, but some, of course, were new Nixon appointees. Drafted with Ellsberg's assistance, the questions focused on topics Nixon and Kissinger wanted addressed: the negotiating environment, enemy capabilities, RVNAF capabilities, the progress of pacification, political prospects in South Vietnam, and the effectiveness of U.S. military operations.

The responses revealed general agreement on several issues. All believed the RVN had been strengthened in recent months, but not enough to enable its armed forces to fight alone successfully against the Vietnamese Liberation Armed Forces (VNLAF) "in the foreseeable future." Although it had improved "its political position in certain respects," the Saigon government continued to be weakest, and the VC/NLF strongest, in the countryside, and so it was "not clear whether it could survive a peaceful competition with the NLF for political power in South Vietnam." Even though the other side had suffered military and political reverses, it was able to replace its losses in South Vietnam through recruitment and infiltration and with supplies and equipment from the Soviet Union and China. The VNLAF was still capable of launching offensives, and it also controlled the initiative in battle and thus the attrition rate of both sides. It seemed, therefore, that the NLF and the DRV were not in Paris to negotiate from weakness, "but rather from a realization that a military victory is not attainable as long as U.S. forces remain in SVN, yet a victory in the political area is very possible."[28]

Despite this unpromising consensus, there were those who slanted their interpretation of facts toward hopefulness. These optimists argued that the enemy's "lower profile on the battlefield" and participation in negotiations were the products of a shift in political and military momentum favoring the United States and South Vietnam. The RVNAF was fighting better, pacification had made real advances, and U.S. operations had been effective—and "with less constraint" could be more so. The RVN was "more stable than at any time since Diem," and it was making progress. American negotiators in Paris should be told that "the tides are favorable."[29]

Others were skeptical. Although improvements had been made in the allied position, the war was essentially stalemated, and "short of unacceptable risks of widening the war," the United States and the RVN "cannot now or in the foreseeable future bring the enemy to his knees." Despite their superior size and more abundant equipment, South Vietnamese armed forces had "great problems." In addition, the optimistic claims made for pacification were inflated, while political progress was inadequate. The other side was not in Paris from political or military weakness, and the strength of the U.S. military position was such that "a compromise settlement is the most likely outcome for Vietnam." The American focus should now be on political actions.[30]

As in the RAND study, most of the optimists were concentrated at the top levels of MACV, the JCS, the U.S. embassy in Saigon, and, to a lesser extent than in the RAND study, in the State Department. The skeptics were to be found among the CIA and civilians in the Pentagon. Opinion varied according to the issues and often was divided between the heads of departments and operatives in the field. In MACV, for example, assessments of progress differed from one military zone to another, but Abrams suppressed the most negative analyses.[31] There were paradoxical divergences, too. Although the CIA and the intelligence divisions of the State Department gave Saigon's armed forces their lowest ratings for improvement and effectiveness, they nonetheless believed that the RVNAF could "hold its own and make some progress" against the PLAF if the latter were not supported by the PAVN.[32]

Kissinger acknowledged that the overall responses in National Security Study Memorandum (NSSM) 1 confirmed the "perplexities" that had given rise to the inquiry in the first place. Very troubling were the "disturbingly large disagreements within the intelligence community over such elementary facts as the size and deployment of enemy forces, and the importance of Cambodia . . . as a supply base." He concluded, "There was no consensus as to facts, much less to policy."[33]

Despite differences between optimists and skeptics, one lesson to be drawn was that, before a complete U.S. withdrawal, the Saigon government needed to eliminate corruption and broaden its political appeal, and its army needed to improve its effectiveness. Both political and military reforms required time, but their accomplishment was plagued by inherent contradictions. The RVNAF was unlikely to improve its performance unless the United States turned over to it the burden of fighting, but if the United States withdrew, the RVNAF's morale might collapse. In a similar Catch-22, government leaders most likely would not attempt serious political reforms unless they were pressured by the United States to do so, but such pressure might undermine their current stability—past U.S. efforts, it was noted, had failed "at directing Vietnamese political life into desired channels."[34] Even with political reforms and military strengthening, the consensus was that neither the Saigon government nor its armed forces would be able to "handle" or "stand up" to Communist forces without American support in the form of monetary aid, logistical assistance, ground troops, and airpower.[35]

Like the participants in the RAND study, NSSM 1 respondents took "victory" to mean the establishment of Thieu's unchallenged sovereignty throughout South Vietnam. But in light of the certainty of American withdrawal, no agency forecast victory coming about as the result of military or diplomatic steps.[36] Instead, they expected hostilities to be ended by a negotiated compromise. The issue for these policy makers had become one of deciding the rate of U.S. withdrawal, the degree of U.S. support for the RVN during withdrawal, and whether U.S. support should be extended past a cease-fire. The JCS and MACV looked "toward continued U.S. support to assure the sovereignty of the GVN." The Department of Defense and the State Department required "only that the South Vietnamese be free to choose their political future without external influence."[37]

Plan of Action

The primary purposes of NSSM 1, however, had not been to elicit agency proposals for alternative national policies or military strategies. Instead, the questions in Kissinger's directive of January 21 had been worded to draw forth agency assessments of political and military conditions in Vietnam and the prospects for either a "victory" or a favorable "compromise" based on options already being considered during the transition period by Nixon and Kissinger. Question 23, for example, had asked what the prospects were for "attaining—at current, reduced, or increased levels of U.S. military effort—either 'victory,' or a strong non-Communist political role after a compromise settlement of hostilities."[38]

The phrase "current levels of U.S. military effort" was a reference to the bombing halt imposed by President Johnson and the "One War, One Strategy" of General Abrams. Initiated in September 1968, the One War operational strategy ended the tacit division of roles and missions between American and South Vietnamese forces, wherein the former had concentrated on attrition and the latter on pacification; now both armies would engage in attrition and pacification—simultaneously searching and destroying, clearing, and providing security.[39] Implicit in other questions—as well as in steps taken and intentions expressed by the new administration—was that current levels of *ground* operations were to be stabilized or gradually reduced; it was also clear that withdrawals of U.S. troops were to be made, even if slowly.[40] Consequently, it was not likely that "increased levels" meant that American GIs would be engaged in big-unit operations in South Vietnam on the scale of those before Tet 1968 (except for those already planned for early 1969) or participate in large-scale invasions of North Vietnam, Laos, and Cambodia—although these latter operations in scaled-down form were probably not yet ruled out and were considered viable options under certain contingencies. The remaining options were to strengthen the RVNAF, switch American troops at some point to small-unit operations, accelerate pacification, and resume and expand aerial bombing. Only the latter option—bombing—translated into significantly increased levels of U.S. military effort. Indeed, the questions Kissinger asked and the answers provided about U.S. military operations had to do mainly with "B-52 effectiveness," air interdiction in Laos, Cambodia, and North Vietnam, and the effect of an "alternative" bombing campaign on the flow of Soviet and Chinese aid.[41]

NSSM 1 had followed the RAND study by two to three months. Agency responses were received in early to mid-February, but a summary was not prepared and circulated to the NSC

Review Group until March 14, and it was revised during the next week in preparation for a March 26 meeting of the NSC.[42] By then, however, Nixon and Kissinger had already begun to implement their strategy to win the war. They had acted before the facts as known and reported by national security agencies in their own comprehensive survey of their own administration had been collated by the NSC staff and discussed by the cabinet. If NSSM 1 served any purpose, it was to provide Nixon and Kissinger by February and March with information about bureaucratic opinion—a map of the bureaucratic terrain, so to speak—and to move the bureaucracy somewhat in the direction of their preexisting covert strategy, or at least to keep them busy while it was being implemented. It may also have been designed, just as Kissinger later said, to buy them time—to postpone criticism from those who were eager to end the war, whether by escalation or de-escalation.

The RAND study, therefore, was probably much more important to the development of their plan than NSSM 1, for it provided Nixon and Kissinger during the transition period with an early and more timely assessment of the difficulties they faced in Vietnam, and also of the range of options available—or at least those options government agencies in the late fall of 1968 believed were available. Like two mechanics collecting used parts to remodel an old car, the president and his assistant had chosen those that best fit their design for winning the peace, although they added Nixon's own ornaments—diplomatic linkage in U.S.-Soviet relations and credible but "mad" threats of escalation. Group A in the RAND options paper had proposed tacit or explicit threats of unrestricted bombing, but the national security agencies had not broached the idea of diplomatic linkage.

Nixon had denied during the presidential campaign that he had in mind what could be called a "plan" for ending the war. He continued these denials after his presidency, asserting he had "never said" he had a "'plan,' much less a 'secret plan' to end the war," for he had recognized "the difficulty of finding a solution" and how "absurd" it would have been at the time of the campaign to reveal a plan even if he had one. "Premature disclosure" would have doomed "even the best-laid plans."[43] He did admit, however, that he had had "strategic ideas" for achieving a peace with honor: "We could use our armed strength more effectively to convince the North Vietnamese that a military victory was not possible, . . . step up our programs for training and equipping the South Vietnamese," and make "adequate use of our vast diplomatic resources" to influence China and the Soviet Union, where "the heart of the problem lay more" than in Vietnam. The actual strategy that eventually did take shape was assembled, he maintained, in "the first months" of his administration. It had five parts: "Vietnamization" of the war; "pacification" of the South Vietnamese countryside; "diplomatic isolation" of North Vietnam; "gradual withdrawal of U.S. troops"; and "peace negotiations." He described the latter as "diplomatic efforts coupled with irresistible military pressure"—an oblique reference to a carrot-and-stick approach, in which the stick was the application of the madman theory. This combined diplomatic-military-political strategy, he explained, was a practical, realistic compromise between the impolitic course of severe military escalation advocated by the military and the naive policy of "peace at any price" advocated by the antiwar opposition. "I was convinced," he wrote, "that unless we backed up our diplomatic efforts with strong military pressure, the North Vietnamese would continue their strategy of talking and fighting until we tired of the struggle."[44] Aerial bombing was to be the central element of that military pressure, for Nixon believed in 1968 and would continue to believe into his presidency that bombing could close "the whole thing down."[45]

This was an accurate retroactive description of the key elements of Nixon's plan but a disingenuous account of the timing of its "taking shape." The strategy— the "secret plan"—that would be followed in 1969 had actually been outlined by Nixon at least as early as August 1968, and its basic elements were set in place by the time of the post-Christmas meetings at the Pierre Hotel between Kissinger, Ellsberg, and Ikle—weeks before NSSM 1. What remained to be completed after the inauguration were the details of implementation and the issuing of orders to commence the implementation: deciding how, when, and where to send verbal and physical signals that credibly threatened the possibility of "mad" escalations; opening a secret, back-channel contact with the Soviets; establishing the U.S. negotiating position vis-à-vis Hanoi; determining the size and timing of U.S. troop withdrawals; attempting approaches to China; and developing alternatives in case of failure. Only in this narrow sense was it true, as he claimed, that the plan "took shape" in the first few months of his administration.[46]

What took shape, therefore, was the "plan of action," as Kissinger described it in conversations with Dobrynin.[47] Because Kissinger was Nixon's implementer of the foreign policy elements of the plan of action, Haldeman, in his notes and diaries, referred to the military and diplomatic aspects of the strategy as "K's plan,"[48] but its essential elements had been designed by Nixon.

Nixon's postwar description of his plan was inaccurate, or at least incomplete, in one other respect: there were aspects of the plan—notably Vietnamization and de-Americanization—that were designed to win victories on the political home front as well. The plan of action, as Kissinger reviewed it later in the year 1969, was three-pronged: "In effect, we are attempting to solve the problem of Vietnam on three highly interrelated fronts: (1) within the U.S., (2) in Vietnam, and (3) through diplomacy."[49] On the home front, Vietnamization and de-Americanization were accompanied by announcements of prospective changes in the draft laws, which served to buy time for the rest of the plan to take hold.[50]

Nixon's and Kissinger's lack of candor about the matter of having or not having a plan before the "first few months" of the administration was in part probably the result of their desire to uphold Nixon's campaign denials, to avoid the charge or appearance of manipulating bureaucratic opinion, to protect their reputations from the taint of misleading the public, and, not least, to put the responsibility for their bombing of Cambodia on the Vietnamese enemy. But intrigue was also their natural modus operandi, becoming part and parcel not only of how they spoke about their plan but of the plan itself. "The only productive negotiations are the private ones," Nixon told his cabinet officers on March 20, and the only "basis for successful negotiating" is "military strength," by which he meant establishing a credible threat of escalation. This was an approach to which "the intellectuals are all opposed," he said, and, which many others in the citizenry, the bureaucracy, and Congress were also opposed. "It's only us nonintellectuals who understand what the game is all about."[51] Although an intellectual, Kissinger was an exception, then, for he understood the strategy: "We had to continue military pressures sufficient to deter Hanoi from turning negotiations into another Panmunjom, but not act so provocatively as to tempt a fight to the finish, [and] our government had to be sufficiently disciplined to speak with the same voice."[52]

National Security Council aide Roger Morris argued in one of his postwar books about Nixinger foreign policy that the president and his assistant did not at any time have anything that could be recognized as a plan for Vietnam. Instead, their approach was one of indecision, equivocation, outward deceit, and inner self-deception—all mixed with personal ambition, power seeking, distrust of the bureaucracy, and an obsession with projecting an image of toughness.[53] However true, the constants of Nixinger strategy toward the Vietnam War remained: big military plays, Vietnamization, pacification, clever negotiating ploys, Soviet linkage, the China card, and counterattacks against domestic opponents. Under pressure from his critics in late 1969, Nixon's public relations line was: "P has a plan, [and] its working." It was the kind of statement he often made, publicly and privately. "All the rest are in doubt," Nixon commented to Haldeman in 1971, "but we know precisely what we're going to do and where we're going to be on Vietnam."[54] He was exaggerating about their precision, but he and Kissinger had plans for Vietnam.

Frequently heard in the White House, the word "plan" was used to convey at least two different but related meanings: it could refer to a scheme of proceeding toward a goal or to a program of specific steps in that direction. There were White House plans for all sorts of things: for press conferences, for trips to San Clemente or Key Biscayne, for sabotaging political opponents, for dealing with Congress, or for international problems.[55] If military plans were the issue, the JCS, with the involvement of Kissinger and the NSC, drew up the programs of specific action, and the president decided what parts were to be implemented. The overall "Vietnam plan," however, was more in the nature of a scheme, with a commitment to particular broad approaches. Throughout the war Nixon and Kissinger would need to decide on specific steps and time lines. They usually proceeded to construct their plan piecemeal after reviewing studies of this or that issue, testing the waters of public, congressional, or bureaucratic opinion, and gauging likely Vietnamese, Soviet, or Chinese reaction. Theirs was not ever a finished plan in the sense of a blueprint—a complete diagram of specific events and time lines. It was a plan in the making, some parts complete, some in the drafting. But those sections of the design that were drawn up from time to time were based on an overall concept—a strategy of key principles that guided their ever-evolving specific plans of action.

For Nixon, if not for Kissinger, the war was yet another personal challenge arising from the tumult of national and international events. Struggle, will, boldness, and creativity—all encapsulated in the president's plan—would again prevail, they believed, as it had in Nixon's prior career and for Kissinger's geniuses of history. Reflecting on this period, Ellsberg was not far off the mark when he said of their attitude: "What was in the mind of the new administration was: We will do it better—and more savagely. . . . Only Nixon and Kissinger—coming in fresh, and thinking we know how to launch a threat campaign—could convince themselves that this was going to do the job."[56] Through winter and spring and into the summer of 1969, Nixon and Kissinger believed that in this manner the war could be ended favorably before the year was out.

At this stage of Nixon's administration, his and Kissinger's hubris was nurtured by their confidence in the plan but also by the flush of electoral victory and the headiness of assuming the presidency. It was, Kissinger remarked, an "innocence and exhilaration of newly acquired power."[57] Haldeman noted in his diary a short time after the inauguration: "For the P, as well as for all of us, life in the White House was like entering an entire new world. . . . It was . . . a totally different position from that of VP. There were lots of new things to learn every day, and he clearly enjoyed the process. . . . He loves being P!"[58]

Optimism, Apprehension, and Timetables

Haldeman also asserted that "from the start of his Presidency," Nixon "fully expected that an acceptable, if not totally satisfactory, solution would be achieved through negotiation within the first six months."[59] Two months after his inauguration, Nixon was still hopeful, if not optimistic. On March 20, shortly after deciding to bomb Cambodia, he "flatly" told his cabinet that "the war will be over by next year."[60] On April 15, with a little more than nine months left in the year, and even as a new crisis flared up in Korea, he assured his cabinet officers and their wives that he "hoped we would have it over in a few months," because he had "some real faith in

[Kissinger's] plan." A decade later, Nixon publicly confirmed that in 1969 he had entered office believing the war could be ended within the year or earlier: "Ideally the war could be over in a matter of months if the North Vietnamese wanted peace. Realistically, however, I was prepared to take most of my first year in office to arrive at a negotiated settlement."[61] For a self-styled realist, his comment uncovered a naive and arrogant assumption: the possibility of ending on his terms in less than one year a war that had been going on for decades, and one that the United States, by the account of most experts, was losing. Such a view of the world's malleability was more presumptuous than realistic.

Kissinger shared Nixon's optimism: "Give us six months, and if we haven't ended the war by then," he told a group of antiwar Quakers in May, "you can come back and tear down the White House fence." He promised his Harvard colleagues, "We'll be out in a matter of months."[62] It was not uncommon for Kissinger to tell others what he assumed they wanted to hear, but Anthony Lake, a member of Kissinger's NSC staff, thought that "Henry was sincere in believing he could negotiate an end to the war, and do it sooner rather than later."[63] In his memoir Kissinger wrote that he had "great hope" and "even thought a tolerable outcome could be achieved within a year."[64]

Although buoyant and optimistic in those early days, Nixon also appreciated the necessity of having to conclude the war in order to deal with the domestic and international crises facing the United States. There was another, more personal necessity as well: "I'm not going to end up like LBJ," he observed in November after his electoral victory, "holed up in the White House afraid to show my face on the street. I'm going to stop that war. Fast."[65] Nixon believed, as did Kissinger, Laird, and other White House advisers, that his honeymoon with public opinion would last only six to nine months. If by then he had not ended the war, it would become, Haldeman noted, "his war."[66] Distinguished outsiders made the same point and used the same timetable. In a thinly veiled warning, Averell Harriman signaled the president that he would find it necessary to oppose him openly if it became "Nixon's War," by which he meant that Nixon would have failed in bringing peace to Vietnam and that antiwar demonstrations would have begun again. Harriman gave the president until October to succeed, or at least show progress.[67] Kissinger felt they were caught between "the hammer of antiwar pressure and the anvil of Hanoi."[68] In response, their strategy was "to walk a fine line . . . between withdrawing too fast to convince Hanoi of our determination and withdrawing too slowly to satisfy the American public."[69] Meanwhile, linkage and threat—made credible by the bombing of Cambodia—would lever the enemy into concessions. Nixon was determinedly optimistic as he began his administration, but things could go wrong, and the war might have to continue in order to ensure an "honorable" exit. He was the steward of American global policy, convinced that the national interest—as he, most of the bureaucracy, and many others in the body politic defined it—rose or fell on the preservation of the Saigon regime.

⪡ 12 ⪢

Bombing Hanoi, Mining Haiphong, and the Moscow Summit

Stephen E. Ambrose

WITH THE OPENING TO CHINA BEHIND HIM, Nixon's next move in establishing triangular diplomacy was his upcoming journey to Moscow. The summit, scheduled for the third week in May [1972], would be the culmination of his diplomacy, marking the completion of his creation of a new era of world power politics. The trip to Peking had been more symbol than reality, the meeting marked by flowery speeches and generalizations rather than direct, specific deals. The trip to Moscow would be just the opposite. And it would be more important, for the simple reason that the U.S.S.R. was incomparably more powerful than the P.R.C. China could be an irritant to the United States in various parts of Asia; the U.S.S.R. could destroy the United States in a flash.

Since 1969, Nixon had moved carefully, cautiously, but steadily toward an arms-control agreement. The obstacles were great: ingrained suspicions of the Soviets, the clamor of the hawks, the economic needs of the military-industrial complex, the war in Vietnam, tension in the Middle East and South Asia, and so forth. But Nixon had persevered, and by the spring of 1972 he was on the verge of prevailing.

He had not created the possibilities all by himself. [Henry] Kissinger's academic brilliance and Metternich-like conceptions had certainly played some role, but more important was the confluence of events and needs. The first of these was the necessity felt by both superpowers to reduce the cost and dangers of the arms race. More specifically, the Soviets had some critical interests at stake. They needed to offset Nixon's Peking trip, for fear of a Sino-American alliance (the beauty of Nixon's triangular diplomacy was that only he could talk to the other two sides of the triangle). Further, the Soviets wanted to promote détente in Europe, which, while progressing, was still in a delicate formative stage. They also wanted expanded trade relations with the United States; indeed they were almost desperate for American grain. In addition, they had long sought a recognition of parity and a compact of equality with the United States.

Nixon was eager to sell the grain and willing to accept détente in Europe. Already playing off the Chinese against the Russians, he now wanted to play off the Russians against the Chinese. But most of all, what he wanted from the summit was credit for an arms-control agreement and progress toward peace in Vietnam. He had already warned Chou [En-lai] that if the North Vietnamese launched a spring offensive, he would react with the full fury of the mad bomber. Now he wanted to let [Leonid] Brezhnev and his pals know that the price for détente was help in ending the war in Vietnam.

For all Nixon's acceptance of the new realities of the world balance of power, however, other more personal things mattered more to him.

As to SALT [Strategic Arms Limitation Talks], Nixon's own words made it clear that he was more concerned with getting credit for an arms-control agreement than he was in reaching an arms-control agreement. He wanted both, of course, but if he had to choose, credit came before reality.

In early March 1972, it appeared that Gerard Smith and the American negotiating team in Vienna were on the verge of completing the SALT treaty, so that when Nixon went to Moscow it would be not to negotiate anything but simply to indulge in a ceremonial signing. Nixon responded with a March 11 memorandum to [H. R.] Haldeman.

"What I am concerned about," he began, "is not that we will fail to achieve the various goals . . . but that when we do make the formal agreements there will be no real news value to them." Nixon insisted that it was "vitally important that no final agreements be entered into until we arrive in Moscow." He instructed Haldeman to "begin a line of pessimism" about progress on SALT, and explained that otherwise "our critics will make it appear that all of this could have been achieved without any summit whatever, and that all we did was to go to Moscow for a grandstand play to put the final signature on an agreement that was worked out by Gerry Smith, State, etc."

As to the policy of détente in general, Nixon was ready to sacrifice it if necessary to avoid what he regarded as humiliation in Vietnam, as his actions in April and May showed, when he came exceedingly close to doing just that in response to a North Vietnamese challenge.

On March 30, the NVA launched the first phase of an offensive against South Vietnam. Using tanks and artillery in numbers never before seen in the war, the Communist forces crossed the DMZ and headed toward Quang Tri. The area had once been defended by U.S. Marines; now it was held by ARVN units that, after some initial resistance, cracked.

On his News Summary for April 3, Nixon underscored the lines that hurt the most: "'Rout,' 'disarray,' 'crushing,' are terms used to describe ARVN retreat in first test of Vietnamization." "GIs quoted by UPI see little chance of ARVN holding at Quang Tri. And several voice strong opposition to the war itself." (The second sentence got a double underscoring plus a marginal order: "K—note!") "CBS and NBC film of thousands of refugees fleeing as enemy uses artillery more intensively than at any time in war. . . . DOD [Department of Defense] feels ARVN was taken by surprise. Situation is expected to get worse."

A catastrophe loomed. It did no good to say that the offensive, after the two-year lull in the fighting in South Vietnam, had long since been anticipated. Nixon had to react. Any hesitation, and he might well face personal as well as national disaster. If the North Vietnamese won the war through force of arms, Nixon's three-year-old policy of Vietnamization would be exposed as a fraud, he would be humiliated and lose the election, and the United States would be disgraced.

Nixon did react, instinctively and immediately. Brushing aside bureaucratic opposition and counsels of moderation, he ordered an all-out counterattack by sea and air power. He sent in B-52s, more fighter-bombers, more aircraft carriers, more cruisers; he took off all budgetary restraints on air sorties; he ordered tactical air strikes up to the eighteenth parallel in North Vietnam; he ordered naval attacks twenty-five miles up the coast of North Vietnam.

In short, he counterattacked with almost everything he had available. What he did not do was launch a counteroffensive. He did not send in troops; he did not even slow the pace of ground forces withdrawal; he did not invade North Vietnam; he did not bomb Hanoi or Haiphong. His relative restraint was all the more remarkable because his anger was boundless. He thought the Communists had played with him for years, using negotiations as a smoke screen to prepare for a massive invasion. He was furious with the Soviets, whose tanks and artillery made the offensive possible. He felt that everything he had worked to achieve was threatened.

But his anger was more understandable than it was justified. In 1970 and 1971 he had been the one to launch offensives in Cambodia and in Laos. Even after they failed, his negotiating stance remained: give back the POWs, pull back your forces to North Vietnam, abandon your gains in Cambodia and Laos, and some months later the United States will complete its withdrawal (although he was never explicit on whether this withdrawal would include American air and sea power). Meanwhile, [Nguyen Van] Thieu would still be in power in Saigon (the promise that he would step down one month before elections was meaningless, as all his appointees would remain in charge and would be the ones to conduct the election).

Nixon, in other words, was demanding that Hanoi surrender its war aims, even as he withdrew American ground forces. How could he have expected the NVA not to attack when its leaders judged the moment to be right?

With regard to the Soviets, Nixon's complaints that they made the offensive possible were certainly true, but he ignored other relevant points. The United States was supplying more material to Saigon than the Soviets were to Hanoi. Soviet control of the actions of the men in Hanoi was never as complete as Nixon assumed it was. The Soviets had not sped the shipment of arms in the winter of '71–'72, nor had they ordered the offensive. The NVA had accumulated the arsenal thanks to the two-year lull on the battlefield, and decided on its own when and how to strike.

Nor did Nixon pay sufficient attention to what the Soviets did *not* do. While they gave Hanoi MiGs and SAMs to defend their airspace, they did not give the NVA fighter-bombers with which to attack the American air bases in Thailand, nor submarines with which to attack the American aircraft carriers in the Gulf of Tonkin. Like Nixon, they exercised some degree of restraint.

Nixon nevertheless had Kissinger tell [Anatoly] Dobrynin on April 3 that Soviet complicity in Hanoi's attack was jeopardizing the summit.

Kissinger was not happy with the assignment. He knew that "Nixon was determined on a showdown," that "he saw no point in further diplomacy until a military decision had been reached." Kissinger, encouraged by Dobrynin to believe that the North Vietnamese would be forthcoming in a scheduled secret meeting between Kissinger and Le Duc Tho on April 24, was not so ready to abandon diplomacy, although he was as one with his boss on the need for an all-out counterattack.

To Nixon's extreme frustration, that attack was slow to get going. According to the Pentagon, bad weather was the cause. Nixon had his doubts. At an afternoon meeting on April 4 with Mitchell and Haldeman, the President said, "Damn it, if you know any prayers say them. . . . Let's get that weather cleared up. The bastards have never been bombed like they're going to be bombed this time, but you've got to have weather."

"Is the weather still bad?" Mitchell inquired.

"Huh!" Nixon answered. "It isn't bad. The Air Force isn't worth a—I mean, they won't fly." He wished he had George Patton.

On April 7, the NVA moved into the second phase of its offensive, attacking from Cambodia to the northwest of Saigon, toward Tay Ninh and An Loc. By then, the American counterattack was under way, as B-52s struck 145 miles north of the DMZ (the first use of B-52s in North Vietnam since early 1968), inflicting heavy casualties. Still the NVA came on; still ARVN failed to do its duty. Nixon had Kissinger's assistant, Al Haig, prepare a contingency plan; if all else failed, it called for bombing all military targets throughout North Vietnam and the mining of North Vietnamese ports.

For all his bellicosity, Nixon was downcast by events. Kissinger told him that even if the worst happened and the remaining American troops pulled out as the NVA won the war, he would still be able to claim credit for ending the war. Nixon said that prospect was "too bleak even to contemplate." He told Kissinger defeat was "simply not an option." But it was certainly a possibility. He expressed his depression in his diary: "If we fail it will be because the American way simply isn't as effective as the Communist way. . . . I have an uneasy feeling that this may be the case. We give them the most modern arms, we emphasize the material to the exclusion of the spiritual and the Spartan life, and it may be that we soften them up rather than harden them up for the battle."

Nixon was also unhappy with Kissinger: "Henry, with all of his many virtues, does seem too often to be concerned about preparing the way for negotiations with the Soviets. . . . Both Haldeman and Henry seem to have an idea—which I think is mistaken—that even if we fail in Vietnam we can still survive politically. I have no illusions whatever on that score, however. The U.S. will not have a credible foreign policy if we fail, and I will have to assume the responsibility for that development."

On April 10, Nixon increased the pressure on the Soviets. Speaking at a State Department ceremony for the signing of an international convention for the banning of biological warfare, with Dobrynin in the audience, he said that every "great power" must follow the principle that it should not encourage "directly or indirectly, other nations to use force or armed aggression against its neighbors."

On the battlefield, meanwhile, the B-52s were dropping hundreds of tons of bombs on the enemy around An Loc, but still ARVN was unable to push back the NVA. Nixon railed at the Pentagon. Why couldn't more be done? He wanted more B-52s sent north, to hit targets that were strategic and diplomatic, as well as tactical targets in the south.

[Melvin] Laird dissented. He feared that the relatively slow and not very maneuverable eight-jet bombers would be easy targets for Hanoi's SAMs. He also feared the congressional uproar that would follow. [William P.] Rogers feared that such an escalation would endanger the summit.

Nixon insisted. He ordered B-52 raids against the oil depots around Hanoi and Haiphong; he even announced them in advance. On April 14, the President said that 150 B-52s, each one carrying thirty tons of bombs (ten times the capacity of the F-4 Phantom fighter-bombers), would hit North Vietnam the following day. It was obvious that such raids would have no effect on the battles around An Loc and Quang Tri; a Pentagon spokesman explained that the purposes were to slow the flow of supplies south, to demonstrate to President Thieu that he could count on Nixon, and to create a bargaining chip.

The next day, April 15, the bombers moved in. They struck inside and outside Hanoi and Haiphong. They caused extensive damage, but the NVA claimed that eleven American planes had been shot down. Still, Nixon was pleased. He told Haldeman, "Well, we really left them our calling card this weekend."

But that same day the North Vietnamese canceled the Paris meeting scheduled for April 24; as this was the meeting at which Dobrynin had hinted the enemy would be forthcoming, the cancellation was a blow. "Henry obviously considered this a crisis of the first magnitude." Nixon wrote in his diary. "I laid down the law hard to him that under these circumstances he could not go to Moscow." Kissinger had been slated to make a secret presummit trip to Moscow to prepare the way for Nixon. The President felt that the Soviets wanted Kissinger to come to discuss SALT, trade arrangements, and the like, when what needed to be discussed was Vietnam.

Nixon realized that his decision to keep Kissinger home "shook him because he desperately wants to get to Moscow one way or the other." But Nixon did not want to discuss SALT; he wanted to "consider our option with regard to imposing a blockade."

On the afternoon of April 15, Nixon had "a pretty candid talk with Henry." The President was depressed. He told Kissinger that if he had to cancel the summit and impose a blockade, "I had an obligation to look for a successor." Nixon speculated on who might replace him; he mentioned [Nelson] Rockefeller, [Warren] Burger, [Ronald] Reagan, and [John] Connally.

Kissinger threw up his hands. He said that "none of them would do," and added that any Democrat was out of the question.

Nixon mused that if Kissinger would stay on, "we could get continuity in foreign policy." Kissinger, not averse to a little flattery himself, "became very emotional." He said Nixon "shouldn't be thinking this way or talking this way. . . . He made his pitch that the North Vietnamese should not be allowed to destroy two Presidents."

Later that evening, Kissinger called Nixon to inform him that Dobrynin was "desperate" to have him come to Moscow, and had promised that Vietnam would be the first item on the agenda. Nixon then reconsidered. He said Kissinger could go to Moscow.

The following day, American bombers hit four Soviet merchant ships at anchor in Haiphong harbor. The Soviets protested, but in a relatively low-key manner, indicating their desire to go ahead with the summit.

Still Nixon had third and fourth thoughts about the wisdom of the Kissinger trip. Kissinger reassured him and Nixon again agreed to let him go. That left the problem of how to inform the Secretary of State. A month earlier Rogers had sent a memo to Nixon saying that he intended to "take personal charge" of the Moscow summit preparations. That was not Nixon's plan at all. He had Haldeman tell Rogers that all communications with the Soviets by the State Department had to be cleared in advance by the White House.

Nixon decided to use a bit of subterfuge in informing Rogers. After Kissinger left for Moscow, Nixon would call Rogers to Camp David to tell him that Kissinger had received a sudden and unexpected summons from Brezhnev to discuss Vietnam. Nixon would assure Rogers that the only subject of discussion would be Vietnam (in the event, when Rogers learned that Kissinger talked about the full range of summit issues, he was "highly indignant." To complete the exclusion of the State Department from this most fundamental of all foreign-policy issues, Kissinger slipped into and out of Moscow without the American ambassador even knowing that he was there. Never before had an American President so personalized basic diplomacy, or so insulted the Department of State).

It was not entirely Nixon's fault. He gave clear oral instructions to Kissinger: Vietnam was to be the first item discussed, and if the Soviets proved "recalcitrant on this point, he should just pack up and come home."

Nixon told Kissinger that while the summit had the potential of being the most important diplomatic encounter "of this century," it was "indispensable" to have "progress" on Vietnam "*by the time of the summit.*" The President instructed his National Security Adviser to insist on a withdrawal of the NVA across the DMZ; he said that action was a "precondition of our ending the bombing of North Vietnam."

Nixon also told Kissinger how to describe the President to Brezhnev: "direct, honest, strong . . . fatalistic—to him election [is] not key. Will not be affected one iota by public opinion. No other President could make SALT agreement while war is still going on."

Kissinger got around this set of orders by the simple expedient of ignoring them. While Kissinger was in Moscow (April 21–24), Nixon was at Camp David with [his friend Bebe] Rebozo ("a conjunction that did not usually make for the calmest reflection," Kissinger noted). Haig was also at Camp David. Nixon bombarded Kissinger with instructions to hang tough, to keep Vietnam up front, and so on. Kissinger in fact brushed past Vietnam, rightly expecting no progress, and plunged into the summit issues. It was the Soviets who insisted on some progress on Vietnam, and Kissinger gave it to them with hints that the United States, for the first time, might be willing to discuss a coalition government, and would not insist on the withdrawal of the NVA from South Vietnam.

Nixon, rightly suspecting that Kissinger was making unauthorized deals, demanded explanations. Kissinger sent a wire: "Brezhnev wants a summit at almost any cost." He told Haig to tell the President, "He must trust me. I have not exactly let him down on other missions." But Nixon feared Brezhnev would cancel the summit, which would be embarrassing: if it was going to be canceled, he wanted to be the one to do it. Further, Haig informed Kissinger, Nixon was in a "starchy mood" because polls indicated his popularity had risen thanks to the bombing campaign. Haig, who to Kissinger's discomfort was becoming one of the Nixon insiders, told Kissinger that the President had telephoned him and said "he views Soviet positions on South Vietnam as frenzied and frivolous and, therefore, is determined to go forward with additional strikes on Hanoi and Haiphong."

In a message of his own to Kissinger, Nixon asserted that SALT was of concern only to "a few sophisticates." The main issue was Vietnam. The President wanted to go all out against the North Vietnamese and was willing to cancel the summit rather than forgo that option. Then, despite the way in which Kissinger had changed the basis of American foreign policy making, from a two-man team to a one-man show, in direct contradiction of clear orders, Nixon praised Kissinger for his "skill, resourcefulness, and determination," and concluded his message, "However it all comes out, just remember we all know we couldn't have a better man in Moscow at this time than Kissinger. Rebozo joins us in sending our regards."

Kissinger speculated that a lot of drinking was going on that weekend at Camp David. Whatever the cause, the result was a set of contradictory presidential messages and orders. Apparently the chief executive of the United States did not know what he wanted, and left it to the National Security Adviser to sort out.

Kissinger returned on April 24. He justified his actions in a long memorandum; in his oral report he made the clinching argument: "If the summit meeting takes place, you will be able to sign the most important arms control agreement ever concluded." Nixon decided not to hold Kissinger to account, perhaps a reflection of the independent power base Kissinger had managed to build, thanks in no small part to the enormously favorable publicity he had received in the past six months. Nixon now needed Kissinger almost as much as Kissinger needed him.

While Kissinger was in Moscow, the North Vietnamese launched the third phase of their offensive, attacking out of Laos and Cambodia into the Central Highlands, toward Kontum and Pleiku. Nixon responded with a televised speech in which he described the NVA attacks as "a clear case of naked and unprovoked aggression across an international border. There is only one word for it—invasion." He "flatly rejected" proposals from dovish senators that he stop the bombing in order to get the enemy back to the negotiating table. "They sold that package to the United States once before, in 1968, and we are not going to buy it again in 1972." He concluded with a bit of Nixonian hyperbole: "If the United States betrays the millions of people who have relied on us in Vietnam . . . it would amount to a renunciation of our morality, an abdication of our leadership among nations, and an invitation for the mighty to prey upon the weak all around the world."

He balanced his bellicosity with some encouraging words. Although Kontum and Quang Tri were surrounded, he asserted that the ARVN was doing well, so well that he could announce a further withdrawal of twenty thousand troops. And he held out hope for negotiations; despite what he said about the bombing, he announced that the canceled April 24 meeting with the North Vietnamese would be held on May 2. There was a further conflicting signal; he greeted a Chinese Ping-Pong team in the Rose Garden.

On the morning of April 30, he called Kissinger on the telephone. He warned again that he intended to cancel the summit "unless the situation militarily and diplomatically substantially improves by May 15. . . . We have crossed the Rubicon and now we must win." He said Hanoi could not be trusted, "they will break every understanding." When Kissinger talked to the North

Vietnamese in Paris, he should be "brutally frank from the beginning—particularly in tone." Tell them, he said, "the President has had enough and now you have only one message to give them—Settle or else!"

Later that morning, Nixon flew down to Floresville, Texas, for a barbecue hosted by John Connally on his ranch, and attended by some two hundred Texas moneymen. George Brown, head of the state's largest construction company, Brown & Root, and LBJ's original backer, was there, as were John Murchison, Dallas oilman, and former Democratic governor Allan Shivers, along with the other key supporters of LBJ throughout his career. These were the same men, Democrats all, who had backed Lloyd Bentsen in his winning senatorial race against George Bush in 1970, and had made Connally governor.

Nixon, delighted to be the guest of honor in a gathering of his old political foes (these were the men who, some thought, had stolen Texas from Nixon for Kennedy in 1960), bubbled over. "I think that I have learned more about Texas on this brief visit than at any other time," he declared. Connally commented. "I have never learned much in politics, but I have learned that you have to fish with live bait. And we are not without some in this gathering this evening."

After the drinks, the beef tenderloin, and the corn on the cob, Nixon answered questions. The Texans wanted to know if he had thought about bombing the dikes in North Vietnam. He said he had, but pointed out that it would cause heavy civilian casualties. Then he added, "We are prepared to use our military and naval strength against military targets throughout North Vietnam, and we believe that the North Vietnamese are taking a very great risk if they continue their offensive in the South." To do less, he said, would insure a "Communist take-over," which would weaken the office of the Presidency, damage respect for the United States around the world, "destroy the confidence of the American people," and lead to further Communist adventures elsewhere.

Those words, in that setting, gave reporters present a sense of *déjà vu*. They had heard it all before, from another President, on another Texas ranch, but before the same audience, between 1965 and 1968. The similarities between LBJ in '68 and Nixon in '72 were growing in size and in number.

Back in Washington, the sense of *déjà vu* increased. Headlines proclaimed that Quang Tri had fallen to the enemy. Nixon had a report on his desk from General [Creighton] Abrams saying that ARVN had evidently lost its will to fight. Adding to Nixon's woes, the newspapers proclaimed that the *New York Times* had won the Pulitzer Prize for the Pentagon Papers.

Kissinger was in the Oval Office on the afternoon of May 1, for last-minute instructions before flying to Paris to meet Le Duc Tho. Don't give an inch, Nixon told him. "No nonsense. No niceness. No accommodations." He also wanted Kissinger to let Dobrynin know that "under no circumstances will I go to the summit if we're still in trouble in Vietnam."

Kissinger flew to Paris, where he found Le Duc Tho "icy and snide." After three fruitless hours, he broke off the talks and headed home.

Nixon was not surprised. He wrote in his diary that Kissinger was so "obsessed with the idea that there *should* be a negotiated settlement" that he failed to see "there really isn't enough in it for the enemy to negotiate at this time."

Nixon recorded that he had a long talk with Haig, who like Kissinger knew that the way to the President's heart was to talk tough. On this occasion, Haig urged Nixon to take stronger action than Kissinger recommended. Nixon further steeled himself in his diary entry: "I must make whatever hard choices have to be made, and take whatever risks need to be taken."

Haig presented the President with an irresistible argument: he "emphasized that even more important than how Vietnam comes out is for us to handle these matters in a way that I can survive in office." That was putting first things first, and moved Haig up even higher in Nixon's esteem. So high, in fact, that the President told [Charles] Colson later that day that Haig and Connally "are the only two men around here qualified to fill this job when I step down."

Haig was as good as Kissinger himself at telling one man one thing, another man another, at backbiting, and at manipulating Nixon. He told Admiral Elmo Zumwalt (Chief of Naval Operations), for example, "that he [Haig] had to exercise considerable dexterity to stiffen the President's backbone when the President was in a bug-out mood, and that he lived in dread that some day the President would be with Henry instead of him when the bug-out mood came on and Henry would be unable to handle it."

Kissinger returned to Washington the evening of May 2. Nixon had a helicopter waiting for him, to bring him to the Washington Navy Yard for a cruise on the *Sequoia*. Haig was also along.

Nixon wanted to launch B-52 strikes against Hanoi and Haiphong on May 5. Kissinger urged caution. He reminded the President that General Abrams wanted to use B-52s inside South Vietnam, to break up the enemy attacks at the point of contact, not hundreds of miles behind the lines, where the effect of the raids would not be felt on the battlefield for months. And he warned Nixon that he could not bomb and have the summit too, that the Soviets would have to cancel, blaming Nixon and the bombing. Then Nixon would really catch it from the doves, who would go after him over the bombing and over the cancellation of the summit.

Nixon acknowledged that "it was hard to see how I could go to the summit and be clinking glasses with Brezhnev while Soviet tanks were rumbling through [South Vietnam]." But he wanted to bomb so badly. But he wanted to go to Moscow so badly. He was in an agony of indecision.

He decided to postpone a decision on Hanoi-Haiphong and the summit until the following week. Meanwhile he ordered plans prepared and told Kissinger to get ready to cancel the summit. If he decided on all-out action, he wanted to preempt the Soviets by canceling first.

Whatever he decided about Hanoi-Haiphong, he was determined to escalate the air war to teach the enemy a lesson. On May 4 he ordered fifty additional fighter-bombers to Southeast Asia, and ordered the fleet brought up to six aircraft carriers on active-duty station. This meant that in the past month he had increased the B-52 force in the war from 80 to 140, the number of fighter-bombers from 400 to 900, the number of carriers from three to six, and the air-navy personnel from 47,000 to 77,000. Meanwhile, he had reduced the number of ground troops from 95,000 to 68,100. None of those figures include the ARVN air force, by 1972 the fourth-largest in the world.

But the enemy could escalate too. On the day Nixon sent in the carriers and the fifty fighter-bombers, the Vietcong announced the establishment of a "provisional revolutionary administration" in Quang Tri City. It was the first time in the war the Communists had succeeded in setting up a government on a provincial level in South Vietnam.

"What will he do, they ask," Max Frankel wrote in the *New York Times*. "What will he do if the North Vietnamese keep coming, the South Vietnamese keep crumbling, the Russians keep stalling and the political risks keep mounting?" Noting Nixon's "propensity for psychic rage and for diplomacy by thunderclap," Frankel reviewed the options. Nixon could hardly increase the air counterattack in the South, as he had already put almost everything available into the battle. He might bomb the dikes, or use nuclear weapons, or invade North Vietnam with marines, but none of that seemed likely. He could pressure the Russians by bombing or mining Haiphong harbor, at a risk to the summit. Or he might make some concessions to the enemy in the hope of achieving a negotiated settlement. But, Frankel concluded lamely, "no one really does know what he might do."

Not even Nixon knew. He continued to waver. He badly wanted and desperately needed advice, not from Kissinger or Haig (he knew their views), not from the Joint Chiefs or the State Department (he saw them as tools, not advisers), but from someone he trusted and respected (and there was almost no one he did).

He decided to turn to John Connally. Connally had once had some military experience; he had served for a few months as Kennedy's Secretary of the Navy. Nixon respected him; he constantly indulged himself in the fantasy that Connally could follow him into the White House. Kissinger acknowledged that Connally had "the best political brain in the Administration." Nixon ordered Haldeman and Kissinger to go to Connally to find out what to do.

Big Jawn did not duck or shirk the responsibility. He was decisive. Haldeman reported to the President that Connally emphatically said, "Most important—the President must not lose the war! And he should not cancel the summit. He's got to show his guts and leadership on this one. Caution be damned—if they cancel, and I don't think they will, we'll ram it right down their throats."

That was what Nixon wanted to hear. Once he knew Connally's views, he asked Connally to join him, Haig, Haldeman, and Kissinger in his EOB office for a council of war.

They reviewed the options, including the possibility of declaring a blockade. They decided a blockade would be too risky, as it carried the danger of having to confront the Soviet Navy. Mining was better.

Nixon pumped himself up. "As far as I'm concerned," he declared, "the only real mistakes I've made were the times when I didn't follow my own instincts." He wished he had bombed North Korea in 1969 after the EC-121 was shot down. He wished he had bombed the hell out of North Vietnam in 1970, when he went into Cambodia. "If we'd done that then, the damned war would be over now. . . . The summit isn't worth a damn if the price for it is losing in Vietnam. My instinct tells me that the country can take losing the summit, but it can't take losing the war."

Kissinger described the commander in chief at this critical moment: "The only symptom of his excitement was that instead of slouching in an easy chair with his feet on a settee as usual, he was pacing up and down, gesticulating with a pipe on which he was occasionally puffing . . . he was playing [General Douglas] MacArthur. . . .

"Nixon then and there decided upon the mining," Kissinger wrote. "It was one of the finest hours of Nixon's Presidency."

Still he needed reassurance. He went up to Camp David for the weekend. Ed and Tricia Cox joined him, as did Julie Eisenhower. He told his daughters of his decision. Julie was worried: would it work? Nixon told her that if he did not do it, "the United States would cease to be a respected great power." She assured him that David would "totally agree." Tricia, Nixon wrote in his diary, "was immediately positive because she felt we had to do something, and frankly didn't know what else we could do to avoid a continued deterioration in the battle areas."

Nixon called John Mitchell. He thoroughly approved.

That left the congressional leadership, the JCS, the DOD, the State Department, and the NSC. None had been consulted, all had to be informed. On Monday morning, May 8, Nixon told the NSC. The meeting lasted more than three hours and the President found it "pretty tough." Laird opposed the decision, Rogers was hesitant, [Senator Jesse] Helms warned that mining Haiphong would not be decisive because the enemy had alternate supply routes available, and the professional military were more interested in fighting the battle in South Vietnam than engaging in strategic projects of dubious immediate benefit in North Vietnam.

Nixon defended his decision. "The real question is whether the Americans give a damn anymore," he said. He warned that if he followed the lead of *Time* magazine, the Washington

Post, the *New York Times*, and the networks and just pulled out, "The U.S. would cease to be a military and diplomatic power. If that happened, then the U.S. would look inward towards itself and would remove itself from the world." But if the United States stayed strong and willing to act, "then the world will remain half-Communist rather than becoming entirely Communist."

With nearly ten thousand atomic weapons, plus all its additional firepower, plus its unrivaled economic strength, it is difficult to see how the United States would have ceased to be a great power if it failed to mine Haiphong harbor, but evidently no one at the NSC protested against Nixon's statement.

The President himself, however, appeared to backtrack later that day. In an afternoon meeting in the EOB with Haldeman and Kissinger, he told Kissinger that Haldeman had raised new questions. Haldeman then described the dire impact that mining Haiphong would have on public opinion; it might lead to Nixon's defeat in November. Kissinger "passionately defended the decision."

Nixon excused himself to go to the bathroom. Kissinger whirled on Haldeman and castigated him for interfering at such a moment. Haldeman, Kissinger later wrote, "grinned shamefacedly, making clear by his bearing that Nixon had put him up to his little speech." When Nixon returned from the bathroom, he signed the order without another word.

Kissinger confessed that he was unable to comprehend why Nixon had played this little game, until a year later when he learned of the taping system. "[This] suggested a possible motive: Nixon wanted me unambiguously on record as supporting the operation." (According to Haldeman, Nixon's motive was to test Kissinger's degree of conviction.)

At 8 P.M., May 8, Nixon met with the joint congressional leadership. He knew what the politicians' advice would be—don't risk the summit, don't escalate—so he did not ask for it. Instead, he told them what he was going to do, and then concluded, "If you can give me your support, I would appreciate it. If you cannot, I will understand." He then walked out of the room.

At 9 P.M., he went on nationwide radio and television. He opened with a review of the military situation. "There is only one way to stop the killing," he said. "That is to keep the weapons of war out of the hands of the international outlaws of North Vietnam." To that end, "all entrances to North Vietnamese ports will be mined. . . . Rail and all other communications will be cut off to the maximum extent possible. Air and naval strikes against military targets in North Vietnam will continue."

He held out one carrot to the North Vietnamese. He would stop the bombing and remove the mines when the POWs were released and there was a cease-fire throughout Indochina. "At that time we will proceed with a complete withdrawal of all American forces from Vietnam within 4 months." Although it was ambiguous, the promise seemed to indicate that (1) "all" included air and naval forces, and (2) by implication, the NVA could hold on to its recent gains and would not be required to simultaneously withdraw from South Vietnam. If that was what he meant, it represented a significant concession on Nixon's part.

To the Soviets, Nixon directed some carefully worded paragraphs: "We respect the Soviet Union as a great power. We recognize the right of the Soviet Union to defend its interests when they are threatened. The Soviet Union in turn must recognize our right to defend our interests.

"No Soviet soldiers are threatened in Vietnam. Sixty thousand Americans are threatened. We expect you to help your allies, and you cannot expect us to do other than to continue to help our allies but let us, and let all great powers, help our allies only for the purpose of their defense, not for the purpose of launching invasions against their neighbors."

He noted the progress that had been made on arms limitation, trade, and other issues. "Let us not slide back toward the dark shadows of a previous age." He said the United States and the Soviet Union were on the threshold of a new relationship. "We are prepared to continue to build this relationship. The responsibility is yours if we fail to do so."

The following morning Nixon, quite full of himself, went after the Pentagon. He regarded the additional bombing proposals the military had put forward as "timid" at best. He sent a memorandum to Kissinger (who had somehow become his executive officer for implementing military decisions). He told Kissinger he was determined to "go for broke. . . . Our greatest failure now would be to do too little too late. . . . I intend to stop at nothing to bring the enemy to his knees. . . . I want the military to get off its backside. . . . We have the power to destroy [the enemy's] war-making capacity. The only question is whether we have the *will* to use that power. What distinguishes me from Johnson is that I have the *will* in spades. . . . For once, I want the military . . . to come up with some ideas on their own which will recommend *action* which is very *strong, threatening,* and *effective.*"

He never meant any of that; he was just puffing himself up. He had already ruled out any truly decisive action, such as reintroducing American ground troops, or invading North Vietnam, or bombing the dikes, or using nuclear weapons. He was making war by temper tantrum, his rage had no sustaining power to it. Mining Haiphong and bombing Hanoi were not decisive acts; they were irritants, major irritants to be sure, but hardly enough to turn back an enemy so determined as the North Vietnamese.

What Nixon had done was demonstrate his determination not to be humiliated. He was hurting Hanoi, not destroying it; he had, in effect, conceded Hanoi's right to keep troops in South Vietnam; what he had not done was agree to abandon Thieu, and made it clear he never would do that. He would even risk the summit, détente, his whole new era of peace, to preserve the government of South Vietnam. He had given Hanoi and Moscow much to think about; he had not changed the course of the War.

The political reaction was predictable. Representative [Gerald] Ford was in full support, as were most Republicans. Senator [George] McGovern called the action "reckless, unnecessary and unworkable, a flirtation with world War III. The only purpose of this dangerous new course is to keep General Thieu in power a little longer, and perhaps to save Mr. Nixon's face a little longer."

Senator [Edward] Kennedy called the mining of Haiphong "a futile military gesture that demonstrates the desperation of the President's Indochina policy. I think his decision is ominous and I think it is folly."

Nixon ignored them. The reaction that mattered was Moscow's. It came quickly enough. The Soviets protested, they demanded, they made accusations—but they never mentioned the summit. Kissinger saw Dobrynin. He wondered why there was no mention of the summit.

"We have not been asked any questions about the summit," Dobrynin replied, "and therefore my government sees no need to make a new decision."

"I think we have passed the crisis," Kissinger reported to Nixon exuberantly. "I think we are going to be able to have our mining and bombing and have our summit too."

Nixon had pulled off one of his great triumphs. Now, if only ARVN could hold on the battlefield, everything had fallen into place, at a perfect time to sustain his re-election bid.

⸎ 13 ⸎

Stabbed in the Back

William Colby

IN THE SPRING OF 1971, I BEGAN TO APPRECIATE a new factor in the war—the virulence of the antiwar movement in the United States. It had erupted earlier, of course, over our incursion into Cambodia in 1970, but that seemed only a faraway and misguided protest against what on the ground was a clearly justified effort to clean out the Communist base areas along the frontier with South Vietnam. The scale of the Khmer Rouge atrocities in Cambodia that were to follow on the Communist victories was a shock to the world when the news finally leaked out of that unhappy land, but this prospect was unperceived in the early 1970s by the antiwar activists, who saw only American and South Vietnamese faults in Indochina.

We in Vietnam were, of course, focused on the situation we saw before us. The Americans were leaving, the pacification program was doing very well, the Vietnamese Army was being strengthened to take over the military defense of South Vietnam, and it finally seemed that a positive outcome from the years (and blood) committed by our Vietnamese friends and by the Americans to the cause of a free South Vietnam was possible. Such incidents in the United States as the killing of four students at Kent State University in Ohio by a National Guard unit in May 1970 certainly demonstrated that there was a major protest at home about the war. We mourned those deaths, as we did so many during those years, and they pressed upon us the fact that the time available to complete our Vietnamization and pacification tasks was, as we knew, short.

Problems related to antiwar sentiment arose in Vietnam itself, giving us concern. One was the rising use of drugs by American troops. Another was the increasing number of incidents of "fragging"—troops surreptitiously attacking their own officers by rolling fragmentation grenades at them. The erosion of national will at home was being reflected in an erosion of discipline and morale among the remaining American troops in Vietnam.

I had a curious personal encounter with the degree to which antiwar sentiments had penetrated even our military in Vietnam. I chatted at dusk one evening with an American soldier standing guard at the rampart around a rural team site I was visiting on one of my nights in the country. He mused that he really didn't understand why we, and he, were in Vietnam. I replied from my World War II perspective that we were protecting our country and our allies against the spread of a Communist threat, and doing it far from home rather than finally at home. He responded that he did not agree with that, and that we should fight only if we were directly engaged. I then asked whether he thought we should fight in Europe or Canada and in each case evoked a "No." Somewhat startled, I asked whether he (from New Jersey) would fight in Maine and got another "No." I gave up at that point, wishing him well as he stood guard over us in that faraway place. I was confident that he would do his duty to protect us while we slept, but I could not help but marvel at the far reach of his negatives.

But my own direct experience of the intensity of the antiwar ferment at home began when I was asked to return to Washington in April 1971 to testify about our assistance to refugees before Senator Edward Kennedy's Subcommittee on Refugees of the Senate Judiciary Committee. In Washington, jurisdiction over refugee programs rested with the Administration for International Development in the Executive Branch and, in the Senate, with the Judiciary Committee, which would presumably control American immigration policy. In Vietnam, the program had been integrated into CORDS [Civil Operations and Revolutionary Development Support] to ensure that it would work in close coordination with the pacification program and the military, with a separate Ministry of the Vietnamese Government managing the refugee centers and dispensing the necessary benefits to the refugees. I was thus the appropriate spokesman to present the situation to the Senate Committee when it wanted to be brought up to date on what was being done for the refugees in Vietnam with American support. In preparation, I had spent several days just before the trip home visiting each of the refugee centers that I knew the Committee's staff had focused on so that I could testify about them from personal knowledge.

As I testified, in the rear of the hearing room a group of antiwar veterans in beards and camouflage uniforms hooted denunciations of me as lying or supporting an American policy of genocide. This did not particularly bother me, especially as Kennedy made it clear that he insisted on order at his hearing.

What was unnerving was the surreal atmosphere of discussing American and South Vietnamese actions as though there were no enemy at all in Vietnam. Kennedy repeatedly tried to make the point that refugees were generated by U.S. military action. When I made it clear that most of the cases he referred to involved South Vietnamese military action in response to Communist attacks (many American forces having gone home by then), he turned to using the term "U.S.-supported actions," to which I replied "Vietnamese action primarily." He referred to one incident as "in the area of My Lai" (the site of the 1968 murder of Vietnamese civilians by an American unit), and I had to point out that the incident was some thirty or forty kilometers from My Lai, which made the reference irrelevant, however dramatic. I also had to point out the elemental fact that the greatest surge in refugees came at the time of the Tet attacks in 1968.

When I tried to stress that millions of refugees had been cared for at least to some degree by the Vietnamese Government's programs over the past several years and that the program had been expanded to cover "war victims" (people who had been hurt but were still in their own homes) rather than only refugees, Kennedy turned to the small scope of South Vietnam's civilian social welfare program, which we had been able to broaden in the preceding year but which could hardly match that of Massachusetts.

At one moment, I had to ride over his question to insist on the full story:

> MR. COLBY: In June 1970, Senator, in Quang Tri Province, what that stemmed from was an effort by about three companies of North Vietnamese to sally down into the lowlands.
>
> SENATOR KENNEDY: Doesn't it appear that those are the ones . . .
>
> MR. COLBY: When they got there the friendly forces, including the local self-defense and local territorial forces, held them and fought with them and the ARVN [South Vietnamese Army] came and chased them out and destroyed them. In the course of that kind of fight you do get that kind of damage to the houses, because there was a lot of shooting going on and a lot of shooting done by our forces and the Vietnamese forces. I don't think there were any American forces involved in that one. But I think that is the origin of that particular incident in Quang Tri Province.

We then got into a theological discussion of whether populations should ever be relocated so that their isolated settlements would not be involved in our battles with North Vietnamese forces. When I tried to stress President [Nguyen Van] Thieu's policy of moving security to the people rather than the people to security wherever possible, and his requirement that relocation be conducted only with high-level approval and with proper preparation, a few cases of inadequate handling (which our officers had reported and which we were trying to correct) were adduced as evidence sufficient to denounce the entire effort. My reference to the fact that many nations had relocated populations in wartime situations (e.g., the Japanese-Americans from California in 1942) was set aside as not justifying the action in a more enlightened today.

I had brought along a Chinese 82-millimeter mortar fin I had picked up in one refugee camp in the highlands to illustrate the Communist practice of attacking refugees in order to drive them back into Communist areas to serve as porters and food growers. But I decided that displaying it would just be contentious, have no effect on the overall atmosphere, and detract from, rather than strengthen, the impression I was trying to project that the situation was by no means perfect, but that the Vietnamese and the Americans on the spot were working on it and fully understood its moral dimensions. My approach seemed to pay off to a degree when Kennedy summed up saying that I had done "an excellent job in attempting to defend an indefensible policy." But the gulf between the reality of making progress in the myriad problems in Vietnam and the American insistence on immediate perfection still persisted; everything bad was blamed on American and South Vietnamese actions.

On June 13, 1971, more fuel was added to the fire directed against our efforts in Vietnam by the start of publication of the so-called Pentagon Papers, followed by the Supreme Court decision, over the Nixon Administration's objections, allowing their publication in full. I had no real problem with their accuracy, but I did with their scope, their coverage ending in May 1968, just when CORDS had begun its work. They thus focused on the Diem period and his overthrow, the revolving-door governments that followed him, the major American military buildup, and the dramatic Communist Tet 1968 offensive. Their description of the formation of CORDS ended on the hopeful note that "at least the Mission was better run and better organized than it ever had been before, and this fact may in time lead to a more efficient and successful effort" (Gravel edition II, 622). The years that followed certainly showed this to be an accurate statement. But the main effect of the publication of the Papers was once again to call attention to the confused and ineffective conduct of the war prior to the period of success that followed 1968, and to reinforce the feeling of futility about Vietnam, which by then had become fixed.

At the end of June 1971, I returned from Vietnam to Washington for the last time. My daughter Catherine was extremely sick. Some critics have alleged that her sickness and later death in 1973 was a protest against my work in Vietnam and particularly my direction of the Phoenix program. I know this to be false, as she was invariably supportive of my efforts on behalf of Vietnam, where she was perhaps happiest during her childhood. After my return she had a series of good and bad periods, but her epilepsy and her depression gradually slipped into anorexia, which finally took her life in 1973 despite the efforts of the medical experts in Washington and at Johns Hopkins in Baltimore.

When I left Vietnam, I turned CORDS over to my most helpful Deputy, George Jacobson, who had begun his service in Vietnam as a military officer, had left, returned in the early 1960s, and had been there since. George enjoyed some fame for leaning out of an upstairs window next door to the Embassy during the 1968 Tet attack to ask that a friend throw him a pistol, with which he then disposed of an attacker heading up the stairs toward him—the incident making great television drama. He was to lead CORDS until its dissolution at the time of the 1973 Peace Treaty, but he stayed thereafter until the last days in 1975.

My return in 1971 fully opened my eyes to the intensity of the antiwar movement. In July the Subcommittee on Foreign Operations and Government Information of the House of Representatives Committee on Government Operations decided to hold hearings on our assistance program in Vietnam, and I took the full impact of the new atmosphere. The Committee began on the somewhat mundane subject of accounting for the budgets devoted to the CORDS effort. A General Accounting Office team had recently visited Vietnam to examine the subject and had been startled at my statement that I did not know in dollar terms what my program cost. Being an intelligent team, they soon understood that I did know about the funds we actually managed in the field but that the full cost of our programs frequently included the costs of weapons or other equipment that were written off when shipped from the United States and delivered to the Vietnamese Government. Also, some assistance programs were handled by different agencies in the United States and in Saigon, but by CORDS at the rural level. The GAO examiners even accepted my statement that we had been putting our efforts into fighting the war rather than into accounting, extracting in return my concession that things were in fact now going well enough that it was appropriate for us to devote some attention to better accounting and financial controls.

The House Subcommittee huffed and puffed a bit about this problem and then repeated much of Senator Kennedy's concern over refugees and the civilian victims of the war. Two congressmen bored in, however, on Phoenix. One, Paul McCloskey of California, had been to Vietnam, where he was escorted around by one of the best of the CORDS officers, Frank Scotton, on detail to CORDS from the USIA [United States Information Agency]. Scotton spoke Vietnamese fluently and operated under my instruction to let the Congressman see anything he wanted to, to tell him the truth even if it hurt, but to try to give him some sense of proportion and of the wartime reality in which we carried on our work. McCloskey was having little of that, however, and focused on nuggets he could use to denounce the program.

The other Congressman, Ogden Reid of New York, concentrated on whether Phoenix met the standards of American Constitutional due process, with right to counsel, court procedures, etc. Since my Constitutional law studies were as good as his (we both graduated from Columbia University Law School), I frankly said that they did not, but that we were doing all we could to improve the procedures under which this necessary program of the war would be carried out. My defense that a war clearly involves an attempt to achieve the capture, the surrender, or the death of the enemy cut little ice with my critics, whose simplistic position was that a war should not be going on in Vietnam and would not be if the Americans were not there.

While I had opened my description of Phoenix with the fact that the Viet Cong terrorism that it was designed to combat had killed some 6,000 South Vietnamese local leaders and ordinary citizens during the past year, the statistics that caught the attention of the press in its accounts of my testimony were those of the effects of Phoenix on the enemy. I recounted that during the years since it began in 1968, the Phoenix program had brought about the capture of some 28,978 Communist leaders in the Viet Cong Infrastructure [VCI], that some 17,717 had taken advantage of the amnesty program, and that some 20,587 had been reported as killed. I made it quite clear that those killings occurred "mostly in combat situations" and supported that statement with the further details that some 87.6 percent of those killed were killed by regular or paramilitary forces, and only 12.4 percent by police or irregular forces. Mr. Reid then asked, "Can you state categorically that Phoenix has never perpetrated the premeditated killing of a civilian in a noncombat situation?"

"No," I replied, "I could not say that, but I do not think it happens often. I certainly would not say never," adding, "Phoenix, as a program, I say, has not done that. Individual members of it, subordinate people in it, may have done it. But as a program, it is not designed to do that." Reid then tried to get me to make an admission in specific numbers of people who may have been inaccurately identified as members of the VCI, which I successfully resisted. I did not know the answer, and I understood that he was seeking a good headline.

We then had a direct debate over Mr. Reid's contention that the United States should cut off its assistance to the program. I countered this by stating that if we did not approve, we should go further—we should use our influence to have the program stopped. But I said that the program was designed to eliminate the problems he was concerned about and should be continued. Then I said:

> Mr. Congressman, I have said on several occasions that unfortunately the Vietnamese are not going to live happily ever after. They are going to face a security threat from North Vietnam and from the Viet Cong over a number of years. They are going to lose a few and they are going to win a few. But I believe that the probabilities are very clear that they will be able to sustain themselves in the future without the U.S. presence there that there has been in the past.

My testimony was followed a day or so later by an account by a former American soldier who presented the most sensational and bloody picture of his "role as it was peripheral to the Phoenix program" and "associated with both military intelligence and the CIA." Mr. K. Barton Osborn never did say precisely with which unit he had served, but he claimed he had worked with the U.S. Marines and Army and that he did not "work with the Vietnamese in any capacity"—a clear indication that he could not in reality have worked with Phoenix, which was by definition a Vietnamese program with our U.S. military Phoenix advisers in a support capacity. Mr. Osborn also indicated that he left Vietnam in 1968, when the Phoenix program had just begun to work as part of the Accelerated Pacification Program, again indicating that whatever he may have done had nothing to do with Phoenix. But his lurid testimony of throwing Communist captives and suspects from helicopters and my report of the numbers affected by this struggle cast in concrete one of the most repulsive, and flatly wrong, images of the Vietnam war, namely, that the Phoenix program under my control had murdered some 20,000 Vietnamese.

This was despite my emphasis that the deaths involved were mostly during military actions and had been identified on the battlefield after the fight as known members of the Communist apparatus. My problem was that I could not and would not say that no wrongful death had ever occurred, so that the sensational item for the press was my admission that some had happened. The Congressmen also did not pick up the key facts about their witnesses, which any attorney would have caught as affecting their credibility, but instead wallowed in the accounts of bloody misdeeds, with the media recording it all. A small solace was that the next day's report in the *New York Times*, while repeating my statistics, gave a straightforward account of the hearing, headlining that I had defended the program "despite killings of civilians" and stating that with "quiet persistence" I had argued that "the program was designed to protect the Vietnamese people from terrorism."

But the fact that Phoenix was reducing the arbitrary way in which the war had been fought was lost in the impression of wrongful death. The fact that the figures were only supplemental to those I had reported during my testimony to Senator [J. William] Fulbright in early 1970, and not different in proportion, was more a mark of the different atmosphere that had grown up around the question of Vietnam than of the figures themselves. I was moved to consider the words of the moralist that if one is not concerned with the death of each person, one is not concerned with the death of any, and thought my critics were concerned primarily with the political capital that could be made of the statistics.

Over a year after this dramatic testimony, the Subcommittee submitted its report on the hearings, which was more significant for what it did not say than for what it did, so it received practically no media coverage. The sole recommendation dealing with the Phoenix testimony was that the Secretary of Defense investigate the allegations of crimes committed by U.S.

military personnel against civilians. The Subcommittee also recorded its concern over the problems of the Phoenix program about which I had testified and that our advisory terms were working to overcome. But no recommendation issued from the Subcommittee that the program or its American support be halted.

The Subcommittee and its staff apparently concluded, on a conscientious review of the full record, that the sensational allegations of the witness did not really stand up as an indictment of the Phoenix program, although some of the incidents may have happened and should be prosecuted. But this is a rather subtle conclusion to be drawn from the report, and it drew no attention from the media or the antiwar movement, both of which continued to repeat the sweeping charges of the witness and to apply them to Phoenix as a whole. It was clear from the experience surrounding the testimony that many Americans, including my two Congressional interrogators, were totally opposed to what we were trying to accomplish in Vietnam. They wanted, in the slogan used by the antiwar movement, "America Out of Vietnam!"—without condition and without consideration of what the Vietnamese might want.

In this account of the Vietnam War, I have omitted any discussion of the various diplomatic efforts that were made to settle it. This was not from inadvertence, nor was it from the fact that the subject never really fell within my responsibilities either in Vietnam or in Washington. Rather, it reflects my belief, then and now, that the process was largely irrelevant to the struggle in the countryside. I was convinced that the North Vietnamese Communist leadership was determined to conquer South Vietnam and would accept nothing less than victory in any negotiations that might take place. They had certainly given full evidence of their determination to prosecute the war, whatever their casualties on the battlefield: I was certain they would not be turned from their objectives by diplomatic persuasion or bargaining.

At various stages, the political leadership of the United States—President Johnson, President Nixon, Henry Kissinger, their aides and diplomats—thought that approaches to the Soviet Union could produce pressures on the North Vietnamese to get them to accept some compromise solution. My own view was that this did not give sufficient weight to North Vietnamese determination and that it missed the most interesting of the balancing acts that occurred during the Vietnam conflict—the exquisite skill of the North Vietnamese in manipulating their Soviet and Chinese sources of supply to extract the maximum from each. Locked as the two Communist giants were in rivalry between Mao's [Mao Tse-Tung] Cultural Revolution and Moscow's revisionism for leadership of the Communist cause worldwide, the North Vietnamese involved them in a competition in which each sought to demonstrate superior credentials as fellow Communists—the gauge being support of Hanoi.

Some of the CIA's counterintelligence personnel considered this Sino-Soviet ideological dispute a charade to confuse the West and advance the cause of Communism, but I accepted it at face value as reflective of an internal theological dispute, and of the national antagonisms that had characterized Russian and Chinese relations for centuries. The North Vietnamese correctly saw in the dispute a chance to play each supporter off against the other and to derive a rich reward in military hardware therefrom. The one thing that seemed obvious to me was that in this situation the Soviets did not have enough influence over the North Vietnamese to halt their operations against South Vietnam. With the frustrations Americans suffered trying to make the South Vietnamese conform to American ideas of what was good for them, I saw little chance that the Soviets could control their far more tough-minded and determined cousins in the North.

I accordingly paid slight attention to the various secret probes and intermediaries or to the direct approaches to Moscow that diverted high-level concentration from the war in the South during the mid-1960s. Even when formal negotiations began in Paris in 1968, it was plain to me that no compromise solution was possible through diplomatic channels. The North Vietnamese had the French model to sustain them. Their steely determination had finally worn down French willingness to continue the war effort in 1954, leading to concessions from Paris far beyond what the Communists had actually won at Dien Bien Phu. And in that performance lay at least one of the factors that kept the North Vietnamese to a hard line in the 1960s and 1970s. It was that they had actually compromised in Geneva in 1954 under the pressure of the Soviets and China, only to see their hope for subsequent "inevitable" total victory frustrated by the unexpected ability of Ngo Dinh Diem, with American support, to revive South Vietnam.

The principal North Vietnamese negotiators in the 1968–1973 period often were quite frank in their references to the strength of the American antiwar movement as a principal factor that would force the United States to withdraw from the war in South Vietnam and cease its support of the Thieu Government. This was put directly to Kissinger by senior North Vietnamese negotiator Le Duc Tho. Despite Kissinger's sharp replies that Tho had no idea of how to deal with an opposition and that Kissinger would not discuss American public opinion with him, the many contacts of the North Vietnamese with Americans in Europe and visiting North Vietnam convinced them that they had only to be intransigent and the Americans would give in. The North Vietnamese attitude was perhaps best expressed by their suggestion at one point that the principal obstacle to a "solution" to the impasse that persisted between the parties could be removed by the simple act of assassinating President [Nguyen Van] Thieu—perhaps in their view a fair comment on how the Americans had treated his predecessor, President [Ngo Dinh] Diem, when he failed to follow American direction.

We in Vietnam were well aware of this firm attitude by our enemies across the battle lines and were fearful that the North Vietnamese were correct, so the only hope was to build up the South sufficiently rapidly so that it could sustain itself against the North without American participation. But we knew it would need American logistics and air support, as we had provided in 1972.

The invisible participant at the negotiating table, on which the North Vietnamese depended to split the American delegation from its South Vietnamese negotiating partner was the American antiwar movement. The North Vietnamese assiduously courted its members through contacts in Europe, visits to Hanoi, and appeals to liberal sympathy with anticolonialism. This was immensely assisted by the American media's full access to South Vietnam and their inability to penetrate North Vietnam's tight security screen, thus providing the American public with a rich diet of stories of the failures and imperfections of the South Vietnamese regime and little or nothing about North Vietnam beyond the image Hanoi wished others to see. What the American public saw, read, and heard was, on balance, another element in the pressures the North counted on the antiwar movement to put on the American Government to ultimately withdraw from Vietnam and, as the French Government did in 1954, leave South Vietnam to its fate.

The most difficult aspect of the antiwar sentiment for us in Vietnam to understand was the fact that when public interest in Vietnam declined with the withdrawal of American troops and the consequent reduction of American casualties, prevailing liberal and antiwar opinion shifted its emphasis from halting American military action to stopping the Vietnam war entirely—at the cost of North Vietnamese victory if need be. Indeed, many antiwar leaders actually believed that a North Vietnamese victory would be the best possible outcome.

These pressures weighed especially heavily on President Richard Nixon and his National Security Assistant, Henry Kissinger. Nixon faced the election campaign in 1972 opposed by George McGovern's flat call for an end to all American involvement in South Vietnam. Kissinger realized that the only possible answer to that challenge was to bring about a peace agreement, and he searched insistently for a formula that would satisfy the North Vietnamese, yet allow President Nixon to assert that the United States had achieved an honorable settlement.

The North Vietnamese had an additional card to play in the persons of the American military captives held in North Vietnam, mostly Air Force and Navy airmen shot down there. Their captors cynically exploited them at the same time they abused them, parading them before antiwar activists like Jane Fonda in order to add this public pressure on President Nixon to yield to their demands. Their own spectacular courage and discipline under pressure (one blinking out the Morse Code letters T-O-R-T-U-R-E with his eyelids before the television cameras recording such a meeting; a group giving a rude hand signal to the still photographers, which *Life* magazine had the bad taste to publish, thus ensuring punishment for the captives) were hardly recognized by a nation that had decided that what they had done in the service of their country was flawed, and that they should be repatriated out of charity, not pride. The effect of this cynical manipulation of these prisoners was summed up in a remark Kissinger later made to me (I had no role in the negotiation from my administrative post in the CIA) when I commented that I could never understand how anyone could have believed that the North Vietnamese would comply with the "Peace" Agreement they finally signed: "You have no idea of the pressure we were under to get the POWs out."

The fundamental issue in the negotiations came down to whether Hanoi could maintain the presence in South Vietnam that they had lost to Thieu's pacification campaigns. Thieu saw this as an impossible outcome, as he fully realized that a peace agreement would mean only one thing—that the United States would end its involvement and support of South Vietnam while the North Vietnamese would return to the attack as soon as the situation seemed propitious. North Vietnam's assistance from its Soviet and Chinese allies would certainly continue, but America's to South Vietnam would as certainly dry up. Thieu thus resolutely refused to accept continued North Vietnamese presence in the South, which would give the North a clear advantage for the succeeding, and inevitable, attack.

Kissinger's accomplishment in the negotiations of finally obtaining North Vietnam's acceptance of the authority of the Thieu Government as an equal to the Communist "Provisional Government" in South Vietnam was of no value to Thieu, who knew that the war would resume as soon as the Americans were removed from the scene, and that the balance of forces without the Americans would certainly favor the Communists and their allies. Kissinger was seeking the best possible compromise with the Communists, trading agreement for their continued presence in South Vietnam, albeit with a promise that they would stop further infiltration, for acceptance of a continued role for the Thieu government. He asserts in his *White House Years* that he assumed that the South Vietnamese Army, with American support, could handle minor violations of the agreement and that the United States would return to aid against major ones in the way it had done in the spring of 1972. He did not contemplate only a "decent interval" between an American departure and a South Vietnamese defeat.

Thieu was both suspicious and resentful during his dealings with Kissinger. In later interviews for Nguyen Tien Hung and Jerrold L. Schecter's *The Palace File*, a book based on the many assurances he received of American support if he would agree to the "peace" conditions Kissinger had arranged with the North Vietnamese, Thieu recounted the various and sometimes petty and denigrating ways in which Nixon and Kissinger handled him very much as a colonial dependent, meeting him in Midway rather than Honolulu and giving him a smaller chair than Nixon (which Thieu changed), keeping from him some of the critical negotiations with the North Vietnamese, and even presenting only an English text of an agreement they had negotiated when the crucial question was the meaning of some of its key phrases in Vietnamese. The pressures to which Thieu was subjected understandably raised in his mind the image of the two Ngo brothers [Ngo Dinh Diem and Ngo Dinh Nhu] as the victims of an American-encouraged coup, lying finally in their own blood in a Vietnamese Army vehicle.

Kissinger recounts his version of the final negotiations in great detail. He had to overcome Thieu's resistance to allowing the North Vietnamese to remain in the South (which Kissinger had already conceded to the Communists), and his first try was to assert to Thieu that later elections to be arranged by the two Vietnamese parties could gauge the balance between the rival authorities. Kissinger's problem was that the conditions he had obtained in his secret bargaining with the North Vietnamese were better from the viewpoint of the South than the ones Thieu had previously authorized him to offer, so that Kissinger knew that the political consequences in the Untited States, particularly from the antiwar movement, would be severe if he did not now secure Thieu's agreement to the settlement. Thieu's problem was that he had indeed given Kissinger such authorization but had done it when the prospects of a favorable outcome of the negotiations through Hanoi's acceptance of any future whatsoever for Thieu's government seemed remote. Now that an agreement appeared logically imminent because of the concessions Kissinger had extracted from the North, it was clear to Thieu, as it was to the North, that any agreement that left the North in the South would only mean a resumption of the war without American support, with defeat almost a certainty. Thieu thus dug in his heels and used every stratagem possible to avoid agreement with Kissinger's program.

While President Nixon made it clear that Kissinger's negotiations should not be affected by the forthcoming American Presidential election, both of them were in fact pressed by the manifest evaporation of American public and Congressional support for Vietnam, and were anxious to extract a peace agreement to forestall a unilateral suspension of American assistance. The North Vietnamese were equally anxious for an agreement to fix an American withdrawal, which they correctly foresaw would bar any return, and made a series of concessions, such as agreeing to withdraw from Laos and Cambodia, to obtain it.

Thus the two actual negotiators had come to an agreement, but were unable to complete it because Thieu was resisting. Even the promise of a pretruce massive infusion of military supplies to South Vietnam, which could thereafter under the agreement be replaced on a one-for-one basis, did not overcome Thieu's resistance. He judged that the key question was continued American will and involvement, which he correctly thought would melt away, rather than the words on the paper of the agreement. Thus he reacted with a combination of hysterical tears, fears that the United States was planning a coup to overthrow him, rudeness to the American envoys, and intransigent rejection of the carefully constructed agreement, despite President Nixon's strongly worded expressions that American support would be forthcoming if the agreement were violated but that he would be unable to maintain American support if the agreement were not signed. The impasse with Thieu became obvious to the North Vietnamese, who then decided they would hold up the agreement to get better terms than those they had already agreed to.

The situation was opened up only by a forceful thrust against both Vietnamese parties. The North Vietnamese were subjected to a powerful bombing attack at Christmas 1972 at President Nixon's express order to make clear to them that this attack was different from the delicately applied, gradual bombing campaigns that had characterized the 1960s. Its force, despite the hysterical opposition aroused among the antiwar factions in the United States, was both precise and effective. The North Vietnamese massively publicized the destruction of a hospital in Hanoi but omitted reporting that it was across the street from the railway yards. They made a mistake in announcing the death toll as 1,300 to 1,600, which to anyone familiar with World

War II bombing casualties in urban communities indicated clearly that the attack had been no "carpet bombing."

And it worked. The North Vietnamese quickly requested a resumption of the negotiations they had stalled, with a view to coming to a final peace agreement along the lines of the concession they had made. Nixon has since stated that he regretted not having hit the North Vietnamese as hard in 1969 as he did in 1972. He is right.

President Nixon's forcefulness was equally effective with President Thieu and the South Vietnamese. To convince him that the Christmas bombing did not reflect any change in the U.S. determination to make an agreement with the North Vietnamese along the lines that had been negotiated, Nixon advised Thieu that "you must decide now whether you desire to continue our alliance or whether you want me to seek a settlement with the enemy which serves U.S. interests alone." Thieu gave a response that withdrew some of his objections but said that he could not "accept" the continued presence of North Vietnamese troops in the South. He thought this formulation would not stop the Americans from the negotiations but would have kept his conscience clear that he had not acquiesced in a provision that he accurately foresaw could lead to the defeat of his country. Nixon then supplemented his forceful letter to Thieu with another that offered his "assurance of continued assistance in the post-settlement period and that we [the U.S.] will respond with full force should the settlement be violated by North Vietnam." And Kissinger returned to Paris to wrap up the arrangement with the North Vietnamese.

When the final Agreement had been settled in Paris and was taken to Saigon for Thieu's acceptance, it was accompanied by a Nixon letter saying that he would sign the Agreement "if necessary, alone. In that case I shall have to explain publicly that your Government obstructs peace. The result will be an inevitable and immediate termination of U.S. economic and military assistance." Despite a flurry of last-minute attempts to salvage something for his country, Thieu accepted the American decision. The die was cast for "peace" in Vietnam. The Peace Agreement was initialed in Paris on January 23, 1973, and finally signed on January 27. The day was marked by the announcement that the American draft was ended, perhaps a more important concession to antiwar movement adherents than the Peace Agreement itself. An emotional television bath followed the return of the POWs from Hanoi, giving them the honor they were due, but clearly putting the final stamp on the fact that America's war, and interest, in Vietnam was over.

It was plain that the Peace Agreement was not a formal treaty, which could have engaged the United States Senate in a ratification vote, with presumably some responsibility for ensuring compliance. To the North Vietnamese, the Agreement was no different from the others they had signed, as was their violation of it in a matter of days after the signing by shipping further military forces and supplies south. The American military had flooded South Vietnam with as much military equipment as it could before the ban of the Peace Agreement was effective so that it could be legally replaced one-for-one while the Agreement was in effect. The North Vietnamese were less concerned with such legalities, for their supplies were to continue in defiance of the Agreement.

PART II

IN COUNTRY

Chapter 5

Allies and Enemies

BY THE LATE 1960S, AMERICANS REGARDED VIETNAM as their war. The Vietnamese, understandably, never thought of it that way. The Americans lost 58,000 dead to the war; up to 3 million Vietnamese perished, soldiers and civilians both. The outcome of the conflict was largely determined in the end by the efforts of the Vietnamese themselves. As Chapter Two indicates, in 1954, the Americans pinned their hopes for a stable, non-communist, and even (someday) democratic southern Vietnam on Ngo Dinh Diem. The "sovereign of discord," as Frances FitzGerald called him, divided contemporaries, and historians too: Seth Jacobs regards him as a disaster and laments that the Eisenhower administration failed to heed the warnings of General J. Lawton Collins about Diem's serious limitations, while Philip Catton, who does not underestimate Diem's liabilities, nevertheless insists that we take him seriously as a thinker and a political leader; he was no American puppet.

The determination of the Americans' enemy, the National Liberation Front and its supporters in North Vietnam, was decisive to the U.S.-South Vietnamese defeat. On the battlefield, in world capitals, and at the negotiating table, Ho Chi Minh and his advisers fought and talked with extraordinary skill. William Duiker, author of the definitive English-language biography of Ho Chi Minh, illuminates the relationship between the North's battlefield strategy and its diplomacy, especially with regard to its reluctant allies in Moscow and Beijing. The chapter's final selection, by Tom Mangold and John Penycate, is an imaginative and compelling story of an NLF soldier who fought the Americans within the vast system of underground tunnels that his comrades had constructed in the south. This passage vividly contrasts the confidence of the NLF and technocratic blunderings of the American troops, who struggled to master tunnel warfare, and it suggests the difficulty of fighting an enemy convinced of its own righteousness and fully attuned to its environment.

⋞ 14 ⋟

Ngo Dinh Diem, the Impossible Ally

Seth Jacobs

THE HISTORIAN FRANCES FITZGERALD OBSERVES that "in going into Vietnam, the United States was . . . entering a world qualitatively different from its own. . . . [T]here was no more correspondence between the two worlds than between the atmosphere of the earth and that of the sea." While overdrawn, FitzGerald's analogy points up the difficulty U.S. policymakers encountered in seeking to impose their concepts of good governance on the anarchy that prevailed in Saigon in the mid-1950s. What was an American diplomat to make of a city where the chief of police was also the leader of a gang of murderers, pimps, racketeers, and drug dealers? How could a coalition be effected between two South Vietnamese groups when one was led by a former seminarian living on high principle and the other by a pirate who fed welshers to his pet tiger? The Eisenhower administration's most consequential venture in nation-building could not have been undertaken in an environment less susceptible to Age-of-Consensus political philosophy. As FitzGerald, whose *Fire in the Lake* remains the most penetrating exploration of the cultural divide between Vietnamese and Americans, notes, "The effort of translation was too great."[1]

General J. Lawton "Lightning Joe" Collins proved more successful at translating Vietnamese politics into the language of Washington statecraft than most of his contemporaries. Indeed, Collins was the first, and for a long time the only, top-level policymaker to recognize the flaws in America's Diem experiment. As U.S. "special representative" in South Vietnam from late 1954 through mid-1955, Collins determined that Ngo Dinh Diem's government was incapable of winning broad indigenous support and would always require American aid to stay afloat. There was no possibility of a Diem-led South Vietnam becoming secure or stable enough to allow the United States to scale back its involvement in this Cold War outpost; rather, the opposite was true: as long as Diem remained in charge, escalation of the U.S. commitment to Vietnam was unavoidable. When President Dwight Eisenhower overruled Collins's recommendations that Diem be abandoned, he narrowed the range of options for future U.S. presidents attempting to cope with Vietnam. By the time the White House came to share Collins's views in 1963 and engineered the overthrow of the Diem regime, it was too late. The United States had sunk too much money and prestige into South Vietnam to permit a graceful exit, and Diem's nine-year reign of terror had obliterated moderate anticommunist alternatives to his administration. Most important, the manner in which Diem went about squelching dissent increased popular resentment of the Saigon government and made South Vietnam's countryside a fertile recruiting ground for the communists.

The "Collins mission," as it was referred to at the time, represented the last chance for Washington to detach itself from a losing proposition. Eisenhower's refusal to heed his special representative's advice made the cataclysm that followed, if not inevitable, at least more difficult to escape. "[T]he decision to back Diem," Secretary of State John Foster Dulles cabled Collins in April 1955, had "gone to the point of no return. . . . [E]ither he had to succeed or the whole business would be a failure." Collins's attempt to pull his country back from that point of no return was one of the pivotal episodes in America's longest war.[2]

When Collins arrived in Saigon in November 1954, the Diem experiment could not have been in greater peril. Diem's was a government in name only. Emperor Bao Dai had little confidence in the new premier and gave him only lukewarm support. This pleased French Prime Minister Pierre Mendès-France, who found Diem's Francophobia alarming at a time when France was attempting to retain influence in its former Indochinese colonies. Mendès-France informed Dulles that he believed other South Vietnamese politicians had "much better records than Diem" and that the United States would "be forced to consider [the] replacement [of] Diem . . . within [a] few months." French generals and diplomats unanimously expressed their belief that Diem would fail.[3]

Clearly, Diem could not count on much assistance from Paris. This was a problem because the French Expeditionary Corps (FEC) was the most powerful military force south of the 17th parallel, and an indispensable tool in maintaining order. Worse, Diem's own military, the Vietnamese National Army (VNA), was essentially under French command, headed by officers chosen and trained by the French. The VNA chief of staff, General Nguyen Van Hinh, was a French citizen who had graduated from the French Air Academy, served with French colonial forces in Algeria, and married a French woman. Not coincidentally, Hinh loathed Diem and repeatedly disobeyed him.

With no army to enforce his rule, Diem had little hope of giving South Vietnam a strong, unified government. The ordinance with which Bao Dai conferred civil and military powers on Diem meant nothing in the countryside, where control was exercised by various dueling parties. The Cao Dai religious sect reigned over the northwestern Mekong Delta. A syncretic faith that wove together Taoism, Buddhism, Confucianism, and Christianity, Cao Daism had over two million followers. Pham Cong Tac, the Cao Dai pope, commanded an armed force of twenty-five thousand troops. The Hoa Hao, a sect that practiced a species of reformed Buddhism, claimed around one million adherents. Its army of several thousand men controlled the region southwest of Saigon. Thirty-odd Montagnard tribes occupied the Central Highlands, where they had lived for centuries as a distinct cultural group, rejecting Vietnamese political authority. France permitted these factions substantial autonomy when Vietnam was part of the French empire, and they were unlikely to surrender time-honored prerogatives just because a new premier had taken up residence in the Norodom Palace. And then there were the communists. Although the Viet Minh had signed the Geneva Accords and moved thousands of their troops out of the south, they left behind a network of cadres to harass the Diem government through acts of sabotage and assassination. Some experts estimated that the Viet Minh dominated as much as one-third of South Vietnam, including most of the border with Cambodia.

If Diem's lack of influence in the provinces was distressing, conditions in Saigon were cause for despair. The South Vietnamese premier could not even control his own capital city, which was in the grip of the Binh Xuyen, Vietnam's preeminent criminal organization. Named after a village south of Saigon, the Binh Xuyen consisted of approximately forty thousand heavily armed thugs. Their leader was Le Van "Bay" Vien, a figure of gargantuan corruption who presided over an empire of vice without parallel in Asia; among his many establishments were the Hall of Mirrors, the world's largest brothel; Le Grande Monde, a gambling complex that occupied several city blocks; and an opium factory that refined a product for distribution throughout Indochina. The compound from which Vien directed the Binh Xuyen's operations seemed stage-managed to scandalize Western observers: it was surrounded by an alligator-filled moat; pythons slithered around the columns on the front porch; a leopard stood guard outside the bedroom door; and a Siberian tigress lived in a nearby cage. Vien's bodyguards frequently had to clean bits of clothing and human bones out of the cage after their boss exacted retribution from those who failed to make protection payments.

In a characteristically self-serving maneuver, Bao Dai transferred control of the Sureté—the national police—to the Binh Xuyen in mid-1954. The emperor received forty-four million piasters (about $ 1.25 million) from Vien in exchange for this transaction, but, as the American embassy complained, he also created a situation in Saigon analogous to the "city of Chicago placing its police force in [the] hands of [the] Al Capone gang during [the] latter's heyday." After sealing his bargain with the emperor, Vien levied a take on commercial traffic in and out of Saigon and continued to run his gambling casinos, houses of prostitution, and drug factories without fear of legal reprisal. Diem seemed powerless to combat him. CIA Station Chief William Colby recalled that the premier "only controlled the space of his [own] palace grounds."[4]

Diem nearly lost even that authority less than three months after the Geneva Conference adjourned. In August 1954, Chief of Staff Hinh began a series of public attacks against Diem, proclaiming that South Vietnam needed a "strong and popular" leader like himself and bragging about the coup he was arranging. Hinh's coup attempt might have succeeded if not for Colonel Edward Lansdale, whose assignment in late 1954 was to coordinate a propaganda campaign north of the 17th parallel. While he and his team of CIA operatives wreaked some havoc in Ho Chi Minh's republic, the colonel found his services more urgently required in the south. Recognizing the threat to Diem's leadership posed by Hinh, Lansdale persuaded Philippine President Ramon Magsaysay to offer the chief of staff's officers an all-expenses-paid tour of Manila's nightclubs. Most of Hinh's henchmen were flown to the Philippines on the eve of insurrection, and the general called off the coup.[5]

In addition to Lansdale, Diem had one other American partisan whose assistance proved crucial during the closing months of 1954. Senator Mike Mansfield, Congress's foremost authority on Asia, made two decisive contributions to the Diem experiment in that time. First, he joined Dulles in Manila to help establish the Southeast Asia Treaty Organization (SEATO), a collective defense alliance including the United States, Great Britain, France, Australia, New Zealand, the Philippines, Thailand, and Pakistan. Dulles wanted, in his words, to erect a "'no trespassing' sign" that warned the Soviets and Chinese not to expand their influence in the Western Pacific, and SEATO met that symbolic requirement. Militarily, the pact lacked teeth. Unlike the North Atlantic Treaty Organization (NATO), SEATO did not require a response from all members if one were attacked; each nation merely pledged to "consult" in the event of aggression and "act to meet the common danger in accordance with its constitutional processes." Despite such timid language, Dulles worried about obtaining the constitutionally required two-thirds vote for ratification of the treaty in the Senate. He therefore decided to sweeten the pill by inviting two Senators—the Republican Alexander Stephens and the Democrat Mansfield—to accompany him at the Manila Conference.[6]

Dulles's strategy worked. Even though any "Southeast Asia Treaty" that did not include India, Burma, and Indonesia—each of which preferred an unaligned status in 1954—was hardly worthy of the name, the Senate ratified SEATO by a vote of eighty-two to one. Dulles had wanted to include South Vietnam, Laos, and Cambodia as treaty members, but Paris objected on the grounds that the Geneva Accords neutralized Indochina and barred its states from joining military alliances. The Americans found a way around this by attaching a protocol to the SEATO agreement that extended its provisions to those areas, projecting what Dulles called an "umbrella of protection" over them. Cambodia and Laos repudiated the protocol, but Diem accepted informal membership in SEATO. A decade later, the protocol would furnish a justification for American military intervention to save South Vietnam.[7]

Of more immediate consequence was Mansfield's "Report on Indochina," delivered to the Senate Foreign Relations Committee after the SEATO treaty was finalized. Mansfield visited Saigon on his way to and from the Manila Conference, and the experience convinced him it was either Diem or defeat for America's grand design in Indochina. When Mansfield addressed his fellow legislators in mid-October 1954, he bound Washington much more tightly to its Diem experiment. He depicted Saigon as an Indochinese Gomorrah, "seeth[ing] with intrigue and counter-intrigue," controlled by "gangsters, pirates, and extortionists." In Mansfield's view, only Diem offered any hope of establishing a regime deserving of U.S. support. Given that the "alternatives to Diem" were "not promising," the Senator argued, Washington's course was clear: "In the event that the Diem government falls, . . . I believe that the United States should consider an immediate suspension of all aid to Vietnam." Diem had one hundred thousand copies of the report printed up and distributed within days of Mansfield's appearance before the committee. Although the Eisenhower administration never formally endorsed it, Mansfield's recommendation was widely construed as American policy.[8]

Mansfield's support was an invaluable asset, but it did little in the short run to improve conditions in Saigon, where political storm clouds continued to gather. Nine members of Diem's government resigned during Hinh's abortive bid for power, and Bao Dai recommended that Diem resign as well. Hinh still commanded the VNA and had not abandoned his plans to unseat Diem. The Binh Xuyen still controlled the police. The French encouraged Diem's rivals in their intrigues against him. Diem, by his own reckoning, had only one battalion on whose loyalty he could depend. Foreign correspondents predicted daily that the Diem regime would fall and that all of Vietnam would come under communist rule.

Eisenhower, a believer in the maxim that long faces do not win wars, complained to Dulles that he was "weary" of the tenor of panic in reports from South Vietnam. Dulles suggested that Eisenhower send a high-ranking general to serve as Washington's "special representative" in Saigon—someone "in whom the president . . . would have full confidence." Eisenhower approved of the idea, and remarked that J. Lawton Collins was "the best qualified U.S. Army officer" he could think of. Collins had served with distinction in both the Pacific and European theaters of World War II, and his postwar resume included stints as army chief of staff and U.S. representative on the NATO Military Committee and Standing Group. He had considerable experience in Asia; indeed, he had even visited Vietnam in 1951, which made him virtually unique among American soldier-statesmen. Lightning Joe, the president assured Dulles, possessed "outstanding qualifications" for this assignment.[9]

When Dulles gave Collins his marching orders, he informed the general that the "chance of success" of his mission was "only one in ten," but that the "importance of checking the spread of communism" made the effort necessary. Eisenhower's directive to his special representative gave Collins carte blanche "to direct, utilize, and control all the agencies and resources of the United States Government" in South Vietnam. The president stressed that the "immediate . . . requirement" facing America was to "assist in stabilizing and strengthening the legal government of Vietnam under the premiership of Ngo Dinh Diem."[10]

Within a week of receiving his assignment, Collins was in South Vietnam, proclaiming at his first press conference: "I am here to give every possible aid to the government of Ngo Dinh Diem and to his government only." Collins brought a reputation for toughness that stood in pleasing contrast to what many Washington policymakers perceived as irresolution on the part of previous ambassadors. Collins's nickname "Lightning Joe" had been acquired as a consequence of his decisive leadership during World War II, and the administration anticipated that a jolt of that lightning would be just the thing to resuscitate America's fortunes in Southeast Asia.[11]

Eisenhower and Dulles were accordingly surprised by the tenor of Collins's "first general impressions and recommendations." "Diem is a small, shy, diffident man with almost no personal magnetism," Collins noted. "I am by no means certain [that] he has [the] inherent capacity to manage [the] country during this critical period." Collins went on to address what he considered the two outstanding difficulties facing South Vietnam's government. First, and most important, the cabinet had to be broadened: Diem was juggling the duties of minister of the interior and minister of defense, in addition to his job as premier. This was an impossible burden. Second, the VNA lacked skilled officers. It had been part of France's colonial policy to reserve positions of military command either for Frenchmen or for Vietnamese who acquired French citizenship. Consequently, Collins warned, "if [the French] Expeditionary Corps were withdrawn prematurely, [the] results could be disastrous." All of the weaponry Washington could muster would not help South Vietnam defend itself until it cultivated some native leadership.[12]

This was a candid distillation of Collins's first days in South Vietnam. The mission did not get off to an auspicious start. General Ely had decided long before Collins's arrival that Diem would have to be replaced, and he was not reticent about so informing the special representative. He told Collins that Diem was "a losing game" and bluntly asserted, "at [the] present time there is no government in Vietnam." Collins's first meeting with Diem was an exercise in frustration, as the premier subjected Collins to a two-hour jeremiad about the "insubordinate attitude of General Hinh," protesting that "Hinh was utterly untrustworthy . . . and that [the] only solution was his departure from Vietnam." Collins had no luck focusing Diem's attention on such pressing matters as cabinet reorganization, disbursement of U.S. funds to the North Vietnamese refugees, and American training and supply of the VNA. As he would learn over the coming months, it was impossible to divert the premier once he fixed on a subject.[13]

Collins bowed to Diem's demands and urged Hinh to leave South Vietnam, although he advised Dulles that "means should be found to save Hinh's face." The chief of staff was granted a two-week grace period to make his departure look like a voluntary relocation. On 19 November, Hinh handed over control of the VNA to General Nguyen Van Vy and left for Paris. He went on to enjoy a successful career as an officer in the French Air Force. Diem had won the feud, but had done little to persuade Collins that he represented the best political talent in Saigon.[14]

With the crisis in civil-military relations resolved, Collins began collaborating with Ely on a seven-point program to improve South Vietnam's prospects for independence. Point one dealt with reforming the VNA: the two generals recommended a reduction of manpower strength from 170,000 to 77,000 by mid-1955, with half the remaining troops to be deployed against a possible invasion from the north and the remainder used to provide internal security. In its most striking departure from French policy, the new plan mandated that South Vietnamese officers command the entire VNA. Other points included refugee resettlement, economic adjustments, establishment of a national assembly as a step toward representative government, and provisions for psychological warfare.

While Diem's pro-Catholic bias disposed him favorably toward any program that gave more assistance to the refugees from the north, most of the Collins-Ely program did not sit well with him. First of all, Diem was concerned about the Binh Xuyen, Hoa Hao, and Cao Dai soldiers who had been integrated into the VNA and were drawing their paychecks from the government. Diem intended to break the power of the sects, but until his own base was more secure he saw no profit in antagonizing sect leaders by firing thousands of their troops. Collins eventually compromised by allowing the VNA to retain ninety thousand soldiers rather than the proposed seventy-seven thousand. Still, his annoyance showed in his cables back to Washington. He did not want Diem to get the impression that, as he put it, "we are just going to give him a bunch of money and let him go ahead and spend it any way he wants."[15]

More worrisome, from Collins's perspective, was Diem's hoarding of power. "None of his subordinates is delegated sufficient authority to work," Collins complained. "Diem wishes to do everything himself." Despite the premier's industriousness—he spent as much as twenty hours a day dealing with government affairs—this could not help but result in a sluggish administration, especially since Diem seemed unable to recognize the difference between doing business and being busy. He would sit up half the night deliberating whether or not to reassign a civil servant or approve a passport application while a cyclone of intrigue whirled around him. No matter how frantically Collins pleaded with him to focus on the big picture, Diem could not tear himself away from minor matters to attend to major ones. Collins determined that his most urgent task was to persuade Diem to broaden his cabinet by appointing men with administrative experience.[16]

Such men did exist in South Vietnam. Chief among them was Phan Huy Quat, whom Collins considered the ablest politician he encountered. Quat was eager to serve in the administration, preferably in his former capacity as defense minister, and Collins recommended that Diem appoint him to that post. Diem resisted the suggestion, protesting that Quat would be intolerable to the Hoa Hao, Cao Dai, and Binh Xuyen. During his tenure in the defense ministry, Quat had attempted to curb the sects' military autonomy and thereby earned their mistrust. Collins responded that Diem himself was endeavoring to co-opt the sect armies into the VNA, and that he and Quat should therefore be natural allies. After some dithering, Diem agreed to abide by Collins's wishes, but then reversed himself on the grounds that sect opposition to Quat would make it impossible for him to function effectively as a cabinet member.

Collins found this rationale preposterous. The real reason for Diem's decision to deny Quat the ministry, he informed Washington, was "fear of Quat as [a] potential successor." If Quat became defense minister, Collins argued, he might acquire "greater stature in [the] public eye," which would render him "more eligible for [a] higher post" if it were "found necessary [to] replace Diem." As far as Collins was concerned, such replacement was overdue. Diem's choice "not to appoint Quat defense minister," he declared, "is [the] final development that convinces me that Diem does not have [the] capacity to unify [the] divided factions in Vietnam, and that unless some such action is taken, . . . this country will be lost to communism." Collins recommended that the United States "[s]upport [the] establishment of another government" and identified Quat as the Vietnamese best qualified to head it.[17]

This was not what Washington wanted to hear. Dulles responded the day before Christmas with a dressing-down, insisting that while the pace of government consolidation "may not please us," Collins should remember that "major changes" in Asia came "more slowly than in [the] West." The secretary concluded that "[u]nder present circumstances, . . . we have no choice but to continue our . . . support of Diem. There [is] no other suitable leader known to us."[18]

Dulles's message marked the beginning of an anomalous stage of the Collins mission during which the special representative tailored his conduct to conform to a reconceptualization of his assignment. Collins had assumed that the mandate he received from Eisenhower gave him discretion to recommend a replacement for Diem if he determined that another politician might prove more effective. While Collins knew that such a demarche would not be received with open arms by Washington, he believed its issuance fell within the purview of his mission.

Dulles's response to the call for Diem's ouster, however, made clear that Collins did not have a wide enough berth to advocate abandonment of the Diem experiment.

Although Collins never persuaded Diem to adopt a more decentralized system of government, he could report a few signs of progress as the new year, 1955, began. The Saigon regime enjoyed economic independence from the French Union's franc zone as of 1 January, when South Vietnam became the direct beneficiary of American aid. This meant that Diem, for the first time, controlled the purse strings of the VNA, which resulted in greater army loyalty to the government. Some American policymakers concluded that since Diem no longer had to worry about a VNA insurrection, he might "feel secure enough to delegate more responsibility to his ministers and carry out meaningful reforms." Collins, while noting that Diem's leverage over VNA funds could backfire if he used this newfound power to precipitate a clash with his rivals, nonetheless concluded that "prospects are brighter" in Saigon.[19]

Collins's mood of forced buoyancy carried over into Dulles's first visit to South Vietnam in February. The secretary privately assured Diem that Washington had "a great stake" in him and announced at a press conference, "today I do not know of any responsible quarter which has any doubts about backing Diem as the head of this government." This was an outrageous assertion; apart from the French officials in Saigon and Paris who had been urging Diem's removal, Dulles was aware that Collins harbored considerable doubts about Diem's political viability. Yet Dulles portrayed the Diem experiment as a success to the assembled correspondents, and Collins, standing at Dulles's side, held his tongue.[20]

Dulles's visit seems to have been interpreted by Diem as a guarantee of U.S. support against all adversaries. Shortly after the secretary's departure, Diem set in motion the chain of events that would culminate weeks later in the Battle for Saigon. Disdaining Collins's advice, he moved to narrow, not expand, the range of factions wielding administrative power. He refused to renew the Binh Xuyen's license for their gambling enterprises and announced that the French policy of subsidizing the Cao Dai and Hoa Hao as anti-Viet Minh allies would be terminated. In response, Binh Xuyen leader Bay Vien hosted a meeting of sect leaders and told them that if the Binh Xuyen, Hoa Hao, and Cao Dai could unite long enough for a joint political act, they could demand and receive the ministries in Diem's cabinet necessary to control the fiscal and human resources of the country. If Diem refused to accept their demands, a united sect front would have sufficient strength to topple the government. Cao Dai and Hoa Hao leaders, fed up with Diem, assented, and the "United Front of All Nationalist Forces" called a press conference at which Cao Dai pope Pham Cong Tac inveighed against Diem's "dictatorship."[21]

The United Front represented a formidable challenge. Ely suggested to Collins that Diem make whatever fence-mending gesture was necessary to defuse the situation. "[The] worst tactic for Diem to adopt," Ely insisted. "would be to turn his back on Bay Vien." Diem seemed bent on doing just that. In reply to Tac's diatribe, Diem tripled his palace guard and deployed VNA troops around Cholon. On 21 March, the United Front issued an ultimatum, insisting that Diem "undertake *within five days* [a] complete re-organization of the cabinet and its replacement by a new cabinet acceptable to the United Front National Forces." Sect leaders did not state what they would do if Diem failed to comply with their demands, but Vien had never been loath to resort to bloodshed when threats failed. Collins counseled Diem to open negotiations with the United Front. Diem refused to budge. The Binh Xuyen positioned mortars around the palace. Vien, it seemed, was spoiling for a fight.[22]

The same could not be said for members of Diem's cabinet. Foreign Minister Tran Van Do resigned in anticipation of the regime's defeat by the sects. Nguyen Van Thoai, Diem's own cousin, caused a sensation by announcing his withdrawal from the government while serving on the South Vietnamese delegation at the Bandung Conference of Non-aligned Nations. Collins took the occasion of these defections to again urge Diem to take Quat into his cabinet. He noted that Diem had previously objected to making Quat defense minister because of potential "troubles with the sects," but that he could hardly have "any more troubles with the sects than he has now." Diem, Collins reported, "made no reply." Instead, he took to the airwaves. "To sow or maintain dissension is contrary to our aspirations," Diem broadcast over Saigon radio, "and nobody is entitled to do so." There would be no softening of the government's position.[23]

A typical head of state, operating without any popular mandate and subject to the whims of an absentee emperor and a superpower sponsor, would have been relieved when the United Front's five-day deadline passed without incident, and would have redoubled his efforts to avoid such confrontations in the future. Diem, however, was not typical. Believing that he had gone eyeball-to-eyeball with Vien and forced him to blink, Diem determined to break the Binh Xuyen's power once and for all. He summoned his remaining cabinet ministers and informed them that he had decided to revoke Bao Dai's grant of police powers to the Binh Xuyen; he would dismiss Vien's hand-picked police chief and replace him with someone loyal to the government. Defense Minister Ho Thong Minh advised Diem to postpone any action until his plan had been approved by the cabinet. When Diem refused, Minh resigned and went to Collins's headquarters to report his defection.

Collins could not condone Diem provoking the Binh Xuyen, especially since the premier had not bothered to consult with his American advisors before installing his own man as police chief. The special representative's concern turned to fury when Ely informed him that Diem had ordered the VNA to seize the headquarters of the Saigon police, a heavily fortified building in one of the more densely populated areas of the city. Ely persuaded Diem to suspend his order, but not before advance units of the VNA occupied the periphery of the headquarters while the Binh Xuyen remained in the HQ compound. South Vietnam had come to the brink of civil war as a consequence of a policy that Diem had initiated without informing the U.S. president's special representative.

This was too much for Collins. In a stormy meeting with Diem—the memorandum of which seems to have been dictated in a voice still choked with fury—Collins threw down the gauntlet. "I told Diem that in my judgment if his orders had been carried out there would have been severe fighting within [the] city," Collins reported. When Diem tried to blame Ely for obstructing a VNA triumph, Collins shot hack that Ely had had no choice, that if the VNA bad been permitted to move against the Binh Xuyen "warfare could have been expected to break out . . . and would have resulted in far greater losses than gains." Collins demanded that Diem employ "political means . . . without fighting" to resolve the crisis, and then issued his own ultimatum: "I said that if he continued his present course we would be under heavy pressure to support a change in government." Collins commanded Diem to "consult with Ely and me before taking any additional critical steps whatever. Diem sullenly responded that "he would think over [the] situation."[24]

He did not have much time to think. That midnight, 29-30 March, explosions rocked Saigon. In response to Diem's removal of the police chief, Vien ordered an assault on VNA headquarters by two hundred Binh Xuyen troops. For three-and-a-half hours into the morning of 30 March, the VNA and Binh Xuyen clashed. The hostilities were inconclusive, but they exacted a heavy toll. The VNA suffered six killed and thirty-four wounded, the Binh Xuyen ten killed and twenty wounded. The bodies of innocent bystanders littered the sidewalk.

If Dulles's reprimand on Christmas Eve 1954 signaled the onset of a second phase in the Collins mission, during which Collins tried to harmonize the administration's commitments to both Diem and a free South Vietnam, the battle on the morning of 30 March 1955 ushered in phase three. Collins concluded that the two commitments were irreconcilable: if Diem remained premier South Vietnam would be lost. "You and the president are entitled to my judgment," Collins wrote Dulles. "I must say now that . . . it is my considered judgment that this man lacks . . . the executive ability successfully to head a government." Collins was not ready to give up on the prospect of preserving a noncommunist state in Indochina. He felt that the economic situation was favorable, the population anticommunist, and the VNA progressing nicely under Franco-American tutelage. He was convinced, however, that unless Diem was removed from office all of these positive conditions would no, would not be enough to keep South Vietnam from retiring behind the Iron Curtain. "I say this with great regret," wrote Collins, "but with firm conviction."[25]

The administration initially seemed inclined to take its special representative's advice. Eisenhower told Dulles that "you can't send this fellow [Collins] down there and have him work on it if his judgment is the way it is. We just have to go along with it." Dulles reluctantly concluded that "the rug is coming out from under the fellow in Southeast Asia. . . . [W]e have to cow-tow [sic] to the BX [Binh Xuyen]. . . . The gangsters will have won"[26]

From Collins's perspective, the sooner Washington yanked the rug, the better. South Vietnam was sliding toward chaos. Government troops and Binh Xuyen thugs bivouacked on opposite sides of Saigon's streets close enough to hurl insults – and the occasional grenade – at one another. French soldiers had built their own strong points throughout the city, laying miles of barbed wire and parking tanks on sidewalks and in traffic circles. Binh Xuyen gunboats, bristling with artillery, prowled the waterfront. None of these circumstances gave Collins cause for cheer, but most infelicitous was the fact that Diem's government had shrunk to a junta composed of members of the Ngo family. Collins was not optimistic about reversing this descent into Caesarism. Diem, he insisted, had to go.

Still, the stridency of Collins's cables did not translate into prompt action on the part of the administration. Dulles, for one, was in no hurry to "cow-tow" to gangsters. Despite Eisenhower's disinclination to overrule the verdict of his lieutenant in Saigon, Dulles delayed responding to Collins until he had an opportunity to discuss the ambassador's conclusions with Mansfield. If recent events had caused the senator to waver in his support of Diem, it would be easier for the administration to consider Collins's demands. If, on the other hand, Mansfield refused to moderate his pro-Diem stance then Collins would have to be reminded of the likely Senate reaction to Diem's removal. The Democrats had recaptured Congress in the midterm elections of 1954, and Dulles was trying to maintain bipartisan congressional support for the president's foreign policy. Moreover, many of Eisenhower's top-priority domestic programs were stalled in committee and at the mercy of a legislature dominated by the opposition party. It was not a good time for the White House to confront the Democrats over Indochina.

Mansfield's reaction, when presented with Collins's messages, was predictable "The U.S. should stick to its guns in continuing to support Diem," the senator advised. "He is the only truly nationalist leader . . . who has any chance of saving Free Viet-Nam." Dulles relayed Mansfield's views to the Saigon embassy, reminding Collins that any change of premiers would be a leap in the dark; there was no guarantee that Diem's successor would manage affairs more competently. Collins responded by insisting that he understood conditions in South Vietnam better than Mansfield did, that Quat could hardly fail to be an improvement over Diem, and that Diem had to be divested of authority at the earliest possible opportunity. "If left to his own devices," Collins warned, "Diem would attack [the] Binh Xuyen ... headquarters in [the] heart of Saigon. . . . If this is done, there will be considerable bloodshed, destruction of property, wounds will be created which will be impossible to heal, and civil war may well result."[27]

Eisenhower was troubled by the contradictory advice he was receiving about the Diem experiment. Whom should he trust: Collins or Mansfield? The former was Washington's highest-ranking official in South Vietnam and, ostensibly, its most authoritative source of intelligence, but the latter was the Senate's Indochina sage. Dulles recommended that Collins be summoned to the White House to make the case for Diem's removal in person. Eisenhower agreed, and the State Department dispatched a cable ordering the special representative home.

The morning after his plane touched down in Washington's National Airport, Collins delivered a tour de force performance before a debriefing panel consisting of representatives of the Defense Department, CIA, Treasury, Foreign Operations Administration, and the U.S. Information Agency. His point-by-point evisceration of the Diem experiment was, according to the officer who composed the minutes of the meeting, "emphatic," "vigorous," and "forceful." Diem, Collins maintained, was leading the United States to disaster in Southeast Asia. The premier had no interest in seeking a peaceful resolution to Saigon's state of emergency—on the contrary, he welcomed a shootout with the Binh Xuyen—and he was even less interested in re-organizing his government by sharing power with leading South Vietnamese politicians. Not that any of those men would agree to serve under him anyway: his policies had so discouraged patriots like Quat and former foreign minister Tran Van Do that they would only resume their government careers if Diem were out of the picture. Such disunity could not be allowed to continue, Collins argued, or South Vietnam was finished. The only way to defeat the Viet Minh was for all noncommunist elements in the country to work together, but Diem alienated precisely those men whose support he needed if his country was to survive. In short, Collins declared, "no solution in Vietnam is possible as long as Diem remains in office."[28]

Meeting with Eisenhower for lunch at the White House that same day, Collins was even more vehement. He rattled off numerous "instances wherein Diem had been persuaded at only the last moment not to do some utterly foolish thing." Most egregious, Collins claimed, was Diem's repeatedly stated intention to attack the Binh Xuyen-held police headquarters "in the heart of Saigon . . . when the streets were full of pedestrians." But this represented only one example of Diem's unsuitability for command; Collins chronicled "many other instances," venting months of frustration, before concluding that "the net of it is . . . this fellow is impossible."[29]

Eisenhower was impressed, but he also had to consider the weight of congressional support for Diem. He advised Collins to try to sway legislators like Mansfield and Representatives Walter Judd and Edna Kelly. While Collins did his best, Congress proved more intransigent than the president. Mansfield found Lightning Joe's case against Diem flimsy, and remarked to his aide after conferring with the special representative: "Collins really doesn't know much." The Senate Foreign Relations and House Foreign Affairs Committees were unsympathetic when Collins addressed them. By coincidence, hearings on foreign aid were ongoing at the time of Collins's recall to Washington, and many in the administration worried that abandonment of Diem would make future U.S. aid to South Vietnam a target for the congressional budget axe.[30]

Yet Collins had the debating advantage of having actually been in Vietnam for almost half a year. (Mansfield, despite his reputation as an Indochina expert, had only spent six days in Vietnam in 1953 and six days in 1954.) This advantage proved crucial when Collins confronted Dulles on 23 April. As Kenneth Young of the State Department reported, a "basic shift in our approach was taken at a long luncheon meeting with the secretary. . . . [Collins] reiterated even more vigorously and firmly his view . . . that Diem must be replaced." Dulles accepted this "basic shift" in principle, but tried to hold out for interim retention of Diem "until . . . genuinely

Vietnamese elements turn up another acceptable solution." Collins informed Dulles that this was an "impossible condition." The secretary laid down his arms. On 27 April, Dulles sent top-secret cables to the embassies in Paris and Saigon setting forth the steps by which Diem was to be eased from office.[31]

Six hours after the cables left Washington, Dulles received notification from Lansdale that fighting had erupted between the Binh Xuyen and the VNA. The "Battle for Saigon" was underway.

Upon receipt of Lansdale's message, Dulles cabled both Paris and Saigon, directing the embassies there to disregard the previous telegrams "until further instructions." Randolph Kidder, chargé d'affaires of the Saigon embassy, did better than that. Worried that Diem's enemies might seize on any evidence of flagging American support for the premier, he ordered Dulles's earlier telegrams burned. The secretary followed up his "blocking" cables with instructions to supply the department with as much information as possible on the fighting to enable the National Security Council (NSC) to make sound judgments about what the U.S. response should be. The NSC was scheduled to meet the following morning, 28 April, and Dulles did not want to be flying blind when he briefed his fellow policymakers.[32]

Kidder strove to keep the State Department posted, but the pace of events in Saigon had accelerated to such a dizzying speed since the first, inconclusive reports of combat that it was impossible to determine what was happening, much less assign responsibility. Fighting began around noon on 27 April and quickly escalated from small arms and mortar exchanges to include the heaviest artillery in the VNA's arsenal. By evening it had engulfed a large part of the city. No one could say for certain whether Vien's gangsters or government troops had fired the first shot, but the most plausible scenario is that Diem seized a vanishing opportunity to stave off dismissal by Washington. The timing of the military engagement was too favorable to Diem's cause to be mere coincidence. Diem probably learned of the Eisenhower administration's intention to oust him and elected to take a now-or-never gamble by engaging the Binh Xuyen.

The results were dramatic. Saigon was in frenzy by the morning of 28 April. Numerous explosions and house-to-house combat drove thousands of people into the streets. A square mile of the city became a free-fire zone. Artillery and mortars obliterated Saigon's poor districts, killing five hundred civilians and leaving twenty thousand homeless. It was difficult to discern any strategy on the part of either the government or the Binh Xuyen, as both sides relied on meat-grinder attrition to break the will of the adversary. In one of the few maneuvers that could be called tactical, the VNA tried to cut the Binh Xuyen off from reinforcements by knocking out the bridge across the canal linking Saigon and Cholon, but the rebels foiled this stratagem by throwing pontoon bridges across the canal. The conflict, it appeared, would be decided on the basis of which side was capable of absorbing and inflicting the most punishment, and neither side was deficient in those capacities. One thousand or so Binh Xuyen and VNA soldiers were killed during the first day alone.

On the morning of 28 April, Dulles telephoned Collins to inform him of the decision to suspend instructions for replacing Diem. The administration "should not act until we have further information," Dulles declared, and cited reports that the VNA "had responded pretty effectively." Washington's decision, he implied, could well turn on whether "Diem is losing control or possibly emerging as a hero." Dulles carried this theme into an NSC meeting later that morning, although Collins attended as well and thus had one more opportunity to make his case for ousting Diem before flying back to Saigon. The secretary argued that the best policy was to let events in South Vietnam run their course, to play for time and see whether "something occurs in the Saigon disorders out of which Diem will emerge as a hero." Collins vehemently dissented. He reiterated his view that "the attempt to destroy the Binh Xuyen by military action" would "produce civil war" and that a "political solution" was therefore imperative. Furthermore, he insisted, no feasible coalition government could be formed so long as Diem played any administrative role. Politically, Collins declared, "Diem's number was up." The NSC listened respectfully but paid no heed. Rather, they ratified Dulles's approach. Eisenhower observed that he could "not see what else we could do at this time."[33]

Just as the Battle for Saigon gave hope to pro-Diem figures in the administration like Dulles, so it invigorated Diem's advocates in Congress. As he had in his 1954 report to the Senate Foreign Relations Committee, Mansfield demanded an end to all aid to South Vietnam if Diem were overthrown. Senator Hubert Humphrey proclaimed that "Premier Diem is an honest, wholesome, and honorable man. He is the kind of man we ought to be supporting, rather than conspirators, gangsters, and hoodlums . . . who are diabolical, sinister, and corrupt." Through Congresswoman Edna Kelly, members of the House Foreign Affairs Committee registered their opposition to the administration's withdrawing support from Diem. Representative Thomas Dodd demanded that Collins be fired and "replaced by someone who measures up to the needs of the hour."[34]

The ardor with which the legislature rallied around Diem was surpassed by the American press. *U.S. News and World Report* described Diem as "the defiant, honest little premier" who was opposed by "an unholy alliance . . . between . . . gangsters, racketeers, soldiers of fortune, and religious fanatics." Publisher Henry Luce's weekly editorial in *Life* proclaimed: "Every son, daughter, or even distant admirer of the American Revolution should be overjoyed and learn to shout, if not to pronounce, 'Hurrah for Ngo Dinh Diem!'" Diem's decision to confront the "Binh Xuyen gangsters," Luce declared, "immensely simplifies the task of U.S. diplomacy in Saigon. That task is, or should be, simply to back Diem to the hilt." The *New York Times* predicted, "If Premier Ngo Dinh Diem should be overthrown by the combination of gangsters, cultists, and French colonials who have been gunning for him, the communists will have won a significant victory."[35]

As Collins made his globe-spanning return flight to Saigon, that city continued to tear itself apart. After forty-eight hours of house-to-house combat, the VNA began to gain the upper hand. Le Grande Monde, previously Vien's largest gambling establishment and now serving as a Binh Xuyen citadel, was overrun by Diem's paratroopers after defenders and attackers suffered heavy losses. Diem's forces then stormed one of Vien's most heavily fortified strongholds, the Petrus Ky High School building in Cholon, and overran that as well. By the time Collins arrived back in South Vietnam on 2 May, the battle was nearly over. The Binh Xuyen forces were broken and running for refuge. All of Vien's command posts in Saigon were reduced to rubble. Across the Arroyo Chinois in Cholon, Vien's headquarters, with its menagerie, was in ruins, his pythons, tigers, and crocodiles killed by mortar and artillery fire. Vien himself managed to escape to Paris and live out his days in moneyed obscurity. The Cao Dai pope fled to Cambodia. Most Hoa Hao leaders surrendered.

While the VNA pursued fleeing Binh Xuyen troops into the Mekong Delta and west toward the Cambodian border, throngs of people gathered outside Diem's residence and chanted "*Da Dao Bao Dai!*" ("Down with Bao Dai!"). Dulles cabled Collins on his return to the U.S. embassy, "Events in [the] past few days have put [the] Vietnamese situation in a . . . different perspective than when you were here." Diem's triumph over the Binh Xuyen, Dulles observed, "would appear to overtake some of the principal reasons previously advanced for [the] U.S. to support Diem's removal. . . . For us at this time to participate in a scheme to remove Diem would not only be domestically impractical but highly detrimental to our prestige in Asia." In other words, despite the arguments that Collins had been drumming into Washington's ear, despite the fact that Diem had laid waste to his own capital, and despite the irrelevance of the Battle for Saigon to America's goal of containing communism in Southeast Asia, the Diem experiment would endure.[36]

The Collins mission, however, was almost over. Collins had been eager to return to his NATO assignment for some time, and the administration was happy to accommodate him in the wake of Diem's victory. The White House issued a press release announcing Collins's relief as special representative and replacement by a regular ambassador. There was no mention of Collins's difficulties with Diem.

If Collins's views had lost credibility in Washington, they echoed sentiments in Paris, where the Diem experiment, never popular, now stirred French policymakers to new heights of pique. At a foreign ministers' conference shortly after the Battle for Saigon, French premier Edgar Faure declared, "Diem is not only incapable but mad. . . . Diem is a bad choice . . . with no chance to succeed." In case Dulles, Faure's American counterpart at the conference, was inclined to dismiss this as empty rhetoric, Faure backed it up by threatening to withdraw the FEC from Vietnam if Diem were not removed. Dulles, taken aback, cabled the White House that Faure was "not bluffing." How should Washington respond to this ultimatum? Was preservation of the Diem experiment worth a rush of one hundred thousand French troops from South Vietnam, with obvious implications as to whose soldiers would succeed them?[37]

The Eisenhower administration determined that it was. Although some voices of alarm were raised, most policymakers were inclined to shoot the works. The National Security Council Planning Board issued a report claiming that withdrawal of the FEC "would clearly disengage us from the taint of colonialism. . . . [W]e should be happy to see the French leave." Dulles concurred. Although he got Faure to endorse a public statement promising continued Franco-American cooperation against the Viet Minh, the handwriting was on the wall. By spurning French demands that Diem be replaced, the Eisenhower administration absolved Paris of its responsibilities in Vietnam and demolished the illusion that the United States and France were equal partners in the enterprise to contain Southeast Asian communism. It was a true crossing of the Rubicon. Diem rubbed salt in French wounds by ordering his army to adopt American-style uniforms and the American salute, and South Vietnamese officers even held a ceremonial burning of their French-style insignia of rank. The formerly French-led VNA was renamed the Army of the Republic of Vietnam (ARVN)—or "Arvin," as American servicemen came to call it. Vietnam was well on its way to becoming an American war.[38]

15

Ngo Dinh Diem, Modernizer

Philip E. Catton

Bernard Fall, a veteran observer of the wars in Indo-China, once noted that information on Ngo Dinh Diem, South Vietnam's president between 1955 and 1963, consisted 'either of totally uncritical eulogy or of equally partisan condemnation'.[1] On the one hand, there were the hagiographies. These included potted histories and official biographies, as well as articles in US newspapers and magazines which had originally praised the Vietnamese leader as 'the tough miracle man of Vietnam'.[2] On the other hand, there were the condemnations, particularly those made by Diem's Communist opponents and the growing number of Western critics. The Vietnamese Communists branded Diem as a reactionary and traitor, a tool of US imperialism: their wartime propaganda referred to him as *tay sai* (a lackey) and his regime as *My-Diem* (American-Diem).[3]

While most Western critics did not see Diem as a puppet, particularly in light of the enormous difficulty that the United States experienced in influencing him, they portrayed his regime as hopelessly conservative. Diem, in this view, had no political agenda of his own, except perhaps an outdated mandarin authoritarianism and a determination to preserve his power by blocking attempts at reform. Frances FitzGerald's is the most forthright expression of this view; in her Pulitzer Prize-winning book on Vietnam, she describes Diem as a Confucian/Catholic reactionary, violently opposed to things Western and modern, and bent on restoring an idealized version of traditional Vietnamese kingship.[4]

Of all the images of Diem, those of the power-hungry autocrat and the backward-looking 'last of the mandarins'[5] have exercised the most lasting influence on Western views of the Saigon regime. Although they continue to dominate the scholarly literature, appearing in widely read historical surveys and in a variety of more specialized treatments of the war,[6] they are false images and obscure our understanding. Diem's government, in fact, had its own views of how to deal with the related issues of counter-insurgency and nation building, forward-looking ideas which, although deeply flawed, constituted a distinct vision of modernity and presented an alternative to the political agenda of both his regime's US ally and his Communist opponent.

Diem's ideas were most clearly embodied in the strategic hamlet programme, the last and most ambitious of the regime's attempts to lead a non-Communist revolution and establish the basis for a modern and independent nation state. Although strategic hamlets aimed to separate the Communist-led guerrillas from the peasantry by regrouping and fortifying thousands of rural settlements, they were not merely a device to defeat the armed insurgency. Diem also saw them as a way of mobilizing the population politically and generating support for his regime; they were the centre-piece of the government's plans to modernize the Republic of Vietnam (RVN) and simultaneously free it from dependence on the United States.

The ideological blueprint for strategic hamlets, as well as most of the Diem government's other major initiatives, was Personalism (*Nhan vi*). Personalism drew much of its inspiration from the Catholic doctrine of the same name, which Diem's brother, Ngo Dinh Nhu, probably first encountered in France in the 1930s. The Vietnamese version also reflected the ethical concerns of various Asian philosophies, notably Confucianism. The Ngo family's Personalism sought a middle way between liberalism and Communism, and between the rights of individuals and their responsibilities towards the community; this third way offered an acceptable route in developing the state, a road to modernity that was 'neither the liberal method considered too slow, nor the Communist method considered too inhumane'.[7] Instead, both individual rights and the needs of the state could be satisfied by generating a desire among the people to do voluntarily what was necessary for the common good. A spirit of self-sacrifice and group solidarity would enable the regime to mobilize the people against the Communists and in support of the government's attempts to modernize Vietnamese society.[8]

Personalism provided the ideological inspiration for a series of large-scale rural projects which culminated in the strategic hamlet programme. The first of these schemes was a land development project in 1957, whose aim was to relocate tens of thousands of Vietnamese—inhabitants of the lowlands, demobilized soldiers, and 'released' political prisoners—in new land development centres (*khu dinh dien*) on uncultivated or abandoned tracts of land in the highlands of the centre and the south, and in the Mekong Delta. At the same time, the scheme encouraged the montagnard populations in highland areas to give up their 'uncivilized' nomadic lifestyle by moving into the new settlements.[9] For strategic reasons, Diem hoped to construct a 'human wall' along South Vietnam's vulnerable frontiers, especially in the delta's Plain of Reeds and in the Central Highlands; economically, the new centres would benefit the country by bringing more land under cultivation. Finally, by opening up new lands, Diem reasoned that the programme would advance the regime's Personalist revolution by fostering a spirit of communal solidarity and national loyalty among a new generation of Vietnamese pioneers.[10]

By mid-1959, the government had established eighty-four land development centres with a population of more than 125,000.[11] Yet, although the programme continued after this time, it was evidently not an adequate solution to the regime's mounting problems. Insurgent activity perceptibly increased in 1958 and 1959, to which the regime responded by formally launching a new rural scheme in July 1959, the agroville programme. Agrovilles (*khu tru mat*), accompanied by smaller agro-hamlets (*ap tru mat*), were to regroup thousands of peasants in the Mekong Delta into newly constructed model settlements in order to provide their inhabitants with security and modern amenities, and to stimulate local and regional development. As with its land development scheme, Diem also saw the new programme as another way to promote his Personalist agenda. In return for the benefits the programme would supposedly confer, the peasants were expected to build and develop agrovilles, and this would, in turn, generate social cohesion and a spirit of collective self-sacrifice.[12]

Only about twenty agrovilles were completed. In practice, the programme dissolved in many places into the large-scale conscription of reluctant peasants to work on the project and the forced resettlement of others. The ensuing popular discontent badly hampered the programme's execution, as did the burgeoning guerrilla war in the countryside. In the first half of 1960, the Communist-led insurgents brought the programme to a standstill.[13] The formation of the National Liberation Front (NLF) and the rapid expansion of the rebels' influence at the end of the year reflected the increasingly organized nature of the resistance to the Diem regime. By April 1961, the regime estimated that less than half of the country was in government hands; the rest falling under varying degrees of guerrilla control.[14]

As the guerrilla war increased, and the agroville programme ended, Diem looked around for other ways to strengthen South Vietnam's rural apparatus and bolster support among the peasants. New rural campaigns in mid-1960 aimed at increasing the number of officials at the grassroots, establishing intelligence nets, and reviving village-level organizations. The regime paid particular attention to mobilizing rural youth, who, according to Diem, constituted the 'backbone of [the] country' and would protect villages, help to develop communities, and provide a fresh infusion of rural leadership.[15] Above all, Diem stressed the need to build the 'democratic infrastructure' in the villages. In early 1961, the regime started to root out corrupt officials in the provinces and to reintroduce local elections, beginning with the selection of members of the government-sponsored republican youth movement to serve on village councils. Diem argued that if people did not choose those responsible for organizing local activities, they would not take part in them.[16]

Such thinking represented a significant change in the regime's conception of the civil war. With increasing urgency, Diem sought ways to win not simply the *passive* loyalty of peasants but their *active* participation in the anti-Communist struggle. At the same time, this kind of popular involvement held out the promise of mobilizing the population in support of the broader goal of modernization, as the president's brother and counsellor, Ngo Dinh Nhu, wished. Critical of Diem's emphasis on the more concrete aspects of development, Nhu was fascinated by the less tangible techniques of mass mobilization, as perfected by the Communists. As well as seeking to turn these methods against the regime's opponents, he also wanted to use them to advance the regime's Personalist revolution.[17]

Through 1960 and 1961, the government searched for a suitable strategic vehicle to carry its hopes. In October 1960, Nhu outlined to an unnamed US official a strategy of 'strength lines', the first attempt at systematic pacification of the countryside, which served as a rough guide to the operations in the Mekong Delta at the end of 1960 and the beginning of 1961.[18] The regime also encouraged the involvement of its provincial subordinates in formulating new approaches. During the summer of 1961, the secretary of state for the interior, Bui Van Luong, asked the provinces for suggestions about how to strengthen the regime's presence in the villages; instructed them to make plans to pacify their areas; and himself took the chair at a number of provincial conferences.[19] As a result of the high-level interest in a new strategy, and a series of provincial initiatives, the strategic hamlet programme began to emerge in the second half of 1961.

Prototype strategic hamlets first appeared in the middle of the year as a number of provincial experiments with the fortification of settlements, the organization of their inhabitants, and the strengthening of local administrations. Although many localities, encouraged by the regime's call to action, were involved, Luong singled out the three provinces of Tay Ninh, Quang Ngai, and Vinh Long as the key examples.[20] By far the most extensive and influential of these operations was that initiated by Major Le Van Phuoc, the province chief of the delta's Vinh Long. He established three model 'strategic hamlets' (*ap chien luoc*), which became showplaces for officials from Saigon and other provinces, and compiled a series of instructional manuals on the creation of strategic hamlets for distribution to local officials, copies of which he dispatched to Saigon. Phuoc stressed that if the regime sought to strengthen the 'democratic infrastructure', and simultaneously strangle the NLF, the hamlet, a number of which made up the larger village, was the place to start.[21] By late 1961, with the regime's blessing, most provinces were constructing strategic hamlets.

Notably absent from this flurry of activity was the regime's superpower patron, the United States. The Americans were not entirely unaware of the regime's plans. The US Military Assistance Advisory Group (MAAG) knew something of the new rural experiments, as General Lionel C. McGarr noted in a report at the beginning of September 1961. So, too, did the

CIA station in Saigon. William Colby, the station chief, met regularly with Nhu to discuss matters of security and the broader problems of nation building. Moreover, the government and the CIA collaborated on several local self-defence projects in 1960 and 1961, including the organization of militia among montagnard communities in the Central Highlands. These projects used concepts and techniques later incorporated into strategic hamlets.[22] Yet, although the United States eventually supported the hamlet scheme, most US officials were 'somewhat bewildered by the sudden appearance of a major activity that had not been processed through their complex co-ordinating staffs'. While US officials had been developing a series of counter-insurgency proposals in 1960 and 1961, the Diem regime had proceeded to fashion its own response to South Vietnam's problems, without seeking to align its plans with those of its superpower ally.[23]

This was not a new pattern in the government's approach to foreign advice. The Ngos were well aware from past experience that US support came with a variety of strings attached; conditions that often offended their sovereign pride and clashed with their own ideas. There had been considerable allied wrangling, for example, over the implementation of the land development programme in the late 1950s, and to avoid a repetition of this conflict, the regime had pointedly forgone discussion of the agroville scheme with the Americans.[24] Not surprisingly, Diem sought to limit foreign involvement in the hamlet programme as well, especially as the United States put a great deal of pressure on the regime in 1961 to accept US policy prescriptions for defeating the insurgents. Such demands only further convinced the Diem regime that its ally was overbearing and meddlesome; indeed, US pressure encouraged the Ngos to see the hamlet programme as a way to free South Vietnam from dependence on the United States for economic and military aid, as well as a way to satisfy their other political goals.

The regime's highly selective approach to accepting foreign support also bedevilled its receipt of advice from the small British Advisory Mission (BRIAM) led by Robert Thompson, a veteran of the Malayan Emergency. For several years, there had been a series of diplomatic and military exchanges between Kuala Lumpur and Saigon, and Thompson had visited Vietnam once before in the spring of 1960. He returned to Saigon in September 1961 and is often credited with influencing the development of the hamlet scheme.[25] Yet BRIAM arrived when Saigon's ideas were well formed and a fledgling hamlet programme already under way. Nor did many of Thompson's proposals for top-down administrative controls complement the regime's ideas about transforming the state from the bottom up. As a result, British officials would report with increasing exasperation the gap between their advice and South Vietnamese policies. They came to suspect, as did US officials, that Saigon flirted with BRIAM's proposals in order to stymie US attempts to promote an American plan of action, as well as to lend intellectual weight to Diem and Nhu's own ideas.[26]

By the end of 1961, those ideas were far enough advanced for Saigon to extend central direction to the various efforts already made by its provincial subordinates. Luong drafted a study document for discussion of the hamlet scheme at an internal security council conference on 8 January 1962. The meeting established strategic hamlets as a national policy and agreed to organize a committee responsible for formulating plans and coordinating construction throughout the country. An inter-ministerial committee for strategic hamlets (*uy-ban lien-bo dac-trach ap chien-luoc*) officially came into being on 3 February 1962 and met weekly to discuss the programme's problems and progress.[27] Although Luong was the committee's secretary-general, Nhu, who later described himself as 'both the originator and the prime mover' of the hamlet programme, ran its meetings.[28] He was the key figure in formulating its goals and methods, Diem broadly concurring with Nhu's ideas and supporting his leadership of the programme.

As with its previous rural projects, Saigon conceived of strategic hamlets as a solution, in fact the ultimate solution, to multiple problems. The regime frequently referred to these difficulties as a trio of enemies: 'Communism, Underdevelopment, and Disunity' (*Cong san, Cham tien va Chia re*), or sometimes 'Colonialism, Feudalism, and Communism' (*Thuc dan, Phong kien va Cong san*). To overcome such formidable opponents required a transformation in the life of South Vietnam. Thus, the regime named its new scheme the 'strategic' (*chien luoc*) hamlet policy, rather than choosing a term such as 'combat' (*chien dau*) hamlet, which official documents had also used in the programme's infancy. As Luong explained, the word 'combat' implied too narrow a concern with the security situation, whereas 'strategic' referred to military, social, political, and economic solutions.[29] The programme was, in fact, the most elaborate articulation of the regime's vision of a modern Vietnam.

Given its importance, the regime described the programme in grandiose terms. Nhu, who once expressed his preference for being an 'archivist-paleographer' rather than a policy-maker,[30] set strategic hamlets within a panoramic vision of Vietnamese history: 'Behind us, behind our people is a heritage of struggle and of march toward progress; in front of us, in front of our people opens a long road which calls us forth.' Strategic hamlets, he explained, were the next frontier in this struggle, the third wave of Vietnamese history. The first stage of that history was the prehistoric 'march to the North of the "One Hundred Viets tribes"'; the second phase, the 'march to the South of our people' from the Middle Ages onwards that carved out a Vietnamese state running from north to south. Strategic hamlets would be equally monumental, sweeping away the last vestiges of feudalism and colonialism and smashing the Communist threat. The ultimate destination of the movement, the regime even suggested, was the liberation of North Vietnam. According to this view, the advance of the strategic hamlet programme, and the exodus of montagnards fleeing the war in the Central Highlands, would meet each other on a single road going north.[31]

Such historical allusions, Nhu was at pains to point out, did not aim to satisfy a 'few intellectual bourgeois whims', but reflected the government's belief that mass mobilization at the village level was the key to its struggle with its enemies, just as a series of mass communal movements in the past created and developed the Vietnamese state. As Diem proclaimed: 'The national policy of strategic hamlets is the quintessence of our truest traditions. It is the pure outgrowth of our ancestral virtues.'[32] To meet the current crisis in all its forms, villagers had to be roused to emulate the exploits of their forefathers. The regime constantly emphasized the importance of struggle (*dau tranh*) if its enemies were to be overcome, just as the Vietnamese Communists used the same term to describe their own efforts to promote revolutionary change. Diem lauded the 'capacity of invention and the tenacity of our people, upon whom the geopolitical situation has imposed for centuries a persistent struggle to survive'.[33] In a study document written for government cadres in late 1961, Lieutenant Colonel Nguyen Van Chau, the director of the bureau of psychological warfare, explained that only by confronting obstacles could a nation develop the material and moral strength necessary to prosper, and warned that a people who did not struggle could not expect their nation to last much longer.[34]

The regime's emphasis on the value of 'struggle' manifested itself in one of the central themes of the strategic hamlet programme: the need for self-sufficiency, Government pronouncements repeatedly stressed that the people must take the initiative and carry the burden of defeating the nation's enemies; the role of the authorities was only to provide the stimulus to action and the minimum of support necessary to initiate the programme. Such self-sufficiency, Nhu argued, was the key issue for Vietnam and, indeed, for all under-developed countries.[35] Though he often expressed this idea in elaborate, Confucian-like formulations, which frequently confused or bemused his listeners,[36] the regime had a clear view of the value of self-reliance, which it considered both a virtue and a necessity.

The Ngos deemed self-reliance a virtue because they believed that people forced back upon their own resources would develop the inner strength and common bonds of unity necessary to defeat the nation's enemies. As an official publication put it: 'Being Personalist requires a militant democratic spirit which conceives liberty as a conquest over oneself and exterior obstacles.' Struggle in adversity would be the handmaiden to personal and collective liberation.[37] Self-sufficiency was also deemed a necessity because of the government's limited resources, unless South Vietnam was prepared to depend on the United States. To the Ngos, however, reliance on foreign aid was not only incompatible with the notion of national sovereignty but also threatened to sap the moral fibre required to build a new society. Why was it, Nhu complained, that every time the Vietnamese discussed the problem of finances, they could only think about American aid? If the people became dependent on outside support, or overly reliant on their own government for that matter, how would they ever be able to nurture the personal and collective strength necessary to develop a modern independent nation? 'Our freedom', Nhu concluded, 'is the result of our struggle, not a gift from Santa Claus, from our government, or from any foreign government.'[38]

As an organizational framework for promoting this struggle, the hamlet programme sought to generate a revolution in four areas: military, social, political, and economic. Militarily, strategic hamlets hoped to reverse the deteriorating situation on the battlefield, where South Vietnam's existing forces had proven incapable of defeating the insurgents, or of controlling the population; when dispersed to defend isolated camps and forts, they lacked the numbers, and also apparently the will, to protect surrounding villages and their inhabitants. What was the purpose of military posts, Nhu asked, if their defenders did not dare to leave them?[39] Yet, when the regular army (ARVN) concentrated its big battalions and ventured into the countryside, the Communist insurgents usually evaded battle or simply melted away into the population. Such large-scale sweeps reminded Lieutenant Colonel John Paul Vann of a ship moving through the ocean, temporarily displacing water which flowed right back into place as soon as the vessel sailed on.[40] Besides yielding few results, conventional sweeps could also be self-defeating: 'Since we did not know where the enemy was,' Nhu observed, 'ten times we launched a military operation, nine times we missed the Vietcong, and the tenth time, we struck right on the head of the population.' The result was popular hostility towards the military, as well as frustration within the ranks of the armed forces.[41]

Strategic hamlets, however, promised to establish a conventional front line in the contest between the government and the guerrillas. Rather than giving the NLF unrestricted access to the population, the new hamlets would create physical and psychological barriers between it and the peasantry. This point reflected Saigon's belief that most villagers agreed to NLF demands for support only because they were terrified or tricked into doing so, not out of sympathy for the insurgents' cause; meanwhile, any disgruntled guerrilla would not desert the NLF's ranks for fear of retribution. Inside strategic hamlets, however, peasants would be able to stand up to the NLF and disillusioned guerrillas find safe havens. Consequently, the insurgents would be compelled to attack hamlets in order to maintain access to their bases of support and prevent their cause from collapsing; by doing so, they would reveal themselves, even to the most gullible of peasants, as the true enemies of the people. Physically and morally isolated, Diem argued, the guerrillas would eventually be reduced to the status of 'a foreign expeditionary corps facing a hostile population'. With the enemy forced into fighting a conventional conflict, moreover, the ARVN would be free to defeat a cornered quarry, instead of chasing shadows.[42]

The primary responsibility for the defence of the country would thus rest with a hamlet-based citizen militia, with the regular army and provincial forces reduced to a supporting role, providing initial protection for fledgling hamlets and hunting down the remnants of the enemy. According to Nhu, this arrangement represented a fundamental change in the spirit of the war, in line with the regime's call for popular struggle and self-sufficiency. He argued that South Vietnam could no longer afford to fight a conventional, or counter-guerrilla, conflict against the insurgents, for that style of warfare was not only tactically bankrupt but also kept the regime dependent on the United States for the support of the RVN's lavishly equipped forces. National pride, and real independence, demanded that South Vietnam develop an alternative defence posture, one better suited to the conditions of an under-developed country. Nhu envisaged a defence policy eventually founded on a smaller regular army, a variety of special forces units (*Biet cach*), and, at the centre, a guerrilla substructure of approximately 700,000 hamlet militia. Thus, just as strategic hamlets would compel the insurgents to switch to conventional fighting, they would also allow the Diem regime to wage an anti-Communist version of a 'people's war', based on a militarily and politically mobilized population.[43]

A further advantage of this military strategy related to a second area of concern: revolutionary social change. By placing the primary responsibility for military defence on the general populace, the regime hoped to kindle a sense of communal solidarity and national consciousness. The government did not expect the overnight conversion of people into model citizens and superpatriots; Nhu, for example, warned government cadres that, when organizing strategic hamlet defences, they should not lecture the inhabitants about world affairs or great ideological disputes, which would only bore or mystify them. However, if villagers began to see that their own personal interests coincided with those of the community arid the nation, then strategic hamlets might change social attitudes.[44]

By protecting their homes, the Ngos reasoned, hamlet residents would be defending not only themselves and their families but also their communities and their country. Hence, the anti-Communist struggle might forge links between people that would gradually overcome the isolated and atomized nature of rural life. Backward peasant attitudes, mired in a narrow concern for individual and family interests, would slowly give way to broader commitments. Indeed, the belief that mutual hardship could foster communal solidarity suffused all aspects of the establishment of strategic hamlets, from the building of their fortifications to plans for their economic development: 'Using difficulty as a springboard,' Diem declared in October 1962, 'the soul of the nation is forging its unity in the trials of war.'[45]

Nowhere were the regime's expectations of this popular mobilization better illustrated than in Nhu's ambitious ideas about strategic hamlet defence. He evidently expected inhabitants to wage their own guerrilla war against the Communists; residents would assume the responsibility for hamlet security after the completion of fortifications, the division of the population into various social groups, and the creation of a militia, usually known as combat youth (*thanh nien chien dau*). Nhu believed that the latter was capable of defending the hamlet from a small band of insurgents; however, in the event of an attack by a platoon or larger unit, its role was only to retard and harass the enemy's advance. During this delaying action, the other inhabitants would hide food and money, and the young people would disappear into secret cellars. Thus, the guerrillas would enter a hamlet composed only of old people and children, while the combat youth would fire at the enemy from their hideouts. If the intruders tried to remain in the strategic hamlet, secret cells organized during its construction would conduct sabotage operations and contact nearby posts or settlements.[46] In effect, the NLF would find itself in the same kind of hostile environment that the ARVN encountered in its sweeps through the countryside. To emphasize further the active role that the regime expected ordinary people to play in the nation's defence, it proposed to lend weapons to hamlet defenders only for a period of six months, during which time they had to capture their own guns from the insurgents.[47]

The considerable commitment of peasants to the defence of their homes could only be expected if they believed that their strategic hamlet deserved protecting in the first place. The regime's programme, Madame Nhu observed, 'is valid only if the life on the inside of the hamlet is worth living, and therefore worth being protected and defended, for it must be remembered that it is always the population of the hamlet itself which closes the hamlet gates and no one else'.[48] To secure this commitment, and give meaning to its social revolution, the regime planned to create a new set of social classes, based on contributions to the 'defence and welfare of the nation'. The three-tier system comprised, first, combatants and their families: second, hamlet leaders and locally elected officials; and, third, poor peasants and workers. Rank in this social order would entitle holders to certain privileges, such as priority in the distribution of riceland, and better access to education and medical treatment.[49] Everyone would be given equal opportunity to benefit from the new scale of values, depending on their contribution to defeating 'Communism, Underdevelopment, and Disunity'. The new system would represent the perfect embodiment of Personalism's attempt to combine individual rights with collective responsibility.

Naturally, there would be 'losers' as well as 'winners' in the reshuffling of the social order. The losers would be the existing elite, whose privileges derived from wealth and education. Clearly, the social revolution was not only an attempt to promote service to the nation but also a direct assault on the established social structure. The well-off, who concerned themselves only with their own private affairs, were 'parasites', Nhu stated; the feudal and colonial orders had bred injustice, subjecting ordinary people to 'the law of the powerful and the rich'.[50] The first duty of government cadres, Nhu told a class of strategic-hamlet trainees, was not to defend the current order but to overthrow it: 'the traditional system, product of a backward political, economic, and social structure . . . would give place to a more progressive, revolutionary one.' Far from seeking to protect and bolster the existing order, then, as its critics generally allege, the regime had set out to dismantle it.[51]

The goal was more fully expressed in the third aspect of the hamlet scheme: political revolution. The peasants, clearly unwilling to fight for the old order, would only rally to the government's side if the rewards of the new social system were backed by political change. 'If fortifications were built around the hamlets while injustice prevailed inside,' Luong observed, 'the people would [simply] believe that they were [being] imprisoned.'[52] Strategic hamlets sought to provide the necessary political framework through local elections and the establishment of the rule of law at the hamlet and village level.

Although Vietnam had a long history of local democracy and representation, when the Diem regime first came into power it preferred to appoint officials directly. The proposed new system of elections sought to restore and extend traditional practice. The most important of the newly elected bodies were the hamlet management committee (usually called the *ban tri su ap*) and the village council (*hoi dong xa*). The hamlet management committee consisted of the hamlet chief and three or four commissioners; the youth delegate was to be chosen by members of the Republican Youth movement, while the other commissioners were to be elected by a secret ballot of all residents over the age of eighteen. The village council included five officials, elected indirectly by members of each village's hamlet committees and the leaders of its hamlets' social organizations.[53] Existing officials, Nhu complained, were usually cronies of the district chiefs, with little or no connection to the villages they ran, who commanded no respect or support among the population, and drove some peasants into the arms of the insurgents. New elections would promote local self-government, encourage political participation as well as enthusiasm for popularly elected authorities, and nurture a new generation of leaders.[54]

Nhu dismissed suggestions that it was dangerous in a time of war to permit elections and to depend on a new group of inexperienced officials, Popular elections, particularly speedy establishment of hamlet committees, would demonstrate to the people the government's intentions. The Diem regime, of course, did not intend to allow known Communists to stand for these offices; moreover, it inadvertently invited electoral abuse by advising local officials to endorse informally the candidacies of those residents who demonstrated most enthusiasm during the building of strategic hamlets. Foreign observers often took such measures to mean that elections were merely a centrally controlled sham; Nhu, however, frequently criticized RVN officials who suggested that voting was only for form's sake and the idea was to make sure that the 'right' people won. He asserted that without free elections, there could be no political change. Strategic hamlets were a revolutionary concept, not simply a policy for restoring security, and the population must be able to witness, and participate in, that political revolution.[55]

A similar concern, both to embody and demonstrate political change underlay the establishment of new legal codes, called communal rules (*huong uoc*). Based upon a government model but adaptable to the customs and concerns of different localities, these regulations were to be drawn up and voted into effect by local residents. Each set of rules enshrined the regime's call for 'democratic law' (*dan chu phap tri*), 'collective development' (*cong dong dong tien*), and 'social justice' (*cong binh xa*) in the countryside, and represented the new social values in action, outlining the rights and responsibilities of hamlet residents.[56] One point often emphasized in regard to residents' rights was the need to stop local abuses of power, especially the arbitrary arrest and imprisonment of political suspects; several officials had warned the regime that local misrule, and the failure to discriminate between NLF adherents and former members of the Viet Minh, fuelled the insurgency. The regime seemed at last to have taken some of this seriously. As with his support for elections, Nhu ignored criticism that introducing new laws might be disruptive of security in a time of war. The regime was bringing security to the countryside *in order to* apply the law there. Communal rules aimed at guaranteeing a democratic regime at the grassroots level, he argued, not in chaining the people.[57]

Besides unleashing and energizing the population, Saigon also expected these laws and elections to help eliminate the influence of those groups it viewed as obstacles to revolutionary change. The chief targets were the existing rural and urban élites, regarded by the Ngos as the backward remnants of feudalism and colonialism. The regime's disdain for the French-trained metropolitan elite was long-standing, and partly reflected in its reluctance to share power with anyone outside its inner circle. The Ngos viewed this class, with its colonial associations, as a self-interested and unpatriotic fifth column, ready to sell out its country to the Americans as it had once done to the French.[58] Although the strategic hamlet programme focused primarily on the countryside, the regime envisaged that it would also cleanse the body politic of this colonial residue, as the political revolution swept into the upper reaches of the system. The regime never fully spelled out the mechanism for achieving this change, but apparently envisaged the gradual extension of elections to progressively higher administrative levels. 'Starting from the hamlets,' an official description of the programme proclaimed, 'the movement must necessarily reshape the entire superstructure.'[59]

As the key battleground was in the countryside, however, Saigon concentrated its attention on rural politics. Until the hamlet programme, the regime largely confined its criticism of local administration to occasional campaigns against corruption, but in a speech to the Saigon Lions Club in May 1962, Luong went further. He publicly admitted that the regime made a mistake after 1954 in preserving the position of the existing rural élite merely because it possessed administrative experience. The regime should have followed the example of the Communists in creating a new class of cadres, free of old feudal and colonial attitudes.[60] Nhu repeated these points at inter-ministerial committee meetings, his numerous talks with officials, and encounters with foreign diplomats. During a discussion with a British embassy official in January 1962, Nhu attacked village elders and local notables, whose anti-Communism, he claimed, stemmed only from the desire to maintain their local power and privileges.[61]

There were significant drawbacks in attacking such figures, as well as the French-trained élite manning the government's offices; after all, the regime depended on these people to implement its policies. Nhu noted this problem in a discussion with US officials in September 1962.[62] Perhaps this concern accounts partly for the difficulty experienced by RVN officials in fully comprehending Nhu's turgid explanations of the hamlet programme's purpose: 'They couldn't figure [out] what the hell he was talking about,' Colby recalled of the meetings between Nhu and the programme's administrators. 'He wasn't that clear—let's face it—because what he was really saying underneath is, 'We're going to replace all you guys."'[63]

If this housecleaning represented the ultimate political goal, it also promised to lay the foundations for the fourth and final pillar of the regime's revolution: economic change. At the beginning of the hamlet programme, this issue received much less attention than the scheme's military, social, and political aspects. Although there were certain elements within the regime that hoped from the outset to incorporate the provision of schools, hospitals, and other amenities into the construction of strategic hamlets,[64] Nhu believed that there could be no economic development without first establishing security in the countryside. He argued, moreover, that, until the social and political revolutions gathered momentum, improved local amenities would principally benefit the rich, who were in a better position to take advantage of them.[65] Thus, the regime subordinated its economic concerns until late 1962, when the hamlet programme was well under way.[66]

For Nhu, economic development was intimately related to the regime's social and political revolutions. Talking to government cadres in mid-1963, he referred to Walt Rostow's stages of economic growth and the need to put an end to 'traditional society' before being able to proceed to the point of economic 'take-off'. The government, he observed, must free people from the bonds of the *ancien régime* and instil in them a revolutionary spirit. Without the individual and collective liberation essential to build an industrial society, South Vietnam would remain a terminally ill patient, kept alive only by the drip feed of foreign aid.[67]

This concept strongly influenced Nhu's attitude towards government or foreign economic support of strategic hamlets. To lavish aid on the peasantry, in his view, would undermine the spirit of self-reliance necessary for the promotion of economic progress in an under-developed country; hamlet residents must bear the primary responsibility for developing their economic life, just as they bore the major burden for the defence of their homes. At a ceremony to inaugurate a new strategic hamlet, for example, a delegation of village elders asked Nhu for assistance in building a school. He refused: 'The government's means are stretched now to their limit. Do not rely on outside aid. First build a revolution within yourself. Then build the school with your own hands.' Nhu parried the protests of the Americans in attendance, who tended to see the hamlet programme as a way for the government to extend a helping hand to peasants: 'You do not understand these villagers. Satisfy one demand and they would return with ten more.'[68]

Nhu preferred small economic projects, such as the development of local cottage industries; endeavours that required minimal outside support, could be sustained without continued government backing, and might generate income to pay for hamlet and village administration. Such considerations underlay the regime's agreement with the Americans to provide hamlets with 20,000 piastres (about $300) for small-scale local initiatives.[69] As well as encouraging self-sufficiency, the regime believed such projects would school peasants in the rights and responsibilities of local democracy. Saigon intended residents to choose, debate, and then vote on 'self-help' projects before they could be undertaken: this programme 'not only permits the rural population to raise its voice in matters affecting the local welfare, but it also draws the people into the processes of self-government, and gives them a personal stake in the future of their country.'[70]

What, finally, was 'the future of their country' that this multifaceted revolution – military, social, political, and economic – was to bring about? To the Ngos, the strategic hamlet programme represented an authentic national revolution, which drew upon the vitality of the village in Vietnamese life. The villages, as Nhu argued in his excursions into history, were the source of the country's strength, the guardians of its national spirit. That vitality, in turn, was the product of their unique place in the traditional administrative system. As a government publication explained, in the past Vietnamese society was composed of two ostensibly opposing systems: a centralized monarchy and 'a popular, autonomous and representative democracy' in the countryside. The two coexisted because of the limits of imperial power embodied in the adage 'the laws of the emperor bow before the customs of the village' (*phep vua thua le lang*); 'therefore, the Vietnamese nation was like a federation composed of numerous and small communal states in a superstate.'[71] The hamlet programme hoped to tap into the latent energy that was believed to exist in these robust corporate communities and, through the development of local self-rule and self-sufficiency, create a modern version of this traditional Vietnamese democracy.[72]

The Ngos had harboured an interest in this sort of modernization at least since their accession to power. Shortly before returning to Vietnam in 1954 from a self-imposed exile abroad, for example, Diem wrote an article analysing the potential for Vietnamese traditions to be updated into a more modem democratic form.[73] This interest in tradition strengthened the critics' view of Diem as the backward-looking 'last of the mandarins'. Diem, however, regarded history as a source of strength and inspiration, not something to be recreated. There was also a notable ambivalence in the Ngos' attitude towards the past. While the regime praised certain aspects of Vietnamese history, it simultaneously tried to rid the country of other vestiges of the feudal and colonial orders. Diem told the journalist Marguerite Higgins: 'We are not going to go back to a sterile copy of the mandarin past. But we are going to adapt the best of our heritage to the modern situation.'[74]

Strategic hamlets represented the regime's fullest expression of this thinking, although it never painted a detailed picture of the proposed new Vietnam. Certainly, the Ngos contemplated a major renovation of the state, which would affect their own political future as well. While he would not be the first ruler in history to do so, Nhu stated that the regime's revolution was effectively 'working for [the] destruction of my family'. He even told an astonished Mieczyslaw Maneli, a Polish delegate to the International Control Commission, that strategic hamlets 'will become the real nucleus of national organization, and then the state itself – as Marx said – will wither away'.[75] The regime harboured equally ambitious notions about its proposed revolution's role in the process of national reunification. Confronted by the success of the south's democratic modernization, Ho Chi Minh's government in the north would be forced to tighten its grip over an increasingly disgruntled population, and through a process of 'attraction', Diem asserted, 'the North Vietnamese regime will disintegrate'.[76]

So impressed was the Diem regime with its concept of a rural-based revolution that it even believed the approach possessed a wider applicability beyond the frontiers of Vietnam. According to the Ngos, newly independent states faced two equally unappetizing routes to development: Western-style democracy, or dictatorship. The former initially attracted many nationalist leaders but proved a recipe for chaos and disorder, given the social divisions bequeathed by colonialism. The latter brought order but at the expense of freedom. 'Taken in their extremes,' noted the *Times of Viet Nam Magazine*, "these trends would lead to anarchy on the one hand and to a monolithic totalitarianism on the other.' Strategic hamlets, however, by simultaneously promoting democratic decentralization, fostering independent rural communities, and building a strong and united nation state, seemed to solve this dilemma. The programme, Nhu contended, provided the under-developed world with a strategy for development, and the Free World a solution to the problem of Communist guerrilla warfare.[77]

Such pronouncements appear surreal in light of the Diem regime's disintegration in 1963. The publicly articulated theory of the strategic hamlet programme did not match the reality of its progress in the countryside. Communist tracts frequently denounced strategic hamlets as disguised prisons or concentration camps.[78] While suitably overblown for propaganda purposes, this description was probably closer to the mark than the regime's illusions of popular mobilization. Tran Van Giau, a historian and veteran party activist, even argued that the broadly expressed objectives of strategic hamlets were only a cover for a much narrower military goal: the elimination of the NLF's armed forces.[79] This latter charge, however, is wide of the mark. The chasm between the theory and practice of the hamlet programme was a problem of translating the regime's ideas into reality, not the result of a hidden agenda. While material signs of the programme sprang up all over the countryside, the regime found it much more difficult to generate popular enthusiasm for it.

Three principal problems plagued the scheme's execution.[80] First, the regime set an unrealistic pace for hamlet construction. Nhu originally proposed to complete all sixteen thousand of the south's hamlets within twelve months. While the programme's progress in 1962 exposed this wild optimism, the regime's emphasis on speed overwhelmed its provincial subordinates and inevitably led to the sacrifice of quality for quantity. Second, the regime's ambitious schedule not only outstripped provincial resources but also encouraged the authoritarian inclinations of local officials. To try to satisfy their superiors' unreasonable demands, provincial officials coerced the rural population into providing the money and manpower to complete the physical requirements of the programme. As a result, peasants became passive instruments in the mere fortification of hamlets, rather than active participants in a popular revolution.

Finally, the programme ran headlong into opposition from peasants and resistance from the NLF. Notwithstanding the coercion that came to characterize strategic hamlets, the fundamental problem with the regime's ideas about mobilizing peasants was the exaggerated expectations of the enterprise's potential. The regime expected its officials to march into the villages, raise the banner of the Republic and, in the four or five weeks it would theoretically take to establish a strategic hamlet, plant the seeds of a rural revolution. Unlike the slow and painstaking way in which the insurgents built up their organization, the regime expected to spark support almost spontaneously with broad appeals to the value of strategic hamlets and the Personalist revolution. Above all, the Ngos placed their faith in revitalizing a supposedly pre-existing communal solidarity among peasants that was not, in fact, characteristic of the south's rural population. An absence of a co-operative spirit was particularly marked in the strategically vital Mekong Delta, where the widely dispersed pattern of settlement discouraged the corporate solidarity evident in other parts of the country.[81] The regime, in short, misunderstood peasants and the nature of rural life.

Like other South-East Asian élites, the Ngos held a nostalgic vision of peasant life, of a time when primeval village democracies dotted the landscape, isolated behind their bamboo hedges.

However, as Jan Breman explains, the image of the corporate peasant community in Asia is a myth, first derived from colonial stereotypes but then also 'doggedly maintained' by the newly independent nation states of South and South-East Asia: 'The understandable wish to denounce the injurious effects of colonial rule gave the vanguard of the nationalist movement good reason to hark back to a supposedly better past.'[82] Yet, in seeking to revitalize and update this image of rural life, the Ngos adopted a fatally flawed version of the past. By placing its faith in the communal feelings supposedly residing in the hamlets and villages, the Diem regime demonstrated an important reason why it failed to compete successfully with the Communists. The patient organizational methods of the insurgents more effectively mobilized support among the rural population than the regime's grand scheme.

Even so, the ideas outlined by the Ngos for the strategic hamlet programme deserve attention. The stress laid by the regime on self-sufficiency and national independence contrasts starkly with the picture of Diem as a tool of the Americans, regularly painted in Communist commentaries on the war. Moreover, Diem's portrayal in most Western accounts as recalcitrant and backward-looking is at odds with the notions of popular mobilization, political change, and the construction of a modern state that underlay the hamlet programme. Perhaps historians have all too often preferred to read history backwards, inferring from their eventual triumph that the Communists were the only serious contenders for Vietnamese leadership with any coherent political vision. This problem has been compounded by the usual focus on the US side of the war, which obscures the motives of the Diem regime and falls back on the familiar image of the mandarin despot. The ideas behind the hamlet programme, however, suggest that these views need to be revised.

Through the hamlet programme in particular, the Ngos presented an alternative vision of a post-colonial state. Consequently, an examination of the hamlet scheme suggests that we need to be more careful about the way we characterize the war in Vietnam. The conflict was not one between the nationalists in Hanoi and the puppets in Saigon, or between the modern nationalists in the north and the mandarin patriots in the south; the struggle was between different brands of modern Vietnamese nationalism. At the same time, however, the failure of strategic hamlets demonstrates the Diem regime's inability to realize its vision of a modern Vietnam, Hence, an appreciation of the ideas of the Ngos can lead to a more sophisticated understanding of why their non-Communist agenda and brand of nationalism was unsuccessful. That its best-laid plans should fail so miserably says much about the underlying organizational and conceptual weaknesses of the Saigon regime, the corresponding strengths of its Communist opponents, and the nature and broader patterns of the war in Vietnam.

16

The Foreign Policy of North Vietnam

William J. Duiker

WHY DID THE COMMUNISTS WIN THE VIETNAM WAR? That question has tormented many Americans—and undoubtedly many Vietnamese as well—for over a quarter of a century. As a general rule, the answer usually has focused on the alleged mistakes committed by U.S. policymakers in prosecuting the war, such as a lack of political will or a faulty military strategy. It is past time to recognize that, whatever the errors committed in Washington or Saigon, the communist victory in Vietnam was a stunning achievement and a testimony to the strategic and tactical genius of the war planners of the Hanoi regime (formally known as the Democratic Republic of Vietnam, or DRV) as well as to the patience and self-sacrifice of millions of their followers throughout the country.

There are undoubtedly a number of explanations for the outcome of the war. Some are rooted in Vietnamese history and culture, while others are more subjective in nature, among which were the superior organizational ability of the communist leadership, its imaginative program and strategy, and the charismatic quality of the revolutionary movement's great leader, Ho Chi Minh. Yet there is little doubt that Hanoi's ability to manipulate the international and diplomatic environment to its own advantage was a key factor in its success. For two decades, North Vietnamese leaders were able to maneuver successfully through the shoals of a complex international situation—including a bitter dispute between their two major allies and a worldwide diplomatic offensive by the United States—in such a manner as to outwit their adversaries, win the often-reluctant support of their squabbling allies, and earn the sympathy and support of peoples on continents throughout the world.

How could a government that for many years was virtually isolated from the international community (and even in the mid-1960s possessed only limited experience in the diplomatic arena) manage to outwit and outmaneuver the statesmen who enacted official policy in the great capital cities of the world? As with so many aspects of the Vietnam conflict, the explanation must be sought in events that took place long before the first U.S. combat troops landed on Vietnamese soil in the spring of 1965. The diplomatic strategy that was applied by DRV leaders during the Vietnam War had been devised over an extended period of time that dates back to the first stages of the Indochina conflict before the end of World War II. Only by studying the experience of Ho Chi Minh and his colleagues during and immediately after the Pacific war will we be able to understand how and why they applied the lessons of that experience with such success in the decades that followed.

Seeking the Moment of Opportunity

Up until the beginning of the Pacific war, the Vietnamese revolution had been only marginally affected by the international situation. It was not, however, for lack of trying. Early in the twentieth century, shortly after the consolidation of French colonial authority throughout Indochina, anticolonialist firebrands had turned their eyes to Japan in the hope that the imperial government in Tokyo, which had just won a stunning victory over tsarist Russia at Port Arthur, would provide assistance to emerging nationalist movements in Southeast Asia. After that gambit failed, their attention rapidly shifted to China, where in 1911 revolutionary forces under Sun Yat-sen had brought about the collapse of the decrepit Manchu empire. Those hopes, too, proved abortive when Sun's party was forced to cede power to the warlord general Yuan Shikai. But Vietnamese nationalists, perhaps influenced by the long tributary relationship between the two countries, did not despair of future Chinese support, and during the next few years hundreds of Vietnamese revolutionary activists fled across the northern border to seek Chinese assistance in the liberation of their country from foreign rule.[1]

The fascination of early Vietnamese nationalists with the chimera of foreign assistance was carried on after the formation of the Vietnamese Communist Party in 1930. The founder of the organization, Ho Chi Minh, had become convinced as a young man that his country could be liberated from the clutches of French imperialism only with help from abroad. Shortly after settling in Paris at the end of World War I, he became attracted to the ideas of the Bolshevik leader Vladimir Lenin, whose revolutionary program envisaged a global revolt by the oppressed peoples of the world against their colonial masters. After joining the French Communist Party in 1920, Ho received training as a communist agent in Moscow, and then went on to South China, where he established the Revolutionary Youth League, the first Marxist-Leninist revolutionary organization in colonial Indochina. Five years later it was transformed into the Indochinese Communist Party (ICP). But although the new party received training and other forms of assistance from local members of the Chinese Communist Party (CCP), the relationship was short-lived. When in the late 1920s CCP activities were suppressed by the Nationalist government of Chiang Kai-shek, ICP units operating in South China were forced into hiding. For the next decade, the Vietnamese revolutionary movement was essentially isolated from the outside world and reduced to a sheer struggle for survival.[2]

The coming of World War II, however, brought help from an unexpected source when, in the fall of 1940, Japanese military forces occupied Indochina in preparation for a future advance throughout Southeast Asia. Although the French colonial administration, which had just fallen under the control of the pro-Axis Vichy French, was left in place, French authority was significantly weakened, thus providing ICP leaders with the opportunity to build up their forces for an uprising to evict the French after the end of the Pacific war.

Ho Chi Minh, who had sharpened his understanding of international politics during nearly two decades as an agent of Lenin's revolutionary outreach organization, the Communist International, was well aware that his party's grasp for power would face better odds for success if it had support and recognition from the international community. Unfortunately, he could expect little help from the Soviet Union, since Moscow's interest in the Vietnamese revolution was obviously minimal. But if the wartime "Grand Alliance" that had been established among the Soviet Union, the United States, and other antifascist countries could be exploited, broad public support from the United States—and perhaps from Nationalist China and other allied countries as well—might be expected for the liberation of his country from French colonial rule after the expected Allied victory. Ho had carefully noted public remarks by U.S. President Franklin D. Roosevelt that the French should not be permitted to return to Indochina after the end of the Pacific war.

Recognition of the revolutionary movement as the legitimate voice of Vietnamese national aspirations by the victorious Allies—and by moderate elements within Vietnamese society itself—could be anticipated, however, only if the communist character of its leadership was carefully disguised. As a consequence, in the spring of 1941 Ho had set the stage by forming a broad multiparty alliance called the League for the Independence of Vietnam, popularly known as the Vietminh Front. The ICP was listed as a component of the front, but its leading role in the organization was not generally known. Ho Chi Minh then set out to win recognition and support for the movement from the Nationalist government in China and from the United States.

Ho's initial attempts to link the Vietminh Front with the Allied cause were derailed in August 1942, when he was arrested by Chinese authorities under suspicion of being a Japanese agent. But after his release a year later he resumed his efforts, and during the last months of the war he was able to establish an amicable working relationship with Chinese Nationalist commanders in South China as well as with U.S. military intelligence operatives in the area, who agreed to provide the Vietminh with limited technical assistance in return for their cooperation in providing intelligence information on Indochina to the Allies.[3]

At the end of the war, Vietminh forces occupied Hanoi and Ho Chi Minh declared the formation of a new independent republic, with himself as provisional president. But he was less successful in seeking international recognition for his new government as the legitimate representative of the Vietnamese people. Despite his tireless efforts to portray himself as a moderate nationalist and a fervent admirer of American democratic principles (primed with his offers for possible future U.S. economic and military concessions in the DRV), Ho's letters to Roosevelt's successor, Harry S. Truman, went unanswered. Similar appeals to London and Moscow also went without response.[4]

Opportunity Lost?

In later years, Ho Chi Minh's appeal for support from the United States was cited by many observers as a lost opportunity for Washington to woo him from his allegiance to Moscow and transform him into an "Asian Tito." In retrospect, the Truman administration might indeed have been advised to test the willingness of the new Vietnamese state to embark on an independent course in world affairs. At that time, it had few true friends in the international arena and might have been sorely tempted to tailor its policies to those of any generous benefactor. On the other hand, there are ample grounds for skepticism that Ho Chi Minh (who was quite adept at flattering would-be allies or adversaries) was entirely sincere in his overtures to the United States. As a longtime practitioner of the Leninist strategy of the united front, Ho was quite willing to make tactical alliances with potential adversaries in the full understanding that such arrangements might be only temporary in character.

Ho Chi Minh's actual motives in seeking U.S. support were perhaps best disclosed in a speech on the international political environment that he presented to colleagues at the close of the Pacific war. In comments remarkable for their prescience, Ho analyzed the fluidity of the postwar international situation as well as the contradictions that might be turned to the advantage of the new Vietnamese government. If the wartime alliance between Moscow and Washington survived into the postwar era, he noted, the United States (and Nationalist China as well) might decide to oppose the European colonial powers and throw its support to the cause of Vietnamese independence. But if tensions erupted between the United States and the Soviet Union, the former probably would decide to support the French in Indochina in order to prevent the spread of communism in Asia. To limit the impact of such a possible contingency, which would virtually isolate the new Vietnamese state on the world's stage, Ho stressed the importance of placating the Americans and the Chinese as much as possible in order to use them against the French.[5]

Ho Chi Minh thus appeared to have little confidence that the anticolonialist sentiments expressed by President Roosevelt during World War II would continue into the postwar era, when the fundamentally imperialist nature of U.S. foreign policy would presumably be reasserted. Ho hinted as much in a letter that he wrote to Charles Fenn, a U.S. military intelligence officer whom he had met in South China earlier in 1945. "The war is finished," he remarked, but the upcoming departure of the Americans from the region "means that relations between you and us will be more difficult." In the end, he predicted, the Vietnamese would have to fight in order to earn their share in "the victory of freedom and democracy."[6]

As it turned out, Ho Chi Minh's attempt to apply the tactics of the united front on the world stage had only limited success. As tensions between Moscow and Washington increased in Europe, the Truman administration (as he had feared) reluctantly decided to support the restoration of French sovereignty in Indochina. The Nationalist government in China was still hoping to force the French out of Southeast Asia, but—like Washington—it was suspicious of Ho's communist leanings and, through the actions of its military representatives in northern Indochina, lent its support to his non-communist rivals. The Soviet Union, the ICP's natural ally, was of no use at all, as Soviet leader Joseph Stalin, like Harry Truman, hoped to curry favor with Paris, where upcoming national elections might bring the communists to power in France.

By midsummer of 1946, Ho Chi Minh's worst premonitions had become reality. During peace talks at Fontainebleau, French representatives rejected his proposal for a compromise solution to the Indochina dispute. Lacking any visible support on the international scene, Ho reluctantly signed a modus vivendi to postpone additional peace talks until the following year, but the move was primarily tactical in nature, as he and his colleagues sought to buy time in order to make preparations for war.

Lean to One Side

When Vietminh forces launched their surprise attack on French installations in North Vietnam on December 19, 1946, the first Indochinese war got under way. Ho Chi Minh did not despair of an eventual negotiated settlement, and in the early months of 1947 he sent out diplomatic feelers to Paris suggesting a resumption of peace talks. When they were rejected, the DRV sent covert signals to Washington stressing the moderation of its domestic and foreign policy objectives. But the Truman administration was increasingly suspicious of the communist leanings of the Vietminh, and it too ignored the overtures.[7]

For the time being, then, the Vietminh were forced to fight alone. In Moscow, Joseph Stalin was suspicious of Ho Chi Minh's ideological orthodoxy and virtually ignored the spreading conflict in far-off Southeast Asia. The DRV's most promising potential source of support was the Communist Party in China, many of whose leaders had become acquainted with Ho during the 1920s and watched the Vietnamese revolution with sympathetic eyes. But the CCP headquarters was now based in North China, where it was mired in its own civil war with Chiang Kai-shek's Nationalist government. A few communist military units—popularly known as the People's Liberation Army (PLA)—were based in the southern provinces and gave some secret assistance to Vietminh forces operating in the vicinity of the frontier.

With its peace feelers rejected, Vietminh war planners lacked an alternative and turned to a policy of self-reliance, based on the Maoist strategy of protracted war. Their hope was to build up the political and military strength of the movement in preparation for an eventual general offensive to drive the enemy into the sea. A description of Vietminh strategy written at the time by ICP General Secretary Truong Chinh made only a brief reference to the possibility of a diplomatic solution, noting that "false negotiations" might be used to distract the enemy and undermine French morale.[8]

By the end of the 1940s, however, the situation changed dramatically, as the communist victory in the Chinese civil war brought a potentially powerful ally to the very northern border of Indochina and provided the Vietminh, for the first time, with a clear prospect of outside assistance. But there was a price to pay for the new relationship. Whereas in the past Vietminh leaders had deliberately downplayed their ties with socialist countries in a bid to win the support of moderates at home and abroad, the new government in Beijing now demanded that they publicly avow their allegiance to the principles of Marxism-Leninism in return for diplomatic recognition and military assistance. Recognition from the Soviet Union followed shortly after, but Moscow established a clear division of labor in carrying out socialist bloc assistance to the DRV, as Stalin assigned primary responsibility for the task to China. Vietnamese leaders were quick to return the favor. In succeeding months, Vietminh news sources publicized the new relationship with China and declared that they would formulate their war strategy and their approach to nation-building on the Chinese model.[9]

The new posture was a gamble, for in drawing closer to the nations of the socialist camp, the DRV ran the risk of drawing the United States into the war on the side of the French. As the prospects for victory in Indochina seemed steadily to recede, Paris began to seek U.S. military assistance, and in March 1949 it had created an autonomous government in Vietnam under the titular rule of former emperor Bao Dai in a bid to win support from Washington. The Truman administration, which remained distrustful of French intentions in Indochina, placed stringent political and military conditions on any prospective aid agreement. But the communist victory in China later that year inflamed anticommunist sentiment in the United States, and with the DRV now moving steadily into the socialist camp, pressure increased on the White House to enter the lists on the side of the French. Within days of Moscow's recognition of the DRV, Washington announced formal ties with the new Bao Dai government. Economic and military assistance, to be channeled through the French, soon followed.

With its decision to identify more closely with the Sino-Soviet bloc, the DRV was for the first time positioned directly on the global ideological divide. Vietnam's new prominence as a major factor in the Cold War had been signaled in a speech by Chinese Premier Liu Shaoqi in December 1949, when he declared that the new China would give its firm support to struggles for national liberation elsewhere in Asia and specifically referred to the one in Indochina. In all likelihood, Liu's comments were greeted with some discomfort by Ho Chi Minh, who for years had tried to avoid identifying his movement directly with the socialist bloc not only in the hope of maximizing its internal appeal, but also in the hope of preventing U.S. intervention. However, the hardening of ideological position of the Cold War and the obvious lure of Chinese aid had been impossible to resist.

It did not take long for the new strategy to bear fruit. In a dramatic battle in the fall of 1950, Vietminh forces defeated French units along the Sino-Vietnamese border and thus opened up the entire border area to Chinese assistance. With the help of Chinese advisors, Vietminh units gradually improved their performance on the battlefield, and in 1951 the high command ordered a major offensive on French-held territories on the fringes of the Red River delta. But for once Ho Chi Minh had overreached, and the Vietminh attacks were driven back with high casualties.

The results of the 1951 campaign sobered Ho's war planners, who were now forced to realize that massive frontal attacks had only minimal success in the face of the enemy's superior firepower. In succeeding years they adopted a more cautious strategy in the hope of dividing the enemy's forces and undermining morale in France, where discontent with the course of the war in Indochina was on the rise. In neighboring Laos and Cambodia, where autonomous royal governments had just been established by the French, ICP leaders sponsored the formation of new revolutionary movements (popularly known as the Pathet Lao and the Khmer Rouge respectively) to operate under Vietminh tutelage. Vietnamese strategists now became increasingly aware of the benefits of waging a protracted war to wear down a more powerful enemy.

In later years, Vietminh commanders would learn how to combine battlefield successes with diplomatic overtures designed to win friends and influence adversaries. Now, however, isolated in their mountain fastness and perhaps temporarily giddy over the prospects for a total victory, they made little use of the weapon of diplomacy as a means of influencing public opinion. When asked by the occasional visiting journalist about the possibility of a negotiated settlement, Vietminh sources consistently downplayed the prospects for peace talks and insisted that the war could come to an end only with a complete victory on the battlefield. Even Ho Chi Minh appeared to believe in the prospects for a total military victory, declaring to one visiting French communist that the DRV was willing to enter peace talks but would make no major concessions.[10]

Devil's Bargain

But the Vietminh were about to be presented with the bill for the Faustian arrangement they had entered into three years earlier. With Indochina now squarely placed within the socialist camp, the DRV was now increasingly vulnerable to the blandishments of its major allies. At first, China had provided active support and encouragement to the Vietminh in the belief that a direct confrontation with the United States in East Asia was sooner or later inevitable. But by the fall of 1953, Beijing had learned the high costs of its own military intervention in Korea and sought a negotiated settlement in Indochina in order to reduce military expenditures and channel scarce resources into domestic projects. In Moscow, a new post-Stalin leadership under Georgyi Malenkov was determined to follow a similar path. With the Indochina conflict at a virtual stalemate on the battlefield, Moscow and Beijing saw few advantages in extending the war and began to pressure the DRV to accept a compromise settlement that could bring an end to the hostilities before they escalated into a global confutation among the major powers.

DRV leaders were initially skeptical. In a speech to intellectuals about the cease-fire reached on the Korean peninsula in July, Ho Chi Minh warned his audience that they should harbor no illusions about the immediate prospects for a satisfactory peace settlement in Indochina. The French must be thoroughly defeated, he declared, so that they would meet Vietnamese conditions and withdraw. Yet Ho always was careful to avoid alienating potential benefactors, and in a lengthy interview with a Swedish reporter in October, he expressed a cautious willingness to listen to French proposals for the restoration of peace in Indochina, although he warned his colleagues in a speech shortly after that conditions were not yet entirely favorable for a settlement.[11]

Moscow and Beijing quickly followed up on Ho Chi Minh's remarks, and in January 1954 plans were launched to hold multilateral talks on the Indochina question at a peace conference to convene in Geneva in May. When Ho visited Moscow and Beijing in April to formulate a common negotiating strategy, he was advised by his hosts to be realistic and flexible in his demands. To sweeten the pot for their Vietnamese allies, Chinese leaders promised to increase the level of their military assistance to Vietminh forces to help bring about a major victory on the battlefield and thus strengthen the DRV's position at the conference cable. The focus of that effort was to take place at the border post at Dien Bien Phu, recently occupied by French forces to hinder the movement of Vietminh units into neighboring Laos.

At Geneva, Chinese and Soviet delegates publicly supported Vietminh demands for the complete withdrawal of French forces and the total independence of all three Indochinese states. But privately they urged their allies to compromise on key issues. At a short meeting with Chinese Foreign Minister Zhou Enlai at Liuzhou in early July, Ho Chi Minh reluctantly agreed on a peace settlement that would call for the temporary division of Vietnam into two separate regroupment zones and a recognition of the royal governments in Laos and Cambodia as the legitimate authorities of two neutral and independent states. In return, Zhou promised that Chinese aid to the DRV would be increased, and he assured Ho that unification surely would come about within a few years. Some of Ho's colleagues were angry at his decision to bow to Chinese advice (Pham Van Dong, the chief DRV negotiator at Geneva, had to be ordered to accept the agreement by the party politburo), but eventually Ho had his way.[12]

What did DRV leaders learn from their experience at Geneva? There was certainly some bitterness in Vietminh circles, particularly among those fighting in the South, that Vietnamese national interests had been betrayed by their allies. But Ho Chi Minh, despite his own evident reluctance to accept a compromise peace, recognized the logic of Zhou Enlai's advice, and at a meeting of the Vietnam Workers' Party (VWP) Central Committee in July, he warned that "some comrades" did not see the United States behind the French. Still, it took all of Ho's persuasive efforts to convince his colleagues that they needed strong and powerful allies and that without a peace settlement in Indochina, the United States would inevitably intervene. In the end, Ho had his way, but the legacy of the Geneva agreement hovered like a shadow over the later history of the Vietnamese revolution and undoubtedly heightened the reluctance of many party leaders to make compromises as they pursued their goal of national reunification.[13]

Disillusionment

A political declaration drawn up at the Geneva Conference had called for national elections to unite the two regroupment zones two years after the close of the conference. The document had not taken the form of a binding commitment on the administrative authorities in each zone, however, but was merely a statement of intent, approved by a verbal agreement among delegations at the conference. Even then representatives of the United States and the Bao Dai government—now to serve as the governing authority in the South—had refused to give their assent. Washington's refusal to commit itself to the provisions of the Geneva agreement undoubtedly worried many of Ho's supporters (Pham Van Dong was quoted as remarking "You know as well as I do that the elections will never take place"). But Ho Chi Minh, placing his confidence in Zhou Enlai's pledge of support in July, expressed optimism that a political solution ultimately would be found. In preparation for such a contingency, the DRV leadership, which had returned to Hanoi in October, left a small infrastructure of supporters in the South to promote national elections. In case elections were not held, these followers would provide the nucleus for a return to armed struggle.

By the summer of 1955, any optimism in Hanoi that pressure from Moscow and Beijing would help to bring about national reunification had dissipated. That spring the prime minister of Bao Dai's government in Saigon—the veteran Catholic politician Ngo Dinh Diem—had announced that he had no intention of holding consultations with representatives from the North on possible future elections. The Eisenhower administration was uneasily aware that Diem's adamant refusal to hold elections contravened the spirit of the Geneva agreement, but, fearing that Ho's popularity would tilt the results of such elections in Hanoi's favor, it was no less anxious to avoid them, and eventually the White House decided to back Saigon in its decision. Diem now proceeded with plans to form an independent state, known as the Republic of Vietnam (RVN), in the South.

Diem's rebuff of Hanoi's offer of consultations, combined with his government's vigorous efforts to suppress all opposition to his rule in South Vietnam, aroused considerable anger in the North, especially among those southerners (variously estimated at 70,000 to 80,000 in number) who had been sent north after the cease-fire as part of the exchange of refugees called for by the accords. For many party leaders, still bitter at the compromises imposed on them at Geneva, Diem's action was no surprise, and preparations were intensified to expose many of these "regroupees" (as the refugees from the South were named) to training in agitprop activity and guerrilla war, in the event that renewed hostilities broke out in the near future. But Ho Chi Minh did not yet despair of a political solution and urged his colleagues to use diplomatic means to turn the new situation to their advantage. To split Paris from Washington, the DRV offered cultural and economic concessions in the North to the French. Then Ho embarked on a trip to Moscow and Beijing to seek bloc support for a demand to reconvene the Geneva conference. But Chinese and Soviet leaders continued to seek a reduction in Cold War tensions and gave only lukewarm support to the Vietnamese appeal. In a public speech on his return to Hanoi, Ho thanked Moscow and Beijing for their support but warned his audience that reunification would come about only through a policy of self-reliance.[14]

Indeed, the new situation presented Hanoi with a knotty dilemma. Discontent within the ranks over the situation in the South needed to be dealt with, but several factors militated against the adoption of a more aggressive policy designed to bring about reunification by forceful means. In the first place, living conditions in the North were depressed, and the national economy badly needed an infusion of foreign capital and technology to lay the foundation for a modern industrial society. At the same time, the North Vietnamese armed forces needed to be modernized to prepare for a possible future confrontation with the Diem regime in South Vietnam. Under the circumstances, a policy of caution appeared in order. In a public letter to the Vietnamese people, Ho Chi Minh promised eventual victory, but only after the DRV had built a strong foundation.

In the meantime, party leaders began to intensify their lobbying efforts to win the support of Hanoi's allies for a future advance toward national reunification. At international conferences held in the Soviet Union and Eastern Europe during the late 1950s, Vietnamese delegates publicly praised the new Soviet policy of "peaceful coexistence" but privately argued that a policy of revolutionary violence might be required in societies where the imperialists refused to concede power in a peaceful manner. But to the anger and frustration of militant elements in Hanoi, Moscow continued to turn a deaf ear to their appeal. Vietnamese pleas for support encountered a more receptive hearing in Beijing, which in 1958 had begun to enter a more radical phase in its foreign as well as in its domestic policy. Still, Chinese leaders were equally reluctant to sanction a strategy that could lead to a Cold War crisis in Indochina, and urged Vietnamese comrades to be patient in pursuing their goal of national reunification.[15]

Call to Action

By the end of the 1950s, pressure was building among Vietminh sympathizers in the South for a more aggressive posture in defending the revolution. The Diem government in Saigon had intensified its efforts to suppress all opposition, and thousands of southerners who were suspected of allegiance to Hanoi were convicted at drumhead tribunals throughout the country and imprisoned or executed. Although Hanoi had authorized its local operatives in South Vietnam to build up their self-defense forces, in some areas the movement was at skeleton strength or had been virtually wiped out. In January 1959 the issue was raised for discussion by the party Central Committee (in 1951 the ICP was renamed the Vietnam Workers' Party [VWP]). Some VWP leaders were opposed to action, not only because it would irritate Hanoi's chief allies, but also on the grounds that the North had just begun its march to socialism with a three-year program to launch the collectivization of agriculture throughout the countryside. Ho Chi Minh advised caution in order to avoid provoking the United States. But Le Duan, a figure of increasing prominence in Hanoi and soon to be named VWP first secretary, had just completed a secret inspection visit to the South and argued strongly for action. In the end party leaders reached a compromise, approving a resumption of revolutionary war in the South, but with the degree of political and military struggle to be applied left unresolved.[16]

After the conference adjourned, Ho Chi Minh left Hanoi on a mission to Beijing and Moscow to explain the decision and plead for bloc support. Bur despite his formidable diplomatic skills, the reaction of Soviet and Chinese leaders was disappointing. Moscow was noncommittal, and Chinese leaders, although sympathetic, were cautious. Conditions in Indochina and around the world, Mao Zedong warned his guest, were not yet ripe. Indeed, it might take up to 100 years to bring about Vietnamese national reunification. It was hardly a message that Ho's more zealous colleagues in Hanoi wished to hear.[17]

One powerful motive for a policy of caution, of course, was the need to determine the attitude of the United States. After the Geneva Conference of 1954, the Eisenhower administration had given its firm support to the government of Ngo Dinh Diem, and Diem was invited to Washington, D.C., on a formal state visit in 1957. At that time, conditions in the RVN appeared stable, inspiring some enthusiastic U.S. commentators to remark that Diem was America's answer to Ho Chi Minh. By the end of the decade, however, such pronouncements rang hollow, as the increasing effectiveness of anti-Diem forces (popularly known in the West as the Viet Cong, or Vietnamese Communists), combined with a bitter conflict between the rightists within the royal Lao government and the Pathet Lao, aroused rising concern in Washington and provoked the White House to consider U.S. military intervention in Laos to prevent a communist victory. Concerned at the prospects of a direct U.S. military presence in Indochina, Hanoi warned Pathet Lao leaders not to exacerbate the situation to the point of threatening the survival of the shaky royal government in Vientiane.

In the meantime, DRV leaders had an additional problem elsewhere, as an ideological dispute was beginning to flare up between Moscow and Beijing over the threat or use of force to protect and extend the socialist community throughout the world. Ho Chi Minh, who feared that the growing tensions between his country's two major allies would hinder Hanoi's effort to achieve unified bloc support for the Vietnamese revolutionary cause, tried to maintain an even-handed stance between the two powers. In a visit to China in August 1960, he suggested bilateral talks to resolve Sino-Soviet differences. Both sides, he chided Mao, were at fault. But Ho's remarks were not appreciated in Beijing, where Foreign Minister Chen Yi remarked that Ho was unable to stand up to the Soviets. Ho had no better luck in Moscow, where Soviet party chief Nikita Khrushchev rebuffed his plea to adopt a conciliatory posture, on the grounds that China was now a big power whose pride had to be taken into account.[18]

Still, Ho Chi Minh was temporarily successful in helping to keep the dispute from coming into the open. At a conference of Communist parties held in Moscow in November 1960, he persuaded an angry Liu Shaoqi to return to the meeting, thus avoiding a public rupture between China and the Soviet Union. But Ho's attempt to maintain good relations with both countries aroused irritation in Hanoi, where some of his more militant colleagues began to remark privately that Ho was too inclined to defer to Moscow. Their concerns may have had some justification, for Ho was increasingly suspicious of Mao Zedong's imperial pretensions and tended to support the Soviet view on most international issues.

The continuing desire of most DRV leaders to maintain friendly relations with both of their country's chief benefactors undoubtedly complicated Hanoi's attempt to formulate a coherent policy to bring about reunification with the South. In September 1960 the VWP had held its Third National Congress. The conference focused its primary attention on the domestic scene, when it approved a five-year plan to enter the stage of transition to a fully socialist economy during the early 1960s. No changes were announced in the party's strategy toward the South, as the conference declaration simply affirmed the current uneasy balance between political and military struggle and stated that reunification would have equal billing with domestic concerns in future years. Representatives from both China and the Soviet Union attended the congress and (undoubtedly to Ho Chi Minh's relief) did not engage in mutual polemics during the meeting.

Still, changes in the regime's approach to national reunification were in the wind. Responding to the rapid growth of local revolutionary forces in the South, Hanoi ordered the creation of a new united front—to be known as the National Liberation Front for South Vietnam—to lead the movement there. Henceforth the NLF, as it was popularly known, would play a role similar to the old Vietminh Front as a broad-based alliance of all forces opposed to the Diem regime. Its stated objective was to bring about the departure of U.S. advisors and the formation of a coalition government dedicated to maintaining peace and neutrality. To reassure foreign observers and moderate elements in the South, there was no mention of communism or of direct future ties with the DRV.

If one of the purposes of the creation of the NLF was to allay U.S. suspicions of the links between the insurgent movement in the RVN and the North, it had little success, for the growing effectiveness of the Viet Cong aroused concern in Washington. Shortly after his accession to the White House in January 1961, President John F. Kennedy ordered the creation of a task force to assess the situation in South Vietnam and recommend measures to prevent a communist takeover in Saigon. Later that year he ordered a dramatic increase in U.S. military assistance to the GVN. But of more immediate concern to Washington was the situation in Laos, where Pathet Lao operations against the rightist government in Vientiane threatened to bring that country under communist rule. Unwilling to commit U.S. military forces to landlocked Laos, Kennedy opted for new peace talks in Geneva to bring about a cease-fire and the formation of a new neutralist government there.

Tiger Trap

Washington's decision to take the crisis in Laos to the conference table was a welcome sign to Hanoi that the United States was looking for a way out of the morass in Indochina. In party meetings, Ho Chi Minh had argued that the United States, which lacked vital security interests in the area, was simply trying to save face in Indochina. Although Duan, along with other militant elements, was increasingly critical of Ho's penchant for seeking diplomatic solutions, in this case he agreed. In a letter to a leading party operative in South Vietnam, Duan predicted that Washington eventually would back down in Indochina, as it had done previously in Korea and in China. In that belief, Hanoi sought to find a means of easing the United States out of South Vietnam through negotiations to create a coalition government that ostensibly would be neutralist but surreptitiously would be dominated by the communists.[19]

Hanoi's optimism about the mood in Washington was misplaced, however, for distrust of communism and a fear of falling dominoes in Southeast Asia continued to dominate the political scene in the United States. Although tentative feelers between U.S. and DRV officials took place in the summer of 1962, the White House lost interest once it became clear that the North Vietnamese had no intention of honoring Soviet assurances at Geneva that the DRV would not take advantage of the Laos agreement to increase the infiltration of personnel and supplies through Laos into the RVN. According to historian Robert Brigham, author of an impressive new study on the diplomatic activities of the NLF, Hanoi also may have decided to withdraw its peace feelers as a result of protests from senior party representatives in the South, ever wary of compromises that might delay once again the final goal of national reunification. The moment of opportunity thus died stillborn.[20]

Hanoi's failure to lure the United States into a face-saving peaceful solution to the conflict in South Vietnam did not deter party leaders from their belief that Washington could be lured into withdrawing from South Vietnam short of an all-out war. During the spring and summer of 1963, Ngo Dinh Diem's police suppressed demonstrations by Buddhists who were protesting what they alleged to be Diem's pro-Catholic bias. This Buddhist Crisis climaxed in the self-immolation of monks in South Vietnam. DRV leaders, perhaps expecting that the White House would decide to withdraw its support from the RVN as a result of the crisis, reacted cautiously to the rising tensions between Washington and Saigon over the issue. When Diem was deposed by a military coup in early November, Hanoi quietly issued peace feelers to the new leadership in Saigon to explore the possibility of a negotiated settlement. But when those overtures were rejected, party leaders concluded that President Lyndon B. Johnson, who had just replaced Kennedy in the White House, was not yet ready to accept Hanoi's terms for a settlement.

Between Moscow and Beijing

With prospects for a U.S. withdrawal from South Vietnam temporarily foreclosed, Hanoi returned to the military option. In December 1963 the party Central Committee gave urgent consideration to a proposal by militants to escalate the military pressure on the South in the hopes of achieving a quick victory before Washington could decide whether to intervene. Any such decision, however, raised the distinct possibility of a wider war. An intensification of the conflict would not cause major problems with Beijing, which was now willing to take risks in order to win Hanoi's support in the Sino-Soviet dispute, but it could anger the Soviet Union, anxious now more than ever, since the 1962 Cuban Missile Crisis, to improve relations with the United States.

The debate was heated, since many senior party leaders, including Ho Chi Minh himself, were still reluctant to offend Moscow or provoke Washington, but Duan and his allies were now in the ascendant in Hanoi, and eventually the proposal was approved. To appease doubters, it was decided that no North Vietnamese regular force troops would be dispatched to take part in the fighting in the South. Although some of the more militant elements in the party leadership appeared willing to risk a total break with the Soviet Union, Duan had no desire to cut all ties to Moscow, and the VWP sent a circular letter to bloc parties that promised that the war could be contained within the boundaries of South Vietnam. At Duan's urging, a critical reference to Soviet "revisionism" (a direct slap at Soviet leader Nikita Khrushchev) was deleted from the letter. Still, the message was clear. North Vietnamese officials suspected of pro-Soviet views were purged from the ranks of the party and the government, and articles critical of alleged "revisionism" appeared in the official press. For the first time, the regime had broken from its careful policy of neutrality in the Sino-Soviet dispute.[21]

In its hope that the United States might react to the heightened conflict in South Vietnam by reducing its role there, however, Hanoi had miscalculated the mood in Washington. As the political and military situation in the South deteriorated in the months following the coup, the Johnson administration showed no signs of weakening resolve and approved measures that threatened to increase the U.S. role in the conflict. When, in early August of 1964, North Vietnamese naval units responded to clandestine operations by South Vietnamese guerrillas in the southern provinces of the DRV by attacking U.S. warships operating in the nearby coastal waters of the Tonkin Gulf, the White House quickly ordered retaliatory air strikes on DRV territory. To party leaders, the U.S. response demonstrated conclusively that Washington had no intention of seeking a face-saving exit from South Vietnam. A few weeks later, the VWP Politburo approved plans to dispatch the first North Vietnamese combat units to the South. The decision further soured relations with Moscow, but it received approval in Beijing, which promised to step up its military assistance and even offered to send Chinese troops if they should become necessary. Chinese leaders, however, did not want to get lured by Hanoi (at the possible instigation of Moscow) into a confrontation with Washington, and Mao warned Duan not to overreact to U.S. provocations.[22]

In October 1964 Nikita Khrushchev was overthrown by a cabal of his rivals in the party Presidium and a new leadership led by Leonid Brezhnev and Alexei Kosygin took power in the Kremlin. Although the coup had little effect in easing the polemics between China and the Soviet Union, it had a significant impact in Hanoi, since the new leaders in Moscow, hoping to isolate China within the socialist camp, seemed more receptive to DRV appeals for increased military assistance. For the remainder of the war, the Soviet Union became an irreplaceable source of advanced military equipment, such as MiG fighters and surface-to-air missiles, that enabled the regime to defend DRV airspace against U.S. air attacks. In return, Hanoi assured Soviet leaders that it would not permit the conflict in Indochina to get out of hand.[23]

It was one thing to restore a measure of balance in the DRV's relations with its two major benefactors; it was another to maintain it. The Chinese were irritated at Hanoi's decision to accept increased military aid from the Soviet Union and did not hesitate to say so. From Beijing's point of view, close relations between Hanoi and Moscow represented a blatant gesture of ingratitude by the former for the considerable amount of assistance that China had provided to the Vietnamese revolution over four decades. When Deng Xiaoping visited Hanoi in December, he demanded that the DRV refuse any future offers of military assistance from Moscow and to rely entirely on Beijing. His hosts flatly refused, and Chinese leaders, fearful that the Vietnamese would shift further reward Moscow, backed down. Hanoi was finally learning how to use the split to its own advantage. But the seeds of later difficulties with Beijing had been sown.

Four Points for Peace

Backed with reasonably firm support from its chief allies, so long as the war could be kept from spreading beyond the borders of South Vietnam, Hanoi had earned some precious breathing room to deal with the rapidly evolving situation in South Vietnam. In the winter of 1964–1965, the political situation in Saigon descended to the point of chaos, as one regime followed another with bewildering rapidity. In the countryside, Viet Cong forces took advantage of the disarray and adopted more aggressive tactics against the demoralized South Vietnamese armed forces. According to U.S. intelligence estimates, the NLF now controlled over 80 percent of the total land area of the RVN. Such signs of progress in the South led to a brief moment of euphoria in Hanoi that victory was at hand. Even the ever-cautious Ho Chi Minh predicted that negotiations with the United States might not be necessary, since victory in the South was imminent. At a meeting of the VWP Central Committee in February 1965, party leaders decided not to send additional North Vietnamese troops down the Ho Chi Minh Trail in the hope that local Viet Cong forces could bring about a collapse of the Saigon regime by midsummer. Even when the White House reacted to a Viet Cong attack on a U.S. Special Forces base in the Central Highlands by ordering bombing raids over the North, Hanoi initially concluded that Washington was simply escalating in order to improve its situation on the battlefield and lay the groundwork for a negotiated withdrawal.

With that in mind, Hanoi returned to the diplomatic offensive in April, when Prime Minister Pham Van Dong issued his famous "Four Points," calling for a settlement based on a withdrawal of U.S. forces, a return to the provisions of the Geneva agreement, a peace settlement based on the program of the NLF, and the peaceful reunification of the two zones without foreign interference. But the proposal was soon embroiled in controversy, as a "five-point" program issued almost simultaneously by the NLF appeared to demand a U.S. withdrawal before negotiations could even get under way. U.S. officials also were concerned that point 3 of Hanoi's Four Points might require the total surrender of the current government in Saigon. Washington sought to clarify the situation through diplomatic contacts with DRV officials, but Hanoi was evasive, and after several meetings in midsummer, Hanoi suddenly broke off the contacts.[24]

According to historian Robert Brigham, North Vietnamese officials had drawn back from negotiations primarily out of deference to the views of their followers in the South, who (rightly or wrongly) feared the possibility of another sellout by Hanoi and its allies. But another factor was undoubtedly Duan's conclusion that Washington—which had now begun to introduce U.S. combat troops into South Vietnam—was not yet prepared to make major concessions at the conference table. As Duan remarked in a letter to southern commanders in May, Hanoi did not wish to enter peace talks until the situation on the battlefield was clearly favorable to the revolutionary forces. "Only when the insurrection [in South Vietnam] is successful," he remarked, "will the problem of establishing a 'neutral central administration' be posed again. In the meantime, the lure of negotiations could be used to win sympathy within the international community and seduce the Johnson administration into further concessions."[25]

By late summer, however, it had become clear that the current Viet Cong offensive would not succeed in toppling the South Vietnamese government, while the steady increase in the number of U.S. combat troops in the South forced Hanoi planners to realize that only a drastic increase in the number of their own troops could avoid a stabilization of the Saigon regime. The leading exponent of this view was General Nguyen Chi Thanh, the newly appointed commander of North Vietnamese forces in the South, who had devised an aggressive strategy to pressure U.S. and South Vietnamese forces throughout the RVN to force them to surrender. Hanoi did not close off the negotiating track entirely—during the fall and winter DRV sources continued to refer to the possibility of a negotiated solution to the conflict—but Duan and his allies within the party leadership had decided that the times were not favorable for negotiations. At a meeting of the Central Committee in November, Duan declared that Hanoi's offer of peace talks was primarily intended as a lure to "tantalize the United States." As a test of U.S. intentions, and to reassure hard-liners who opposed any consideration of the diplomatic option, DRV sources posed two conditions for the opening of talks: a total bombing halt of the North and U.S. acceptance of point 3 of the Four Points.[26]

Stab in the Back

The escalation of the war, a process that was now under way on both sides, made it ever more vital for Hanoi to achieve crucial support from its allies. Moscow could be kept in line so long as Hanoi prevented the war from spreading beyond the borders of South Vietnam and indicated an interest in a possible future diplomatic settlement. Soviet officials did express frustration, however, that Vietnamese leaders refused to consult with them about DRV war plans. The Soviet military attaché in Hanoi was consistently informed by North Vietnamese officials that DRV strategists had "their own views" on the formulation of strategy in the South.[27]

As always, relations with Beijing were more complicated. Party leaders in Hanoi wanted China to serve not only as a key source of military assistance but also as a powerful deterrent to dissuade the United States from expanding the war beyond the borders of South Vietnam. During the early months of 1965, Beijing had promised Vietnamese leaders that China would serve as the "great rear" of the Vietnamese revolution, providing military equipment, technical assistance, and, if necessary, even combat troops to help their Vietnamese comrades to achieve their objectives. In April the two countries signed an aid agreement providing for the dispatch of Chinese support troops to North Vietnam. Two months later bilateral discussions in Beijing reached agreement that China would respond in kind to any further U.S. escalation of the war.

In fact, however, some Chinese leaders were becoming increasingly concerned that they might get dragged into a direct confrontation with the United States, and Beijing began to signal Washington that, while it was quite willing, if necessary, to intervene directly in the Vietnam conflict to protect its national interests, it had no intention of provoking a conflict with the United States. If Washington did not directly threaten China, the messages hinted, the latter would not involve itself directly in the war. After a bitter midsummer debate among party leaders in Beijing, China rejected Hanoi's request for Chinese combat pilots and rebuffed a Soviet proposal for united action to provide assistance to the DRV. An article allegedly written by Chinese Minister of Defense Lin Biao that was published in September implicitly advised party leaders in Hanoi to adopt a policy of self-reliance and protracted war in the South.[28]

To North Vietnamese war planners, China's decision to limit its commitment in Vietnam represented a "stab in the back," which seriously hindered their ability to dissuade the United States from using its technological superiority to seek a total victory in the war.[29] Early the following year, Duan responded to China's unsolicited advice as conveyed in Lin Biao's article, retorting that "it is not fortuitous that in the history of our country, each time we arose to oppose foreign aggression, we took the offensive and not the defensive."[30]

Duan's testy response was a blunt message to Beijing that Hanoi intended to follow its own dictates in drafting war strategy. Still, although Vietnamese party leaders were reluctant to admit it, China had become one of their most potent weapons in facing down the United

States. Although Chinese leaders had been careful to qualify the degree of their commitment to the DRV, the implicit threat of Chinese intervention was undoubtedly a major factor in constraining the Johnson administration from undertaking a more aggressive approach to the war. Moreover, during the next few years, Chinese military assistance to North Vietnam increased dramatically, while the number of Chinese civilian and military personnel serving in Vietnam reached to over 100,000.[31]

But even the steady flow of Chinese personnel and equipment into the DRV did not resolve differences between Beijing and Hanoi, in part because the expanding Chinese presence was a growing irritant among the people of North Vietnam. The situation was exacerbated during the late 1960s, when visiting Red Guards began to spout the slogans of the Great Proletarian Cultural Revolution to their Vietnamese hosts. Party leaders in Hanoi had their own way of signaling their displeasure, as articles about the tradition of Chinese "feudal aggression" began to appear in the official press. The none-too-subtle hint was soon picked up in Beijing. If our presence is irritating to you, Deng Xiaoping remarked to Duan in April 1966, "we will withdraw at once."[32]

Fight and Then See

Meanwhile, on the battlefield, the cost in both human and material terms of Nguyen Chi Thanh's aggressive strategy was enormous, with potential benefits that were as yet unclear. By early 1967 dissent against existing policy was being expressed in both civilian and military circles in Hanoi. Some apparently even expressed a renewed desire to pursue the negotiating track. With the peace movement in the United States and around the world growing rapidly, there was some optimism in Hanoi that the Johnson administration might be prepared to offer major concessions to bring an end to the war. In January 1967 DRV foreign minister Nguyen Duy Trinh signaled Washington that if the U.S. bombing campaign over North Vietnamese territory were to be halted unconditionally, prospects for the opening of peace talks would improve. Hanoi's previous condition—that the United States must accept its Four Points as a precondition for opening negotiations—had thus been tacitly abandoned. To White House officials, however, the ambiguity of Hanoi's message (did "there could be talks" mean the same thing as "there will be talks"?) aroused suspicions that were not clarified in succeeding contacts, and eventually Washington rejected the proposal as inadequate.

The Johnson administration had not lost interest in opening peace talks, however, and by June further contacts were under way, as the White House pushed a new proposal—known variously as the Pennsylvania or the San Antonio formula. The plan called for a halt in U.S. bombing of the North, provided that peace talks began and that DRV officials gave assurances that they would not take advantage of the cessation to escalate their military operations in the South. In Hanoi there was some interest in the proposal, but since plans were already under way for a major military offensive in South Vietnam sometime early in the following year, DRV sources eventually rejected the offer. War planners hoped that a major assault could further destabilize the situation in the RVN and lay the groundwork for major U.S. concessions. If necessary, the U.S. proposal could be revived later.[33]

The Tet Offensive broke out throughout South Vietnam at the end of January 1968. There has been considerable debate among historians over the objectives of the campaign, but Vietnamese sources make it clear that policymakers themselves were not certain of the likely outcome, thus reflecting Duan's view (citing Lenin) that "we must fight and then see." Hanoi's maximum goal was to use a combination of armed attacks and popular uprisings to bring about the collapse of the Saigon regime, leading to immediate negotiations and an early withdrawal of U.S. military forces. But its minimum objective was to destabilize the situation in the South sufficiently to force the United States to seek negotiations under unfavorable conditions. As it turned out, the results of the Tet Offensive were mixed. Viet Cong forces sustained heavy losses and did not succeed in toppling the Saigon regime. But the campaign did have a significant effect on public support for the war in the United States, and in persuading many American officials that the war could not be won at an acceptable cost. The White House reluctantly decided to launch heightened efforts to bring about peace talks.[34]

Fight and Talk

The first breakthrough came in early April, when Hanoi agreed to open discussions with U.S. representatives to seek agreement on an unconditional U.S. bombing halt as a means of bringing about the beginning of negotiations. Hanoi's decision created immediate problems with China, which for the past three years had been warning Hanoi not to abandon the Four Points as a precondition for engaging in peace talks. In a discussion with Pham Van Dong that same month, Zhou Enlai criticized the Vietnamese for considering a partial bombing halt, charging that it would cause the revolutionary forces in South Vietnam to lose the initiative. Dong retorted that the DRV was simply trying to use adroit diplomatic tactics in order to mobilize world opinion against the United States and force Washington into concessions. When Zhou noted that the Chinese had more experience in dealing with the United States than had Vietnamese negotiators, Dong thanked him for his opinion while noting that "we are the ones who are fighting against the U.S. and defeating them." So, he concluded, it is we who should be responsible for undertaking both military and diplomatic activities.[35]

Chinese leaders reiterated their criticisms in the autumn, when the DRV agreed to open peace negotiations with representatives of the United States, the RVN, and the NLF in Paris. Beijing charged that Hanoi thus had given the Saigon regime a degree of international legitimacy that it had never possessed in reality. By now, however, the atmosphere in Sino-Vietnamese discussions had become increasingly strained. North Vietnamese officials bluntly rejected Beijing's suggestions, pointing out that the DRV had made a mistake by listening to Chinese advice at Geneva in 1954. Eventually Mao Zedong gave his imprimatur to Hanoi's fight-and-talk strategy, while warning Vietnamese visitors to be wary of U.S. tricks.[36]

For the moment, then, strains between Beijing and Hanoi had been papered over, with both sides skeptical of an early diplomatic solution. North Vietnamese leaders continued to use the peace talks in Paris primarily as a forum for swaying public opinion while simultaneously attempting to build up their armed forces in the South for another assault on the Saigon regime. When the neutralist government of Prince Norodom Sihanouk in Cambodia was overthrown by a military coup led by General Lon Nol in 1970, the two countries were able to cooperate in setting up a fragile alliance between Sihanouk's supporters and the Khmer Rouge.

But although Mao had given his blessing to Hanoi's fight-and-talk strategy, Chinese leaders were still free with their advice, counseling their Vietnamese counterparts to adopt a protracted war strategy on the battlefield and warning against putting too much confidence on the negotiations in Paris. In September 1970 Pham Van Dong assured Zhou Enlai that DRV war planners had no illusions about a diplomatic settlement at that point (the talks in Paris, he remarked, are just "a play of words"), since Washington was still seeking a victory in the war.

Hanoi's current conditions for a settlement (establishing a timetable for the full withdrawal of U.S. troops and the removal of South Vietnamese President Nguyen Van Thieu prior to the formation of a coalition government) were not intended for serious consideration, but only to "corner" the Americans and build up popular sympathy for the revolutionary movement inside South Vietnam and around the world. The diplomatic struggle, he insisted, thus played a useful role along with the military effort on the ground.[37]

The Nixon Shock

But in the early 1970s, policymakers in Hanoi suddenly were faced with an uncomfortable new reality when China decided to seek a rapprochement with the United States. For much of Asia, the prospects for improved Sino-U.S. relations were a welcome indication that the Cold War in the region was finally beginning to thaw. But for party leaders in Hanoi, the step was a stunning setback to their war strategy, since the latter had been based on the premise that China's hostility to the United Stares was a stable factor in world affairs. Now the DRV was faced with the disagreeable possibility that Chinese leaders (who had once urged toughness in the struggle against the imperialist forces) would now collude with Washington to deprive the Vietnamese of the fruits of their revolutionary struggle.

As Chinese leaders undoubtedly argued, the possibility did exist that improved relations between Beijing and Washington could prove advantageous to the cause of Vietnamese reunification, since it would serve to reduce U.S. concerns about communist expansion in Southeast Asia and enable the White House to focus attention on other parts of the world. But that view was not shared in Hanoi, where North Vietnamese leaders feared that the projected visit of President Richard M. Nixon to China—first announced on July 15, 1971—would undercut their own efforts to undermine public support for the war in the United States and that China now would actively promote a compromise peace settlement in Indochina in order to satisfy its own changing security interests.[38]

Hanoi's fears that Beijing would begin to pressure the North Vietnamese to accept a compromise peace settlement soon took on substance, for Chinese leaders had become convinced that Washington was planning to seek an honorable withdrawal from Indochina. North Vietnamese war planners now focused their own hopes for success on plans for a new general offensive in South Vietnam that could further erode the authority of the Saigon regime and bring about further U.S. concessions in peace talks. The Easter Offensive, launched in late March 1972, vividly displayed the superiority of North Vietnamese forces against South Vietnamese units—now operating without U.S. ground support. Still, U.S. air strikes blunted the offensive, and the RVN, although severely shaken, remained in place.

For the next several months, North Vietnamese leaders assessed the situation in light of the new realities. In July Zhou Enlai advised Le Duc Tho to be more flexible in the peace talks and, if necessary, to recognize Nguyen Van Thieu as a potential member of the future tripartite coalition. Tho was skeptical, because Nixon's major opponent in the 1972 presidential campaign, Democratic Senator George McGovern, was campaigning on a platform of immediate U.S. withdrawal from South Vietnam. But by early fall it had become clear that Senator McGovern was going to be soundly defeated in the presidential elections, while Nixon was threatening to escalate U.S. military pressure in Vietnam after the election if a peace settlement did not appear a likely possibility.

On October 8 Tho abandoned Hanoi's demand for the resignation of Nguyen Van Thieu and the formation of a coalition government as a condition for a peace agreement. Instead, he accepted a plan calling for a "ceasefire in place" and the recognition of two administrative entities in South Vietnam—the Saigon regime under President Nguyen Van Thieu and the Provisional Revolutionary Government, or PRG (a shadow government created by Hanoi to serve as its representative in the South in 1969). U.S. military forces were to be withdrawn, while a tripartite subdiplomatic organization called the National Council of Reconciliation and Concord (NCRC) and composed of representatives of the PRG, the RVN, and neutralist forces in the South was to be created to smooth the way for a future coalition government and national elections. The final treaty embodying these terms was finally signed in Paris in January 1973.

To many members of the NLF, the Paris agreement was ominously reminiscent of the betrayal that had taken place at Geneva two decades previously, and VWP leaders went to considerable lengths to assure them that the cause of reunification had not been forgotten. In fact, however, Hanoi appeared to feel no sense of urgency to complete national reunification. Now that U.S. military forces had been withdrawn from the RVN, North Vietnamese leaders were confident that victory in the South was only a matter of time. In talks held in Beijing in June, Zhou Enlai suggested that "during the next 5 to 10 years, South Vietnam, Laos, and Cambodia should build peace, independence, and neutrality." Duan appeared to agree, remarking to Zhou that the DRV was in no hurry to transform the current government in Saigon into a socialist one (he mentioned the possibility of ten to fifteen years), so long as it had been transformed into "a democratic and a nationalist one."[39]

As it turned out, it did not take nearly that long to complete the reunification of North and South Vietnam. When the Thieu regime balked at carrying out the provisions of the Paris agreement and aggressively attacked enemy-held areas in South Vietnam, DRV leaders revised their plans and launched a major offensive in the South beginning in early 1975. The decision aroused some anxiety in Moscow and Beijing, but when Washington did not react (Nixon had been replaced by President Gerald Ford in August 1974, and the latter had no stomach for resuming the war), South Vietnamese resistance rapidly crumbled, and Saigon fell to a North Vietnamese assault on April 30, 1975. Reunification took place a year later, and the regime drafted plans to complete socialist transformation throughout the country by the end of the decade.

Conclusion

In the months and years that followed the fall of Saigon, official sources in Hanoi ascribed victory to a variety of factors: the firm and astute leadership provided by the party, the unyielding patriotism and heroism of the Vietnamese people, and the personality and strategical genius of its great leader, Ho Chi Minh. Relatively little credit was assigned to the role of diplomacy or to the assistance provided by Hanoi's chief allies. To the contrary, Vietnamese leaders, now locked in an increasingly bitter dispute with China, consistently downplayed the support that they had received over the decades from outside sources, and especially from Beijing, whose assistance to the DRV was now portrayed as having been motivated by self-seeking purposes.[40]

In fact, however, diplomacy had been a weapon of crucial importance to the party in its struggle to bring about national reunification on its own terms. Like the ancient Chinese military strategist Sun Tzu, Vietnamese war planners had recognized at an early stage of their struggle that a pragmatic understanding of their own strengths and weaknesses, as well as those of their adversaries, would be a key prerequisite for final victory. And they had realized that the international environment would have to be artfully managed to isolate their enemy and maximize support for the revolutionary cause.

In formulating their diplomatic approach, the weapon of choice was the Leninist concept of the united front, which the Bolshevik leader had devised as a means of rallying support for the revolutionary forces against a more powerful adversary. Like Lenin, Vietnamese leaders applied the concept both internally, against their nationalist rivals, and in foreign affairs, where they sought to drive a wedge between their chief adversaries of the moment (first the French and later the United States) from other interested governments on the world scene. Neutral forces were carefully cultivated, even though their long-term sympathy for the party's ultimate objectives was decidedly limited.

Such tactics were not uniformly successful. Ho Chi Minh's persistent efforts to win U.S. support for the cause of Vietnamese national independence after World War II were fruitless. His later confidence that Washington could be persuaded not to intervene directly in South Vietnam was equally not borne out by events. Such miscalculations were obviously a major factor in his declining influence at the height of the Vietnam War. Similarly, DRV leaders had only limited success in coordinating assistance from their chief allies to their best advantage. Despite Ho's best efforts to mediate the Sino-Soviet dispute, relations between Moscow and Beijing deteriorated rapidly during the 1960s and hindered Hanoi's ability to present Washington with a united front.

Once the scope of the challenge had been made clear, however, Vietnamese strategists were adept in finding solutions. The united front approach originally devised by Ho Chi Minh in the 1920s proved highly effective in winning worldwide sympathy for the cause of Vietnamese national liberation. Vietnamese leaders learned to effectively manipulate the Sino-Soviet dispute to gain crucial military and diplomatic support from both Moscow and Beijing. Finally, Vietnamese policy planners effectively orchestrated the issue of opening peace talks in a manner that presented a public impression of flexibility while actually refusing meaningful negotiations until a time of Hanoi's choosing.

In the end, of course, Hanoi made a number of significant compromises to bring about the peace agreement that was signed in January 1973. For Vietnamese strategists, however, the concessions made at Paris were more apparent than real, since they realized, better than their counterparts in Washington, that once the U.S. shield had been removed from the South, the Saigon regime would be no match for its adversary to the North. DRV leaders apparently expected a lengthy period of time to elapse before the final victory and were prepared to accept a compromise settlement in the form of a coalition government dominated by the NLF. But the resignation of President Nixon in August 1974 brought an unexpected dividend when his successor proved reluctant to intervene to counter the 1975 spring offensive. In the end, Hanoi's strategy had succeeded even more than party leaders had anticipated.

Much of the credit for the party's diplomatic success must go to Ho Chi Minh, whose astute grasp of international affairs compensated for the lack of experience of many of his colleagues. A clear measure of his importance is that after his death in 1969 Hanoi's relations with China rapidly deteriorated, leading to the Sino-Vietnamese War a decade later and a series of foreign policy reverses that were not fully rectified until the 1990s. Although Ho had made a number of errors in his assessment of the international environment during the era of the Cold War, his sage advice was a major factor in enabling the party to vanquish its adversaries in the thirty-year struggle for total power in Vietnam.

⋞ 17 ⋟

The National Liberation Front and the Land

Tom Mangold and John Penycate

He heard the tracks of the armored personnel carriers long before the malignant clouds of dust came into view. Nam Thuan lay very still, trying to count the number, but in his eyes and ears was only the fusion of squeaky steel belts and the approaching halo of dirt as the American armor moved busily out of the early morning sun and straight toward him.

As Communist party secretary of Phu My Hung village with its six small hamlets, Nam Thuan was automatically political commissar of the village defense force, a small unit already much depleted by action and promotions to the regional fighting forces. His small platoon that morning comprised a good deputy commander and a couple of village farm boys. His orders had been simple enough: He was to delay any American thrust on Phu My Hung by luring the enemy into engagement. He would destroy them if possible; if not, his diversionary battle would allow ample time for the village to be evacuated and the arms and guerrillas to be hidden.

It was August 1968; the war against the Americans was three years old. The great Tet offensive seemed to have taken many lives, yet South Vietnam had still not been reunited with the North. If anything, Thuan thought, the Americans seemed more confident and more powerful than ever. But at least they were predictable—it was a necessary consolation as the small armored column rattled nearer; the Americans always came when expected, came noisily, and came in strength.

He counted thirteen M-113 carriers. It was a larger force than he had expected. Thuan needed to move quickly if he was to draw the column toward him and toward the tunnels. To fight with he had just two remote-controlled mines which he would detonate, and a boxful of captured American M-26 grenades. In the confusion, he would retreat and escape down the tunnel, but not so quickly that the Americans would not see him.

Things went wrong from the beginning. He detonated the first DH-10 mine prematurely and it exploded harmlessly just ahead of the lead American APC. The second mine failed to go off. The column was still too far away for Thuan to hurl the grenades. He stood up, deliberately breaking cover, and began to run awkwardly toward the tunnel entrance—its position marked by the open trapdoor—hugging the box of grenades. The lead APC spotted him and changed course to follow. Thuan wondered whether the Americans would now fire the turret-mounted machine gun; even if they did, it was improbable that a bumping gun would hit a small running target. Hands reached out of the open tunnel trapdoor to take the box of grenades. Thuan vaulted into a shaft and closed the door above his head. Blinded by the sudden change from sunlight to darkness, Thuan remained still for a few moments, crouching in the three-foot-deep shaft, gathering breath, waiting for images to return to his retinas. At the bottom of the shaft in which he stood and almost at a right angle to it began a sixty-foot communication tunnel. Thuan wriggled easily into its secure embrace. He realized he could no longer hear the noisy tracks of the APCs. Control of the battle had now passed from his hands to those of an American above ground. If the carriers passed overhead it would be impossible to rechallenge them before they reached Phu My Hung. He had been ordered not to allow that to happen.

For a few moments Thuan considered his environment. He had just entered the shaft that connected with the communication tunnel. At the end of the communication tunnel was a second shaft going down another three feet and at the end of that was a second communication tunnel. If he crawled along that, he would eventually reach a similar shaft and tunnel system leading up and out. However, the exit point for this system was some 120 feet away from the place where the Americans had seen him. It was crucial to his plan that they never discover the second exit. It was only sparsely camouflaged, but he had his own man hidden there who could tell him with minimum delay what the Americans were doing above ground while Thuan was below.

The tunnel was still cool from the evening air of the night before. Thuan crawled carefully into a small alcove dug some four feet into the first communication tunnel. As he hunched inside, he heard a muffled explosion followed by a blast, and a sudden beam of dust-filled sunlight pierced the shaft. The Americans had hit the tunnel trapdoor, blowing it clean away. It was what he had prayed for. The column was bound to stop while the tunnel system was fully explored and then destroyed by the Americans. As the dust and debris stung his eyes, Thuan squinted through the gloom and picked up his AK-47 automatic rifle, hugged it to his chest, and waited quietly in the alcove.

He waited over an hour. When he heard the first American helicopter he knew there would be no attempt to explode the tunnel without exploration. As the machine clapped and whirred its noisy way to the ground, Thuan assumed that the Americans had flown in their special tunnel soldiers, trained to fight in the honeycomb of underground tunnels and caverns that spread beneath the protective clay of the district of Cu Chi.

Thuan's observer, secreted above ground in the second hidden tunnel exit, had sent a messenger through the tunnels to Thuan in the alcove. The message was wholly predictable. The Americans had indeed brought more men by helicopter. They were small. They were tunnel soldiers.

The first GI did not even approach the open tunnel entrance for another hour. Earlier, Thuan had heard some conversation above his hiding hole, but nothing for about thirty minutes. Whatever happened, only one American could come in at a time. Both the first entrance shaft and the second long communication tunnel were only just wide enough for one thin man. The tunnel soldiers were thin; they fought well, but unlike Nam Thuan and his small village platoon of Communist guerrillas, they had not spent years inside the tunnels of Cu Chi; they had not fought many battles in their dank blackness.

Thuan could not conceive of failure. He had already been awarded one Victory Medal third class and one Victory Medal second class. He was about to earn another. Small even by Vietnamese standards, naturally slender, Thuan had never known peace in his land. His father had fought the French from similar tunnel complexes in Cu Chi when Thuan was still a child. Thuan had been allowed occasional tunnel sorties, playing soldiers with his friends. The enemy had been other village boys, ludicrously made up to look like the French soldiers, with charcoal mustaches and charcoaled arms, in an attempt to ape the perpetual wonder of hirsute Westerners.

As he grew up, it was the Americans who took the place of the French, and their hairy arms and large frames were no joke to the handful of village children who had been selected by the Communist party to receive a full education. He soon hated the Americans. A friend from Hanoi had told him the Americans called the village fighters Viet Cong, to him an insulting and derogatory term. Now, at thirty-three and still unmarried, Thuan was waiting for the call to join the regular soldiers, but the party had deliberately kept him as a village commander of the part-time self-defense force. He had fought a brave war. He was cunning and ruthless and, above all, he was one of the few cadres who knew the geography of all the eight miles of underground tunnels that the villagers had built in the area. Sometimes he was the only man who could guide the soldiers from Hanoi along the tunnels on their secret journeys through Cu Chi; the men from the North marveled at being able to travel safely under the Americans' noses.

A small earth-fall from the exposed tunnel entrance warned Thuan that the first American tunnel soldier was descending. He had purposely ordered that the first shaft be dug just over three feet deep; it meant the American would have to descend feet first and then wriggle awkwardly into the long communication tunnel where Thuan waited, hidden in an alcove. In the past, as a GI's feet had touched the bottom, Thuan had stabbed the soldier in the groin with his bayonet. This time, as the green-and-black jungle boots descended, Thuan leaned out of his alcove and, using the light from the tunnel entrance, shot the soldier twice in the lower body.

Above ground, the Americans were now in trouble. They could not drop grenades down the shaft because their mortally wounded comrade jammed the hole—anyway, he might still be alive. Slumped in the narrow shaft, he prevented other soldiers from making their way down to chase Thuan. He guessed it would take the Americans at least thirty minutes to get the ropes slipped under the dying man's arms and then haul him out. The Americans' concern for their dead and wounded remained a source of bewilderment and relief to the Communist soldiers. Anything that delayed the battle inevitably favored the weaker side and allowed reloading, regrouping, and rethinking.

Once the American's body had been removed from the shaft, Thuan anticipated that his comrades would probably drop a grenade or two down the hole, wait for the smoke to clear, then climb into the shaft and crawl quickly into the first communication tunnel, firing ahead with their pistols. They would be smarter this time and they would be angrier. He would not wait where he was.

His next fighting position was the second shaft, some four feet deep, which connected the first communication tunnel with the second lower one. There was a trapdoor at the top of the second shaft, but Thuan had to remove it for his next operation to succeed. He prayed the Americans would not be using gas at this early stage to flush him out. If they did not, and he was very lucky, the Americans would follow him, using flashlights. Thuan hid in the second shaft, its trapdoor off. He crouched low enough to be invisible to the Americans as they groped their way along the communication tunnel toward him. And yes, they were using flashlights. They might as well have been using loudspeakers to announce their intentions.

The tunnel soldiers had not thrown grenades but they had fired their pistols in volleys to clear the tunnel ahead. From his crouching position in the shaft at the end of this tunnel, Thuan could look up and feel sharp splinters of clay falling on his face as the bullets struck the end of the tunnel above the open shaft. The noise of the firing was deafening. Now the tunnel soldiers were slowly advancing. As soon as their flashlights saw an open shaft entrance ahead, they would roll a grenade down it and Thuan would be blown to pieces. The timing was now critical. He waited for a pause in the pistol volleys and then popped his head and shoulders out of the shaft. He saw at least two flashlights, they blinded him. As a foreign voice shouted, he fired the first clip from his AK-47, loaded the second by touch, and fired that, too. The tunnel exploded in a roar of noise, orange light, and screams of the wounded. He ducked back into the shaft, picking up the trapdoor from the bottom and replacing it above his head. He wriggled down the shaft and slipped along the second communication tunnel far enough for safety should the Americans be able to remove the trapdoor and throw grenades down after him. He lay breathless and sweating on the earth.

From his hiding place above ground at the top of the secret shaft, about 120 feet away from the American position, Thuan's observer watched as the Americans slowly brought out their dead and wounded from Thuan's attack. Three helicopters arrived for the victims. Thuan carefully noted all the information the messenger brought him from above ground. It gave him the basic material to make this next plan for below ground. Thuan's deputy was convinced that now, surely, the Americans would dynamite the tunnel. Thuan was not so sure. It was four in the afternoon, and the Americans would want to leave, spend the night in Dong Zu base, next to Cu Chi town, and return by helicopter at first light. They still had not discovered the second secret tunnel entrance; they had lost surprise; they had lost men. They might hope there was a tunnel complex large enough to be worth exploring for documents or Communist military equipment. Thuan still had his box of grenades and a perfect escape route behind him. He gambled on another battle.

That night Thuan developed a mild fever and went to a small sleeping hole inside the tunnel. Just large enough for one man but with the luxury of a specially dug air ventilation hole leading in from the surface three feet above, the hole was also used for the wounded before they could be taken by tunnel on the longer trip to the underground tunnel hospital at Phu My Hung. Indeed, there were still bloodstained bandages in the hole. The guerrillas had been unable to burn them or bury them since the last battle. The incessant heavily armored sweeps mounted by the 25th Division from their huge fortress next to Cu Chi town had kept the Communist defense forces pinned inside their tunnels for weeks on end. Sometimes there had been surprise raids by the tunnel soldiers; sometimes there had been many deaths. As Thuan sweated his way through the night, he assumed the new tunnel soldiers would be more careful and cautious than the last squad. Success would depend on the Americans' not knowing the layout of the system, and anticipating that the Communists had now fled.

This time, he would allow the Americans to crawl forward without any impedance and let them travel much farther than they had gone before. Their journey would take them down the first shaft and along the first communication tunnel, then down the second shaft (scene of the previous day's attack) and along the second, or bottom, communication tunnel. They would then reach a third shaft, one that led up. The tunnel soldiers would know what Nam Thuan knew, that this was the most dangerous and critical moment of any tunnel exploration. Thuan would be waiting for them.

He called one of the village boys and ordered him to fill a bag with earth. Then he checked and rechecked his grenades. The American ones were infinitely superior to the homemade ones or even the grenades the Chinese had sent, but tunnels had a way of destroying sensitive mechanisms. In the kind of war that Nam Thuan fought in the tunnels, there were only first chances—never seconds.

The Americans came, as they always seemed to, shortly after eight in the morning. A team crawled with exaggerated care through the tunnel system that had seen such havoc the day before. They moved by inches, looking for tunnel booby traps, but Thuan had dismantled everything—he wanted the soldiers dead, not saved through their own vigilance. He waited until the first dim hint of light announced they were now on their way along the second, the lower, communication tunnel. The leader would find himself facing the shaft at the end of the tunnel. He would shine his flashlight up. He might even have time to see the grenade that would fall to end his life.

In the five seconds before the grenade exploded in the middle of the Americans—Thuan never knew how many there were—he had time to slam the trapdoor shut and heave the heavy bag of earth on top and himself on top of the bag. The explosion just managed to lift the trapdoor with its extra weight. Afterward there was complete silence.

Before American soldiers later destroyed the tunnel with Bangalore torpedoes—chains of explosives linked by detonating cord—Thuan's men had time to retrieve four working pistols, all .38s, and two broken flashlights left by the Americans. His platoon escaped from the secret exit. In fact, the explosions destroyed only some seventy feet of the tunnel complex, and the system was usable again within a few weeks.

Fourteen months later, Nam Thuan was invited to join the regular forces as an officer. He became fully responsible for the defense of the six hamlets of Phu An village. Three years later, in November 1973, the Americans were gone and the war was being fought only by the South Vietnamese army; Thuan was a member of the district party committee when the guerrilla forces of Cu Chi, strengthened by regular troops from North Vietnam, went on the offensive for the first time in five years. They wiped out forty-seven South Vietnamese military posts in one month alone. Two years later, on 28 March 1975, Thuan was with the forces who raised the flag of the Communist National Liberation Front over the town of Cu Chi. He is now a major in the People's Army of Vietnam.

Chapter 6
The Battlefield

Most Americans who went to Vietnam in the 1960s and 1970s—either to join the battle, report on it, or attempt to repair its ravages—described it as a lushly beautiful place in which it was impossible to fight a civilized war. The heat was literally breathtaking. Soldiers who slogged through the jungle or rice paddies were almost never dry or clean, and they suffered a variety of ailments from trench foot to dysentery to fevers that would not break. They were bitten by insects and snakes and sucked by leeches. The human enemy, often unseen for days, turned up suddenly, firing from a village only recently "pacified" by the Americans. Women and children, caught between warring sides, frequently helped the Viet Cong, or were the Viet Cong. Trails were booby-trapped with horrific devices, the mere thought of which jangled the nerves of the toughest GI.

The most powerful American writing about the Vietnam War was done by those who experienced or witnessed it firsthand. Philip Caputo was a gung-ho Marine from Chicago who arrived in Vietnam with the first infantry units in March 1965. By the time he led his patrol down Purple Heart Trail, Caputo had changed his thinking about the nobility of the war, as the excerpt here indicates. The chapter's second piece is the story of 1st Lieutenant Archie "Joe" Biggers, as told by himself to Wallace Terry. Biggers was an African-American Marine platoon leader from Texas whose tale is straightforward, but his message is as harrowing as Caputo's. Lynda Van Devanter went to Vietnam in 1969 because she wanted to help people in need. Like all American nurses there she found more than she bargained for, but what shocked her most was the hostility with which she was greeted by her fellow Americans when she returned to "the real world" the following year. Tim O'Brien also went to Vietnam. His contribution to this chapter is an excerpt from his brilliant novel *Going After Cacciato*, in which the title character decides to run away from the war and head for Paris. Finally, Michael Bilton and Kevin Sim reconstruct the terrible events in the hamlet of My Lai on the morning of March 16, 1968. The killing of innocents began early that day in the war.

≼ 18 ≽

Getting Hit

Philip Caputo

THE PLATOON REACHED HILL 92 IN THE MIDAFTERNOON. The men were worn out by that time, their shoulders aching from the weight of rifles, packs, and flak jackets. They had been under one kind of fire or another for twenty-four hours and were dazed with fatigue. Rigging shelters against the drumming rain, they lay down to rest. Some did not bother to build shelters. They had ceased to care even for themselves. I walked around, checking their feet. A few had serious cases of immersion foot, their shriveled skin covered with red pustules and blisters. It amazed me that they could walk at all. We ate lunch. Our rations were the same as the Viet Cong's: cooked rice rolled into a ball and stuffed with raisins. The riceballs were easier to carry than the heavy C-ration tins and alleviated the diarrhea from which we all suffered. Eating the rice on that desolate hill, it occurred to me that we were becoming more and more like our enemy. We ate what they ate. We could now move through the jungle as stealthily as they. We endured common miseries. In fact, we had more in common with the Viet Cong than we did with that army of clerks and staff officers in the rear.

I was putting on dry socks when Captain Neal called on the radio. A Christmas cease-fire had gone into effect. The operation had been secured. My platoon was to return to friendly lines as quickly as possible. Why not lift us out with helicopters? I asked. No, Neal said, that was out of the question. I passed the word and the troops cheered. "Hey-hey. We're gonna get some slack. Merry fuckin' Christmas."

"No, no. I want to stay out here," said PFC Baum. "I just love it out here in the mud and the rain and the shit."

Shouldering our packs, we tramped down to Purple Heart Trail, the quickest route back. The trail forked near Dieu Phoung, a hamlet several hundred yards west of Charley Hill. The right fork led along the river, the left over the foothills toward the outpost. We took the latter because it was shorter and less likely to be mined or ambushed.

Outside the hamlet was a flooded rice paddy with a steep embankment at its far end. A barbed wire fence, anchored at one end to a dead tree, ran along the length of the embankment. The trail climbed through a hole in the fence near the tree. The lead squad, Sergeant Pryor's, Jones, and I crossed the rice paddy. The water was cold and chestdeep in places, and the rain dimpled the water in a way that reminded me of an evening rise on a trout stream. That was how the Ontonogan River looked in the evenings, in the place where it made a slow, wide bend around a wooded bluff upstream from the rocky, white-water narrows at the Burned Dam. There, the river had been deep and smooth where it curved, and the big trout rising made rings in the copper-colored water. Bill, my fishing buddy, and I used to cast for browns in the deep pool at sunset. We never caught many, but we had a fine time, casting and talking about the things we were going to do when we left school, about all that awaited us in the great outside world, which seemed so full of promise. We were boys and thought everything was possible. The memory sent a momentary pang through me: not so much a feeling of homesickness as one of separation—a distancing from the hopeful boy I had been, a longing to be like that again.

Pryor's squad climbed the embankment, the men slipping on the muddy trail, slipping and falling into each other until they were bunched in a knot. The rest of the platoon waded through the rice paddy behind us, holding their rifles in the air. A snake made a series of S's in the black water as it slithered between two men in the column. On dry ground again, Pryor's marines picked up their interval and hiked up the ridgeline that rose above the embankment. The Cordillera loomed in the distance, high and indomitable. The last two squads started to struggle up the bank, bunching up as one man after another slipped and slid into the man behind him.

Standing by the dead tree, I helped pull a few marines up the trail. "Pass it back not to bunch up," I said. To my left, a stream whispered through a brushy ravine. "Don't bunch up," a marine said. "Pass it back." On the other side of the paddy, the rear of the column was filing past a hut at the edge of the hamlet. Smoke started to roll from the hut and a woman ran out yelling.

"Bittner," I called to the platoon sergeant, who was bringing up the rear, "what the hell's going on?"

"Can't hear you, sir."

"The hut. Who the hell set fire to the hut?"

"Somebody said you passed the word to burn the hut, sir."

"What?"

"The word came back to burn the hut, sir."

"Jesus Christ. I said, 'Don't bunch up.' DON'T BUNCH UP. Put that fire out."

"Yes, sir."

I stood by the leafless tree, watching the marines douse the fire with helmets full of water. Fortunately, the thatch had been wet to begin with and did not burn quickly. Turning to walk back toward the point squad, I saw Allen stumbling on the trail.

"Allen, how're you doing?" I asked, extending my arm. Taking hold of it, he hauled himself over the lip of the embankment.

"Hackin' it, lieutenant. I'm hackin' it okay," Allen said, walking beside me. Ahead, I could see Pryor's squad trudging up the ridge and the point man briefly silhouetted on the ridgeline before he went down the other side. "But this here cease-fire's come along at the right time," Allen was saying. "Could use a little slack. This here cease-fire's the first slack. . . ."

There was a roaring and a hot, hard slap of wind and a needle pricking my thigh and something clubbed me in the small of the back. I fell face down into the mud, my ears ringing. Lying on my belly, I heard an automatic carbine rattle for a few seconds, then someone calling "Corpsman! Corpsman!" Because of the ringing in my ears, the shots and voice sounded far away. "Corpsman! Corpsman!" Someone else yelled "Incoming!" I got to my hands and knees, wondering what fool had yelled "incoming." That had not been a shell, but a mine, a big mine. Who the hell had yelled "incoming"? You did, you idiot. It was your voice. Why did you say that? The fence. The barbed wire fence was the last thing you saw as you fell. You had fallen toward the fence, and it was like that time when you were six and walking in the woods with your friend Stanley. Stanley was nine, and he had been frightening you with stories about bears in the woods. Then you had heard a roaring, growling sound in the distance and, thinking it was a bear, you had run to the highway, tried to climb the barbed wire fence at the roadside, and caught your trousers on the barbs. Hanging there, you had cried, "Stanley, it's a bear! A bear, Stanley!" And Stan had come up laughing because the growling noise you had heard was a roadgrader coming up the highway. It had not been a bear, but a machine. And this roaring had not been a shell, but a mine.

I stood, trying to clear my head. I was a little wobbly, but unmarked except for a sliver of shrapnel stuck in one of my trouser legs. I pulled it out. It was still hot, but it had not even broken my skin. Allen was next to me on all fours, mumbling. "What happened? I don't believe it. My God, oh my God." Some thirty to forty feet behind us, there was a patch of scorched, cratered earth, a drifting pall of smoke, and the dead tree, its trunk charred and cracked. Sergeant Wehr was lying near the crater. He rose to his feet, then fell when one leg collapsed beneath him. Wehr stood up again and the leg crumpled again, and, squatting on his good leg, holding the wounded one straight out in front of him, he spun around like a man doing a cossack dance, then fell onto his back, waving one arm back and forth across his chest. "Boom. Boom," he said, the arm flopping back and forth. "Mah fust patrol, an' boom."

Allen got to his feet, his eyes glassy and a dazed grin on his face. He staggered toward me. "What happened, sir?" he asked, toppling against me and sliding down my chest, his hands clutching at my shirt. Before I could get a grip on him, he fell again to all fours, then collapsed onto his stomach. "My God what happened?" he said. "I don't believe it. My head hurts." Then I saw the blood oozing from the wound in the back of his head and neck. "Dear God my head hurts. Oh it hurts. I don't believe it."

Still slightly stunned, I had only a vague idea of what had happened. A mine, yes. It must have been an ambush-detonated mine. All of Pryor's squad had passed by that spot before the mine exploded. I had been standing on that very spot, near the tree, not ten seconds before the blast. If it had been a booby trap or a pressure mine, it would have gone off then. And then the carbine fire. Yes, an electrically detonated mine set off from ambush, a routine occurrence for the rear-echelon boys who looked at the "overall picture," a personal cataclysm for those who experienced it.

Kneeling beside Allen, I reached behind for my first-aid kit and went numb when I felt the big, shredded hole in the back of my flak jacket. I pulled out a couple of pieces of shrapnel. They were cylindrical and about the size of double-O buckshot. A Claymore, probably homemade, judging from the black smoke. They had used black powder. The rotten-egg stink of it was in the air. Well, that shrapnel would have done a fine job on my spine if it had not been for the flak jacket. My spine. Oh God—if I had remained on that spot another ten seconds, they would have been picking pieces of me out of the trees. Chance. Pure chance. Allen, right beside me, had been wounded in the head. I had not been hurt. Chance. The one true god of modern war is blind chance.

Taking out a compress, I tried to staunch Allen's bleeding. "My God, it hurts," he said. "My head hurts."

"Listen, Allen. You'll be okay. I don't think it broke any bones. You'll be all right." My hands reeked from his blood. "You're going to get plenty of slack now. Lotsa slack in division med. We'll have you evacked in no time."

"My God it hurts. I don't believe it. It hurts."

"I know, Bill. It hurts. It's good that you can feel it," I said, remembering the sharp sting of that tiny sliver in my thigh. And it had done nothing more than raise a bump the size of a beesting. Oh yes, I'll bet your wounds hurt, Lance Corporal Bill Allen.

My head had cleared, and the ringing in my ears quieted to a faint buzz. I told Pryor and Aiker to form their squads into a perimeter around the paddy field. Casualty parties started to carry the wounded out of the paddy and up to the level stretch of ground between the embankment and the base of the ridgeline. It was a small space, but it would have to do as a landing zone.

A rifleman and I picked up Sergeant Wehr, each of us taking one of the big man's arms. "Boom. Boom," he said, hobbling with his arms around our necks. "Mah fust patrol, lieutenant, an' boom, ah got hit. Gawd-damn." A corpsman cut Wehr's trouser leg open with a knife and started to dress his wounds. There was a lot of blood. Two marines dragged Sanchez up from the paddy. His face had been so peppered with shrapnel that I hardly recognized him. Except for his eyes. The fragments had somehow missed his eyes. He was unconscious and his eyes were half closed; two white slits in a mass of raspberry red. Sanchez looked as if he had been clawed by some invisible beast. The marines fanned him with their hands.

"He keeps going out, sir," said one of the riflemen. "If he don't get evacked pretty quick, we're afraid he'll go out for good."

"Okay, okay, as soon as we get the others up."

"Rodella, sir. Get Rodella up. Think he's got a sucking chest wound."

I slid down the embankment and splashed over to where the corpsman, Doc Kaiser, was working to save Corporal Rodella. There were gauze and compresses all over his chest and abdomen. One dressing, covering the hole the shrapnel had torn in one of his lungs, was soaked in blood. With each breath he took, pink bubbles of blood formed and burst around the hole. He made a wheezing sound. I tried talking to him, but he could not say anything because his windpipe would fill with blood. Rodella, who had been twice wounded before, was now in danger of drowning in his own blood. It was his eyes that troubled me most. They were the hurt, dumb eyes of a child who has been severely beaten and does not know why. It was his eyes and his silence and the foamy blood and the gurgling, wheezing sound in his chest that aroused in me a sorrow so deep and a rage so strong that I could not distinguish the one emotion from the other.

I helped the corpsman carry Rodella to the landing zone. His comrades were around him, but he was alone. We could see the look of separation in his eyes. He was alone in the world of the badly wounded, isolated by a pain none could share with him and by the terror of the darkness that was threatening to envelop him.

Then we got the last one, Corporal Greeley, a machinegunner whose left arm was hanging by a few strands of muscle; all the rest was a scarlet mush. Greeley was conscious and angry. "Fuck it," he said over and over. "Fuck it. Fuck it. Fuck the cease-fire. Ain't no fuckin' cease-fire, but they can't kill me. Ain't no fuckin' booby trap gonna kill me." Carrying him, I felt my own anger, a very cold, very deep anger that had no specific object. It was just an icy, abiding fury; a hatred for everything in existence except those men. Yes, except those men of mine, any one of whom was better than all the men who had sent them to war.

I radioed for a medevac. The usual complications followed. How many wounded were there? Nine; four walking wounded, five needing evacuation. *Nine?* Nine casualties from a single mine? What kind of mine was it? Electrically detonated, black-powder, a homemade Claymore probably. But what happened? Goddamnit, I'll tell you later. Get me a medevac. I've got at least one, maybe two who'll be DOW if we don't get them out of here. How big was the mine? Four to five pounds of explosive, plenty of shrapnel. It was placed on an embankment and the platoon was down in a rice paddy below it. Most of the shrapnel went over their heads. Otherwise, I'd have several KIAs. Okay? Now get me those birds. "Boom. Boom," said Sergeant Wehr. "Mah fust patrol an' boom, ah get hit." Charley Two, I need the first letter of the last names and the serial numbers of the WIAs needing evac. Now? Yes, now. Rodella and Sanchez had lapsed into unconsciousness. The corpsmen and some marines were fanning them. Doc Kaiser looked at me pleadingly.

"Hang loose, doc," I said. "The birds'll be here, but the assholes in the puzzle-palace have to do their paperwork first. Bittner! Sergeant Bittner, get me the dog tags of the evacs, and hustle."

"Yes, sir," said Bittner, who was one of the walking wounded. A green battle dressing was wrapped around his forehead. One of the walking wounded. We were all walking wounded.

Bittner gave me the dog tags. I tore off the green masking tape that kept the tags from rattling and gave Captain Neal the required information. Then the radio broke down. Jones changed batteries and started giving long test-counts: "Ten-niner-eight-seven. . . ." I heard Neal's voice again. Did I have any serious casualties? For Christ's sake, yes, why do you think I'm asking for a medevac?

"Charley Two," said Neal, "you must have not been supervising your men properly. They must have been awfully bunched up to take nine casualties from one mine."

"Charley Six," I said, my voice cracking with rage. "You get me those birds now. If one of these kids dies because of this petty bullshit I'm going to raise some kinda hell. I want those birds."

There was a long pause. At last the word came: "Birds on the way."

The helicopters swooped in out of the somber sky, landing in the green smoke billowing from the smoke grenade I had thrown to mark the LZ. The crew chiefs pushed stretchers out of the hatches. We laid the casualties on the stretchers and lifted them into the Hueys, the rain falling on us all the time. The aircraft took off, and watching the wounded soaring out of that miserable patch of jungle, we almost envied them.

Just before the platoon resumed its march, someone found a length of electrical detonating cord lying in the grass near the village. The village would have been as likely an ambush site as any: the VC only had to press the detonator and then blend in with the civilians, if indeed there were any true civilians in the village. Or they could have hidden in one of the tunnels under the houses. All right, I thought, tit for tat. No ceasefire for us, none for you, either. I ordered both rocket launcher teams to fire white-phosphorus shells into the hamlet. They fired four altogether. The shells, flashing orange, burst into pure white clouds, the chunks of flaming phosphorus arcing over the trees. About half the village went up in flames. I could hear people yelling, and I saw several figures running through the white smoke. I did not feel a sense of vengeance, any more than I felt remorse or regret. I did not even feel angry. Listening to the shouts and watching the people running out of their burning homes, I did not feel anything at all.

« 19 »

Feeling Cold

Wallace Terry

THE FIRST ONE I KILLED REALLY GOT TO ME. I guess it was his size. Big guy. Big, broad chest. Stocky legs. He was so big I thought he was Chinese. I still think he was Chinese.

We were on this trail near the Ashau Valley. I saw him and hit the ground and came up swinging like Starsky and Hutch. I shot him with a .45, and I got him pretty good.

He had an AK-47. He was still holding it. He kicked. He kicked a lot. When you get shot, that stuff you see on Hoot Gibson doesn't work. When you're hit, you're hit. You kick. You feel that stuff burning through your flesh. I know how it feels. I've been hit three times.

That's what really got to me—he was so big. I didn't expect that.

They were hard core, too. The enemy would do anything to win. You had to respect that. They believed in a cause. They had the support of the people. That's the key that we Americans don't understand yet. We can't do anything in the military ourselves unless we have the support of the people.

Sometimes we would find the enemy tied to trees. They knew they were going to die. I remember one guy tied up with rope and bamboo. We didn't even see him until he shouted at us and started firing. I don't know whether we killed him or some artillery got him.

One time they had a squad of sappers that hit us. It was like suicide. They ran at us so high on marijuana they didn't know what they were doing. You could smell the marijuana on their clothes. Some of the stuff they did was so crazy that they had to be high on something. In the first place, you don't run through concertina wire like that. Nobody in his right mind does. You get too many cuts. Any time you got a cut over there, it was going to turn to gangrene if it didn't get treated. And they knew we had the place covered.

Another time this guy tried to get our attention. I figured he wanted to give up, because otherwise, I figured he undoubtedly wanted to die. We thought he had started to *chu hoi* [defect]. And we prepared for him to come in. But before he threw his weapon down, he started firing and we had to shoot him.

And, you know, they would walk through our minefields, blow up, and never even bat their heads. Weird shit.

But I really thought they stunk.

Like the time we were heli-lifted from Vandergrift and had to come down in Dong Ha. There was this kid, maybe two or three years old. He hadn't learned to walk too well yet, but he was running down the street. And a Marine walked over to talk to the kid, touched him, and they both blew up. They didn't move. It was not as if they stepped on something. The kid had to have the explosive around him. It was a known tactic that they wrapped stuff around kids. That Marine was part of the security force around Dong Ha, a lance corporal. He was trying to be friendly.

I think it stinks. If those guys were low enough to use kids to bait Americans or anybody to this kind of violent end, well, I think they should be eliminated. And they would have been if we had fought the war in such a manner that we could have won the war. I mean total all-out war. Not nuclear war. We could have done it with land forces. I would have invaded Hanoi so many times, they would have thought we were walking on water.

The people in Washington setting policy didn't know what transpired over there. They were listening to certain people who didn't really know what we were dealing with. That's why we had all those stupid restrictions. Don't fight across this side of the DMZ, don't fire at women unless they fire at you, don't fire across this area unless you smile first or unless somebody shoots at you. If they attack you and run across this area, you could not go back over there and take them out. If only we could have fought it in a way that we had been taught to fight.

But personally speaking, to me, we made a dent, even though the South did fall. Maybe we did not stop the Communist takeover, but at least I know that I did something to say hey, you bastards, you shouldn't do that. And personally I feel good about it. People like Jane Fonda won't buy that, because they went over there and actually spent time with the people that were killing Americans. That's why I feel that I shouldn't spend $4 to see her at the box office. She's a sexy girl and all that other kind of stuff, but she's not the kind of girl that I'd like to admire. She was a psychological letdown, and she definitely should not have been allowed to go to Hanoi.

I learned a lot about people in my platoon. I learned you have to take a person for what he feels, then try to mold the individual into the person you would like to be with. Now my platoon had a lot of Southerners, as well as some Midwesterners. Southerners at the first sign of a black officer being in charge of them were somewhat reluctant. But then, when they found that you know what's going on and you're trying to keep them alive, then they tried to be the best damn soldiers you've got. Some of the black soldiers were the worse I had because they felt that they had to jive on me. They wanted to let me know, Hey, man. Take care of me, buddy. You know I'm your buddy. That's bull.

As long as a black troop knows he's going to take a few knocks like everybody else, he can go as far as anybody in the Corps. Our biggest problem as a race is a tendency to say that the only reason something didn't go the way it was programmed to go is because we are black. It may be that you tipped on somebody's toes. We as blacks have gotten to the place now where we want to depend on somebody else doing something for us. And when we don't measure up to what the expectations are—the first thing we want to holler is racial discrimination. My philosophy is, if you can't do the job—move.

Let's face it. We are part of America. Even though there have been some injustices made, there is no reason for us not to be a part of the American system. I don't feel that because my grandfather or grandmother was a slave that I should not lift arms up to support those things that are stated in the Constitution of the United States. Before I went to Vietnam, I saw the "burn, baby, burn" thing because of Martin Luther King. Why should they burn up Washington, D.C., for something that happened in Memphis? They didn't hurt the white man that was doing business down there on 7th Street. They hurt the black man. They should have let their voices be known that there was injustice. That's the American way.

I still dream about Vietnam.

In one dream, everybody has nine lives. I've walked in front of machine guns that didn't go off. When they pulled the trigger, the trigger jammed. I've seen situations where I got shot at, and the round curved and hit the corner. I'd see that if I had not made that one step, I would not be here. I think about the time where a rocket-propelled grenade hit me in the back, and it didn't go off. We were in a clear area and got hit by an enemy force. The RPG hit me. Didn't go off. Didn't explode. We kept walking, and five of us got hit. I got frays in the lower back and right part of the buttocks. I didn't want to go back to the hospital ship, so I just created the impression that I could handle it. But the stuff wouldn't stop bleeding, and they had to pull the frays out. There was this doctor at Quang Tri, Dr. Mitchell, who was from Boston, a super guy. He painted a smile on my rear end. He cut a straight wound into a curve with stitches across so it looks as if I'm smiling. When I drop my trousers, there's a big smile.

I dream about how the kids in my platoon would come to talk to you and say things about their families. Their families would be upset when they heard I was black. But then some guy would give me a picture of his sister. He would say, "She's white, but you'd still like her. Look her up when you get back to the States." And there would be the ones who did not get a letter that day. Or never got a letter their whole tour. In those cases, I would turn around and write them letters and send them back to Vandergrift.

And you dream about those that you lost. You wonder if there was something you could have done to save them. I only lost two kids. Really.

Cripes was a white guy. I think he was from St. Louis. He was a radio operator. You could tell him. "Tell the battalion commander that everything is doing fine." He would say, "Hey, Big Six. Everything is A-okay. We are ready, Freddie." You know, he had to add something to whatever you said. Otherwise, he was a very quiet guy. But one big problem he had was that he wanted to get into everything. He was trying to prove something to himself. If he saw somebody move, he was going to follow him. No matter what you could do to tell him not to fire, he'd fire. One night, after we got out to Fire Support Base Erskine, we got hit. It was about eleven. Cripes got shot. We don't know if he got hit by our fire or their fire. I just know he crawled out there. He must have seen something. Cripes just had a bad habit of being in the wrong place at the wrong time.

Lance Corporal Oliver was a black kid from Memphis. He carried an automatic rifle. He had been with us maybe three months. He was a very scary kid. He was trying to prove a lot of things to himself and to his family, too. So he was always volunteering to be point. It was very difficult to appoint someone as a point man. A lot of times when you had a feeling you were going to be hit, you asked for volunteers. Oliver always volunteered.

We were on Operation Dewey Canyon. In February of 1969. We had been told the NVA was in there that night. One platoon had went out and got hit. And we got the message to go in next. I got the whole platoon together and said, "Listen. I'm going to walk point for you." My troops said, "No, sir, you don't need to walk. We will arrange for someone to walk point." So the next day the whole platoon got together and said, "Who wants to walk point today?" Oliver stuck up his hand. I said, "I'll be the second man."

Now we had this dog to sniff out VC. Normally he would walk the point with the dog handler. His handler, Corporal Rome from Baltimore, swore Hobo could smell the Vietnamese a mile away. If he smelled one, his hair went straight. You knew something was out there.

One time, when we were walking a trail near Con Thien, this guy was in this tree. At first we thought he was one of the local indigenous personnel, like the ARVN. He turned out to be something else. He had his pajamas on and his army trousers. He wasn't firing. He was just sitting there. Hobo just ran up in that tree, reached back, and tore off his uniform. He was armed with an AK-47. Hobo took that away from him, threw him up in the air, and grabbed him by the neck and started dragging him. We learned a lot from that guy. You put a dog on a guy, and he'll tell you anything you want to know.

Another time at Vandergrift, Hobo started barking in the officers' hootch. We had sandbags between us. And Hobo just barked and barked at the bags. Nobody could figure out what was wrong. Finally I told Hobo to shut up, and I walked over to the sandbags. There was this viper, and I took a shotgun and blew its head off.

We used to dress Hobo up with a straw hat on his head and shades on. All of us had shades. And we used to take pictures of Hobo. And sit him on the chopper. And he'd be in the back of the chopper with his shades on and his hat, and he would smile at us.

We got to the place where we could feed him, and put our hands in his mouth. We would give him Gravy Train or Gainsburgers. If we ran out on patrol, we would give him our C-rations. He really liked beef with spice sauce.

Hobo was so gullible and so lovable that when you had a problem, you ended up talking to him. You could say, "Hobo, what the hell am I doing here?" Or, "Hey, man. We didn't find nothin' today. We walked three miles and couldn't find nothin'. What the hell are you doing walking this way?" And he'd look at you and smile, you know, in his own little manner. And he'd let you know that he should really be here to understand all this shit we're putting down. Or he would do things like growl to let you know he really didn't approve of all this bullshit you're talking. It's hard to explain. But after eight months, Hobo was like one of the guys.

Hobo signaled the ambush, but nobody paid any attention. We walked into the ambush. A machine gun hit them. Oliver got shot dead three times in the head, three times in the chest, and six times in the leg. Rome got hit in the leg. Hobo got shot in the side, but even though he was hit, he got on top of Rome. The only person that Hobo allowed to go over there and touch Rome was me.

It never got better. It seemed like everyday somebody got hurt. Sometimes I would walk point. Everybody was carrying the wounded. We had 15 wounded in my platoon alone. And the water was gone.

Then on the twelfth day, while we were following this trail through the jungle, the point man came running back. He was all heated up. He said, "I think we got a tank up there." I told him, "I don't have time for no games." The enemy had no tanks in the South.

Then the trail started converging into a really well-camouflaged road, about 12 feet wide and better made than anything I had ever seen in Vietnam. Then I saw the muzzle of this gun. It was as big as anything we had. And all hell broke open. It was like the sun was screaming.

I thought, my God, if I stay here, I'm going to get us all wiped out.

In front of us was a reinforced platoon and two artillery pieces all dug into about 30 real serious bunkers. And we were in trouble in the rear, because a squad of snipers had slipped in between us and the rest of Charlie Company. My flanks were open. All the NVA needed to finish us off was to set up mortars on either side.

Someone told me the snipers had just got Joe. He was my platoon sergeant.

That did it. I passed the word to call in napalm at Danger Close, 50 meters off our position. Then I turned to go after the snipers. And I heard this loud crash. I was thrown to the ground. This grenade had exploded, and the shrapnel had torn into my left arm.

The Phantoms were doing a number. It felt like an earthquake was coming. The ground was just a-rumbling. Smoke was everywhere, and then the grass caught fire. The napalm explosions had knocked two of my men down who were at the point, but the NVA were running everywhere. The flames were up around my waist. That's when I yelled, "Charge. Kill the gooks. Kill the motherfuckers."

We kept shooting until everything was empty. Then we picked up the guns they dropped and fired them. I brought three down with my .45. In a matter of minutes, the ridge was ours. We had the bunkers, an earth mover, bunches of documents, tons of food supplies. We counted 70 dead NVA. And those big guns, two of them. Russian-made. Like our 122, they had a range of 12 to 15 miles. They were the first ones captured in South Vietnam.

Well, I ordered a perimeter drawn. And since I never ask my men to do something I don't do, I joined the perimeter. Then this sniper got me. Another RPG. I got it in the back. I could barely raise myself up on one elbow. I felt like shit, but I was trying to give a command. The guys just circled around me like they were waiting for me to tell them something. I got to my knees. And it was funny. They had their guns pointed at the sky.

I yelled out, "I can walk. I can walk."

Somebody said, "No, sir. You will not walk."

I slumped back. And two guys got on my right side. Two guys got on my left side. One held me under the head. One more lifted my feet. Then they held me high above their shoulders, like I was a Viking or some kind of hero. They formed a perimeter around me. They told me feet would never touch ground there again. And they held me high up in the air until the chopper came.

I really don't know what I was put in for. I was told maybe the Navy Cross. Maybe the Medal of Honor. It came down to the Silver Star. One of those guns is at Quantico in the Marine Aviation Museum. And the other is at Fort Sill in Oklahoma. And they look just as horrible today as they did when we attacked them.

Rome lost his leg. From what I'm told, they gave him a puppy sired by Hobo. So Hobo survived Dewey Canyon. They wanted to destroy him at first, but he got back to the kennel. If anybody would've destroyed that dog, it would have been me.

But Hobo didn't get back to the States. Those dogs that were used in Vietnam were not brought back. The Air Force destroyed all those dogs. They were afraid of what they might do here.

If I had Hobo right now, he wouldn't have to worry about nothing the rest of his life. He was a hell of a dog. He could sense right and wrong. I would have trusted Hobo with my own children. If somebody got wrong or was an enemy of my family, Hobo would have brought his ass to me. There ain't no doubt about it. Yet he was a nice dog. He would give me a kiss on the jaw. I loved that dog.

But the thing that really hurt me more than anything in the world was when I came back to the States and black people considered me as a part of the establishment. Because I am an officer. Here I was, a veteran that just came back from a big conflict. And most of the blacks wouldn't associate with me. You see, blacks are not supposed to be officers. Blacks are supposed to be those guys that take orders, and not necessarily those that give them. If you give orders, it means you had to kiss somebody's rear end to get into that position.

One day I wore my uniform over to Howard University in Washington to help recruit officer candidates. Howard is a black school, like the one I went to in Texas, Jarvis Christian College. I thought I would feel at home. The guys poked fun at me, calling me Uncle Sam's flunky. They would say the Marine Corps sucks. The Army sucks. They would say their brother or uncle got killed, so why was I still in. They would see the Purple Heart and ask me what was I trying to prove. The women wouldn't talk to you either.

I felt bad. I felt cold. I felt like I was completely out of it.

« 20 »

Nursing and Disillusionment

Lynda Van Devanter

I WENT UP-COUNTRY WITH TWO OTHER SECOND LIEUTENANTS, Michelle Neuman and Coretta Jones, flying in a six-passenger single-engine plane to Nha Trang and hopping a supply helicopter from there to Pleiku. Michelle was a petite blonde, with blue eyes, a pageboy haircut, and the face of an elf. From the time she was an infant, everyone had called her Mickie, a name that seemed to fit perfectly her bubbly personality. She had been raised near Boston, but had gone to a nursing school in San Jose, California, to get away from home. When she laughed, it sounded more like a giggle. She was a whirlwind of undirected energy, and she was one of the most fun people I'd every known. She was forever trying to tell jokes and usually forgetting the punch lines. Even when she remembered them, she would giggle so hard that she wouldn't be able to get the words out. Of course, Mickie's punch lines never mattered. Her giggle was so infectious that it would be impossible not to laugh with her. If I didn't know better, I would have sworn that she had invented the word "cute." Everybody liked her immediately.

Coretta was far more subdued than her outgoing friend. She had gone to the same nursing school as Mickie, but since Coretta was two years ahead, they hadn't got to know each other until recently, as the result of a one in a million coincidence. Ten days earlier, they had found themselves the only women on the same plane out of Travis, headed for Vietnam. Coretta was three years older than Mickie and two years older than I. She had worked in the emergency room of a hospital in Oakland, California, her hometown, before deciding to join the Army to "find something better." She was tall and black, with a body that was slightly overweight but very attractive. Although at that point, I thought of myself as a girl, there was no question in my mind that Coretta was a woman. She carried herself with a quiet confidence and seemed to be one of the few people who really listened when others talked. However, the thing that stood out the most was her compassion. There wasn't anything about her that you could point to and say made her compassionate, but her concern for others always came through. Maybe it was an expression given off by those big brown eyes or from her warm smile. Whatever it was, I knew instinctively that she was a person who could be counted on in a crunch.

When we arrived at the 71st Evac Hospital, we were met with an enthusiasm that was hard to believe. I don't think I've ever felt so welcome anywhere. But everyone had a strange habit of referring to us as "turtles" or "FNGs."

"Why turtles?" I asked.

"Because it took so long for you to get here," one of the nurses said. "The people you're replacing have waited a whole year."

"And what's an FNG?"

"What else?" she said. "A Fucking New Guy. Welcome to the war. We could use some new blood around here."

There was a list in the emergency room [ER] that had the name of every person assigned to the hospital. Next to each name was the person's blood type. When the hospital ran out of blood, someone would go immediately to that list. As a result, replacements were more than just people who could take over some of the workload; they were, literally, new blood.

We all experienced a degree of shock when we saw the hospital compound for the first time. Coretta made her evaluation less than five minutes after we had left the helicopter. "This is the damnedest hospital I've ever seen," she said. That was probably an understatement.

After signing in at headquarters, we got an abbreviated tour. The 71st consisted of a group of ramshackle wooden buildings and metal Quonset huts, all covered with a layer of red dust and protected by a fence, barbed wire, bored guards, and Vietnamese soldiers in tanks. The ER was about fifty yards from the helipad and was connected to the post-op/intensive care unit and the operating room [OR]—actually six operating cubicles, three on each side of an open hallway and divided from each other by five-and-a-half-foot-tall cabinets. The building housing them was called the surgical-T, because of its shape. Next door to the surgical-T was the morgue. As we walked past it, a nurse wheeled a gurney through its double doors. I felt like I wasn't supposed to look.

Our guide was a six-foot-four-inch hulk of a man who must have weighed 250 pounds and who looked like he could lift a tank with one arm. He wore dirty, wrinkled fatigues and his jungle boots were coated with a layer of red dust. His clothes hung on him. I had the feeling that he was the kind of man who would have looked sloppy even in a tux. He appeared to enjoy the role of tour guide, and he seemed to like the three of us instantly, although he didn't bother to tell us his name.

When we were finished with the business part of the tour, our guide offered to show us the "important sights," which were the park, the banana trees, and the pool. The park was a narrow strip of ground behind the headquarters building and between a couple of other buildings he referred to as hooches. It was called the Bernard J. Piccolo Memorial Peace Park, in honor of the popular commander who had just left. The banana trees were a couple of scrawny things near the commanding officer's trailer. The signs in front of them identified them as the Bernard J. Piccolo Memorial Banana Tree and the Elizabeth L. Piccolo Memorial Banana Tree. He said both names fully, as if to combine them into the Bernard J. and Elizabeth L. Piccolo Trees would have been highly irreverent. And God pity anyone who had the nerve to call them Bernie and Liz. Such sacrilege would never be permitted. It was important to always respect Bernard J. because he had been "a truly wonderful man," and Elizabeth L., because she had waited faithfully back in the world while her husband "did his duty for God, apple pie, and country. Amen."

Our last stop was the pool. "Only evac hospital in-country with our very own pool," he said proudly.

"Don't tell us," I said. "You call it the Bernard J. Piccolo Memorial Swimming Pool."

He laughed. "No, actually the people around here were thinking of calling it the Captain Bubba L. Kominski Memorial Swimming pool, in honor of just possibly the second best neurosurgeon on the entire continent of Asia, with perhaps the exception of Upper Mongolia. But Bubba Kominski is far too modest to allow anything like that."

"Why Bubba L. Kominski?" I asked.

"Because the good captain just happened to save the life of an infantry lieutenant who just happened to be the son of an engineer colonel who just happened to be grateful enough to the 71st to donate some men and machinery to our noble effort to make life on this planet more meaningful. In short, Captain Bubba L. Kominski, gentleman, scholar, neurosurgeon of distinction, and father of the six-month-old Glenda Lee Kominski, just happened to be the man responsible for getting this pool built."

"Sounds impressive," I said teasingly. "And when do we just happen to get to meet this wonderful Captain Bubba L. Kominski?"

Our guide smiled broadly, put his enormous, meaty hands around my waist, and lifted me more than a foot off the ground until I was at eye level with him. "You're looking at the man," he said. "Captain Bubba L. Kominski at your service."

Bubba got us temporarily set up with cots in the living room of Colonel Bernard J. Piccolo's trailer, which was vacant until a new commander arrived. "They're gonna have to kick a couple of doctors out of a hooch so you girls can have more permanent quarters," he said.

The next day, Mickie, Coretta, and I started to work. Coretta was assigned to the emergency room. Mickie and I joined the operating room staff. None of us was quite ready for duty at the 71st.

That first shift was a shock. There were *only* fifteen wounded soldiers who needed surgery. I saw young boys with their arms and legs blown off, some with their guts hanging out, and others with "ordinary" gunshot wounds. In addition, at least another twenty-five DPCs—delayed primary closures—were scheduled for the OR. These were guys who had been brought in with wounds a few days earlier. Since wounds coming into the 71st were usually dirty, and the possibilities of infection high, doctors would stop the bleeding, remove the metal fragments or bullets, and clean the wound during the initial surgery. Then, rather than close the outer skin immediately, they would leave the wound covered with sterile fine mesh gauze and antibiotics for a few days to make sure infections didn't get a chance to start. Later, when the risk of infection was lessened, the guy would be brought back into the OR for a DPC.

My first case was a D & I, debridement and irrigation, with Bubba Kominski. "I bet you thought us world-renowned neurosurgeons were above mere donkey work like this," he said. "Well, Van, lesson number one is that everybody around this death factory is a jack of all trades." The D & I was probably the most common operation in Vietnam. When a soldier got a frag wound, he would usually have little holes all over his body, where fragments had broken the skin. Our job, after we stopped the bleeding, was to remove the metal fragments and cut away any dead skin—debridement—and then to clean the wound with sterile saline solution to reduce the risk of infection—irrigation. Bubba called it, "making big holes out of little holes." He said our kid had stepped on a Bouncing Betty.

"A Bouncing Betty?" I asked.

"It's a land mine," he answered. "An explosive charge bounces up to about waist level before going bang. The V.C. like it because it tends to deprive our upstanding young men of a part of their anatomy that usually spends a lot of time at attention when it's in the presence of unclothed beautiful women. Fortunately, this young trooper had his back to the charge. Family jewels all in place, but it sure took a bite out of his ass."

The next lesson that Bubba taught me was to forget most of the things I had learned in nursing school and at the OR school, starting with the arrangement of my instrument tray. "You can always tell the FNGs by the way they set up their Mayo stands," he said. In almost every OR, there are specific ways to organize the instruments. Every item has a place, and the best scrub nurses can find things blindfolded. The system is based on the idea that the only person using the tray will be the scrub. She normally hands the surgeon what he needs. If he forgets this rule, he is usually reminded with a quick rap across his knuckles.

However, as Bubba quickly pointed out, we had neither the time nor personnel for us to follow these standards. Stateside operations are usually performed by a surgeon with at least one assistant plus a scrub. In Vietnam, I would be expected to be both scrub nurse and assistant, and sometimes would find myself without a free hand with which to give instruments. He proved his point immediately. "Get on the other side of the table," he said. "You're going to start cutting with me."

"I don't know how to cut," I said.

"That's why I'm going to teach you, Van. Welcome to med school."

Bubba was an excellent teacher and I learned quickly. From that case, we went to a neuro case, one in which a nineteen-year-old boy had gotten a bullet lodged in his back, pressing against his spinal cord. As Bubba cut down to the vertebrae and started working his way to the spinal cord, I saw another facet of his personality. He became very intense, and concentrated every ounce of his being on the delicate work that had to be done. It would have been obvious to even an untrained observer that Captain Bubba L. Kominski was a virtuoso with a knife. He may very well have been accurate in calling himself "the second best neurosurgeon in Asia."

The wounded soldier had been brought in paralyzed, but Bubba hadn't been quite sure if it was because the spinal cord had been cut or only bruised. Although a bruise could also be serious enough to cause permanent paralysis, it would leave some hope.

It turned out that our kid's spinal cord was moderately bruised, with the bullet lodged against it. "No question about it," Bubba said. "We got us some damage here." He used his tiny instruments to slowly and meticulously cut away pieces of vertebrae and remove the bullet, taking special care not to do any further damage to the spinal cord. "Hey, Van, we got a bleeder that let loose. Could you give me some suction while I tie it off?" I was extremely nervous. One mistake could end whatever small chances this guy might have to walk again. Finally, Bubba dropped a bullet into the specimen bowl.

As he finished the surgery, I asked, "Do you think he'll walk again?"

"Hard to tell," he said. "But if he does or doesn't we'll never know. We just patch them up and send them away. We never hear what happens after they're gone."

"Isn't it frustrating?"

"You'll get used to it, Van. This is an assembly line, not a medical center."

One thing I knew I'd never get used to was something I encountered later in the day when I had to work with another doctor on my first serious burn case. The soldier, whose entire body had been charred beyond recognition, had been at the 71st for the past three days. His patrol had been accidentally attacked by one of our own helicopters. Of the ten men, he was the only survivor. In spite of the work that was being done to keep him alive, he was undoubtedly going to die. Almost his entire body, except for his feet, had been seared by napalm, a jellied petroleum substance that oozes down the skin and into the pores, carrying flames with it. By now, he was covered with a sickly blue-green slime, called pseudomonas, a common bacterial infection among severely burned patients. I could barely look at the kid while we scraped away the infected dead tissue, trying to get down to a viable area so he might have some chance of healing. Long after we were finished with him, I was unable to get the smell of pseudomonas and napalm out of my nose. It seemed to be in my clothes, my hair, and even the pores of my skin. I would live with that smell for the next year. It was disgusting.

When I went to the mess hall that night, all the food smelled like the burned soldier. I had managed to control my stomach during the surgery, but twice that evening, when I thought about it, I retched. . . .

Once Carl [a Vietnam boyfriend] was gone, I tried to bury my loneliness in work. I missed him, probably more than I've ever missed anyone in my life. A few times, I thought of breaking my promise and writing him a letter. But I didn't want to interfere in his other life. He was back in the real world with his wife and kids, where all of us wanted to be. What could I possibly offer him now?

I checked that mail each day for a card, a letter, some sort of reminder that I was not forgotten. Carl never sent a word. Maybe it was best that way.

However, I could still hear his voice telling me I had to be tough to survive. And as each day passed, I found myself developing a harder shell to protect my emotions. For the first few weeks after he went home, I drank heavily and used more grass. But after a while, I started avoiding them because they lowered my defenses. Before, they had effectively deadened all pain and kept me from feeling the suffering of others. Now, they only made me feel it more. I was getting tired. This war was beginning to look different than the one I had believed in only a few weeks earlier. I started listening to the local discontents who railed against Nixon, Congress, the Joint Chiefs of Staff, and the whole U.S. government. Every time another person died on my table, I came one step closer to agreeing with them. I still tried to remind myself that we were in Vietnam to save people who were threatened by tyranny, but that became more and more difficult to believe as I heard stories of corrupt South Vietnamese officials, U.S. Army atrocities, and a population who wanted nothing more than to be left alone so they could return to farming their land. I saw kids—American eighteen- and nineteen-year-olds and little Vietnamese and Montagnard kids—who were dying of diseases that I thought had been eliminated from the face of the earth. There were cases of malaria, polio, typhoid, cholera, and tetanus. One day, I saw some dead American soldiers lying outside the morgue. They had been ambushed by an NVA unit. The butchers had cut off our soldiers' penises and stuffed them into the GIs' mouths. I was outraged by the scene, but not as outraged as I became when I later saw a similar scene, only this time with dead Viet Cong. It was the first time I realized that our clean-cut, wholesome American boys could be as brutal as the "godless communists."

Neither group was as bad as the ROKs. The ROKs were soldiers from the Republic of Korea. They were part of a token international force that had been assembled in South Vietnam so the U.S. need not claim this as a solely American war. The ROKs handled most of the interrogations in our area and were some of the hardest soldiers there. They practiced every conceivable kind of torture, and often the interrogations ended in death regardless of whether the person was a V.C. or just an innocent Vietnamese who happened into the wrong place at the wrong time. One of the favorite forms of torture was referred to as the "Bell Telephone Hour." They would connect electrical wires from a field telephone set to the victim's testicles or vagina. If presented with an answer they didn't like, they would crank the phone to produce a shock. The pain must have been excruciating. Yet that wasn't the worst type of interrogation.

The preferred technique was far more gruesome. I saw the results of that method on a night when we received an unconscious V.C. suspect for surgery. He had been scalped. It wasn't a quick scalping. It had taken place over a number of hours, a little at a time, to bring about the maximum amount of suffering. They had made the man stand on his toes while they attached his flesh to a hook. Each time he moved an inch, he was in agony.

By the time we got that case, I was already insensitive enough to the suffering to laugh when one of our own surgeons lifted the flap of scalp and said, "No sense wasting this. Know any bald guys?"

During those months after Carl left, I lost my direction and found myself becoming a person I would never have been before Vietnam. Maybe he would have said I was merely getting tough. Like thousands of Americans, I began calling the Vietnamese—both friendly and enemy—"gooks." I would have thought I was above that sort of racism; after all, hadn't I marched in the United States for civil rights like a good Catholic girl who believed all oppression was wrong?

I began to understand how many of my friends had felt during my early months there. I had looked down on them for displaying just the kind of attitude I was beginning to develop. Now, I saw the Vietnamese as nothing more than a group of thieves and murderers. It was especially difficult because V.C. looked the same as anyone else. Rather than try to distinguish between the friends and enemies, I learned to hate all of them. They were the ones who kept killing American soldiers. Why should we bother saving them?

Once, in the middle of a push, I was directed to scrub on a belly case. When I looked at the chart, I realized I would be working on a prisoner of war, an NVA lieutenant colonel. I was furious. I stormed up to the nurse in charge. "We still have GIs out there," I said. "What the fuck are we doing this guy for?"

"We're following triage protocol," she said. "This soldier is next."

"But twenty minutes ago, this jerk was out there trying to blow us away."

"And now he's wounded and needs our help, Van. Get to work."

"If you're such a gook lover, why don't you scrub on the case?"

"Because I've ordered you to do it."

In addition to being upset, I was extremely confused by the whole episode. I could understand that as a human being, he had a right to proper care, but every bone in my body told me that he wasn't worth the effort. In fact, he could have been the officer who had ordered Father Bergeron's execution, or the battalion commander who was responsible for every single case we got that day. I wanted to spit in his face. Instead, I spit in my hands. That was how I scrubbed for the case before donning sterile gloves. If he died of an infection, fuck him.

A part of me knew that after it was over, I would be ashamed. I had taken a vow as a nurse to help all human beings no matter what race, creed, color, or sex. According to that vow, they were all entitled to quality care. But my bitterness far outweighed any vows I had spoken in a graduation ceremony. I did what I had to do for that POW and not one bit more. All the time we worked on him, I wished that he would die.

But he didn't.

When we were finished and it was apparent that the NVA colonel would live, the surgeon suggested we literally charge an arm and a leg for the operation. I offered to get the saw and we all laughed hysterically. Some day, I would hate myself for having laughed. But not now. . . .

When the soldiers of World War II came home, they were met by brass bands, ticker-tape parades, and people so thankful for their service that even those who had never heard a shot fired in anger were treated with respect. It was a time when words like honor, glory, and duty held some value, a time when a returning GI was viewed with esteem so high it bordered on awe. To be a veteran was to be seen as a person of courage, a champion of democracy, an ideal against which all citizens could measure themselves. If you had answered your country's call, you were a hero. And in those days, heroes were plentiful.

But somewhere between 1945 and 1970, words like bravery, sacrifice, and valor had gone out of vogue. When I returned to my country in June of 1970, I began to learn a very bitter lesson. The values with which I had been raised had changed; in the eyes of most Americans, the military services had no more heroes, merely babykillers, misfits, and fools. I was certain that I was neither a babykiller nor a misfit. Maybe I was a fool.

There are those among the poets, philosophers, and psychologists who believe that the root of all unhappiness is unfulfilled expectation. Many people, they argue, have unrealistic expectations. If you learn not to expect too much, their logic goes, you won't be disappointed. Therefore, you'll be happier. Perhaps they're right. Perhaps if I hadn't expected anything at all when I returned to the States, I would not have been disappointed. Maybe I would have been contented simply to be on American soil. Maybe all of us who arrived at Travis Air Force Base on June 16 had unrealistic expectations.

But we didn't ask for a brass band. We didn't ask for a parade. We didn't even ask for much of a thank you. All we wanted was some transportation to San Francisco International Airport so we could hop connecting flights to get home to our families. We gave the Army a year of our lives, a year with more difficulties than most Americans face in fifty years. The least the Army could have done was to give us a ride.

At Travis we were herded onto buses and driven to the Oakland Army Terminal where they dumped us around 5 A.M. with a "so long, suckers" from the driver and a feeling that we were no more than warm bodies who had outlived their usefulness. Unfortunately, San Francisco International was at least twenty miles away. Since most of us had to get flights from there, wouldn't it have been logical to drop us at the airport? Or was I expecting too much out of the Army when I asked it to be logical?

I checked into commercial buses and taxis, but none were running. There was a transit strike on, and it was nearly impossible to get public transportation of any kind. So I hung one of my suitcases from my left shoulder, hefted my duffel bag onto my right shoulder, grabbed my overnight case with my left hand and my purse with my right, and struggling under the weight, walked out to the highway, where I stuck out my thumb and waited. I was no stranger to hitchhiking. It was the only way to get around in Vietnam. Back in 'Nam, I would usually stand on the flight line in my fatigues, combat boots, jungle hat, pigtails, and a smile. Getting a ride there was a cinch. In fact, planes would sometimes reach the end of the runway, then return to offer me a lift.

But hitchhiking in the real world, I was quickly finding out, was nowhere near as easy—especially if you were wearing a uniform. The cars whizzed past me during rush hour, while I patiently waited for a good Samaritan to stop. A few drivers gave me the finger. I tried to ignore them. Some slowed long enough to yell obscenities. One threw a carton of trash and another nearly hit me with a half-empty can of soda. Finally, two guys stopped in a red and yellow Volkswagen bus. The one on the passenger side opened his door. I ran to the car, dragging the duffel bag and other luggage behind me. I was hot, tired, and dirty.

"Going anywhere near the airport?" I asked.

"Sure am," the guy said. He had long brown hair, blue eyes framed by wire-rimmed glasses, and a full curly beard. There were patches on his jeans and a peace sign on his T-shirt. His relaxed, easy smile was deceptive.

I smiled back and lifted my duffel bag to put it inside the van. But the guy slammed the door shut. "We're going past the airport, sucker, but we don't take Army pigs." He spit on me. I was stunned.

"Fuck you, Nazi bitch," the driver yelled. He floored the accelerator and they both laughed uncontrollably as the VW spun its wheels for a few seconds, throwing dirt and stones back at me before it roared away. The drivers of other passing cars also laughed.

I looked down at my chest. On top of my nametag sat a big gob of brownish-colored saliva. I couldn't touch it. I didn't have the energy to wipe it away. Instead, I watched as it ran down my name tag and over a button before it was absorbed into the green material of my uniform.

I wasn't angry, just confused. I wanted to know why. Why would he spit on me? What had I done to him? To either of them? It might have been simple to say I had gone to war and they blamed me for killing innocent people, but didn't they understand that I didn't want this war any more than the most vocal of peace marchers? Didn't they realize that those of us who had seen the war firsthand were probably more antiwar than they were? That we had seen friends suffer and die? That we had seen children destroyed? That we had seen futures crushed?

Were they that naive?

Or were they merely insensitive creeps who used the excuse of my uniform to vent their hostility toward all people?

I waited a few more hours, holding my thumb out until I thought my arm would fall off. After awhile, I stopped watching people as they hurled their insults. I had begun noticing the people who didn't scream as they drove by. I soon realized they all had something in common. It was what I eventually came to refer to as "the look." It was a combination of surprise at seeing a woman in uniform, and hatred for what they assumed I represented. Most of them never bothered to try to conceal it. "The look" would start around the eyes, as if they were peering right through me. Their faces would harden into stone. I was a pariah, a nonperson so low that they believed they could squash me underfoot; I was as popular as a disease and as untouchable as a piece of shit.

While I stood there alone, I almost wished I was back in 'Nam. At least there you expected some people to hate you. That was a war. But here, in the United States, I guess I wanted everything to be wonderful. I thought that life would be different, that there would be no more pain. No more death. No more sorrow. It was all going to be good again. It had to be good again. I had had enough of fighting, and hatred, and bitterness.

Around 10:30 A.M., when I had given up hope and was sitting on my duffel bag, a passing driver shouted three words that perfectly illustrated my return to the world:

"Welcome home, asshole!"

A few minutes later, an old black man in a beat-up '58 Chevy stopped and got out of his car. He walked with a limp and leaned forward as if he couldn't stand straight. His clothes were frayed and his face deeply lined. He ran his bony fingers through his gray-black hair, then shook his head and smiled. "I don't know where you're going, little girl," he said. "But I been by here four times since early morning and you ain't got a ride yet. I can't let you spend your whole life on this road." He was only headed for the other side of Oakland, but he said he'd rather go out of his way than see me stranded. He even carried my duffel bag to the trunk. As we drove south on 101, I didn't say much other than thank you, but my disillusionment was obvious.

"People ain't all bad, little girl," he said. "It's just some folks are crazy mixed up these days. You keep in mind that it's gotta get better, 'cause it can't get any worse."

21

"They Did Not Know Good from Evil"

Tim O'Brien

"*LUI LAI, LUI LAI*!" STINK WOULD SCREAM, pushing them back. "*Lui lai*, you dummies. . . . Back up, move!" Teasing ribs with his rifle muzzle, he would force them back against a hootch wall or fence. "*Coi Chung*!" he'd holler. Blinking, face white and teeth clicking, he would kick the stragglers, pivot, shove, thumb flicking the rifle's safety catch. "Move! *Lui lai*. . . . Move it, go, go!" Herding them together, he would watch to be sure their hands were kept in the open, empty. Then he would open his dictionary. He would read slowly, retracing the words several times, then finally look up. "*Nam xuong dat*," he'd say. Separating each word, trying for good diction, he would say it in a loud, level voice. "Everybody . . . *nam xuong dat*." The kids would just stare. The women might rock and moan, or begin chattering among themselves like caged squirrels, glancing up at Stink with frazzled eyes. "Now!" he'd shout. "*Nam xuong dat*. . . . Do it!" Sometimes he would fire off a single shot, but this only made the villagers fidget and squirm. Puzzled, some of them would start to giggle. Others would cover their ears and yap with the stiff, short barking sounds of small dogs. It drove Stink wild. "*Nam xuong* the fuck down!" he'd snarl, his thin lips curling in a manner he practiced while shaving. "Lie down! *Man len*, mama-san! Now, goddamn it!" His eyes would bounce from his rifle to the dictionary to the cringing villagers. Behind him, Doc Peret and Oscar Johnson and Buff would be grinning at the show. They'd given the English-Vietnamese dictionary to Stink as a birthday present, and they loved watching him use it, the way he mixed languages in a kind of stew, ignoring pronunciation and grammar, turning angry when words failed to produce results. "*Nam thi xuong dat*!" he'd bellow, sweating now, his tongue sputtering over the impossible middle syllables. "*Man len*, pronto, you sons of bitches! Haul ass!" But the villagers would only shake their heads and cackle and mill uncertainly. This was too much for Stink Harris. Enraged, he'd throw away the dictionary and rattle off a whole magazine of ammunition. The women would moan. Kids would clutch their mothers, dogs would howl, chickens would scramble in their coops. "*Dong* fuckin' *let thit*!" Stink would be screaming, his eyes dusty and slit like a snake's. "*Nam xuong dat*! Do it, you ignorant bastards!" Reloading, he would keep firing and screaming, and the villagers would sprawl in the dust, arms wrapped helplessly around their heads. And when they were all down, Stink would stop firing. He would smile. He would glance at Doc Peret and nod. "See there? They understand me fine. *Nam xuong dat*. . . . Lie down. I'm gettin' the hang of it. You just got to punctuate your sentences."

Not knowing the language, they did not know the people. They did not know what the people loved or respected or feared or hated. They did not recognize hostility unless it was patent, unless it came in a form other than language; the complexities of tone and tongue were beyond them. Dinkese, Stink Harris called it: monkey chatter, bird talk. Not knowing the language, the men did not know whom to trust. Trust was lethal. They did not know false smiles from true smiles, or if in Quang Ngai a smile had the same meaning it had in the States. "Maybe the dinks got things mixed up," Eddie once said, after the time a friendly-looking farmer bowed and smiled and pointed them into a minefield. "Know what I mean? Maybe . . . well, maybe the gooks cry when they're happy and smile when they're sad. Who the hell knows? Maybe when you smile over here it means you're ready to cut the other guy's throat. I mean, hey . . . didn't they tell us way back in AIT that this here's a different culture?" Not knowing the people, they did not know friends from enemies. They did not know if it was a popular war, or, if popular, in what sense. They did not know if the people of Quang Ngai viewed the war stoically, as it sometimes seemed, or with grief, as it seemed other times, or with bewilderment or greed or partisan fury. It was impossible to know. They did not know religions or philosophies or theories of justice. More than that, they did not know how emotions worked in Quang Ngai. Twenty years of war had rotted away the ordinary reactions to death and disfigurement. Astonishment, the first response, was never there in the faces of Quang Ngai. Disguised, maybe. But who knew? Who ever knew? Emotions and beliefs and attitudes, motives and aims, hopes—these were unknown to the men in Alpha Company, and Quang Ngai told nothing. "Fuckin beasties," Stink would croak, mimicking the frenzied village speech. "No shit, I seen hamsters with more feelings."

But for Paul Berlin it was always a nagging question: Who were these skinny, blank-eyed people? What did they want? The kids especially—watching them, learning their names and faces, Paul Berlin couldn't help wondering. It was a ridiculous, impossible puzzle, but even so he wondered. Did the kids *like* him? A little girl with gold hoops in her ears and ugly scabs on her brow—did she feel, as he did, goodness and warmth and poignancy when he helped Doc dab iodine on her sores? Beyond that, though, did the girl *like* him? Lord knows, he had no villainy in his heart, no motive but kindness. He wanted health for her, and happiness. Did she know this? Did she sense his compassion? When she smiled, was it more than a token? And . . . and what *did* she want? Any of them, what did they long for? Did they have secret hopes? His hopes? Could this little girl—her eyes squinting as Doc brushed the scabs with iodine, her lips sucked in, her nose puckering at the smell—could she somehow separate him from the war? Even for an instant? Could she see him as just a scared-silly boy from Iowa? Could she feel sympathy? In it together, trapped, you and me, all of us: Did she feel that? Could she understand his own fear, matching it with hers? Wondering, he put mercy in his eyes like lighted candles; he gazed at the girl, full-hearted, draining out suspicion, opening himself to whatever she might answer with. Did the girl see the love? Could she understand it, return it? But he didn't know. He did not know if love or its analogue even existed in the vocabulary of Quang Ngai, or if friendship could be translated. He simply did not know. He wanted to be liked. He wanted them to understand, all of them, that he felt no hate. It was all a sad accident, he would have told them—chance, high-level politics, confusion. He had no stake in the war beyond simple survival; he was there, in Quang Ngai, for the same reasons they were: the luck of the draw, bad fortune, forces beyond reckoning. His intentions were benign. By God, yes! He was snared in a web as powerful and tangled as any that victimized the people of My Khe or Pinkville. Sure, they were trapped. Sure, they suffered, sure. But, by God, he was just as trapped, just as injured. He would have told them that. He was no tyrant, no pig, no Yankee killer. He was innocent. Yes, he was, he was innocent. He would have told them that, the villagers, if he'd known the language, if there had been time to talk. He would have told them he wanted to harm no one. Not even the enemy. The enemy! A word, a crummy word. He *had* no enemies. He had wronged no one. If he'd known the language, he would have told them how he hated to see the villages burned. Hated to see the paddies trampled. How it made him angry and sad when . . . a million things, when women were frisked with free hands, when old men were made to drop their pants to be searched, when, in a ville called Thin Mau, Oscar and Rudy Chassler shot down ten dogs for the sport of it. Sad and stupid. Crazy. Mean-spirited and self-defeating and wrong. Wrong! He would have told them this, the kids especially. But not me, he would have told them. The others, maybe, but not me. Guilty perhaps of hanging on, of letting myself be dragged along, of falling victim to gravity and obligation and events, but not—not!—guilty of wrong intentions.

After the war, perhaps, he might return to Quang Ngai. Years and years afterward. Return to track down the girl with gold hoops through her ears. Bring along an interpreter. And then, with the war ended, history decided, he would explain to her why he had let himself go to war. Not because of strong convictions, but because he didn't know. He didn't know who was right, or what was right; he didn't know if it was a war of self-determination or self-destruction, outright aggression or national liberation; he didn't know which speeches to believe, which books, which politicians; he didn't know if nations would topple like dominoes or stand separate like trees; he didn't know who really started the war, or why, or when, or with what motives; he didn't know if it mattered; he saw sense in both sides of the debate, but he did not know where truth lay; he didn't know if Communist tyranny would prove worse in the long run than the tyrannies of Ky or Thieu or Khanh—he simply didn't know. And who did? Who really did? He couldn't make up his mind. Oh, he had read the newspapers and magazines. He wasn't stupid. He wasn't uninformed. He just didn't know if the war was right or wrong. And who did? Who really *knew*? So he went to the war for reasons beyond knowledge. Because he believed in law, and law told him to go. Because it was a democracy, after all, and because LBJ and the others had rightful claim to their offices. He went to the war because it was expected. Because not to go was to risk censure, and to bring embarrassment on his father and his town. Because, not knowing, he saw no reason to distrust those with more experience. Because he loved his country and, more than that, because he trusted it. Yes, he did. Oh, he would rather have fought with his father in France, knowing certain things certainly, but he couldn't choose his war, nobody could. Was this so banal? Was this so unprofound and stupid? He would look the little girl with gold earrings straight in the eye. He would tell her these things. He would ask her to see the matter his way. What would *she* have done? What would *anyone* have done, not knowing? And then he would ask the girl questions. What did she want? How did she see the war? What were her aims—peace, any peace, peace with dignity? Did she refuse to run for the same reasons he refused—obligation, family, the land, friends, home? And now? Now, war ended, what did she want? Peace and quiet? Peace and pride? Peace with mashed potatoes and Swiss steak and vegetables, a full-tabled peace, indoor plumbing, a peace with Oldsmobiles and Hondas and skyscrapers climbing from the fields, a peace of order and harmony and murals on public buildings? Were her dreams the dreams of ordinary men and women? Quality-of-life dreams? Material dreams? Did she want a long life? Did she want medicine when she was sick, food on the table and reserves in the pantry? Religious dreams? What? What did she *aim* for? If a wish were to be granted by the war's winning army—any wish—what would she choose? Yes! If LBJ and Ho were to rub their magic lanterns at war's end, saying, "Here is what it was good for, here is the fruit," what would Quang Ngai demand? Justice? What sort? Reparations? What kind? Answers? What were the questions: What did Quang Ngai want to know?

In September, Paul Berlin was called before the battalion promotion board.

"You'll be asked some questions," the first sergeant said. "Answer them honestly. Don't for Chrissake make it complicated—just good, honest answers. And get a fuckin haircut."

It was a three-officer panel. They sat like squires behind a tin-topped table, two in sunglasses, the third in skintight tiger fatigues.

Saluting, reporting with his name and rank, Paul Berlin stood at attention until he was told to be seated.

"Berlin," said one of the offficers in sunglasses. "That's a pretty fucked-up name, isn't it?"

Paul Berlin smiled and waited.

The officer licked his teeth. He was a plump, puffy-faced major with spotted skin. "No bull, that's got to be the weirdest name I ever run across. Don't sound American. You an American, soldier?"

"Yes, sir."

"Yeah? Then where'd you get such a screwy name?"

"I don't know, sir."

"Sheeet." The major looked at the captain in tiger fatigues. "You hear that? This trooper don't know where he got his own name. You ever promoted somebody who don't know how he got his own fuckin name?"

"Maybe he forgot," said the captain in tiger fatigues.

"Amnesia? "

"Could be. Or maybe shell shock or something. Better ask again."

The major sucked his dentures halfway out of his mouth, frowned, then let the teeth slide back into place. "Can't hurt nothin'. Okay, soldier, one more time—where'd you find that name of yours?"

"Inherited it, sir. From my father."

"You crappin' me?"

"No, sir"

"And just where the hell'd he come up with it . . . your ol' man?"

"I guess from his father, sir. It came down the line sort of." Paul Berlin hesitated. It was hard to tell if the man was serious.

"You a Jewboy, soldier?"

"No, sir."

"A Kraut! Berlin . . . by jiminy, that's a Jerry name if I ever heard one!"

"I'm mostly Dutch.'

"The hell, you say."

"Yes, sir."

"Balls!"

"Sir, it's not—"

"Where's Berlin?"

"Sir?"

The major leaned forward, planting his elbows carefully on the table. He looked deadly serious. "I asked where Berlin is. You heard of fuckin' Berlin, didn't you? Like in East Berlin, West Berlin?"

"Sure, sir. It's in Germany."

"Which one?"

"Which what, sir?"

The major moaned and leaned back. Beside him, indifferent to it all, the captain in tiger fatigues unwrapped a thin cigar and lit it with a kitchen match. Red acne covered his face like the measles. He winked quickly—maybe it wasn't even a wink—then gazed hard at a sheaf of papers. The third officer sat silently. He hadn't moved since the interview began.

"Look here," the major said. "I don't know if you're dumb or just stupid, but by God I aim to find out." He removed his sunglasses. Surprisingly, his eyes were almost jolly. "You're up for Spec Four, that right?"

"Yes, sir."

"You want it? The promotion?" "Yes, sir, I do."

"Lots of responsibility."

Paul Berlin smiled. He couldn't help it.

"So we can't have shitheads leadin' men, can we? Takes some brains. You got brains, Berlin?"

"Yes, *sir*."

"You know what a condom is?" Paul Berlin nodded.

"A condom," the major intoned solemnly, "is a skullcap for us swingin' dicks. Am I right?"

"Yes, sir."

"And to lead men you got to be a swingin' fuckin' dick." "Right, sir."

"And is that you? You a swingin' dick, Berlin?" "Yes, sir!"

"You got guts?" "Yes, sir. I—"

"You 'fraid of gettin' zapped?" "No, sir."

"Sheeet." The major grinned as if having scored an important victory. He used the tip of his pencil to pick a speck of food from between his teeth. "Dumb! Anybody not scared of gettin' his ass zapped is a dummy. You know what a dummy is?"

"Yes, sir." "Spell it." Paul Berlin spelled it. The major rapped his pencil against the table, then glanced at his wristwatch. The captain in tiger fatigues was smoking with his eyes closed; the third officer, still silent, stared blankly ahead, arms folded tight against his chest.

"Okay," said the major, "we got a few standard-type questions for you. Just answer 'em truthfully, no bullshit. You don't know the answers, say so. One thing I can't stand is wishy-washy crap. Ready?"

"Yes, sir."

Pulling out a piece of yellow paper, the major put his pencil down and read slowly.

"How many stars we got in the flag?" "Fifty," said Paul Berlin.

"How many stripes?"

"Thirteen."

"What's the muzzle velocity of a standard AR-15?" "Two thousand feet a second." "Who's Secretary of the Army?"

"Stanley Resor."

"Why we fightin' this war?"

"Sir?"

"I say, why we fightin' this fuckin-ass war?"

"I don't—"

"To win it," said the third, silent officer. He did not move. His arms remained flat across his chest, his eyes blank. "We fight this war to win it, that's why."

"Yes, sir."

"Again," the major said. "Why we fightin' this war?"

"To win it, sir."

"You sure of that?"

"Positive, sir." His arms were hot. He tried to hold his chin level.

"Tell it loud, trooper: Why we fightin' this war?"

"To win it."

"Yeah, but I mean why?"

"Just to win it," Paul Berlin said softly. "That's all. To win it."

"You know that for a fact?"

"Yes, sir. A fact."

The third officer made a soft, humming sound of satisfaction. The major grinned at the captain in tiger fatigues.

"All right," said the major. His eyes twinkled. "Maybe you aren't so dumb as you let on. *Maybe.* We got one last question. This here's a cultural type matter . . . listen up close. What effect would the death of Ho Chi Minh have on the population of North Vietnam?"

"Sir?"

Reading slowly from his paper, the major repeated it. "What effect would the death of Ho Chi Minh have on the population of North Vietnam?"

Paul Berlin let his chin fall. He smiled.

"Reduce it by one,sir."

In Quang Ngai, they did not speak of politics. It wasn't taboo, or bad luck, it just wasn't talked about. Even when the Peace Talks bogged down in endless bickering over the shape and size of the bargaining table, the men in Alpha Company took it as another bad joke—silly and sad—and there was no serious discussion about it, no sustained outrage. Diplomacy and morality were beyond them. Hardly anyone cared. Not even Doc Peret, who loved a good debate. Not even Jim Pederson, who believed in virtue. This dim-sighted attitude enraged Frenchie Tucker. "My God," he'd sometimes moan in exasperation, speaking to Paul Berlin but aiming at everyone, "it's your *ass* they're negotiating. Your ass, my ass. . . . Do we live or die? That's the issue, by God, and you blockheads don't even talk about it. Not even a *lousy opinion*! Good Lord, doesn't it piss you off, all this Peace Talk crap? Round tables, square tables! Idiotic diplomatic etiquette, power plays, maneuvering! And here we sit, suckin' air while those mealy-mouthed sons of bitches can't even figure out what kind of table they're gonna sit at. Jesus!" But Frenchie's rage never caught on. Sometimes there were jokes, cynical and weary, but there was no serious discussion. No beliefs. They fought the war, but no one took sides.

They did not know even the simple things: a sense of victory, or satisfaction, or necessary sacrifice. They did not know the feeling of taking a place and keeping it, securing a village and then raising the flag and calling it a victory. No sense of order or momentum. No front, no rear, no trenches laid out in neat parallels. No Patton rushing for the Rhine, no beachheads to storm and win and hold for the duration. They did not have targets. They did not have a cause. They did not know if it was a war of ideology or economics or hegemony or spite. On a given day, they did not know where they were in Quang Ngai, or how being there might influence larger outcomes. They did not know the names of most villages. They did not know which villages were critical. They did not know strategies. They did not know the terms of the war, its architecture, the rules of fair play. When they took prisoners, which was rare, they did not know the questions to ask, whether to release a suspect or beat on him. They did not know how to feel. Whether, when seeing a dead Vietnamese, to be happy or sad or relieved; whether, in times of quiet, to be apprehensive or content; whether to engage the enemy or elude him. They did not know how to feel when they saw villages burning. Revenge? Loss? Peace of mind or anguish? They did not know. They knew the old myths about Quang Ngai—tales passed down from old-timer to newcomer—but they did not know which stories to believe. Magic, mystery, ghosts and incense, whispers in the dark, strange tongues and strange smells, uncertainties never articulated in war stories, emotion squandered on ignorance. They did not know good from evil.

≺ 22 ≻

My Lai: The Killing Begins

Michael Bilton and Kevin Sim

SOON AFTER FIRST LIGHT, CHARLIE COMPANY lined up on the landing field inside the defended perimeter of LZ [Landing Zone] Dottie, waiting for the "Dolphins" and the "Sharks" to appear out of the sky.* Some of the men were bleary-eyed. They had talked long into the night about what the next day would be like, before finally snatching a few hours' sleep, only to be ushered from their bunks before dawn, at 5:30 A.M., and told to gather up their gear.

Platoon commanders distributed ammunition. More than a hundred men and several tons of fighting gear were about to be shipped 11 miles in an operation they hoped would take the enemy completely by surprise. The target of their first full-scale combat assault was less than fifteen minutes' flying time away. The troops could hear the distant *whop-whop-whop-whop* of the nine liftships and gunships from the 174th Helicopter Assault Company before the aircraft emerged from behind the tree line. They landed close by, kicking up clouds of fine dust from the downdraft of spinning rotors.

The "Slicks," the troop-carrying helicopters, were to move the company in two lifts. First they would take [Capt. Ernest] Medina's command group, the 1st Platoon, and as many of the 2nd Platoon as they could manage. These would then secure the landing zone for the remainder of the company. Also to be carried on the second lift were a few additional men from other brigade units temporarily assigned to Charlie Company for the Pinkville operation. They included Lieutenant Dennis Johnson, a military intelligence officer, and his Vietnamese interpreter. Demolition engineers Jerry "Hotrod" Hemming and Calvin Hawkins had volunteered for the operation only the day before. Finally, an Army photographer and a reporter from the public information outfit were being taken along as well.

Weighed down by extra clips of ammunition, machine-gun bandoleers, grenades, flak jackets, water canteens, ropes, flashlights, .45 pistols, medical bandages, grenade launchers, and K-rations, the men on the first lift waited at the departure point. The additional equipment they needed for battle meant an extra heavy load for the liftships. Radio operators stuck close to their platoon command groups; ammo bearers were joined as if by an umbilical cord to the machine-gun teams. When the choppers touched down, the men in the first lift clambered into the vibrating compartments of the doorless cargo holds. Waiting for them on either side of the aircraft were two gunners, crouched beneath a metal covering enclosing the helicopter's transmission and hydraulic system, directly beneath the rotor mast.

The pilots sat in heavily armored seats of half-inch-thick steel wrapped in an aluminum frame. They throttled every last percent of available power on the gauge, making mental notes against checklists of radio call signs and frequencies. They had already made their calculations of the likely weight they were carrying, judging down to the last few hundred pounds how high and how

* "Dolphins"/"Sharks": radio call signs of the liftships and gunships of the 174th Helicopter Assault Company.

fast they could fly the aircraft, men, and equipment. Behind them turbine fans spun gases from a jet engine and caused the machines to shudder violently. The pilots waited for the point when the 48-foot-long rotors were spinning fast enough to give the aircraft lift. They then pulled on the control stick, adjusted the rotor wings, and allowed the aircraft to rise slowly off the ground.

Watching this at a distance, the remnants of Charlie Company left behind on the ground inhaled the sweet smell of kerosene filtering from engine exhausts. Finally the "Dolphins" and "Sharks" staggered from their parking slots and gradually lifted into the air. They lumbered, nose tilted forward, along the ground until the pilots judged they had enough power to climb higher. Rising above the tree line, they gathered up into a "V" formation before heading south, hugging the edge of Highway One.

On the ground the Army photographer began work. Ron Haeberle had been in the fourth year of college as a photography major in his home town of Cleveland, Ohio, when he was drafted. The Army quickly recognized his talent with a camera and assigned him to the Public Information Detachment at brigade headquarters at Duc Pho. Haeberle and Jay Roberts, a PID reporter from Arlington, Virginia, were assigned to write a morale-boosting piece on Task Force Barker's campaign to root out the Viet Cong from the Batangan Peninsula. Their usual procedure, developed after similar missions with other outfits, was to prepare a press release and photograph that would be used in *Stars and Stripes* and many other Army newspapers. The MACV [Military Assistance Command, Vietnam] information office in Saigon circulated their stories, and often they made it onto the AP [Associated Press] wire and into the papers back home. Now, Haeberle's service-issue Leica, with its black-and-white film, stayed unused as he focused his own 35-mm Nikon on the slowly rising helicopters. He had captured the first image of the day on Ektachrome color film.

Several hundred feet above, the pilots lined up behind the aircraft they were designated to follow in the formation. By 7:22 A.M. the first lift of troops had left Dottie behind and was well on its way. "Coyote Six," Frank Barker's command-and-control helicopter, was already on station. "Skeeter," a tiny bubble helicopter, was *en route* from Chu Lai. During the battle it would skip low over the trees, reconning the battle ground, ferreting out the enemy positions, drawing fire for the high and low gunships to engage. Off the coastline away out to the east on the South China Sea, *News Boy India Two Zero*, a high-powered Swift boat of the "Brown Water Navy," which operated among South Vietnam's inshore waters and rivers, moved into position. It was all going like clockwork.

In the hamlet, which the Americans had labeled My Lai 4 on their military maps, the day had begun several hours earlier with the lighting of fires. This was women's work. Every household had a fire in their dirt yard, sheltered from the wind and shared with dogs, pigs, ducks, and chickens. With luck the dying embers from the night before were enough to give a flame to a freshly applied handful of dried twigs. A pan of water was boiled constantly on the lighted fire and replaced only when a meal was to be heated up. It was an early morning routine which had gone on for generation after generation. Most of the farmers, who were heads of households, were already out in the fields. Some of the older children had gone to fetch water from wells, or check how many fish they had netted in the river.

Seven kilometers away, the pilots swung their aircraft round in a long semicircle and made their final run-in to approach the landing zone from the southwest. They scanned the horizon, looking for smoke: not the fine wisps of blue smoke from household fires, but thick, heavy, white smoke, the kind that accompanied the booming sounds of surface detonating rounds as high explosive and white phosphorus shells whumped and burst onto the western edge of the settlement. For three minutes, just before 7:30 A.M., a small group of artillerymen sweated and strained to deliver their first barrage of the day from four 105-mm guns. D company, 6/11th Artillery Battalion, had fired thousands of rounds into Quang Ngai Province during its time at the fortified fire base at LZ Uptight, across the Diem Diem River only 6 miles north of My Lai 4. To the artillerymen firing the guns the target was merely a set of coordinates, though they knew perfectly well that when the shells landed they would kill anything within a radius of 35 meters on unobstructed flat ground.

The impact of the artillery fire was being monitored that morning by Lieutenant Dennis Vasquez, an observer aboard Frank Barker's "Charlie Charlie" aircraft. Covering a similar route to the one they had taken on their fly-by recce the day before, Barker's observation team were still several miles away from the LZ. In the distance Vasquez could see smoke popping around what he took to be the landing zone. When the shells thundered in toward their target the people of My Lai 4 fled underground into crude bomb shelters or tunnels dug beneath their homes.

Virtually unobserved, the artillery barrage was tantamount to blind firing. No spotter was close enough to adjust the fire away from the village. What was intended as an artillery preparation for the paddy fields 400 meters northwest of the village turned instead into something else. In those three minutes 120 rounds fell not only among the dikes and fields but also very close to the fragile dwellings spread out around the hamlet. Eventually they strayed over into the inhabited area itself, sending shrapnel flying, snapping trees like twigs, causing terror and panic.

Blind firing was nothing new to the province of Quang Ngai. Hundreds of thousands of rounds had been lobbed across the region, from the mountains in the west right down to the wide coastal plain. Mostly it was harassment and interdiction fire intended to unsettle the Viet Cong and to keep them on their toes at night. Some of these barrages were fired by an artillery unit at a fire base perched on top of a mountain overlooking the Song Ve Valley. In August the previous year, B Battery of the 2nd Battalion of the 320th Artillery celebrated the firing of its 250,000th round with a brief ceremony, complete with pennants flying and a color guard standing to attention.

In his command-and-control chopper, the "Charlie Charlie" ship, Barker sat at a homemade console of radios. At the flick of a switch he could contact the ground troops and the gunships. Sitting next to Barker, Lt. Vasquez didn't bother to adjust the artillery fire which was intended to clear the drop zone for the helicopters. Barker was keen to keep down the heads of any Viet Cong defensive positions. Every one and a half seconds a shell exploded close to the village. So powerful was the roar of the artillery it could be clearly heard several miles away by the members of Charlie Company who remained waiting on the ground at Dottie.

At LZ Uptight, where the rounds of the preparatory artillery barrage were being fired the mortar platoon members left behind manning the direction-finding radar listened in on their radios. Over in Task Force Barker's tactical operations center at Dottie, and further to the south in the operations room of the brigade headquarters at Duc Pho, more radio operators waited to monitor news of the battle.

As the liftships neared their arrival point, the men of Charlie Company were shaken by the sudden fusillade of machine guns pouring tracer fire down onto the landing zone. Martin Fagan, with Medina's command group in the fourth helicopter, sat next to the port door gunner. The deafening clatter as the machine gun opened up scared the hell out of him. To Dennis Conti, who was with Lt. [William] Calley's command group, the gunner nearest him appeared to be firing almost straight down as they dropped through thick smoke low over the landing zone.

The paddy field was bone dry. As they hit the ground Calley shouted: "Let's go!" and everyone but Conti jumped out. He had caught his mine sweeper in the seats behind him. Eventually freeing himself, he jumped down into the long elephant grass. Conti was considered by everyone in the platoon to be a street-smart Italian. Joe Cool. Ladies' man. But now, with the smoke from the fires still drifting around, he became disoriented. He couldn't tell which way the rest of the platoon had gone. To his right he heard a machine gun open up and saw what he thought was a farmer running with his cattle. He fired a round from an M-79 grenade launcher—but the man was too far away.

Machine gunners Robert Maples and James Bergthold jumped out of their "slick" when it was still six feet off the ground. Hitting the paddy, Maples stumbled under the weight of the machine gun he was carrying and lost his helmet. He scrambled around trying to find the steel pot and then ran to the irrigation dike. Bergthold, carrying a .45 pistol, three hand grenades, his pack, and about six hundred rounds of machine-gun ammunition, struggled along behind. Hemming and Hawkins, the demo men from the engineering battalion, also made a dash for the safety of the dike. Hawkins then had to run back to find a roll of detonation cord his partner dropped when jumping out of the liftship. He found the cord and rejoined Hemming.

The "Dolphins" took off again and the leadship announced over the air the landing zone was "cold." The "Sharks" continued pouring all kinds of fire onto the fringes of the village with machine guns, grenade launchers, and rockets. Barker acknowledged the message from "Dolphin Lead" and relayed it back to the operations center at Dottie. The information surprised him. Against all the odds the LZ was cold. There was no enemy fire. Just then the "Warlord" aeroscouts took up a chase of several armed men in black pajamas running below them. "We got a couple of dinks with weapons," the pilot of the lead ship radioed as another chopper headed off to block an escape route. From different parts of My Lai 4 villagers were trying to get to safety a few hundred yards away down a road which led in one direction to Quang Ngai City and in the other to the coast. The rest of the villagers stayed hiding in their bunkers or simply took shelter in their homes.

The next twenty minutes saw intense aerial activity as the helicopters continued searching for signs of enemy positions. The fifty troops on the ground spread out and secured defensive positions, running to the bank of an irrigation ditch. Out in the fields another farmer frantically raised his hands by way of both greeting and to show he had no weapon. He was immediately felled by a burst from a machine gun. The first lift held their defensive positions and waited for the rest of the 2nd and 3rd platoons to join them.

The second lift had a quicker journey across country to the LZ. There was no longer any reason to follow a circuitous route; the element of surprise had only been required for the first lift. John Smail, a squad leader with the 3rd Platoon, nearly didn't make it at all. His assigned chopper on the landing field at Dottie quickly filled up. He approached to get on board but there was no room for him and he had a few anxious moments as he quickly raced round searching for another ship to board. As they lifted off at 7:30 A.M., the other men began joking with him about almost being left behind before the start of Charlie Company's most important mission.

Soon they were over the landing zone. The door gunners in the "slick" carrying Diego Rodriguez, of the 2nd Platoon, opened up with yet more tracer fire. Already nervous about what lay ahead, Rodriguez sat by the starboard door. Suddenly spent shells flew up from the machine gun and struck him in the face. In another ship, meanwhile, Haeberle took a couple of more shots with his Nikon of the approach to the landing zone.

When the second lift hit the LZ they too quickly spread out as they ran to take up defensive positions with the others. Mortars were set up and a 3rd Platoon squad led by Steven Grimes was sent to recover a VC weapon spotted by one of the aeroscouts who had marked it with a smoke canister. Other members of the platoon saw a woman carrying a child in the brush some distance away. A tall soldier from Chicago named Charles West stood up and with his M-16 on full automatic began loosing off a burst of fire from the hip. Smail, his squad leader, got angry and shouted out how stupid the soldier had been to fire in the direction of where Grimes's men had gone searching for the VC weapon. He could have killed their own men.

To Michael Bernhardt what was happening already confirmed his worst fears about Medina's instructions the night before. Along with the gunships, almost everyone in the 1st and 2nd platoons were firing their weapons, and now the 3rd Platoon was joining in. The moment a Vietnamese was spotted, volleys of fire were loosed off, and the "enemy" fell wounded or dying. It was apparent to Bernhardt, as it was to virtually everyone gathered there on the ground, that they were receiving no return fire at all. There was no incoming.

The 1st and 2nd platoons got ready to move into the village in separate groups. Spread out "on line" in a typical infantry formation, they moved forward, over the dike, through another paddy, and entered the village firing from the hip. The 3rd Platoon and Medina's command group stayed behind, forming a defensive perimeter on the western edge of the village, about 150 meters from the tree line. Twenty minutes after they arrived Medina wanted Bernhardt to check out a suspicious-looking ammo box someone had found. Among his equipment Bernhardt carried a long rope. To make sure it wasn't booby-trapped he tied the rope round the box and jerked it several times. When it failed to explode, he opened the lid and found inside a small Sony radio and various pieces of a medical kit. Bernhardt kept hold of the box for the rest of the day.

Shortly before 8 A.M., Medina radioed the operations center via the "Charlie Charlie" ship that they had fifteen confirmed VC killed. It was his first lie of the day. It was impossible to have a battle and not have enemy killed.

Over the course of the next three hours Charlie Company moved through My Lai 4 and also entered several other subhamlets, small pockets of homes grouped together and known in the neighborhood by a particular local name. The place the Americans called My Lai 4 was in fact called Tu Cung by the Vietnamese who lived there. It had a number of subhamlets—including Binh Tay and Binh Dong. Tu Cung, along with three other hamlets—My Lai, Co Luy, and My Khe—spread over two or three square kilometers as far as the coast to the west and the Tra Khuc River to the south. Collectively this formed an area the locals called Son My village. The whole of Son My was the target for Task force Barker over the next three days.

The totality of what happened in My Lai 4 that morning was not known to any single individual who took part in Charlie Company's combat operation. As they assaulted the village each platoon split into separate squads and soon these too became broken down, as numerous groups of men, often in ones and twos, moved through the hamlet. Occasionally they crossed each other's paths and squads from different platoons intermingled. At the end of the day a number of soldiers remarked that it had been a miracle none of them was caught in any crossfire. Parts of the village were covered in thick foliage, bamboo trees, banana trees, and other vegetation. No single group of GIs had the opportunity to see what everyone else was doing. But they could all hear firing, often long bursts of automatic fire from M-16s and machine guns. Hand grenades were thrown and the M-79 launchers hurled small bomblets 100 meters or more through the air.

A few geographical features gave Charlie Company some sense of direction. A main trail ran approximately north–south for the whole of the village. Another ran west–east forming a "T" junction of sorts where the two trails met almost in the middle of the settlement. An irrigation ditch formed in a discontinuous semicircle around the furthest southern fringes of the village several hundred meters beyond the tree line, separated from the inhabited area by rice paddies.

Lt. Col. Barker's plan provided for two platoons initially to sweep through the village, quickly taking out any enemy opposition they encountered. Half an hour later the 3rd Platoon would come in behind, mopping up, killing the livestock, and burning hootches. Capt. Medina and his command group would direct operations from the rear.

Calley's 1st Platoon edged into the southern portion of My Lai 4 in three separate squads, line abreast. Calley and his radio operator, Charles Sledge, held back, maintaining a discreet distance from the troops advancing in front of them. Prisoners or Viet Cong suspects were to be sent back to the platoon commander for screening.

Greg Olsen fired his M-60 machine gun as they moved forward, trying to hit a man running away. The weapon suddenly jammed while Lenny Lagunoy was feeding him a belt of ammunition. Lagunoy grabbed the gun from Olsen, recocked it so as to clear the obstruction, and fired once more on the fleeing villager. All around them troops were firing on anything that moved. Olsen shot at animals, pigs, chickens, ducks, and cows. Soldiers yelled inside small dwellings for people to come out, using hand signals if they appeared. If there was no answer, they threw grenades into the shelters and bunkers. Others didn't bother to find out if the bunkers were empty and threw the grenades in regardless. Small clusters of people were being gathered into one larger group of fifty or sixty old men, women, children, and babies in arms, some so badly wounded they could hardly walk. Olsen noticed one elderly woman shot in the hip. Several of the troops saw their buddies behaving in ways which shocked them.

For Robert Maples it was not the first time he had seen things he disapproved of, but this was something altogether different. A quiet, mild-mannered, and thoughtful Negro from Englishtown, a rural area of New Jersey, he had enlisted almost two years before out of a sense of curiosity about Vietnam instead of waiting to be drafted. Not long after he arrived in the country, Maples and some of the other men saw a personnel carrier with twenty human ears strung like trophies on its radio antenna. Everyone in the company soon heard about it. Then, on one of their first patrols up in the mountains, they discovered they were being followed. A couple of the guys set up an ambush and killed those shadowing them. To prove it, they cut off their ears and brought them back for the rest to see. Maples was disgusted. He thought the episode gross and unwarranted. Now, minutes after they entered My Lai 4, he and Bergthold came across a hut which had been raked with bullets. Inside, Bergthold discovered three children, a woman with a flesh wound in her side, and an old man squatting down, hardly able to move. He had been seriously wounded in both legs. From six feet Bergthold aimed his .45 pistol and pulled the trigger, causing the top of the man's head to fly off. It was a sight that would be forever etched in Maples's memory. Bergthold claimed to have shot the old man as an act of mercy.

Two other members of the same squad, Roy Wood and Harry Stanley, were taken by surprise when a woman came out of a bamboo hut. Wood whirled and fired, creasing the woman in the side, slightly injuring her. The woman had two children, one a baby in arms, the other only just able to walk. They sent her back to Calley for screening. In another hut they found a man, his wife, a teenage girl, and a younger girl. Wood grabbed the terrified man and shouted: "VC?" Holding his hands in the air, as if to plead for his life, the man replied: "No VC." Then Wood saw the pitiful sight of an elderly woman who had been wounded, staggering down a path toward them. She had been shot with an M-79 grenade which had failed to explode and was still lodged in her stomach. An old man wearing a straw coolie hat and no shirt was with a water buffalo in a paddy 50 meters away. He put his hands in the air. Several members of the platoon opened fire as Calley watched. Harry Stanley saw that the fleeing villagers were offering no resistance. His friend Allen Boyce, who lived in New Jersey only a couple of miles from Maples, came up behind him with a Vietnamese farmer, aged between 40 and 50 years, in custody. He wore black pajamas and his shirt hung open so that Stanley could see his chest. Boyce pushed the man forward to where Stanley was standing beside the trail. Suddenly, and for no reason, Boyce stabbed the man with the bayonet attached to the end of his rifle. He fell to the ground gasping for breath. Boyce killed him and then grabbed another man being detained, shot him in the neck, and threw him into a well, lobbing an M-26 grenade in after him.

"That's the way you gotta do it," he told [Varnado] Simpson, who had considered Boyce a close friend during jungle training in Hawaii. This sort of deranged behavior profoundly affected many of those who witnessed it and refused to take part. Maples, who was standing nearby, said to Stanley: "That Boyce has gone crazy."

Even Robert Lee, the platoon medic, joined in the frenzy but confined his efforts to slaughtering animals. He killed a cow that had been injured. Lee was from a farming community and "didn't want to see the beast suffer." Up in front, he and the platoon sergeant, Isaiah Cowan, could see women and children being slain. They were stunned by what was happening all around them. The further they went into the village, the more bodies they found.

Dennis Conti stayed for a while with Calley's command group but occasionally wandered off on his own, zigzagging across the path which ran west to east through the village as far as the main trail. He stuck close to Calley in case the platoon leader needed the mine sweeper. He helped round up people for questioning, a normal procedure when they searched villages. He gave his mine sweeper to an old man to carry while he moved some of the Vietnamese toward the platoon command group. To Conti the men appeared all psyched up when they landed. The shooting, once it began, created almost a chain reaction. He joined in, without killing anyone. Inside the village his comrades appeared out of control. Families had huddled together for safety in houses, in the yards and in bunkers only to be mown down with automatic weapon fire or blown apart by fragmentation grenades. Women and children were pushed into bunkers and grenades thrown in after them. But if Conti discovered anyone alive he brought them back to the trail. He and Paul Meadlo collected a group of about twenty-five people—mostly women and children. Still more were brought over by other members of the platoon. At one point, wandering off on his own, Conti found a woman aged about 20 with a 4-year-old child. He forced her to perform oral sex on him while he held a gun at the child's head, threatening to kill it. Just at that moment Calley happened along and angrily told him to pull on his pants and get over to where he was supposed to be.

Amid all this mayhem the first and second platoons overlapped on occasions when the right flank of Lieutenant Stephen Brooks's 2nd Platoon crossed paths with the left flank of the 1st Platoon. Half a dozen people from both platoons then witnessed a stocky, blond-haired 2nd Platoon soldier from Kansas City called Gary Roschevitz become hysterical when troops from the 1st Platoon were walking a small group of villagers back for screening. Roschevitz, aged 25, was older than most of the grunts in the company. Standing almost six feet tall and weighing close to 230 pounds, he made a surprise grab for Roy Wood's M-16 and demanded the weapon as a trade for his M-79. But Wood wasn't having any.

"Don't turn them over to the company," Roschevitz appealed to those gathered there. "Kill them!"

Wood, who was physically by far the smaller of the two men, held tightly onto his rifle. Roschevitz then snatched hold of Varnado Simpson's M-16, turned, and shot a Vietnamese farmer in the head. Wood began feeling sick at the sight of the man's brains spilling onto the ground and turned away. Roschevitz shot two more peasants in the head before handing the gun back to Simpson.

As far as the outside world knew, a firefight against a large Viet Cong force was underway in the village. Barker and [Col. Oran] Henderson were back on the scene briefly in their respective helicopters. By about 8:30 A.M., Barker had checked once more with Medina to find out how things were going. Medina told him that the body count was 84 enemy killed, and Barker relayed the additional 69 KIA [killed in action] to the tactical operations center. In fact the death toll was far higher, but still no shots had been fired at Charlie Company and they had yet to kill a single enemy soldier.

In the northern portion of the village the 2nd Platoon had also run berserk. Employing the routine combat assault technique used by Calley, Stephen Brooks's men also approached line abreast in three squads. Firing as they moved, they came to dwellings and yelled out "Lai Dai" in Vietnamese ("Come here") at the villagers sheltering in homemade shelters or bunkers. Fragmentation grenades were tossed inside; homes were sprayed with automatic fire. Children aged only 6 or 7 came toward them with their hands outstretched, saying "Chop chop." They asked for the food and candy they had received from other American soldiers on two previous visits to the village. The soldiers scythed them down. After one group of Vietnamese were killed in front of a hut, the first squad leader, Sergeant Kenneth Scheil, began telling the men with him that he didn't like what they were all doing but that he had to obey orders. The villagers had huddled together for safety, but the Americans poured fire into them, tearing their bodies apart, one man firing a machine gun at random, others using their M-16s on automatic.

Dennis Bunning informed his squad leader, Sgt. Hodges, he wasn't going to fire on women and children. Hodges ordered him to get right out on the far left flank, beyond the tree line and into the rice paddies. Brooks's radio operator, Dean Fields, witnessed Varnado Simpson shoot a woman with a baby from a distance of about 25 meters. Her right arm was shot almost completely off at the wrist. All that held it on was a fragile piece of flesh. She ran into a hootch and someone yelled an order for her and the baby to be killed.

Max Hutson, the weapons squad leader, formed a machine-gun team with Floyd Wright. As soon as they passed the tree line they were confronted less than 30 feet away by a middle-aged woman climbing out of a tunnel using both hands. She was unarmed but they opened fire and she fell back into the tunnel. Hutson and Wright took turns on the machine gun. Whenever they came across any Vietnamese they opened fire, killing them. Hutson could see people firing all around him—the whole scene was one of chaos and confusion, with people moving, yelling, and shouting. Some of the troops were afraid they would be shot by their own men.

The other machine-gun team, Charles Hutto and Esequiel Torres, were also firing at everything that moved—Hutto with the M-60 and Torres with his rifle. After thirty minutes Tores demanded they swap. By this time Hutto, growing weary of all the killing, was glad to hand over the heavier and more powerful weapon.

Jay Buchanon, the platoon sergeant, was also over on the extreme left flank of the platoon, almost on the edge of the tree line. He quickly realized the whole assault was a complete mess. Amid the thick undergrowth he knew there was no opposition but it sounded like a pitched battle was going on. He yelled: "Keep moving, keep moving—fire when fired upon. Stay on line, keep moving. If you receive fire, return it."

Away to his right, closer to where Brooks was moving forward, a slaughter was taking place. Thomas Partsch, a sensitive soul who made regular entries in his diary whenever the platoon took a break, could see that Brooks had totally lost control. As soon as villagers emerged with their hands held up, the troops shot them down. Partsch and Gary Crossley came to a building.

It was a well-made house, 20 feet by 10 with a small extension on the side measuring about 8 feet by 6, which gave it an L-shaped appearance. The dwelling was of good quality, a permanent structure made of mud and clay. It had an elevated floor about one step up from the ground and a roof which overhung the house by about two feet over the entrance door, with bamboo windows either side, providing shade from the tropical sun. An old man appeared dressed in black pajamas. Without hesitating Crossley shot the old man in the left arm, just below the elbow. The shot severed the arm, causing it to hang down. Attempting to put his hands in the air, the old man yelled: "No VC! No VC!" A woman wearing black pajama bottoms and a white shirt came out carrying a baby. She frantically shouted in Vietnamese at the two Americans, then proceeded to drag the man inside. Partsch noticed that Crossley looked physically pale and was shaking nervously. He hadn't fired again. When Partsch asked him why, he said that he didn't know.

"Why didn't you finish the job?" Partsch asked again. Crossley replied that he just couldn't bring himself to pull the trigger a second time, he only wanted to see what it was like to shoot someone. Just then two men—Hutson, the weapons squad leader, and Wright, carrying the machine gun—went in after the Vietnamese couple and opened up with a burst of fire.

Occasionally Partsch was close enough to Lt. Brooks and his radio operator to hear Medina calling: "What the hell is going on over there?" At times the static was so bad that Brooks couldn't make contact. After receiving one such message the platoon leader ushered Partsch away from the radio. Overhead, Partsch saw Frank Barker flying low over the treetops in his helicopter—clearly recognizable in his white flying helmet, sitting in his normal position, right near the edge of the door next to the machine gunner.

When he sat down for a rest, Partsch got out his diary and wrote in pencil his account of the day's proceedings so far:

> Got up at 0530 and we left 0715. We had nine choppers, two lifts. We started to move slowly through the village, shooting everything in sight, children, men, women, and animals. Some was sickening. Their legs were shot off and they were still moving. They were just hanging there. I think their bodies are made of rubber. I didn't fire a single round yet and didn't kill anybody, not even a chicken. I couldn't. We are now supposed to push two more villages. It is about 10.00 hours and we are taking a rest before going in. We also got two weapons, one M-I and a carbine.

Those in My Lai 4 that day had a choice whether or not to take part in what was happening. Many followed what they believed were their orders. Some appeared even to enjoy the activity. Only a handful offered any real help or compassion to the Vietnamese. The platoon medic, a Mexican-American named George Garza, found a little boy aged 6 or 7 with an arm injury and bandaged it. Harry Stanley and another Negro, Herbert Carter, the 1st Platoon tunnel rat, located a second child. Carter admired Stanley, describing him often as a "sharp dude." He believed he cared more for the Vietnamese than his fellow Americans. Stanley urged the boy to keep quiet and stay hidden.

Another who refused to take part in the slaughter, Leonard Gonzalez, was also assigned to the extreme left flank of the 2nd Platoon, beyond the tree line. He patrolled in a rice paddy at the far northwest corner of the village. On the edge of the field Gonzalez discovered a young girl aged 11 or 12, wounded in the chest. She was lying on her back, dressed in black pajamas with a white top, crying and moaning with pain. Gonzalez got his canteen and poured water on the girl's forehead and tried to get her to drink some water. There was little more he could do for her and he got up to leave. Gonzalez had only gone a few paces when he heard a shot; he turned to see that she had been killed.

An order came telling the squad to close up. This meant that Gonzalez and Bunning, who was about 25 meters away, had to move over out of the paddy, through the trees and into the village itself. In a clearing near a small hootch a group of fifteen Vietnamese had been gathered, four women in their thirties, three in their fifties, three girls in their late teens and five children aged between 3 and 14. Standing around were seven or eight soldiers from two different squads including Hutto, Torres, and Roschevitz. Gonzalez heard someone yell that if anyone was behind the Vietnamese to take cover because they were going to open fire. A shot rang out and a bullet penetrated the head of a young child being carried by its mother, blowing out the back of its skull. Others began firing also until the entire group was dead. Gonzalez could stand no more; he turned away and vomited. Few words were spoken until someone said: "Let's move out."

Roschevitz later fired two rounds from his M-79 grenade launcher at a group of Vietnamese sitting on the ground. The first bomblet missed; the second landed among them with devastating effect, but against the odds it failed to kill them all. Someone finished off those left alive. A soldier stopping over a tunnel yelled for the occupants to come out. Gonzalez moved closer and could hear people responding as if they were about to comply, whereupon the soldier threw in a grenade and yelled: "Fire in the hole!'"—telling everyone to stand clear.

Behind the 1st and 2nd platoons Medina's command group had formed a security line out in the paddy fields beyond the western perimeter of My Lai 4. Some forty-five minutes had elapsed since the first troops entered the village and Medina was waiting to send in the 3rd Platoon, led by a recent arrival, a young lieutenant named Geoffrey LaCross. This was LaCross's very first combat mission. From Lake Leelanau, Michigan, he had joined the company and taken command of the platoon only three weeks before, on February 26. . . . Medina hoped the savvy of the platoon sergeant, Manuel Lopez, would make up for LaCross's inexperience. It helped that the 3rd Platoon had been given the less taxing role of mopping up.

For Medina, the best way to clear a village was to send a sweep team through very rapidly, clearing people out of the hootches as quickly as possible. The search teams would then go from hootch to hootch, checking bunkers and tunnels looking for any enemy who might be hiding. One added refinement today was that LaCross's men were also to burn the village. Medina received the instruction to let the Zippo squads loose from Frank Barker directly. Barker said he had arranged for this to be cleared with the Vietnamese authorities in Quang Ngai through the senior district advisor to the 2nd ARVN Division. The truth was that since the area was controlled by the Viet Cong the government officials didn't care what happened to people in the villages. Medina knew Barker regularly met with the Vietnamese and the American province advisors. The burning of villages was supposed to be strictly controlled. As far as Medina was concerned, the burning of villages was always carried out with the approval of the South Vietnamese.

Some distance away Sergeant Grimes's squad from the 3rd Platoon searched for Viet Cong weapons. They set off through the paddy fields and then followed the line of the irrigation ditch which ran around the village. Grimes's men crossed over a bamboo footbridge and saw a tiny bubble aeroscout reconning low over the ground drop a smoke grenade. They recrossed the bridge, moved toward a clump of foliage, and found an M-1 and a rifle.

More rifles were found when the 2nd Platoon located the bodies of two VC killed by the gunships and marked with smoke. The VC, each about 20 years old, were not in uniform but carried an American pack, pistol belts, and ammo pouches. They had been armed with an M-1 and a carbine, which was now full of mud and still loaded.

Deeper into the village the 1st Platoon collected a large group of about sixty Vietnamese. They were made to squat down. An alert Conti spotted a 4-year-old child running away toward a hootch. Dropping his gear, he sprinted after the child, which managed to escape him. He discovered a woman with a baby in a hootch and a much older female he took to be the grandmother in a nearby underground shelter. Conti escorted the young woman and her child back to the holding point and then returned for the old woman who had refused to move. He then teamed up with Meadlo. Once more they guarded the squatting Vietnamese. Calley appeared with his radio operator, Charles Sledge.

Calley had been called twice that morning on the radio by an anxious Medina. "What is happening over there?" Medina demanded to know, challenging the slow progress of the 1st Platoon. He wanted Calley to get his men back on line and keep moving. This made the young platoon commander nervous. Throughout his time with the company he had frequently been made the butt of Medina's jokes. Medina knew Calley couldn't command the respect of his men. Now, under pressure, Calley replied that the large groups of civilians they had gathered were slowing the platoon down. Never one to accept excuses, Medina told Calley simply to get rid of them. So when Calley came across Meadlo and Conti in the clearing and said: "Take care of them," his intention was clear. It was his way of getting Medina off his back.

Conti thought nothing of the implications of Calley's request when he replied simply: "OK." Like many in the company he regarded the man as a joke and resented the way Calley tried to suck up to the men one minute, calling them by their first names, and then shouted and bawled at them the next. Conti felt his platoon commander had absolutely no leadership ability.

Among the squatting Vietnamese were ten to fifteen men with beards and ten women, as well as a handful of very elderly, gray-haired women who could hardly walk. The rest were children of all ages—from babies up to early teens.

Calley, who was carrying a bandolier of ammunition around one shoulder, said: "I thought I told you to take care of them."

Meadlo somewhat naively responded: "We are. We're watching over them."

"No," reposted Calley. "I want them killed." He moved over to where Conti was standing beside Meadlo. "We'll get on line and fire into them."

Conti and Meadlo looked at each other and backed off, neither of them wanting a part in what was about to happen. Calley, losing his temper, beckoned them toward him: "Come here . . . come here. Come on, we'll line them up; we'll kill them."

Conti, searching for an excuse, pointed out that he was carrying a grenade launcher and he didn't want to waste ammunition. Perhaps he should keep guard over by the tree line in case anyone tried to get away, he suggested.

Calley turned to Meadlo: "Fire when I say 'Fire.' "

Conti stood behind them as Calley and Meadlo, standing side by side, blazed away. They stood only ten feet from their hapless victims, changing magazines from time to time. The Vietnamese screamed, yelled, and tried to get up. It was pure carnage as heads were shot off along with limbs; the fleshier body parts were ripped to shreds. Meadlo had taken twenty-three fully loaded magazines for his M-16 in his pack when they left Dottie. He fired in a spraying motion. He noticed one man dressed in red fall dead as he fired the rifle on automatic until the magazine was exhausted. Then he reloaded. He then switched to semiautomatic fire and loaded the third magazine.

After a minute or so Meadlo couldn't continue. Tears flooded down his cheeks. He turned, stuck his rifle in Conti's hand, and said: "You shoot them." Conti pushed the weapon back: "If they are going to be killed, I'm not doing it. Let him do it," he said, pointing at Calley, By this time Conti could see that only a few children were left standing. Mothers had thrown themselves on top of the young ones in a last desperate bid to protect them from the bullets raining down on them. The children were trying to stand up. Calley opened fire again, killing them one by one. Conti swore at him. Finally, when it appeared to be all over, Calley calmly turned and said: "OK, let's go." Suddenly someone yelled out that more Vietnamese, five women and six children some distance away, were making a break for the tree line. Calley burst out: "Get them, get them! Kill them!" Conti waited until they reached the tree line before letting loose with his grenade launcher, firing above them into the top of the trees. He asked Calley if he should pursue the fleeing villagers, but Calley replied no.

The urgency now was to push on to the far end of the village. Calley cajoled his men forward. They split up once more and continued to come across still more Vietnamese hiding in bunkers, shelters, and their fragile homes, terrified. Gathered in groups they were marched to the far side of the village, toward the paddy fields and the irrigation ditch. By the time Conti arrived at the edge of the ditch there were already a number of Vietnamese standing there, guarded by some of the soldiers, who squatted down and took a rest. Conti approached Charles Hall, from Chicago, a Negro soldier in the first squad who was standing near a small wooden bridge which crossed the ditch. The Italian boasted how Calley had earlier caught him with his pants down and his penis out trying to get a blow job from the Vietnamese woman, while threatening her child with a gun. Nothing surprised any of them about Conti. He and a half a dozen members of the company were notorious for fooling with the local women—so much so that medics administered shots of penicillin to him while they were on operations in the field. Nick Capezza, the company medic, used to joke how he nearly exhausted his supplies of the antibiotic drug giving Conti his shots for venereal disease.

Meadlo's face was flushed. His eyes were still full of tears when he arrived with Grzesik at the ditch site and found Calley sitting down. "We've got another job to do," he said looking up at them. About ten members of the platoon were guarding forty to fifty Vietnamese. Babies were crying and crawling around. James Dursi, a heavy-set Irish-Italian from Brooklyn, was looking at a man in white robes with a goatee beard, whom he took to be a Buddhist monk, praying over an elderly woman. She was seriously ill and had been carried through the village on a narrow wooden platform which the Vietnamese use as a bed. Calley was now on his feet. Harry Stanley appeared on the scene and tried to question the monk, who was crying and bowing as he tried to make himself understood. Calley couldn't understand him. Grzesik, who had attended Vietnamese language classes in Hawaii, tried more questions and got nowhere. Calley was getting more and more impatient. Where had the Viet Cong gone? Where were the weapons? Where were the NVA?

When the man shook his head, Calley struck him in the mouth with his rifle butt.

Just then a child, aged about 2 years and parted from its mother, managed to crawl up to the top of the ditch. Dursi watched horrified as Calley picked the child up, shoved it back down the slope, and shot it before returning to question the monk. The villagers pleaded for the holy man's life. Stanley asked the bearded man the same questions in Vietnamese that Calley was asking in English in an effort to defuse the situation. But the monk vainly replied that there were no North Vietnamese soldiers in the village. There were no weapons. Stanley translated these replies. Immediately Calley grabbed the monk, pulled him round, hurled him into the paddy, and opened fire with Meadlo's M-16. As the elderly *mama-san* lying prostrate tried to get up, she too was killed.

More Vietnamese shepherded by soldiers were arriving on the scene, and Calley indicated to Meadlo and Boyce he wanted everyone killed. He began pushing the peasants into the irrigation channel. Others joined in, using their rifle butts to shove the wailing Vietnamese down the steep slope. Some jumped in by themselves; others sat down on the edge, moaning and crying, clearly aware that disaster was imminent. It was a pitiful sight.

Up until the time all the firing started, Herbert Carter had been kneeling beside Dursi, quietly playing with a couple of children. Dursi said incredulously: "I think Calley wants them all killed." Carter said: "Oh, no."

"He can send me to jail but I am not going to kill anybody," said Dursi, beginning to move away, wondering what would happen to him for refusing to fire. Dursi was another one who liked to play with the children. Earlier in the day he had been devastated after he opened fire and killed someone running from the village. It turned out to be a woman carrying a baby and Dursi was horrified and ashamed by what he had done. Olsen had seen he was really cut up about it.

A woman standing next to Robert Maples showed him a bullet wound in her left arm. He felt helpless. There was nothing he could do for her. Calley shoved her in the ditch and told Maples: "Load your machine gun and shoot these people."

Maples shook his head and replied: "I'm not going to do that." Calley turned his M-16 on Maples as if to shoot him there and then. Maples was surprised and relieved when some of the other soldiers interposed to protect him. Calley backed off. Seconds later he and Meadlo began firing. A machine gun opened up and one of the squad leaders tried to usher the men into line so they could all fire simultaneously. Dursi stood completely frozen, watching disbelievingly, as the Vietnamese tried frantically to hide under one another, mothers protecting babies. Screaming at Dursi above the sounds of M-16s on full automatic, Meadlo continued pouring shell into the ditch. Crying hysterically once more, he stopped for a second: "Why aren't you firing?" he pleaded with Dursi, "Fire, why don't you fire?" The onlookers saw the remnants of shredded human beings, hundreds of pieces of flesh and bone, flying up in the air as the shallow ravine was repeatedly sprayed with bullets. Magazine after magazine was reloaded during the mass execution.

PART III

CONTROVERSIES AND CONSEQUENCES OF AMERICAN INVOLVEMENT

Chapter 7

International Dimensions of the War

Remote as Southeast Asia seemed to be to many Americans, the Vietnam War had enormous ramifications for the international system during the Cold War. The Americans tried to pull their allies into the war, hoping to win public support for their cause and to attract troops from other nations to bear some of the burden of the fighting. Vietnam's neighbors, Laos and Cambodia, were drawn deeply into the conflict, as the next chapter will suggest. And the North Vietnamese worked strenuously to secure economic and especially military aid from the leading communist nations, the Soviet Union and China. This proved a delicate business, as excerpts here from Ilya Gaiduk (on the Soviet Union) and Qiang Zhai (the PRC) indicate. Both the Soviets and Chinese viewed the U.S. escalation in Vietnam during 1964–1965 with apprehension. Ideological solidarity seemed to demand a generous response to Vietnamese pleas for help, and to some extent the growing acrimony between Moscow and Beijing created a competition to show which nation could help North Vietnam more—a situation obviously of benefit to Hanoi. At the same time, neither communist power wished for a confrontation with the United States over Southeast Asia. Despite American fears, Soviet and Chinese leaders did not believe that Vietnam was worth a wider war.

The final piece in the chapter comes from Odd Arne Westad's study of the Cold War as a global event. The Soviet Union and China again figure prominently in Westad's account, but so do real or would-be revolutionaries in Indonesia, the Philippines, Western Europe, the United States, and Cuba, all of whom looked to events in Vietnam as possible harbingers for their own radical hopes and plans.

⋞ 23 ⋟

The Soviet Union and American Escalation

Ilya V. Gaiduk

WITH PRESIDENT JOHNSON'S DECISION to begin sustained reprisals against North Vietnam, the conflict in Indochina entered a new phase. Now military actions on both sides dictated a logic of their own to the participants. From March 1965 on, scenarios were already being written on the battlefield. Events between March and July 1965 proved that both Washington and Hanoi, contrary to their declarations in support of peaceful negotiations, saw military conflict as the only means to their ends.

The eleventh plenum of the Lao Dong party [Workers' Party of Vietnam], held in March, confirmed the course of Vietnamese Communists on a military victory over "American imperialism." Meanwhile, decisions of the Johnson administration on the deployment of U.S. combat forces in South Vietnam, and the expansion of the air war against the DRV, showed American determination to suppress insurgency in the South and its supporters in the North. And new developments in Southeast Asia had repercussions in the capitals of friends and allies of the participants of the conflict; Moscow was among those who viewed events in Indochina with apprehension and uncertainty.

Because Soviet efforts to achieve a diplomatic settlement of the conflict had failed, Moscow was apparently inclined, at least for the time being, to concentrate instead on consolidating DRV defenses and meeting Chinese accusations of "betrayal" of the interests of socialism. In March Beijing intensified its campaign against the Soviet Union as a response to the conference of Communist and Workers' parties held in Moscow at the beginning of the month and to the first signs of rapprochement between the Soviets and the North Vietnamese after [Alexei] Kosygin's visit to Southeast Asia. The discontent of Chinese leaders had been demonstrated in an incident near the American embassy in Moscow on March 4. The next day *Pravda* informed its readers that a demonstration by foreign students who were studying in Soviet universities had been held in front of the American embassy, reportedly protesting U.S. aggression against Vietnam.[1] The report was brief and would have gone unnoticed if a week later, on March 13, *Pravda* had not published a note from the USSR Ministry of Foreign Affairs to the Chinese ambassador, in which Soviet authorities condemned the "vociferous propaganda campaign" unfolding in China and related to the March 4 demonstration. The note presented the Soviet version of that day's events and called the behavior of Chinese students during the demonstration an "attempt prepared in advance to provoke violent actions directed both against a foreign embassy and representatives of the Soviet authorities."[2] *Pravda* claimed that more than thirty militia and military had been beaten and four seriously injured by the Chinese.[3] When the Chinese government honored the students who were involved in this and a later incident, in ceremonies in Beijing after the students returned home, it seemed clear to Soviet leaders that Chinese authorities had been behind this "provocation."[4]

These events demonstrated that the rift between the two Communist giants not only had not been repaired after the American escalation in Vietnam, it had broadened despite Soviet efforts to create a "unified front" of socialist countries. The Soviet leadership now began to take vigorous steps to develop Soviet–North Vietnamese relations.

First, Moscow undertook to strengthen cooperation between the two countries in economic and military areas. The first important shipments of Soviet aid to Hanoi evidently took place in March as a consequence of agreements concluded during the February visit of the Soviet delegation to the DRV. Moscow initially used sea transport and confined its aid to supplies of food and equipment, but after a protocol between the USSR and China on the transit of Soviet aid through Chinese territory was concluded on March 30[5] (a minor concession by Beijing to the demands of the "united front"), growing amounts of arms and ammunition were moved from the Soviet Union for the People's Army of Vietnam.

Moscow meanwhile maintained a hard public line on the situation in Southeast Asia. Soviet propaganda intensified during March as the Kremlin spared no opportunity to declare its adherence to the "just cause" of the Vietnamese people and issued numerous statements condemning U.S. aggression. Moreover, Soviet leaders added a new wrinkle to their pronouncements in support of Hanoi. On March 24 [Leonid] Brezhnev spoke on Red Square to honor the just-returned Soviet cosmonauts of Voskhod II. Suddenly turning to the problem of the Vietnam War, Brezhnev routinely condemned "American imperialism" for its assault on the independence and territorial integrity of a socialist country. Then he noted that many Soviet citizens had volunteered to go to Vietnam to fight for freedom. The Soviet leader assured his audience that he understood "feelings of fraternal solidarity and socialist internationalism" which were finding their expression in these appeals of the Soviet people. His country, he emphasized, would fulfill its international obligation toward the DRV.[6]

Brezhnev's statement alarmed officials in Washington who feared nothing more than direct Soviet participation in the war. U.S. Ambassador [Foy] Kohler in Moscow assessed the speech as the "opening gun in political and propaganda campaign designed to undermine U.S. position in Vietnam before the world, to alarm world opinion as to imminent escalation of hostilities . . . and thus persuade the world that the only alternative to serious deterioration of the situation is a conference on Soviet terms." Yet Kohler perceived the reference to volunteers only as a cover to allow Moscow to dispatch Soviet personnel to man sophisticated weaponry sent by the USSR to Hanoi.[7]

But this was scarcely Brezhnev's only purpose. While his principal motive was to demonstrate Soviet readiness to assist a fraternal socialist country by all possible means, his claim about Soviet volunteers was also aimed at Chinese accusations that "revisionists" in Moscow were ready to provide only halfhearted support to their allies so as not to spoil their relations with the "imperialists." And another clear objective was to strengthen the Soviet position in Hanoi, which called for a whole complex of Soviet efforts, not just "volunteers."

Sending volunteers to Vietnam was certainly not considered practical by Moscow in March 1965 (and, as we shall see, later as well). Brezhnev's reference was a response to the appeal of the National Liberation Front of South Vietnam on March 22 for assistance—including volunteers—from socialist countries in its struggle against "American imperialism." The real meaning of this appeal was revealed four days later in a conversation between the Soviet ambassador to Hanoi and DRV Deputy Foreign Minister Hoang Van Loi. Hoang confirmed that the campaign for volunteers played a "political role of expressing revolutionary solidarity and friendship of the peoples of the socialist countries." The NLF was grateful for Soviet support but did not yet need volunteers. They would be requested when necessary.[8]

For Hanoi, however, such a "necessity" was complicated by the Chinese factor. North Vietnamese leaders understood that they would be obliged to invite volunteers from the People's Republic of China as well as from the Soviet Union and other socialist countries. Despite close relations between the two Asian countries, there was an undercurrent of suspicion in Hanoi toward its "great northern neighbor" conditioned by experience. The North Vietnamese tried to cloak this "credibility gap" by referring to the rivalry between Moscow and Beijing as the principal obstacle in the question of volunteers and other logistical problems. One North Vietnamese expert also mentioned the question of subordinating volunteers to the Vietnamese command.[9] Though important, this problem could be resolved much more easily than Hanoi's fear of finding itself under Beijing's command.

Soviet volunteers and other aspects of Soviet–North Vietnamese relations were discussed during the April 1965 visit to Moscow of a DRV delegation headed by Le Duan. This visit appeared to be the last in a series of high-level meetings of leaders of the two countries that determined the direction and forms of cooperation under wartime conditions.

Information about the arrival of the North Vietnamese delegation was withheld by Soviet media until after the delegation left Moscow, attesting to the secret nature of the visit. Instead Soviet newspapers were filled with reports about the visit of a high-level delegation from Mongolia. Only on April 18 did *Pravda* publish the joint Soviet–North Vietnamese communiqué with information about the visit.

The communiqué informed the Soviet people that Le Duan, with DRV Minister of Defense Vo Nguyen Giap and Foreign Minister Nguyen Duy Trinh, had met with the highest Soviet authorities from April 10 to 17. The agenda of these negotiations was not revealed, but it could be inferred from the communiqué that the main item was Soviet-DRV cooperation in the North Vietnamese struggle against "American aggressors."

The communiqué contained two paragraphs that were important for an understanding of the negotiations. The first was a clear warning that, in the event U.S. aggression against the Democratic Republic of Vietnam continued, the Soviet government, "in accordance with the feelings of proletarian internationalism," would permit the departure to Vietnam of those Soviet citizens who expressed a desire to "fight for the just cause of the Vietnamese people, for preservation of socialist achievements" in the DRV, provided the government of North Vietnam requested volunteers. Second, the parties noted "with satisfaction" that the "earlier understanding" on "strengthening the defense potential of the DRV" was being carried out according "to the envisaged extent and procedure."[10]

Soviet leaders' satisfaction with the results of the negotiations was confirmed by Premier Kosygin several days later during a meeting honoring the Mongolian delegation. Kosygin told his audience about the visit of the North Vietnamese to Moscow and emphasized that negotiations between the Soviet and Vietnamese leaders had been a success. "They brought about positive results and helped to work out coordinated positions on the problems of forms and means of the struggle against the aggressive policy of American imperialism, of further strengthening the defense capacity of the socialist Vietnam as well as of a settlement of the problems of Indochina on the basis of the Geneva Accords."[11]

The April visit of the North Vietnamese to Moscow did not go unnoticed by Washington. The Johnson administration was anxious to learn of the outcome of the talks; the principal question was Soviet–North Vietnamese military cooperation. According to a special memorandum from the Board of National Estimates, the USSR would "almost certainly" provide Hanoi with weaponry for antiaircraft defense. It would include surface-to-air missile batteries for areas around Hanoi, Haiphong, and other vital centers, and fighter aircraft—though the planes would be difficult to ship by rail without Chinese collaboration. As to military personnel, U.S. intelligence assumed the Soviets might dispatch "some pilots and technicians" under the guise of "volunteers." It questioned the likelihood of the Soviets deploying to Vietnam military forces that would include air defense units, ground units, a variety of other technical personnel, coastal naval vessels, and even submarines. Rather, the CIA and other intelligence suggested, the Soviet Union would choose a middle course between full-scale involvement and total disengagement, and "some sort of middle course" was "probably what emerged out of the April meeting in Moscow." But, the memorandum warned, if the crisis persisted at current or higher levels of risk and complication, "the middle way may not survive."[12]

The visit of Le Duan and his colleagues to Moscow may also have helped to resolve problems of transportation of Soviet aid through Chinese territory, and the stopover of the DRV delegation in Beijing on its way home probably had to do with arranging delivery of the aid. In fact, the CIA informed authorities in Washington in May that most of the problems relating to the Soviet aid had been settled and that "the arrival of the long expected Soviet military aid in North Vietnam may be imminent."[13] Later that month, on May 25, American intelligence reported the first signs of Soviet modern weapons in Vietnam: fifteen MIG 15/17s, probably sent to Vietnam by rail through China, in addition to one hundred armored personnel carriers equipped with antiaircraft guns.[14] Next day the State Department informed the American embassy in Moscow about the arrival in Vietnam of IL-28 light bombers, which the U.S. military had considered an offensive weapon during the 1962 Cuban missile crisis. Although State Department officials believed that the "preferred role of the aircraft in Moscow's view would be deterrence for the time being," they noted the determination of Soviet leaders to support their allies in North Vietnam by all possible means, even to the detriment of détente.[15]

Indeed, in the spring of 1965 Moscow demonstrated an unwillingness even to discuss prospects of a peaceful settlement in Vietnam. It seemed that Soviet leaders had renounced their earlier efforts to find a political solution to the dangerous situation. They flatly rejected any proposals that did not include the total cessation of American bombing of North Vietnamese territory.

While visiting London from March 16 to 20, Foreign Minister [Andrei] Gromyko, though he was "friendly and reasonably constructive" on problems of Soviet-British relations, was equally adamant with regard to a Vietnam settlement. He stonewalled every proposal to recall the Geneva Conference or any type of conference with the participation of the Soviet Union. His response was a "flat repetition" of the Soviet denunciation of the United States and a demand for unconditional withdrawal of American troops, equipment, and advisers.[16] Doubtless this attitude took into account the position of North Vietnam. Hanoi was ready to negotiate only on its own terms and was in no hurry to go to the conference table, preferring to gain military advantage and then to negotiate from a position of strength. The U.S. attitude was essentially the same.

Soviet leaders had been informed of the decisions of the eleventh plenum of the Lao Dong party as well as the intention of the United States to expand the presence and role of American forces in Vietnam. Soviet newspapers regularly provided their readers with the details of American plans during March and April 1965. In this situation Moscow apparently chose to strengthen its positions in the DRV and await further developments—a policy that seemed inadequate to Washington. While members of the Johnson administration believed the United States could always get to the conference table when necessary, and that there was "no great hurry about it right now,"[17] they felt pressure from various circles at home and abroad "to make explorations toward the possibility of talks" and considered the Soviet Union a potential ally in these explorations. Furthermore, American leaders hoped to keep channels of communication with Moscow open and get the Soviets involved in various peace initiatives as a guarantee against Soviet military involvement in the conflict. Finally, Washington viewed the Soviets as a welcome counterweight to Beijing in Southeast Asia and thus was ready to take some steps, however symbolic, to meet Soviet desires for a peaceful settlement of the Vietnam War. In this vein James Thomson and Chester Cooper of the National Security Council staff argued the case for a conference on Cambodia, proposed by Prince Sihanouk and supported by Moscow, in their memorandum to McGeorge Bundy on April 21.[18] These recommendations as well as those of other presidential advisers were clearly taken into account by the administration in April and early May as it pondered a bombing pause.

The May 1965 attempt to find a diplomatic solution of the conflict went forward when neither Washington nor Hanoi was ready to agree on a serious compromise of its objectives. From the outset it was thus doomed to failure. Nevertheless it proved useful as the first substantial test of attitudes of the countries involved in the conflict.

Project Mayflower, the code name of the first U.S. bombing pause, has been analyzed extensively by many scholars.[19] Here our analysis is confined to a brief account of the principal events of May 10–18 with emphasis on the role of the Soviet Union.

As mentioned earlier, pressure on the Johnson administration to move toward a peaceful settlement of the conflict in Indochina had mounted since the escalation of the war in February-March 1965. Not only was public opinion in the United States and abroad clamoring for a bombing halt and negotiations, but leaders from various countries were also calling for decisive peace moves. In Washington there was no consensus either. As Brian VanDeMark has noted, demands for a bombing halt came from the left as well as the right, for different reasons. While the left opposed further bombing in order to facilitate peace talks, "military and especially intelligence officials, doubting Rolling Thunder's ability to coerce North Vietnam into a settlement, began prodding LBJ to halt bombing briefly to test Hanoi's interest in negotiations, only to resume even more intense bombing thereafter."[20]

Johnson responded to this pressure by deciding on a bombing pause and ordering a simultaneous approach to the North Vietnamese with an offer to negotiate. He explained his decision in a May 10 cable to Ambassador Maxwell Taylor in Saigon. "You should understand," the president declared, "that my purpose in this plan is to begin to clear a path either toward restoration of peace or toward increased military action, depending upon the reactions of the Communists. We had amply demonstrated our determination and our commitment in the last two months, and I now wish to gain some flexibility."[21]

In its attempt to contact Hanoi, Washington counted on Soviet help. Moscow was to be approached in order to sound out the Kremlin's position toward diplomatic contacts between the warring parties and its possible role in arranging them. With this in mind, Secretary of State Rusk summoned Soviet Ambassador [Anatoli] Dobrynin to his office on May 11 and informed him of the U.S. initiative along the lines of a message he planned to send to Kohler in Moscow the same day.

The cable to Kohler instructed the American ambassador to deliver a message to the North Vietnamese ambassador in Moscow, explaining that the United States was suspending its air attacks on North Vietnam for seven days beginning May 12. The ambassador was to emphasize the U.S. conviction that the "cause of trouble" in Southeast Asia was armed action against the South Vietnamese government by forces directed from North Vietnam. The American government would note whether during the bombing pause there were "significant reductions in such armed actions by such forces." Only in this case would an opportunity arise to bring a permanent end to American attacks on North Vietnam.[22]

Dobrynin's reaction to this information from Rusk reflected the attitude of the Soviet government at the time. According to Rusk, the Soviet ambassador "*was clearly relieved we [were] not asking them to act as intermediary*."[23] Apparently Soviet leaders were not eager to act as mediators between Hanoi and Washington, and Dobrynin knew this full well. Events confirmed this attitude.

When Kohler failed in his efforts to transmit a message to the North Vietnamese ambassador, he tried to reach any high-level official in the Soviet Foreign Ministry to ask for help in communicating with the North Vietnamese. The only official Kohler was able to meet with was Deputy Foreign Minister Nikolai Firyubin, who flatly declined his government's role as an intermediary and went on to lecture Kohler about the aggressive policy of the United States in Vietnam. Firyubin, who was responsible for Soviet relations with Asian countries, was acquainted with reports that the Soviet embassy in Hanoi sent to Moscow and therefore was acutely aware of North Vietnamese views on the prospects of the war and the Soviet role. These views were similar to those expressed in a later conversation between a member of the Vietnamese politburo, Le Duc Tho, and a French journalist. Le Duc Tho did not conceal his satisfaction with the economic and military aid and moral support rendered to the DRV by the Soviet Union. He noted, however, that Soviet leaders did not seem to believe in an ultimate victory of North Vietnam in the war, ". . . and this encourages them to search for a solution of the South Vietnamese question by means of negotiations; as to us, we think that conditions for negotiations have not yet ripened."[24]

Moscow could not fail to consider North Vietnamese suspicion of Soviet intentions with respect to a settlement of the Vietnamese conflict, and Firyubin was especially cautious not to jeopardize Moscow's efforts in March and April to create a solid ground for the Soviet position in Vietnam. Accordingly, his attacks on the U.S. position during his conversation with Kohler, his warnings that the American aggression would not "go unpunished without response," his defense of the struggle in South Vietnam as a natural outcome of popular protest against oppression by the "Saigon puppets," seemed to be part of a ritual designed to avoid possible blame for "softness" on the part of Moscow.

But Firyubin, while refusing to be a "postman" between the two warring parties, "made no effort to return" the text of the oral communication which Kohler had handed him at the beginning of the conversation.[25] It may have been a deliberate move by the Soviets to see that Hanoi would eventually receive the U.S. offer at least from the hands of Soviet comrades.

This was Kohler's understanding of Firyubin's behavior, and the ambassador remained surprisingly optimistic after his conversation. In a message to the State Department he confessed that he "could understand, if not sympathize with, Soviet sensitivity." He expressed a hope that Firyubin's reaction would not be viewed in Washington as evidence of a conscious hardening of the Soviet attitude. "It may simply be [a] reflection of [the] bind Soviets find themselves in at moment." Kohler was sure the U.S. message was already in DRV hands and that Washington should be on the alert for reaction from the other side.[26]

The ambassador's optimism had some basis. Just one day before the bombing pause, the Soviets had authorized a contact between "two somewhat shadowy officials" and Pierre Salinger, former press secretary to Presidents Kennedy and Johnson, who was in Moscow at the time on private business. Salinger was invited to dinner by Mikhail Sagatelyan of the Telegraph Agency of the Soviet Union. During the dinner Sagatelyan speculated at length on possible solutions to the conflict in Vietnam. Two nights later Salinger and Sagatelyan again met for dinner, this time joined by a Soviet Foreign Ministry representative identified only as Vasily Sergeyevich. The Soviets confirmed their interest in a resolution in Vietnam and informed Salinger that the

Soviet government had received the U.S. proposal to North Vietnam but would not answer it or act upon it until Soviet leaders were sure that something substantive would come from these meetings with Salinger.

"Throughout conversation," Kohler reported to Washington, "Soviets made clear to Salinger that because of sensitive Soviet position any progress toward political settlement Vietnam problem must be initiated and carried through, at least in preliminary stage, on basis unofficial contacts, clear implication being if leak should occur or if scheme should go awry, Soviet Government would be in position to disavow whole affair."[27] Sagatelyan clearly acted with the knowledge of the Soviet leadership, otherwise there was no reason for a Soviet journalist to touch upon the subject of Vietnam during a meeting with Salinger. Since Soviet officials were obliged to report on all meetings with Westerners, it might even be dangerous for Sagatelyan to raise this subject without prior authorization by his superiors.

One may therefore wonder about the purpose of Soviet officials who authorized the meetings with Salinger. Apparently Sagatelyan's task was twofold: to convey to the Americans Moscow's concern over developments in Vietnam and its desire to see the conflict settled, and to let Washington know that under the circumstances the Soviets had little room for maneuver, though the situation might change for the better. Perhaps the Kremlin was also probing the substance of the American proposals to North Vietnam. In any event, their interest in Sagatelyan's contacts waned.

A "brief Kaffeeklatsch" between Secretary Rusk and Foreign Minister Gromyko in Vienna on May 15 rounded off Soviet interest in Project Mayflower. During this "chat" Gromyko stated plainly that Moscow would not negotiate on Vietnam, that it viewed the temporary suspension of bombing as "insulting," and that the United States itself would have to find ways of establishing contact with North Vietnamese leaders. In light of the foreign minister's words, Rusk concluded that "Gromyko wanted me to believe that they are not prepared to work toward a settlement in Hanoi and Peiping and that, indeed, unless we abandon our effort in South Viet-Nam there will be very serious consequences ahead."[28]

Meanwhile, as officials in Washington had expected, Hanoi's response to the American initiative was far from positive. Yet there were encouraging steps by Hanoi, notably a statement of the North Vietnamese National Assembly and an approach by the head of the DRV economic delegation in Paris, Mai Van Bo, to French diplomats. This approach, however, was made after the bombing resumed and was therefore too late to influence American decisions.[29]

Considering that Washington's objectives in the bombing pause were negative—to prove that Hanoi was not inclined toward a peaceful settlement—the results of the pause were confirming. Some months later Defense Secretary McNamara admitted: "Our first pause was a propaganda effort."[30] The substance of motives determines the substance of results in a situation where, to paraphrase Ralph Waldo Emerson, "war is in the saddle and rides mankind."

Meanwhile the scope of Soviet aid to North Vietnam was continuing to expand. The war's increasing demands forced Hanoi to ask for additional help from its socialist allies, first from the Soviet Union and China. The North Vietnamese thus sent a new delegation, headed by Pham Van Dong's deputy Le Thanh Nghi, to Moscow, Beijing, and the capitals of the Eastern European countries.

Pravda reported on the DRV delegation's arrival in Moscow on June 5, 1965, without referring to the goals of the visit.[31] But its importance became clear when news spread that Le Thanh Nghi was received first by Kosygin and then by Brezhnev. The talks, which took place between Kosygin's deputy Vladimir Novikov and the North Vietnamese, extended until July 10, with a break to allow Le Thanh Nghi to travel to Eastern Europe with the clear intention of coordinating socialist aid to the "fighting people of heroic Vietnam." In a communiqué issued after the visit and published by *Pravda* on July 13, the participants proclaimed that agreements had been reached on Soviet assistance in developing the people's economy and strengthening the defense capability of the Democratic Republic of Vietnam. They contained provisions on additional Soviet aid to North Vietnam beyond that already in the pipeline.[32]

Neither the amount nor the conditions of this aid were revealed by the negotiators, but the DRV council of ministers was "glad to note significant results in many areas achieved during these visits and negotiations."[33] Clearly North Vietnamese leaders were generally satisfied with the socialist countries' attitude toward aid to the DRV.

These negotiations in Moscow in June and July demonstrated that the Soviet Union was becoming more and more deeply involved in the conflict in Southeast Asia. Moreover, this involvement was not confined to defending North Vietnam in its encounter with the United States. Soviet leaders were fully aware that arms and ammunition produced in the USSR were being channeled to South Vietnamese "patriots" in direct conflict with Washington.[34] They seemed ready to take this risk. At least the Kremlin did not conceal its well-disposed attitude toward Viet Cong representatives in the Soviet capital.

The Soviet Union had agreed in December 1964 to open a permanent NLF mission in Moscow, but only in late April 1965 did the mission's staff arrive in the city. Kosygin received Dang Quang Minh, the head of the mission, on June 3, emphasizing the importance which the Soviet leadership attributed to its relations with the NLF.[35] At the same time this was a clear demonstration of Soviet determination to support the war in South Vietnam.

Yet Moscow was not willing to exceed certain limits of that risk. Soviet leaders could not fail to perceive the danger of an encounter with the United States, especially if Washington chose to resort to nuclear weapons to suppress the insurgency in South Vietnam. This seemed to be a real nightmare for Moscow because in the summer of 1965 reports on such a possibility reached the Kremlin regularly. For example, in June Soviet intelligence informed the Kremlin that in a conversation with Italian Foreign Minister Amintore Fanfani, Secretary of State Rusk had admitted that the prospect of using tactical nuclear weapons in Vietnam was on the agenda of American policymakers.[36] The USSR ministers of defense and foreign affairs and the KGB, in their report for the Soviet leadership in August, seriously considered the question of U.S. readiness to wage a thermonuclear war and the Johnson administration's intentions in this regard.[37]

Moscow could not neglect other pitfalls inherent in the USSR's involvement in Vietnam, such as the financial burden of aid to the DRV aggravation of relations with the West, and incorrigible waywardness of the North Vietnamese comrades who viewed support of their struggle as the only duty of the Soviet people. All these factors pushed Soviet leaders to turn their eyes once again to relations with the United States—easier to do after Moscow had proved its adherence to the cause of North Vietnam.

For their gesture toward the United States, Soviet leaders used a reception arranged by the American embassy in Moscow in honor of a prominent diplomat and scholar, godfather of the cold war doctrine of "containment," and former ambassador to the Soviet Union, George F. Kennan, who was visiting in June apparently for his usual "sentimental journey" to the place of his youth. Foy Kohler invited to lunch at his residence, the famous Spaso House, several well-known Soviet officials, historians, and academicians, among them Foreign Minister Gromyko. Gromyko initially declined the invitation but then "suddenly" changed his mind and accepted while other invitees "suddenly" declined.

The conversation that took place on June 25 was significant from many points of view. According to Kohler, it "ranged over wide spectrum and throughout Gromyko was affable and gave impression of genuine desire to resume dialogue on basic issues which initiated in post-Cuba period."[38] After general discussion with Kennan on the problems of national liberation movements, Gromyko somewhat unexpectedly expressed a desire to convey to the American ambassador "two basic points": first, that the Soviets were not authorized and could not negotiate on behalf of North Vietnam, and, second, that it had been and continued to be "fundamental Soviet policy to seek improvement in U.S.-Soviet bilateral relations."

Developing the first statement, Gromkyo stressed that the Vietnamese situation had to be discussed directly with the DRV. The Soviet position was to support the four-point statement of Pham Van Dong of April 8. As in his conversation with Rusk in Vienna, Gromyko "cautioned" the Johnson administration that no progress could be made if future approaches to the DRV were cast in such "insulting" terms as they had been earlier.

As to Soviet-American relations, Gromyko noted that the Soviet government was disappointed by the "drastic change" in U.S. policy since the 1964 elections. He compared some measures of the Johnson administration to those that had been endorsed by Barry Goldwater in his electoral campaign.

Kohler tried to convince his counterpart that Washington understood quite well the difficulties faced by the Soviet government in dealing with the Vietnamese situation, first of all because of the attitudes of Hanoi and Beijing. But the Johnson administration remained hopeful that Moscow "would be prepared to bring its influence to bear on Hanoi in effort to bring about peaceful settlement of Vietnamese problem" which the United States did not wish to see escalated to a dangerous degree. The ambassador defended his country's actions in South Vietnam as consistent with previous U.S. policy and assured Gromyko that thus far there had been no change in the U.S. attitude toward relations with the Soviet Union. "We have consistently taken the position," stated Kohler, "that despite current difficulties, particularly in Vietnam, we desire continuing improvement in U.S.-Soviet relations on which such a significant start had been made in 1963."[39]

Gromyko apparently came to Spaso House not simply to reiterate that the Soviets were not in a position to play the role of intermediary between the United States and North Vietnam. His intention was also to reaffirm the Soviet interest in maintaining good relations with Washington. Kohler understood this and received the Soviet foreign minister's assurances enthusiastically, promising Gromyko that the U.S. government would do its part in developing relations between the two countries. In Kohler's report to Washington, he noted the fact of Gromyko's appearance at Spaso, his positive remarks on the U.S.-Soviet relationship, his affable mood, and his "almost wistful" recall of the atmosphere in 1963. Kohler concluded that there was "perhaps some new flexibility in Sov[iet] posture."[40]

Kohler's cable was received in Washington with mixed feelings. On one hand, as a staff member of the State Department's Bureau of Intelligence and Research observed in a memorandum to Llewellyn Thompson, Gromyko's visit as well as "other recent talk about channels of communication" suggested that "at the very least the Soviets might be getting worried that our relations are drifting out of control."[41] The fact that Gromyko refrained from objections during Kohler's pleas for Soviet pressure on Hanoi to negotiate was seen in Washington as another positive indication.

On the other hand, U.S. policymakers also noted Soviet efforts to outdo the Chinese in Southeast Asia in "revolutionary militancy" and some signs of Soviet hardening toward other international problems. Some members of the Johnson administration believed that the time had come for the USSR to move responsibly to reduce tensions in sensitive areas, primarily in Vietnam.

In light of Gromyko's assurances in his meeting with Kohler, Washington decided to probe the Soviet position more fully. This task was presumably in Secretary Rusk's mind when he called in Dobrynin on the eve of the latter's departure for Moscow, since this was a good opportunity to use the ambassador to carry home with him the American government's ideas on cooperation toward resolution of the conflict in Southeast Asia. This was all the more urgent for the Johnson administration because it was seriously considering plans for further Americanization of the war in Vietnam. Thus a discussion with Dobrynin could avoid a "misunderstanding" on the part of the Soviet leadership and could persuade the Kremlin that Washington was eager to find ways to end the war as soon as possible.

Rusk began his conversation with Dobrynin by restating his government's desire to see relations with the Soviet Union improved, a desire that remained unchanged despite sharp personal attacks on President Johnson in the Soviet press. The secretary of state then noted that "in the broadest sense" the key problem between the two countries was that of Southeast Asia. The U.S. government was ready to discuss this problem with the Soviets but was uncertain about the other side's attitude toward such a discussion.

After these introductory remarks Rusk speculated on the possibility of maintaining an "informal channel" of communication between Washington and Moscow on the problem of Vietnam. He understood Soviet concern about a possible disclosure of secret contacts between the two countries, Rusk said, but he was positive that private talks could be arranged and secured. Rusk concluded: "We understand that it is difficult for Moscow to bring this matter [i.e., the war in Vietnam] to its peaceful conclusion. There are also difficulties on our side. However, despite the existence of millions of Chinese, *there are only two countries, the Soviet Union and the United States, that can keep the peace.* We are puzzled as to how to proceed, assuming that both of us really want peace."[42]

To reinforce this conversation with the Soviet ambassador, Washington was planning to send W. Averell Harriman to Moscow to persuade the Soviets to take a more active role in negotiations. Harriman's name meant much in the history of Soviet-American relations. His experience in dealing with the Soviets went back to the early twenties when, as a young businessman and heir to one of the great American fortunes, he had received from Stalin's regime a concession for mining manganese in Soviet Georgia. Harriman's Georgian Manganese Company was an important part of the Soviet plan to win American recognition of the USSR through economic relations with the world's most developed capitalist country.

Harriman had come to Moscow for the first time in 1926 to meet with such famous Bolsheviks as Maxim Litvinov and Leon Trotsky. His next trips to the Soviet Union occurred during World War II, first as a special envoy of President Roosevelt, then as American ambassador to the Soviet Union. Harriman met with Stalin several times and gained vast experience in dealing with the dictator and his minions. Indeed, he won such respect in the USSR that his name became forever linked with the Soviet-Western alliance and victory over Hitler. Stalin himself paid special attention to the U.S. ambassador.

After the war Harriman remained a prominent figure in Soviet-American relations. He knew personally Khrushchev and Mikoyan. He met Kosygin when the latter was only one of Stalin's functionaries. As Harriman noted in a letter to President Johnson just after the 1964 election, "Presidents Roosevelt, Truman, and Kennedy used me as a pinch hitter for special negotiations, in addition to my regular duties. By luck or good fortune, my batting average has been surprisingly good."[43] Thus when the problem of finding appropriate channels of communication with the Soviets arose, Harriman seemed a logical candidate to be sent to Moscow—and he himself vigorously promoted this decision.

Harriman privately doubted the wisdom of U.S. involvement in Vietnam and believed in the need for a political settlement of the conflict. In his view, the road to peace in Indochina led through Moscow.[44] Harriman's confidence was based upon his estimate of the new Soviet leadership. Just after Khrushchev's ouster, Harriman confided to John McCloy, one of Johnson's close associates, that he knew Kosygin well and believed the new Soviet premier to be pragmatic.[45] This implied that for Kosygin, who was preoccupied with problems of the Soviet economy, the war in Indochina was an irritating obstacle that diverted money and other means for a needless imbroglio. Therefore, Harriman believed, Washington's desire to resolve the conflict as quickly as possible was in the Kremlin's interest, and it would be useful to maintain reliable channels of communication with Moscow and to ask the Soviet leaders for assistance in this matter. He was ready to go privately to Moscow on a reconnaissance mission.

He broached this subject with Ambassador Dobrynin in June and asked him to find out whether Moscow would approve his trip. Gromyko's conversation with Kohler and Kennan strengthened Harriman's determination to visit the Soviet Union, though, as he stressed in his telephone conversation with the Soviet ambassador, he did not wish to go unless Soviet leaders welcomed him.[46] Finally Dobrynin called on Harriman on July 1, 1965, and informed him that Soviet leaders had consented to meet with the former "special envoy to Churchill and Stalin."[47] Harriman, unlike Kennan, did not intend to take a "sentimental journey." In order to preserve the confidential nature of his visit, however, he announced his trip as an ordinary vacation.

Apparently this venture was wholly Harriman's initiative, but Johnson and Rusk then supported the idea of the ambassador at large (Harriman's official State Department title, though he preferred to be called "Governor," a legacy of his tenure as governor of New York). Rusk defined the goals of Harriman's visit in his conversation with Dobrynin on July 3. "The Secretary said he wished to make clear that he was not suggesting that Governor Harriman intended to get into formal negotiations" on the problems of Vietnam. "He said that Governor Harriman was, of course, aware of the United States position and familiar with our bilateral relations and would be glad to discuss them with the Soviet authorities." But his main task, said Rusk, was to determine Moscow's attitude toward contacts between the two capitals regarding U.S. involvement in the Vietnamese conflict."[48]

Neither the administration nor Harriman intended to reveal the true purpose of the mission. On the eve of the ambassador's departure, the State Department reminded him of the need to "discourage press speculation" about the trip, especially the Moscow portion, "as much as possible." Officially Mr. and Mrs. Harriman were on vacation. If the question arose as to whether Harriman expected to meet with Soviet authorities during his visit, the reply would not exclude such a possibility "in view of his position and personal acquaintance with officials of the French, Soviet and other governments."[49] The itinerary included Paris, Moscow, Brussels, West Germany, Rome, Belgrade, and London.

On July 8 Harriman arrived in Paris. There he discussed the principal aim of his trip with French Foreign Minister Couve de Murville. As soon as the French learned of the background of Harriman's mission, Couve drew the ambassador's attention to Moscow's difficult position. He noted that the Soviets "sincerely wanted peace but had no way to exercise any influence in this direction." They could not let the DRV down, Couve explained, but, on the other hand, they did not wish to risk increasing conflict.[50] With this discomforting information, Harriman left Paris for Moscow on July 12.

Harriman's announced purpose in Moscow was to attend an international film festival, though he had not entered a movie theatre in years and could barely remember a few films that had been shown for Stalin after banquets in the Kremlin.[51] As might be expected, this incongruity in the governor's behavior evoked interest among journalists, who asked administration representatives and even President Johnson about it. At his news conference on July 13, the president was asked whether Harriman's trip to Moscow had any connection with the Soviet position in Vietnam. Johnson stressed that Harriman was on vacation and had not been sent by the administration, though the president "approved heartily of his [Harriman's] statement that he would be glad to visit with any people that cared to visit with him."[52] Not surprisingly, Premier Kosygin was among those people.

Two meetings between Kosygin and Harriman took place in Moscow on July 15 and 21. On both occasions *Pravda* published brief information about these meetings without revealing details. Harriman, said the reports, was in the Soviet Union as a private citizen and had initiated these conversations.[53] Unlike *Pravda*'s dreary prose, however, discussions between the two men seemed to be lively and emotional.

According to Harriman's report to Washington, Kosygin struck him as a sincere believer in communism and its ultimate victory. The premier "looked me squarely in the eye," wrote Harriman, when he talked about communism, liberation movements, and the U.S. endangering world peace. At the same time the American envoy found Kosygin pragmatic and not doctrinaire. He had enormous concern for the success of the Soviet economy. He made frank and sober statements about the international situation and how the Soviets understood it. In all, Harriman concluded that the premier had "conviction, determination, and courage."[54]

The subject of the talks ranged from Vietnam to Berlin to problems of nuclear weapons and bilateral relations. The Soviet premier complained that Johnson had changed course after the 1964 election, a recurrent Soviet remonstrance that showed itself in the depth of disappointment Moscow felt with regard to developments in Vietnam. The Soviets had figuratively voted for Johnson in the last election, Kosygin said, but the American president had not come up to their expectations.[55] Harriman tried to change this opinion of Johnson and may have succeeded, for Kosygin became "increasingly cordial in his expressions of desire" to meet the president.[56]

But the principal theme of the discussion was the Vietnamese conflict. Kosygin made it clear that the situation in Vietnam, though small in itself, affected relations between Moscow and Washington. However much Kosygin wished to see the Vietnam problem disappear, he nevertheless supported Pham Van Dong's four points and remained unconvinced by Harriman's assertions that the National Liberation Front was not the voice of the people of South Vietnam. He was clearly concerned about the Soviets' delicate position and sought to convey to Harriman that the row with Beijing was a most serious influence on Soviet policy toward Indochina.

Although he rejected the role of intermediary in the U.S.-DRV dispute, the Soviet premier was positive in his desire for a settlement in Vietnam and the retention of the 17th parallel as the demarcation line. This suggested that the Soviets did not object to the existence of two Vietnams, one of which would remain nonsocialist and perhaps with limited American forces on its territory.

His conversations with Kosygin left Harriman with contradictory feelings. As he stated in his report to Washington, "Visit to Moscow achieved somewhat more than the minimum I had expected and less than my highest hopes."[57] Certainly Harriman's arrival in the Soviet capital and his meetings with Kosygin proved to be useful in themselves. As Harriman noted, this was the first meeting of a representative of the Johnson administration with a member of the USSR ruling triumvirate since its coming to power in November 1964, except for incidental talks at receptions. The discussions helped clarify some problems of bilateral relations and of the world situation, and American leaders "gained some insight" into Soviet leaders' thinking, attitudes, and foreign affairs objectives.

What Harriman had not achieved was a firm Kremlin guarantee to exert pressure on Hanoi to negotiate on American terms. Special Assistant McGeorge Bundy remained skeptical about Harriman's accomplishments. It seemed "striking" to Bundy that Kosygin's comments were "rather routine": a standard list of disarmament objectives, a standard speech in favor of national liberation movements, a standard exchange on Vietnam.[58] The premier had apparently expressed an agreed Soviet position. But even in this position there were promising nuances for the United States.

The State Department's director of intelligence and research, Thomas Hughes, cited such nuances in a memorandum to Rusk. "Most suggestive" were Kosygin's remarks that the United States had to "counterpropose" something to Pham Van Dong's four points. This suggestion had "no precedent in authoritative Soviet or North Vietnamese comment." Hughes evaluated the Soviet premier's phraseology on Vietnam as a "serious suggestion and not simply as a means of washing his hands of the subject."[59] Kosygin implied that Hanoi did not rule out a political settlement and that its four points might be open to adjustment.

In a broader sense, Hughes wrote, the Soviet premier demonstrated that Soviet leaders were ready to discuss with Washington any problems which might seem appropriate. A "standard list" of Soviet declarations did not mean that it would remain unchanged forever, and Kosygin's apparent wish to see the Vietnamese conflict resolved, as well as his urging the United States to get together with North Vietnam in disregard of Beijing, implied that Moscow would move toward this end. But Washington had to take steps to facilitate this Soviet movement.

This idea of a U.S. adjustment dominated Harriman's conversation with Yosip Broz Tito, the Yugoslavian leader, when the old negotiator arrived in Belgrade after visits to Moscow, Brussels, Bonn, and Rome. Tito told Harriman that his impression from Moscow leaders was that the Indochinese situation was particularly difficult for the Soviet Union because of the U.S. bombing of North Vietnam. "The Soviet Union cannot fail in its stand of solidarity with Hanoi since it would otherwise expose itself to the danger of isolating itself in Southeast Asia and Communist parties elsewhere," explained Tito. As a Communist dictator, though an independent one, he understood Soviet concern full well. If the United States wanted Moscow's assistance, Tito stressed, it was first necessary to cease bombing the DRV.[60]

But the Johnson administration was not inclined to slow its military action against Hanoi. On the contrary, in July it was planning further escalation of the war in Vietnam. The same day Harriman met with Kosygin, Johnson held a meeting in the White House to discuss McNamara's recommendations to send an additional 200,000 U.S. troops to Vietnam.[61] These discussions among the administration and congressional leaders lasted until July 28 when the president announced his decision to raise the total of American forces in Vietnam from 75,000 to 125,000, stressing that additional forces would be sent later as requested.[62] The air war against North Vietnam was likewise to be intensified.

Although Kosygin could not have known of these plans when he spoke with Harriman, his posture took into account the possibility of further escalation of the war. Under such circumstances, Soviet leaders could not afford to take on any obligations with regard to settlement of the conflict. Besides, the Soviets knew that Hanoi's irreconcilable position was only strengthened by aggressive U.S. actions. The Johnson administration sought Moscow's assistance while undermining the basis for it.

Moscow's irritation showed itself on August 6 during a reception at the Kremlin honoring the Afghan king. Kosygin's speech included "unacceptable remarks about 'American imperialistic aggression in Viet-Nam,'" according to Kohler's report to Washington.[63]

Thus in the spring and summer of 1965 the war in Indochina approached a new, more dangerous phase despite attempts to prevent the fatal course of events. Peace initiatives failed to bring the warring parties to the negotiating table—and even some of those initiatives were little more than propaganda. Hanoi and Washington had not yet exhausted their bellicose potential.

24

China and the American Escalation

Qiang Zhai

IN THE FIRST HALF OF 1964, THE ATTENTION of American officials was shifting increasingly toward Hanoi. This trend reflected a mounting U.S. concern over the infiltration of men and supplies from the north and a growing dissatisfaction with a policy that allowed Hanoi to encourage the insurgency without punishment. In addition to expanding covert operations in North Vietnam, including intelligence over flights, the dropping of propaganda leaflets, and OPLAN 34A commando raids along the North Vietnamese coast, the Johnson administration also conveyed to Pham Van Dong through a Canadian diplomat on June 17 the message that the United States was ready to exert increasingly heavy military pressure on the DRV to force it to reduce or terminate its encouragement of guerrilla activities in South Vietnam. But the North Vietnamese leader refused to yield to the American pressure, claiming that Hanoi would not stop its support for the struggle of liberation in the South.[1]

During this period, tensions were also increasing in Laos. On April 19, a coup took place led by two right-wing generals, Kouprasith Abhay and Siho Lamphouthacoul. Although short-lived, the coup caused chaos in the Lao government. In the wake of the incident, Souvanna Phouma reorganized the government by excluding the Communists. The topsy-turvy nature of Lao politics manifested itself in the fact that the Pathet Lao was now turning against Kong Le. Considering the Geneva Accords irrelevant, the Lao Communists mounted an attack on Kong Le's forces on the Plain of Jars on May 13, which alarmed Washington and Souvanna. The Lao prime minister permitted unarmed U.S. reconnaissance flights over the Plain of Jars. After Communist antiaircraft guns shot one down on June 6, the United States retaliated three days later by using F-100s to strike the Communist antiaircraft battery at Xieng Khouang. Apparently without U.S. authorization, Thai-piloted Royal Lao Air Force T-28s assaulted the Pathet Lao headquarters at Khang Khay and hit the Chinese Economic and Cultural Mission, killing one Chinese and wounding five others.[2]

Chinese leaders watched these developments closely and apprehensively. At a reception hosted by a visiting Tanzanian delegation in Beijing on June 16, a disturbed Zhou Enlai condemned the U.S. bombing of the Pathet Lao headquarters and the Chinese mission as a violation of the Geneva Accords and an escalation of the conflict in Indochina.[3] He told the Burmese leader Ne Win in Rangoon on July 10 that if the United States wanted to wage a Korean-style war, China must be prepared.[4]

To confront the increasing U.S. pressure in Indochina, Beijing stepped up its coordination with the Vietnamese and Laotian parties. On June 21–24, General Van Tien Dung, chief of staff of the PAVN, visited Beijing, where he discussed with Mao and Zhou Enlai China's military aid to the DRV.[5] Mao told Dung on June 24 that if the United States invaded North Vietnam, China would send troops to the DRV in the form of volunteers.[6] He assured the Vietnamese envoy that "our two parties and two countries must cooperate and fight the enemy together. Your business is my business and my business is your business. In other words, our two sides must deal with the enemy together without conditions."[7]

Between July 5 and 8, Zhou Enlai led a CCP delegation to Hanoi to meet with leaders from the DRV and the Pathet Lao, who described how the United States was using South Vietnam as a base to attack socialism and as a test site for its counterinsurgency warfare. After noting that Southeast Asia was the area in the world where "conflicts are most concentrated, struggle most fierce, and revolutionary conditions most ripe," Zhou pointed out two possible military developments in the region: the United States might intensify the counterinsurgency warfare; or it might turn the counterinsurgency warfare into a local war with a direct deployment of American troops in South Vietnam and Laos or with bombing or invasion of North Vietnam. No matter what approach the United States adopted, Zhou pledged, China would surely intervene to support the struggle of the Southeast Asian people. As to concrete measures that the VWP and the Pathet Lao might take, Zhou suggested a combination of political and military struggles: on the political front, to adhere to the two Geneva Accords, exploit Franco-American disagreements, and organize a broad international united front to lay bare the U.S. violations of the two agreements in the military area, to strengthen armed forces, consolidate base areas, and win battles of annihilation. "Our principle for the struggle," Zhou concluded, "should be to do everything we can to limit the war to the current scale while preparing for the second possibility" of American intervention. Should that second possibility occur, China would match American actions: if the United States sent troops, China would do likewise.[8] Here Zhou reiterated China's willingness to dispatch combat soldiers into North Vietnam if the United States used ground troops to invade it.[9]

On August 2, North Vietnamese patrol boats opened fire on U.S. destroyers in the Gulf of Tonkin. Two days later, the White House claimed that a second assault took place. President Johnson ordered air strikes against North Vietnamese installations as a reprisal, and then used the alleged attack as a pretext for sending Congress what became the Gulf of Tonkin Resolution, which authorized the president to use military forces as necessary to protect U.S. lives and interests in Southeast Asia.

The Gulf of Tonkin incident prompted Chinese and North Vietnamese leaders into close consultation. Zhou Enlai and Luo Ruiqing cabled Ho Chi Minh, Pham Van Dong, and Van Tien Dung on August 5, asking them to "investigate the situation, work out countermeasures, and be prepared to fight."[10] Le Duan journeyed to Beijing and met with Mao on August 13. He told Mao that the first incident of August 2 was the result of the decisions made by the DRV commander on the spot. The CCP leader informed Le Duan that according to Beijing's intelligence, the second incident of August 4 was "not an intentional attack by the Americans" but caused by "the Americans' mistaken judgment, based on wrong information."[11]

In response to the crisis in Vietnam, China increased military preparations in its southern provinces and stepped up military aid to the DRV. Shortly after the Gulf of Tonkin incident, the leaders in Beijing instructed the Kunming and Guangzhou Military Regions and the air force and naval units stationed in south and southwest China to begin a state of combat readiness. Four air divisions and one antiaircraft division were dispatched into areas adjoining Vietnam and put on a heightened alert status.[12] In August, China also sent approximately fifteen MIG-15 and MIG-17 jets to Hanoi, agreed to train North Vietnamese pilots, and began to build new airfields in areas adjacent to the Vietnamese border, which would serve as sanctuary and repair and maintenance facilities for Hanoi's jet fighters.[13] By moving new air force units to the border area and constructing new airfields there, Beijing intended to deter further U.S. expansion of war in South Vietnam and bombardment against the DRV. Between August and September

1964, the PLA also sent an inspection team to North Vietnam to investigate the situation in case China later needed to dispatch support troops.[14]

On October 5, Mao discussed with Pham Van Dong and Hoang Van Hoan in Beijing the possible expansion of the war by the United States against North Vietnam. The CCP leader asked the Vietnamese Communists to copy the Chinese, who, during the Korean War constructed defensive works along the coast so as to prevent the enemy from pushing into the interior. If the Americans were determined to invade the interior, Mao advised the North Vietnamese not to deploy their main forces in a head-on confrontation in order to preserve strength.[15]

The first months of 1965 witnessed a significant escalation of the American war in Vietnam. On February 7, 9, and 11, U.S. aircraft struck North Vietnamese military installations just across the seventeenth parallel, ostensibly in retaliation for Viet Cong attacks on American barracks near Pleiku and in Qui Nhon. On March 1, the Johnson administration stopped claiming that its air attacks on North Vietnam were reprisals for specific Communist assaults in South Vietnam and began continuous air bombing against the DRV. On March 8, two battalions of marines armed with tanks and eight-inch howitzers landed at Danang.[16]

The U.S. escalation of the war made the DRV desperate for help. Le Duan and Vo Nguyen Giap rushed to Beijing in early April to ask China to increase its aid and send troops to the DRV. Duan told Chinese leaders that Hanoi needed "volunteer pilots, volunteer soldiers, as well as other necessary personnel, including road and bridge engineers." The North Vietnamese envoys expected Chinese volunteer pilots to perform four functions: to limit U.S. bombing to south of the twentieth or nineteenth parallel, to defend Hanoi, to protect several major transportation lines, and to boost morale.[17] On behalf of the Chinese leadership, Liu Shaoqi replied to the North Vietnamese visitors on April 8 that "it is the obligation of the Chinese people and party" to support the Vietnamese struggle against the United States. "Our principle is," Liu continued, "that we will do our best to provide you with whatever you need and whatever we have. If you do not invite us, we will not go to your place. We will send whatever part [of our troops] that you request. You have the complete initiative."[18]

In April, China signed several agreements with the DRV concerning the dispatch of Chinese support troops to North Vietnam.[19] Between April 21 and 22, Giap discussed with Luo Ruiqing and Yang Chengwu, first deputy chief of staff, the arrangements for sending Chinese troops.[20] In May, Ho Chi Minh paid a secret visit to Mao in Changsha, the chairman's home province, where he asked Mao to help the DRV repair and build twelve roads in the area north of Hanoi. The Chinese leader agreed to Ho's request and instructed Zhou Enlai to see to the matter.[21]

In discussions with Luo Ruiqing and Yang Chengwu, Zhou said: "According to Pham Van Dong, U.S. blockade and bombing has reduced supplies to South Vietnam through sea shipment and road transportation. While trying to resume sea transportation, the DRV is also expanding the corridor in Lower Laos and roads in the south. Their troops would go to the south to build roads. Therefore they need our support to construct roads in the north." Zhou decided that the Chinese military should be responsible for road repair and construction in North Vietnam. Yang suggested that since assistance to the DRV involved many military and government departments, a special leadership group should be created to coordinate the work of various agencies. Approving the proposal, Zhou immediately announced the establishment of the "Central Committee–State Council Aid Vietnam Work Team," with Yang and Li Tianyou as director and vice director, respectively. In the meantime, an "Aid Vietnam Leadership Group" led by Luo Ruiqing was established within the Central Committee to supervise the operations of the work team.[22]

In early June, Van Tien Dung held discussions with Luo Ruiqing in Beijing to flesh out the general Chinese plan to assist North Vietnam. According to their agreement, if the war remained in its current conditions, the DRV would fight the war by itself and China would provide various kinds of support as the North Vietnamese needed. If the United States used its navy and air force to support a South Vietnamese attack on the north, China would also provide naval and air force support to the DRV. If U.S. ground forces were directly used to attack the north, China would use its land forces as strategic reserves for the DRV and conduct military operations whenever necessary. As to the forms of Chinese–North Vietnamese air force cooperation, Dung and Luo agreed that China could (1) send volunteer pilots to Vietnam to operate Vietnamese aircraft; (2) station both pilots and aircraft in North Vietnam airfields; or (3) fly aircraft from bases in China to join combat in Vietnam and to land on North Vietnamese bases only temporarily for refueling. The third option was known as the "Andong model" (a reference to the pattern of Chinese air force operations during the Korean War). In terms of the methods of employing Chinese ground troops, the two military leaders agreed that the Chinese forces would either help to strengthen the defensive position of the North Vietnamese troops to prepare for a counteroffensive or launch an offensive themselves to disrupt the enemy's deployment and win strategic initiatives.[23]

But despite Liu Shaoqi's April promise to Le Duan, and Luo Ruiqing's agreement with Van Tien Dung, China in the end failed to provide pilots to Hanoi. According to the Vietnamese *White Paper,* the Chinese General Staff on July 16, 1965, notified its North Vietnamese counterpart that "the time was not appropriate" to send Chinese pilots to Vietnam.[24] China's limited air force capacity may have caused leaders in Beijing to have second thoughts. Beijing's intention to avoid a direct confrontation with the United States may also have played a role. Whatever the reasons for China's decision, the failure to satisfy Hanoi's demand must have greatly disappointed the North Vietnamese, since the control of the air was so crucial for the DRV's effort to protect itself from the ferocious U.S. bombing, and must have undoubtedly contributed to North Vietnam's decision to rely more on the Soviet Union for air defense.

Beginning in June 1965, China sent ground-to-air missile, antiaircraft artillery, railroad, engineering, minesweeping, and logistic units into North Vietnam to help Hanoi defend the DRV. The total number of Chinese troops in North Vietnam between June 1965 and March 1968 amounted to over 320,000.[25] The peak year was 1967, when 170,000 Chinese soldiers were present.[26] They operated antiaircraft guns, built and repaired roads, bridges, and rail lines, and constructed factories. They enabled the PAVN to send large numbers of troops to South Vietnam for the fighting. When the last Chinese troops withdrew from Vietnam in August 1973, 1,100 soldiers had lost their lives and 4,200 had been wounded.[27]

One agreement between the PLA's Kunming Military Region and the PAVN's North Western Military Region on June 11, 1967, indicated the magnitude of Beijing's aid to the DRV. According to the agreement, in 1967 China would provide material assistance to the PAVN troops stationed in upper Laos. There were 1,890 North Vietnamese soldiers there, a figure provided by the Vietnamese side. Aside from weapons and other military equipment, China agreed to equip the North Vietnamese troops right down to the articles for daily use, including 5,670 sets of uniforms (three sets per person annually), 5,670 pairs of shoes (three pairs per person annually), 567 tons of rice (0.8 kilogram per person daily), 20.7 tons of salt, 55.2 tons of meat, 20.7 tons of fish, 20.7 tons of sesame and peanuts, 20.7 tons of beans, 20.7 tons of lard, 6.9 tons of soy sauce, 20.7 tons of white sugar, 8,000 toothbrushes, 11,100 tubes of toothpaste, 24,700 bars of regular soap, 10,600 bars of scented soap, and 109,000 cases of cigarettes. In total, the agreement included 687 different items, covering such goods as table tennis balls, volleyballs, harmonicas, playing cards, pins, fountain pen ink, sewing needles, and vegetable seeds.[28]

Both Mao and Zhou Enlai followed events in Vietnam closely and often issued instructions regarding Chinese aid to the DRV. After reading a report about the difficult living conditions of the Vietnamese Communist troops in the mountain regions in the south prepared by a group of Chinese journalists who had visited there in 1965, Mao instructed in November 1965 that China "must give mosquito nets, clothes, canned food, dried meats, medicine, waterproof cloth, hammocks and other materials in large quantities" to the Vietnamese.[29] Zhou Enlai specified that Chinese equipment sent to the south be designed in the way that was "easy to use, easy to carry, and easy to hide." For this purpose, he demanded specifically that each piece of equipment not weigh over thirty kilograms so that Vietnamese women would have no difficulty in carrying it on their heads or on their shoulders.[30]

To supervise the transportation of materials to the DRV, Beijing in 1965 established a special leadership group. Luo Ruiqing was appointed director. Materials provided by China, the Soviet Union, and other socialist countries were shipped by rail to cities near the Vietnamese border (like Ping Xiang, Guangxi province), where they were transported into the DRV either by rail or by trucks. The materials soon overwhelmed the North Vietnamese transportation capacity, and Chinese railway stations and warehouses became overstocked with supplies. Beginning in 1967, China employed over 500 trucks to help carry supplies into the DRV.[31]

To facilitate moving supplies into South Vietnam, China created a secret coastal transportation line to ship goods to several islands off central Vietnam for transit to the south. A secret harbor on China's Hainan Island was constructed to serve this transportation route.[32] Beijing also operated a costly transportation line through Cambodia to send weapons, munitions, food, and medical supplies to the National Liberation Front in South Vietnam.[33] Between 1965 and 1967, Chinese weapons for 50,000 soldiers arrived by ship via Sihanoukville.[34] Some of the Chinese arms went to equip the Cambodian army.[35]

China's shipment of military materials to North Vietnam increased rapidly in 1965. In comparison with 1964, the delivery of guns increased 2.8 times, from 80,500 to 220,767; pieces of artillery increased about 3 times, from 1,205 to 4,439; gun bullets increased nearly 5 times, from 25.2 million to 114 million; and artillery shells increased almost 6 times, from 335,000 to 1.8 million. Between 1966 and 1967, China's supply of military goods to the DRV dropped slightly from the 1965 level before reaching its peak in 1968. In 1969–70, a sharp decrease occurred at the same time that Beijing withdrew all its support troops from the DRV. Not until 1972 would there be another major increase of China's military shipment to the DRV, but for reasons very different from the ones behind Beijing's rising and falling aid from 1965 to 1969.[36]

The newly available Chinese documents clearly indicate that Beijing provided extensive support (short of volunteer pilots) to Hanoi during the Vietnam War and in doing so risked war with the United States. As one China specialist has perceptively observed, the deployment of Chinese troops in Vietnam was not carried out under maximum security against detection by Washington. The Chinese troops wore regular uniforms and did not disguise themselves as civilians. The Chinese presence was intentionally communicated to U.S. intelligence through aerial photography and electronic intercepts. The presence of troops, along with the large base complex that China built at Yen Bai in northwest Vietnam, provided credible and successful deterrence against an American invasion of North Vietnam.[37]

While increasing aid to the DRV and making war preparations at home in the first half of 1965, Chinese leaders, determined to avoid war with the United States, also issued clear and repeated warnings to Washington through multiple channels, including the Sino-American ambassadorial talks at Warsaw, third-party leaders, and the British charge in Beijing. The Chinese ambassador to Poland, Wang Guoquan, told John M. Cabot, his American counterpart, that the United States would surely lose in Vietnam and that the "Chinese people will not sit idly by and we know how to deal with your aggression."[38]

Zhou Enlai, during his visit to Pakistan on April 2, asked Pakistani president Ayub Khan, who was scheduled to visit the United States later in the month, to convey to President Johnson a four-point message, which stated that: (1) China would not take the initiative to provoke a war with the United States; (2) it meant what it said and would honor its international commitment; (3) it was prepared; (4) if the United States bombarded China without constraints, China would not sit there waiting to die. If the Americans came from the air, China would fight back on the ground. Bombing would mean war, and the war would have no boundaries.[39]

Ayub Khan, however, did not deliver the Chinese message as Zhou had hoped because just nine days before his scheduled arrival in the United States, President Johnson, dismayed by his flirtation with China, suddenly canceled his invitation.[40] On June 8, Zhou Enlai asked President Julius Nyerere of Tanzania to forward the same message to the United States.[41] A similar signal was sent to the Americans by Foreign Minister Chen Yi during his conversation with the British charge in Beijing a week before, on May 31. Chen declared that "China will not provoke war with the United States" but that "what China says counts." China was prepared for war and that "if the United States bombs China, that would mean war and there would be no limits to the war."[42]

These were the most serious warnings issued by the Chinese government to the United States, and there is evidence that American officials took them seriously. Taking note of Chen Yi's May 31 statement, William P. Bundy, assistant secretary of state for Far Eastern affairs, told Secretary of State Dean Rusk on June 5, 1965, that the Chinese foreign minister had drawn a line for the United States. If the United States limited its assaults to the air over North Vietnam, did not approach China, and did not directly attack China, Beijing would not come into the war. But the PRC would "go all the way if it did come in" to the war. Bundy also informed Rusk that he had told the British the previous day that "they could tell Chen Yi we had received the message."[43]

The specter of Chinese intervention in a manner similar to China's involvement in the Korean War was a major factor in shaping President Johnson's gradual approach to the Vietnam War. He wanted to forestall Chinese intervention by keeping the level of military actions against North Vietnam controlled, exact, and below the threshold that would provoke a direct Chinese entry. He had clearly learned a lesson from the Korean War, when the Truman administration's failure to heed Beijing's warning against crossing the thirty-eighth parallel led to a bloody confrontation between the United States and China. In his discussion with the Joint Chiefs of Staff in July 1965 of whether to send an additional 100,000 soldiers to South Vietnam, for example, the president asked, "If we come in with hundreds of thousands of men and billions of dollars, won't this cause them [China and Russia] to come in?" General Harold Johnson, army chief of staff, replied that he did not think so. When the president then reminded the general that "MacArthur didn't think they would come in [to Korea] either," General Johnson countered that the circumstances were different. But the president persisted that he had to "take into account" that the Chinese would send their troops into the war.[44]

This China-induced U.S. strategy of gradual escalation was a great help for Hanoi, for it gave the Vietnamese Communists time to adjust to U.S. bombing and to develop strategies to frustrate U.S. moves. As the China expert John Garver has aptly noted, "By helping to induce Washington to adopt this particular strategy, Beijing contributed substantially to Hanoi's eventual victory over the United States."[45]

The United States made plain its intention to avoid war with Beijing when it informed China at the Warsaw talks that it had no plan either to destroy North Vietnam or to invade the PRC.[46] Thus through public pronouncements, private messages, and mutual signals, Beijing and Washington came to understand the scope and limits of each other's involvement in the Vietnam War. During the latter part of 1965 and early 1966 they developed a tacit understanding that so long as the United States did not invade North Vietnam or China, nor seek to destroy the DRV as a viable nation, then Beijing would limit its military involvement in the conflict.[47]

Mao's Complex Calculations

Mao's decision to aid Hanoi is closely linked to his perception of U.S. threats to China's security, his commitment to national liberation movements, his criticism of Soviet revisionist foreign policy, and his domestic needs to transform the Chinese state and society. These four factors were mutually related and reinforcing.

Sense of Insecurity

Between 1964 and 1965, Mao worried about the increasing American involvement in Vietnam and perceived the United States as posing a serious threat to China's security. The CCP leader viewed the United States as "the most ferocious enemy of the people of the world," committing neocolonialist aggression against Asian, African, and Latin American countries and seeking "peaceful evolution" against socialist states. In Asia, Mao contended, the United States was occupying Taiwan, turning South Korea and South Vietnam into its colonies, exercising actual control and partial military occupation of Japan, undermining Laotian neutrality and independence, plotting subversion of the Cambodian government, and likewise interfering with other Asian countries. Mao believed that American escalation of war in Vietnam constituted a link in Washington's chain of encirclement of China. For him, support for North Vietnam was a way of countering the U.S. containment of China. The Communist success in South Vietnam would prevent the United States from moving closer to the Chinese southern border.[48]

On several occasions in the first part of 1964, Mao talked about U.S. threats to China and the need for China to prepare for war. During a party conference held between May 15 and June 17, the chairman contended that "so long as imperialism exists, the danger of war is there. We are not the chief of staff for imperialism and have no idea when it will launch a war. It is the conventional weapon, not the atomic bomb that will determine the final victory of the war."[49] On June 16, Mao delivered a speech to a conference at the Ming Tombs (Shisanling) Reservoir on the outskirts of Beijing, asking the party to prepare for war. Mao's address was later known as "the Ming Tombs Speech."[50] Defense Minister Lin Biao talked with Yang Chengwu twice, on July 10 and 12, stressing the importance of reorienting the PLA's strategy and military planning in accordance with the "carefully considered" speech made by Mao at the Ming Tombs Reservoir.[51]

At first Mao did not expect that the United States would attack North Vietnam directly.[52] The Gulf of Tonkin incident came as a surprise to him. Mao had originally planned to take a horse ride to inspect the Yellow River in the second part of 1964. On August 6, he told Wang Dongxing, head of the Guard Bureau of the CCP Central Committee, that "war is coming and I have to reconsider my activities."[53] The crisis in Vietnam caused Mao to cancel his planned trip to the Yellow River, and on October 22, he again pointed out that China must base its work on war and make active preparations for an early, large-scale, and nuclear war.[54]

To deal with what he perceived as U.S. military threats, Mao took several domestic measures in 1964, the most important of which was the launching of the massive Third Front project, a major strategic action designed to provide an alternative industrial base that would enable China to continue production in the event of an attack on its large urban centers. This program called for heavy investment in the remote provinces of southwestern and western China and envisaged the creation of a huge self-sustaining industrial base area to serve as a strategic reserve. The project had a strong military orientation and was directly triggered by the U.S. escalation of war in Vietnam.[55]

On April 25, 1964, the War Department of the PLA General Staff drafted a report for Yang Chengwu on how to prevent an enemy surprise attack on China's economic system. The report listed four factors that made China vulnerable to such an attack: (1) China's industry was over concentrated. About 60 percent of the civil machinery industry, 50 percent of the chemical industry, and 52 percent of the national defense industry were concentrated in fourteen major cities with over one million inhabitants. (2) Too many people lived in cities. According to the 1962 census, fourteen cities each had a population over one million, and twenty cities a population between 500,000 and one million. Most of these cities were located in the coastal areas and very vulnerable to air strikes. No effective mechanisms existed at the moment to organize anti-air works, to evacuate urban populations, to continue production, and to eliminate the damages of an air strike, especially a nuclear strike. (3) Principal railroad junctions, bridges, and harbors were situated near large and medium-size cities and could easily be destroyed when the enemy attacked the cities. No measures had been taken to protect these transportation points against an enemy attack. In the early stage of war, they could become paralyzed. (4) All of China's reservoirs had a limited capacity to release water in an emergency. Among the country's 232 large reservoirs, 52 were located near major transportation lines, and 17 were close to important cities. In its conclusion, the report made it clear that "the problems mentioned above are directly related to the whole armed forces, to the whole people, and to the process of a national defense war." It asked the state council "to organize a special committee to study and adopt, in accordance with the possible conditions of the national economy, practical and effective measures to guard against an enemy surprise attack."[56]

Yang Chengwu presented the report to Mao, who returned it to Luo Ruiqing and Yang on August 12 with the comment: "It is an excellent report. It should be carefully studied and gradually implemented." Mao urged the newly established state council's special committee in charge of the Third Front to begin its work immediately.[57] Mao's approval of the report marked the beginning of the Third Front project to relocate China's industrial resources to the interior. It is important to note the timing of Mao's reaction to the report—right after the Gulf of Tonkin incident. The U.S. expansion of the war to North Vietnam had confirmed Mao's worst suspicions about American intentions.

Deputy Premier Li Fuchun became director and Deputy Premier Bo Yibo and Luo Ruiqing became vice directors of the special committee. On August 19, they submitted to Mao a detailed proposal on how to implement the Third Front ideas.[58] In the meantime, the CCP secretariat met to discuss the issue. Mao made two speeches at the meetings on August 17 and 20. He asserted that China should be on guard against an aggressive war launched by imperialism. At present, he continued, factories were concentrated around big cities and coastal regions, a situation deleterious to war preparation. Factories should be broken into two parts. One part should be relocated to interior areas as early as possible. Every province should establish its own strategic rear base. Departments of industry and transportation should move, as should schools, science academies, and Beijing University. The three railroad lines between Chengdu and Kunming, Sichuan and Yunnan, and Yunnan and Guizhou should be completed as quickly as possible. If there was a shortage of rails, the chairman insisted, rails on other lines could be dismantled. To implement Mao's instructions, it was decided at the meetings to concentrate China's financial, material, and human resources on the construction of the Third Front.[59]

While emphasizing the "big Third Front" plan on the national level, Mao also ordered provinces to precede with their "small Third Front" projects. The chairman wanted each province to develop its own light armament industry capable of producing rifles, machine guns, cannons, and munitions.[60] The Third Five-Year Plan was revised to meet the strategic contingency of war preparation. In the modified plan, a total of three billion yuan was appropriated for small Third Front projects. This was a substantial figure, but less than 5 percent of the amount that was set aside for the big Third Front in this period.[61]

In addition to his apprehension about a strike on China's urban and coastal areas, Mao also feared that the enemy might deploy paratroop assault forces deep inside China. In a meeting with He Long, deputy chairman of the Central Military Commission, Luo Ruiqing, and Yang Chengwu on April 28, 1965, Mao called their attention to such a danger. He ordered them to prepare for the landing of enemy paratroopers in every interior region. The enemy might use paratroops, Mao contended, "to disrupt our rear areas, and to coordinate with a frontal assault. The number of paratroops may not be many. It may involve one or two divisions in each region, or it may involve a smaller unit. In all interior regions, we should build caves in mountains. If no mountain is around, hills should be created to construct defense works. We should be on guard against enemy paratroops deep inside our country and prevent the enemy from marching unstopped into China."[62]

It appears that Mao's attitudes toward the United States hardened between January and April 1965. On January 9, Mao had an interview with Edgar Snow, an American journalist whom he had first met in the 1930s. Mao expressed confidence that Washington would not expand the war to North Vietnam because Secretary of State Rusk had said so. He told Snow that there would be no war between China and the United States if Washington did not send troops to attack China.[63] Two days later, the CCP Central Military Commission issued the "Six-Point Directive on the Struggle against U.S. Ships and Aircraft in the South China Sea," in which it instructed the military not to attack American airplanes that intruded into Chinese airspace in order to avoid a direct military clash with the United States.[64]

In April, however, Mao rescinded the "Six-Point Directive." Between April 8 and 9, U.S. aircraft flew into China's airspace over Hainan Island. On April 9, Yang Chengwu reported the incidents to Mao, suggesting that the order not to attack invading U.S. airplanes be lifted and that the air force command take control of the naval air units stationed on Hainan Island. Approving both of Yang's requests, Mao said that China "should resolutely strike American aircraft that overfly Hainan Island."[65] It is quite possible that the further U.S. escalation of war in Vietnam in the intervening months caused Mao to abandon his earlier restrictions against engaging U.S. aircraft. On April 12, the Chinese air force command prepared the "Combat Plan for Dealing with the Provocation of American Aircraft," which stated that the air force should "not only be ready to engage U.S. aircraft in aerial battles and intercept U.S. bombers in the border region but also be prepared to fight U.S. fighter planes and bombers on a larger and more protracted scale in interior regions."[66]

On the same day, Liu Shaoqi chaired an expanded meeting of the politburo to discuss the situation in Vietnam and war preparation at home, and a directive on strengthening the work of war preparation was passed.[67] Mao approved the directive the next day, and the CCP Central Committee on April 14 distributed the document throughout the party structure above the county level. The instruction alerted party cadres to the grave danger posed by the American escalation of the war in Vietnam and stressed the urgency of war preparation. The U.S. expansion of the war in Indochina and the direct attack on the DRV, the directive pointed out, "are seriously threatening the security of our country. We have already indicated to the whole world our solemn and just position that we cannot ignore this threat and that we are ready at any time to fight together with the Vietnamese people. We must also be prepared to deal with the spread of the war by U.S. imperialism to our territory." The directive asked the party cadres to monitor closely the development of the war in Vietnam and take seriously the possibility of enemy aggressions.[68]

It is important to point out that the entire Chinese leadership, not just Mao, took the strategic threat from the United States very seriously during this period. Zhou Enlai told Spiro Koleka, first deputy chairman of the Council of Ministers of Albania, on May 9, 1965, in Beijing that China was mobilizing its population for war. Although it seemed that the United States had not made up its mind to expand the war to China, the Chinese premier continued, war had its own law of development, usually in a way contrary to the wishes of people. Therefore China had to be prepared.[69] Zhou's remarks indicated that he was familiar with a common pattern in warfare: accidents and miscalculations rather than deliberate planning often lead to war between reluctant opponents.

In an address to a Central Military Commission war planning meeting on May 19, 1965, Liu Shaoqi called for the development of the Third Front as well as the atomic bomb, the hydrogen bomb, and long-range missiles. With these preparations, Liu claimed:

> Even if the United States has bases in Japan, Taiwan, and the Philippines, its ships are big targets out on the sea and it is easy for us to strike them. The enemy's strength is in its navy, air force, atomic bombs, and missiles, but the strength in navy and air force has its limits. If the enemy sends ground troops to invade China, we are not afraid. Therefore, on the one hand we should be prepared for the enemy to come from all directions, including a joint invasion against China by many countries. On the other, we should realize that the enemy lacks justification in sending troops. . . . This will decide the difference between a just and an unjust war.[70]

Zhu De remarked at the same meeting that "so long as we have made good preparations on every front, the enemy may not dare to come. We must defend our offshore islands. With these islands in our hands, the enemy will find it difficult to land. If the enemy should launch an attack, we will lure them inside China and then wipe them out completely."[71]

Scholars have argued over Beijing's reaction to the threat posed by U.S. intervention in Vietnam. Much of this argument focuses on the supposed "strategic debate" that took place in 1965 between Luo Ruiqing and Lin Biao. Various interpretations of this "debate" exist, but most contend that Luo was more sensitive to American actions in Indochina than either Lin or Mao and that Luo demanded greater military preparations to deal with the threat, including accepting the Soviet proposal of a "united front."[72]

There is nothing in the recently available Chinese materials to confirm the existence of the "strategic debate" in 1965.[73] The often cited evidence to support the hypothesis consists of Luo Ruiqing's May 1965 article celebrating the defeat of Germany in World War II and Lin Biao's September piece, "Long Live the Victory of People's War."[74] In fact, although published in Lin's name, the latter article was prepared primarily by the writing group organized by Luo in the General Staff. The final version of the "People's War" article also incorporated opinions from the writing team led by Kang Sheng. (Operating in the Diaoyutai National Guest House, Kang's team was famous for writing the nine polemics against Soviet revisionism.) Although the article included some of Lin Biao's previous statements, Lin himself was not involved in its writing. When Luo asked Lin for his instructions about the composition of the article, the defense minister said nothing. Zhou Enlai and other standing politburo members read the piece before its publication.[75] The article was approved by the Chinese leadership as a whole and was merely published in Lin's name. Luo was purged in December 1965 primarily because of his dispute with Lin over domestic military organization and petty personal squabbles rather than over foreign policy issues.[76]

Luo Ruiqing did not oppose Mao on Vietnam policy. In fact he carried out loyally every Vietnam-related order issued by the chairman. Mao completely dominated the decision making. In the authoritarian Chinese political culture, Mao's power was absolute. Once the "great leader" spoke, the party obeyed. Whatever private opinions were held, the only viable option was to follow the course dictated by Mao. Petty individual hatreds and jealousies rather than disputes over large policy issues characterized political life in China around the time of the Cultural Revolution.[77] The origins of the "People's War" article point to the danger of relying on public pronouncements to gauge inner-party calculations and cast doubts on the utility of the faction model in explaining Chinese foreign policymaking.[78]

It is possible that the two articles published in Luo Ruiqing's and Lin Biao's names were written primarily in response to the Soviet argument on war and peace. On January 30, 1965, Mao asked Yang Chengwu and Lei Yingfu, deputy director of the Combat Department of the General Staff, to find a person well versed in political and military issues to prepare a commentary on the book *Military Strategy*, edited by Soviet chief of staff V. D. Sokolovsky and published by the Soviet Defense Ministry's Military Press in 1962.[79]

The "People's War" article may have been designed mainly to counter Soviet views on war and peace, but its call for the surrounding of the world cities (industrialized nations) by the world rural areas (developing countries) through militant local revolutions greatly alarmed American policymakers, who viewed the article as a Chinese *Mein Kampf*, committing Beijing to undermine vulnerable colonial and newly independent nations.[80] U.S. defense secretary Robert McNamara later recalled: "The Johnson administration—including me— interpreted the speech as bellicose and aggressive, signaling an expansionist China's readiness to nourish 'local' forces across the world and to give a helping pushing when the time came. Lin's remarks seemed to us a clear expression of the basis for the domino theory."[81]

Commitment to National Liberation Movements

The second factor that shaped Mao's decision to support the DRV was his need to form a broad international united front against both the United States and the Soviet Union. To Mao, national liberation movements in the Third World were the most important potential allies in the coalition that he wanted to establish.[82] Between 1963 and 1964, the CCP chairman developed the concept of "Two Intermediate Zones." The first zone referred to developed countries, including capitalist states in Europe, Canada, Japan, Australia, and New Zealand. The second zone referred to underdeveloped nations in Asia, Africa, and Latin America. These two zones existed between the two superpowers. Mao believed that countries in these two zones had conflicts with the United States and the Soviet Union and that China should make friends with them to create an international united front against Washington and Moscow.[83]

Mao initially developed the idea of the intermediate zone during the early years of the Cold War. The CCP leader first broached the idea in a discussion with Anna Louise Strong, an American journalist, in 1946. He claimed that the United States and the Soviet Union were "separated by a vast zone including many capitalist, colonial and semi-colonial countries in Europe, Asia, and Africa" and that it was difficult for "the U.S. reactionaries to attack the Soviet Union before they could subjugate these countries."[84] In the late 1940s and throughout the greater part of the 1950s, Mao leaned to the side of the Soviet Union to balance China against the perceived American threat. But beginning in the late 1950s, with the emergence of Sino-Soviet differences, Mao came to revise his characterization of the international situation. He saw China confronting two opponents: the United States and the Soviet Union. To oppose these two foes and break China's international isolation, Mao proposed the formation of an international united front.

Operating from the principle of making friends with countries in the "Two Intermediate Zones," Mao promoted such anti-American tendencies as French president De Gaulle's break with the United States in the first zone and championed national liberation movements in the second zone. For Mao, the Vietnam conflict constituted a part of a broader movement across Asia, Africa, and Latin America, which represented a challenge to imperialism as a whole. China reached out to anticolonial guerrillas in Angola and Mozambique, to the "progressive" Sihanouk in Cambodia, to the leftist regime under Sukarno in Indonesia, and to the anti-U.S. Castro in Cuba.[85] In the former socialist camp dominated by the Soviet Union, Mao encouraged Albania to persuade other East European countries to separate from Moscow.[86]

During this increasingly radical period of Chinese foreign policy, Mao singled out three anti-imperialist heroes for emulation by Third World liberation movements: Ho Chi Minh, Castro, and Ben Bella. In a speech to a delegation of Chilean journalists on June 23, 1964, Mao remarked: "We oppose war, but we support the anti-imperialist war waged by oppressed peoples. We support the revolutionary war in Cuba and Algeria. We also support the anti-U.S.-imperialist war conducted by the South Vietnamese people."[87] In another address to a group of visitors from Asia, Africa, and Oceania on July 9, Mao again mentioned the names of Ho Chi Minh, Castro, and Ben Bella as models for anticolonial and anti-imperialist struggle.[88]

Envisioning China as a spokesperson for the Third World independence cause, Mao continued to believe that the Chinese revolutionary experience provided a model for the struggle of liberation movements in Asia, Africa, and Latin America. By firmly backing the Vietnamese struggle against the United States, he wanted to demonstrate to Third World countries that China was their true friend. A victorious, China-supported North Vietnam in its war of national unification would demonstrate Beijing's revolutionary credentials and show the political wisdom of Mao's more militant strategy for coping with U.S. imperialism and the incorrectness of Khrushchev's policy of peaceful coexistence.[89]

A number of Chinese anti-imperialist initiatives, however, ended in a debacle in 1965. First Ben Bella was overthrown in Algeria in June, which led the Afro-Asian movement to lean in a more pro-Soviet direction due to the influence of Jawaharlal Nehru in India and Josip Broz Tito in Yugoslavia. The fall of Ben Bella frustrated Mao's bid for leadership in the Third World by setting the agenda at the Algiers conference of Afro-Asian leaders. In September, war broke out between India and Pakistan, a Chinese ally, over the territory of Kashmir. China's effort to deter India's advance failed, and New Delhi won the conflict. The net result, strategically, was a gain for Moscow and a loss for Beijing. On September 30, Sukarno was toppled in a right-wing countercoup, derailing Mao's plan to maintain a militant "Beijing-Jakarta" axis.[90]

Chinese behavior, nevertheless, did convince leaders in Washington that Beijing was a dangerous gambler in international politics and that American intervention in Vietnam was necessary to undermine a Chinese plot of global subversion by proxy. Robert McNamara wrote in his memoirs: "In retrospect, one can see the events of autumn 1965 as clear setbacks for China. . . . But, blinded by our assumptions and preoccupied with a rapidly growing war, we—like most other Western leaders—continued to view China as a serious threat in Southeast Asia and the rest of the world."[91] That misperception, in turn, may have constituted a missed opportunity for the U.S. to re-evaluate its prior assumptions about the consequences of a U.S. defeat in Vietnam for the rest of Southeast Asia and thus to reconsider the American commitment to "pay any price" to assure the survival of a non-Communist South Vietnam.

Criticism of Soviet Revisionism

Mao's firm commitment to Vietnam also needs to be considered in the context of the unfolding Sino-Soviet split. By 1963, Beijing and Moscow had completely parted ways after three years of increasingly abusive polemics. The conclusion of the Partial Nuclear Test Ban Treaty in July 1963 was a major turning point in Sino-Soviet relations. Thereafter the Beijing leadership publicly denounced any suggestion that China was subject to any degree of Soviet protection and directly criticized Moscow for collaborating with Washington against China. The effect of the Sino-Soviet split on Vietnam soon manifested itself as Beijing and Moscow wooed Hanoi to take sides in their ideological dispute.

After the ouster of Khrushchev in October 1964, the new leadership in the Kremlin invited the CCP to send a delegation to the October Revolution celebrations. Beijing dispatched Zhou Enlai and Marshal He Long to Moscow for the primary purpose of sounding out Leonid Brezhnev and Alexei Kosygin on the many issues in dispute, namely, Khrushchev's long-postponed plan to convene an international Communist meeting, China's support for revolutionary movements, the Soviet Union's desire for peaceful coexistence with the United States, the two countries' attitudes toward Tito, and "revisionist" domestic policies within the Soviet Union. The Chinese discovered during their tour between November 5 and 13 that nothing basic had changed in the Soviet position: the new leaders in Moscow desired an improvement in Sino-Soviet relations with the condition that Beijing stop its criticisms and limit competition in foreign policy, probably in return for the resumption of Soviet economic aid.[92]

Instead of finding an opportunity to improve mutual understanding, the Chinese visitors found their stay in Moscow unpleasant and China's relationship with the Soviet Union even worse. During a Soviet reception, Marshal Rodion Malinovsky suggested to Zhou Enlai and He Long that just as the Russians had ousted Khrushchev, the Chinese should overthrow Mao. The Chinese indignantly rejected this proposal. Zhou registered a strong protest with the Soviet leadership, referring to Malinovsky's remarks as "a serious political incident."[93] Zhou told the Cuban Communist delegation during a breakfast meeting in the Chinese embassy on November 9 that Malinovsky "insulted Comrade Mao Zedong, the Chinese people, the Chinese Party, and myself" and that the current leadership in the Kremlin inherited "Khrushchev's working style and way of thinking."[94]

Before Zhou's journey to Moscow, the Chinese leadership had suggested to the Vietnamese Communists that they also send people to travel with Zhou to Moscow to see whether there were changes in the new Soviet leaders' policies. Zhou told Ho Chi Minh and Le Duan later in Hanoi on March 1, 1965, that he was "disappointed" with what he had seen in Moscow and that "the new Soviet leaders are following nothing but Khrushchevism."[95] Clearly, Zhou wanted the Hanoi leadership to side with China in the continuing Sino-Soviet dispute. Beijing's extensive aid to the DRV was designed to keep Hanoi within China's orbit.

The collective leadership that succeeded Khrushchev was more forthcoming in support of the DRV. During his visit to Hanoi on February 7-10, Soviet premier Alexei Kosygin called for a total U.S. withdrawal from South Vietnam and promised Soviet material aid for Ho Chi Minh's struggle. The fact that a group of missile experts accompanied Kosygin indicates that the Kremlin was providing support in that crucial area. The two sides concluded formal military and economic agreements on February 10.[96] Clearly, the Soviets were competing with the Chinese to win the allegiance of the Vietnamese Communists. Through its new gestures to Hanoi, Moscow wanted to offset Chinese influence and demonstrate its ideological rectitude on issues of national liberation. The new solidarity with Hanoi, however, complicated Soviet relations with the United States, and after 1965, the Soviet Union found itself at loggerheads with Washington. While Moscow gained greater influence in Hanoi because of the North Vietnamese need for Soviet material assistance against U.S. bombing, it at the same time lost flexibility because of the impossibility of retreat from the commitment to a brother Communist state under attack by imperialism.

Before late 1964, Hanoi was virtually on China's side in the bifurcated international Communist movement. After the fall of Khrushchev and the appearance of a more interventionist position under Kosygin and Brezhnev, however, Hanoi adopted a more balanced stand. Leaders in Beijing were nervous about the increase of Soviet influence in Vietnam. According to a Vietnamese source, Deng Xiaoping, secretary-general of the CCP, paid a secret visit to Hanoi after the Gulf of Tonkin incident with the promise of one billion Chinese yuan in aid if the DRV refused all aid from the Soviet Union.[97]

China's strategy to discredit the Soviet Union was to emphasize the "plot" of Soviet-American collaborations at the expense of Vietnam. During his visit to Beijing on February 11, 1965, Kosygin asked the Chinese to help the United States to "find a way out of Vietnam." Chinese leaders warned the Russians not to use the Vietnam issue to bargain with the Americans.[98] Immediately after his return to Moscow, Kosygin on February 16 proposed to Beijing and Hanoi that an international conference on Indochina be called without preconditions. The Chinese condemned the Soviet move, asserting that the Russians wanted negotiation rather than continued struggle in Vietnam and were conspiring with the Americans to sell out Vietnam.[99] The Chinese criticism of the Soviet peace initiative must have confirmed the American image of China as a warmonger.

In the spring of 1965, Moscow asked Beijing to grant an "air corridor" through which a Soviet airlift could be conducted in defense of the DRV and to cede a base in Yunnan, where hundreds of Soviet military personnel could be stationed to assist Hanoi's war effort. Accusing the Russians of taking advantage of the war in Vietnam to violate Chinese sovereignty, the Chinese turned down the Soviet request. While rejecting this kind of coordination, Beijing did allow the Soviet Union to transport its aid to the DRV through the Chinese rail corridor, which remained a major supply route for the Vietnamese war effort between 1965 and 1968.[100] According to one Chinese account, by the end of 1965 China helped the Soviet Union transport 43,000 tons of military supplies to North Vietnam.[101]

Beijing would spurn any proposal that would grant Moscow access to China. It consented to the transshipment of Soviet military goods through China by rail precisely because it could control it. This situation soon led to Soviet accusations of Chinese tampering and deliberate delays. During 1966–67, Beijing and Moscow exchanged charges regarding whether China had hampered the shipment of Soviet military aid to the DRV.[102] Whether Beijing intentionally blocked the transportation of Soviet military supplies to North Vietnam remains a question. What is certain is that during the Cultural Revolution those supply trains were often attacked and robbed of weapons and munitions by feuding factions. The attacks occurred most frequently in Guangxi province, where the Cultural Revolution seriously divided mass organizations. Between 1967 and 1968, Zhou Enlai held numerous meetings in Beijing with representatives from the feuding factions in Guangxi, urging them to stop fighting, to return the arms they had seized, and not to block the transportation of aid materials to North Vietnam. He also ordered the PLA to take over the control of the railway system.[103] Clearly, the politics of the Cultural Revolution at the mass level affected China's dealings with North Vietnam.

The Sino-Soviet rivalry over Vietnam certainly provided leaders in Hanoi an opportunity to obtain maximum support from their two Communist allies, but one should not overstate the case. Sometimes the benefits of the Sino-Soviet split for the DRV could be limited. For example, the Hanoi leadership wanted Moscow and Beijing to agree on common support actions, particularly on a single integrated logistical system. They failed to achieve this objective, however, primarily because of China's objection.[104]

Domestic Need to Transform the Chinese State and Society

Beginning in the late 1950s, Mao became increasingly apprehensive about the potential development of the Chinese revolution. He feared that his life's work had created a political structure that would eventually betray his principles and values and become as exploitative as the one it had replaced. His worry about the future of China's development was closely related to his diagnosis of the degeneration of the Soviet political system and to his fear about the effects of U.S. secretary of state John Foster Dulles's strategy of "peaceful evolution." Mao took Dulles's statements about encouraging liberalization in socialist countries seriously. He believed that Dulles's plan to induce a peaceful evolution within the socialist world through cultural infiltration was taking effect in the Soviet Union, given Khrushchev's fascination with peaceful coexistence with the capitalist West. Mao wanted to prevent that from happening in China.[105]

The problem of succession preoccupied Mao throughout the first half of the 1960s. His acute awareness of impending death contributed to his sense of urgency. He perceived the emergence of new ruling elite in China, who, through its centralized control of the economic system, provided little scope for popular participation in the process of development. Mao disliked the economic retrenchment policy followed by Liu Shaoqi and Deng Xiaoping after the Great Leap Forward, viewing them as "taking the capitalist road." While learning from the Great Leap that mass mobilization was not the key to rapid economic growth, Mao retained faith in popular participation as a tool of ideological renewal, social transformation, and rectification.[106]

The U.S. escalation of war in Vietnam made Mao all the more eager to put his own house in order. He was afraid that if he did not nip what he perceived to be revisionist tendencies in the bud and if he did not choose a proper successor, after his death China would be in the hands of Soviet-like revisionists, who would "change the color" of China, abandon support for national liberation struggles, and appease U.S. imperialism. Mao was a man who believed in dialectics. Negative things could be turned into positive matters. The American presence in Indochina was a threat to the Chinese revolution. But on the other hand, Mao found that he could turn the U.S. threat into an advantage by using it to intensify domestic anti-imperialist feelings and mobilize the population against revisionists. Mao had successfully employed that strategy against Chiang Kai-shek during the civil war. Now he could apply it again to prepare the masses for the Great Cultural Revolution that he was going to launch. Accordingly, in the wake of the Gulf of Tonkin incident, Mao unleashed a massive "Aid Vietnam and Resist America" campaign across China.[107]

In sum, aiding Vietnam served four primary purposes for Mao: it countered U.S. threats to China's security, demonstrated Beijing's credibility as a true supporter of Third World nationalist liberation movements, allowed China to compete with the Soviet Union for leadership in the international Communist camp and for influence in Indochina, and drummed up domestic support for Mao's fundamental reshaping of the Chinese state and society.

Sino-Vietnamese Discords

Signs of Sino-Vietnamese differences emerged in the early days of China's intervention in the Second Vietnam War. Vietnamese historical pride and cultural sensitivity was one major factor that complicated Beijing-Hanoi interactions. When Chinese troops went to North Vietnam in 1965, they found themselves in an awkward position. On the one hand, the Hanoi leadership wanted their service in fighting U.S. aircraft and in building and repairing roads, bridges, and rail lines. On the other hand, the Vietnamese authorities tried to minimize their influence by restricting their contact with the local population. For instance, Vietnamese officials blocked Chinese medical teams' efforts to treat Vietnamese civilian patients.[108] They objected to the Chinese practice of distributing among Vietnamese villagers materials (written in Vietnamese) on achievements of China's economic construction.[109] They also prohibited their people from accepting and wearing Mao badges.[110] Informed of such incidents, Mao urged Chinese troops in the DRV to "refrain from being too eager" to help the Vietnamese.[111] While Chinese soldiers were in North Vietnam, the Vietnamese media reminded the public that in history China had invaded Vietnam. The journal *Historical Studies* published articles in 1965 describing Vietnamese resistance against Chinese imperial dynasties in the past.[112]

The increasing Vietnamese resentment against the Chinese presence in the DRV prompted Deng Xiaoping to confront Le Duan directly on this issue at a meeting in Beijing on April 13, 1966. The barely five-foot-tall Deng was famous for a temperament as peppery as the cuisine of his native Sichuan province. With characteristic bluntness, he told Duan that Mao had criticized Chinese officials for showing "too much enthusiasm" on the Vietnam question. After mentioning the presence of 130,000 Chinese troops in the DRV, the stationing of Chinese soldiers along the Vietnamese border, and the Sino-DRV discussions about joint fighting if the United States invaded North Vietnam; the CCP secretary-general posed straightforwardly the question of distrust before his North Vietnamese counterpart: "Are you suspicious of us because we have so much enthusiasm? Do the Chinese want to take control over Vietnam? We would like to tell you frankly that we don't have any such intention. . . . If we have made a mistake thus making you suspicious, it means that Comrade Mao is really farsighted." Deng also brought up the incident of a Chinese ship that requested entry to a Vietnamese port during U.S. bombing but was refused. Duan, claiming to be unaware of the ship incident, reassured the Chinese that Hanoi had always appreciated their assistance and that "the more enthusiasm you have, the more beneficial it is for us. Your enthusiastic assistance can help us to save the lives of 2 or 3 million people."[113]

The increasing rivalry between Beijing and Moscow also hampered Sino-DRV cooperation. The Chinese and Soviet efforts to win Hanoi's allegiance put the North Vietnamese in a dilemma. On the one hand, the change of Russia's attitude of reluctance toward Vietnam to active assistance in late 1964 and early 1965 made the North Vietnamese more unwilling to echo China's criticisms of revisionism. On the other hand, they still needed China's assistance and deterrence. But Mao's rejection of the Soviet proposal of a "united action" on Vietnam ruled out the possibility of a closer coordination within the international Communist camp in support of the DRV.

During Kosygin's visit to Beijing in February 1965, he proposed to Mao and Zhou that China and the Soviet Union end their mutual criticisms and cooperate on the issue of Vietnam. But Mao dismissed Kosygin's suggestion, asserting that China's argument with the Soviet Union would continue for another 9,000 years.[114] On April 3, Moscow proposed to Beijing a DRV-Chinese-Soviet summit meeting, but China rejected the suggestion. In a further reply to the

Soviet Communist Party on July 10, the CCP Central Committee, with Mao's approval, retorted that on the Vietnam issue the Soviet Union had adopted appeasement toward the United States. Moscow's proposal for a "united action" on Vietnam, the committee continued, was designed to subordinate fraternal parties to the Soviet party and to turn those parties into Russian tools in the USSR's plot to dominate the world with the United States.[115] Mao's arrogance and strongly held ideological convictions eliminated any possibility of reconciliation between Beijing and Moscow. His veto of a joint action with the Soviet Union in support of the DRV made the Vietnamese Communists realize that China's conflict with Moscow was more important to Mao than assisting Hanoi in its fight against the United States.

During February and March 1966, a Japanese Communist Party delegation led by Secretary-General Miyamoto Kenji visited China, the DRV, and North Korea to encourage a "joint action" between China and the Soviet Union to support North Vietnam. Miyamoto first broached the idea with the CCP delegation led by Liu Shaoqi, Zhou Enlai, Deng Xiaoping, and Peng Zhen in Beijing. The two sides worked out a communiqué that included only points of agreement between the two delegations. The communiqué condemned U.S. aggression in Vietnam and pledged support for the Vietnamese people. On the issue of attitudes toward the Soviet Union, the communiqué emphasized the importance of the struggle against modern revisionism in waging the struggle against U.S. imperialism but failed to mention the USSR by name. When Miyamoto came to see Mao in Shanghai on March 28, the chairman burst into a rage, insisting that the communiqué mention the Soviet Union by name in its condemnation of modern revisionism. Miyamoto disagreed, so the Beijing communiqué was torn up."[116] Clearly, by this time Mao had connected the criticism of Soviet revisionism with the domestic struggle against top party leaders headed by Liu, Deng, and Peng. It was no wonder that these officials soon became leading targets for attack when the Cultural Revolution swept across China a few months later.

In the meantime the Vietnamese Communists made clear their different attitude toward Moscow by deciding to send a delegation to attend the Twenty-third Congress of the Communist Party of the Soviet Union, which was to be held between March 29 and April 8. The Chinese had chosen not to participate in the congress. The North Vietnamese were walking on a tightrope at this time. On the one hand, they relied on the vital support of Soviet weapons; on the other hand, they did not want to break their ties with China. Thus Hanoi at this time made a special point of refuting Moscow's accusations that Beijing was blocking Soviet weapons shipment to the DRV. Pham Van Dong, speaking before the North Vietnamese National Assembly, praised China for its "devoted help in the transit of the aid from the Soviet Union and other fraternal East European countries according to schedule."[117] In February 1967, Hanoi again denounced Western "slanders" based on Soviet broadcasts that Beijing had hijacked missiles sent by Moscow to the DRV.[118]

By carefully navigating among the shoals of Sino-Soviet rivalry, Hanoi eventually succeeded in early 1967 in getting Beijing and Moscow to agree on a new arrangement for transporting Soviet arms through China to the DRV. The agreement provided for the North Vietnamese to receive the shipments at the Sino-Soviet border before escorting them through Chinese territory. This arrangement had the advantage of minimizing chances of Chinese-Russian quarrels over weapons transportation and was undoubtedly meant by both powers as a gesture of support for Hanoi's war endeavor rather than as a prelude to a Sino-Soviet rapprochement.[119]

25

The Vietnamese and Global Revolutions

Odd Arne Westad

The superpower conflict over Vietnam had not been eagerly sought by either Moscow or Washington, but had been brought about by the interventionist mindset of both powers in responding to the dynamics of the Vietnamese revolution. After the Korean War the United States had made it clear that it would not accept a unified Vietnam under Communist leadership, and that it would rather intervene than see Ho Chi Minh succeed in his aims. Viewing Ho's Hanoi government as an extension of Soviet and Chinese power in Southeast Asia, both the Eisenhower and Kennedy administrations believed that the fall of the weak South Vietnamese state—set up after the 1954 Geneva Accords and completely dependent on US support—could set off a domino effect through which not only neighboring Laos and Cambodia, but also the much more important states of Thailand, Malaya, and Indonesia would face successful challenges for power by their Communist parties supported by an aggressive Chinese regime. Although preventing the unification of Vietnam—even through nationwide elections—was not in itself an aim for either Eisenhower or Kennedy, it became the *sine qua non* of US policy since the only force powerful enough to unify the country by the ballot or the bullet was Ho's Communist-led Workers' Party of Vietnam. By the early 1960s the prospect of a direct US intervention loomed increasingly large on the horizon, as the South Vietnamese government seemed both unwilling to follow US prescriptions for internal reform and incapable of containing the leftwing rebellion spreading on their side of the supposedly temporary 1954 demarcation line.

Judging from the new sources we now have access to, the American view of South Vietnam's role in Communist thinking within Southeast Asia was largely correct. After 1954 and especially after the rebellion in the south started in 1960, Vietnam became a benchmark for what other Communist parties could hope to achieve domestically and what kind of support they could hope to receive from Moscow and Beijing. The 1954 division of Vietnam sent the signal that the immediate prospect for extending the pattern of socialist revolutions was not good. US intervention in the Korean War, China's war-weariness symbolized by Zhou Enlai's careful diplomacy, and the Soviet post-Stalin mixture of theoretical dogmatism and *détente* toward the West had created a sense of retrenchement [sic] among many Communist leaders in Southeast Asia. This attitude was perhaps best exemplified by the Malayan Communist Party's leader, Chin Peng, who remembers that by 1953–55 "neither Moscow nor Peking saw value in an armed struggle dragging on in Malaya. A military victory . . . it had been decided for us, was out of the question."[1] At the same time, the Indonesian Communist Party began feeling its way toward an electoral and parliamentary involvement in its country's politics—a strategy which, by the late 1950s, had proved spectacularly successful, to both Beijing's and Moscow's surprise.

The 1959–66 VWP decision to give its blessing to an armed rebellion in the south was the clearest indication that this period of caution was over. Hanoi's decision was its own, but it was taken after much pressure from southern Communist cadre and, as we shall see, against advice from both Moscow and Beijing. The northern-based party's new-found determination to reunify the country by force first and foremost came out of desperation with the lack of any international or country-wide process that pointed in the direction of the reunification promised at Geneva. On the contrary, the US-supported regime of Ngo Dinh Diem seemed at least in economic terms to be entrenching itself in the south.[2] As is so often the case in revolutionary situations, it was fear that the existing regime would improve its fortunes that forced the revolutionaries to take action. The southerners in the VWP leadership were instrumental in shaping a strategy that saw a 10,000 Communist cadre from the north infiltrate the south during the year 1960, with the aim of helping to organize a broad-based National Liberation Front (NLF) inside the Republic of Vietnam.[3]

But while the contemporary US view may be right about the influence Vietnamese decisions had within Southeast Asia in the late 1950s and early 1960s, it was certainly wrong about the roles Moscow and Beijing had in shaping Vietnamese strategy. To the Soviets the aim in the 1950s had been to help build a viable socialist state in the northern half of Vietnam, which in due course would be economically successful and politically and militarily strong. When Hanoi had adopted the necessary (Soviet) models of development and harvested the fruits from them, then the people in the country as a whole would "opt for socialism." This strategy for "socialism in half a country" was the only possible solution for Vietnam, Soviet advisers insisted in the 1950s, and was the only one Moscow was willing to support. The problem was the "independent Vietnamese friends, working in South Vietnam, who believed it was necessary to organize separate attacks against the Diem regime as a means of inspiring the masses to fight. This manifested an oversimplified, un-Marxist approach to the situation and to the question of armed insurrection," the Soviet leadership complained to their Chinese colleagues in 1957.[4]

When representatives of the VWP met with the Soviets and the Chinese in Moscow in May 1960 to prepare the upcoming 3rd Congress of the Vietnamese party, both of its big allies warned against an "insurrectionist" policy in the south. Even so, the VWP Congress sanctioned in broad outline the policy of armed struggle that the party leadership had decided on the previous year, while covering the new policy in phrases about eventual "peaceful reunification" that would be close to the Soviet heart. It was therefore the Vietnamese decisions—not the Sino-Soviet split, as often claimed—that broke the Geneva stalemate and set the country on course for war. New Chinese evidence shows that even after the beginning of the open split with the Soviets in the summer of 1960, Beijing remained lukewarm to the idea of a war of liberation in South Vietnam, while increasingly providing it both with rhetorical and military support. Mao's problem was that although he wanted to assist the Vietnamese party—no other foreign revolution was as important to Mao as that in Vietnam—the timing for a war in the south was exceptionally bad from a Chinese perspective. The self-inflicted wounds of the Great Leap Forward had left the Chinese economy severely weakened, while leaving behind sores that would continue to fester in Chinese politics for years to come. Chairman Mao wanted to deal with the problems through dramatic political changes within China. While the support of revolutionary parties elsewhere was part of that agenda, having a full-blown war and a possible US intervention next door to China was not.

The Sino-Soviet split was therefore a setback and not an advantage for the Vietnamese Communists. They attempted assiduously to stem the tide of dissolution in the world Communist movement, even to the point of trying to get Ho Chi Minh to mediate in the conflict in person. Consultations between the North Vietnamese, the North Koreans, and the Mongolians up to 1965 show that all of the three smaller Asian socialist states viewed the split as a potential threat to them, even though Hanoi and Pyongyang were substantially closer to Beijing in ideological terms than was Ulaanbaatar. When the conflict between Moscow and Beijing intensified in 1963, North Vietnam found itself sharing many positions with the Chinese, while still vying for Soviet support in waging a civil war against South Vietnam. Mao's stress on Third World solidarity, on revolutionary action, and on short, massive campaigns appealed to the Vietnamese leaders, as did his strong anti-imperialist rhetoric. By late 1963 Moscow saw Hanoi as firmly in the Chinese camp as far as ideology went, and Soviet diplomats reported that it was just a question of time before Hanoi would come out openly as an ally of Beijing.

Given the high hopes the Soviets had for the development of socialism in Vietnam, and also their substantial investments of time and money there, Hanoi's Chinese leanings shocked the Kremlin almost as much as the collapse of its relations with Beijing had done a few years earlier. Both before and after the fall of Nikita Khrushchev in October 1964, the Soviet party leadership attempted to rationalize Hanoi's political direction. Sadly, their conclusions were often racial rather than political: both being "Orientals," the Chinese and the Vietnamese would naturally draw together in their views and their policies, many Soviet leaders thought. This fundamental misunderstanding of the Chinese-Vietnamese relationship clouded Soviet policy during the crucial 1964–66 period in Vietnam, and gave rise to policy recommendations—both during Khrushchev's regime and after—that made Moscow steadily lose influence in Hanoi. When the US military intervention in 1964 convinced a majority within the new Soviet leadership that they would have to dramatically increase their aid to Vietnam, they did so without having much of a hope of influencing Hanoi's military or political strategy, at least in the short run. To the Soviets, their aid to Vietnam was an ideological duty and a response to US aggression, as well as an answer to China's and Vietnam's rhetoric.

To Mao Zedong, the Johnson administration's bombing raids and its sending of US ground troops to Vietnam came as a surprise. Since the late 1950s the Chairman had been preaching that the United States was a superpower in decline, afraid of taking on new involvements in the Third World and increasingly incapable of maintaining its hegemony over the capitalist countries. Indeed, much of Mao's domestic and international policy had been based on this assumption, including the break with the Soviet Union. By 1964–66 there were many voices within the CCP that felt China to be dangerously isolated at a time when its southern neighbor was coming under attack from the United States. But Mao's response, as was often the case when under pressure, was to take a step to the Left: only if China carried out a "continuous revolution" that would purge it of "rightists, revisionists, and all kinds of traitors" could the country face up to its external challenges. The Chairman realized, however, that while this Cultural Revolution was going on, China should attempt to avoid a war with the imperialists. The PRC's foreign policy in the mid-1960s was therefore high on rhetoric but low on action: even though Mao had decided to respond militarily to an all-out US ground attack across the 1954 demarcation line, China's continued involvement in Vietnam was the exception that confirmed the rule . . . China's general direction during the Great Proletarian Cultural Revolution was inward and away from engaging foreign revolutions.

In spite of Washington's views to the contrary, there was around 1965 a strong sense both in Moscow and Beijing that things were not going well in their conflict with imperialism. The initial euphoria over decolonization had worn out and the United States seemed to be resurgent, confronting the Soviets over Cuba, intervening in Vietnam, and dealing with some of its domestic problems, such as poverty and race. The new leadership in Moscow was disappointed over the fate of many of its potential Third World allies, which had been replaced through military coups in the mid-1960s, and seemed to turn away from most increases in its involvement in Third World affairs, except as far as Vietnam was concerned. Ironically, the Soviet and Chinese reluctance (for differing reasons, as we have seen) to step up their aid to other countries may have been a blessing for the Vietnamese revolution, concentrating the assistance to one country at the time when it was most needed—even if neither Moscow nor Beijing thought that Hanoi could win militarily against the Americans. One particular reason for this rising preoccupation with assisting the Vietnamese Communists was the brutal crushing of the Indonesian Left in 1965, perhaps the greatest setback for Communism in the Third World in the 1960s and—seemingly—a signal victory for US abilities to influence Asian affairs.

By the early 1960s Sukarno's regime in Indonesia was as much a puzzle for Moscow and Beijing as it was for Washington. While welcoming the Indonesian leader's increasingly strident anti-Western rhetoric and his willingness to confront the remnants of colonialism in Southeast Asia, the Soviets worried about Indonesia's economic decline, about the regime's and the Indonesian Communist Party's (PKI's) closeness to China, and about what they saw as Sukarno's unpredictability. Mao Zedong, on his side, was becoming increasingly intolerant of "bourgeois" Third World regimes, even when they tried to be close to China, and suspected Sukarno of trying to use Beijing to achieve his own hegemony in the Southeast Asia region. While Beijing welcomed the PKI's public support for its ideological positions, it viewed the Indonesian party as such as thoroughly infected with revisionist practices. Ironically, while moving into its ultra-left mode, Beijing also resented what they saw as bad treatment of the Chinese in Indonesia (who, of course, in most cases were badly treated because they were merchants or capitalists).

But if the Communist states saw trouble brewing in Indonesia, their alarm was nothing compared to Washington's views. "The road ahead for Indonesia is a troubled one of domestic deterioration, external aggression, and overall Communist profit," a US national security estimate concluded in July 1964. In spite of President Johnson's unwillingness to cut all ties with Sukarno—and thereby with the Indonesian military, which the president saw as a counterweight to the PKI—he had concluded that the leader of the fifth most populous country in the world was a threat to the stability of the whole region. "I don't trust him. I don't think he is any good," the Texan confided to Senator Richard Russell. By mid-1964 the covert operations program against Communist influence in Indonesia—originally sanctioned by President Kennedy in December 1961—had moved into high gear. Although we still do not know precisely what methods the CIA used or who their Indonesian collaborators were, the aims were clear:

> Portray the PKI as an increasingly ambitious, dangerous opponent of Sukarno and legitimate nationalism and instrument of Chinese neo-imperialism. Provide covert assistance to individuals and organizations capable of and prepared to take obstructive action against the PKI. Encourage the growth of an ideological common denominator, within the framework of Sukarno's enunciated concepts, which will serve to unite non-Communist elements and create cleavage between the PKI and the balance of the Indonesian society. Develop black and grey propaganda themes and mechanisms for use within Indonesia and via appropriate media assets outside of Indonesia in support of the objectives of this program. Identify and cultivate potential leaders within Indonesia for the purpose of ensuring an orderly non-Communist succession upon Sukarno's death or removal from office.

A key cause of US concern was Sukarno's policy of confrontation—*konfrontasi*—with neighboring Malaysia, a country that he regarded with some right as a British neocolonial creation, set up to prevent the unification of all Malays in one Indonesian state. In 1963 and 1964 Jakarta dithered on the brink of war with Malaysia and its British ally, while the Johnson administration tried to defuse the tension so as not to strengthen the PKI and its allies.[5] But for Sukarno the US attitude was one of betrayal. In his view, while the Kennedy administration had helped Indonesia gain possession of Dutch-occupied Irian Jaya, its successor now schemed to keep

Malaysia under British control. Confronted with Washington's threats of cutting off all aid to the faltering economy, Sukarno responded in characteristic style:

> All I have really wanted from America was friendship. . . . Maybe she didn't see how our revolution paralleled hers? OK, America. Don't try to win my heart. But don't try to break it either. . . . Don't publicly treat Sukarno like a spoiled child by refusing him any more candy unless he's a good boy because Sukarno has no choice but to say "to hell with your aid."[6]

With the economy in free fall, mainly because of his regime's financial incompetence, and with internal unrest on the rise, Sukarno moved to the left politically. In a speech on Independence Day, 17 August 1964, he stressed who his supporters were:

> There are still people, who accuse Sukarno of "taking sides," who accuse Sukarno of "favoritism." Sukarno taking sides, taking sides with whom? If it is against imperialism, feudalism, and the enemies of the revolution in general, yes! Certainly Sukarno has favorites, that is, he sides with the people and he sides with the revolution itself. . . . I have been accused of bringing advantage to one group only among our big national family. My answer is also, yes. Yes, I am giving advantage to one group only, namely—the revolutionary group! I am a friend of the nationalists, but only of the *revolutionary* nationalists! I am a friend of the religious group, but only the *revolutionary* religious group! I am a friend of the Communists, because the Communists are *revolutionary* people.[7]

In October, during the Non-Aligned summit meeting in Cairo, Sukarno explained to [Josip Broz] Tito that his current purpose was to drive all of Indonesian politics to the left and thereby to neutralize the "reactionary" elements in the army that could be dangerous for the revolution. He did not intend to give up the long-term alliance between nationalists, religious progressives, and Communists, but to ensure that the alliance, as he put it, "would be able to defend itself."[8]

The end of Sukarno's year of living dangerously came in September 1965. In the overheated political atmosphere in Jakarta, where rumors of plots and coups circulated daily, a group of young radical officers attempted to crush the army leadership, whom they claimed were against Sukarno and the revolution. In spite of killing six of the leading generals and—belatedly—getting the support of the PKI Politburo, the so-called "30 September Movement" failed to seize control of the country. After a day of chaos, during which Sukarno refused to commit himself to either side, the army and its Islamic and nationalist allies struck back furiously. With the head of the Army Strategic Reserve, General Suharto, in command, more than half a million Communists and left-wing sympathizers were massacred in an orgy of violence during the months that followed. Sukarno's political project was also dead—the "great leader of the revolution" was repeatedly humiliated by the generals and forced to resign, ignominiously, in 1967.

The end of the Indonesian revolution came as a shock to the Soviets, who blamed Chinese scheming and the PKI's ineptness for the defeat of the Left. Already in January 1964, PKI leader Aidit had charged Moscow with building capitalism and claimed that some day it "would fully revert back to capitalism."[9] Moscow's relationship with the PKI leadership had been deteriorating fast since the beginning of 1965, with the main Indonesian Communist newspaper accusing the Soviets of being part of the NEKOLIM (neocolonialist, colonialist, and imperialist) forces that Sukarno and the PKI so detested.[10] The Soviet embassy, on its side, increasingly found its main contacts among officers and moderate nationalists rather than in the PKI. In a 1964 report to Moscow on the Chinese hold on the PKI, the embassy even quoted the heads of the Islamic Nahdlatul Ulama Party as saying that the "PKI is working against the Soviet Union and the Soviet Union is a friend of Indonesia. Therefore PKI should be taken care of."[11] The Soviet ambassador's postmortem on the 30 September events accused the PKI leaders of having been held hostage to events rather than trying to steer them, and thereby having brought disaster upon themselves. The ambassador suspected Chinese complicity in the coup, especially since it was directed against the army chief of staff, Nasution, with whom the Soviets had been on increasingly good terms.[12] For the United States, the crushing of the coup, the sidelining of Sukarno, and the gradual imposition of General Suharto's pro-US dictatorship was a result of the Indonesian political crisis that was almost too good to be true. Granted, something along these lines was what the Americans had been working toward since the early 1960s, but only twelve months before Suharto's coming to power the US embassy's prediction had been that the army's "strength and unity of purpose under non-Communist leadership will inevitably erode."[13] In November 1965 the CIA advocated US support for the army's efforts to exterminate Communism:

> Now that it has seized upon the fortuitous opportunity afforded by PKI's error in the 30 September affair and is asking for covert help as well as understanding to accomplish that very task, we should avoid being too cynical about its motives and its self-interest, or too hesitant about the propriety of extending such assistance provided we do so covertly, in a manner which will not embarrass them or our embarrass our government.[14]

Even though the full extent of US support for Suharto and Islamist groups in hunting down the Communists in 1965 and 1966 is not known, it is clear that the United States—as well as Britain and Australia—provided the Indonesian Army with lists of members of the Communist Party, and that they thereby, at least indirectly, became complicit in mass murder of monstrous proportions.[15]

For the main advisers in the Johnson administration, what mattered most after the military takeover in Indonesia was the effect it would have on the rest of the region. "It is hard to overestimate the potential significance of the army's apparent victory over Sukarno," Robert Komer wrote to the president in March 1966. "Indonesia has more people—and probably more resources—than all of mainland Southeast Asia. It was well on the way to becoming another expansionist Communist state, which would have critically menaced the rear of the whole Western position in mainland Southeast Asia. Now . . . this trend has been sharply reversed."[16] In the National Security Council, Johnson's ambassador to South Vietnam, Henry Cabot Lodge, claimed that "the recent overthrow of the Communists in Indonesia is a direct result of our having taken a firm stand in Vietnam."[17] In Moscow—while crying few tears for the PKI leadership—many key foreign policy advisers felt "a sense of shame" for not having done more for the Indonesians. For the Soviets, too, the overthrow of Sukarno increased the importance of Vietnam—if the Communist Party lost there, then Soviet positions would have been forced out of Southeast Asia altogether.

After late 1966 both China and the Soviet Union began changing their estimates of North Vietnam's endurance, the Communists' fighting abilities in the south, and the Johnson administration's political ability to increase the intensity of US warfare up to a point that would make Hanoi amenable to a return to *status quo ante.* For China, this change in its Vietnam estimate did not mean much in terms of foreign policy, since the country was already consumed by the Cultural Revolution (although it did prepare the ground for Mao's normalization of relations with the United States after 1969). For Moscow, the unexpected successes for Vietnamese arms and the ensuing difficulties for Lyndon Johnson presented opportunities for a great victory, but also conjured up the danger of a Hanoi that would go too far and a United States that would respond by increasing pressure against other socialist states, including those in Europe. The

Kremlin therefore viewed itself increasingly as a peacemaker, willing to bargain for the best possible settlement for North Vietnam (but at the same time desperately afraid that others would uncover its real lack of decisive influence within the VWP leadership). The American insistence on trying to deal with Hanoi through Moscow was therefore a particular comfort to Brezhnev and Kosygin—not only did it confirm in their own minds that Moscow was at the head of a world revolution, but it also provided the Soviets with leverage in other areas of world politics.

Within Vietnam's immediate neighbors, Laos and Cambodia, which had shared its fate as part of the French colonial empire, the beginning military successes of the Vietnamese Communists against the United States emboldened the Left to launch offensives of its own. In Laos, where renewed civil war between the Communist-led Pathet Lao and the neutralist government broke out in 1963, North Vietnamese military support (at first against the wishes of the Soviet Union) led to increasing successes for the Pathet Lao toward the end of the 1960s. At the same time the Laotian Left came increasingly under Vietnamese direction and control. In Cambodia, however, the main radical party—an intensely nationalist group known in French as Khmer Rouge—had an uneasy relationship with Vietnam from its inception in the early 1960s. Their chances of success seemed slim in a country led by a prince—Noroddom Sihanouk—who not only had allowed the North Vietnamese and the NLF to set up supply bases on Cambodian territory, but who, in 1965, had broken diplomatic relations with the United States. But the start of US bombing of Cambodia, in 1969, and the brief US ground invasion the following year completely changed the picture. Prince Sihanouk was overthrown in a coup, while the Khmer Rouge began attracting a large following based on its strange mix of Marxist and nativist ideas. While condemning Vietnamese interference in his revolution at every turn, the Khmer Rouge leader Saloth Sar—calling himself Pol Pot—began receiving military aid from Hanoi from 1969 onwards in order to help defeat the Americans and the Cambodian military regime they supported.

During its war against the United States, Vietnam never engaged in the kind of socialist internationalism outside its own immediate region that we see in the case of Cuba. The Vietnamese revolution therefore became an indirect inspiration for others in the Third World, and—as we shall see—in the pan-European world as well. Vietnam became a symbol of successful resistance to the United States, of revolutionary heroism, of David battling Goliath. For many *tiermondistes*—especially those who had begun their journey toward disillusionment over corruption and mismanagement in newly independent states—Vietnam was a shining example of the good guerrilla [war] (sufficiently far away geographically for most of them that the real consequences of the Vietnamese revolution would not have to be taken into account). Che Guevara, just back from a humbling defeat in Congo and working his way into an even more disastrous defeat in Bolivia, sent a message to the 1967 Tricontinental Conference in Havana where he cried out for two, three, many Vietnams:

> What greatness has been shown by this people! What a stoic and courageous people! And what a lesson for the world their struggle holds. . . . The peoples of three continents are watching and learning a lesson for them in Vietnam. Since the imperialists are using the threat of war to blackmail humanity, the correct response is not to fear war. Attack hard and without let-up at every point of confrontation—that must be the general tactic of the people.

But Che also chided those who had not done enough to help the Vietnamese:

> The solidarity of the progressive world with the Vietnamese people has something of the bitter irony of the plebeians cheering on the gladiators in the Roman Circus. To wish the victim success is not

> enough; one must share his fate. One must join him in death or in victory . . . guilty are those who at the decisive moment hesitated to make Vietnam an inviolable part of socialist territory—yes, at the risk of a war of global scale, but also compelling the US imperialists to make a decision. And also guilty are those who persist in a war of insults and tripping each other up, begun quite some time ago by the representatives of the two biggest powers in the socialist camp.

For Che and for many other leftists around the globe—including, as we shall see, some in the industrialized countries—Cuba and Vietnam contributed to inspiring a New Left, which saw both the Soviet development model and Soviet foreign policy as too dogmatic, too self-satisfied, and too timid. Often claiming to criticize the Soviets from a more radical Marxist position, a small number of these groups and parties viewed Maoist China as a new lodestar, but far more claimed that Cuba and Vietnam were showing the way to a more comprehensive and quicker victory over imperialism. While the Cubans engaged some of these movements directly, both in Latin America and Africa, the Vietnamese served as example more than support. Hanoi's military and political success against the US, especially after the 1968 Tet Offensive, created a revolutionary resurgence in Southeast Asia, in which parties claimed to have learnt from the North Vietnamese and the NLF how to wage a new form of revolutionary guerrilla warfare. Since very few of their leaders had studied the actual Vietnamese experience (not to mention its military tactics, which tended to be increasingly conventional forms of warfare), one may talk of these "Vietnam-inspired" rebellions as a form of creative misunderstanding, often led by intellectuals worshipping the heroic peasant guerrilla.

Malaysia, Thailand, and the Philippines all saw revolutionary upswings led by such groups in the wake of the North Vietnamese offensives against the United States and the South Vietnamese government. In Malaysia the Communist guerrilla movement of the late 1960s was based on the MCP [Malayan Communist Party] remnants and took over many of that party's weaknesses, including remaining an almost exclusively ethnic Chinese movement. As a result, the Malaysian Communists remained isolated, without any real chance of challenging the Malay establishment, which struck back by in effect disenfranchising the whole Chinese community in 1969. After China cut off its support in 1974 the Malaysian party quickly became defunct. In Thailand the 1971 and 1976 military coups—which the military juntas claimed were undertaken in response to ethnic and student unrest—drove left-wing activists underground, from where they for a time seemed set to launch a successful guerrilla war against the government and against US bases. But the Thai Left soon fragmented, under pressure from a massive US aid program to the government. With no viable military strategy of their own and without support either from Vietnam or China, the majority of the movement's leaders soon found their way back to the cities, abandoning the peasants and ethnic minority groups they had claimed to lead to the fury of the Bangkok military junta.

In the Philippines, the New People's Army (NPA) and the Communist Party of the Philippines (Marxist-Leninist; CPP [m-1]) followed a somewhat different trajectory. Originally a China-oriented breakaway from the Soviet-oriented Communist Party, the CPP (m-l) group began assassinating officials of Ferdinand Marcos' dictatorship in 1970 and acquired weapons by ambushing troops around its original base in northern Luzon. By the mid-1980s the NPA had an army of more than 20,000 men organized in guerrilla groups throughout the Philippine archipelago and underground party cells in many small towns and villages. Its leader, Jose Maria Sison, was an intellectual who has studied not only Marxism-Leninism, but also Western theories of revolution. Coming from a family of big landowners in Luzon, Sison was inspired by the example of leaders such as Lumumba and Castro, and—like many New Left intellectuals in the West—came into conflict with the authorities for the first time when protesting against the Vietnam War. Having studied in Indonesia in the early 1960s, Sison believes that the PKI failed because its underground organization in the countryside was too weak, and he has been determined not to repeat the same mistake in the Philippines. But while the rural strategy may have helped the CPP to survive up to today, it also isolated it from the main opposition groups in the cities. When the Marcos dictatorship fell in 1986 the CPP was unable to take advantage of the political changes and became increasingly marginalized toward the end of the Cold War, as a more pluralistic political system took hold in the Philippines.[18]

Vietnamese resistance to the United States inspired not only Third World radicals but also—for the first time—made the Cold War in the Third World a central part of left-wing mobilization within the pan-European world itself. The Western European and American students who demonstrated in the streets and occupied their universities in the late 1960s found the "old" Left—both socialists and Communists—too timid on domestic reform and too placid in dealing with the problems of the Third World. Only "direct action" from below, through an alliance of students and workers, could break the impasse in Western politics, the New Left radicals believed. The NLF or Che Guevara—or even China's Cultural Revolution—became symbols of the impassioned action demanded by student protesters. "The Third World taught us the concept of an uncompromising and radical policy, different from the shallow, unprincipled bourgeois *Realpolitik*" Hans-Jürgen Krahl, one of the leaders of the West Berlin student revolt, told his judges from the dock in 1968.

> Che Guevara, Fidel Castro, Ho Chi Minh, and Mao Zedong are revolutionaries who teach us the political ethics of the uncompromising policy, which enables us to do two things: first, to reject the policies of peaceful coexistence, such as is being conducted as *Realpolitik* by the Soviet Union, and, second, to see clearly the terror that the United States, assisted by the Federal Republic [of Germany], is carrying out in the Third World.[19]

Placing the "new anti-imperialism" at the heart of the struggle for change in the West may have been a popular view among student protesters, but it infuriated some West European socialists such as the German author Günther Grass, who accused the students of solidarizing themselves with the Third World while forgetting Communist oppression inside Europe itself. Protesting the Soviet invasion of Czechoslovakia in August 1968 was less attractive to the students than attacking US behavior in Vietnam, he argued. To the students of Berlin or Paris, Grass claimed, "the attempted reform in Prague proved to be sketchy and unattractive.

> Or in other words: Alexander Dubcek's attentively formulated programme for democratic socialism could not compete with the cult of Che Guevara. A sober process, hampered at the time by the necessary compromises, interrupted today by power politics, drowned in the rhythmic clapping and the argument-less cheers for Ho Chi Minh.[20]

The New Left in the end had only a limited influence on West European or US politics, but the protests they organized did help convince many within the American elite that the Vietnam War could not be won at an acceptable cost—at home and abroad. When Lyndon Johnson declared that he would not seek reelection in order to open the way for a peaceful settlement of the Vietnam conflict, opponents of US policy, be they in New York, Paris, Moscow, or in the Third World, were truly astounded. For the first time a conflict in the Third World had brought down an American president and imposed limits on what only a few years before was seen as an unbound—if not boundless—pattern of intervention. And while Johnson's successor, Richard

Nixon, in no way subscribed to a noninterventionist foreign policy, he too soon realized that the war in Vietnam was unwinable, and chose to withdraw (although only after copying the North Vietnamese in expanding the war to Cambodia). The slow end to the Vietnam War was a watershed in Cold War history, from which lessons were drawn that, in the 1970s, came to implicate the Third World more, not less, in the global conflict between the United States and the Soviet Union.

Ironically, the end to the war *inside* Vietnam, when it finally came in 1975—two years after the Paris Peace Accords and the US withdrawal—was a highly conventional military offensive by the North, patterned more on the Soviet victory over German forces at Kursk in 1943 or the CCP's offensive across the Yangzi in 1949 than on slogans of "people's war." South Vietnam saw no bloodbath in defeat, but rather a slow strangling of the southern non-Communist forces that had cooperated with the Hanoi regime as part of the NLF. From the late 1970s onwards hundreds of thousands of people fled by sea, or, in the strangest of twists, across the border to China to escape from a doctrinaire northern regime that seemed to offer few opportunities for those who were not in the service of the Party. By 1979 Vietnam found itself at war not only with a genocidal Khmer Rouge regime in neighboring Cambodia (which the Vietnamese themselves had helped to power), but also with its former Chinese allies, with whom relations had been deteriorating since the beginning of China's Cultural Revolution. To Washington and Moscow—whose fear of Beijing's influence in Hanoi had motivated much of their Vietnam policy—the Third Indochina War ought to have served as a *memento mori* for their Third World policies overall. But . . . superpower interventionism did not receive a profound setback through the Vietnam War and its aftermath. Their only impact was on the form such interventions were to take in the 1970s.

Chapter 8
Laos and Cambodia

FRENCH INDOCHINA INCLUDED NOT JUST Vietnam but its neighbors to the west, Laos and Cambodia. For brief periods—Laos in 1960–1961, Cambodia in 1970—these places made front-page news in the United States when the Kennedy and Nixon administrations tried, with decidedly limited success, to keep them out of Communist hands. Otherwise, Laos and Cambodia were for Americans sites of the sideshow war, adjunct to the conflict on the main stage. Part of the Ho Chi Minh Trail, used by the North Vietnamese to supply NLF and northern troops in the south, ran through Laos; Communist war materiel transited Cambodia on its way to South Vietnam, and communist troops found sanctuary there. Both places had their own Communist "liberation" movements: the Pathet Lao in Laos, the Khmer Rouge in Cambodia. And both countries were bombed heavily by the United States.

The readings in this chapter shed light on the sideshow wars. Historian Timothy Castle summarizes and evaluates U.S. policy toward Laos from 1955 to 1975. While the Americans were committed to keeping an anti-Communist force of Hmong fighters in the field, Ho Chi Minh and his generals were equally determined to maintain Laos as a conduit for North Vietnamese troops and supplies heading south. The other two readings are excerpts from books by the British scholar William Shawcross and former National Security Adviser and Secretary of State Henry Kissinger, offering strikingly different interpretations of the Nixon administration's secret decision to bomb North Vietnamese sanctuaries inside Cambodia in 1969. The Shawcross-Kissinger debate remains one of the most bitter from the period and raises troubling questions. Was bombing Cambodia legal? Was it a risk worth taking, or should Nixon have anticipated that it might expand and prolong the war? Was the secrecy of the bombing justified? And finally, does the Nixon administration bear any responsibility for the ultimate victory of the Khmer Rouge, and is it therefore tainted by association with the unspeakable crimes of the Communist regime in Cambodia from 1975 to 1978?

« 26 »

The War in Laos

Timothy N. Castle

THE AMERICAN MILITARY AID PROGRAM in Laos began as an adjunct to other U.S. security initiatives in the region. Rejecting the 1954 Geneva settlement as inadequate to preclude communist aggression in Southeast Asia, the Eisenhower administration orchestrated the creation of the Southeast Asia Treaty Organization. When the United States succeeded France in training the South Vietnamese armed forces, it also began providing military assistance to the French Military Mission in Laos. America's "can do" spirit was, however, inconsistent with the lax French colonial work ethic and the United States moved immediately to take charge of Lao military training.

Initial U.S. efforts at Lao military assistance, which began in 1955, fell miserably short. The Programs Evaluations Office was encumbered by a staff of military retirees and former or would-be military personnel; it lacked direction, experienced great difficulty with the French military, and was hampered by the convoluted Lao political situation. Nevertheless, Washington allowed the PEO to muddle along for more than three years before deciding that the program required the attention of a senior active-duty military officer. The arrival of Brigadier General [John A.] Heintges in February 1959 signaled Washington's decision to begin a full-fledged military aid program and, therefore, an even greater departure from the 1954 agreements.

Although it was not planned, General Heintges's assignment coincided with Prime Minister Phoui Sananikone's announcement that the Royal Lao government viewed the 1954 Geneva Agreements as fully implemented. This declaration, and the recent replacement of Pathet Lao cabinet members by right-wing army officers, touched off increased military contact between the Pathet Lao and the Lao army. The Royal Lao Army acquitted itself in its usual desultory fashion, evidence that the PEO had accomplished little, and the Phoui government publicly requested greater U.S. military aid.

Washington responded quickly to the Lao request and Heintges soon had several hundred U.S. Army Special Forces trainers and Filipino contract technicians assigned to the PEO. The arrival of these additional personnel and an increased budget still did not markedly improve the fighting capabilities of the Royal Lao Army. The Green Berets were frustrated by the short length of their tours in Laos and the refusal of Lao officers to take part in any training programs. And, while the integration of Filipino technicians into the Lao military seemed expedient at the time, it inculcated a reliance on foreigners that stifled later efforts to make the Lao armed forces more self-sufficient.

The expanded American presence in Laos provided opportunities for enormous graft and malfeasance within the royal government. Pathet Lao propagandists rightly pointed to suddenly wealthy civil servants, while the Lao people waited futilely for promised roads, schools, and clinics. The Lao army's enlisted force was exploited by their officers, who often short-changed the men in their pay and food rations and sold newly arrived U.S. military equipment. A sincere, but naive attempt by Captain Kong Le to redress these injustices and end foreign influence in his country elevated the Laotian civil war into a confrontation of superpowers.

Kong Le's 1960 coup and the installation of Souvanna Phouma as prime minister were immediately and firmly opposed by the United States and Thailand. Since the 1954 signing of the Manila Pact, Washington and Bangkok had been united in their efforts to oppose the inclusion of the Pathet Lao in any Lao coalition government. This anticommunist fervor caused the United States and Thailand to overlook the copious shortcomings of General Phoumi [Nosavan]'s military leadership and his financial misdeeds, while precipitously dismissing anyone who considered involving the Pathet Lao in a political settlement.

The Thai blockade of Vientiane, the suspension of American military aid to Souvanna's government, and blatant PEO assistance to General Phoumi's forces only exacerbated the situation. For five years the U.S. had enjoyed the advantage of resupplying the Lao military through Thailand by air transport and highway shipment. In contrast, support for the Pathet Lao from China and North Vietnam had to make its way into Laos via time-consuming truck convoys. When Souvanna countered these actions by accepting Soviet military aid he dramatically balanced the military assistance scales. Suddenly, the United States and its new president were faced with an unprecedented Soviet airlift and the realization that the Russians had decided to test America's resolve in Southeast Asia.

The Laotian crisis, escalating in the first days and months of the Kennedy administration, threatened to undercut the young president's international credibility, his foreign policy agenda, and force the United States into a war with the Soviets. Kennedy insisted that he would not be "humiliated" by the Soviets, but the president and his advisors knew enough about the land and people of Laos to decide that the United States should avoid, if possible, a conventional war in Laos. The White House decided to pursue a strategy of tough military "signaling" to the Soviets, while expanding the Lao military assistance program and ordering the development of a secret and unconventional military force in Laos.

Earlier U.S. military assistance efforts in Laos were covert in deference to the 1954 Geneva Accords and mostly focused on the training and support of a conventional army. The Kennedy administration, beginning in 1961, greatly expanded America's involvement in Laos. Since the Royal Lao Army had repeatedly shown its ineptitude, the United States simply recruited a group that would fight. Emphasizing the dangers the communists posed to the Hmong way of life, the CIA was able to develop a surrogate army for the lowland Lao. Determined to make Laos a bastion of freedom, Washington chose to ignore the consequences of supporting a government that was often reluctant to shed blood in its own defense. Although diplomatic maneuvering would prompt a brief respite in U.S. military activity, America's covert Lao war policy was set.

The 1962 Geneva Agreements allowed the United States and the Soviet Union to back away from military confrontation, but the diplomats did little to solve the Lao kingdom's security concerns. President Kennedy, despite the knowledge that North Vietnamese forces remained in Laos, complied with the Geneva terms and ordered a complete withdrawal from Laos of the U.S. Military Assistance Advisory Group. The president acted at the urging of Ambassador W. Averell Harriman, who firmly believed the Soviets could ensure North Vietnamese adherence to the accords. Harriman's faith was misplaced, and perhaps the Kremlin truly misjudged its sway over Hanoi. In any case, Ho Chi Minh never had any intention of abandoning his Laotian highway to South Vietnam.

In addition to Harriman's Soviet "guarantee," there was also a State Department judgment that Hanoi's forces would be circumspect in their violations of Laotian neutrality. This is a critical point in understanding America's Lao policy.

Because the North Vietnamese were transiting Laos en route to make war in South Vietnam, the White House was now conceding that American intervention, if necessary, should occur in South Vietnam and not Laos. In addition, the administration believed that as long as the North Vietnamese denied their presence in Laos, the U.S. could also undertake "nonattributable" military action in the kingdom without fear of international condemnation. Accordingly, Washington could then move its focus to Vietnam where, administration experts predicted, the U.S. could more easily defend the region against communist expansion.

The CIA experienced little difficulty in implementing this covert war policy. Vang Pao and his Hmong clans, driven off their mountains by continuing communist pressure and facing hostility in the lowlands, had little choice but to fight. Air America's experienced pilots and unparalleled repair facilities promised professional and durable air support. Once USAID [Agency for International Development] was directed by the president to assist the CIA with refugee relief and "cover" for agency operatives, the team was complete. The training of the lowland Lao army was left to DEPCHIEF [Deputy Chief, Joint U.S. Military Advisory Group, Thailand], the U.S. military attachés in Laos, and the USAID Requirements Office.

Without Thai air bases and Thai manpower the United States could not have supported a meaningful covert war in Laos. Bangkok, anxious to see the United States stem communism on the far side of the Mekong, allowed the basing of hundreds of American aircraft—which flies missions over Laos, Cambodia, and the Vietnams—and established "Headquarters 333" to work in concert with the CIA. At no financial cost the astute Thais were able to gain increased border security and hundreds of millions of dollars in military and economic aid. Moreover, the American presence guaranteed the Thai a powerful and immediate buffer against any large-scale communist aggression.

The political implications of the United States conducting a secret war in a neutral country left no doubt that the American ambassador to Laos would have to have strict control over the operation. Even though the "Kennedy letter" enunciated the ambassador's authority over the embassy's "Country Team," the State Department was quite judicious in the selection of its senior Vientiane diplomat. Leonard Unger became the first ambassador to undertake the extraordinarily difficult job of publicly proclaiming American adherence to Lao neutrality, while secretly directing a prohibited military assistance program. Ambassador Unger was more than equal to the task and was subsequently posted to Bangkok where he continued to be an active participant in arranging Thai support for the Lao war.

Ambassador William Sullivan was the most important and influential man in the twenty-year history of America's military assistance program in Laos. For more than four years Sullivan ran the Vientiane Country Team and the Lao war with virtual impunity. His experience in Geneva and support in Washington provided Sullivan with formidable foreign policy insight and political clout. Ambassador Sullivan established himself as the supreme and unquestioned arbiter of all U.S. activities in Laos. His personal attention and involvement in every aspect of the American Mission insured its smooth and professional operation; Sullivan's flaw was an undisguised distrust of the American military.

Ambassador Sullivan believed that U.S. policy objectives in Laos dictated that the U.S. military presence there be minimal. As the war in Vietnam intensified, Sullivan was under increasing pressure from the U.S. military command in Saigon to ease these restrictions. The ambassador was correct in refusing to delegate all of his military authority to COMUSMACV [Commander of the U.S. Military Assistance Command, Vietnam]. America's announced respect for the 1962 Geneva Accords would have looked foolish, indeed, if Laos had been designated a part of COMUSMACV's theater of operations. Nonetheless, Sullivan could have allowed COMUSMACV, through the 7/13th Air Force, a much greater role in the direction of the air war. Professional military advice on aerial operations would not have exposed America's true military involvement in Laos and it might have improved the air campaign.

Sullivan's decision to exclude COMUSMACV and the 7/13th Air Force from almost all decision making elevated the military role of the CIA. In particular, through the ambassador, the CIA exercised considerable control over American military air power. As evidenced by the recollections and writings of many senior U.S. Air Force officers, CIA officers were mostly untrained in the employment of sophisticated bomber aircraft. Also questionable was the Agency's direction of Air America and U.S. Air Force helicopters in the insertion and extraction of large numbers of troops. In defense of the CIA role, William Sullivan and William Colby have both pointed to the Agency's long experience in Laos as compared to the usual one-year U.S. military tour of duty. Still, Sullivan could have directed a closer association between the CIA and the 7/13th AF that might have capitalized on the expertise of both organizations. It is obvious the CIA wanted air power on demand, with no outside interference.

Ambassador Sullivan also insisted that DEPCHIEF play a minor role in Lao operations. The USAID Requirements Office was staffed by dedicated people, mostly former military men. But the RO, even with the addition of Project 404 personnel, was able neither to gauge the effectiveness of the Lao military nor adequately supervise Lao use of American aid. The results were sloppy training, abuse of military equipment, opportunities for wholesale malfeasance, and an ineffective army. If the DEPCHIEF commander had been given a responsible place on the embassy Country Team, the RO workers and their colleagues in Thailand might well have developed more effective training programs. Such a collaboration offered the chance of some real improvement in the Lao military.

The military situation in Laos began to change in the late 1960s. America's covert paramilitary war in Laos was fast escalating into a conventional conflict with enormous human and financial costs. The increased aggressiveness of the North Vietnamese dry-season campaigns, a new administration in Washington, and a growing antiwar feeling in the American Congress brought change, albeit slowly, to America's Lao policy.

Ambassador G. McMurtrie Godley, who enjoyed close associations within the CIA, initially retained most of William Sullivan's management policies. The CIA station chief continued to serve as the ambassador's principal military advisor and DEPCHIEF and the 7/13th AF were largely ignored. As the war in Laos accelerated, Godley and his Country Team found themselves increasingly involved in large-scale military operations. The Hmong, who for years had effectively served as guerrilla fighters, were now regularly employed against sizable North Vietnamese forces. Marginally equipped and poorly suited for conventional combat, the Hmong suffered horrific casualties. The kingdom's defense began to depend almost entirely on massive aerial bombing and the infusion of additional Thai artillery and infantry units. Nevertheless, Godley clung to the policies of the past and allowed his staff to dictate military requirements to a wholly exasperated 7/13th AF and COMUSMACV.

After years of effort, in 1972 the Pentagon convinced the State Department that DEPCHIEF required the attention of a general officer. Brigadier General Vessey's performance quickly won Godley's confidence, and, for the first time since the departure of Major General Tucker in October 1961, there was a professional military leader in Laos. Vessey's expertise and recommendations led the way for much improved relations between the U.S. embassy in Vientiane and senior U.S. military officials in Thailand and South Vietnam. Visits to Laos by U.S. general officers, unthinkable in the past, began to occur with some frequency. Increased understanding, on both sides of the Mekong, measurably improved cooperation on military matters.

However, public revelations about the true extent of America's involvement in the kingdom brought about stiff reductions, mandated by the U.S. Congress, in Lao military aid. By late 1972 there was little question that the United States would soon disengage from the war in Vietnam. The U.S. military had "joined" the Vientiane Country Team a little late.

The war in Laos was always fought in the shadow of Vietnam, so when Hanoi and Washington concluded a settlement there was no doubt that the Lao conflict would soon end. Dr. [Henry] Kissinger's recollections notwithstanding, the Royal Lao government had no choice but to complete a cease-fire agreement with the Pathet Lao. Nevertheless, Prince Souvanna Phouma was hardly an unwitting victim of American foreign policy. By late 1964 the prince was fully aware of America's covert Lao ground and air campaigns. For more than eight years Souvanna had accepted, and often requested, U.S. military activity in Laos. During much of this period, the prince also maintained close contact with his brother, Prince Souphanouvong. The prime minister and Henry Kissinger might well have enjoyed a mutual discussion on Metternich.

The February 1973 Vientiane Agreement stopped U.S. bombing in Laos and, once a new Lao coalition government was formed, mandated the expulsion of Air America and the Thai SGUs [Special Guerrilla Units]. Although some in Washington hoped that the new Lao government would allow the retention of a small U.S. military assistance program, America's covert war in Laos was at an end.

Over the next year, as the Pathet Lao and the royalists attempted to form a new government, the United States continued to supply the Royal Lao Army with military aid. It was a wasted effort. For too many years, with U.S. acquiescence, the Lao military had been content to sit out the war and allow the Americans to pay the Hmong and Thais to defend the kingdom. Now, even with the imminent cancellation of the U.S. military aid program, there was no sense of urgency. Some senior Lao military officers believed Souvanna and Souphanouvong would come to a compromise and, as before, the communists would only be part of a new government. Others, reflecting a traditional Lao perspective, were resigned to their fate. The Lao were not, and could never be, "Turks."

The formation of the Lao Provisional Government of National Union resulted in the complete withdrawal by late May 1974 of the remaining Thai SGUs and the departure of all non-accredited U.S. military personnel from Laos. The United States had fully complied with the Ventiane Agreement, even though President Nixon, like President Kennedy in 1962, knew that the North Vietnamese remained in Laos. Unlike Kennedy, however, Nixon was not thinking about a future U.S. covert return to Laos. On May 9, 1974, the U.S. House Judiciary Committee had opened impeachment hearings on the president of the United States. Regardless of North Vietnamese duplicity, U.S. military involvement in Laos and the rest of Indochina had come to an end.

When the North Vietnamese forces entered Saigon on April 30, 1975, the Pathet Lao knew their victory was also near. Plans for any future U.S. military aid program in Laos completely evaporated, and the U.S. embassy in Vientiane was drawn down to a skeleton staff. The military assistance program in Laos was ended.

This study began with a basic question: Why was Laos of importance to the United States? The answer inheres in the geopolitical foundation of the containment strategy. The engine that drove America's overall post–World War II involvement in Southeast Asia was its determination to halt communist expansion before it consumed the entire continent. Laos, which uniquely bordered all the region's other states, was a key component of any successful communist movement in South Vietnam, Thailand, and Cambodia. The preservation of a truly neutral Laos, which would deny communist trespass of the kingdom, therefore figured prominently in the

U.S. containment strategy. This examination has shown, however, that Laotian neutrality was never achieved. Communist violations of the 1954 and 1962 Geneva Agreements were countered by the establishment of a covert U.S. military assistance program for Laos, also a clear violation of Laotian neutrality.

Was American policy toward Laos, therefore, a failure? The answer depends upon one's criteria. State Department official Roger Hilsman, in *To Move a Nation*, has called President Kennedy's containment stratagem of neutralizing Laos a "triumph of statecraft." Hilsman and successive White House advisors discerned the political, military, and physical tangle of Laos; the chaotic, land-locked country was no place to fight another Asian ground war. To this end, America's objective of shifting the conventional military confrontation with the communists to Vietnam was both pragmatic and adept. For more than a decade the United States successfully maintained the façade of Laotian neutrality and focused its armed forces on winning the public war in Vietnam.

The geographic imperative of Laos nevertheless remained. Official neutrality notwithstanding, Laos was essential to the spread of communism in Southeast Asia. The kingdom's eastern provinces were Hanoi's critical avenues to the south. In response, U.S.-controlled Hmong and Thai ground forces worked hard to disrupt these resupply activities. Increasingly, American bombers rained the Ho Chi Minh Trail with tons of bombs. Yet, both sides wisely avoided a full-scale war in Laos. The North Vietnamese army and their Pathet Lao allies could have struck at many of the important Laotian river cities, including Luang Prabang. Washington could have ordered American troops inserted into Laos and placed along the Trail. In either case the result would have been an immediate and bloody escalation of the war. Both countries refrained from direct confrontation and precipitous military action, so that "nonattributable war" exacted relatively few American casualties.

By avoiding direct military intervention in Laos, America also relinquished an opportunity to sever Hanoi's pipeline to South Vietnam. Despite harassment by the "secret army" and massive American bombing, the North Vietnamese continued to make their way south. The United States, unwilling to commit American ground forces to Laos, constrained by a war-weary and disillusioned public, and allied with an ineffective South Vietnamese military, could not defeat the North Vietnamese. Ultimately, Laotian "Neutrality" worked to the advantage of Hanoi and doomed U.S. objectives.

Washington could take some solace in the fact that relatively few American lives were lost in Laos, and the majority of the Lao Lum and their cities escaped the fighting, but one Laotian group suffered greatly. For the Hmong of northeastern Laos there was no neutrality. Their horrific casualties were payment in advance for the promise of a better life, free of communist or lowland Lao controls. Americans solicited these highland guerrilla fighters; still, U.S. policymakers cannot be held completely responsible for the Hmong losses. The elite of Vientiane and Luang Prabang, who openly viewed the mountain people as little more than savages, were quite willing to sit back and allow their Hmong surrogates to fight the communist trespassers. After all, the lowland Lao army rarely possessed the determination to stand and fight effectively against the North Vietnamese. Moreover, communist proscriptions were anathema to the Hmong way of life. U.S. involvement increased the level of violence, but even without American assistance most of Van Pao's Hmong clans would have resisted the North Vietnamese.

A final legacy of America's Laotian policy is that it cemented Thai-U.S. relations. A major confrontation in Laos would have quickly spread across the long and porous Thai-Lao border. Anxious to assist in the containment of communism, Bangkok permitted the United States to build critical air facilities and to recruit manpower for the "secret army." As the war expanded these nominally Royal Thai Air Force bases became the cornerstone of the American bombing campaigns in Laos, Cambodia, and North Vietnam. The U.S.–paid Thai forces increasingly took the place of the decimated Hmong guerrillas. Thailand acquired enormous economic and military benefits from the American presence, and the Untied States obtained what some observers have termed an "unsinkable aircraft carrier."

America's war in Laos, hidden from public view for so long, deserves greater study. The unique relationships, among the Departments of State, Defense, and the Central Intelligence Agency, along with the cooperation of the Royal Thai government, and the sacrifices of the Hmong people, all merit further examination. America's longest war cast a long shadow and, nearly twenty years later, there is still much to be learned.

27

Bombing Cambodia: A Critique

William Shawcross

THE FIRST REQUEST WAS UNPRETENTIOUS. On February 9, 1969, less than a month after the inauguration of Richard Nixon, General Creighton Abrams, commander of United States forces in South Vietnam, cabled General Earle G. Wheeler, Chairman of the Joint Chiefs of Staff, to inform him that "recent information, developed from photo reconnaissance and a rallier gives us hard intelligence on COSVN HQ facilities in Base Area 353."

COSVN HQ was the acronym for the elusive headquarters—"Central Office for South Vietnam"—from which according to the United States military, the North Vietnamese and Viet Cong were directing their war effort in South Vietnam. Until then, Abrams remarked, the military had placed COSVN in Laos. Now he was certain the headquarters was much farther south, in one of neutral Cambodia's border states which were being used by the Communists as bases and sanctuaries from the fighting in Vietnam. Abrams wanted to attack it.

> The area is covered by thick canopy jungle. Source reports there are no concrete structures in this area. Usually reliable sources report that COSVN and COSVN-associated elements consistently remain in the same general area along the border. All our information, generally confirmed by imagery interpretation, provides us with a firm basis for targeting COSVN HQs.

Already Abrams had been instructed by the new administration to discuss United States troop withdrawals with the South Vietnamese. Now he reminded Wheeler that he had predicted a large-scale enemy offensive around Saigon in the near future. An attack on COSVN, he argued, "will have an immediate effect on the offensive and will also have its effect on future military offensives which COSVN may desire to undertake." An appropriate form of assault would be "a short-duration, concentrated B-52 attack of up to 60 sorties, compressing the time interval between strikes to the minimum. This is more than we would normally use to cover a target this size, but in this case it would be wise to insure complete destruction."

Abrams seems to have understood some of the implications of this request. Prince Norodom Sihanouk, Cambodia's ruler, had long been trying to keep his country out of the war in Vietnam. Abrams assured Wheeler that "there is little likelihood of involving Cambodian nationals if the target boxes are placed carefully. Total bomber exposure over Cambodian territory would be less than one minute per sortie." (Put another way, sixty sorties would take about one hour.) The general also thought it necessary to point out that "the successful destruction of COSVN HQs in a single blow would, I believe, have a very significant impact on enemy operations throughout South Vietnam." He asked for authority for the attack.

The Joint Chiefs sent Abrams's memo up to Melvin R. Laird, a former Wisconsin Republican Congressman, who was the new Secretary of Defense. Laird passed it to the White House, where it received the immediate attention of the new President and his National Security Affairs adviser, Dr. Henry Kissinger.

Two days later General John P. McConnell, the acting chairman in Wheeler's absence, sent a reply that must have cheered Abrams; it indicated that Washington was taking the idea even more seriously than Abrams himself. His request to Wheeler had not been highly classified, but simply headed "Personal for Addressees." McConnell's answer, however, was routed so that almost no one but he and Abrams could see it and was plastered with classifications: "Top Secret"—"Sensitive"—"Eyes Only"—"Delivery during Waking Hours"—"Personal for Addressee's Eyes Only."

McConnell told Abrams that his request had been presented to "the highest authority." In the conventions of cable language, this meant that President Nixon himself had seen it. The President had not rejected the idea; Abrams was told that "this matter will be further considered." The cable went on:

> 2. The highest authority desires that this matter be held as closely as possible in all channels and in all agencies which have had access to it.
>
> 3. The highest authority also wants your estimate on the number of Cambodian civilians who might become casualties of such an attack.
>
> 4. It will not, repeat not, be necessary for you to send a briefing team to Washington. However, it will be important for you to keep me informed on any further developments from your viewpoint. Warm regards.

Despite McConnell's advice, Abrams did send a briefing team to Washington. Two colonels arrived at the Pentagon, and a special breakfast meeting was arranged at which they could explain Abrams' proposals to a number of senior officials. These included Melvin Laird, General Wheeler, Colonel Robert Pursley, Laird's military assistant, and Lieutenant General John Vogt, then the Air Force's Assistant Deputy Chief of Staff for Plans and Operations. The meeting was also attended by a representative from Dr. Kissinger's National Security Council staff, Colonel Alexander Haig.

The colonels outlined their argument with conviction. This time, they claimed, it really was true: Viet Cong and North Vietnamese headquarters had been located. Base Area 353 was in the so-called Fish Hook, a corner of Cambodia that jutted into South Vietnam, northwest of Saigon. Even without COSVN, it was considered one of the most important Communist sanctuaries in Cambodia. Several regiments were based there and it also contained military hospitals and large caches of food and arms.

Over the next five weeks Abrams's request was frequently discussed by the National Security Council staff and at Presidential meetings in the Oval Office of the White House. Understandably perhaps, the Joint Chiefs were enthusiastic in support of the proposal. Melvin Laird was more skeptical. But he acknowledged that if COSVN had really been discovered it should be destroyed and argued that it could be publicly justified as an essential precondition to troop withdrawal. Nixon and Kissinger, however, were adamant that if it were done, it had to be done in total secrecy. Normal "Top Secret" reporting channels were not enough. Later, General Wheeler recalled that the President said—"not just once, but either to me or in my presence at least half a dozen times"—that nothing whatsoever about the proposal must ever be disclosed.

Before a final decision was made, the Chiefs cabled Abrams to tell him that he could make tentative plans for launching the strike on the early morning of March 18. He was told of the demands for secrecy and was given a code name for the operation—"Breakfast," after the Pentagon briefing.

The cable set out in detail the way in which the raids were to be concealed. The planes would be prepared for a normal mission against targets in Vietnam. If the Joint Chiefs sent the signal "Execute repeat Execute Operation Breakfast," they would then be diverted to attack the Cambodian base area. No announcement would be made. "Due to sensitivity of this operation addressees insure that personnel are informed only on a strict need-to-know basis and at the latest feasible time which permits the operation to be conducted effectively."

Abrams made the necessary dispositions, and on March 17 Wheeler cabled him: "Strike on COSVN headquarters is approved. Forty-eight sorties will be flown against COSVN headquarters. Twelve strikes will be flown against *legitimate* targets of your choice in SVN not repeat not near the Cambodian border." (Emphasis added.)

The strikes were to take place almost at once, between three o'clock and seven o'clock on the morning of March 18, unless Abrams received a priority "Red Rocket" message "Cancel repeat Cancel Operation Breakfast."

The cable described how the press was to be handled. When the command in Saigon published its daily bombing summary, it should state that, "B-52 missions in six strikes early this morning bombed these targets: QUOTE Enemy activity, base camps, and bunker and tunnel complexes 45 kilometers north-east of Tay Ninh City. UNQUOTE. Following the above, list two or more other B-52 targets struck (12 sorties)."

Wheeler continued:

> In the event press inquiries are received following the execution of the Breakfast Plan as to whether or not U.S. B-52s have struck in Cambodia, U.S. spokesman will confirm the B-52s did strike on routine missions adjacent to the Cambodian border but state that he has no details and will look into this question. Should the press persist in its inquiries or in the event of a Cambodian protest concerning U.S. strikes in Cambodia, U.S. spokesman will neither confirm nor deny reports of attacks on Cambodia but state it will be investigated. After delivering a reply to any Cambodian protest, Washington will inform the press that we have apologized and offered compensation.

Finally, Wheeler reminded Abrams and the B-52 commanders, "Due to the sensitivity of this operation all persons who know of it, who participate in its planning, preparation or execution should be warned not repeat not to discuss it with unauthorized individuals."

Many of the B-52s used in Indochina were based at Anderson Air Force Base in Guam. The planes had been built in the 1950s as an integral part of the United States' nuclear deterrent, but since 1965 more than a hundred of them had been adapted to carry dozens of conventional 750-lb. bombs in their bellies and under their wings. They were still controlled by Strategic Air Command but were at the disposition of the Commander of U.S. Forces in South Vietnam. Abrams could call upon sixty planes a day. Each plane could carry a load of approximately thirty tons of bombs.

Before takeoff, the crews of the B-52s were always briefed on the location of their targets in South Vietnam. After Wheeler's March 17 "Execute Operation Breakfast" order was received, the pilots and navigators of the planes to be diverted were taken aside by their commanding officer and told to expect the ground controllers in Vietnam to give them the coordinates of new targets—they would be bombing Cambodia.

That evening the heavily laden planes rumbled off the long runway, rose slowly over the Russian trawlers, which almost always seemed to be on station just off the island, and climbed to 30,000 feet for the monotonous five-hour cruise to Indochina. There was little for the six-man crew to do—except watch for storm clouds over the Philippines and refuel in mid-air—until they were above the South China Sea approaching the dark line of the Vietnamese coast.

At this point they entered the war zone and came under control of the ground radar sites in South Vietnam. But even now there was little reason for concern. There were no enemy fighter planes to harass and chivvy them, no antiaircraft fire, no ground-to-air missiles. A ground radar controller gave the navigator the coordinates of the final bomb run. Then the controller watched on his radar screen as the planes, in cells of three, approached the target; as they did so he counted down the bombardiers with the words "Five—four—three—two—one—*hack*."

Twenty times that night the ground controllers, sitting in their air-conditioned "hootches" in South Vietnam, cans of Coke or 7-Up by their elbows, called out *hack*. Sixty long strings of bombs spread through the dark and fell to the earth faster than the speed of sound. Each plane load dropped into an area, or "box," about half a mile wide by two miles long, and as each bomb fell, it threw up a fountain of earth, trees and bodies, until the air above the targets was thick with dust and debris, and the ground itself flashed with explosions and fire. For the first time in the war, so far as is known, forty-eight of such boxes were stamped upon neutral Cambodia by the express order of the President.

One group of men was especially delighted by the event. Since May 1967, when the U.S. Military command in Saigon became concerned at the way the North Vietnamese and Viet Cong were evading American "search and destroy" and air attacks in Vietnam by making more use of bases in Laos and Cambodia, the U.S. Special Forces had been running special, highly classified missions into the two countries. Their code name was Daniel Boone.

The Daniel Boone teams entered Cambodia all along its 500-mile frontier with South Vietnam from the lonely, craggy, impenetrable mountain forests in the north, down to the well-populated and thickly reeded waterways along the Mekong river. There was a quality of fantasy about the missions. They usually contained two or three Americans and up to ten local mercenaries, often recruited from the hill tribes of the area. All the Americans were volunteers, and they were enjoined to the strictest secrecy; the release they had to sign subjected them to a $10,000 fine and up to ten years' imprisonment for disclosing details of the forays. Because the missions were supposed to be what the Army called "sterile," the Americans either wore uniforms that could not be traced to any American unit or were disguised in the black pajamas of the Viet Cong. They carried what had become by the middle '60s the universal symbol of revolution, the Soviet-designed AK-47 automatic rifle made in China. Deaths were reported to relatives as having occurred "along the border."

These and other precautions helped conceal the work from the American press and the Congress. But black pajamas do not really hide well-fed Caucasians prowling around Southeast Asian jungles. Teams often found that, within two hours of being "inserted" by helicopter (parachutes were not used, because the Americans fell so much faster than the Vietnamese), their opponents had put trackers onto them. Their reconnaissance mission abandoned, they had to flee through the jungle or crawl through the thick fifteen-foot grass, evading their stalkers until they could find a suitable clearing to call helicopter support for rescue.

Randolph Harrison, who saw himself then as a "gung-ho lieutenant," arrived at the Special Forces headquarters in Ban Me Thuot, in the Central Highlands, in August 1968. He was given command of one of the reconnaissance companies, and he made his first mission into Cambodia on November 17, 1968, just after the American people, in the hope of peace, narrowly elected Nixon. At this time there was no consensus within the Untied States' intelligence establishment on the extent to which the North Vietnamese and Viet Cong were using Cambodia as a sanctuary or as a supply route, but Harrison was shocked by the evidence he saw of the enemy's insouciance just across the border from his own camp.

"There were hard-surface roads, those concrete reinforced bunkers. I personally found some abandoned base camps that were acres in size," he said later. "When you get an opportunity to see that blatant an example of their presence there, you scream and beg and do everything you can to get somebody to come in there and blast them." What he and his friends wanted most of all, he said, were B-52 "Arclight" strikes—"We had been told, as had everybody . . . that those carpet bombing attacks by B-52s [were] totally devastating, that nothing could survive, and if they had a troop concentration there it would be annihilated." They were enthusiastic when, on the morning of March 18, Major Michael Eiland, the Daniel Boone Operations officer, came up from Saigon to tell them of Operation Breakfast. He ordered a reconnaissance team into Area 353 by helicopter to pick up any possible Communist survivors. "We were told that . . . if there was anybody still alive out there they would be so stunned that all [we would] have to do [was] walk over and lead him by the arm to the helicopter."

Captain Bill Orthman was chosen to lead this team; he was given a radio operator named Barry Murphy and eleven Vietnamese. All were confident and rather excited. They were flown over the border and landed in rubble and craters. After the helicopters had taken off, the Daniel Boone men moved toward the tree line in search of their dead or dazed enemy. But within moments they were, in Harrison's words, "slaughtered."

The B-52 raid had not wiped out all the Communists as the Special Forces men had been promised. Instead, its effect, as Harrison said, had been "the same as taking a beehive the size of a basketball and poking it with a stick. They were mad."

The Communists fired at them from behind the trees on three sides. Three of the Vietnamese soldiers were immediately hit and Orthman himself was shot both in the leg and in the stomach. The group split apart and Orthman stumbled toward a bomb crater. Then a C.S. gas grenade in his rucksack burst into flames, searing the flesh of his back and his left arm. Barry Murphy threw himself into another crater and radioed frantically for the helicopters to return. Back at base they heard his call, "This is Bullet. We've got four wounded and are taking fire from all directions. We don't . . . Oh god! I'm hit!, hit! I'm hit! My leg! Ow! I'm . . . again! My back ahh can't move!" His last scream was indecipherable.

Eventually one helicopter managed to come back down through the automatic-weapons fire to pick up the survivors. Orthman was saved because a friend jumped out and rushed across the ground to carry him aboard. Three of the Vietnamese made it to the helicopter; Barry Murphy's body was not recovered.

Despite the setback, another reconnaissance team was immediately ordered to take off for Cambodia to gather "dazed" Viet Cong. Their earlier enthusiasm for the mission was now gone and in a rare breach of discipline the Daniel Boone men refused. Three of them were arrested. "You can't be court-martialed for refusing to violate the neutrality of Cambodia," Randolph Harrison reassured them. They were not.

As the night fell over Indochina, day was beginning in Washington. In his basement office in the White House, Henry Kissinger was discussing a point of policy with Morton Halperin, a young political scientist who had worked in the Pentagon during the previous administration and was now Kissinger's assistant for planning.

As the two men were talking, Colonel Alexander Haig came into the room and handed Kissinger a paper. As he read it, Halperin noticed, Kissinger smiled. He turned to Halperin and said that the United States had bombed a base in Cambodia and the first bomb-damage assessment showed that the attack had set off many secondary explosions. What did Halperin think of that? Halperin, who knew nothing of Breakfast, made a noncommittal answer. Kissinger told him that he was placing great trust in him and he must respect the confidence; almost no one else knew about the attack and no one else must know.

In his February 9 cable, Abrams had asked for a single attack to destroy COSVN headquarters. But once the decision had been made in principle that Communist violations of Cambodia's neutrality justified aggressive reciprocal action, it was not difficult to repeat the performance. The first mission had not been discovered by the press, nor had Cambodia protested. Indeed, it would now have been hard for the White House to insist on only one attack: Base Area 353 was, according to Abrams's headquarters, the Military Assistance command, Vietnam (MACV), only one of fifteen Communist sanctuaries.

Over the next fourteen months 3,630 B-52 raids were flown against suspected Communist bases along different areas of Cambodia's border. Breakfast was followed by "Lunch," "Lunch by "Snack," Snack by "Dinner," Dinner by "Dessert," Dessert by "Supper," as the program expanded to cover one "sanctuary" after another. Collectively, the operation was known as "Menu."

In 1973, after the bombing was finally discovered, both Nixon and Kissinger maintained, and still maintain, that the secrecy was necessary to protect Sihanouk, who was variously described as "acquiescing in," "approving," "allowing" or even "encouraging" the raids, so long as they were covert. They maintained that the areas were unpopulated and that only Vietnamese Communist troops, legitimate targets, were there. When he was confirmed as Secretary of State in 1973, for example, Kissinger declared that "It was not a bombing of Cambodia, but it was a bombing of North Vietnamese in Cambodia," and "the Prince as a minimum acquiesced in the bombing of unpopulated border areas." In 1976 he stated that "the government concerned [Sihanouk's] never once protested, and indeed told us that if we bombed unpopulated areas they would not notice." In fact, the evidence of Sihanouk's "acquiescence" is at least questionable, and the assertion that no Cambodians lived in these areas not only was untrue, but was known to be untrue at the time. The Joint Chiefs themselves informed the administration as early as April 1969 that many of the sanctuary areas were populated by Cambodians who might be endangered by bombing raids. The White House was to ignore this reservation.

The Chiefs' description of the bases is contained in a memorandum of April 9, 1969, written for the Secretary of Defense, in which they advocated invasion as well as bombing of Cambodia. Its conclusions were based on "Giant Dragon" high-altitude overflights, "Dorsal Fin" low-level aerial surveys and the Daniel Boone ground forays, among other evidence. It described the military purpose as well as the nature of each of the fifteen bases they had identified, and went on to estimate the number of Cambodians they contained. The figures are worth considering.

Base Area 353, Breakfast, covered 25 square kilometers and had a total population of approximately 1,640 Cambodians, of whom the Joint Chiefs reckoned 1,000 to be peasants. There were, according to the Chiefs, thirteen Cambodian towns in the area. (Villages would be a more accurate description.)

Base Area 609, Lunch, was north, near the Laotian border, in wild country without any towns. The Chiefs asserted that there were an estimated 198 Cambodians there, all of them peasants.

Base Area 351, Snack, covered 101 square kilometers and had an estimated 383 Cambodians, of whom 303 were considered peasants. There was one town in the area.

Base Area 352, Dinner, had an estimated Cambodian population of 770, of whom 700 were peasants. It contained one town.

Base Area 350, Dessert, had an estimated Cambodian population of 120, all peasants.

The Chiefs believed that all these "sanctuaries" should be attacked. They attempted to estimate how many Cambodians would be killed; they maintained that, as the Cambodians lived apart from the Vietnamese troops, their casualties would be "minimal." But they conceded that such calculations depended on many variables and were "tenuous at best." There was no pretense that the raids could occur without danger to the Cambodians—"some Cambodian casualties would be sustained in the operation." And they agreed that "the surprise effect of attacks could tend to increase casualties, as could the probable lack of protective shelters around Cambodian homes to the extent that exists in South Vietnam." Cambodian peasants, unlike the Vietnamese, had little experience of being bombed.

Some scruples, however, were brought to bear. Three of the fifteen sanctuaries—base areas 704, 354 and 707, which had "sizeable concentrations of Cambodian civilian or military population" in or around them—were not recommended for attack at all. (The definition of "sizeable" is not known; presumably it was higher than the 1,640 Cambodians living in the Breakfast site, which they had approved.) The Chiefs' warning seems to have made no difference. Base Area 704 appeared on the White House's Menu as Supper. In the course of events, 247 B-52 missions were flown against it.

Because of Nixon's repeated insistence on total secrecy, few senior officials were told about Menu. The Secretary of the Air Force, Dr. Robert Seamans, was kept in ignorance; since he is not in the chain of command, this was not illegal, but General Wheeler later said that, if necessary, he would have lied to him and denied that the raids were taking place. The Chief of Staff of the Air Force, General John Ryan, was not informed; nor were the Cambodian desk officers on Abrams's intelligence arm in Saigon, the Office of Strategic Research and Analysis. None of the Congressional committees, whose duty it is to recommend appropriations and thus enable the Congress to fulfill its constitutional function of authorizing and funding war, was notified that the President had decided to carry war into a third country, whose neutrality the United States professed to respect. Instead, only a few sympathetic members of Congress, who had no constitutional authority to approve this extension of war, were quietly informed.

But if Congress and the public were easily kept in ignorance, the official record-keeping system required more sophisticated treatment. The Pentagon's computers demanded, for purposes of logistics, a complete record of hours flown, fuel expended, ordnance dropped, spare parts procured. In response to Nixon's demands for total and unassailable secrecy, the military devised an ingenious system that the Joint Chiefs liked to describe as "dual reporting."

Whether they flew from Guam, from Okinawa, or from Thailand, most B-52 missions over South Vietnam were guided to their targets by the "Skyspot" ground radar controllers at one of four radar sites in the country. The controllers received details—known as the "frag"—of the proposed strike after it had been approved in Washington. From the "frag," they calculated the range and bearing of the target from the radar site and the altitude, airspeed and ballistics of the bomb load. They then guided the planes down a narrow radar beam to target.

After missions were completed, B-52 crews reported what primary or secondary explosions they had seen to their debriefing officer at base, and the ground controllers sent their own poststrike reports to Saigon. Both reports entered the Pentagon computers and the official history of the war.

The procedures for Menu were modeled on Operation Breakfast. After a normal briefing on targets in Vietnam, the pilots and navigators of the planes that were to be diverted that night were told privately to expect the ground controllers to direct them to drop their bombs on a set of coordinates that were different from those they had just received. It was not a wide diversion; the South Vietnamese cover targets were usually selected so that the planes could simply fly another few kilometers beyond, until they were over the Cambodian target.

Major Hal Knight of Memphis was, for much of 1969, supervisor of the radar crews for the region of Vietnam that lay between Saigon and the Cambodian border. Every afternoon before a Menu mission, a special Strategic Air Command courier flight came to Bien Hoa airbase, where he worked, and he was handed a plain manila envelope containing an ordinary poststrike report form on which target coordinates had already been filled in. He locked it in his desk until evening and then, when the shift had assembled, gave the coordinates to his radar crew. They fed them through their Olivetti 101 computers to produce the details of the final bombing run for the new Cambodian target. These were called to the navigators when the B-52s arrived on station overhead in the early-morning dark.

After the bombs were released, the plane's radio operator—who was not supposed to know of the diversion—called his base by high-frequency radio to say that the mission had been accomplished. At base, the intelligence division, which also knew nothing of the change, entered the original South Vietnamese coordinates on the poststrike report. When the crews landed and were debriefed they were asked routine questions about malfunction, bomb damage and weather. The pilots and navigators were to make no mention of the new target—they had, after all, been forewarned, so it did not really count as a diversion.

At Bien Hoa itself Knight was under instructions to gather up every scrap of paper and tape with which the bombing had been plotted and lock them in his desk until daybreak. Only then (his superiors were afraid that pieces of paper might be dropped in the dark) was he to take the documents to an incinerator behind the hut and very carefully burn them. He was then to call a Saigon number he had been given—it was at Strategic Air Command Advanced Echelon—in order to tell the unidentified man who answered the telephone that "the ball game is over." The normal poststrike reports from the radar site were filled out with the coordinates of the original South Vietnamese cover target and sent, in the ordinary way, to Saigon by security mail. The night's mission over Cambodia entered the records as having taken place in Vietnam. The bombing was not merely concealed; the official, *secret* records showed that it had never happened.

The system worked well by he book, but it took no account of the attitudes of the men who were expected to implement it. Hal Knight, for example, accepted the military logic of bombing Cambodia but intensely disliked this procedure. Strategic Air Command is responsible for the nation's nuclear defense, and falsification of its reporting process was for him, alarming; Knight had been trained to believe that accurate reporting was "pretty near sacred." He was especially concerned that he was violating Article 107 of the Military Code of Justice, which provides that anyone "who, with intent to deceive, signs any false record, return regulation, order or other official document, knowing the same to be false . . . shall be punished as a court-martial may direct."

Red tape protects as well as restricts, and Knight feared that the institutional safeguards and controls that are integral to the maintenance of discipline and of a loyal, law-abiding army were being discarded. He did not know at what level the bombing had been authorized or whom these unprecedented procedures were supposed to deceive; but he did appreciate, to his dismay, that the practice gave him horrifying license.

A normal target was known to many people at the radar site, to the entire B-52 crew, to the intelligence unit at the plane's base and to dozens of Pentagon officials; a Menu mission was known only to him and a very few others. There was nothing to stop him from choosing the coordinates of a town in South Vietnam or Cambodia and having it bombed. Indeed, "if someone could have punched the right number into the right spot they could have had us bombing China," he observed later.

Knight discussed the falsification with other radar operators on other sites; they too found it hard to explain. If confidentiality were so important, why not simply raise the classification from "Secret" to "Top Secret"? He asked his commanding officer, Lieutenant Colonel David Patterson about it; he was told not to do so.

"So I said, well, what is the purpose of it?"

Patterson replied "Well, the purpose is to hide these raids."

"Who from?" asked Knight.

He was apparently told, "Well, I guess the Foreign Relations Committee."

The Foreign Relations Committee did not find out about the unauthorized and illegal extension of the war into a neutral country until 1973, when Knight himself wrote to Congress to complain. But even under the restrictions imposed, the campaign was, to paraphrase Dean Rusk, known to the President, two members of the NSC, a couple of State Department officials and three hundred colonels in the Pentagon.

One evening soon after the raids began, the pilot of a Forward Air Control plane (FAC), which guided fighter bombers to their targets in South Vietnam, was sitting outside his hootch at An Loc, a few miles from the Cambodian border. "We saw beacons going overhead to the West," said Captain Gerald Greven later. "We saw the flames in the distance and the trembling of the ground from what appeared to be B-52 strikes." He was surprised, because he knew of no targets in that area. The next morning he flew to find the craters, and "to my astonishment they were on the West side of the river separating the borders of South Vietnam and Cambodia."

Greven was impressed by the amount of destruction the raids had caused, but puzzled, "I went back to my commander and he said he had no knowledge of the strike and why it had taken place." He spoke to the regional commander for the Forward Air Controllers— "he also declared to have no knowledge." He then went on to Air Support headquarters at Bien Hoa and spoke to the commanding officer. "I was told, with a slight smile, that obviously my 'maps were in error.' " Greven correctly took that to mean that he "did not have a need to know." He asked no more questions. But eventually he, too, contacted Congress.

William Beecher was the *New York Times* Pentagon correspondent, a diligent reporter. After Nixon's victory in November 1968, Beecher asked his contacts in the Defense Department how they would advise the new President to extricate American troops from Vietnam. He was told that one possible way of "buying time" would be to bomb the sanctuaries. Beecher noted this hypothesis and by April 1969 began to suspect that it was being carried out. The Pentagon was reporting its bombing strikes in South Vietnam near the Cambodian border, but he knew that no targets were there. And, despite the special "security precautions," information began to leak almost at once. On March 26, one week after the Breakfast mission, the *New York Times* reported briefly but accurately that Abrams had requested B-52 strikes against the sanctuaries. Ronald Ziegler, the White House Press Secretary, was quoted as giving a "qualified denial" to the reports. "He said that to his knowledge no request had reached the President's desk." This story was followed by comments—in *U.S. News & World Report* and by columnist C. L. Sulzberger in the *New York Times*—urging that Nixon do what he had in fact already begun. But only Beecher took the trouble to follow the obvious lead that any "qualified denial" offers. He revisited those to whom he had talked at the end of 1968, and on May 9 he revealed in the *Times* that "American B-52 bombers have raided several Viet Cong and North Vietnamese supply dumps and base camps in Cambodia for the first time, according to Nixon Administration sources, but Cambodia has not made any protest."

Beecher wrote that the bombing had started because of the increase in supplies reaching South Vietnam by sea and through Cambodia, supplies that "never have to run any sort of bombing gauntlet before they enter South Vietnam." He claimed that Prince Sihanouk had dropped hints that he would not oppose American pursuit of Communist forces which he was himself unable to dislodge. Perhaps most important, Beecher stated that the bombing was intended "to signal" Hanoi that the Nixon administration, "while pressing for peace in Paris, is willing to take some military risks avoided by the previous Administration . . . to demonstrate that the Nixon Administration is different and 'tougher.' . . ."

The revelation aroused no public interest. Four years later, this same account was to cause at least a short-lived uproar and spark demands for impeachment, but at the time it had little obvious effect. There was no press follow-up, and no members of the Senate Foreign Relations Committee, the Senate Armed Services Committee or the Appropriations committees voiced concern. In Key Biscayne, however, where Nixon and Kissinger and their staffs were working on the first of Nixon's major Vietnam speeches, the article provoked reactions that verged on hysteria.

After reading the story with Nixon, Kissinger spent much of his morning on the telephone with FBI Director J. Edgar Hoover. According to Hoover's detailed memoranda of the conversations, Kissinger asked him, in his first call at 10:35 A.M., to make "a major effort to find out where [the story] came from." A half hour later Kissinger telephoned again to say that while the FBI was about it they should try to find the sources of previous Beecher stories as well. Hoover replied that he would call back the next day with any information they had managed to gather. But within two hours Kissinger was on the line again, this time to ask Hoover to be sure he was discreet "so no stories will get out." Just how the Director liked being told how to protect his beloved FBI is not recorded, but Hoover assured Kissinger that discretion would be maintained; he had decided, he said, not to contact Beecher directly but to try to divine the source of the story from other reporters.

That afternoon, relaxing by the swimming pool with other members of the National Security Council staff, Kissinger invited his aide Morton Halperin to walk with him down the beach. Strolling along the sand, Kissinger told him of the great concern he felt over the Beecher leak. Halperin knew Kissinger well; they had been together at Harvard. He recalls that Kissinger assured him of his personal trust in him but reminded him that there were others in the Nixon administration who were suspicious of Halperin's New York and Harvard background and the fact that he had worked in [Robert] McNamara's Pentagon. It was he who was suspected of leaking to Beecher. Halperin replied that he could not have been the source; after all, it was only by chance (and Kissinger's indiscretion) that he knew anything about the bombing. Kissinger apparently agreed that this was so, but said that he was under great pressure from other members of the administration and the White House.

Kissinger now proposed an ingenious way of justifying his confidence in Halperin to the others. So that he could not possibly be held responsible for any future leaks, Kissinger suggested that he be taken off the distribution list for highly classified material. Then when a leak next occurred, he would be above suspicion and also retroactively cleared.

Halperin did not find the arrangement amusing; he had been dealing with classified materials for years and had never been asked to prove his loyalty. But Kissinger was such an old friend and presented his case with such charm and solicitousness, Halperin recalls, that he agreed to the proposal.

Kissinger and Hoover talked once more that day. At 5:05 P.M. the FBI director telephoned to report his progress. To judge by Hoover's memo, it was a bizarre conversation.

Hoover told Kissinger that Beecher "frequented" the Pentagon press office (hardly a surprising piece of information, in view of the fact that he was a Pentagon correspondent). There were still many pro-Kennedy people in the Pentagon, Hoover remarked, and they all fed Beecher with information. But on this occasion he was convinced that Morton Halperin was the culprit. According to FBI files, Halperin believed the United States had "erred in the Vietnam commitment"; moreover, the Canadian Mounted Police had discovered that he was on the mailing list of a Communist publication, "Problems of Peace and Socialism." Both Halperin and Beecher were members of the "Harvard clique" (as, of course, was Kissinger), and it was clear where the blame must lie. At the end of his memo Hoover noted, in words which resonate down the years, "Dr. Kissinger said he appreciated this very much and he hoped I would follow it up as far as we can take it, and they will destroy whoever did this if we can find him, no matter where he is."

That same afternoon the FBI placed a wiretap on Halperin's home in Bethesda, a bedroom suburb of Washington. This tap was immediately followed by others. In important, specific detail, these taps infringed the limits of the law. They marked the first of the domestic abuses of power now known as Watergate.

Night after night through the summer, fall, and winter of 1969 and into the early months of 1970 the eight-engined planes passed west over South Vietnam and on to Cambodia. Peasants were killed—no one knows how many—and Communist logistics were somewhat disrupted. To avoid the attacks, the North Vietnamese and Viet Cong pushed their sanctuaries and supply bases deeper into the country, and the area that the B-52s bombarded expanded as the year passed. The war spread.

⊰ 28 ⊱

Bombing Cambodia: A Defense

Henry A. Kissinger

THE 1968 UNDERSTANDING WITH THE NORTH Vietnamese that led to the bombing halt included the "expectation" that there would be no attacks on major cities or across the DMZ [Demilitarized Zone]. When we took office, however, enemy infiltration was mounting, which strongly indicated that a new offensive was in the offing.

The only plan we found for such a contingency was for renewal of bombing of the North. On November 24, 1968, Secretary of Defense Clark Clifford had declared on ABC-TV's "Issues and Answers": "If they, at some time, show us that they are not serious and that they are not proceeding with good faith, I have no doubt whatsoever that the President will have to return to our former concept and that is to keep the pressure on the enemy and that would include bombing if necessary." Averell Harriman made the same point in a White House briefing on December 4, 1968. General Earle Wheeler, Chairman of the Joint Chiefs, was only following inherited doctrine when he told Nixon at the NSC [National Security Council] meeting of January 25, 1969, that everything possible was being done in Vietnam "except the bombing of the North."

No one in the new Administration, however, could anticipate a resumption of the bombing of the North with anything but distaste. We were savoring the honeymoon that follows the Inauguration of a new President; Nixon had never previously enjoyed the approval of the media. None of us had the stomach for the domestic outburst we knew renewed bombing would provoke—even if it were the direct result of North Vietnamese betrayal of the understandings that had led to the bombing halt. Above all, we had not yet given up hope, in the first month of the new Presidency, of uniting the nation on an honorable program for settlement of the war.

Unfortunately, alternatives to bombing the North were hard to come by. On January 30, I met in the Pentagon with [Melvin] Laird and Wheeler to explore how we might respond should there be an enemy offensive in South Vietnam. Wheeler reiterated that American forces within South Vietnam were already fully committed; the only effective riposte would be operations in the DMZ or renewed bombing of the North. Laird demurred at the latter suggestion, emphasizing that the bombing halt had encouraged public expectations that the war was being wound down. Nor did I favor it, because I was eager to give negotiations a chance. On February 1, Nixon sent me a note: "I do not like the suggestions that I see in virtually every news report that 'we anticipate a Communist initiative in South Vietnam.' I believe that if any initiative occurs it should be on our part and not theirs." But my request to the Joint Chiefs for suggestions elicited the now familiar response outlining various levels of air or naval attacks on North Vietnamese targets and Mel Laird's (and my) equally standard reluctance to accept the recommendation.

Thought then turned to bombing of the North Vietnamese sanctuary areas in Cambodia, for reasons exactly the opposite of what has been assumed; it was not from a desire to expand the war, but to avoid bombing North Vietnam and yet to blunt an unprovoked offensive which was costing 400 American lives a week.

Revisionists have sometimes focused on the Nixon Administration's alleged assault on the "neutral" status of a "peaceful" country. These charges overlook that the issue concerned territory which was no longer Cambodian in any practical sense. For four years as many as four North Vietnamese divisions had been operating on Cambodian soil from a string of base areas along the South Vietnamese border. In 1978 the Communist victors in Cambodia put the uninvited North Vietnamese presence in northeastern Cambodia in 1969–1970 at 300,000, which far exceeded our estimates. Cambodian officials had been excluded from their soil; they contained next to no Cambodian population.* They were entirely controlled by the North Vietnamese. From these territories North Vietnamese forces would launch attacks into South Vietnam, inflict casualties, disrupt government, and then withdraw to the protection of a formally neutral country. It requires calculated advocacy, not judgment, to argue that the United States was violating the neutrality of a peaceful country when with Cambodian encouragement we, in self-defense, sporadically bombed territories in which for years no Cambodian writ had run, which were either minimally populated or totally unpopulated by civilians, and which were occupied in violation of Cambodian neutrality by an enemy killing hundreds of Americans and South Vietnamese a week from these sanctuaries.

The first suggestion came from General Wheeler. When Laird on January 30 had expressed doubt that a renewed bombing of the North was politically supportable, Wheeler proposed, as an alternative, attacks on the complex of bases that the North Vietnamese had established illegally across the border in Cambodia. On February 9, General [Creighton] Abrams cabled General Wheeler from Saigon that recent intelligence from a deserter, as well as photo reconnaissance, showed that the Communist headquarters for all of South Vietnam was located just across the Cambodian border. (As a novice I was more impressed by such seemingly definitive evidence than I would be later on. As it turned out, the Communist leaders in Phnom Penh eight years later also confirmed that the deserter's information had been accurate on that score.) Abrams requested authority to attack the headquarters from the air with B-52s. Ambassador [Ellsworth] Bunker endorsed the idea in a separate cable through State Department channels.

These recommendations fell on fertile ground. In the transition period on January 8, 1969, the President-elect had sent me a note: "In making your study of Vietnam I want a precise report on what the enemy has in Cambodia and what, if anything, we are doing to destroy the buildup there. I think a very definite change of policy toward Cambodia probably should be one of the first orders of business when we get in." General [Andrew J.] Goodpaster had drafted a reply for my signature with detailed information about the North Vietnamese base areas along the Cambodian border. He reported that "our field command in South Vietnam is convinced that the vast bulk of supplies entering Cambodia come in through Sihanoukville.... What we are doing about this is very limited.... The command in the field has made several requests for authority to enter Cambodia to conduct pre-emptive operations and in pursuit of withdrawing forces that have attacked us. All such requests have been denied or are still pending without action."

The importance of Sihanoukville was one of the contested issues in the NSSM [National Security Study Memorandum] I study. The US military command in Saigon was convinced that between October 1967 and September 1968 some ten thousand tons of arms had come in through Sihanoukville. But CIA and State disputed this. According to them the flow of supplies

---

* The communist deserter who helped pinpoint the location of the North Vietnamese headquarters reported that no Cambodians were permitted in the headquarters area. General [Creighton] Abrams reported this to the President in February along with an assurance that the target was at least a kilometer distant from any known Cambodian hamlets.

down the Ho Chi Minh Trail through Laos was more than adequate to take care of the external requirements of *all* Communist forces in South Vietnam. At stake in this analysts' debate, of course, was whether the Cambodian sanctuaries were so crucial a target that they should be attacked; as happens all too frequently, intelligence estimates followed, rather than inspired, agency policy views. Those who favored attacks on the sanctuaries emphasized the importance of Sihanoukville; those who were opposed depreciated it. (When U.S. and South Vietnamese forces moved into these sanctuaries in April 1970, documents in Communist storage dumps indicated that shipments through Cambodia far exceeded even the military's highest estimates.)

But whatever the dispute about whether the matériel traveled through Sihanoukville or down the Ho Chi Minh Trail, there was no dispute about the menace of the North Vietnamese bases in Cambodia to American and South Vietnamese forces. On February 18, I received a briefing by a two-man team from Saigon, together with Laird, Deputy Secretary [David] Packard, General Wheeler, and Laird's military assistant, Colonel Robert E. Pursley. I reported to the President the conviction of General Abrams that no Cambodian civilians lived in the target area. Nevertheless, I advised against an unprovoked bombing of the sanctuaries. We should give negotiations a chance, I argued, and seek to maintain public support for our policy. We could review the situation again at the end of March—the classic bureaucratic stalling device to ease the pain of those being overruled. Nixon approved that recommendation on February 22, the day before he was to leave on his trip to Europe.

On the very day of Nixon's decision to defer action against the sanctuaries, the North Vietnamese transformed vague contingency planning into a need to deal with a crisis. After weeks of preparation antedating the new Administration, Hanoi launched a countrywide offensive. Americans killed in action during the first week of the offensive numbered 453, 336 in the second week, and 351 in the third; South Vietnamese casualties were far heavier, averaging over 500 a week. It was an act of extraordinary cynicism. No substantive negotiating sessions had been held in Paris with our new delegation, headed by Henry Cabot Lodge; the new Administration could hardly have formed its policy. Whether by accident or design, the offensive began the day before a scheduled Presidential trip overseas, thus both paralyzing our response and humiliating the new President. It occurred despite the fact that Nixon had communicated with the North Vietnamese in the transition period (as we shall see below), emphasizing his commitment to settle the war on the basis of the self-respect and honor of all parties involved. Without even testing these professions of intent, the first major move of Hanoi was to step up the killing of Americans. I noted in a report to the President that the North Vietnamese had been "able to achieve a relatively high casualty rate among US and South Vietnamese forces while not exposing their own main units."

Nixon received a military briefing on the enemy offensive in the Oval Office surrounded by piles of loose-leaf briefing books compiled by my staff and the State Department for each country he was about to visit. (Nixon later came to use the Oval Office mostly for ceremonial occasions; he usually preferred to work in his informal office in the Executive Office Building.) Nixon was going through the books, committing them to memory, grumbling about the effort he had to make to do so. He was also seething. All his instincts were to respond violently to Hanoi's cynical maneuver. For years he had charged his predecessors with weakness in reacting to Communist moves. But he was eager also that his first foreign trip as President be a success. American retaliation might spark riots in Europe; passivity might embolden our adversary. He did not resolve this dilemma immediately. The only White House reaction on the day the offensive started was a phone call by me to Soviet Ambassador [Anatoly] Dobrynin. The President wanted Moscow to understand, I said, that if the North Vietnamese offensive continued we would retaliate.

But the next day, on February 23, while in the air en route from Washington to Brussels, Nixon made up his mind; he suddenly ordered the bombing of the Cambodian sanctuaries. It seemed to me that a decision of this magnitude could not be simply communicated to Washington and to Saigon by cable from *Air Force One* without consulting relevant officials or in the absence of a detailed plan for dealing with the consequences. I therefore recommended to Nixon to postpone the final "execute" order for forty-eight hours and sent a flash message to Colonel Alexander Haig, then my military assistant in Washington, to meet me in Brussels, together with a Pentagon expert. I wanted to go over the military operations once again and to work out a diplomatic plan.

Haig, [H. R.] Haldeman (representing Nixon, who could not attend without attracting attention), the Pentagon planning officer, and I met on board *Air Force One* at Brussels airport on the morning of February 24, just before the president spoke at NATO headquarters. The plane that Nixon used had been built to Johnson's specifications. Directly behind a stateroom for the President was a conference area with an oversized chair fitting into a kidney-shaped table; both the chair and the table were equipped with buttons that enabled them to develop a life of their own. The chair could assume various positions; the table could move hydraulically up and down. If one pressed the wrong button the table would slowly sink, pinning one helplessly in the chair; the situation could turn critical if the chair was rising at the same time. In this awesome setting we worked out guidelines for the bombing of the enemy's sanctuaries: The bombing would be limited to within five miles of the frontier; we would not announce the attacks but acknowledge them if Cambodia protested, and offer to pay compensation for any damage to civilians. In the short time available, we developed both a military and a diplomatic schedule as well as guidance for briefing the press. Haig and the Pentagon expert left immediately for Washington to brief Laird. Nixon later in London gave [William P.] Rogers a cryptic account of his thinking but no details.

Before the day was out, Laird cabled his reservations from Washington. He thought that it would be impossible to keep the bombing secret, the press would be difficult to handle, and public support could not be guaranteed. He urged delay to a moment when the provocation would be clearer. It was symptomatic of the prevalent mood of hesitation, the fear to wake the dormant beast of public protest. In retrospect, it is astonishing to what extent all of us focused on the legal question of whether the understanding had been violated, and not on the four hundred American deaths a week by which Hanoi sought to break our will before we could develop any course of action. Even more astonishing now is that during this entire period no serious consideration was given to resuming the bombing of North Vietnam: the bombing halt, entered to speed a settlement, was turning into an end in itself.

I agreed with Laird's conclusions about the Cambodian bombing, if not with his reasoning. I thought that a failure to react to so cynical a move by Hanoi could doom our hopes for negotiations; it could only be read by Hanoi as a sign of Nixon's helplessness in the face of domestic pressures; it was likely to encourage further military challenges, as North Vietnam undertook to whipsaw Nixon as it had succeeded with Johnson. But the timing bothered me. I did not think it wise to launch a new military operation while the President was traveling in Europe, subject to possible hostile demonstrations and unable to meet with and rally his own government. I also did not relish the prospect of having Vietnam the subject of all our European press briefings or of privately trying to offer explanations to allied governments not always eager to reconcile their private support of our Vietnam efforts with their public stance of dissociation. I said as much to the President. The following day, while we were in Bonn, Nixon canceled the plan.

The so-called mini-Tet exposed the precariousness of our domestic position. The enemy offensive surely must have been planned over many months. It occurred when we were barely four weeks in office and before the enemy could possibly know what we intended—since we did not know ourselves. Yet the *New York Times* on March 9 blamed the new Administration for having provoked Hanoi by presuming to spend a month in studying the options in a war involving an expeditionary force of over 500,000 men: "The sad fact is that the Paris talks have been left on dead center while Ambassador Lodge awaits a White House go-ahead for making new peace proposals or for engaging in private talks out of which the only real progress is likely to come. Everything has been stalled while the Nixon Administration completes its military and diplomatic review." This theme soon was repeated in the Congress.

The President adopted a restrained posture in public while champing at the bit in private. At a news conference on March 4 he declared:

> We have not moved in a precipitate fashion, but the fact that we have shown patience and forbearance should not be considered as a sign of weakness. We will not tolerate a continuation of a violation of an understanding. But more than that, we will not tolerate attacks which result in heavier casualties to our men at a time that we are honestly trying to seek peace at the conference table in Paris. An appropriate response to these attacks will be made if they continue.

On March 4, I passed on to the President without comment a Laird memo recommending against proposals by the Joint Chiefs to attack North Vietnam. Laird was far from a "dove"; in normal circumstances his instincts were rather on the bellicose side. He would have preferred to aim for victory. But he was also a careful student of the public and Congressional mood. He was a finely tuned politician and as such he had learned that those who mount the barricades may well forgo a future in politics; he was not about to make this sacrifice. He therefore navigated with great care between his convictions, which counseled some military reaction, and his political instinct, which called for restraint. He opposed bombing North Vietnam; he became a strong supporter of the attack on the Cambodian sanctuaries. (His only disagreement had to do with public relations policy; he did not think it possible to keep the bombing secret, on practical, not on moral, grounds.) The President, following a similar logic, ordered a strike against the Cambodian sanctuaries for March 9. On March 7, Rogers objected because of prospects for private talks in Paris.

Nixon retracted his order a second time. With each time he marched up the hill and down again, Nixon's resentments and impatience increased. Like Laird he kept saying that he did not want to hit the North, but he wanted to do "something." On March 14, Nixon was asked at a news conference whether his patience was wearing thin. He replied:

> I took no comfort out of the stories that I saw in the papers this morning to the effect that our casualties for the immediate past week went from 400 down to 300. That is still much too high. What our response should be must be measured in terms of the effect on the negotiations in Paris. I will only respond as I did earlier. . . . We have issued a warning. I will not warn again. And if we conclude that the level of casualties is higher than we should tolerate, action will take place.

Next day the North Vietnamese fired five rockets into Saigon—a further escalation and violation of the understanding. There were thirty-two enemy attacks against major South Vietnamese cities in the first two weeks of March. At 3:35 P.M. the day the rockets hit Saigon I received a phone call from the President. He was ordering an immediate B-52 attack on the Cambodian sanctuaries. Capping a month of frustration, the President was emphatic: "State is to be notified only after the point of no return. . . . The order is not appealable." ("Not appealable" was a favorite Nixon phrase, which to those who knew him grew to mean considerable uncertainty; this, of course, tended to accelerate rather than slow down appeals.)

I told the President that such a decision should not be taken without giving his senior advisers an opportunity to express their views—if only to protect himself if it led to a public uproar. No time would be lost. A detailed scenario would have to be worked out in any event, and to prepare instructions would require at least twenty-four hours. A meeting was therefore scheduled for the following day in the Oval Office. I consulted Laird, who strongly supported the President's decision. To prepare for the meeting, I wrote a memo for the President listing the pros and cons. The risks ranged from a pro forma Cambodian protest to a strong Soviet reaction; from serious Cambodian opposition to explicit North Vietnamese retaliation—though it was hard to imagine what escalation Hanoi could undertake beyond what it was already doing. Finally, there was the risk of an upsurge of domestic criticism and new antiwar demonstrations. I recommended that our Paris delegation ask for a private meeting on the day of the bombing so as to emphasize our preference for a negotiated solution. I urged the President to stress to his associates that the proposed bombing was *not* to be a precedent. What my checklist did not foresee (what none of our deliberations foresaw) is what in fact happened: no reaction of any kind—from Hanoi, Phnom Penh, Moscow, or Peking.

The meeting on Sunday afternoon, March 16, in the Oval Office was attended by Rogers, Laird, Wheeler, and myself. It was the first time that Nixon confronted a concrete decision in an international crisis since becoming President; it was also the first time that he would face opposition from associates to a course of action to which he was already committed. He approached it with tactics that were to become vintage Nixon. On the one hand, he had made his decision and was not about to change it; indeed, he had instructed me to advise the Defense Department to that effect twenty-four hours before the meeting. On the other hand, he felt it necessary to pretend that the decision was still open. This led to hours of the very discussion that he found so distasteful and that reinforced his tendency to exclude the recalcitrants from further deliberations.

The Oval Office meeting followed predictable lines. Laird and Wheeler strongly advocated the attacks. Rogers objected not on foreign policy but on domestic grounds. He did not raise the neutral status of Cambodia; it was taken for granted (correctly) that we had the right to counter North Vietnam's blatant violation of Cambodia's neutrality, since Cambodia was unwilling or unable to defend its neutral status. Rogers feared that we would run into a buzz saw in Congress just when things were calming down. There were several hours of discussion during which Nixon permitted himself to be persuaded by Laird and Wheeler to do what he had already ordered. Having previously submitted my thoughts in a memorandum, I did not speak. Rogers finally agreed to a B-52 strike on the base area containing the presumed Communist headquarters. These deliberations are instructive: A month of an unprovoked North Vietnamese offensive, over a thousand American dead, elicited after weeks of anguished discussion exactly *one* American retaliatory raid within three miles of the Cambodian border in an area occupied by the North Vietnamese for over four years. And this would enter the folklore as an example of wanton "illegality."

After the meeting, the Joint Chiefs sought to include additional attacks on North Vietnamese troop concentrations violating the Demilitarized Zone. Laird and I agreed that it was more important to keep Rogers with us and the proposal was not approved.

The B-52 attack took place on March 18 against North Vietnamese Base Area 353, within three miles of the Cambodian border. For this strike the Pentagon dug into its bottomless bag of code names and came up with "Breakfast"—as meaningless as it was tasteless. When an air attack hits an ammunition or fuel depot, there are always secondary explosions that provide nearly conclusive evidence of a successful raid. The initial assessment by the crew of the March 18 Breakfast strike reported "a total of 73 secondary explosions in the target area ranging up to five times the normal intensity of a typical secondary."

Originally the attack on Base Area 353 was conceived as a single raid. Nixon ordered another strike in April 1969 partly because there had been no reaction from either Hanoi or Phnom Penh to the first, partly because the results exceeded our expectations, but above all because of an event far away in North Korea. Nixon had wanted to react to the shooting down of an unarmed American reconnaissance plane by bombing North Korea. (He had severely criticized Johnson for his failure to take forceful measures in response to the capture by North Korea of the electronic ship *Pueblo.*) Nixon had refrained, primarily because of the strong opposition of Rogers and Laird. But as always when suppressing his instinct for a jugular response, Nixon looked for some other place to demonstrate his mettle. There was nothing he feared more than to be thought weak; he had good foreign policy reasons as well for not letting Hanoi believe that he was paralyzed.

In May, Nixon ordered attacks on a string of other Cambodian base areas, all unpopulated and within five miles of the border. The strike on Base Area 350 was given the code name of "Dessert"; Base Area 351 was "Snack," Base Area 740 was "Supper," Base Area 609 was "Lunch," and Base Area 352 was "Dinner." On the theory that anything worth doing is worth overdoing, the whole series was given the code name of "Menu." From April through early August 1969 attacks were intermittent; each was approved specifically by the White House. Afterward, general authority was given; raids were conducted regularly. The map, defining the narrow strip of base areas within a few miles of the border, refutes the charges of "massive bombing of neutral Cambodia" that impelled twelve members of the Hosue Judiciary Committee in 1974 to propose an article of impeachment on the theory that Nixon had concealed from Congress this "presidential conduct more shocking, and more unbelievable than the conduct of any president in any war in all of American history," as Representative Robert Drinan imagined it. Neither Cambodia nor North Vietnam ever claimed that there were Cambodian or civilian casualties. The statistics of tonnage dropped during these raids, so often invoked as an example of Administration barbarity, conveniently omit this salient fact or that it was confined to a strip only a few miles wide along the border. The series continued until May 1970, when strikes began openly in support of U.S. And South Vietnamese ground operations against the North Vietnamese bases.

Periodic reports on the Menu strikes were sent to the President. In November 1969, he wrote on one, "continue them." In December 1969 and February 1970, he asked for an evaluation of their usefulness. Each time, Laird reported that General Abrams and Ambassador Bunker were convinced (as he reported on one occasion) that "Menu has been one of the most telling operations in the entire war." General Abrams credited the Menu operations with disrupting enemy logistics, aborting several enemy offensives, and reducing the enemy threat to the whole Saigon region. Laird endorsed the Joint Chiefs' and General Abrams's view that the Menu strikes "have been effective and can continue to be so with acceptable risks."

The original intention had been to acknowledge the Breakfast strike in response to a Cambodian or North Vietnamese reaction, which we firmly anticipated. For example, the CIA predicted in memoranda of February 20 and March 6 that Hanoi would "certainly" or "almost certainly" seek to derive propaganda advantages from charging an American expansion of the conflict. The Defense Department doubted that the attacks could be kept secret; my own view on that subject was agnostic. In a conversation with Nixon on March 8, I said: "Packard and I both think that if we do it, and if silence about it doesn't help, we have to step up and say what we did." The President agreed. A formal acknowledgment was prepared for the contingency of a Cambodian protest. It offered to pay damages and asked for international inspection.

Our initial reticence was to avoid *forcing* the North Vietnamese, Prince Sihanouk of Cambodia, and the Soviets and Chinese into public reactions they might not be eager to make. A volunteered American statement would have obliged Hanoi to make a public response, perhaps military retaliation or interruption of the peace talks. It would have required Sihanouk to take a public stand, tilting toward Hanoi as he tried to walk a tightrope of neutrality. It could have prompted reactions from the Soviet Union and China in the midst of our serious pursuit of triangular diplomacy.

But Hanoi did *not* protest. In fact, its delegation in Paris accepted Lodge's proposal for private talks on March 22 within seventy-two hours of our request. And Sihanouk not only did not object; he treated the bombing as something that did not concern him since it occurred in areas totally occupied by North Vietnamese troops and affected no Cambodians; hence it was outside his control and even knowledge.

In fact, our relations with Cambodia improved dramatically throughout the period of the bombing. Sihanouk's subtle and skillful balancing act between domestic and foreign pressures had been a cause of wonderment for a decade. An hereditary prince, Norodom Sihanouk had managed to obtain a mass support among the population that appeared to make him unassailable. He had established his country's independence and acquired the aura of indispensability. He had maneuvered to keep his country neutral. After the Laos settlement of 1962, he had concluded that the Communists, whom he hated, would probably prevail in Indochina. He adjusted to that reality by acquiescing in the North Vietnamese establishment of base areas in his country. In 1965 he found a pretext to break diplomatic relations with us. Yet his collaboration with the Communists was reluctant; Hanoi was encouraging the Khmer Rouge (Cambodian Communists), who began guerrilla activity long before there was any American action in Cambodia; Sihanouk sentenced the Communist leaders to death in absentia. For all these reasons I strongly supported a Rogers recommendation to the President in February 1969 that we approach Sihanouk with a view to improving relations.[†] These overtures were eagerly received. Our Embassy in Phom Penh reopened, headed by a chargé d'affaires.

Sihanouk's acquiescence in the bombing should have come as no surprise. As early as January 10, 1968, during the previous Administration, he had told Presidential emissary Chester Bowles:

> We don't want any Vietnamese in Cambodia. . . . We will be very glad if you solve our problem. We are not opposed to hot pursuit in uninhabited areas. You would be liberating us from the Viet Cong. For me only Cambodia counts. I want you to force the Viet Cong to leave Cambodia. In unpopulated areas, where there are not Cambodians,—such precise cases I would shut my eyes.

On May 13, 1969, nearly two months after the bombing had begun, Sihanouk gave a press conference which all but confirmed the bombings, emphatically denied any loss of civilian life, and to all practical purposes invited us to continue:

[†] Interestingly enough, these diplomatic overtures to Cambodia were opposed by the Department of Defense and the Joint Chiefs of Staff, who feared that they might interfere with possibilities of bombing the Cambodian sanctuaries. I received a memorandum from Defense warning against such "diplomatic action which implies a restraint or inhibition in any expansion of current operating authorities designed to protect our forces in South Vietnam." This was signed by Paul Warnke, then still Assistant Secretary of Defense for International Security Affairs.

> I have not protested the bombings of Viet Cong camps because I have not heard of the bombings. I was not in the know, because in certain areas of Cambodia there are no Cambodians. . . .
>
> Cambodia only protests against the destruction of the property and lives of Cambodians. All I can say is that I cannot make a protest as long as I am not informed. But I will protest if there is any destruction of Khmer [Cambodian] life and property.
>
> Here it is—the first report about several B-52 bombings. Yet I have not been informed about that at all, because I have not lost any houses, any countrymen, nothing, nothing. Nobody was caught in those barrages—nobody, no Cambodians. . . .
>
> That is what I want to tell you, gentlemen. If there is a buffalo or any Cambodian killed, I will be informed immediately. But this is an affair between the Americans and the Viet Cong–Viet Minh without any Khmer witnesses. There have been no Khmer witnesses, so how can I protest? But this does not mean—and I emphasize this—that I will permit the violation by either side. Please note that.

On August 22, 1969, Sihanouk said the same to Senator [Mike] Mansfield[‡] (according to the reporting cable):

> there were no Cambodian protests of bombings in his country when these hit only VC's and not Cambodian villages or population. He declared that much of his information regarding U.S. bombings of uninhabited regions of Cambodia came from U.S. press and magazine statements. He strongly requested the avoidance of incidents involving Cambodian lives.

And on July 31, 1969, after four and a half months of bombing of North Vietnamese sanctuaries inside Cambodia, Sihanouk warmly invited President Nixon to visit Cambodia to mark the improvement of U.S.–Cambodian relations. Relations continued to improve until Sihanouk was unexpectedly overthrown.

No one doubted the legality of attacking base areas being used to kill American and friendly forces, from which all Cambodian authority had been expelled and in which, according to Sihanouk himself, not even a Cambodian buffalo had been killed. We saw no sense in announcing what Cambodia encouraged and North Vietnam accepted. The reason for secrecy was to prevent the issue from becoming an international crisis, which would almost certainly have complicated our diplomacy or war effort. The war had been expanded into Cambodia four years earlier by the North Vietnamese, who occupied its territory. The war had been escalated within Vietnam from February 22 on, with North Vietnamese attacks on cities in violation of the 1968 understandings. To bomb base areas from which North Vietnamese soldiers had expelled all Cambodians so that they could more effectively kill Americans—at the rate of four hundred a week—was a minimum defensive reaction fully compatible with international law. It would surely have been supported by the American public. It was kept secret because a public announcement was a gratuitous blow to the Cambodian government, which might have forced it to demand that we stop; it might have encouraged a North Vietnamese retaliation (since how could they fail to react if we had announced we were doing it?). The North Vietnamese kept silent because they were not eager to advertise their illegal presence on Cambodian soil. Our bombing saved American and South Vietnamese lives.

This is why the press leaks that came from American sources struck Nixon and me as so outrageous. Accounts of B-52 or other air strikes against sanctuaries in Cambodia appeared in the *New York Times* (March 26, April 27) and *Washington Post* (April 27); a detailed story by William Beecher appeared in the *New York Times* on May 9; there was another in the *Wall Street*

---

‡ Senator Mansfield did not know of the Menu program and undoubtedly assumed Sihanouk was speaking of accidental bombings.

Journal on May 16; a widely disseminated UPI [United Press International] story appeared in the *Washington Post* on May 18; *Newsweek* reported it on June 2.

The conviction that press leaks of military operations were needlessly jeopardizing American lives, which I shared, caused the President to consult the Attorney General and the Director of the FBI about remedial measures. J. Edgar Hoover recommended wiretaps, which he pointed out had been widely used for these (and other much less justified) purposes by preceding administrations. The Attorney General affirmed their legality. Nixon ordered them carried out, in three categories of cases: officials who had adverse information in their security files; officials who had access to the classified information that had been leaked; and individuals whose names came up as possibilities in the course of the investigation according to the first two criteria. On the basis of these criteria, seventeen wiretaps were established by the FBI on thirteen officials and also four newsmen, lasting in some cases only a few weeks and in other cases several months. (My office was not aware of all of them.) Contrary to malicious lore, senior officials did not spend time pruriently reading over lengthy transcripts of personal conversations. What was received were brief summaries (usually about a page in length) of what the FBI considered discussions of sensitive military or foreign policy matters. The FBI's threshold of suspicion tended to be much lower than the White House's. In May 1971, Nixon cut off the reports sent to my office; thereafter, they went only to Haldeman, who had been receiving them all along. . . .

I wish to record that I went along with what I had no reason to doubt was legal and established practice in these circumstances, pursued, so we were told, with greater energy and fewer safeguards in previous administrations. The motive, which I strongly shared, was to prevent the jeopardizing of American and South Vietnamese lives by individuals (never discovered) who disclosed military information entrusted to them in order to undermine policies decided upon after prayerful consideration and in our view justified both in law and in the national interest. I believe now that the more stringent safeguards applied to national security wiretapping since that time reflect an even more fundamental national interest—but this in no way alters my view of the immorality of those who, in their contempt for their trust, attempted to sabotage national policies and risked American lives.

At the same time, we were wrong, I now believe, not to be more frank with Congressional leaders. To be sure, President Nixon and I gave a full briefing in the Oval Office on June 11, 1969, to Senators John Stennis and Richard Russell, Chairmen of the Sentate Armed Services and Appropriations committees. Senate Minority Leader Everett Dirksen was also informed. In the House, Representatives Mendel Rivers and Leslie Arends, the Chairman and a ranking minority member of the House Armed Services Committee, as well as Minority Leader Gerald Ford, were briefed. Laird briefed key members of the Armed Services and Appropriations committees of both houses. Not one raised the issue that the full Congress should be consulted. This was at that time the accepted practice for briefing the Congress of classified military operations. Standards for Congressional consultation, too, have since changed, and this is undoubtedly for the better.[§]

Nor is it true that the bombing drove the North Vietnamese out of the sanctuaries and thus spread the war deep into Cambodia. To the extent that North Vietnamese forces left the sanctuaries it was to move back into Vietnam, not deeper into Cambodia—until after Sihanouk was

[§] The Pentagon's double-bookkeeping had a motivation much less sinister than that described in revisionist folklore. To preserve the secrecy of the initial (originally intended as the only) raid, Pentagon instructions were kept out of normal channels. The purpose was not to deceive Congress (where key leaders were informed) but to keep the attack from being routinely briefed to the Saigon press. The procedure was continued by rote when bombing became more frequent two months later. When Congressional committees asked for data four years later, new Pentagon officials, unaware of the two reporting channels, unwittingly furnished data from the regular files. This was a bureaucratic blunder, not deliberate design.

unexpectedly overthrown a year later. Then, North Vietnamese forces deliberately started to overrun Cambodian towns and military positions in order to isolate Phnom Penh and topple Sihanouk's successor.** And the widened war caused by that new act of North Vietnamese aggression, while searing and tragic, was not secret. It was fully known by our public, debated in the Congress, and widely reported in the press. Our air operations then were conducted under strict rules of engagement, supervised by our Ambassador in Phnom Penh and aided by aerial photography, designed to avoid areas populated by Cambodian civilians to the maximum extent possible. The "secret" bombing concerned small, largely uninhabited territories totally occupied by the North Vietnamese. The picture of a warlike, bloodthirsty government scheming to deceive is a caricature of the reality of harassed individuals, afraid alike of capitulation on the battlefield and more violent escalation, choosing what they considered a middle course between bombing North Vietnam and meekly accepting the outrage of a dishonorable and bloody offensive. The attacks on the enemy sanctuaries in Cambodia were undertaken reluctantly, as a last resort, as a minimum response, when we were faced with an unprovoked offensive killing four hundred Americans a week. We attacked military bases unpopulated by civilians and at most only five miles from the border. We would have been willing to acknowledge the bombing and defend it had there been a diplomatic protest. There was no protest; Cambodia did not object, nor did the North Vietnamese, nor the Soviets or the Chinese. Proceeding secretly became, therefore, a means of maintaining pressure on the enemy without complicating Cambodia's delicate position, without increasing international tensions in general, and without precipitating the abandonment of all limits.

** Sihanouk in a conversation with me on April 25, 1979, in front of witnesses denied that our bombing had had any effect in pushing the North Vietnamese to move westward. Our bombing "did not impress them," he said jovially.

Chapter 9

Interpreting the War

STUDENTS OF HISTORY EVENTUALLY MUST try to explain why the United States became involved in Vietnam and why it stayed so long in the war; there are no more fundamental and important questions than these. Even as the war raged, policymakers, scholars, and journalists were offering their interpretations of U.S. intervention. Some concluded that the United States had been sucked into Vietnam step by unthinking step: well intentioned but naïve Americans had walked unwittingly into a quagmire. Others, such as Frances FitzGerald in the excerpt reprinted here, assert that American values and assumptions were inappropriate in Vietnam's cultural landscape and necessarily led to tragedy. Gareth Porter argues, to the contrary, that the United States was all but invited to intervene in Vietnam by the preponderance of its own power during the Cold War; the conflict between the parties in Vietnam offered an opportunity to members of the national security bureaucracy (often resisted by the presidents they served) to assert U.S. power in a unipolar world. Radical critics of the war, prominent among them the noted linguist Noam Chomsky, indicted neither culture nor power as such but American ideology. The Vietnam War, they claimed, was the awful but logical result of U.S. imperialism, undertaken by the state and authorized by liberal intellectuals.

Beginning in the late 1970s and early 1980s, a "revisionist" interpretation of the war emerged. Led by the neo-conservative intellectual Norman Podhoretz, the revisionists criticized the opponents of the war and generally defended civilian policymakers and military officials. The war, according to presidential candidate Ronald Reagan in 1980, was "a noble cause." A turn, or perhaps return, to interest in the cultural underpinnings of the war gave rise to interpretations like that of historian Robert Dean, who emphasizes in this selection the need, felt by presidents Kennedy and Johnson, to show toughness and manliness in their Vietnam policies; standing up to the communists was the only possible course for men who might otherwise be judged timid, soft, and effeminate.

Historical interpretation is always difficult, and the passions that continue to surround the Vietnam War make the work of its chroniclers particularly hazardous. The various schools of thought on the U.S. intervention have different approaches to evidence, different disciplinary perspectives, and different ideas about how to weigh the importance of individual policymakers against that of national culture or ideology or the institutions of decision making. It may be frustrating to confront the multiplicity of interpretations of the U.S. involvement in Vietnam, but it is also the highest responsibility of historians.

❮ 29 ❯

A Clash of Cultures

Frances FitzGerald

SOMEWHERE, BURIED IN THE FILES of the television networks, lies a series of pictures, ranging over a decade, that chronicles the diplomatic history of the United States and the Republic of Vietnam. Somewhere there is a picture of President Eisenhower with Ngo Dinh Diem, a picture of Secretary McNamara with General Nguyen Khanh, one of President Johnson with Nguyen Cao Ky, and another of President Nixon with President Thieu. The pictures are unexceptional. The obligatory photographs taken on such ceremonial occasions, they show men in gray business suits (one is in military fatigues) shaking hands or standing side-by-side on a podium. These pictures, along with the news commentaries, "President Nixon today reaffirmed his support for the Thieu regime," or "Hanoi refused to consider the American proposal," made up much of what Americans knew about the relationship between the two countries. But the pictures and news reports were to a great extent deceptions, for they did not show the disproportion between the two powers. One of the gray-suited figures, after all, represented the greatest power in the history of the world, a nation that could, if its rulers so desired, blow up the world, feed the earth's population, or explore the galaxy. The second figure in the pictures represented a small number of people in a country of peasants largely sustained by a technology centuries old. The meeting between the two was the meeting of two different dimensions, two different epochs of history. An imagined picture of a tributary chieftain coming to the Chinese court represents the relationship of the United States to the Republic of Vietnam better than the photographs from life. It represents what the physical and mental architecture of the twentieth century so often obscures.

At the beginning of their terms in offfice President Kennedy and President Johnson, perhaps, took full cognizance of the disproportion between the two countries, for they claimed, at least in the beginning, that the Vietnam War would require only patience from the United States. According to U.S. military intelligence, the enemy in the south consisted of little more than bands of guerrillas with hardly a truck in which to carry their borrowed weapons. The North Vietnamese possessed antiaircraft guns and a steady supply of small munitions, but the United States could, so the officials promised, end their resistance with a few months of intensive bombing. In 1963 and 1965 few Americans imagined that a commitment to war in Vietnam would finally cost the United States billions of dollars, the production of its finest research and development laboratories, and fifty-five thousand American lives. They did not imagine that the Vietnam War would prove more politically divisive than any foreign war in the nation's history.

In one sense Presidents Kennedy and Johnson had seen the disproportion between the United States and Vietnam, but in another they did not see it at all. By intervening in the Vietnamese struggle the United States was attempting to fit its global strategies into a world of hillocks and hamlets, to reduce its majestic concerns for the containment of Communism and the security of the Free World to a dimension where governments rose and fell as a result of arguments between two colonels' wives. In going to Vietnam the United States was entering a country where the victory of one of the great world ideologies occasionally depended on the price of tea in a certain village or the outcome of a football game. For the Americans in Vietnam it would be difficult to make this leap of perspective, difficult to understand that while they saw themselves as building world order, many Vietnamese saw them merely as the producers of garbage from which they could build houses. The effort of translation was too great.

The televised pictures of the two chiefs of state were deceptive in quite another way: only one of the two nations saw them. Because of communications, the war was absurd for the civilians of both countries—but absurd in different ways. To one people the war would appear each day, compressed between advertisements and confined to a small space in the living room; the explosion of bombs and the cries of the wounded would become the background accompaniment to dinner. For the other people the war would come one day out of a clear blue sky. In a few minutes it would be over: the bombs, released by an invisible pilot with incomprehensible intentions, would leave only the debris and the dead behind. Which people was the best equipped to fight the war?

The disparity between the two countries only began with the matter of scale. They seemed, of course, to have come from the same country, those two figures in their identical business suits with their identical pronouncements: "The South Vietnamese people will never surrender to Communist tyranny," "We are fighting for the great cause of freedom," "We dedicate ourselves to the abolition of poverty, ignorance, and disease and to the work of the social revolution." In this case the deception served the purposes of state. The Chinese emperor could never have claimed that in backing one nomad chieftain against another he was defending the representative of Chinese civilization. But the American officials in supporting the Saigon government insisted that they were defending "freedom and democracy" in Asia. They left the GIs to discover that the Vietnamese did not fit into their experience of either "Communists" or "democrats."

Under different circumstances this invincible ignorance might not have affected the outcome of the war. The fiction that the United States was defending "freedom and democracy" might have continued to exist in a sphere undisturbed by reality, a sphere frequented only by those who needed moral justification for the pursuit of what the U.S. government saw as its strategic interests. Certain "tough-minded" analysts and officials in any case ignored the moral argument. As far as they were concerned, the United States was not interested in the form of the Vietnamese government—indeed, it was not interested in the Vietnamese at all. Its concerns were for "containing the expansion of the Communist bloc" and preventing future "wars of national liberation" around the world. But by denying the moral argument in favor of power politics and "rational" calculations of United States interests, these analysts were, as it happened, overlooking the very heart of the matter, the issue on which success depended.

The United States came to Vietnam at a critical juncture of Vietnamese history—a period of metamorphosis more profound than any the Vietnamese had ever experienced. In 1954 the Vietnamese were gaining their independence after seventy years of French colonial rule. They were engaged in a struggle to create a nation and to adapt a largely traditional society to the modern world. By backing one contender—by actually creating that contender—the United States was not just fighting a border war or intervening, as Imperial China so often did, in a power struggle between two similar contenders, two dynasties. It was entering into a moral and ideological struggle over the form of the state and the goals of the society. Its success with its chosen contender would depend not merely on U.S. military power but on the resources of both the United States and the Saigon government to solve Vietnamese domestic problems in a manner acceptable to the Vietnamese. But what indeed were Vietnamese problems, and did they even exist in the terms in which Americans conceived them? The unknowns made the whole enterprise, from the most rational and tough-minded point of view, risky in the extreme.

In going into Vietnam the United States was not only transposing itself into a different epoch of history; it was entering a world qualitatively different from its own. Culturally as geographically Vietnam lies half a world away from the United States. Many Americans in Vietnam learned to speak Vietnamese, but the language gave no more than a hint of the basic intellectual grammar that lay beneath. In a sense there was no more correspondence between the two worlds than that between the atmosphere of the earth and that of the sea. There was no direct translation between them in the simple equations of X is y and a means b. To find the common ground that existed between them, both Americans and Vietnamese would have to re-create the whole world of the other, the whole intellectual landscape. The effort of comprehension would be only the first step, for it would reveal the deeper issues of the encounter. It would force both nations to consider again the question of morality, to consider which of their values belong only to themselves or only to a certain stage of development. It would, perhaps, allow them to see that the process of change in the life of a society is a delicate and mysterious affair, and that the introduction of the foreign and the new can have vast and unpredictable consequences. It might in the end force both peoples to look back upon their own society, for it is contrast that is the essence of vision.

The American intellectual landscape is, of course, largely an inheritance from Europe, that of the Vietnamese a legacy from China, but in their own independent development the two nations have in many respects moved even further apart from each other. As late as the end of the nineteenth century Americans had before them a seemingly unlimited physical space—a view of mountains, deserts, and prairies into which a man might move (or imagine moving) to escape the old society and create a new world for himself. The impulse to escape, the drive to conquest and expansion, was never contradicted in America as it was in Europe by physical boundaries or by the persistence of strong traditions. The nation itself seemed to be less of a vessel than a movement. The closing of the frontier did not mean the end to expansion, but rather the beginning of it in a new form. The development of industry permitted the creation of new resources, new markets, new power over the world that had brought it into being. Americans ignore history, for to them everything has always seemed new under the sun. The national myth is that of creativity and progress, of a steady climbing upward into power and prosperity, both for the individual and for the country as a whole. Americans see history as a straight line and themselves standing at the cutting edge of it as representatives for all mankind. They believe in the future as if it were a religion; they believe that there is nothing they cannot accomplish, that solutions wait somewhere for all problems, like brides. Different though they were, both John Kennedy and Lyndon Johnson accepted and participated in this national myth. In part perhaps by virtue of their own success, they were optimists who looked upon their country as willing and able to right its own wrongs and to succor the rest of the world. They believed in the power of science, the power of the will, and the virtues of competition. Many Americans now question their confidence; still, the optimism of the nation is so great that even the question appears as a novelty and a challenge.

In their sense of time and space, the Vietnamese and the Americans stand in the relationship of a reversed mirror image, for the very notion of competition, invention, and change is an extremely new one for most Vietnamese. Until the French conquest of Vietnam in the nineteenth century, the Vietnamese practiced the same general technology for a thousand years. Their method of rice culture was far superior to any other in Southeast Asia; still it confined them to the river-fed lowlands between the Annamite cordillera and the sea. Hemmed in by China to the north and the Hindu kingdom of Champa to the south, the Vietnamese lived for the bulk of their history within the closed circle of the Red River Delta. They conquered Champa and moved south down the narrow littoral, but by American or Chinese standards they might have been standing still, for it took them five centuries to conquer a strip of land the length of Florida. The Vietnamese pride themselves less on their conquests than on their ability to resist and to survive. Living under the great wing of China, they bought their independence and maintained it only at a high price of blood. Throughout their history they have had to acknowledge the preponderance of the great Middle Kingdom both as the power and as the hub of culture. The Vietnamese knew their place in the world and guarded it jealously.

For traditional Vietnamese the sense of limitation and enclosure was as much a part of individual life as of the life of the nation. In what is today northern and central Vietnam the single form of Vietnamese settlement duplicated the closed circle of the nation. Hidden from sight behind their high hedges of bamboos, the villages stood like nuclei within their surrounding circle of rice fields. Within the villages as within the nation the amount of arable land was absolutely inelastic. The population of the village remained stable, and so to accumulate wealth meant to deprive the rest of the community of land, to fatten while one's neighbor starved. Vietnam is no longer a closed economic system, but the idea remains with the Vietnamese that great wealth is antisocial, not a sign of success but a sign of selfishness.

With a stable technology and a limited amount of land the traditional Vietnamese lived by constant repetition, by the sowing and reaping of rice and by the perpetuation of customary law. The Vietnamese worshiped their ancestors as the source of their lives, their fortunes, and their civilization. In the rites of ancestor worship the child imitated the gestures of his grandfather so that when he became the grandfather, he could repeat them exactly to his grandchildren. In this passage of time that had no history the death of a man marked no final end. Buried in the rice fields that sustained his family, the father would live on in the bodies of his children and grandchildren. As time wrapped around itself, the generations to come would regard him as the source of their present lives and the arbiter of their fate. In this continuum of the family "private property" did not really exist, for the father was less of an owner than a trustee of the land to be passed on to his children. To the Vietnamese the land itself was the sacred, constant element: the people flowed over the land like water, maintaining and fructifying it for the generations to come.

Late in the war—about 1968—a Vietnamese soldier came with his unit to evacuate the people of a starving village in Quang Nam province so that the area might be turned into a "free fire zone." While the villagers were boarding the great American helicopters, one old man ran away from the soldiers shouting that he would never leave his home. The soldiers followed the old man and found him hiding in a tunnel beside a small garden planted with a few pitiful stunted shrubs. When they tried to persuade him to go with the others, he refused, saying, "I have to stay behind to look after this piece of garden. Of all the property handed down to me by my ancestors, only this garden now remains. I have to guard it for my grandson." Seeing the soldiers look askance, the old man admitted that his grandson had been conscripted and that he had not heard from him in two years. He paused, searching for an explanation, and then said, "If I leave, the graves of my ancestors, too, will become forest. How can I have the heart to leave?"

The soldiers turned away from the old man and departed, for they understood that for him to leave the land would be to acknowledge the final death of the family—a death without immortality. By deciding to stay he was deciding to sacrifice his life in postponement of that end. When the soldiers returned to the village fourteen months later, they found that an artillery shell had closed the entrance to the tunnel, making it a grave for the old man.[1]

Many American officials understood that the land and the graves of the ancestors were important to the Vietnamese. Had they understood exactly why, they might not have looked upon the wholesale creation of refugees as a "rational" method of defeating Communism. For the traditional villager, who spent his life immobile, bound to the rice land of his ancestors, the world was a very small place. It was in fact the village or *xa*, a word that in its original Chinese roots signified "the place where people come together to worship the spirits." In this definition of society the character "earth" took precedence, for, as the source of life, the earth was the basis for the social contract between the members of the family and the members of the village. Americans live in a society of replaceable parts—in theory anyone can become President or sanitary inspector—but the Vietnamese lived in a society of particular people, all of whom knew each other by their place in the landscape. "Citizenship" in a Vietnamese village was personal and untransferable In the past, few Vietnamese ever left their village in times of peace, for to do so was to leave society itself— all human attachments, all absolute rights and duties. When the soldiers of the nineteenth-century Vietnamese emperors came to the court of Hué, they prayed to the spirits of the Perfume River, "We are lost here *[dépaysés]* and everything is unknown to us. We prostrate ourselves before you [in the hope that] you will lead us to the good and drive the evil away from us."[2] The soldiers were "lost" in more than a geographical sense, for without their land and their place in the village, they were without a social identity. To drive the twentieth-century villager off his land was in the same way to drive him off the edges of his old life and to expose him directly to the political movement that could best provide him with a new identity.

During the war the village *dinh* or shrine still stood in many of the villages of the south as testimony to the endurance of the traditional political design of the nation. In prehistoric times, before the advent of national government, the *dinhs* referred to the god of the particular earth beneath the village. In assuming temporal power, the emperors of Vietnam took on the responsibility to perform the rites of the agriculture for all the Vietnamese villages and replaced the local spirits with the spirits of national heroes and genii. Under their reign the *dinh* contained the imperial charter that incorporated the village into the empire, making an ellision between the ideas of "land," "Emperor," and "Vietnamese." The French brushed away the sacred web of state, but they did not destroy this confluence of ideas. The Vietnamese call their nation *da nuoc*, "earth and water"—the phrase referring to both the trickle of water through one rice field and the "mountains and rivers" of the nation.

Like the Celestial Empire of China, the Vietnamese empire was in one aspect a ritual state whose function was to preside over the sacred order of nature and society. At its apex the emperor stood as its supreme magician-god endowed with the responsibility to maintain the harmonious balance of the *yin* and the *yang*, the two related forces of the universe. His success in this enterprise (like that of the villagers in the rites of ancestor worship) depended upon the precision with which he followed the elaborate set of rituals governing his relations with the celestial authorities and the people of the empire. To act in conformity with the traditional etiquette was to insure harmony and prosperity for the entire nation. In A.D. 1129 the Emperor Ly Than Tong proclaimed to the court: "We have little virtue; we have transgressed the order of Heaven, and upset the natural course of events; last year the spring was blighted by a long rain; this year there is a long drought. . . . Let the mandarins examine my past acts in order to discover any errors or faults, so that they may be remedied."[3] In analyzing these disasters the emperor blamed them on his deviation from Tao, the traditional way, which was at once the most moral and the most scientific course.

As Americans are, so to speak, canted towards the future, the traditional Vietnamese were directed towards the past, both by the small tradition of the family and the great tradition of the state. Confucianism—the very foundation of the state—was not merely a "traditional religion," as Judaism and Christianity are the traditional religions of the West. Originating in a society of ancestor worshipers, it was, like ancestor worship itself, a sacralization of the past. Unlike the great Semitic prophets, Confucius did not base his teachings on a single, contemporary revelation. "I for my part am not one of those who have innate knowledge," he said. "I am simply one who loves the past and is diligent in investigating it."[4] According to tradition, Confucius came to his wisdom through research into the great periods of Chinese civilization—the Chou empire and its predecessors in the distant past. Tradition presents the Master not as a revolutionary but as a true reactionary. Arriving at certain rules and precepts for the proper conduct of life, he did not pretend to have comprehended all wisdom, but merely to have set up guideposts pointing towards the Tao or true way of life. For him the Tao was the enlightened process of induction that led endlessly backwards into the past of civilization. The Tao may have been for him a secular concern, a matter of enlightened self-interest. ("The Master never spoke of the spirits," reported his disciples, leaving the question moot.) But for later Confucians it had a sacred weight reinforced by magic and the supernatural.

For traditional Vietnamese, formal education consisted of the study of the Confucian texts—the works of the Master and the later commentaries. To pass beyond the small tradition of the family and the village was therefore not to escape the dominion of the past, but to enter into it more fully. The mandarins, the literate elite, directed all their scholarship not towards invention and progress, but towards a more perfect repetition of the past, a more perfect maintenance of the status quo. When a French steamship was sighted off the shores of Vietnam in the early nineteenth century (or so the story goes) the local mandarin-governor, instead of going to see it, researched the phenomenon in his texts, concluded it was a dragon, and dismissed the matter.[5]

As long as Vietnamese society remained a closed system, its intellectual foundations remained flawless and immobile. Quite clearly, however, they could not survive contact with the West, for they were based on the premise that there was nothing new under the sun. But the coming of the French posed a terrible problem for the Vietnamese. Under the dominion of the old empire the Vietnamese were not members of a religious community (like the Christians of Byzantium or the Muslims of the Abbasid caliphate) but participants in a whole, indivisible culture. Like the Chinese, they considered those who lived outside of its seamless web to be by definition barbarians. When the Vietnamese conquered peoples of other cultures—such as the Chams—they included these people within the structure of empire only on condition of their total assimilation. The peoples they could not assimilate, they simply surrounded, amoeba-like, and left them to follow their own laws. The various montagnard tribes that lived beyond the zone of wet-rice cultivation retained their own languages, customs, and governments for thousands of years inside Vietnam. But with the arrival of the French forces in the nineteenth century the Vietnamese confronted a civilization more powerful than their own; for the first time since the Chinese conquest in the second century B.C. they faced the possibility of having to assimilate themselves. Confucianism was, after all, not merely a religion or an arbitrary morality, but a science that operated inside history. Confucius said, "If it is really possible to govern countries by ritual and yielding, there is no more to be said. But if it is not really possible, of what use is ritual?"[6] The rituals and the way of life they confirmed did not help the Vietnamese defend themselves against the French, and thus certain mandarins concluded they had to be abandoned. As the French armies swept across the Mekong Delta, Phan Thanh Giang, the governor of the western provinces, reconciled this logic with his loyalty to the nation by committing suicide and ordering his sons not to serve the French but to bring up their children in the French way.[7]

Similarly, those mandarins who decided to resist the French saw the foreign armies as a threat not only to their national sovereignty and to their beliefs, but to their entire way of life. The southern patriots warned their people:

> Our country has always been known as a land of deities; shall we now permit a horde of dogs and goats to stain it?
>
> The moral obligations binding a king to his subjects, parents to their children, and husbands to their wives were highly respected. Everyone enjoyed the most peaceful relationships.
>
> Our customs and habits were so perfect that in our country, in our ancestors' tombs, and in our homes, all things were in a proper state.
>
> But from the moment they arrived with their ill luck, happiness and peace seem to have departed from everywhere.[8]

And the mandarins were correct: the French occupation changed the Vietnamese way of life permanently. Since the Second World War the Vietnamese have been waging a struggle not merely over the form of their state but over the nature of Vietnamese society, the very identity of the Vietnamese. It is the grandeur of the stakes involved that has made the struggle at once so intense and so opaque to Westerners.

Just before the fall of the Diem regime in 1963 the American journalists in Vietnam wrote long and somewhat puzzling analyses of the Buddhist demonstrations, in which they attempted to explain how much the rebellion against Diem owed to "purely religious" motives, how much to "purely political" ones. Like most Westerners, these journalists were so entrenched in their Western notion of the division of church and state that they could not imagine the Vietnamese might not make the distinction. But until the arrival of the European missionaries there was never such a thing as a church in Vietnam. Shaped by a millennium of Chinese rule and another of independence within the framework of Southeast Asia, the "Vietnamese religion" was a blend of Confucianism, Taoism, and Buddhism sunken into a background of animism. More than a "religion" in any Western sense, it was the authority for, and the confirmation of, an entire way of life—an agriculture, a social structure, a political system. Its supernatural resembled one of those strange metaphysical puzzles of Jorge Luis Borges: an entire community imagines another one which, though magical and otherworldly, looks, detail for detail, like itself. In the courts of Hué and Thanglong, organization-minded genii presided over every government department and took responsibility for the success or failure of each mandarin's enterprise. (During a long period of drought in the seventeenth century the Emperor Le Thai Ton ordered his mandarins: "Warn the genii on my behalf that if it doesn't rain in three days, I will have their tablets boiled and thrown in the river so as to prevent my people from uselessly throwing away their money on them.")[9] In the villages the peasants recognized hosts of local spirits and ghosts as well as the official genii delegated by the mandarins. In Paul Mus's words, religion was the "spiritualization of the community itself" and "the administration of Heaven." The "religion," in some sense, was the state and vice versa— except that the emperor was not the representative of God on earth, but rather a collective moral personality, a representation of the sacred community to itself.

For the Vietnamese today as in centuries past, each regime—each state or political movement—has its own "virtue," its own character, which, like that of a human being, combines moral, social, and political qualities in a single form. Whether secular parties or religious sects, all modern Vietnamese political movements embrace a total design for the moral life of the individual and the social order of the nation. With Ngo Dinh Diem, for instance, this spherical Confucian universe showed up continually through the flat surfaces of Western language. He spoke of himself as the chosen of Heaven, the leader elected to defend Vietnamese morality and culture. The

Buddhist leaders had much the same pretensions, and even for the Vietnamese Communists, the heirs to nineteenth-century Western distinctions between church and state, between one class and another, the society retains its moral impulse, its balanced Confucian design.

Never having known a serious ideological struggle in their history, many Americans persisted in thinking of the Vietnamese conflict as a civil war, as a battle between two fixed groups of people with different but conceivably negotiable interests. But the regional conflict existed only within the context of a larger struggle that resembled a series of massive campaigns of conversion involving all the people in the country and the whole structure of society. Owing to the nature of the old society, the struggle was even more all-encompassing than the European revolutionary wars. Americans, and indeed most Westerners, have lived for centuries with a great variety of institutions—with churches, with governments, with a patriarchal family, with industrial concerns, trade unions and fraternities, each of which offered a different kind of organization, different kinds of loyalties—but the Vietnamese have lived with only three: the family, the village, and the state."[10] As the family provided the model for village and state, there was only one type of organization. Taken together, the three formed a crystalline world, geometrically congruent at every level. The mandarins, for instance, were known as the "fathers of the people," and they stood in the same relationship to the emperor (himself the "son of Heaven") as the Vietnamese son stood to his father. Recruited by competitive examination, they moved closer to the emperor, that is, higher in the great imperial family, as they passed through the grades of the examination system. The village was a more informal organization—a Vietnamese deviation from the orthodox Chinese model—but it reflected a similar hierarchical design. The "government" of the family, the village, and the empire derived from one single set of instructions. Thus a change in one implied a change in all the others.[11]

To American officials throughout the war it seemed absolutely unreasonable that the non-Communist sects and political factions could not come to some agreement, could not cooperate even in their opposition to the Communists. But then the Americans had been brought up in a pluralistic world, where even the affairs of the family are managed by compromise between its members. In the traditional Vietnamese family— a family whose customs survived even into the twentieth century—the father held absolute authority over his wife (or wives) and children. The Vietnamese woman by custom wielded a great deal more power than her Chinese sister, but the traditional Chinese-based law specified that the patriarch governed his wife and children as he governed his rice fields. In theory, though not by customary practice, he could dispose of them as he wished, and they had no recourse against him.[12] The emperor held a similar power over the great family of the empire. By law the trustee of all the rice lands,[13] he held them for the villages on condition of their productivity and good behavior. Without a priesthood or independent feudal aristocracy to obstruct the unified field of his power, he exercised authority through a bureaucracy of mandarins totally dependent on him. Though Vietnam was often divided between warlord families, the disputes were never resolved by a sharing of power—by treaties such as the dukes of Burgundy made with the kings of France—but always by the restoration of an absolute monarch. Even after Vietnam had been divided for two centuries between the Trinh dynasty in the north and the Nguyen in the south, the Vietnamese would not acknowledge the legitimacy of both sovereigns. To do so would have been to assert that the entire moral and social fabric of the community had dissolved. As a family can have only one father, so the nation could have only one emperor to preside over its one Tao or way of life.

> Good conduct, then contentment; thus calm prevails. Hence there follows the hexagram of PEACE. Peace means union and interrelation.

In the *I Ching*, the ancient Chinese Book of Changes, lie all the clues to the basic design of the Sino-Vietnamese world. As the commentary to the verse explains, the Chinese character translated as "peace" implies not only the absence of conflict, but a positive union conducive to prosperity and contentment. To the Vietnamese of the twentieth century "peace" meant not a compromise between various interest groups and organizations, but the restoration of a single, uniform way of life. The Vietnamese were not interested in pluralism, they were interested in unanimity.

Since the Second World War one of the main reasons for the hostility of American intellectuals to Communism has been the suppression of intellectual freedom by Communist leaders in the Soviet Union and the Eastern European countries. In an attempt to rally Americans to the Vietnam War U.S. officials and their sympathizers took pains to argue that the Vietnamese Communists came from the same totalitarian mold. The difficulty with their argument was, however, that the non-Communist Vietnamese leaders believed in intellectual freedom no more than the Communists—a fact that would seem to indicate that their attitudes were founded not in ideology but in culture.

Intellectual freedom, of course, implies intellectual diversity. Westerners tend to take that diversity for granted, for the Western child, even of the narrowest background, grows up with a wide variety of authorities—parents, teachers, clergy, professional men, artists, scientists, and a host of other experts. The traditional Vietnamese child, however, grew up into a monolithic world composed of the family and its extensions in the state. For him there was no alternative to the authority of the father and no question of specialized knowledge. The education of a mandarin was greater, but hardly more diverse, than that of the rice farmer, for the Confucian tradition provided a personal philosophy, a religion, a technology, and a method of managing the state. For the mandarin there was no such thing as "pure science" or "knowledge for its own sake." There was (somewhere) a single correct answer to every question; the mandarin therefore studied in order to learn how to act.

The Vietnamese have lived with diversity for over a century, but the majority—including many of those brought up with French education—still perceive the intellectual world as uniform and absolute. While teaching at the Saigon university in 1957 one young American professor discovered at the second session of his course on comparative government that several students had memorized large sections of their first reading assignment. Pleased but somewhat bewildered, he asked them to finish their work on Machiavelli and turn to Montesquieu. The next day after class the students came to him in open rebellion. "What do you mean?" they asked angrily. "What do you mean by teaching us one thing one day and one thing the next?" The students could not conceive that government could be a matter of opinion. Either a government had worked or it had not, and if it had not worked, then it was not a proper subject for study. Ho Chi Minh said in answer to the question "What is the aim of study?": "One must study in order to remould one's thinking . . . to foster one's revolutionary virtues. . . . Study is aimed at action: the two must go hand in hand. The former without the latter is useless. The latter without the former is hard to carry through."[14]

In trying to teach comparative government, the American professor had, of course, assumed that his Vietnamese students possessed certain analytical tools: a conceptual framework, for instance, that allowed them to abstract the idea "government" from all the various instances of government that have existed in the world. In his course he would often be working from the general to the particular by a process of deductive logic. (A republic has certain characteristics, this state has the same characteristics, therefore it must be a republic.) What he did not realize was that his logic was hardly more universal than the forms of government he was discussing, and that most Vietnamese have an entirely different organization of mind.

The Chinese system of orthography, used by the Vietnamese until the mid-nineteenth century,[15] was not, like the Roman alphabet, composed of regular, repeatable symbols. It was built of particulars. The ideograms for such abstract notions as "fear" or "pleasure" were composed of pictures of concrete events (the pictures of a man, a house, and so on) and to the highly literate these events were always visible within the larger word. The writing was therefore without abstraction, for each word has its own atmosphere, impossible to translate into Western languages and irreducible to categories. Each word was a thing-in-itself.[16] Traditional Vietnamese education accorded with its medium. The child did not learn "principles" from his parents, he learned how to imitate his father in his every action. Confucius said, "When your father is alive, discover his project and when he is dead, remember his actions. If in three years you have not left the road followed by your father, you are really a son full of filial piety."[17] In his formal education the child encountered not a series of "disciplines" but a vast, unsystematized collection of stories and precepts. In the Confucian texts instructions on how to dress and write poetry were juxtaposed with injunctions to such virtues as patience and humility. Each precept, independently arrived at by a process of induction (the Confucian researches into the past), had its own absolute importance for the proper conduct of life. Phrased, perhaps, as a moral absolute, the precept still depended for authority on the success it was thought to have conferred in the past. Confucian logic was, in a sense, pure pragmatism applied over a vast distance in time. In reading the Confucian precepts the child arrived not at a theory of behavior but at a series of clues to the one true way of life.

At the end of his scholarly book, *Viet Cong*, Douglas Pike, an American official and the leading government analyst of the National Liberation Front, breaks out of his neutral tone to conclude: "The NLF and the people it influenced lived in a muzzy, myth-filled world of blacks and whites, good and evil, a simplistic world quite out of character with the one to which the Vietnamese was accustomed. . . . Here, one felt, was tomorrow's society, the beginning of 1984, where peace is war, slavery is freedom, the nonorganization is the organization."[18] American officials might, perhaps, legitimately criticize the National Liberation Front, but they have had, as in this instance, a curious tendency to criticize what is most typically and essentially Vietnamese. A world where there is no clear air of abstraction, no "principles" and no "theories," cannot but seem "muzzy" and "myth-filled" to Westerners. The Vietnamese Communist leaders differ from the non-Communists only in that they have successfully assimilated the Western conceptual framework and translated it into a form of intellectual organization that their less educated compatriots can understand. Like Mao's *Thoughts*, the NLF's "Three Silences" and "Six Duties of a Party Member" correspond exactly to the Confucian precepts. Taken together, they do not form an "ideology" in the Western sense, but the elements of a Tao, or, as the Vietnamese now call it, a "style of work," a "style of life." As for the NLF being "tomorrow's society, the beginning of 1984, where peace is war, slavery is freedom," it is not perhaps so different from the United States government—at least on the subject of Vietnam. In 1970, for instance, President Nixon called the American invasion of Cambodia a "step towards peace" and his firm stand behind President Thieu a firm stand "for the right of all the South Vietnamese people to determine for themselves the kind of government they want."[19] The difference between the two is simply that Americans have traditionally distinguished between objective truth and political persuasion, description and project, whereas the Vietnamese have not—at least not in the same manner.

Westerners naturally look upon it as sinister that the children of North Vietnam and the NLF zones of the South learn to read and do arithmetic from political material. But "politics," or "government" in the widest sense of the word, was also the basis for the traditional education. Confucianism was, first and foremost, a philosophy of social organization. The Confucian texts, for instance, provided the foundation for the imperial law. (Is not the law . . . true virtue? asked one of the nineteenth-century intellectuals. "In the law we can . . . find complete expositions of the three duties [of a prince, a father, and a husband] and of the five constant virtues [benevolence, righteousness, propriety, knowledge, and sincerity] as well as the tasks of the six ministries [of the central government].")[20] As one historian has pointed out, the texts established a social contract between the government and the governed, for in order to claim legitimacy the emperor would have to echo Confucius's "I invent nothing, I transmit," thus acknowledging the limitations on his personal power. To learn how to read was therefore already to learn the management of the state. Because the Confucian texts formed the whole of civil education, the bias of the intellectuals was towards these "human sciences," towards practical instruction in the governing of society. To the traditional Confucian scholars all knowledge led back into the political and moral world of man. Mathematics and the physical sciences were no exceptions for, as scientists, the Confucians understood the universe as a unified "field" in which the movements of heaven and earth directly affect human society. The aim of the physical sciences was to plot these movements, these changes, so that man might put himself in tune with the world and with his fellow men. The mandarins, for instance, studied astrology in order to learn the political outlook for the nation: the appearance of comets or the fall of meteorites presaged the smaller disturbances of man. While man could do nothing by himself, he could with intelligence discern the heavenly movements and put his own smaller sphere in accord with the larger one. In China, after a dynastic struggle, the new emperor coming to power would break the instruments of the court musicians in the conviction that they, like the old dynasty, were out of tune with the universe—that they had in some sense caused the rebellion. Similarly, the new emperor would initiate the "rectification of names" so that the words he used for the affairs of state should (unlike those of his predecessor) perfectly accord with the magical etiquette governing the relations of man and nature.

At the time of the Buddhist struggle in 1966 the Buddhist leaders claimed, "Ninety percent of the Vietnamese are Buddhists . . . the people are never Communists," while the NLF leaders claimed by contrast, "The struggle of the religious believers in Vietnam is not separate from the struggle for national liberation." The two statements were mutually contradictory, and an American might have concluded that one or both of their proponents was telling an untruth. But neither the Buddhists nor the NLF leaders were actually "lying," as an American might have been under similar circumstances. Both groups were "rectifying the names" of the Vietnamese to accord with what was no longer the "will of Heaven" but "the laws of history" or "the spirit of the times." They were announcing a project and making themselves comprehensible to their countrymen, for whom all knowledge, even the most neutral observation, is to be put to use.[21]

With this intellectual framework in mind it is perhaps easier to see why the pilots of the People's Republic of China should read Mao's *Thoughts* in order to learn how to fly an airplane. The Vietnamese Communists look upon technology as an independent discipline in certain respects, but they insist that political education should be the basis for using it. During the period of conflict and change in their society, this emphasis on politics is not, perhaps, as unreasonable as it seems to most Americans. Without political education it proved useless or destructive for the cadets of the Saigon air force to learn how to fly airplanes.

For Americans the close relationship the Vietnamese draw between morality, politics, and science is perhaps more difficult to understand now than at any other time in history. Today, living in a social milieu completely divided over matters of value and belief, Westerners have come to look upon science and logic alone as containing universal truths. Over the past century Western philosophers have worked to purge their disciplines of ethical and metaphysical concerns; Americans in particular have tended to deify the natural sciences and set them apart from their social goals. Under pressure from this demand for "objective truth," the scholars of human affairs have scrambled to give their own disciplines the authority and neutrality of science. But because the social scientists can rarely attain the same criteria for "truth" as physicists or chemists, they have sometimes misused the discipline and taken merely the trappings of science as a camouflage for their own beliefs and values. It is thus that many American "political scientists" sympathetic to American intervention in Vietnam have concluded that the NLF's subordination of science and "objective truth" to politics has its origins in Communist totalitarianism.

For Westerners who believe in the eternal verity of certain principles the notion of "brainwashing" is shocking and the experience is associated with torture. But in such societies as those in Indonesia, China, and Vietnam, it is in one form or another an activity of every political movement. Under the traditional Vietnamese empire there was only one truth, only one true way. And all modern Vietnamese parties have had to face the task of changing the nature of the "truth." Among people with an extremely pragmatic cast of mind, for whom values depend for their authority upon success, the task has implied a demonstration that the old ways are no longer useful, no longer adapted to the necessities of history. During the course of the war both the Saigon government and the NLF held "reeducation" courses for defectors and prisoners, with varying degrees of success. Those Americans who objected to the process (and most Americans singled out the NLF) saw it in European terms as the forcible destruction of personality, a mental torture such as Arthur Koestler described in *Darkness at Noon*. But to the Vietnamese, Communist and non-Communist, it did not imply torture at all, for the reason that they have a very different kind of commitment to society than do Westerners.

And it is this commitment that lies at the basis of intellectual organization. Unlike the Westerner, the Vietnamese child is brought up not to follow certain principles, but to accept the authority of certain people. The "Three Net Ropes" of the traditional society consisted in the loyalty of the son to his father, of the wife to her husband, and the mandarin to his emperor. The injunctions to filial piety and conjugal obedience were unconditional. Traditional Vietnamese law rested not upon the notion of individual rights, but the notion of duties—the duty of the sovereign to his people, the father to his son, and vice versa. Similarly, the Confucian texts defined no general principles but the proper relationship of man to man. Equal justice was secondary to social harmony. This particular form of social contract gave the individual a very different sense of himself, of his own personality. In the Vietnamese language there is no word that exactly corresponds to the Western personal pronoun I, *je, ich*. When a man speaks of himself, he calls himself "your brother," "your nephew," "your teacher," depending upon his relationship to the person he addresses. The word he uses for the first person *(toi)* in the new impersonal world of the cities originally denoted "subject of the king."[22] The traditional Vietnamese did not see himself as a totally independent being, for he did not distinguish himself as acutely as does a Westerner from his society (and by extension, the heavens). He did not see himself as a "character" formed of immutable traits, eternally loyal to certain principles, but rather as a system of relationships, a function of the society around him. In a sense, the design of the Confucian world resembled that of a Japanese garden where every rock, opaque and indifferent in itself, takes on significance from its relationship to the surrounding objects.

In central Vietnam, where the villages are designed like Japanese gardens, a young Vietnamese district chief once told this writer that he had moved a group of villagers from a Liberation village to his headquarters in order to "change their opinions." He had not lectured the villagers on the evils of Marxism and he did not plan to do so; he would simply wait for them to fall into relationship with his political authority. Had the villagers, of course, received an adequate political education, his waiting would be in vain. A "hard-core" NLF cadre would understand his community to include not only the village or the district but all of Vietnam. His horizons would be large enough in time and space to encompass a government-controlled city or years of a harsh, inconclusive war. But with regard to his refugees, the district chief was probably right: the old people and the children had left their NLF sympathies behind them in the burning ruins of a village only two miles distant.

In the old society, of course, a man who moved out of his village would find in his new village or in the court of Hué the same kind of social and political system that he had left behind him. During the conflicts of the twentieth century, however, his movement from one place to another might require a change of "ideology," or of way of life. In 1966 one American official discovered an ARVN soldier who had changed sides five times in the war, serving alternately with three NLF units and three GVN battalions. Clearly this particular soldier had no political education to speak of and no wider sense of community. But even for those that did, the possibility of accommodation and change remained open. When asked by an American interviewer what he thought of the GVN, one Front defector found it necessary to specify that "with the mind of the other regime" (i.e., that of the NLF) he felt it was bad for the people. At that point he was preparing himself to accept a new interpretation.

Such changes of mind must look opportunistic or worse to Westerners, but to the Vietnamese with their particular commitment to society it was at once the most moral and the most practical course. Indeed, it was the only course available, for in such situations the Vietnamese villager did not consider an alternative. In the old language, a man depended upon the "will of Heaven"; it was therefore his duty to accommodate himself to it as well as possible. In a letter to his subordinates of the southern provinces Phan Thanh Giang described this ethic of accommodation in the most sophisticated Confucian terms:

> It is written that he who lives according to Heaven's will is in the right way; he who departs from Heaven's will is wrong. To act according to Heaven's will is to act according to one's reason. Man is an intelligent animal created by Heaven. Each animal lives according to its proper nature, like water which seeks its own level or fire which spreads in dry places. . . . Man to whom Heaven has given reason should endeavor to live according to that reason.[23]

In conclusion Phan Thanh Giang requested that his officials surrender without resistance to the invading French forces. "The French," he wrote, "have huge battleships, full of soldiers and armed with powerful cannons. . . . It would be as senseless for you to assail [them] as for the fawn to attack the tiger. You would only draw suffering upon the people whom Heaven has entrusted to your care."[24] Loyal to the Vietnamese emperor, Phan Thanh Giang could not so easily accommodate himself to necessity. Branding himself as a traitor, he chose the same course that, throughout history, his predecessors had taken at the fall of dynasties. Suicide was the only resolution to the unbearable conflict between loyalty to the emperor and obligation to what he saw as the will of Heaven, to the will of the community as a whole.

But such protests against the will of Heaven were only for the mandarins, the moral leaders of the community. They were not for the simple villager, for as Confucius said, "The essence of the gentleman is that of wind; the essence of small people is that of grass. And when a wind passes over the grass, it cannot choose but bend."[25] In times of political stability the villager accommodated himself to the prevailing wind that clearly signaled the will of Heaven. Only in times of disorder and uncertainty when the sky clouded over and the forces of the world struggled to uncertain outcome, only then did the peasant take on responsibility for the great affairs of state, and only then did the leaders watch him carefully, for, so went the Confucian formula, "The will of Heaven is reflected in the eyes and ears of the people."

This ancient political formula clarified the basis on which twentieth-century Vietnamese, including those who no longer used the old language, would make their political decisions. Asked which side he supported, one peasant from a village close to Saigon told a Front cadre in 1963: "I do not know, for I follow the will of Heaven. If I do what you say, then the Diem side will arrest me; if I say things against you, then you will arrest me, so I would rather carry both burdens on my shoulders and stand in the middle." Caught between two competing regimes, the peasant did not assert his right to decide between them, rather he asked himself where his duty lay. Which regime had the power to claim his loyalty? Which would be the most likely to restore peace and harmony to his world? His decision might be based on personal preference (a government that considered the wishes of the people would be more likely to restore peace on a permanent basis). But he had, nonetheless, to make an objective analysis of the situation and take his gamble, for his first loyalty lay neither with the Diem regime nor the NLF but with the will of Heaven that controlled them both. At certain periods *attentisme* was the most moral and the most practical course.

As a warning to Westerners on the difficulties of understanding the twentieth-century conflict in Vietnam, Paul Mus told an ancient Chinese legend that is well known to the Vietnamese. There was trouble in the state of Lu, and the reigning monarch called in Confucius to ask for his help. When he arrived at the court, the Master went to a public place and took a seat in the correct way, facing south, and all the trouble disappeared.[26]

The works of Vo Nguyen Giap are but addenda to this legend, for the legend is the paradigm of revolution in Vietnam. To the Vietnamese it is clear from the story that Confucius was not taking an existential or exemplary position, he was actually changing the situation. Possessed of neither godlike nor prophetic authority, he moved an entire kingdom by virtue of his sensitivity to the will of Heaven as reflected in the "eyes and ears of the people." As executor for the people, he clarified their wishes and signaled the coming—or the return—of the Way that would bring harmony to the kingdom. For the Hoa Hao and the Cao Dai, the traditionalist sects of the south that in the twentieth century still believed in this magical "sympathy" of heaven and earth, political change did not depend entirely on human effort. Even the leaders of the sects believed that if they, like Confucius, had taken "the correct position," the position that accorded with the will of Heaven, all Vietnamese would eventually adopt the same Way, the same political system that they had come to.

Here, within the old spiritualist language, lies a clue as to why the Vietnamese Communists held their military commanders in strict subordination to the political cadres. Within the domestic conflict military victories were not only less important than political victories, but they were strictly meaningless except as reflections of the political realities. For the Communists, as for all the other political groups, the vehicle of political change was not the war, the pitch of force against force, but the struggle, the attempt to make manifest that their Way was the only true or "natural" one for all Vietnamese.* Its aim was to demonstrate that, in the old language, the Mandate of Heaven had changed and the new order had already replaced the old in all but title. When Ho Chi Minh entered Hanoi in August 1945, he made much the same kind of gesture as Confucius had made in facing south when he said (and the wording is significant, for he was using a language of both East and West), "We, members of the Provisional Government

* The English word 'struggle,' a pale translation of the Vietnamese term *dau tranh*, fails to convey the drama, the awesomeness, the totality of the original." (Douglas Pike, *Viet Cong*, p. 85.)

of the Democratic Republic of Viet-Nam solemnly declare to the world that Viet-Nam has the right to be a free and independent country—and in fact it is so already. The entire Vietnamese people are determined to mobilize all their physical and mental strength, to sacrifice their lives and property in order to safeguard their independence and liberty."[27] His claims were far from "true" at the time, but they constituted the truth in potential—if he, like Confucius, had taken the "correct position." For the Confucians, of course, the "correct position" was that which accorded with the will of Heaven and the practice of the sacred ancestors. For Ho Chi Minh the "correct position" was that which accorded with the laws of history and the present and future judgment of the Vietnamese people.

30

An Opportunity for Power

Gareth Porter

It was not Cold War ideology or exaggerated notions of the threat from communism in Southeast Asia that paved the U.S. road to war in Vietnam but the decisive military dominance of the United States over the Soviet Union. The extremely high level of confidence on the part of national security officials that the United States could assert its power in Vietnam without the risk of either a major war or a military confrontation with another major power conditioned the series of decisions that finally led to war. To put it another way, the imbalance of power so constrained the policies of Moscow and Beijing toward Vietnam (and toward the peripheral countries more generally) that it created incentives for ambitious U.S. objectives in that country.

The imbalance of power did not have the same influence on all the actors involved in U.S. policy making on Vietnam. The values, attitudes, and interests of the national security bureaucracy were focused overwhelmingly on U.S. power and influence abroad, so it is not surprising that the signals of highly unequal power relations had a very direct influence on their policy preferences. The same cannot be said, however, of the presidents who were in office during the period under study. Eisenhower, Kennedy, and Johnson saw no reason to commit U.S. forces against an internal insurgency in South Vietnam. For those three presidents, other political values, including the avoidance of war, outweighed the desire to score a Cold War victory over the Communists. Although all three presidents were well aware of the stark imbalance of power, therefore, it did not incline them to go to war in Vietnam. During the 1961–65 period, U.S. dominance led to a consistent pattern of struggle between the president and the national security bureaucracy over Vietnam.

During 1954–55, the imbalance of power directly shaped John Foster Dulles's response to the crisis in Indochina, but it did not lead to a decision to intervene, because both Eisenhower and Dulles thought such intervention would be a disastrous course. However, the imbalance of power did lead Dulles to exploit the *threat* of military intervention to exert pressure on the USSR and the PRC in regard to Indochina. Even more important, after the Geneva Accords, the unequal configuration of power encouraged him to carry out a "covert operation" to support the repression of the Viet Minh political organization in South Vietnam and to cast aside the Geneva Accords provisions for national elections to reunify Vietnam. The latter decision, made without consulting Eisenhower, discarded a policy on Vietnamese elections based on consistency with broader U.S. ideology and Cold War policy. We now know that North Vietnam was prepared to agree to virtually everything the United States demanded, not only on guarantees of a free election, but on continuation of a separate regime in South Vietnam for an indefinite period. The tragedy of Dulles's decision is compounded by the fact that Eisenhower had already ruled out U.S. military intervention to save South Vietnam from just the kind of internal Communist insurgency that arose in 1960 in response to the U.S.-instigated repression.

By the time Kennedy entered the White House, the initial U.S. assessment of Soviet and Chinese acquiescence in the U.S. assertion of power in South Vietnam had hardened into a fundamental assumption of U.S. policy. When the new Communist insurgency suddenly became a potentially serious threat to the Diem regime, therefore, national security officials believed that the United States had a free hand to employ U.S. military power in South Vietnam to suppress it before it could become too powerful. The Soviet Union was considered irrelevant to the Vietnam issue, China was mired in starvation and disorder, and both the Chinese and North Vietnamese were seen as intimidated by the destructive power of the United States. The absence of any external constraint led Kennedy's principal advisers to advocate the use of U.S. forces in South Vietnam with little or no debate.

Kennedy, on the other hand, explicitly rejected the overall U.S. power advantage as the framework for approaching the issue. He was inclined by his personal knowledge of the historical background to the conflict to avoid a U.S. military commitment in South Vietnam. But he was also afraid to reject his advisers' recommendation completely. The result was a compromise on the third major decision in late 1961 that allowed a major U.S. role in the counterinsurgency war by U.S. pilots but ruled out open combat by U.S. troops. Meanwhile, the earlier effect of the imbalance of power—the rejection of the Geneva Accords and of any political-diplomatic compromise with the North Vietnamese—continued to operate. Kennedy's efforts to initiate diplomatic contacts with Hanoi were resisted by the national security bureaucracy in the firm belief that South Vietnam was a place where the United States could and should effectively exert its power.

When Lyndon Johnson ascended to the White House, a fourteen-month struggle began over the third major decision—whether or not to carry out an air war against North Vietnam. As the Communist bloc disintegrated, the power relationship had continued to develop even more favorably for the United States, and U.S. officials had come to view Moscow as a potentially helpful interlocutor in getting Hanoi to retreat. The tenuous character of a series of South Vietnamese governments made bombing the North even more attractive. Because air attacks on the North were a low-risk option, provided the bombing did not threaten the regime or the Chinese border, the case for attacking North Vietnam did not even depend on the prospects for forcing Hanoi to withdraw from the war. It could also be useful as a bargaining chip, and even in the worst case, it would demonstrate that the United States was willing to use its power to punish its adversaries for challenging U.S. interests in East Asia. U.S. military dominance was thus central to the rationale for the bombing of North Vietnam.

Lyndon Johnson had strong reservations about bombing the North from the beginning, but the pattern of pressures, resistance, and compromise that had defined the major policy decision on Vietnam in the Kennedy administration repeated itself under Johnson. Johnson's advisers repeatedly pressed him to commit himself to a strategy of military pressure on North Vietnam; he refused but tried to keep his advisers "on board" his policy by suggesting that he had not rejected their recommendation completely. After Johnson's landslide election victory, the pressure on him intensified, until a compromise was finally reached between the president and his advisers in February 1965 limiting the scope of the bombing much more narrowly than the advisers had wanted by ruling out even the threat of bombing civilian targets.

The causal linkage between the imbalance of power and the fourth major policy decision on the limited deployment of ground troops in South Vietnam is more complex than in earlier decisions. When Rolling Thunder began, McNamara and McGeorge Bundy understood that the South Vietnamese government might suffer serious reverses and go rapidly downhill at any time, and they had grave doubts about whether U.S. forces could actually defeat the Vietnamese insurgency. Nevertheless, they could still imagine a peace agreement or tacit understanding that would not involve any explicit political compromise with Hanoi. They proposed to increase U.S. ground strength in South Vietnam significantly, which, they hoped, in combination with the northward movement of the bombing of North Vietnam, would signal to Hanoi the seriousness of the U.S. commitment to stay in South Vietnam. This was extremely wishful thinking on their part, which they could have entertained only because of the extraordinary U.S. power advantage. They believed U.S. ability to destroy much of North Vietnam at will would deter Hanoi from committing regular troops to the South, and a stalemate in the war was therefore possible.

The notion that the ability of the United States to threaten North Vietnam with vast destruction could be used to control Hanoi's role in the war in the South still had a strong hold on the thinking of Johnson's advisers in March-April 1965. It was based on a historical reality: the North Vietnamese had constrained their role in the South for years out of fear of U.S. retaliation. Those advisers failed to consider two new realities, however: first, the major escalation of the war in the South—and of American military involvement in it—meant that Hanoi's leaders had reached a threshold where they regarded the failure to send North Vietnamese troops to the South as having potentially irreversible consequences. Thus they were willing to accept some increased risk of U.S. bombing by late 1964 and early 1965 in order to achieve an improved military balance in the South.

Second, the U.S. threat to North Vietnam had already been considerably diluted by the beginning of the actual bombing campaign—which was very far from the kind of devastation Hanoi had feared all along—and by Lyndon Johnson's refusal to threaten devastation to cow the North Vietnamese. Even after the purpose of the bombing was officially designated as interdiction rather than pressure on Hanoi's political will on April 1, 1965, Bundy, McNamara, and Rusk seem to have relied on the residual threat to remove the existing restrictions on the bombing of the DRV to deter a large-scale North Vietnamese troop presence in the South—hence, McNamara's dabbling in nuclear threat in April.

On a path to war strewn with cruel ironies, perhaps the greatest irony is that the fifth and final decision, namely, to give the military leaders all the troops they wanted in mid-1965, was the least affected by the unequal power relationship. For McNamara and Bundy, at least, exaggerated expectations of the efficacy of dominant power in constraining Hanoi's options, while enhancing those of the United States, were still alive and well in April, but those expectations had come crashing down by early June. The prospect of either relatively short-term defeat or a long, bloody war if the United States did not choose to settle was no longer deniable. Facing that truth, Johnson, Bundy, and McNamara were all gravitating in early and mid June toward a limited commitment option that they all knew meant the acceptance of a possible defeat. Like Kennedy before him and Johnson himself during the previous year and a half, Johnson never referred directly to the acceptance of defeat either in meetings or in phone conversations with McNamara. He spoke of the need to meet the U.S. treaty obligation in Vietnam, but not of preventing the fall of the Saigon government regardless of the cost.

Johnson still hoped to avoid escalation to an open-ended ground war by establishing an upper limit on troop deployments, while hoping for an evolution of congressional sentiment that would make possible a negotiated exit from the war. But his hope of avoiding a big war depended on having the active support at least of his principal advisers, and especially of McNamara, in order to face the inevitable accusations of having lost South Vietnam. McNamara initially supported the limited commitment option, but he abandoned it within a few days when he realized that Johnson was considering an option that would make everyone associated with it even more vulnerable to the charge that he was following a "no-win" policy. Ultimately, it was the presidential need for collective responsibility for a politically unpalatable decision and his primary national security advisers' fear of taking such responsibility that put the administration on the path to an open-ended war in Vietnam.

Dysfunctional Policy Making on Vietnam

The Cold War consensus explanation for the Vietnam War implies that the national security institutions and the processes of policy making on Vietnam worked the way they should in a democratic system. The theme of the first major assessment of Vietnam policy making after the war was that "the system worked," because the policy consistently reflected the presumed consensus on the goal of containing Communism.[1] The present study suggests, however, that the process of making policy toward Vietnam resulted in policy decisions that did *not* reflect the best judgment of the president about Vietnam. Instead, the policy was skewed by the aggressive role of the national security bureaucracy in pushing its own policy preferences.

Students of U.S. foreign policy have long observed that the president's actual power over foreign policy does not match his formal authority. More than four decades ago, Richard Neustadt portrayed the president as able to get his way with his subordinates only by persuading them to follow his lead, suggesting that a degree of independence was inherent in their positions as heads of bureaucracies with their own interests.[2] The bureaucratic politics model of foreign policy making views foreign policy decisions as the result of "conflict and consensus-building," in which the different goals and values of the president and leading policy makers are reconciled.[3]

Such anodyne descriptions of the process of making foreign policy fail, however, to convey the seriousness of the struggles between the presidents and their national security advisers from 1961 to 1965 over the issue of going to war in Vietnam. The idealized image of White House meetings at which the president seeks to bring his subordinates around to his viewpoint bears no relationship to the reality of the policy-making process revealed in this study. In fact, the process in respect to Vietnam was just the reverse of this image: the Defense Department, the State Department, the JCS, and even the White House national security staff played the role that students of foreign policy making have always attributed to the president, and Presidents Kennedy and Johnson were hard put to maintain control over Vietnam policy.

The tendency of national security advisers to lobby aggressively for military action did not begin with the Kennedy administration. It was already evident, albeit at a lower level of intensity, even in the Eisenhower administration in 1954. Chairman of the JCS Admiral Arthur Radford and former CIA Director Walter Bedell Smith used their positions on a task force created by Eisenhower to put pressure on him to intervene in Indochina, despite the president's explicit directive to them to provide alternative options to such intervention. Eisenhower was not really vulnerable to such pressures, because they did not represent a consensus among national security offcials, and because he knew that public opinion would not support intervention in Indochina on behalf of the French. He was able to manage the pressures from the national security bureaucracy for war without the need for any substantive compromise with the hawks. Even so, he felt obliged to make the argument that intervention would risk a war with the Soviet Union and China, which appears to have been created out of whole cloth.

Not all the decisions on the road to war in Vietnam directly involved the question of using military force. U.S. policy on the Geneva settlement was one issue that involved force only indirectly, insofar as it was realized that the decision might provoke a military response by the

Vietnamese Communists. For that reason, Eisenhower did not follow the issue as closely as he would have had it more obviously been a question of war and peace. As a result, Dulles was able to take the decision on scrapping the existing policy on national elections under the Geneva Accords out of Eisenhower's hands by ensuring that it was never raised within the NSC.

By the time Kennedy entered the White House, high officials in the Defense and State Departments and the White House Office of National Security Affairs, as well as the JCS, were asserting their primacy in making Vietnam policy. Well before Kennedy had begun to focus on the problem, they had already formulated their own policy, which was to prepare for the introduction of U.S. combat forces into the war, and had begun to seek presidential authorization to carry it out. That pattern only became more pronounced over the course of 1961.

High-ranking bureaucrats and national security advisers expected the president to accede to the policy on Laos and Vietnam that they found necessary to maintain existing U.S. positions of strength in Southeast Asia. When Kennedy began to carry out his own policy of neutralization of Laos in the face of opposition from his advisers, key officials in the State Department, the CIA, and the military were outraged that Kennedy was making an end run around them. Many of them considered that he was selling out a U.S. ally to the Soviet bloc. Determined to hold on to the U.S. positions in both Laos and South Vietnam, Walt Rostow, U. Alexis Johnson, and Maxwell Taylor began meeting in the summer of 1961 to make plans to get Kennedy to drop the negotiation of a compromise on Laos and use military force in both Laos and South Vietnam.

Kennedy responded to the aggressive advocacy role of the national security bureaucracy by carefully avoiding a clear-cut rejection of the use of force in any formal meeting, encouraging his advisers to believe that he was still considering their recommendations. In November 1961, Kennedy compromised with the hawks in his administration by approving the opening wedge of U.S. combat intervention in South Vietnam, but he made it clear that he would approve the use of combat troops only under diplomatic circumstances that everyone knew were prohibitive. That decision shocked his national security advisers. Reflecting the feelings of the inner circle of national security officials, McGeorge Bundy's memorandum to Kennedy about the decision captures the feeling on the part of his advisers that a president should not reject the course of action recommended unanimously by his national security team.

Two months after Kennedy's decision, the JCS openly challenged his policy against the use of combat forces in South Vietnam in an unsolicited letter to McNamara. That action in itself reflected a dramatic change in the norms governing the role of the JCS in relation to the making of foreign policy decisions from those of the early Eisenhower years. When Radford had called a meeting of the JCS on March 31, 1954, to canvass their views on sending Eisenhower a memorandum calling for military intervention in Indochina, Army Chief of Staff Matthew Ridgeway had insisted that, unless requested by "proper authority," such a recommendation would be "clearly outside the proper scope of authority of the JCS" and would "involve the JCS inevitably in politics."[4] By 1962, however, the JCS were no longer constrained from trying to infiuence the president's policy toward Vietnam.

Kennedy soon realized that compromise with his advisers threatened a loss of control over the policy, making him vulnerable to pressures from military and civilian advisers alike for open-ended escalation of the U.S. military role in South Vietnam. He sought to regain control over Vietnam policy by adopting an indirect strategy of withdrawal that would not expose him to political charges of having lost South Vietnam. He exploited McNamara's personal ties with the Kennedys, using his secretary of defense to initiate planning by the military for a strict timetable for withdrawal of U.S. troops. Later, Kennedy exploited his brother's close friendship with Maxwell Taylor, whose cooperation in the plan as chairman of the JCS was vital to its success, to the same end. While the negptiations went forward, Kennedy maintained a public rhetorical stance of staunch opposition to withdrawal from South Vietnam. By drawing McNamara and Taylor into his withdrawal strategy, Kennedy succeeded in regaining a tenuous control over Vietnam policy in October 1963.

Kennedy's fear of opposition and criticism by his own national security bureaucracy and his adoption of a strategy of manipulating policy from behind the scenes limited his ability to lead, even within his own administration. After his efforts to open a diplomatic channel to Hanoi in 1962 encountered stiff resistance from Harriman, Kennedy postponed any such diplomatic probe, waiting to see how the withdrawal plan would develop and whether a diplomatic settlement would be necessary. In the final weeks of his life Kennedy apparently realized that he would have to resort to negotiations in order to avoid being sucked ever deeper into the war.

The assassination of John F. Kennedy and the entrance of a new president into the White House dramatically increased the distorting effects of the aggressive role of national security advisers on Vietnam policy. Kennedy had been able to weaken the national security bureaucracy's power over policy by using both his defense secretary and the chairman of the JCS as stalking horses. When Lyndon Johnson became president, however, neither McNamara nor Taylor was any longer constrained by personal loyalty to the president. Johnson's two top advisers were once again free to push for the use of force on Vietnam, with serious consequences for policy making.

Throughout 1964 and the early part of 1965, McNamara, Taylor, and other principal advisers used a wide range of bureaucratic devices to maneuver Johnson into agreeing to initiate military action against North Vietnam: Joint warnings by the CIA, State, and Defense that Johnson had to act soon to avoid irreversible deterioration; insistence that the loss of South Vietnam would result in a falling-dominoes effect in Southeast Asia; a unanimous recommendation of bombing from his principal advisers, after they had convened as the "Executive Committee" without Johnson's authorization; and the drafting of a congressional resolution that would have formally committed the president to prevent the loss of South Vietnam by force, if necessary. Even more serious was McNamara's deliberate deceit in failing to inform Johnson about the uncertainty surrounding the alleged second attack on U.S. navy vessels [in the Tonkin Gulf] on August 4. McNamara and Rusk tried again in September to mousetrap Johnson into retaliatory strikes over a nonexistent naval attack but this time were rebuffed.

There is surely no parallel in modern history to the twelve separate attempts by the national security bureaucracy over a fourteen-month period to get Johnson to authorize the use of military force against the same state. It is indicative of the acute contradiction between Johnson and his advisers, however, that Johnson rebuffed every one of them, except when he was deprived by McNamara of vital information in the Tonkin Gulf decision. Those attempts can be summarized as follows:

1. November 1963–January 1964: change of wording of NSAM [National Security Action Memorandum]; preparation of plans for covert actions that included U.S. air attacks on North Vietnam
2. February 1964: McGeorge Bundy proposes creation of an interagency group to plan military pressures on North Vietnam to Johnson; creation by Rusk of such a group without presidential authorization
3. March 1964: draft recommendation by McNamara for bombing North Vietnam to be presented to Johnson upon return from South Vietnam
4. May 1964: joint recommendation by McNamara and Rusk for commitment to use force
5. June 1964: proposal for congressional joint resolution on use of force
6. August 1964: withholding of information by McNamara on doubts about the alleged attack on U.S. ships in the Tonkin Gulf

7. September 1964: plans for a strategy of provocation
8. September 1964: effort to convince Johnson that another attack on U.S. ships had taken place
9. November 1964: recommendations for retaliation for attack on the Bien Hoa airbase
10. December 1964: unanimous recommendation for two-phase bombing policy
11. December 1964: recommendations by Taylor, McGeorge Bundy, and others for retaliation for the bombing of Brinks Hotel in Saigon
12. January 1965: McNamara-Bundy letter to Johnson insisting that present policy was unacceptable

Johnson became concerned very early in his presidency about the political implications of the aggressiveness with which the JCS and McNamara were pressing him to go to war. Like Kennedy, he was careful never to put anything on paper that could be cited as evidence of his rejection of the use of force. Once he had discovered arguments he could use to justify rejecting the bombing of North Vietnam (the threat of intervention by China, ineffectiveness in bringing North Vietnam to heel, the fragility of the South Vietnamese government, and the threat of physical harm to U.S. women and children in Saigon), Johnson was willing to defy his advisers on that issue. Johnson also had an additional motive for resisting pressures for war in the opportunity to pass a historic domestic reform program. His preoccupation with his "Great Society" agenda, moreover, came after his election in November 1964, just when his advisers were counting on their unanimous recommendation of a bombing program to finally prevail on him to implement that policy.

Despite Johnson's resistance to actually committing himself to the use of force over Vietnam, his advisers extracted one concession after another from him: first studies of covert pressures on the North, then contingency plans for bombing, then the retaliatory strike over the alleged Tonkin Gulf attacks, then a commitment to retaliate against future incidents. Johnson's advisers drew the noose progressively tighter in anticipation of a decision by the president after the election to approve the bombing program. It was after the election that the tensions between the national security bureaucracy and Johnson over Vietnam became palpable. While the president refused to budge on starting the bombing of North Vietnam week after week in December and January of 1964–65, his advisers became increasingly convinced that he was ready to let South Vietnam go and was hoping that one of the revolving-door governments in Saigon would ask the United States to leave. The reaction of top national security officials to his policy once again revealed the bureaucracy's view of its role in making policy on the defense of U.S. national security interests in Southeast Asia. They considered Johnson's refusal to pursue the policy on which they had agreed, after a long, formal interagency process, to be unacceptable. McGeorge Bundy and McNamara finally used the ultimate leverage of the national security bureaucracy on the president: the implicit threat to disassociate themselves from his policy if it resulted, as they expected, in the loss of South Vietnam.

In the month that followed the McNamara-Bundy letter, Johnson made a series of compromises with his advisers that in large part accepted their policy of systematic bombing of the North and resulted in the Rolling Thunder campaign. That compromise had far-reaching political consequences at home. Despite Johnson's insistence on avoiding any change in declaratory policy, it created the general expectation that the United States would now act to prevent the loss of South Vietnam. It also ushered in a period in which Johnson was suddenly under pressure to approve a substantial ground combat deployment as well, on the basis of quite unrealistic policy assumptions.

The April decision on troop deployment appears to have represented the apogee of influence of Johnson's inner circle of advisers. In June, with the military pressing for an open-ended commitment of troops to the war, Johnson tried to reassert presidential leadership over policy to avoid that outcome. But in the end, he felt that he could not make the decision to reject the full request for troops without the active support of McNamara. The use of force had become, in effect, a collective responsibility shared by the president and his principal advisers.

Thus the dynamics of policy making on Vietnam, in which the national security bureaucracy had powerful leverage on the president to make concessions to their preference for war, undermined a principle that should govern decisions on the use of military force in a democratic society: that such decisions are not only made formally by the president and approved by Congress but actually reflect the considered judgment of the highest elected official. Neither Kennedy nor Johnson had full control over Vietnam policy, because the national security bureaucracy acted as an independent power center within the U.S. government with the right to pressure the president on matters of war and peace.

Underlying the ability of the national security bureaucracy to wrest concessions from the president on Vietnam policy and ultimately, in the case of Lyndon Johnson, to break his resistance to going to war, was the fear on the part of both Kennedy and Johnson of political retribution over a policy decision that might lead to the defeat of the U.S. client regime in South Vietnam. The model for the kind of political attack that both presidents feared, moreover, was not the "Who lost China" campaign, with its search for subversives in the State Department who had allegedly prevented the United States from giving military aid to an anti-Communist ally, but the attack on Kennedy in September–October 1962 over his failure to use military force against the Soviet military presence in Cuba. It was not unreasonable to fear that such a campaign would appeal to public opinion because of the general assumption that the United States should be able to prevail against a third-rate Communist foe.

The perception of anti-Communist critics of U.S. policy toward Vietnam as too "soft" was most dramatically expressed by Senator Thomas J. Dodd (D. Conn.), who declared in a 1961 Senate speech, "If the United States, with its unrivaled might, with its unparalleled wealth, with its dominion over sea and air . . . can be laid in the dust by a few thousand primitive guerrillas, then we are far down the road from which there is no return."[5] The Republican view, still best represented by Eisenhower and Nixon, assumed that U.S. military dominance over the Communist powers and the ability to devastate North Vietnam should have been sufficient to defeat the Communist challenge in Vietnam.

A central conclusion of this study, therefore, is that the aggressiveness of the national security bureaucracy in asserting the necessity for a military approach to Vietnam in both the Kennedy and Johnson administrations was not a function of the specific personalities involved. It was a consequence of the emergence of a dramatic imbalance of power at the global level. The dominant power of the United States created a political atmosphere that encouraged the expression of certain policy approaches and discouraged the expression of others. In that atmosphere, the national security bureaucracy became increasingly self-confident, powerful, and convinced of its own right to define U.S. policy toward Vietnam. The constitutional role of the president in making foreign policy and deciding on the use of force was replaced, in practice, by a system of shared power and responsibility over the decision to use force between presidents and unelected national security managers.

Lessons of Vietnam for the Unipolar Era

Since the end of the Cold War, it has been universally agreed that the international system is "unipolar," meaning that no other state or possible combination of states can counterbalance the power of the United States. Beginning in the 1990s and continuing into the new century, students of international relations and international security have carried on a heated debate over whether the new situation of clear-cut U.S. dominance is likely to endure and whether it is desirable in terms of international peace and stability. Defenders of policies aimed at exploiting the "unipolar moment" have argued that the present structure is likely to be enduring, and that it is more likely than a balance of power to preserve peace, because it minimizes uncertainty. They assert that U.S. dominance ensures that weaker states will not be tempted to challenge even an expansive definition of U.S. security interests around the globe.[6]

Opponents of policies based on unipolarity, on the other hand, argue that a policy aimed at preserving and exploiting U.S. dominance is both futile, because of the fundamental tendency of states to balance against a dominant power, and dangerous, because the exploitation of dominance is likely to be seen as provocative by other states.[7] Paralleling these academic arguments over the unipolar system, of course, are sharp differences of view over the practice of unilateralism in the use of military power by the United States against a weaker "rogue" state in the absence of a consensus of the international community. The Bush administration justified the U.S. invasion and occupation of Iraq in 2003 by alleging a threat of "weapons of mass destmction." Underlying that highly inflammatory—and ultimately deceptive—claim, however, was a more fundamental issue. Defenders of using U.S. dominance to maintain a world order of Washington's own choosing saw the occupation of Iraq as minimizing the likelihood of serious threats to U.S. and international security. Opponents saw the unilateral use of force in Iraq as more likely to increase regional instability and the dangers to U.S. and global security.

These debates on the advantages and disadvantages of unipolarity and of policies that exploit it have assumed that there has never before been anything in the modern state system even remotely similar to the present global structure of power. This assumption reflects the conventional view that there was a rough bipolar balance of power between the United States and the Soviet Union throughout the Cold War. The reinterpretation of the period between the Korean and Vietnam wars offered in this study suggests, however, that the dominance of U.S. power over that period was roughly equivalent to the unipolarity of the post-Cold War period. In the earlier period, U.S. power could not be balanced by that of the Soviet Union and China. By 1964, U.S. offlcials had begun to view the Soviet Union less as a Cold War rival for power than as a potentially useful adjunct to U.S. efforts to impose a settlement in Vietnam at some future date. Several major states today arguably occupy analogous political roles in relation to the issue of unilateral U.S. use of military force.

The insights that can be gleaned from reassessing the dynamics of the political system and of U.S. policy making toward Vietnam during that period are highly relevant, therefore, to the present "unipolar moment." In particular, the U.S. experience on the road to war in Vietnam offers useful lessons about the ways in which the United States is mostly likely to become involved in wars in a unipolar system. The question is whether wars are more likely to arise from states that seek to make a signiflcant change in the international balance of power, or even to disturb a regional status quo, or from the tendency of the United States to extend its power and influence too far and to provoke greater resistance and hostility to U.S. power.

In retrospect, it is clear that U.S. dominance during the interwar period of the Cold War reduced to virtually nil the possibility of wars involving the Soviet Union or China—the only second- or even third-level states in the power hierarchy who at least in theory were hostile to U.S. power interests. Neither Communist great power was willing to take even minimal risks of a military clash with the United States. The extreme imbalance of power ruled out even the encouragement by the USSR or the PRC of a direct challenge by local Communists to U.S. power interests. It is no accident that the Soviet Union and China, whose internal organization and ideology inclined them toward support for such challenges to the existing international order, both gave up their previous policy of backing revolutionary struggles just as the new power configuration emerged at the end of the Korean War. Those effects of the unipolarity of that interwar period can be counted as positive for preventing war.

The lesson of this study of the impact of unbalanced power on the Vietnam issue, however, is that the absence of challenge from second-rank or third-rank states in terms of power does not prevent the occurrence of war on the periphery. The initiative in challenging the U.S. power position in South Vietnam in 1959-60 did not come from either of the major Communist powers, after all, but from the Vietnamese Communists themselves. It was not the North Vietnamese regime, moreover, that initially pushed for an armed uprising aimed at upending the Saigon regime. The party leadership in Hanoi, under pressure from their Communist patrons and cautious in the face of the ever-present threat of U.S. military force, had been prepared to continue to support the Soviet-Chinese strategy of waging only political struggle in South Vietnam. The initiative came from the South Vietnamese victims of the Diemist repression, for many of whom the issue of armed struggle was literally one of life or death. Their motivation in taking up arms had nothing to do with Cold War power politics between the two blocs. These southern Communists and former Viet Minh forced the hand of the North Vietnamese regime by threatening Hanoi with a loss of control over its followers in the South.

In the earlier unipolar power era, then, it was those with the *least* power who were willing to take the initiative to challenge U.S. power, rather than those who were closest to the United States in power capabilities. Although seemingly paradoxical, this historical fact reflected an elementary reality: these local resistance forces had the least to lose and the most to gain from challenging the status quo established by U.S. power. Furthermore, they were the least knowledgeable about U.S. power capabilities. This fact suggests that the debate over the present unipolar power structure has been too narrow in its focus on whether other major powers or potential major powers are likely to challenge U.S. dominance. The previous experience with unipolarity indicates that the United States can probably intimidate second- and third-level states, because the risks of even slight overt resistance to U.S. assertion of power beyond their borders are simply too great. One lesson of the path to war in Vietnam, however, is that war is much more likely to arise, not from a decision by those with the most to lose but from conflicts involving the vigorous assertion by the United States of its power interests abroad, even in the absence of an overt challenge by another state.

A second lesson from the path to war in Vietnam has to do with the roles of force and diplomacy in the ability of the dominant power to exert influence on potential foes. The dominance of the United States in the international politics of the interwar period was based primarily on its ability to manipulate the implicit or explicit threat to use U.S. air and naval power—including the ultimate sanction of the use of nuclear weapons— without having to actually use that power. We now know just how strongly the existence of strategic asymmetry impressed on the Soviet Union and China, as well as North Vietnam, the risks and costs of war with the United States. During the entire period between the Geneva Accords and the major U.S. combat intervention in Vietnam in 1965, the North Vietnamese leaders were ready to make far-reaching compromises on the length of time that an independent non-Communist regime could remain in the South, provided that it was buffered from U.S. political-military power. That position was a direct consequence of the ability of the United States to threaten wholesale destruction of North Vietnamese society. For the same reason, the North Vietnamese also limited participation in the armed struggle to native southerners for the first four years of the war.

Despite the genuine fear of U.S. attack, however, the DRV became increasingly committed to the struggle in the South from 1961 on. Its gradual assumption of increasingly greater risk reflects two factors working in tandem. The first was the fact that the outcome of the struggle in the South bore on the primordial interest of the regime in national independence. The more direct reason for the escalation of North Vietnamese involvement, however, was that the United States completely shut the door on any compromise that could have allowed North Vietnam to end the war honorably.

By rejecting diplomatic negotiation, the United States threw away most of its actual ability to shape the political outcome in South Vietnam through a combination of threat, restraint, and knowing what concessions it could extract from Hanoi, short of giving up the ultimate possibility of reunification. Paradoxically, by attempting to press its advantage too far—and especially by engaging in systematic bombing of North Vietnam while blocking the possibility of diplomatic compromise—the United States sacrificed its considerable influence over Hanoi's choices.

The outcome of U.S. policy can be traced to the reading of power relationships by the national security bureaucracy. In opting to put in a large ground contingent and postponing any diplomatic probe of Hanoi in 1965, Johnson's national security advisers were basing their recommendations on the incentives that they presumed to be inherent in the overwhelming U.S. dominance in the power relationship with Hanoi. In doing so, they completely ignored the much more complex set of actual incentives facing Hanoi.

This episode illustrates the broader problem of the reliance by the national security bureaucracy on the absence of any external countervailing power in using force. It suggests that national security officials in the dominant state are incapable of going beyond crude signals of hierarchical power in thinking about going to war against a weaker state or sociopolitical movement in confiict with U.S. policy. The record of policy deliberations on Vietnam suggests that the advisers were simply unable to recognize that they were pressing their power advantage too far in South Vietnam in that crucial March–May 1965 period. The fateful decisions to deploy more troops and to forgo genuine negotiations were only possible because of the engrained habit of relying so heavily on the U.S. power advantage in Vietnam over a period of years. This is obviously not a tendency that is exclusive to U.S. Vietnam policy in the first half of the 1960s, moreover. It is likely that it is endemic to policy making over a prolonged period of unbalanced power and conflicts with much weaker adversaries.

In documenting the effect of the imbalance of power on U.S. policy toward Vietnam, this study illustrates the most fundamental insight of realist international relations theory: that a rough balance of power is necessary to curb the tendency of the strongest state to exploit its power advantage to the maximum at the expense of weaker states. "Unbalanced power is a danger to weak states," Kenneth Waltz once observed, adding, "It may also be a danger to strong ones."[8] Realist theory generally asserts that the tendency of the strongest state to extend its power and influence continues until it is checked by external forces or by sociopolitical forces at home that weaken its ability to do so.[9]

Until the end of the Cold War, realists generally did not apply this general principle to the United States, but in the present "unipolar moment," the issue of how to restrain the excessive use of U.S. power is unavoidable. It has now become part of the debate over the advantages and disadvantages to the United States and to the world of U.S. dominance of the international system. Waltz, for one, has suggested that peace will require not only external constraints on U.S. power but internal restraints as well.[10] Students of unipolar politics and foreign policy looking at the question of domestic restraint on the deployment of U.S. power abroad would do well to take account of the political dynamics of policy making on the road to war in Vietnam.

The impetus for the assertive use of U.S. military power in Vietnam came overwhelmingly from the national security bureaucracy itself, rather than from the presidency. The policy-making process on Vietnam became dysfunctional because of the refusal of national security advisers to accept a presidential policy that rejected the use of military force in defense of national security interests. That earlier unipolar experience suggests that the problem of inadequate domestic restraints may be exacerbated by the tendency of the national security bureaucracy to assert itself in policy making.

Alongside these parallels between the present unipolar moment and the one that existed for at least twelve years in the 1950s and 1960s, there are obvious differences as well. Perhaps the main one is a far greater pluralism of sociopolitical and intellectual views of national security in the current phase of unipolar power than existed in the earlier period. As long as the unipolar moment persists, however, the political power of the national security bureaucracy, both within the executive branch and in the larger society, will certainly remain a challenge to domestic efforts to restrain the use of military power by the United States.

« 31 »

A Defense of Freedom

Norman Podhoretz

HERE THEN WE ARRIVE AT THE CENTER of the moral issue posed by the American intervention into Vietnam.

The United States sent half a million men to fight in Vietnam. More than 50,000 of them lost their lives, and many thousands more were wounded. Billions of dollars were poured into the effort, damaging the once unparalleled American economy to such an extent that the country's competitive position was grievously impaired. The domestic disruptions to which the war gave rise did perhaps even greater damage to a society previously so self-confident that it was often accused of entertaining illusions of its own omnipotence. Millions of young people growing to maturity during the war developed attitudes of such hostility toward their own country and the civilization embodied by its institutions that their willingness to defend it against external enemies in the future was left hanging in doubt.

Why did the United States undertake these burdens and make these sacrifices in blood and treasure and domestic tranquillity? What was in it for the United States? It was a question that plagued the antiwar movement from beginning to end because the answer was so hard to find. If the United States was simply acting the part of an imperialist aggressor in Vietnam, as many in the antiwar movement professed to believe, it was imperialism of a most peculiar kind. There were no raw materials to exploit in Vietnam, and there was no overriding strategic interest involved. To Franklin Roosevelt in 1941 Indochina had been important because it was close to the source of rubber and tin, but this was no longer an important consideration. Toward the end of the war, it was discovered that there was oil off the coast of Vietnam and antiwar radicals happily seized on this news as at last providing an explanation for the American presence there. But neither Kennedy nor Johnson knew about the oil, and even if they had, they would hardly have gone to war for its sake in those pre-OPEC days when oil from the Persian Gulf could be had at two dollars a barrel.

In the absence of an economic interpretation, a psychological version of the theory of imperialism was developed to answer the maddening question: Why are we in Vietnam? This theory held that the United States was in Vietnam because it had an urge to dominate—"to impose its national obsessions on the rest of the world," in the words of a piece in the *New York Review of Books*,[1] one of the leading centers of antiwar agitation within the intellectual community. But if so, the psychic profits were as illusory as the economic ones, for the war was doing even deeper damage to the national self-confidence than to the national economy.

Yet another variant of the psychological interpretation, proposed by the economist Robert L. Heilbroner, was that "the fear of losing our place in the sun, of finding ourselves at bay, . . . motivates a great deal of the anti-Communism on which so much of American foreign policy seems to be founded." This was especially so in such underdeveloped countries as Vietnam, where "the rise of Communism would signal the end of capitalism as the dominant world order, and would force the acknowledgment that America no longer constituted the model on which the future of world civilization would be mainly based."[2]

All these theories were developed out to a desperate need to find or invent selfish or self-interested motives for the American presence in Vietnam, the better to discredit it morally. In a different context, proponents of one or another of these theories—Senator Fulbright, for example—were not above trying to discredit the American presence politically by insisting that no national interest was being served by the war. This latter contention at least had the virtue of being closer to the truth than the former. For the truth was that the United States went into Vietnam for the sake not of its own direct interests in the ordinary sense but for the sake of an ideal. The intervention was a product of the Wilsonian side of the American character—the side that went to war in 1917 to "make the world safe for democracy" and that found its contemporary incarnations in the liberal internationalism of the 1940s and the liberal anti-Communism of the 1950s. One can characterize this impulse as naive: one can describe it, as Heilbroner does (and as can be done with any virtuous act), in terms that give it a subtly self-interested flavor. But there is no rationally defensible way in which it can be called immoral.

Why, then, were we in Vietnam? To say it once again: because we were trying to save the Southern half of that country from the evils of Communism. But was the war we fought to accomplish this purpose morally worse than Communism itself? Peter L. Berger, who at the time was involved with Clergy and Laymen Concerned About Vietnam (CALCAV), wrote in 1967: "All sorts of dire results might well follow a reduction or a withdrawal of the American engagement in Vietnam. Morally speaking, however, it is safe to assume that none of these could be worse than what is taking place right now." Unlike most of his fellow members of CALCAV, Berger would later repent of this statement. Writing in 1980, he would say of it: "Well, it was not safe to assume. . . . I was wrong and so were all those who thought as I did." For "contrary to what most members (including myself) of the antiwar movement expected, the peoples of Indochina have, since 1975, been subjected to suffering far worse than anything that was inflicted upon them by the United States and its allies."[3]

To be sure, the "bloodbath" that had been feared by supporters of the war did not occur—not in the precise form that had been anticipated. In contrast to what they did upon taking power in Hanoi in 1954 (when they murdered some 50,000 landlords), or what they did during their brief occupation of Hue during the Tet offensive of 1968 (when they massacred 3,000 civilians), the Communists did not stage mass executions in the newly conquered South. According to Nguyen Cong Hoan, who had been an NLF agent and then became a member of the National Assembly of the newly united Communist Vietnam before disillusionment drove him to escape in March 1977, there were more executions in the provinces than in the cities and the total number might well have reached into the tens of thousands. But as another fervent opponent of the war, the *New York Times* columnist Tom Wicker was forced to acknowledge, "what Vietnam has given us instead of a bloodbath [is] a vast tide of human misery in Southeast Asia—hundreds of thousands of homeless persons in United Nations camps, perhaps as many more dead in flight, tens of thousands of the most pitiable forcibly repatriated to Cambodia, no one knows how many adrift on the high seas or wandering the roads."[4]

Among the refugees Wicker was talking about here were those who came to be known as "the boat people" because they "literally threw themselves upon the South China Sea in small coastal craft. . . ."[5] Many thousands of these people were ethnic Chinese who were being driven out and forced to pay everything they had for leaky boats; tens of thousands more were Vietnamese fleeing voluntarily from what Nguyen Cong Hoan describes as "the most inhuman and oppressive regime they have ever known."[6] The same judgment is made by Truong Nhu Tang, the former

Minister of Justice in the PRG who fled in November 1979 in a boat loaded with forty refugees: "Never has any previous regime brought such masses of people to such desperation. Not the military dictators, not the colonialists, not even the ancient Chinese overlords."[7]

So desperate were they to leave that they were willing to take the poor chance of survival in flight rather than remain. Says Nguyen Cong Hoan: ". . . Our people have a traditional attachment to their country. No Vietnamese would willingly leave home, homeland, and ancestors' graves. During the most oppressive French colonial rule and Japanese domination, no one escaped by boat at great risk to their lives. Yet you see that my countrymen by the thousands and from all walks of life, including a number of disillusioned Vietcongs, continue to escape from Vietnam; six out of ten never make it, and for those who are fortunate to make it, they are not allowed to land."[8] Adds one of the disillusioned who did make it, Doan Van Toai: "Among the boat people who survived, including those who were raped by pirates and those who suffered in the refugee camps, nobody regrets his escape from the present regime."[9]

Though they invented a new form of the Communist bloodbath, the North Vietnamese (for, to repeat, before long there were no Southerners in authority in the South, not even former members of the NLF and the PRG) were less creative in dealing with political opposition, whether real or imagined. The "re-education camps" they had always used for this purpose in the North were now extended to the South, but the result was not so much an indigenous system of Vietnamese concentration camps as an imitation of the Soviet Gulag. (*The Vietnamese Gulag*, indeed, was the name Doan Van Toai gave to the book he published about the camps in 1979.) The French journalist Jean Lacouture, who had supported the Communists during the war to the point (as he now admitted) of turning himself into a "vehicle and intermediary for a lying and criminal propaganda, [an] ingenuous spokesman for tyranny in the name of liberty,"[10] now tried to salvage his integrity by telling the truth about a re-education camp he was permitted to visit by a regime that had good reason to think him friendly. "It was," he wrote, "a prefabricated hell."[11]

Doan Van Toai, who had been in the jails over which so much moral outrage had been expended in the days of Thieu, describes the conditions he himself encountered when he was arrested by the Communists: "I was thrown into a three-foot-by-six-foot cell with my left hand chained to my right foot and my right hand chained to my left foot. My food was rice mixed with sand. . . . After two months in solitary confinement, I was transferred to a collective cell, a room 15 feet wide and 25 feet long, where at different times anywhere from 40 to 100 prisoners were crushed together. Here we had to take turns lying down to sleep and most of the younger, stronger prisoners slept sitting up. In the sweltering heat, we also took turns snatching a few breaths of fresh air in front of the narrow opening that was the cell's only window. Every day I watched my friends die at my feet."[12]

Toai adds: "One South Vietnamese Communist, Nguyen Van Tang, who was detained 15 years by the French, eight years by Diem, six years by Thieu, and who is still in jail today, this time in a Communist prison, told me . . . 'My dream now is not to be released; it is not to see my family. My dream is that I could be back in a French prison 30 years ago.' "[13]

No one knows how many people were sent to the Vietnamese Gulag. Five years after the fall of Saigon, estimates ranged from 150,000 to a million. Prime Minister Pham Van Dong, who so impressed Mary McCarthy with his nobility in 1968, told a French magazine ten years later that he had "*released* more than one million prisoners from the camps,"[14] although according to the figures of his own government he had arrested only 50,000 in the first place.

These prisoners naturally included officials of the former government of South Vietnam, but many opponents of the Thieu regime could also be found among them, some of whom were by 1981 known to have died in the camps. One such Thic Thien Minh, "the strategist of all the Buddhist peace movements in Saigon, . . . who was sentenced to 10 years in jail by the Thieu regime, then released after an outpouring of protest from Vietnamese and antiwar protesters around the world," and who died after six months of detention by the Communists in 1979. Another was Tran Van Tuyen, a leader of the opposition to Thieu in the Saigon Assembly. A third was the philosopher Ho Huu Tuong, "perhaps the leading intellectual in South Vietnam," who died in a Communist prison in 1980. All these—along with other opponents of Thieu possibly still alive, like Bui Tuong Huan, former president of Hué University; Father Tran Huu Thanh, a dissident Catholic priest; and Tran Ngoc Chau, whose own brother had been a North Vietnamese agent—were arrested (and of course held without trial) "in order," says Toai, "to preempt any possible opposition to the Communists."[15]

Before the Communist takeover, there had been a considerable degree of political freedom in South Vietnam which manifested itself in the existence of many different parties. After the North Vietnamese conquest, all these parties were dissolved: as for the NLF, "they buried it," in the bitter words of Truong Nhu Tang, "without even a ceremony," and "at the simple farewell dinner we held to formally disband the NLF in late 1976 neither the party nor the government sent a representative." The people of Vietnam, who "want only the freedom to go where they wish, educate their children in the schools they choose and have a voice in their government" are instead "treated like ants in a colony. There is only the opportunity to follow orders strictly, never the opportunity to express disagreement. Even within the [Communist] party, the principle of democracy has been destroyed in favor of the most rigid hierarchy. Stalinism, discredited throughout most of the Communist world, flourishes under the aged and fanatic Vietnamese leadership."[16]

Reading these words, one recalls Susan Sontag, Mary McCarthy, and Frances FitzGerald expending their intellectual energies on the promulgation of theories of Vietnamese culture calculated to deny that the people of Vietnam cared about freedom in the simple concrete terms set forth by Tang. One recalls Sontag saying that "incorporation" into a society like that of North Vietnam would "greatly improve the lives of most people in the world." One also recalls that both Sontag and McCarthy were troubled by the portraits of Stalin they saw all over the North; they were there, Sontag thought, because the Vietnamese could not bear to waste anything. Perhaps that is also how she would explain why portraits of Soviet leaders began appearing in public buildings, schools, and administrative offices throughout South Vietnam after 1975, and why the following poem by To Huu, president of the Communist Party Committee of Culture and a possible successor to Pham Van Dong,[17] was given a prominent place in an anthology of contemporary Vietnamese poetry published in Hanoi in the seventies:

Oh, Stalin! Oh, Stalin!
The love I bear my father, my mother, my wife, myself
It's nothing beside the love I bear you.
Oh, Stalin! Oh, Stalin!
What remains of the earth and of the sky
Now that you are dead?[18]

Written on the occasion of Stalin's death, this poem no doubt earned its place in an anthology twenty years later by virtue of its relevance to the spirit of the new Communist Vietnam. For if the Vietnamese Communist party is Stalinist, so is the society over which it rules. "Immediately after the fall of Saigon, the Government closed all bookshops and theaters. All books published under the former regimes were confiscated or burned. Cultural literature was not exempt, including translations of Jean-Paul Sartre, Albert Camus and Dale Carnegie [!]. . . . The new regime replaced such books with literature designed to indoctrinate children and adults with the idea that the 'Soviet Union is a paradise of the socialist world.' "[19]

As with books, so with newspapers. Under the old regime, under constant attack throughout the world for its repressiveness, there had been *twenty-seven* daily newspapers, three television stations, and more than twenty radio stations. "When the Communists took over," writes the political analyst Carl Gershman, "these were all closed down, and replaced by two official dailies, one television channel, and two radio stations—all disseminating the same government propaganda."[20]

All the other freedoms that existed, either in full or large measure, under the Thieu regime were also eliminated by the Communists. Freedom of movement began to be regulated by a system of internal passports, and freedom of association was abolished to the point where even a large family gathering, such as a wedding or a funeral, required a government permit and was attended by a security officer.

Freedom of religion, too, was sharply curtailed. The Buddhists, who were so effective an element in the opposition to Diem, soon learned that there were worse regimes than his. A Human Rights Appeal drafted by the Unified Buddhist Church and smuggled out by the Venerable Thich Manh Giac when he escaped by boat, charged that the government, "pursuing the policy of shattering the religious communities in our country, . . . has arrested hundreds of monks, confiscated hundreds of pagodas and converted them to government administration buildings, removed and smashed Buddha and Bodhisattva statues, prohibited celebration of the Buddha's birthday as a national holiday, . . . and forbidden monks to travel and preach by ordering restrictions in the name of 'national security.' "[21]

Unlike demonstrations by Buddhists in 1963, this appeal fell on deaf ears; whereas a raid on a Buddhist temple led directly to the overthrow of Diem, a similar raid by the Communist police in April 1977 went unnoticed; and whereas the self-immolation of a single Buddhist monk in 1963 attracted the horrified attention of the whole world, the self-immolation of twelve Buddhist nuns and priests on November 2, 1975, in protest against Communist repression, received scarcely any notice either in the United States or anywhere else.

When all this is combined with the terrible economic hardships that descended upon Vietnam after 1975—hardships that were simultaneously caused by the new regime and used by it to justify resettling millions of people in the so-called New Economic Zones, remote jungle areas where they worked "in collective gangs at such tasks as clearing land and digging canals,"[22] under primitive living conditions with little food and rampant disease—it is easy to see why a sense of despair soon settled over the country. Truong Nhu Tang: "The fact is that today Communism has been rejected by the people and the even many party members are questioning their faith. Members of the former resistance, their sympathizers and those who supported the Vietcong are disgusted and filled with bitterness. These innocent people swear openly that had they another chance their choice would be very different. The commonly heard expression is: I would give them not even a grain of rice. I pull them out of their hiding holes and denounce them to the authorities."[23]

The Buddhist human-rights appeal conveyed much the same impression: "Since the liberation thousands have committed suicide out of despair. Thousands have fled the country in small boats. Hospitals are reserved for cadres: civilians hardly have a chance to be hospitalized in case of sickness, while more than 200 doctors remain in detention. Schoolchildren under fourteen have been assigned to collect pieces of scrap material in big garbage heaps and other places during the summer vacation. . . . A country that used to export rice has no rice to eat, even though the number of 'laborers' has now increased about ten times." The government, the appeal went on to say, prohibits "creative thinking and participation of independent groups. Totalitarianism destroys all possibility of genuine national reconciliation and concord."[24]

Some years after these words were written, a great and angry dispute broke out in the United States over the question of whether there was any practical validity or moral point in the distinction between authoritarianism and totalitarianism. Not surprisingly, those who dismissed the distinction as academic were in general veterans of the antiwar movement, who still refused to see that (as Gershman said in 1978) "for the Vietnamese, the distinction between a society that is authoritarian . . . and one that is totalitarian" turned out to be anything but academic.[25]

Peter L. Berger, one of the few former members of the antiwar movement who recognizes that "the transformation of Saigon into Ho Chi Minh City now offers a crystal-clear illustration of the difference between authoritarianism and totalitarianism, both in terms of political science and political morality," expresses amazement at "the persistent incapacity of even American professors to grasp a difference understood by every taxi driver in Prague." He believes that this incapacity derives in large part from a strong ideological interest in hiding "the fact that totalitarianism today is limited to socialist societies"—a fact that "flies in the face of the socialist dream that haunts the intellectual imagination of the West. . . ."[26]

I have no doubt that Berger is right about this. But where Vietnam in particular is concerned, there is a strong interest not only in protecting the socialist dream in general but, more specifically, in holding on to the sense of having been on the morally superior side in opposing the American struggle to prevent the replacement of an authoritarian regime in the South with a totalitarian system. The truth is that the antiwar movement bears a certain measure of responsibility for the horrors that have overtaken the people of Vietnam; and so long as those who participated in that movement are unwilling to acknowledge this, they will go on trying to discredit the idea that there is a distinction between authoritarianism and totalitarianism. For to recognize the distinction is to recognize that in making a contribution to the conquest of South Vietnam by the Communists of the North, they were siding with an evil system against something much better from every political and moral point of view.

Some veterans of the antiwar movement have protected themselves from any such acknowledgment of guilt by the simple expedient of denying that there is any truth in the reports by refugees like Toai, Coan, and Tang or journalists like Lacouture. Noam Chomsky, for example, speaks of "the extreme unreliability" of these reports,[27] and he is echoed by William Kunstler, Dave Dellinger, and other inveterate apologists for the Vietnamese Communists. Peter Berger compares such people to "individuals who deny the facts of the Holocaust" and rightly considers them "outside the boundaries of rational discourse."[28]

There are, however, others—like the editors of the Socialist magazine *Dissent,* Irving Howe and Michael Walzer—who are fully aware of the horrors that have followed the American withdrawal and the Communist conquest, and who are at least willing to ask, "Were We Wrong about Vietnam?" But of course their answer to this question is No. They were right because they were against both Saigon *and* Hanoi: they were right "in refusing to support the imperial backers of both." What then did they support? "Some of us . . . hoped for the emergence of a Vietnamese 'third force' capable of rallying the people in a progressive direction by enacting land reforms and defending civil liberties." But since, as they admit, there was very little chance of any such alternative, to have thrown their energies into opposing the American effort was tantamount to working for the Communist victory they say they did not want. Nevertheless, they still congratulate themselves on being against the evils on both sides of the war: "Those of us who opposed American intervention yet did not want a Communist victory were in the difficult position of having no happy ending to offer—for the sad reason that no happy ending was possible any longer, if ever it had been. And we were in the difficult position of urging a relatively complex argument at a moment when most Americans, pro- and antiwar, wanted blinding simplicities."[29] This is not moral choice; this is moral evasion—irresponsible utopianism disguised as moral realism. Given the actual alternatives that existed, what did the urging of "a relatively complex argument" avail for any purpose other than to make those who urged it feel pleased with themselves? If it served any purpose at all for the people of South Vietnam, it was to help deliver them over to the "blinding simplicities" of the totalitarianism Howe and Walzer so piously deplore and whose hideous workings they are now happy to denounce and protest against, even though there is no one in Ho Chi Minh City or Hanoi to listen or to hear.

Another veteran of the antiwar movement, Professor Stanley Hoffmann of Harvard, who also sees "no reason not to protest the massacres, arbitrary arrests, and persecutions perpetrated by the regimes that have taken over atter our exit," nevertheless urges "those who condemned the war . . . to resist all attempts to make them feel guilty for the stand they took against the war." It was not, says Hoffmann, the antiwar movement that contributed to these horrors, but rather the people (led by Nixon and Kissinger) who were supposedly fighting to prevent them. True as this was of Vietnam—where "a monstrously disproportionate and self-destructive campaign" only added "to the crimes and degradation of eventual Communist victory"—it was even truer of Cambodia. "All those who, somehow, believe that the sufferings inflicted on the Cambodian people, first by the Pol Pot regime, and now by the Vietnamese, retrospectively justify America's attempt to save Phnom Penh from the Reds" were instructed by Hoffmann in 1979 to read a new book "showing that the monsters who decimated the Cambodian people were brought to power by Washington's policies."[30]

The book Hoffmann was referring to, *Sideshow: Kissinger, Nixon and the Destruction of Cambodia*, by the English journalist William Shawcross, sought to demonstrate that those Americans who fought to stop the Communists from coming to power in Cambodia were responsible for the crimes the Communists committed when the fight against them was lost. They can be held responsible, not as one might imagine because they did not fight as hard as they should have, or because in the end they deserted the field, but on the contrary because they entered the field in the first place. By attacking—first by bombing, then by invading—the North Vietnamese sanctuaries in Cambodia, the Americans (that is, Nixon and Kissinger) not only drove the Communists deeper into Cambodia, thereby bringing the war to areas that had previously been at peace. They also intensified the rage and bitterness of the Khmer Rouge (as the Cambodian Communists under Pol Pot were called), thereby turning them into perhaps the most murderous rulers ever seen on the face of the earth.

Sideshow is a brilliantly written and argued book. Indeed, not since Hannah Arendt's *Eichmann in Jerusalem*—which shifts a large measure of responsibility for the murder of six million Jews from the Nazis who committed the murders to the Jewish leaders who were trying to save as many of their people as they could—has there been so striking an illustration of the perverse moral and intellectual uses to which brilliance can be put.

There are, for example, the clever distortions and omissions that enable Shawcross to charge the Nixon Administration with having destabilized the neutral government of Prince Norodom Sihanouk by bombing the sanctuaries (when in fact Sihanouk welcomed these attacks on the Communist military bases within his own country which he himself was not powerful enough to banish) and with causing large numbers of civilian casualties by the indiscriminate pattern of the bombing raids (when in fact care was taken to minimize civilian casualties). But what is fully on a par of perversity with Hannah Arendt's interpretation of the Jewish role in the genocidal program of the Nazis against them is the idea that Pol Pot and his followers needed the experience of American bombing and the "punishment" they subsequently suffered in the war against the anti-Communist forces of Cambodia to turn them into genocidal monsters.

This idea about the Khmer Rouge can easily enough be refuted by the simple facts of the case. Thus according to Kenneth Quinn, who conducted hundreds of interviews with refugees from Cambodia, the Khmer Rouge began instituting the totalitarian practices of their revolutionary program in areas they controlled as early as 1971.[31] So too Father François Ponchaud, who was in Phnom Penh when the Communists arrived and whose book *Cambodia: Year Zero* Shawcross himself calls "the best account of Khmer Rouge rule":[32] "The evacuation of Phnom Penh follows traditional Khmer revolutionary practice: ever since 1972 the guerrilla fighters had been sending all the inhabitants of the villages and towns they occupied into the forests to live, often burning their homes so they would have nothing to come back for."[33]

Indeed, as Shawcross himself points out, this revolutionary program was outlined in uncannily clear detail in the thesis written at the University of Paris in 1959 by Khieu Samphan, who would later become the Khmer Rouge commander in chief during the war and the head of state afterward. But Shawcross, in line with his own thesis that it was the war that made "the Khmer Rouge . . . more and more vicious,"[34] stresses that "the methods this twenty-eight-year-old Marxist prescribed in 1959 for the transformation of his country were essentially moderate."[35] In support of the same thesis, he quotes Quinn to the effect that "the first steps to change radically the nature of Khmer society" that the Khmer Rouge took in 1971 were "limited."[36]

What Shawcross fails or refuses to see is what Ponchaud understands about such moderate methods and limited steps—namely, that they remained moderate and limited only so long as the Khmer Rouge lacked the power to put them into practice. "Accusing foreigners cannot acquit the present leaders of Kampuchea," Ponchaud wrote (before the Vietnamese invaded Cambodia and replaced the Khmer Rouge Communists with a puppet Communist regime of their own); "their inflexible ideology has led them to invent a radically new kind of man in a radically new society." Or again: "On April 17, 1975, a society collapsed: another is now being born from the fierce drive of a revolution which is incontestably the most radical ever to take place in so short a time. It is a perfect example of the application of an ideology pushed to the furthest limits of its internal logic."[37]

The blindness to the power of ideas that prevents Shawcross from recognizing ideology as the source of the crimes committed against their own people by the Khmer Rouge is his greatest intellectual sin. It is a species of philistinism to which many contemporary intellectuals (who, as intellectuals, might be expected to attribute a disproportionate importance to the role of ideas) are paradoxically prone, and it takes the form of looking for material factors to account for historical developments even when, as in this case, the main causal element is clearly located in the realm of ideas.

But this sin is exceeded in seriousness by the moral implications of Shawcross's book. As Peter W. Rodman (who has been an aide to Henry Kissinger both in and out of government) says in concluding a devastating critique of Shawcross's scholarship: "By no stretch of moral logic can the crimes of mass murderers be ascribed to those who struggled to prevent their coming into power. One hopes that no craven sophistry will ever induce free peoples to accept the doctrine that Shawcross embodies: that resistance to totalitarianism is immoral."[38]

Yet it is just this "craven sophistry" that Stanley Hoffmann reaffirms in the very face of the horrors that have befallen the peoples of Indochina under Communist rule: "As Frances FitzGerald put it," he writes,"our mistake was in creating and building up 'the wrong side,' and we were led by that mistake to a course of devastation and defeat."[39] One can almost forgive

Anthony Lewis for asking "What future possibility could be more terrible than the reality of what is happening to Cambodia now?"[40] since he asked this question before the Khmer Rouge took over. One can almost forgive the *New York Times* for the headline "Indochina without Americans: For Most, A Better Life" on a piece from Phnom Penh by Sydney H. Schanberg[41] since it was written before the Khmer Rouge had begun evacuating the city and instituting a regime that led to the death of nearly half the population of the country. Such writers should have known enough about the history of Communism to know better, and they should now be ashamed of their naïvete and of the contribution they made to the victory of forces they had a moral duty to oppose. Nevertheless, they were not yet aware of what Hoffmann already knew when he *still* described the Communists as the right side in Indochina and still denounced those who resisted them as immoral and even criminal. This is almost impossible to forgive.

In May 1977, two full years after the Communist takeover, President Jimmy Carter—a repentant hawk, like many members of his cabinet, including his Secretary of State and his Secretary of Defense—spoke of "the intellectual and moral poverty" of the policy that had led us into Vietnam and had kept us there for so long. When Ronald Reagan, an unrepentant hawk, called the war "a noble cause" in the course of his ultimately successful campaign to replace Carter in the White House, he was accused of having made a "gaffe." Fully, painfully aware as I am that the American effort to save Vietnam from Communism was indeed beyond our intellectual and moral capabilities, I believe the story shows that Reagan's "gaffe" was closer to the truth of why we were in Vietnam and what we did there, at least until the very end, than Carter's denigration of an act of imprudent idealism whose moral soundness has been so overwhelmingly vindicated by the hideous consequences of our defeat.

32

An Act of Imperialism

Noam Chomsky

AT 8 A.M. ON APRIL 30, 1975, THE LAST U.S. Marine helicopter took off from the roof of the American Embassy in Saigon. Less than five hours later, General Minh made the following announcement over the Saigon radio: "*I, General Duong Van Minh, President of the Saigon Government, appeal to the armed forces of the Republic of Vietnam to lay down their arms and surrender to the forces of the NLF unconditionally. I declare that the Saigon Government, from central to local level, has been completely dissolved.*"[1]

For the United States, these events signaled the end of a quarter-century-effort to maintain Western domination over all or part of Indochina. For the Vietnamese, it meant that the foreign invaders had finally been repelled and their colonial structures demolished, after more than a century of struggle.

With fitting symmetry, history had come full circle. "The first act of armed intervention by a Western power in Vietnam," according to the Vietnamese historian Truong Buu Lam, "is generally held to have been perpetrated in 1845 by a ship of the United States Navy, the *Constitution*," in an effort to force the release of a French bishop.[2] The skipper of "Old Ironsides" was Commander John Percival known as "Mad Jack." Sailors under his command "disembarked at Danang and proceeded to terrorize the local population . . . United States sailors fired on an unresisting crowd and several dozens were killed" before Mad Jack withdrew in failure.[3] A few years later the French navy returned and took Da Nang, and in the years that followed, established their imperial rule over all of Indochina, bringing misery and disaster. The agronomist Nghiem Xuan Yem wrote in 1945 that under French colonization "*our people have always been hungry* . . . so hungry that the whole population had not a moment of free time to think of anything besides the problem of survival."[4] In the northern parts of the country, two million people are reported to have died of starvation in a few months in 1945.[5]

Throughout this period, resistance never ceased. Early French eyewitnesses reported that

> We have had enormous difficulties in imposing our authority in our new colony. Rebel bands disturb the country everywhere.[6] The fact was that the centre of resistance was everywhere, subdivided to infinity, almost as many times as there were Annamese. It would be more exact to consider each farmer busy tying up a sheaf of rice as a centre of resistance.[7]

Meanwhile, the French complained, the only collaborators are

> intriguers, disreputable or ignorant, whom we had rigged out with sometimes high ranks, which became tools in their hands for plundering the country without scruple. . . . Despised, they possessed neither the spiritual culture nor the moral fibre that would have allowed them to understand and carry out their task.[8]

A century later, the imperial overlords had changed, but their complaints never varied. The resistance, however, did significantly change its character over the years:

> At first, the partisans fought to recover the independence of their country to avenge their king, and to safeguard their traditional pattern of life. By the 1900's, as the occupation developed into a systematic exploitation of the colony's economic resources, creating in its wake large-scale social disruptions, slogans of explicit social and political values were added to the original calls for independence from the French. The spontaneous reaction against foreigners, the armed struggle to oust them, had grown into a demand for revolutionary—political and later social—changes.[9]

The August revolution of 1945, led by the Viet Minh, was the culmination of a struggle of revolutionary nationalism. On September 2, President Ho Chi Minh proclaimed the independence of Vietnam:

> Our people have broken the chains which for a century have fettered us, and have won independence for the Fatherland. Viet Nam has the right to be free and independent and in fact it is so already. The entire Vietnamese people are determined to mobilize all their physical and mental strength, to sacrifice their lives and property, in order to safeguard their freedom and independence.[10]

. . . It is important to bear in mind that the United States Government was never in any doubt as to the basic facts of the situation in Vietnam. Intelligence reports describe the "intense desire on the part of the Annamese for independence and thorough hatred by them of the French and any other white people who happen to be in any way supporting or sympathizing with the French."[11] The Headquarters of the OSS, China Theatre, reported to the Chief of the Intelligence Division on September 19, 1945, that Emperor Bao Dai, in an interview, "stated that he had voluntarily abdicated, and was not coerced by the Provisional Government," because he approved "the nationalistic action of the Viet Minh" and preferred to "live as a private citizen with a free people than rule a nation of slaves." On the same date, the same source reported an interview with Ho Chi Minh, "the President of the Provisional Government of Viet Nam," in which Ho assured him that "his people are prepared for a long struggle of ten or twenty years, and are willing to fight for the freedom, not of their own, but of future generations." He reported his personal opinion that "Mr. Ho Chi Minh is a brilliant and capable man, completely sincere in his opinions," and that "when he speaks, he speaks for his people, for I have travelled throughout Tonkin province, and found in that area people of all classes are imbued with the same spirit and determination as their leader." The new government, he reported, "is an outgrowth of the controlling forces in the military resistance"; "Viet Nam looks to America for moral support in their struggle, almost expect it." A "personal observation" of October 17 certifies "to the fact that the great mass of the population supports Ho Chi Minh and his party, and to the anti-Japanese action in which they have engaged . . . In travelling through Tonkin, every village flew the Viet Minh flag . . . The women and children were also organized, and all were enthusiastic in their support." The report continues that American observers "saw how well the majority of the people follow the orders of Ho Chi Minh and the Provisional Government," apart from "some of the wealthy merchants and former high Annamese officials."

As for those at the receiving end of these communications, the State Department's assessment of Ho Chi Minh and the Provisional Government of Vietnam was summed up this way by Abbot Low Moffat, the Chief of the Division of Southeast Asian Affairs:

> I have never met an American, be he military, OSS, diplomat, or journalist, who had met Ho Chi Minh who did not reach the same belief: that Ho Chi Minh was first and foremost a Vietnamese

> nationalist. He was also a Communist and believed that Communism offered the best hope for the Vietnamese people. But his loyalty was to his people. When I was in Indochina it was striking how the top echelon of competent French officials held almost unanimously the same view. Actually, there was no alternative to an agreement with Ho Chi Minh or to a crushing of the nationalist groundswell which my own observations convinced me could not be done. Any other government recognized by the French would of necessity be puppets of the French and incapable of holding the loyalty of the Vietnamese people.[12]

Thus, the United States committed itself with its eyes open and with full knowledge of what it was doing to crushing the nationalist forces of Indochina. "Question whether Ho as much nationalist as Commie is irrelevant," Secretary of State Dean Acheson explained. Quite the contrary, he urged in May 1949, that "no effort should be spared" to assure the success of the French Quisling government, since there seemed to be "no other alternative to estab Commie pattern Vietnam." And on the eve of the Korean war, in March 1950, Acheson observed that French military success "depends, in the end, on overcoming opposition of indigenous population"; we must help the French "to protect IC from further COMMIE encroachments."[13]

Two years earlier, a State Department Policy Statement of September 1948 had spelled out the fundamental "dilemma" which the United States faced in Indochina. It was a "dilemma" which would never cease to haunt American policy makers. The "dilemma" was this. The Communists under Ho Chi Minh had "captur[ed] control of the nationalist movement," thus impeding the "long-term objective" of the United states, namely, "to eliminate so far as possible Communist influence in Indochina." The State Department analysis added that "our inability to suggest any practicable solution of the Indochina problem" was caused by "the unpleasant fact that Communist Ho Chi Minh is the strongest and perhaps the ablest figure in Indochina and that any suggested solution which excludes him is an expedient of uncertain outcome." But to the very end, the United States continued to back former agents of French colonialism, who easily transferred their allegiance to the successor imperial power, against the nationalist movement "captured" (by implication, illegitimately) by the Viet Minh and its successors.

This "dilemma" is absolutely central to the understanding of the evolution of American policy in Indochina. The *Pentagon Papers* historian, considering the situation after the Tet offensive of 1968, asks whether the United States can "overcome the apparent fact that the Viet Cong have 'captured' the Vietnamese nationalist movement while the GVN has become the refuge of Vietnamese who were allied with the French in the battle against the independence of their nation." It does not occur to him to ask whether the United States *should* attempt to "overcome" this fact. Rather, the problem is a tactical one: how can the fact be overcome? In this analysis, the historian reflects quite accurately the tacit assumptions that were unquestioned in the extensive documentary record.

For propaganda purposes, the issue was reformulated. It was our noble task to protect Indochina from "aggression." Thus the *Pentagon Papers* historian, in the musings just cited, continues by observing that the question he raises is "complicated, of course, by the difficult issue of Viet Cong allegiance to and control by Communist China." Again, the historian accurately reflects the mentality revealed in the documents. He does not try to *demonstrate* that the Viet Cong owed allegiance to Communist China or were controlled by Peking. Rather, he adopts the premise as an *a priori* truth, untroubled by the fact that no evidence was ever brought forth to substantiate it.

Not that intelligence didn't try. Elaborate attempts were made to demonstrate that the Viet Minh and its successors were merely the agents of some foreign master. It was, in fact, a point of rigid doctrine that this must be true, and no evidence to the contrary served to challenge the doctrine. Depending on date and mood, the foreign master might be the Kremlin or "Peiping," but the principle itself could not be questioned.

The function of the principle is transparent: it served to justify the commitment "to defend the territorial integrity of IC and prevent the incorporation of the ASSOC[iated] States within the COMMIE-dominated bloc of slave states" (Acheson, October 1950), or to safeguard Vietnam from "aggressive designs Commie Chi" (Acheson, May 1949) by support for the French puppet regime. One of the most startling revelations in the *Pentagon Papers* is that in the twenty-year period under review, the analysts were able to discover only one staff paper (an intelligence estimate of 1961) "which treats communist reactions primarily in terms of the separate national interests of Hanoi, Moscow, and Peiping, rather than primarily in terms of an overall communist strategy for which Hanoi is acting as an agent."

Intelligence labored manfully to provide the evidence required by the doctrine. But their failure was total. It was impossible to establish what had to be true, that Ho Chi Minh was a puppet of the Kremlin or "Peiping."[14] Faced with this problem, American officials in Saigon reached the following casuistic conclusion: "It may be assumed that Moscow feels that Ho and his lieutenants have had sufficient training experience and are sufficiently loyal to be trusted to determine their day-to-day policy without supervision." In short, the absence of evidence that Ho was a puppet was held up as conclusive proof that he "really" was an agent of international communism after all, an agent so loyal and trustworthy that no directives were even necessary.

The whole amazing story gives a remarkable indication of how effective are the controls over thought and analysis in American society. It is a gross error to describe the *Pentagon Papers*, as is commonly done, as a record of government lies. On the contrary, the record reveals that the top policy planners and, for the most part, the intelligence agencies were prisoners of the ideology of our highly ideological society No less than "independent intellectuals" in the press and the universities, they believed precisely those doctrines that had to be believed in order to absolve the United States of the charge of aggression in Indochina. Evidence was—and remains—beside the point.

Not only were the Viet Minh necessarily agents of a foreign power, they were also literally "aggressors." The National Security Council, in February 1950, held that France and the native armies it had assembled "is now in armed conflict with the forces of communist aggression." A presidential commission of early 1954 added that France was fighting "to defend the cause of liberty and freedom from Communism in Indochina" while the cause of the Viet Minh is "the cause of colonization and subservience to Kremlin rule as was the case in China, in North Korea and in the European satellites." Later internal documents refer generally to the VC aggression in the South and describe the Pathet Lao in Laos as "aggressors." Indeed, the Joint Chiefs of Staff went so far as to characterize "political warfare, or subversion" as a form of aggression. And Adlai Stevenson informed the United Nations Security Council that "the United States cannot stand by while Southeast Asia is overrun by armed aggressors," adding that "the point is the same in Vietnam today as it was in Greece in 1947," where the United States was also defending a free people from "internal aggression," a marvelous new Orwellian construction.

By and large the New Frontiersmen were quite at home with this rhetoric. With "aggression checked in Vietnam," writes Arthur Schlesinger, "1962 had not been a bad year."[15] In fact, 1962 was the first year in which U.S. military forces were directly engaged in combat and combat support, the bombing of villages, the gunning down of peasants from helicopters, defoliation, etc. Only three years later, in April 1965, did U.S. intelligence report the presence of the first North Vietnamese battalion in the south.

It is important to recognize that these ridiculous rationalizations for American aggression in Indochina were accepted in their essentials within the American "intellectual community." Left-liberal opinion, regarding itself as "opposing the war," called for a peace settlement between South and North Vietnam with American troops in place in the South; in short, a victory for American imperialism.[16] The war is described in retrospect as a "tragic error," where worthy impulse was "transmuted into bad policy," a case of "blundering efforts to do good." Such assessments are offered even by people who became committed opponents of the war in its latter phases. The plain and obvious fact that the United States was guilty of aggression in Indochina is rejected with horror and contempt; or, to be more accurate, it is simply dismissed as beyond the bounds of polite discourse by liberal commentators. These facts give an important insight into the nature of the liberal opposition to the war which later developed, largely on "pragmatic" grounds, when it became obvious that the costs of the war to us (or, for the more sensitive, to the Vietnamese as well) were too great for us to bear.[17]

The fundamental dilemma, perceived from the start, permitted only two outcomes to the American involvement in Indochina. The United States government might on the one hand choose to come to terms with the Vietnamese nationalist movement, or it might bend its efforts to the destruction of the Viet Minh and its successors. The first course was never seriously contemplated. Therefore, the United States committed itself to the destruction of the revolutionary nationalist forces in Indochina. Given the astonishing strength and resiliency of the resistance, the American intervention in Vietnam became a war of annihilation. In every part of Indochina, the pattern was repeated. As in the days of the early French conquest, "each farmer busy tying up a sheaf of rice" might be "a centre of resistance." Inevitably, the United States undertook to destroy the rural society.

American intellectuals dutifully supplied the rationale. We were engaged in a process of "urbanization and modernization," they explained, as we drove the peasants out of their villages by bombs, artillery and search-and-destroy operations, simultaneously destroying the countryside to ensure that return would be impossible. Or, the United States was helping to control "village thugs" in violent peasant societies where "terrorists can operate largely unmolested whether or not the local population supports them" (Ithiel de Sola Pool). More generally:

> In the Congo, in Vietnam, in the Dominican Republic, it is clear that order depends on somehow compelling newly mobilized strata to return to a measure of passivity and defeatism from which they have recently been aroused by the process of modernization. At least temporarily, the maintenance of order requires a lowering of newly acquired aspirations and levels of political activity, [as] we have learned in the past thirty years of intensive empirical study of contemporary societies.[18]

By the end, even the more cynical and sadistic were driven to silence as the horrendous record of the achievements that they had sought to justify for many years was slowly exposed to public view.

The terminology of the "behavioral sciences" was continually invoked in an effort to delude the public and the colonial administrators themselves. "Counterinsurgency theorists" explained in sober terms that "all the dilemmas are practical and as neutral in an ethical sense as the laws of physics."[19] It is simply a matter of discovering the appropriate mix of aversive conditioning (B-52 raids, burning of villages, assassination, etc.) and positive reinforcement (the detritus of the American presence) so as to overcome the unfair advantage of the revolutionaries—revolutionaries who in fact had won popular support by virtue of their constructive programs,[20] much to the dismay of the social scientists who persisted to the end with claims to the contrary based on "empirical studies" which they never produced.

In a report to President Kennedy after a 1962 study mission in Southeast Asia, Senator Mike Mansfield discussed the "widespread support of the peasants for the Vietcong," and remarked that any "reorientation" of peasant attitudes "involves an immense job of social engineering." He anticipated the unpleasant need of "going to war fully ourselves against the guerrillas—and the establishment of some form of neocolonial rule in South Vietnam," which he "emphatically" did not recommend. Others, however, took up the task of social engineering with zeal and enthusiasm. The Australian social psychologist Alex Carey, who has studied the matter in some detail, concludes that the American pacification program was "neither more nor less than a nation-sized sociological experiment in bringing about changes, desired by American policy, in the attitudes and values of a physically captive population."[21] The more sophisticated analyst went further still. They derided the concern for popular attitudes—such mysticism has no place in a scientific civilization such as ours—and urged instead that we concern ourselves solely with more objective matters, that is, with controlling behavior. This advance to the higher stages of applied science was necessitated by the miserable failure of the colonial agents in their efforts to mimic native revolutionaries.[22]

I cannot survey here the techniques that were attempted. Perhaps the mentality of the "scientists" is sufficiently indicated in one minor experiment in operant conditioning reported in *Congressional Hearings*.[23] An American psychiatrist working in a mental hospital in Vietnam subjected one group of patients to "unmodified electroconvulsive shock" which "produces systemic convulsions similar to a grand mal epileptic seizure and in many patients is very terrifying." Others were offered work "including tending crops for American Special Forces—Green Berets—in Viet Cong territory 'under the stress of potential or actual VC attack or ambush'." Asked about the "research value" of this amusing study; Dr. Veatch, who was testifying, replied that "the entire field of behavior conditioning is of great interest in the treatment of mental patients as well as prisoners." This example, insignificant in context, reveals very clearly who was insane, the patients or the "scientists," just as academic studies on "control of village violence" leave no doubt as to who are the violent individuals who must be somehow controlled in a civilized society.

Commenting on the "experiment" just cited, Alex Carey observes that "To be mentally ill and Asian deprives a man of most of his humanity; to be a communist and Asian deprives him of all of it." He goes on to show how this experiment exhibits in microcosm the major features of the program of social engineering devised by the American descendants of [Heinrich] Himmler's SS and the Nazi physicians as they sought to design a more appropriate culture for the benighted Vietnamese once control had been gained over the population by violence and terror.

While studying the American pacification program, Carey interviewed John Paul Vann, field operations coordinator of the U.S. Operations Mission, who was generally regarded as the most important American official in Vietnam after the Ambassador and the chief military commander.[24] Vann provided him with a remarkable 1965 memorandum, since privately circulated, "in response to a request for material on the concepts and theory that had guided the pacification programme."[25] In this memorandum, Vann noted that a social revolution was in process in South Vietnam, "primarily identified with the National Liberation Front," and that "a popular political base for the government of South Vietnam does not now exist." But it is "naive" to expect that "an unsophisticated, relatively illiterate, rural population [will] recognize and oppose the evils of Communism." Therefore, the United States must institute "effective political indoctrination of the population," under an American-maintained "autocratic government."

Vann was not a brutal murderer of the style of those who designed the military operations. He objected strongly to the ongoing destruction of the civilian society by American terror. His view was that of the benevolent imperialist, the bearer of the White Man's Burden, who urged that "we should make it clear [to the Vietnamese villagers] that we continue to represent that permanent revolution of mankind which the American revolution advanced; and that only the principles of that revolution can ultimately produce the results for which mankind longs." We must overcome "the pseudo-science of communism" by the techniques of the behavioral sciences, "psywar," firm in our conviction that "our system . . . is more in keeping with the fundamentals of human nature," as John F. Kennedy once explained.[26] If the Vietnamese are too stupid to comprehend these well-known facts, then we must drill them in by force—with the most benevolent of intentions. Indeed, it would be immoral to do otherwise, just as we do not permit children of retardates to injure themselves in their innocence.

The United States Government and its agents in the field had to carry out two essential tasks. The first and most crucial was to destroy the society in which the resistance was rooted—the society "controlled by the Viet Cong," in the terminology of the propagandists. In South Vietnam, the primary victim of American aggression, a vast expeditionary force was let loose to accomplish this task. But by the late 1960s, Washington came to understand why earlier imperial aggressors—the French in Indochina, for example—had relied primarily on hired killers or native forces organized under colonial management to conduct a war against a resisting civilian population. To its credit the invading American army had begun to disintegrate, necessitating its withdrawal.[27] The disintegration was in part due to revulsion against its tasks, and in part to the indirect influence of the peace movement at home, which—as apologists for state violence lamented—was "demoralizing American public opinion."[28] Washington's response was to assign the job of destruction to more impersonal agencies—helicopter gunships, bombers, and artillery. American technology devised fiendish devices to maximize the damage done to "enemy personnel." . .

The task of destruction was accomplished with partial success. In South Vietnam, the society was virtually demolished, though the resistance was never crushed. But the aggressors faced a second and more difficult job: to construct a viable Quisling regime out of the wreckage, and to rebuild the society in accordance with the imperial vision. This effort was a dismal failure. Like the French before them, the American conquerors were able to assemble "a crew of sychophants, money-grubbers and psychopaths,"[29] but rarely more. Efforts were made to integrate the ruined societies into the "free world economy" by encouraging American and Japanese investment. Academic studies explained how foreign investment "must be liberated from the uncertainties and obstacles that beset it" so that it might take advantage of the cheap labor offered by a society of rootless atomized individuals driven from their villages by American urbanization, a virtually ideal labor market.[30] It was hoped that with the vast flow of arms and the expansion of the police, the merry crew of torturers and extortionists placed into power by the United States would somehow manage to control the population.

To the very end, the American government was committed to victory, at least in South Vietnam. To fend off liberal criticism, [Henry] Kissinger and his press entourage spoke vaguely of a "decent interval," but there is no evidence that they looked forward to anything short of total victory for the American client regime. Nonetheless, success was beyond their grasp. When Washington was no longer able to call forth the B-52's, the whole rotten structure collapsed from within, virtually without combat. Symbolic of the American failure in its second task—reconstruction of the society it had demolished—was the "fall of Danang," where the foreign aggression began more than a century before. Three intact ARVN divisions with more than 100,000 men and enough ammunition for a six-month siege were stationed in Danang, as of March 26. "Thirty-six hours later, without a single shot having been fired, the ARVN ceased to exist as a fighting unit." What happened is described by a French teacher who remained:

> The officers fled by air taking with them the ground crews so that the pilots that had stayed on could not get their planes started. Left without leaders the army fell apart. On March 28 widespread looting started. The rice stocks were sacked and in the hospitals the army and the local staff stole all the drugs in order to sell them on the black market. Then the army started shooting civilians at random, often to steal their motorcycles. By then half of the army was in civilian clothes, which they had stolen. For 36 hours, with the Vietcong nowhere in sight but with rumors of their arrival constantly spreading, the city became a nightmare. By that time the population had but one hope: that the Vietcong would arrive as quickly as possible to restore order, any order.

Many civilians fled, "because the Americans told us the Communists would kill us," as they explained to reporters. America "left behind in Danang . . . an empty shell and a good deal of hatred, which will probably endure."[31]

The fact of the matter is that there never was any hope for the population of Indochina apart from a victory for the forces of revolutionary nationalism. . . .

The Nazi-like brutality of the American assault on Indochina is the most searing memory of these terrible years. Even though the ideologists and propagandists will labor to erase it, I cannot believe that they will succeed. Nonetheless, it must be understood that the savage programs put into operation by the Government and justified or ignored by much of the intelligentsia did not merely result from some sadistic streak in the American character. To be sure, the element of racism cannot be dismissed. One may doubt whether such maniacal "experiments in population control" would have been conducted—at least, with such self-satisfaction and lack of guilt—on a white population. But in a deeper sense, the savagery of the American attack was a necessary and unavoidable consequence of the general policy that was adopted in the late 1940s—the policy of crushing a revolutionary nationalist movement that was deeply rooted in the population, and that gained its support because of the appeal of its commitment to independence and social reconstruction.

This policy remained in force until the final collapse of the Saigon regime. During the 1950's, the United States hoped to regain control over all of Indochina. The National Security Council in 1956 directed all U.S. agencies in Vietnam to "work toward the weakening of the Communists in North and South Vietnam in order to bring about the eventual peaceful reunification of a free and independent Vietnam under anti-Communist leadership." Policy for Laos was stated in similar terms: "In order to prevent Lao neutrality from veering toward pro-Communism, encourage individuals and groups in Laos who oppose dealing with the Communist [bloc]—Support the expansion and reorganization of police, propaganda and army intelligence services, provided anti-Communist elements maintain effective control of these services—Terminate economic and military aid if the Lao Government ceases to demonstrate a will to resist internal Communist subversion and to carry out a policy of maintaining its independence."[32] In Cambodia as well, the United States made significant efforts (in part, through the medium of its Thai, South Vietnamese and Philippine subordinates) to reverse the commitment to neutralism.[33] A few years later, it was recognized that Viet Minh control over North Vietnam was irreversible, and the imperial managers lowered their sights. The goal was now a "non-Communist South Vietnam" instituted and guaranteed by American military force (since there was no other way), and a Western-oriented Laos and Cambodia.

Given this continuity of policy, it is hardly surprising that many Vietnamese saw the Americans as the inheritors of French colonialism. The *Pentagon Papers* cites studies of peasant attitudes demonstrating that "for many, the struggle which began in 1945 against colonialism continued uninterrupted throughout [Ngo Dinh] Diem's regime: in 1954, the foes of nationalists were transformed from France and Bao Dai, to Diem and the U.S. . . . but the issues at stake never changed." By early 1964, even the U.S.-backed generals were warning of the "colonial flavor to the whole pacification effort," noting that the French in their worst and clumsiest days never tried to control the local society as the Americans were planning to do. But the American leadership saw no alternative, and rejected the objections of their clients as "an unacceptable rearward step." A Systems Analysis study concluded that unless the Viet Cong infrastructure ("the VC officials and organizers") "was destroyed, U.S.-GVN military and pacification forces soon degenerated into nothing more than an occupation army." They did not add that if this "infrastructure" was destroyed, the U.S.-GVN forces would be nothing but a gang of murderers. Both conclusions are, in fact, correct, and reflect the natural consequences of the implementation of the Indochina policy first mapped out in the late nineteen-forties.

It was only after the Tet offensive that American terror was unleashed against South Vietnam in its full fury. What was to come was indicated by the tactics employed to reconquer the urban areas that quickly fell into the hands of Vietnamese resistance forces in January-February 1968. The events in Hué were typical. Here, thousands of people "were killed by the most hysterical use of American firepower ever seen," and then designated "as the victims of a Communist massacre."[34] The "accelerated pacification program" that followed was a desperate effort to reconstruct the shattered American position. It had some success. Describing the "massive" increase in population which had been achieved by August 1970, John Paul Vann estimated that "we control two million more people than we controlled two years ago," although he added that "occupation is only the first step in pacification." As for that second step—the "willing cooperation of the people with the Government and the overt rejection of the enemy"—contrary to the pretense of ignorant social scientists, that step had not been and never would be achieved.[35]

Many people think of My Lai when recalling the post-Tet terrorism. But this is misleading. In fact, My Lai was just one of many such massacres. Some of these massacres, including My Lai, took place during "Operation Wheeler Wallawa." In this campaign, over 10,000 "enemy" were reported killed, including the victims of My Lai, who were listed in the official body count. Speaking of "Wheeler Wallawa," Kevin Buckley, head of the *Newsweek* bureau in Saigon, observed that

> an examination of that whole operation would have revealed the incident at My Lai to be a particularly gruesome application of a wider policy which had the same effect in many places at many times. Of course, the blame for that could not have been dumped on a stumblebum lieutenant. Calley was an aberration, but "Wheeler Wallawa" was not.

The real issue concerning this operation was not the "indiscriminate use of firepower," as often is alleged.[36] Rather, "it is charges of quite discriminating use—as a matter of policy, in populated areas."*

---

* The director of the nearby Canadian hospital, Dr. Alje Vennema, reports that he knew of the My Lai massacre at once but did nothing because it was not at all out of the ordinary; his patients were constantly reporting such incidents to him.[37] In fact, the military panel investigating My Lai discovered that a similar massacre had taken place only a few miles away at the village of My Khe. Proceedings against the officer in charge were dismissed on the grounds that he had carried out a perfectly normal operation in which a village was destroyed and its population was forcibly relocated.[38] The panel's decision tells us all we need to know about "Wheeler Wallawa."

One can gain a better understanding of American post-Tet strategy—strategy brought to its culmination under the management of Henry Kissinger—by considering such operations as "Speedy Express." This campaign was conducted by the U.S. 9th Infantry Division in the Mekong Delta province of Kien Hoa in early 1969. Studied in detail by Alex Shimkin and Kevin Buckley, a partial description of it appeared in *Newsweek* for June 19, 1972. What follows is based on notes supplied to me by Buckley.

For many years, the province had been "almost totally controlled" by the NLF:

> For a long time there was little or no military activity in the delta. The 9th Division did not even arrive until the end of 1966. Front activities went far beyond fighting. The VC ran schools, hospitals and even businesses. A pacification study revealed that an NLF sugar cane cooperative for three villages in the Mo Cay district of Kien Hoa produced revenue in 1968 which exceeded the entire Saigon government budget that year for Kien Hoa.

But the "aggressive military effort carried out by the U.S. 9th Infantry Division" had succeeded in establishing some degree of government control. In the six months of Operation Speedy Express, "a total of some 120,000 people who had been living in VC controlled areas" came under government control. To achieve this result, the 9th Division applied "awesome firepower," including "3,381 air strikes by fighter bombers, dropping napalm, high explosives and antibombs," B-52's and artillery shelling "around the clock" at a level that "it is impossible to reckon." Armed helicopters "scour[ed] the landscape from the air night and day," accounting for "many and perhaps most of the enemy kills." The 9th Division reported that "over 3,000 enemy troops were killed in March, 1969, which is the largest monthly total for any American division in the Vietnam War." All told, 10,899 people were killed and 748 weapons were captured. From these figures alone one can make a fair judgment as to the nature of the "enemy troops" who were killed by bombing and shelling, much of it at night. In the single month of March, the Ben Tre hospital reported 343 people wounded by "friendly" fire as compared with 25 by "the enemy." And as a U.S. pacification official noted, "Many people who were wounded died on their way to the hospitals" or were treated elsewhere (at home, in VC hospitals, or ARVN dispensaries). A senior pacification official estimated that "at least 5,000" of those killed "were what we refer to as non-combatants."

Interviews in the "pacified" areas confirm the grim picture. One VC medic reported that his hospital took care of at least 1,000 people in four villages in early 1969. "Without exception the people testified that most of the civilians had been killed by a relentless night and day barrage of rockets, shells, bombs and bullets from planes, artillery and helicopters." In one area of four villages, the population was reduced from 16,000 to 1,600. Every masonry house was in ruins. Coconut groves were destroyed by defoliants. Villagers were arrested by U.S. troops, beaten by interrogators, and sent off to prison camps. The MACV [Military Assistance Command, Vietnam] location plots for B-52's show that the target center for one raid was precisely on the village of Luong Phu. In the neighboring village of Luong Hoa, village elders estimated that there were 5,000 people in the village before 1969 but none in 1970 "because the Americans destroyed every house in the village with artillery, air strikes or by burning them down with cigarette lighters." About 100 people were killed by bombing, they report. Pounding from the air was "relentless." Helicopters chased and killed people working in fields. Survival was possible in deep trenches and bunkers, but many small children "were killed by concussion from the bombs which they could not withstand even though they were in bunkers," villagers report. An experienced American official compared My Lai and the operations of the 9th Division as follows:

> The actions of the 9th Division in inflicting civilian casualties were worse. The sum total of what the 9th did was overwhelming. In sum, the horror was worse than Mylai. But with the 9th, the civilian casualties came in dribbles and were pieced out over a long time. And most of them were inflicted from the air and at night. Also, they were sanctioned by the command's insistence on high body counts.

He also stated that "the result was an inevitable outcome of the unit's command policy."

While the 9th division was at work in the field, others were doing their job at home. One well-known behavioral scientist, who had long deplored the emotionalism of critics of the war and the inadequacy of their empirical data, wrote this as the campaign ground on: "the only sense in which [we have demolished the society of Vietnam] is the sense in which every modernizing country abandons reactionary traditionalism."[39]

Operation Speedy Express was regarded as a "stunning success." Lauding the commanding General—one must assume, without irony—upon his promotion, General Creighton Abrams spoke of "the great admiration I have for the performance of the 9th Division and especially the superb leadership and brilliant operational concepts you have given the Division." "You personify the military professional at his best in devotion and service to God and country," rhapsodized Abrams, referring specifically to the "magnificent" performance of the 9th Division, its "unparalleled and unequaled performance," during Speedy Express. . . .

Again, it is important to bear in mind that the character of the American war cannot be attributed solely to a sadistic military leadership or to incompetent or deranged civilian advisers. It was a calculated and rational enterprise undertaken to realize goals that could be achieved in no other way: namely, the goal, stated clearly in the 1940s, of preventing Communist domination in a region where it was always understood, the Communists had "captured" the national movement. Furthermore, the tactics employed were by no means novel. To cite only the most obvious analogy, recall the air war in Korea, and significantly, the manner in which it was later analyzed. . . .

Why feign surprise at the bombing of dikes in 1972 when 12,000 peasants (including, it seems, the remnants of My Lai) were driven from their homes in the Batangan Peninsula in January 1969, after having lived in caves and bunkers for months in an effort to survive constant bombardment, and were then shipped to a waterless camp near Quang Ngai over which floated a banner which said, "We thank you for liberating us from communist terror"?[40] Just another episode in which this "modernizing country abandons reactionary traditionalism" under the guidance of its benevolent big brother.

The same fundamental "dilemma" that made inevitable the savagery of the war always compelled the United States to evade any serious moves towards a negotiated settlement, and to reject the "peaceful means" that are required by the "supreme law of the land." In the second Mansfield Report (December 1965), it is explained that:

> negotiations at this time, as a practical matter, would leave the Viet Cong in control of the countryside (much of which, by the way, they have controlled for many years and some of it since the time of the Japanese occupation). The Nationalists (and only with our continued massive support) would remain in control of Saigon, provincial capitals and the coastal base-cities. The status of the district seats would be in doubt.[41]

This conclusion was based on the reasonable assumption that "negotiations merely confirm the situation that exists on the ground."

Thus, despite the massacre of some 200,000 people in the preceding decade, despite the direct engagement of American military forces for four years, and despite the massive invasion and aerial bombardment of 1965, a political settlement was unthinkable, because the National Liberation Front controlled the countryside.[42]

Similar reasoning had impelled the United States to undertake overt aggression earlier in the year. Throughout 1964, the NLF made repeated efforts to arrange a negotiated settlement based on the Laos model, with a neutralist coalition government. But the United States rejected any such "premature negotiations" as incompatible with its goal of maintaining a non-Communist South Vietnam under American control. The reason was quite simple. As American officials constantly reiterated, the NLF was the only significant political force and the U.S.-Imposed regime had virtually no popular base. Only the politically organized Buddhists could even conceive of entering into a coalition with the NLF, and the Buddhists, as General [William] Westmoreland sagely observed, were not acting "in the interests of the Nation." Ambassador [Henry Cabot] Lodge later regarded them as "equivalent to card-carrying Communists," according to the Pentagon historian. Thus, the U.S. Government position was that only General Westmoreland and Ambassador [Maxwell] Taylor understood "the interests of the Nation," all political groupings in South Vietnam thereby being automatically excluded from any possible political settlement. To be sure, as William Bundy explained, we might be willing to consider the peaceful means required by law "after, *but only after*, we have established a clear pattern of pressure" (i.e., military force; his emphasis). As noted earlier, pacification specialist Vann took the same view, as did all other knowledgeable observers.

The United States therefore supported General [Nguyen] Khanh and the Armed Forces Council. But by January 1965, even that last hope went up in smoke. As Ambassador Taylor explained in his memoirs,[43] the United States government "had lost confidence in Khanh" by late January 1965. He lacked "character and integrity," added Taylor sadly. The clearest evidence of Khanh's lack of character was that by late January he was moving towards "a dangerous Khanh-Buddhist alliance which might eventually lead to an unfriendly government with which we could not work." Moreover, as we now know from other sources, he was also close to a political agreement with the NLF.[44] Consequently, Khanh was removed. And in late January, according to the *Pentagon Papers*, Westmoreland "obtained his first authority to use U.S. forces for combat within South Vietnam." The systematic and intensive bombing of South Vietnam (accompanied by a more publicized but less severe bombing of the North) began a few weeks later, to be followed by the open American invasion.

At every other period, much the same was true. The 1954 Geneva Accords were regarded as a "disaster" by the United States. The National Security Council met at once and adopted a general program of subversion throughout the region to ensure that the political settlement envisioned in the Accords would not be achieved.[45] In October 1972, just prior to the U.S. Presidential election, the DRV offered a peace proposal that virtually recapitulated the Geneva Accords and also incorporated the central positions in the founding documents of the NLF. Nixon and Kissinger could not openly reject this offer just prior to the elections, but they indicated clearly that the proposal was unacceptable while claiming deceitfully that "peace was at hand." Abetted by the subservient press, they were able to carry out this charade successfully, but when their later efforts to modify the proposals (including the Christmas bombings) failed utterly, they were compelled to accept the very same offer (with trivial changes in wording) in January 1973.

As in the case of Geneva 1954, this agreement was purely formal. Even before the Paris Agreements of January 1973 were signed, Kissinger explained to the press that the United

States would reject every essential principle in the Agreements. And in fact, the United States at once committed itself to subverting these agreements by intensifying the political repression in South Vietnam and by launching military actions against PRG [Provisional Revolutionary Government (of South Vietnam)] territory through the medium of its client regime, massively supplied with arms. Again, the treachery of the mass media served to delude the public with regard to these events, helping to perpetuate the slaughter.[46]

By mid-1974, U.S. Government officials were reporting enthusiastically that their tactics were succeeding. They claimed that the [Nguyen Van] Thieu regime had conquered about 15 percent of the territory of the PRG, exploiting its vast advantage in firepower, and that the prospects for further successes were great. As in the 1950s, the whole structure collapsed from within as soon as the Communists were so ungracious as to respond.

The point of this brief résumé has been to illustrate the complete refusal of the United States to consider any political settlement. The reason was always the same. It was always understood that there was no political base for the U.S. aggression, so that a peaceful political settlement would constitute a defeat. This was precisely the dilemma of 1948, and it was never resolved. . . .

As I noted earlier, it was after the Tet offensive of early 1968 that the American murder machine really went into high gear in South Vietnam. The reasons were essentially two. It was feared that a political settlement of some sort would be inescapable, given the mounting pressures within the U.S. and in the international arena to limit or terminate the American war. And with the American military forces disintegrating in the field, it was evident that they would soon have to be withdrawn and replaced by native mercenaries. Given all this, it was decided to carry out the maximum amount of destruction possible in South Vietnam in the time remaining. The hope was that a U.S.-imposed regime might maintain control over a sufficiently demoralized and shattered society. As noted, American officials like Vann felt that the post-Tet accelerated pacification campaigns had been partially successful in bringing the population under American "occupation," though "pacification" would, of course, still require substantial efforts.

Imperialist ideologues in the academic community generally shared this analysis. Henry Kissinger, in his last contribution to scholarship before ascending to high office, outlined "the thrust for American policy in the next phase" as follows: "the United States should concentrate on the subject of the mutual withdrawal of external forces and avoid negotiating about the internal structure of South Vietnam for as long as possible."[47] Putting aside his irrelevant rationalizations, the meaning of this prescription is obvious. If American terrorism could succeed in at last demolishing the southern resistance, an American client regime might be able to maintain itself. This would, however, only be possible if the North Vietnamese could be compelled to withdraw (the war planners had always expected that the bombing of the North and the direct American invasion of the South would draw the DRV into the Southern conflict). Then, with North Vietnam out of the way, the United States could bring to bear the socio-economic programs mentioned earlier to maintain the stable, noncommunist South Vietnam it had always sought. Of course, Kissinger's prescription required that the southern resistance be smashed before the withdrawal of American troops. This is why it was under his regime that such operations as Speedy Express were launched against the South Vietnamese, while the air war was stepped up in Laos and Cambodia.

It is not surprising that Kissinger was, for a time, the great hope of American liberals. As I have already noted, left-liberal "opponents" of the war had themselves urged that the solution was a peaceful settlement between South and North Vietnam with American military forces remaining in the South. Indeed, to this day they feel that their proposals to this effect might have occasionally been questionable in "nuance," but nothing more.[48] Thus, it was perfectly natural that Kissinger should have been able to pacify much of the liberal opposition with his analysis of how an American military victory over the South Vietnamese might yet be attained.

To be sure, Kissinger was fully aware of the fundamental dilemma that had always plagued America policymakers. His way of phrasing the problem was as follows:

> The North Vietnamese and Viet Cong, fighting in their own country, needed merely to keep in being forces sufficiently strong to dominate the population after the United States tired of the war. We fought a military war; our opponents fought a political one . . . our military operations [had[little relationship to our declared political objectives. Progress in establishing a political base was excruciatingly slow . . . In Vietnam—as in most developing countries—the overwhelming problem is not to buttress but to develop a political framework . . . One ironic aspect of the war in Vietnam is that while we profess an idealistic philosophy, our failures have been due to an excessive reliance on material factors. The Communists, by contrast, holding to a materialistic interpretation, owe many of their successes to their ability to supply an answer to the question of the nature and foundation of political authority.[49]

Translating to simple prose: our problem is that the Vietnamese live there and we do not. This has made it difficult for us to develop a viable Vietnamese regime, whereas the Viet Minh and their successors had long ago created a functioning and successful social order in which they gained their support. There is no "irony" here. Rather, the problem is one that all imperial aggressors confront when faced with stubborn resistance, magnified in this case by the appeal of the social revolution.

Given the fundamental commitment to destroy the national movement, the United States was compelled to conduct a war of annihilation in South Vietnam and the surrounding region, and to reject any political settlement of the conflict. The question, however, remains: why was it always regarded as necessary to pursue this course? As noted earlier, the fundamental "dilemma" was clearly perceived in 1948, when State Department analysts explained that the "long-term objective" of the United States was "to eliminate so far as possible Communist influence in Indochina." The rationalization offered was that we must "prevent undue Chinese penetration and subsequent influence in Indochina" because of our deep concern "that the peoples of Indochina will not be hampered in their natural developments by the pressure of an alien people and alien interests." Therefore, the United States attempted to restore French rule, in accordance with another "long-term objective": "to see installed a self-governing nationalist state which will be friendly to the U.S. and which . . . will be patterned upon our conception of a democratic state," and will be associated "with the western powers, particularly with France, with whose customs, language and laws [the peoples of Indochina] are familiar, to the end that those peoples will prefer freely to cooperate with the western powers culturally, economically and politically" and will "work productively and thus contribute to a better balanced world economy," while enjoying a rising standard of income.

The subsequent history in Indochina (and elsewhere) reveals just how deep was the American commitment to self-government, to democracy, and to a rising standard of living for the mass of the population. We may dismiss this as the usual imperialist tommyrot.

But the concern that Indochina "contribute to a better balanced world economy" was real enough. There is compelling documentary evidence, from the *Pentagon Papers* and other sources, that this and related concerns dominated all others and impelled the United States on its course in Indochina. As the record clearly demonstrates, American planners feared that the success of revolutionary nationalism would cause "the rot to spread" to the rest of mainland

Southeast Asia and beyond to Indonesia and perhaps South Asia, ultimately impelling Japan, the workshop of the Pacific, to seek an accommodation with the Communist powers. Should this all happen, the United States would in effect have lost the Pacific phase of the Second World War, a phase which was fought in part to prevent Japan from constructing "new order" closed to American penetration.

The mechanism by which the rot would spread was never clearly spelled out. But there is ample evidence that the planners understood that it would not be by military conquest. Rather, the danger was seen to lie in what they sometimes called "ideological successes," the demonstration effect of a successful revolution in Indochina (as in China). To counter this danger, pressure was put on Japan to reject "accommodation" with China. Access to Southeast Asia was promised as a reward for good behavior. And access was granted. By 1975, "Japanese commercial interests in Southeast Asia account for one-third of its U.S. $100,000 million annual trade, more than 90% of the total $4,000 million 'yen credits' and a substantial share of the $10,000 million overseas investment balance,"[50] transactions which "have tended to enrich only a privileged few in Southeast Asia and their business and political counterparts in Japan." It is no surprise, then, "that Japan was the only major country which had fully supported the American war policy in Indochina, including all-out bombing of North Vietnam in [1972]."[51]

In spite of the fact that there is now substantial documentary evidence to support this analysis of American intentions,[52] it cannot be accepted by ideologists.[53] Instead, they emphasize other, peripheral factors—the need to gain French support for American programs in Europe, concern for some mystic "image," etc. To be sure, these factors were real enough. Thus, restoration of European capitalism was the primary objective of American post-war policy, and it was achieved in a manner which (not coincidentally) supported an immense expansion of overseas investment by American-based corporations. And there is no doubt that the United States was concerned to reinforce the image of a grim destroyer that would tolerate no challenge to its global order. But the primary reason why the long-term objective of destroying the Communist-led nationalist movement could not be abandoned is precisely the one that is repeatedly and clearly stressed in the documentary record: the United States could not tolerate the spreading of the rot of independence and self-reliance over Southeast Asia, with its possible impact upon Japan, the major industrial power of the Pacific region.

The precise weight of the motives that led American planners to commit themselves to the destruction of the Vietnamese nationalist movement may be debated, but the extensive documentary record now available, and briefly surveyed here, leaves no doubt that the commitment was undertaken in full awareness of what was at stake. This fact is difficult for many American intellectuals to accept, even those who opposed the war. To cite one striking and not untypical example, Professor John K. Fairbank of Harvard argues that a "factor of ignorance" lies at the source of what he called "our Vietnam tragedy." Lacking "an historical understanding of the modern Vietnamese revolution," we did not "realize that it was a revolution inspired by the sentiment of nationalism while clothed in the ideology of communism as applied to Vietnam's needs. . . . The result was that in the name of being anticommunist, vague though that term had become by 1965, we embarked on an anti-nationalist effort." We misconceived "our role in defending the South after 1965," conceiving it as aimed at blocking aggression from North Vietnam and "forestalling a southward expansion of Chinese communism."[54] As we have seen, this analysis is refuted at every point by the historical record. The top planners knew from the start that the revolution was inspired by nationalism while clothed in the ideology of communism, and consciously embarked on an effort to destroy the national movement. They always understood that intervention from the North was a response to American aggression (which they, like Fairbank, called "defending the South"). "Chinese expansion" was fabricated to provide a propaganda cover for American aggression in Indochina. At the very moment when they were planning the 1965 escalation, William Bundy and John McNaughton noted that unless the United States expanded the war, there would probably be "a Vietnamese-negotiated deal, under which an eventually unified Communist Vietnam would reassert its traditional hostility to Communist China."

As to why scholars choose to ignore the factual record, one may only speculate. We may note that it is convenient to blame the American "failure" on ignorance—a socially neutral concept—thus deflecting analysis of the systematic and institutional factors that brought about the American war.

A study group sponsored by the Woodrow Wilson Foundation and the National Planning Association once defined the primary threat of "communism" as the economic transformation of the Communist powers "in ways which reduce their willingness and ability to complement the industrial economies of the West";[55] American hegemony in "the West" was naturally assumed. The comment is accurate and astute. The United States, as the dominant power in the global capitalist system (the "free world"), will use what means it can muster to counter any move towards independence that will tend to "reduce" this "willingness and ability."

Three-quarters of a century ago, Brooks Adams proclaimed that "Our geographical position, our wealth, and our energy pre-eminently fit us to enter upon the development of Eastern Asia and to reduce it to part of our own economic system."[56] As Oliver Wendell Holmes admiringly commented, Adams thought that the Philippine War "is the first gun in the battle for the ownership of the world."[57] American victory in the Pacific War of 1941–45 appeared to lay the basis for success in achieving this "long-term objective." The United States Government was not prepared to see its vision—which, in the familiar manner, was presented as utterly selfless and benign—threatened by a nationalist movement in a small and unimportant country where the peasants were too naive to understand what was in their best interests. The policy planners and intellectuals, who stood by quietly while hundreds of thousands were slaughtered in Indonesia as the "communist menace" was crushed and the country's riches again flowed towards the industrial powers, or who watched with occasional clucking of tongues as countries of the Western hemisphere fell under the rule of American-backed fascist torturers, could hardly have been expected to react differently in the case of Indochina. Nor did they, until the domestic costs of the war mounted beyond tolerable levels, and a spontaneous movement of protest and resistance threatened to shatter domestic tranquility and authority.

« 33 »

An Assertion of Manhood

Robert D. Dean

PRESIDENT JOHNSON DEPLORED THE COUP and the murder of [Ngo Dinh] Diem. He, too, held the fixed conviction that the United States (and by extension his political fortunes) could not afford the "loss" of South Vietnam to communism. Johnson, a masterful operator in the Senate before his term as vice president, demanded absolute "loyalty" and consensus within his inner circle of national security managers. He inherited Kennedy's foreign policy personnel along with the Vietnamese crisis. His relationship with the "Harvards," as he labeled the Kennedy holdovers, was often uneasy, colored by his fear that their primary allegiance went to Robert Kennedy. Johnson wanted the prestige in foreign affairs that seemed to come with members of the Kennedy team, but he resented the enveloping aura of class privilege they carried.

Sensitive about comparisons between their Ivy League credentials and his education at San Marcos State Teacher's College, Johnson acted to establish dominance and test the loyalty of his privileged subordinates. This sometimes took the form of verbal challenges to their masculinity. In other cases it involved attempts to humiliate or embarrass them through calculated displays of his own body in ways appropriate, perhaps, to the rough-hewn male culture of the Texas hill country, but deliberately inappropriate to eastern establishment bureaucrats. For example, the Brahmin national security adviser McGeorge Bundy was "one of the delicate Kennedyites" Johnson targeted. "You are such a sissy," Johnson declared when Bundy indicated his preference for tennis over an invitation for golf with the president. "What do you want to run out here and play a girl's game for?" President Johnson occasionally conducted business with subordinates while perched upon the toilet "in an attempt to uncover, [to] heighten, the vulnerability of other men," as Richard Goodwin, himself subject to such treatment, later recalled. Unlike Goodwin, McGeorge Bundy failed the test, according to Johnson's account. Bundy, the president claimed:

> came into the bathroom with me and then found it utterly impossible to look at me while I sat there on the toilet. You'd think he had never seen those parts of the body before. For there he was, standing as far away from me as he possibly could, keeping his back toward me the whole time, trying to carry on a conversation. I could barely hear a word he said. I kept straining my ears and then finally I asked him to come a little closer to me. Then began the most ludicrous scene I had ever witnessed. Instead of turning around and walking over to me, he kept his face away from me and walked backwards, one rickety step at a time. For a moment there I thought he was going to fall into my lap. It certainly made me wonder how that man had made it so far in the world.[1]

Whatever his personal doubts about the manhood and loyalty of the Kennedy team, Johnson had opposed the coup that toppled Diem and worried that the factionalism that contributed to it was dangerous to the presidency. Nor did the new president fully appreciate the nuances of the counterinsurgency and development theories that so entranced the Kennedy bureaucrats. In one of the first meetings of the new administration the president directed that the bureaucracy stop the "bickering and any person that did not conform to policy should be removed." Johnson indicated a preference for directly forceful means to maintain the Saigon regime, as John McCone noted for the record: "he was anxious to get along, win the war—he didn't want as much effort placed on so-called social reforms."[2]

Johnson's national security managers were faced with conflicting imperatives. The South Vietnamese regime had to be preserved, even though it amounted to little more than small groups of feuding elites incapable of organizing and running a viable government. Devoid of indigenous political legitimacy, the tottering state of South Vietnam merely provided a fig leaf for the U.S. imperial presence. A massive military intervention was politically undesirable in an election year. So, too, was the prospect of the loss of Vietnam. The solution was to quietly conduct a holding operation—to "maintain the status quo" until the 1964 presidential election, while preparing for escalating levels of force afterward. The warrior-intellectual identity narrative demanded some kind of action, even when the warriors estimated such action had only limited potential for significant effect.[3]

In January 1964, McNamara, Rusk, McCone, and Bundy had Johnson approve a new campaign of "covert operations" against North Vietnam. An expansion of U.S. electronic intelligence gathering, U.S. overflights, and psychological warfare was crowned with OPLAN 34-A: "intensified sabotage operations in North Vietnam by Vietnamese personnel" run by the CIA. It was not the intent of 34-A to have a significant material impact on the North Vietnamese capacity to support the southern insurgency, which, as Secretary Rusk pointed out, was largely indigenous: "98% of the problem is in South Vietnam and not in cross-border operations." Instead, the hoped-for effect was psychological—a message of stoic resolve and "toughness" delivered to enemies—to "persuade Hanoi that we have no intention of quitting." The self-imposed imperative to demonstrate such vigorous and warlike determination demanded reasoning that contradicted their incipient understanding, based on empirical evidence, that the insurgency had strong indigenous nationalist roots. The undeclared war against the north would somehow, the virile bureaucrats argued, "put muscle behind our argument that the trouble comes from the north and that when that trouble stops, our presence in South Vietnam can become unnecessary."[4] Despite the hopes pinned on OPLAN 34-A, Johnson agreed with others outside the inner circle of advisers that "long-range over there, the odds are certainly against us." The ability to articulate one set of propositions about the nature of the problem, and then to recommend actions that logically contradict those propositions, evident here, is a recurrent pattern in the reams of paper expended on policy "options" by the national security managers. The imperative to do so was intimately connected to the maintenance of their identities as active, powerful men relentlessly defending boundaries against enemies, and tied also to the maintenance of political legitimacy and power.[5]

With the palpable failure of the government of South Vietnam to achieve stability and the strength to "pacify" its insurgent populace, U.S. policymakers stepped up contingency planning for an increase of "pressure" on the North Vietnamese state. The heroic and successful confrontation with the Soviets over missiles in Cuba provided the operational model for the war planners. They presumed that a campaign of graduated application of "pain" would induce the North Vietnamese government to see reason and to direct their instruments in the south to renounce the ambition and effort to unite Vietnam. The imperial brotherhood saw the alternative, "a bugout in Southeast Asia," as worrisome and unpalatable.[6]

By May 1964 national security planners had developed schemes for a "major stiffening" of U.S. "effort in South Vietnam, essentially by marrying Americans to Vietnamese at every level," as McGeorge Bundy's gendered metaphor described it. Bundy's language expressed a central aspect of the imperial, masculine identity narrative shared by the foreign policy bureaucrats. This narrative cast the South Vietnamese as weak supplicants, unable to defend themselves against a ruthless enemy without heroic U.S. efforts. "The object of this exercise is to provide what Khanh [then the South Vietnamese dictator du jour] has repeatedly asked for: the tall American at every point of stress and strain."[7]

Despite the implicitly imperial and orientalizing tropes employed by Johnson's national security bureaucrats, they vehemently denied the imputation that meaningful parallels could be drawn between the United States and the French empire thrown out of Vietnam in 1954. Charles Bohlen, ambassador to France, was dispatched to persuade the French leader General Charles de Gaulle to drop his advocacy of "neutralization" of Vietnam, and to line up behind U.S. policy. During the discussion Bohlen dismissed the Frenchman's assertion that the American predicament displayed remarkable similarity to the French imperial experience:

> General de Gaulle said that France did not agree with the U.S. in its analysis of the situation in that it did not consider that there was any real government in Vietnam. . . . He said that the war in essence was the same one that the French had been fighting since the end of the World War II: that the Vietnamese had no taste for this war and that the anti-Communist forces in Vietnam were not up to the task. I interrupted him to tell him . . . it was quite different, one was a colonial war which came out as colonial wars always do and the other was war against aggression directed and maintained from without.[8]

The clear warnings of European allies fell on deaf ears. Domestic politics helped propel the Johnson administration closer to full-scale intervention. A set of related incidents from the spring and summer of 1964 helps illustrate the pervasive politics of masculinity surrounding issues of national security and foreign policy decision making. Lyndon Johnson had learned well the political lessons of the "loss" of China during his tenure in the Senate. He and his high-level foreign policy advisers understood the political vulnerability of the Democratic Party to charges of weakness and "treason" based on the history of the countersubversion and counter-perversion crusades of the 1950s.[9] His greatest political apprehensions concerning American policy toward Vietnam focused on the Right; he feared being blamed for the "loss" of Vietnam. His top advisers, inherited from Kennedy, reinforced these impulses. South Vietnam, counseled McGeorge Bundy, was "both a test of U.S. firmness and specifically a test of U.S. capacity to deal with 'wars of national liberation.'"[10]

Although some prominent journalists questioned the wisdom of deeper military involvement, other strident voices in the press seemed to confirm LBJ's estimation of the political risks inherent in a negotiated settlement. Bundy's friend Joseph Alsop, the Washington columnist, issued repeated shrill warnings of "catastrophe" to befall the empire if the president "duck[ed] the challenges in Viet-Nam." McGeorge Bundy kept Johnson appraised of Alsop's increasing bellicosity. He served as a middleman in his old friends' efforts to apply pressure for more military force, while advising the president how to keep the columnist's support: "Joe Alsop is back [from Saigon] breathing absolute fire and sulfur about the need for war in South Vietnam. I'm going to see him this afternoon and find out just how alarmed he is . . . I have a feeling that the best way to keep him on the reservation is for you to have a few words."[11]

After a long career as an establishment pundit and journalist, Alsop considered his own foreign policy expertise equal to that of anyone in the Johnson administration. His frequent trips to South Vietnam convinced him that without "direct American military pressure on the communist side" a U.S. "defeat in Southeast Asia" loomed. The dominoes would topple and the American imperium would crumble, he cautioned in May. After the loss of the entire

Pacific, including Japan and America's chain of island military bases, "no sane man would bet a nickel on the future of the present regime in India or would expect the eventual stabilization in Africa," he lectured. "Even the American position as an Atlantic power would be gravely undermined. For this kind of staggering failure on one side of the globe never passes unnoticed on the other side." Rather than accept defeat, Alsop prescribed a campaign of aerial bombing "to inflict enough damage on North Vietnam to persuade Ho Chi Minh and his colleagues to abide by the Geneva Treaties."[12]

Alsop's goal was to shape policy, not merely to analyze it. To that end, he cast Johnson's holding operation as a "passive more-of-the-same policy." Only "the more timid Washington policymakers" harbored doubts about the wisdom of escalation, he asserted. Alsop pushed LBJ toward war—represented as the only action that would assure his presidency a heroic place in history. A "neutralist government in the South," Alsop declared, was really "a thinly concealed surrender." The columnist invoked the legacy of the recently martyred president: "for Lyndon B. Johnson, Viet-Nam is what the second Cuban crisis was for John F. Kennedy." To lose the tiny Southeast Asian client, Alsop asserted, meant political doom, just as the loss of China had meant ruin for the Democratic administration a decade earlier: "As President Truman did in China, President Johnson now faces a situation in which taking action will be bad politics now, whereas inaction will be worse politics later." Alsop carefully cast the president's choices as stark polarities. To "neutralize" Indochina and thus allow the Vietnamese to decide their own fate revealed weakness, timidity and surrender; to launch America's powerful technology of death against the (apparently) overmatched North Vietnamese demonstrated strength, heroic leadership, and the realization of the nation's imperial destiny. Alsop's unsolicited advice amounted to the conventional wisdom of the imperial brotherhood, similar in essence to the recommendations of his close advisers. Nonetheless, LBJ came to deeply resent Alsop's unrelenting public demands for war, believing such stridency circumscribed his choices. The journalist's repeated equation of negotiation with cowardice reduced the administration's room for maneuver because Alsop so effectively summarized Johnson's own view of the diplomatic and domestic consequences of "weakness."[13]

But despite recurrent calls to expand the war, President Johnson and some of his political cronies and erstwhile congressional colleagues were deeply pessimistic about the likely outcome of U.S. escalation. At the end of May, when the president sought his opinion, Senator Richard Russell warned his former protégé: "It's a tragic situation. It's just one of those places where you can't win. Anything you do is wrong." The senator from Georgia cautioned that U.S. military intervention would not work: "it would be a Korea on a much bigger scale and a worse scale. . . . If you go from Laos and Cambodia and Vietnam and bring North Vietnam into it too, it is the damnedest mess on earth. The French report that they lost 250,000 men and spent a couple of billion of their money and two billion of ours down there and just got the hell whipped out of them." When Johnson broached his war managers' proposal to bomb infiltration routes or "oil plants" in the North, Russell, bluntly, but with considerable prescience, dismissed an air war as a feasible solution to the dilemma:

> Oh, hell! That ain't worth a hoot. That's just impossible. . . . We tried it in Korea. We even got a lot of old B-29s to increase the bomb load and sent 'em over there and just dropped millions and millions of bombs, day and night, . . . they would knock the road at night and in the morning the damn people would be back traveling over it. We never could interdict all their lines of communication although we had absolute control of the seas and the air, and we never did stop them. And you ain't gonna stop these people either.[14]

Russell regarded Vietnam as a dangerous entanglement, not worth the profound risks of military intervention. Johnson asked him directly, "How important is it to us?" "It isn't important a damn bit," Russell replied forcefully, "with all these new missile systems." American military security was not tied to any strategic imperative to hold Vietnam. Johnson was slightly taken aback: "Well, I guess it's important to us—." "From a psychological standpoint," interjected Russell.[15]

Johnson confided to Russell that he too, had profound doubts about the wisdom of intervention in Vietnam. "I've got a little old sergeant that works for me over at the house and he's got six children and I just put him up as the United States Army, Air Force and Navy every time I think about making this decision and think about sending that father of those six kids in there. And what the hell are we going to get out of his doing it? And it just makes the chills run up my back. . . . I just haven't got the nerve to do it, and I don't see any other way out of it." But Johnson plaintively voiced bigger worries about the domestic political consequences if he failed to enlarge the war in Southeast Asia and thus "lost" territory to communism. "Well, they'd impeach a President though that would run out, wouldn't they? . . . outside of [Senator Wayne] Morse, everybody I talk to says you got to go in, including Hickenlooper, including all the Republicans."[16] Russell warned the president that while intervention "with all the troops" might look "pretty good right now" as a domestic and international political gesture, "it'll be the most expensive venture this country ever went into."[17]

Within minutes of the conclusion of his phone conversation with Richard Russell, LBJ consulted McGeorge Bundy. LBJ confessed that Vietnam "worried the hell out" of him—"I don't think it's worth fighting for and I don't think we can get out. . . . What the hell is Vietnam worth to me? What is Laos worth to me? What is it worth to this country?" Although he understood Vietnam or Laos to be of little intrinsic significance compared to the potential costs of war, the potential psychological effects of "softness" worried him deeply. "Of course, if you start running from the Communists, they may just chase you into your own kitchen." "That's the dilemma," Bundy agreed, "that is what the rest of that half of the world is going to think if this thing comes apart on us." LBJ wavered between his fear of appearing weak to domestic and foreign audiences and the apparent wisdom of those who counseled against escalation, simultaneously endorsing caution and disparaging the unmanly weakness of those who urged it. "Everybody I talk to that's got any sense in there says, 'Oh my God, ple-e-ease give this thought.' Of course, I was reading [Senator Mike] Mansfield's stuff this morning and it's just milquetoast as it can be. He got no spine at all. But this is a terrible thing we're getting ready to do." Bundy prodded Johnson toward a controlled toughness, to be expressed with bombs against North Vietnam: "We really need to do some target folder work, Mr. President, that shows precisely what we do and don't mean here. The main object is to kill as few people as possible while creating an environment in which the incentive to react is as low as possible."[18]

Sensing the president's hesitation to use force, Bundy tentatively ventured a suggestion that might take the political sting out of sending conscripts to fight an unpopular Asian war. The solution to the problem of "saying to a guy, 'You go to Vietnam and you fight in the rice paddies'" was to invoke the imperial brotherhood's tradition of volunteer heroism in war. "What would happen," Bundy mused, if the president were to say in a speech, "'And from now on, nobody goes to this task who doesn't volunteer.' I think we might turn around the atmosphere of our own people out there if it were a volunteer's enterprise." Johnson was skeptical, worried that volunteers would not materialize, fearing that the prospect of war was broadly unpopular. "I don't think it's just [Senators] Morse and Russell and Gruening." Accepting LBJ's diagnosis, Bundy agreed: "I know it isn't, Mr. President. It's 90 percent of the people who don't want any part of this." The heroic burden of leadership, Bundy implied, must be borne by elites willing to ignore the reluctance of the populace to make the sacrifices required by duty.[19]

Johnson continued the circular and strangely schizophrenic behind-the-scenes discourse with his political cronies. In June LBJ again consulted Senator Richard Russell. Yet again he outlined his assessment of the political and military dilemma he faced: "I don't believe that the American people ever want me to run [from Vietnam]. . . . At the same time, I don't want to commit us to a war." Russell, chairman of the Armed Services Committee, agreed that there were no attractive alternatives: "We're just like the damn cow over a fence out there in Vietnam." The president fished for a commitment to intervention, recounting the pugnacious advice to defend boundaries given him by A. W. Moursund, a political crony from Johnson City, Texas.

> "Goddamn [Moursund said] there's not anything that'll destroy you as quick as pulling out, pulling up stakes and running. America wants, by God, prestige and power." I said, "Yeah, but I don't want to kill these folks." He said, "I don't give a damn. I didn't want to kill them in Korea, but if you don't stand up for America, there's nothing that a fellow in Johnson City"—or Georgia or any other place—"they'll forgive you for anything except being weak." Goldwater and all of 'em are raising hell about . . . hot pursuit and let's go in an bomb 'em.[20]

Without hesitation, Russell warned the president of the bloody stalemate he envisioned: "It'd take a half million men. They'd be bogged down there for ten years." But fear of the domestic political consequences of "weakness" gripped the southern senator too, despite his clairvoyance about the contemplated escalation. The "American inclination," Russell believed, was to "shoot back" when U.S. power was challenged. Russell offered equivocal advice to LBJ; the politics of manliness dictated continuing engagement in a losing battle, but the foreseeable damage to the national interest resulting from growing military intervention demanded withdrawal. Russell again outlined the double bind facing Johnson: "I don't know what the hell to do. I didn't ever want to get messed up down there. I do not agree with those brain trusters who say that this thing has got tremendous strategic and economic value and that we'll lose everything in Southeast Asia if we lose Vietnam. . . . But as a practical matter, we're in there and I don't know how you can tell the American people you're coming out. . . . They'll think that you've just been whipped, you've been ruined, you're scared. It'd be disastrous."[21]

LBJ seized upon the part of the senator's counsel that supported his own inclination to use force, proposing his own justification for escalation: "I think that I've got to say that I didn't get you in here, but we're in here by treaty and our national honor is at stake. And if this treaty's [SEATO] no good, none of 'em are any good. Therefore we're there. And being there, we've got to conduct ourselves like men." Johnson and Russell continued tracing circles, hoping to hit upon a politically acceptable solution to the Vietnam crisis. Johnson suggested that a "proposal . . . like Eisenhower worked out in Korea" could offer a way out. Russell then offered another assessment of the political psychology of the American electorate, at odds with his earlier estimate: "I think the people, if you get some sort of agreement all the way around, would understand it. . . . I don't think they'd be opposed to coming out. I don't think the American people want to stay in there. They've got enough sense that it's just a matter of face, that we can't just walk off and leave those people down there."[22]

Despite his very real doubts, LBJ saw no "honorable" alternative to force. The Gulf of Tonkin incidents of August 2 and 4, 1964, provided Johnson with an occasion to rally Congress around the flag by asking their support for an immediate military response to "aggression." Calculations about the domestic political value of a demonstration of military power also entered the equation. Immediately after the second of the real (August 2) and imagined (August 4) North

Vietnamese attacks on the destroyers *Maddox* and *Turner Joy*, the Democratic president summoned the congressional leadership to confer with him.[23] Johnson entered the meeting with his resolve bolstered by political advice from friends that he should "make it look like a very firm stand." Barry Goldwater, Republican nominee for president, posed a special threat to Johnson's ability to project a convincing image of political manliness, they warned. "You're gonna be running against a man who's a wild man," fellow Texan and former treasury secretary Robert Anderson counseled; "if he can show any lack of firmness . . . this fella's gonna play all the angles." LBJ sought approval to bomb North Vietnam from conservative Republicans Bourke Hickenlooper, Charles Halleck, and Everett Dirksen, and from Democrats William Fulbright, Mike Mansfield, and Richard Russell. He posed the problem in terms designed to stir the patriotic impulse to defend boundaries. "We can tuck our tails and run, but if we do these countries will feel all they have to do to scare us is to shoot the American flag."[24]

The congressional leaders responded as the president wished, and he unleashed the waiting bombers to strike North Vietnam. The Gulf of Tonkin resolution subsequently passed by Congress at the president's request gave the executive branch carte blanche for future military action. Johnson's maneuvering was designed, in part, to outflank Goldwater, his presidential rival, and the Republican Right during an election year, by actions designed to seem at once tough but moderate. The "measured" bombing of North Vietnam made Johnson seem to respond strongly to "aggression" without reawakening domestic fears of another Korean-style "ground war in Asia" involving large numbers of American troops. He offered a studied contrast in masculine leadership, an image of reasoned strength, compared to Goldwater's militantly apocalyptic pronouncements.[25]

The Arizona senator was, as Johnson's director of the State Department's Bureau of Intelligence and Research later put it, "not your ordinary civilian presidential candidate." Goldwater projected a formidable image as a manly cold warrior. He was a major general in the air force, the "commander of a reserve unit on Capitol Hill called the 9999th Air Force Reserve Unit." Goldwater political advertisements displayed photographs of the candidate in the cockpit of a military jet aircraft dressed in flight gear, adjacent to the caption "He's a Space-Age Man with a Victory Plan!" In other photographs he appeared in his dress uniform standing at the Berlin Wall, or in a cowboy hat posed against the Arizona landscape. Goldwater's handlers sold him as a "Fighting Man," a "Courageous Man," an "All-American Man . . . THE MAN for President of the United States." The senator's publicists invoked his wartime service: despite a "knee injury" the senator had demanded active duty, and through the "intervention of both Arizona senators" spent World War II flying "multi-engine cargo planes over the China-Burma-India Hump." Goldwater, they boasted, had by then "logged 7,500 air hours as a military pilot." Goldwater's election-year speeches accused the president of "backdownsmanship" in relations with the communists. The Republican candidate taunted Johnson and his advisers as "architects of defeat." Against such an opponent, Lyndon Johnson worked to protect himself in the game of political manliness.[26] Domestically, Johnson used the retaliatory bombing to foreclose opportunities for Goldwater to bait him for "weakness" toward Asian communism. The president played down the likelihood of war during the campaign. He undertook no major initiatives in Vietnam, despite the perilous condition of the U.S. client state.

Johnson played a waiting game during the election season, urging his foreign policy officials to find an answer to the "internal feuding" of the South Vietnamese government, enmeshed in a seemingly endless series of coups and revolving-door juntas. The U.S. proxies in Saigon, however, refused to buckle down and effectively prosecute the war against the insurgents. The national security bureaucrats anticipated the need for "tough decisions" based on the "messed up situation" within the chaotic government of South Vietnam. As collapse in South Vietnam seemed imminent, the frenetic contingency planning began to include more radical solutions. By the end of August, McGeorge Bundy counseled the president that to prevent the loss of their Southeast Asian client, the United States should consider the introduction of ground troops: "A still more drastic possibility which no one is discussing is the use of substantial U.S. armed forces in operations against the Viet Cong. I myself believe that before we let this country go we should have a hard look at this grim alternative, and I do not at all think that it is a repetition of Korea. It seems to me at least possible that a couple of brigade-size units put in to do specific jobs about six weeks from now might be good medicine everywhere."[27]

Johnson, however, did not intend to introduce ground troops during the election campaign. The president, a Texan who claimed descent from ancestors who died at San Jacinto, was caught between the conflicts apparent from the counsel of his warrior-bureaucrats, the saber-rattling of his presidential rival Barry Goldwater, the anticipation of the political unpopularity of an Asian land war, and his own firmly entrenched abhorrence of "appeasement." The counsel of the patrician neo-stoic Bundy may well have struck a chord with him.[28] But his first priority was to win the 1964 election; he strove to position himself as a reasonable but firm leader.

Picking a way through the political dangers on each side led to contradictions between secret government policy and planning and political pronouncements for public consumption. A pattern of deception resulted. LBJ was careful to present an image of controlled power to the American public. The Texan assured midwestern audiences that while the United States would not retreat from South Vietnam, he "was not about to send American boys 9 or 10,000 miles from home to do what Asian boys ought to be doing for themselves."[29] "In Asia," Johnson declared, "we face an ambitious and aggressive China." But the United States was the "mightiest nation in the world," he continued, and such "great power cannot be put into the hands of those who would use it either impulsively or carelessly." Barry Goldwater was a man of the sort who "rattle their rockets some," and who "bluff about their bombs"; just the type of man, he implied, who would "seek a wider war. . . . There are those that say you ought to go north and drop bombs, to try to wipe out the supply lines, and they think that would escalate the war. . . . We don't want to get involved in a nation with 700 million people and get tied down in a land war in Asia."[30] Under Johnson's leadership the United States was not about to "break our treaties" or "walk off and leave people who are searching for freedom," he declared. The solution to the threat to South Vietnam posed by Chinese communism was to "continue to make those people more effective and more efficient and do our best to resolve that situation where the aggressors will leave their neighbors alone. . . . We will not permit the independent nations of the East to be swallowed up by Communist conquest."[31]

In mid-October, less than three weeks before the election, the Republicans opened another salient in the political struggle, guaranteed to revive the Democrats' worst memories of the Red Scare and the politics of countersubversion and counterperversion. Walter Jenkins, Johnson's close and trusted aide for twenty-five years (and, ironically, White House liaison to the FBI), was arrested October 7 in the basement men's room of the YMCA near the White House, a place known as "a gathering spot for homosexuals." Jenkins forfeited the fifty-dollar bond and said nothing to the president or other White House officials.[32]

Alarm bells began ringing in the White House on the morning of October 14, when a local reporter asked Lady Bird Johnson's press secretary to comment on the arrest. It was soon determined that Jenkins had in fact been arrested, and the forfeiture of bond was . . . considered "proof" of guilt. The White House quickly dispatched lawyers Clark Clifford (a "wise man" and the future secretary of defense) and Abe Fortas (another "wise man" and a close adviser on Vietnam and other issues) in an attempt to contain the story. Fortas and Clifford made the rounds of the editorial offices of the Washington *Star*, the *Daily News*, and the *Post*, using their influence to delay the breaking of the story until Jenkins could be hustled into a guarded hospital room and shielded from the press. Dean Burch, chairman of the Republican National Committee, forced the issue into the open with a 6:00 P.M. statement asserting that "there is a report sweeping Washington that the White House is desperately trying to suppress a news story affecting the national security." Within a few minutes of Burch's statement, wire services reported Jenkins's hospitalization.[33]

The president "wavered between despair and anger." Johnson rightly feared that the Goldwater campaign would seize upon the presence of a homosexual presidential aide in an attempt to orchestrate a reprise of the Lavender Scare politics of the McCarthy era. Johnson himself shared stereotyped assumptions about homosexuals and threats to "security" in the State Department, perhaps adding to his distress over the potential political damage of the Jenkins scandal. Just a few months earlier in conversation with aides, LBJ had attributed newspaper leaks to homosexuals in the State Department: "McCarthy said about the State Department that they have to give these things because of sex or some other reason to these papers. And I'm beginning to believe that. 'Cause whenever they give to the papers—*regularly*— *systematically*—important things before even the President even decides them, somebody's got something on 'em."[34]

Johnson immediately and ruthlessly cut his losses and looked for a way to block Goldwater's use of the issue. When apprised of the situation he threatened to immediately fire Jenkins, but was persuaded to allow the devoted aide to proffer his resignation. Johnson refused to appear at a scheduled campaign event that evening until he was notified that Jenkins had resigned. The president put as much distance between himself and his scandal-tainted ex-employee as he could. Clifford later asserted that LBJ "never spoke of Walter Jenkins again: his faithful retainer became a nonperson."[35]

Johnson issued a statement the next day to announce that he had "requested and received Mr. Jenkins' resignation." He disavowed any prior knowledge of "questions with respect to [Jenkins's] personal conduct." To demonstrate his vigilance and resolve and to outflank the Republicans on the homosexuals-in-government issue, Johnson boasted of his decisiveness: "Within moments after being notified last night, I ordered Director J. Edgar Hoover of the FBI to make an immediate and comprehensive inquiry and report promptly to the American people."[36]

Despite the administration's efforts at containment, newspapers across the country gave front-page play to the story of Jenkins's arrest and resignation when the story appeared on October 15. Prominently displayed coverage of the scandal continued until election day. "Lyndon Aide Quits in Morals Case," blared a banner headline in the *Chicago Tribune;* the front pages of the *Washington Post* and the *New York Times also* carried the story. But potentially most damaging to Johnson and his presidential election campaign was the news reported by both the *Times* and the *Tribune* that police vice squad records revealed a previous arrest of Jenkins, five years earlier in the same YMCA men's room on charges of "disorderly conduct (pervert)."[37]

Pundits and commentators predicted that the homosexual scandal "was bound to be seriously detrimental to President Johnson's campaign." The case raised "questions of state," they argued. "There can be no place on the White House staff or in the upper echelons of government for a person of markedly deviant behavior," pronounced the editor of the *New York Times.* At best, Johnson's relationship with Jenkins could be explained as a worrisome lapse of "security"; at worst, as the *Chicago Tribune* declared, it proved that a "cover-up [was] underway." Jenkins, the editors solemnly intoned, had "been installed at the President's elbow, privy to every secret of state and national security." They trotted out the old arguments linking communism, espionage, and "perversion" to condemn LBJ: "It is established Russian tactics to seize every opportunity of homosexuality, drunkenness, and loose character as means of blackmail to obtain secret information." The *Tribune* pronounced it a sex scandal as serious as the recent Profumo Affair that had brought down the British minister of war and badly damaged the Conservative government.[38]

One "stroke of luck" provided Johnson leverage to reduce the political damage. Jenkins had been a member in good standing of the 9999th Air Force Reserve Unit, abolished by McNamara the day after the Republicans nominated Goldwater for president. Johnson, familiar with the politics of sexual blacklisting and the McCarthy-era Lavender Scare from his years in the Senate, looked for something he could use to intimidate his rival. Hoping to fight sexual scandal with sexual scandal, LBJ ordered the FBI to search for "derogatory information" on members of Goldwater's staff. A check of fifteen names turned up nothing. But the White House quickly discovered that all of Jenkins's recent fitness reports had been written by his commanding officer, Major General Barry Goldwater. Newspapers promptly reported the connection. Despite Goldwater's denials, the apparent association restrained the Republican candidate from fully exploiting the issue of Jenkins's homosexuality; both Lyndon Johnson and Barry Goldwater had been "compromised" by association with a "security risk." As Republicans publicized the scandal, Johnson made sure that the newspapers again reported Goldwater's connection to the former White House aide. The press disclosed that FBI agents were dispatched one morning at 6:30 A.M. to question the candidate on his knowledge of "Jenkins' personal habits." Other news, too, helped divert some media attention from the scandal during its first days. The October 16 revelation of Soviet premier Nikita Khrushchev's ouster by rivals in the Politburo, and reports the following day of the first atomic bomb detonation by communist China, competed for front-page attention with the White House homosexual scandal.[39]

Goldwater struck a pose as a high-minded candidate who would not mention the Jenkins scandal "unless he [found] that it involve[d] a question of national security." He largely limited himself to innuendo about the "curious crew" surrounding LBJ, and to general condemnations of moral decay in the White House. But while Goldwater posed on the high road, his campaign aides and Republican allies gleefully gay-baited the White House, predicting that the scandal "would probably have 'a terrific impact' on the election." Dean Burch, Republican national chairman, vice presidential candidate William E. Miller, and former vice president Richard Nixon all took up the task of keeping the homosexual scandal in the headlines. They accused LBJ of a "coverup of corruption so deep that it casts a shadow over the White House itself." When the FBI released its report announcing that Jenkins's homosexuality had caused no breach of security, Dean Burch seized on a passage in the report that suggested that Jenkins "had limited association with some individuals who are alleged to be, or who admittedly are, sex deviates." "The important, unanswered questions," pronounced Burch, were: "Who are these sex deviates? Are they also employed by the federal government? If so, where do they work? When did Mr. Jenkins have 'limited association' with these sex deviates?"[40]

The Republicans repeatedly linked the presence of a homosexual in the White House to their assaults on Johnson's "weak" foreign policy. On the campaign trail, Goldwater's running mate claimed that "no man today can say there has or has not been a security leak," worrying that "Jenkins' arrest was a public police record for everyone to see—including the Communists." Moments later he denounced the "utter confusion" of the administration's Vietnam policy. "They don't know what to do except to instruct American soldiers to do enough to die but not enough to win," Miller seethed. Representative John M. Ashbrook of the House Committee on Un-American Activities decried the presence of Jenkins on the White House staff, fretting that the former aide had "been privy to the most sensitive deliberations of the American government—to our greatest secrets." Replaying the political rhetoric of the previous decade's Lavender Scare, Ashbrook blamed the Democrats for again abetting homosexual infiltration of the State Department. Not only had Jenkins compromised U.S. security, he warned, but "in this connection I would note that the records show that almost three times as many security risks were eliminated from the state department in 1963 as there were in 1960, indicating clearly an increase in the number of those risks." Playing the numbers game, Ashbrook cited executive session testimony by State Department security officials, revealing that in the years 1960-1963 respectively, 18, 24, 24, and 27 Washington employees of the State Department had been fired for homosexuality. Furthermore, press accounts of Ashbrook's statement revealed that "60 of 152 applicants for state department jobs were rejected because they were perverts."[41]

The press corps eagerly pursued the story, largely dispensing with the coded and euphemistic references common in the homosexual panic of the 1950s. The papers named Jenkins's sexual partner arrested with him in the YMCA men's room. They published extensive investigative pieces on the policies and procedures of the Metropolitan Police vice squad, trying to determine how Jenkins slipped through several "security" checks despite his 1959 arrest. Even Lieutenant Roy Blick, recently retired from the morals division, had another fleeting moment in the limelight. The *New York Times* reported that Blick had not notified Senator Johnson of the 1959 arrest, because he had been "burned" in earlier cases involving senators and their families. Feeding the renewed interest in the "question" of "homosexuals in government" a *New York Times* reporter discovered that Jenkins had written a memo admonishing federal officials to "invoke tighter screening procedures" to prevent homosexuals from obtaining government employment. Walter Trohan of the *Chicago Tribune,* an old crony of Joe McCarthy's, reported that Jenkins had once interceded with air force officials to try to reinstate an officer discharged "for a morals offense."[42]

Despite such intense scrutiny by newspapers and the "virtual monopoly on the morality issue" held by Goldwater, public reaction confounded the expectations of Washington insiders. Goldwater supporters, initially "elated" by anticipation of political damage to the Johnson campaign, saw their hopes dashed. President Johnsons political advisers were "greatly concerned" when the story broke, but a week later were relieved to see front-page newspaper stories on voter polls that showed a small *increase* in support for their candidate. Establishment columnist Walter Lippmann expressed distaste for Goldwater's campaign of "innuendo and insinuation, of sly hints and smirks," a form of "sneak attack." Public reaction, as reported by the press, was similar. After distancing himself from Jenkins and imposing stringent new security procedures on the White House, Johnson capitalized on public fears of Goldwater's extremism. On the stump, LBJ claimed to see a "trend away from the Republican party," the result of a "smearlash." "When some people get desperate they get dangerous, and when they are dangerous they are not cautious; and when they get to smearing and fearing some of their own people do not want to go along with them." As the election neared, Johnson counterattacked, asserting that Eisenhower had confronted "a situation similar to the Walter Jenkins episode," but that he had shown a humane forbearance and refused to politically exploit the case: "We Democrats felt sorry for him [i.e., Eisenhower's homosexual appointee]; thought it was a sickness and disease." Richard Nixon and other Republicans responded with outrage and charges of a "smear." Ike blandly told reporters that he didn't recall any 'problem' similar to the Walter Jenkins episode."[43]

The reactions, in 1964, of Johnson and his advisers to "aggressive" Asian communism and to a sudden vulnerability to a homosexual scare were predicated on their memory of the politics of 1949–52. Johnson formulated his response to the related crises to protect his administration from the misfortune and eventual electoral defeat that befell Truman, buffeted by the fallout from countersubversion and counterperversion and the outbreak of the Korean War. The widely publicized Jenkins scandal embarrassed the administration and provided another chastening lesson in the politics of manliness, reinforcing the predisposition toward "toughness" in foreign policy.[44]

During the fall and winter of 1964 the national security planners worked frantically to devise schemes to prevent the fall of Saigon to the insurgents. To the foreign policy bureaucrats, the loss of the Southeast Asian bulwark of containment was almost too painful and too dangerous to contemplate. Even though all estimates predicted the likely collapse of the regime, the bureaucrats approached the need to plan for that contingency with almost pathological wariness. John McNaughton, assistant secretary of defense, asked his new assistant, Daniel Ellsberg, to explore a series of possible scenarios in which South Vietnam did collapse, and to formulate possible U.S. responses to limit the damage. Before undertaking the task, McNaughton warned Ellsberg not to discuss his task with any colleagues in the department, and not to use a secretary to type the reports. A "leak" was perceived to be so dangerous politically and personally that Ellsberg was instructed to type the documents himself. The foreign policy reason of the manly warrior-intellectuals had clear boundaries; Ellsberg stepped very near the outer edge. Even to consider the possibility that the United States might "lose Indochina" conjured up the legacy of the countersubversive purges of the previous decade. "You should be clear," McNaughton cautioned, "that you could be signing the death warrant to your career by having anything to do with calculations and decisions like these. A lot of people were ruined for less."[45]

Much more likely to be rewarded were energetic efforts to devise a winning strategy. Much labor and attention went toward formulating contingency plans for "reprisals" against the North Vietnamese. The bureaucrats believed that the application of the principles of behaviorism to international diplomacy could preserve the South Vietnamese regime. Aerial bombing seemed to offer the promise of the efficient application of American technological superiority to deliver "messages" of "pain" to the men in Hanoi who presumably controlled the insurgents in the South. It was hoped, although never predicted with confidence, that the North Vietnamese leaders would act rationally in response to the graduated campaign of death and destruction; sensing U.S. resolve, they would abandon the war.[46]

In December 1964, as President Johnson conferred with his advisers on the grave situation in Vietnam, he braced for war. All that was needed to trigger American reprisals was an act of enemy "aggression": "DRV [North Vietnam] will bomb Saigon once. Then we are off to the races. . . . Day of reckoning is coming. Want to be sure we've done everything we can." Money was no obstacle to the anticipated escalation. The feeble, feminized South Vietnamese allies must be given all the reinforcement the United States could buy, commanded Johnson. "[I do] not want to send widow woman to slap Jack Dempsey."[47]

The anticipated provocation arrived on February 7, 1965, while National Security Adviser McGeorge Bundy visited South Vietnam. Viet Cong forces attacked the helicopter base and barracks of American military "advisers" at Pleiku in the Vietnamese Central Highlands. Ten days earlier Bundy, with Robert McNamara, had warned the president of "disastrous defeat" if the United States continued to wait for a "stable government" before deploying the "enormous power of the United States." After consultation with the U.S. "Country Team," and before making an inspection visit to the base at Pleiku with its dead and wounded Americans, Bundy recommended the start of the previously planned campaign of reprisal bombings against the North. Within fourteen hours of the raid on Pleiku, the president launched 132 carrier-borne aircraft on bombing sorties over North Vietnam. Johnson directed Maxwell Taylor, ambassador to Saigon, to begin the planned evacuation of American women and children. "We will carry out our December plan for continuing action against North Vietnam with modifications up and down in tempo and scale in the light of your recommendations as Bundy reports them," cabled the president.[48]

Despite the reprisal bombing, the president still hesitated at authorizing sustained aerial bombing of the North. His advisers encouraged him to begin "Phase II" or "Rolling Thunder"—a sustained campaign of bombing designed to "take the initiative" from the communists. McGeorge Bundy cast the situation much as journalist Joseph Alsop had: "The American investment is very large. . . . There is no way of negotiating ourselves out of Vietnam which offers any serious promise at present . . . any negotiated withdrawal today would mean surrender on the installment plan." LBJ hesitated, worried that the instability of the South Vietnamese government could not provide a reliable base for such massive escalation of U.S. military intervention. In late February, another coup abetted by Ambassador Maxwell Taylor and the U.S. mission to Saigon deposed the unreliable General Khanh. On March 2, 1965, with the apparent emergence of a more "dependable" military junta and the mass arrests of South Vietnamese civil servants who supported a negotiated peace, Johnson dispatched the first U.S. aircraft in a campaign of sustained bombing against North Vietnam.[49]

In March, President Johnson demonstrated his resolve to a group of his high-level national security bureaucrats. He promised not to "give in" to "another Munich." If the United States did not defend imperial boundaries in Vietnam, Johnson argued, "then Thailand" would become the battleground. "Come Hell or high water, we're gonna stay there." He urged his cabinet and staff to "beg borrow or steal to get a government" to support the U.S. military presence in South Vietnam. The forced inactivity of the previous year had been frustrating. "We endured this thru a campaign," Johnson griped. But he made it clear that the humiliations of passivity need no longer be tolerated. The president evoked the heroic legacy of the frontier racial war of American myth. With a scrambled metaphor he exhorted his men to war: "You gotta get some Indians under your scalp."[50]

Johnson's war managers began to take large numbers of Vietnamese "scalps" with Rolling Thunder, the ongoing bombing attacks. The onset of the air campaign quickly led to the introduction of substantial numbers of U.S. ground troops, justified by the need to "protect American boys." First, marines were deployed to protect U.S. air installations, then more troops were added to conduct offensive operations in the areas around U.S. air bases to protect soldiers stationed on them. By the summer of 1965 the Pentagon had requested an increase of a hundred thousand troops, bringing levels to between 175,000 and 200,000. They projected needs for another hundred thousand within six months. The escalation that had proceeded headlong since April paused very briefly during July, while the president held a series of meetings with his war managers to "discuss in detail" the "alternatives" facing the United States in Vietnam.

The Social Reason of the Imperial Brotherhood

During 1964 and 1965, some in Congress dissented from the general bureaucratic consensus that the collapse of the proxy regime in Vietnam would represent a crushing blow to America's position as leader of the "free world." Three Democratic senators, Wayne Morse (Oregon), Ernest Gruening (Alaska), and Frank Church (Idaho) spoke publicly against escalation. Many others were dubious, but political loyalty to the president silenced them. Senator Mike Mansfield warned Johnson of the likely course of events in Vietnam and urged him to disentangle the United States from the fruitless enterprise. "We will find ourselves engaged merely in an indecisive, bloody, and costly military involvement," Mansfield cautioned. The adventure was doomed by "the absence of sufficient national interest to justify it to our own people." Mansfield believed that the benefits of maintaining American "prestige" did not justify a war in Asia, in view of the tangible costs he foresaw. The United States had gotten itself embroiled in a futile war in Korea because "we tended to talk ourselves out on a limb with overstatements of our purpose and commitment only to discover in the end that there were not sufficient American interests to support with blood and treasure in a desperate final plunge." Johnson was not receptive. One White House aide described the president's attitude: "He hated Mike Mansfield, just despised him."[51]

Vice President Hubert Humphrey, too, angered the president in mid-February 1965 with arguments against deepening the intervention in Vietnam. As was customary among men who dissented from conventional wisdom but sought to retain "influence" in government, Humphrey prefaced his missive with obsequious oaths of fealty, swearing "loyalty, help, and support." Humphrey eschewed global "strategic" arguments in favor of domestic political ones. He argued that war would be politically unpopular, especially with Democrats, that arguments justifying the intervention were politically barren and could not generate support at home, that the failure of the South Vietnamese government further jeopardized domestic support for war, that the potential for war with China (the Korean analogy) made the war unwise politically. Finally, he suggested that 1965 was the ideal time to "cut losses." "Indeed," Humphrey averred, "it is the first year when we can face the Vietnam problem without being preoccupied with the political repercussions from the Republican right." With remarkable prescience, Humphrey predicted that the administration's "political problems are likely to come from new and different sources (Democratic liberals, independents, labor) if we pursue an enlarged military policy very long."[52]

Morse, Gruening, Mansfield, and Humphrey were outside the inner circle of executive power and decision making, and thus easily dismissed. George Ball, undersecretary of state, had grave reservations about the wisdom of U.S. intervention, and his in-house role as devil's advocate reveals much about the process of reason in the inner circle of the imperial brotherhood. While Ball had spent much of his adult life as a powerful Washington lawyer involved in national and international politics, his upbringing didn't fully conform to the central patterns of the imperial brotherhood in the foreign policy bureaucracy. Although of prosperous and upwardly mobile family origins, Ball was educated in an Illinois public high school and at Northwestern University; he lacked the credentials (elite boarding school, Ivy League, clubman) that many of his associates possessed. Ball did not share the neo-stoic aristocratic or frontier identity narrative of warrior heroism. Youthful reading of the First World War "poetry of disillusion" by Wilfred Owen, Sigfried Sassoon, Robert Graves, and others had engendered in him a distaste for the celebration of hero myth. During World War II Ball did not serve in an elite military combat or operational unit; instead he participated in the Strategic Bombing Survey, conducted to assess the effectiveness of the air campaign against Germany and Japan. His wartime experience did not leave him with a personal narrative of heroic and victorious engagement in battle. Instead, he acquired a deep skepticism about the effectiveness of aerial bombardment, even against nations with a highly developed industrial infrastructure supposedly vulnerable to the crippling effects of air power.[53]

Ball's experience in international law during the forties and fifties had been closely tied to European trade issues. He worked closely with Jean Monnet, French statesman and architect of the European Coal and Steel Community. Ball's career trajectory gave him a distinct

"Atlanticist" outlook. He believed that U.S. power and influence in the world was grounded in the leadership of the Atlantic community. He disdained entanglements in peripheral, politically chaotic, and economically undeveloped Third World nations as potentially wasteful and dangerous diversions from the interests that supported American power. Ball believed that tangible and substantial economic or strategic interests should be the yardstick used to measure the necessity of U.S. involvement in the world. Indonesia, which possessed rich natural resources and a large population and where Western oil corporations did business, was a Southeast Asian nation deserving American concern, Ball argued. Vietnam lacked such significance. Once, when Zanzibar seemed threatened by a "Chinese takeover," Ball twitted his fellow national security managers over their unquenchable zeal for "containment" even in such irrelevant African backwaters with a brief memo: "God watches every sparrow that may fall, so I don't see why we have to compete in that league."[54]

Perhaps most significantly, Ball, unlike his other associates in the national security bureaucracy, had closely followed the French debacle in Indochina. His French law clients had introduced him to the military and civilian architects of the colonial war. He saw firsthand the "self-deception" of leaders "seduced by self-serving arguments" while engaged in *la guerre sale* against a Viet Minh enemy with an "irrational willingness" to "take staggering losses." Over the course of years of transatlantic shuttling, Ball saw the futility of each in a series of new French "tactical schemes—the Navarre Plan, the Salan Plan, the LeClerc Plan, and the de Lattre de Tassigny Plan—that would magically assure victory in a short period."[55]

Ball had warned Kennedy in November 1961 that the Taylor-Rostow plan for the introduction of ground troops would "be a tragic error." "Within five years," Ball predicted, "we'll have three hundred thousand men in the paddies and jungles and never find them again. That was the French experience." Kennedy abruptly cut off the conversation, and Ball pursued it no farther. But in September and October 1964, deeply concerned about the drift of U.S. policy toward major intervention, Ball secretly prepared a memo of sixty-seven single-spaced pages analyzing the costs and benefits of American involvement. He foresaw the potential for disaster, and recommended that the United States "cut its losses" and find a negotiated settlement "under the best conditions obtainable." Ball sent the memo to McNamara, Rusk, and McGeorge Bundy. Their reaction, as Ball recounts it, was not to engage in debate over the challenges raised to U.S. policy, but to regard the existence of the memo itself with some alarm, for fear of "leaks." They treated it "as an idiosyncratic diversion from the only relevant problem: how to win the war." Neither McNamara, Rusk, or Bundy sent the memo on to the president.[56]

Their efforts at bureaucratic containment were only partly successful. Other imperial bureaucrats harbored profound doubts about the likely consequences of escalation. When William Bundy got wind of Ball's argument, he responded with his own forty-two-page memorandum in which he dared to argue that the loss of South Vietnam "could be made bearable." Since the South Vietnamese "had ceased to care strongly about defending themselves," they could take the blame in the eyes of the world. Bundy went farther, openly challenging the legitimacy of the South Vietnamese state, although blaming the French for the mess: "A bad colonial heritage of long standing, totally inadequate preparation for self-government by the colonial power, a colonialist war fought in half-baked fashion and lost, a nationalist movement taken over by Communism ruling in the other half of an ethnically and historically unified country, the Communist side inheriting much the better military force and far more than its share of the talent—these are the facts that dog us today."[57] American withdrawal, with prestige intact, could be accomplished by the use of more violence, Bundy argued. With the next Viet Cong provocation, the United States should respond with large-scale reprisal attacks against

North Vietnam. Because the domino theory was overdrawn, the administration could then agree to international demands for Geneva-style negotiations leading to American withdrawal. But even the solution of "shooting your way out of the saloon," as Daniel Ellsberg phrased it, aroused great alarm within and without the bureaucracy, putting William Bundy's career at risk. When on November 23, after he had sent a memo with the disengagement plan to Rusk and McNamara, they summoned him to squelch the proposal. Bundy's bureaucratic superiors instructed him that "it won't wash." Admiral Mustin of the Joint Chiefs of Staff had been outraged by Bundy's proposal too, and protested vigorously. Bundy dropped his support for Ball's negotiated peace and began planning for escalation.[58]

Ball's heresies and William Bundy's tentative endorsement of a negotiated settlement, when word leaked out, provoked discord within the imperial brotherhood; perhaps in some measure they led to the vigorous suppression of in-house dissent by McNamara and Rusk. On the morning of November 23, Joseph Alsop's column warned that the "Europe minded" George Ball, "whose knowledge of Asia could be comfortably contained in a fairly small thimble, has none the less been signing memoranda advocating a negotiated settlement with the Vietnamese Communists." The only heartening news Alsop could offer was that in contrast to the "concealed surrender" advocated by Ball, "the more courageous and able" of Johnson's chief advisers were on the "do something side." In fact, Alsop asserted, they appeared to "favor doing something pretty drastic" to save South Vietnam. William Bundy, caught that day between the doves and hawks within the administration, wrote an angry letter to his old friend Alsop. "From the most basic of all points of view—straight patriotism—this kind of piece measurably increases the difficulty of serious discussion within the government of grave issues," scolded Bundy. Alsop shot back a "peppery" reply, asserting both his patriotism and his journalistic duty to bring such "discussion with the government" to light. Public scrutiny would "prevent our always numerous scalawags and incompetents in office from advocating cowardly courses and doing dangerous things." It was left to McGeorge Bundy to mend fences with their politically influential imperial brother.[59]

Only in late February 1965, after the reprisal bombing campaign against the North had occurred, did Johnson actually see a copy of Ball's October memo questioning the practical wisdom of aerial bombing and escalation. Johnson did not unequivocally dismiss Ball's arguments. Between March and July, Ball wrote several memos to the president questioning the premises of the justifications for further U.S. intervention. Ball argued that the political and physical "terrain" of Vietnam could not support a large-scale American effort. Using the metaphor of a diseased body, Ball suggested that they "could not be sure how far the cancer has infected the whole body politic of South Viet-Nam"; a war in support of the regime would be like "administering cobalt treatment to a terminal case." Further, contrary to the assumptions of his fellow national security managers, Ball argued that the real danger to U.S. "prestige" lay in loudly proclaiming the vital importance of maintaining a minor client regime, taking on a rag-tag guerrilla army with the full weight of American power, and then encountering stalemate or defeat.[60]

Ball's "cold-blooded calculation" did not sit well with Bundy, McNamara, and Rusk. They worked to contain the spread of such alarming ideas. The president agreed, in early July, to discuss two draft papers, one arguing "Ball's preference for a negotiated withdrawal" and the other "McNamara's recommendation of a substantial increase of military strength." Bundy reported that his two colleagues in the cabinet felt "strongly that the George Ball paper should not be argued with you in front of any audience larger than yourself, Rusk, McNamara, Ball, and me." They feared the political consequences if word reached the public that "withdrawal" was even considered within the realm of the possible: "it is exceedingly dangerous to have this possibility reported in a wider circle." Bundy himself was clearly apprehensive that the president might find Ball's argument persuasive. "My personal, private opinion is that both Rusk and McNamara are too diffident and that it would help you to have a few more people in the meeting."[61]

The practical test of Ball's arguments in the larger culture of the imperial bureaucracy came in late July 1965, as Lyndon Johnson convened his high-level Vietnam advisers to ponder the grave implication of sending U.S. troops in lots of a hundred thousand to fight in Vietnam, as Robert McNamara recommended.[62] George Ball later referred to the reasoning that led to the escalation as "turning logic on its head." More accurately stated, the process reveals the way that deeply ingrained ideologies of elite masculinity, buttressed by individual experience in the competition for power at both the personal and the collective level, created a context of conceivable meanings, a "logic," that made Ball's proposed course of action quite literally unthinkable.[63]

The July meetings were conducted along formally rational lines. They were designed to resolve the president's genuine doubts about the requested escalation by bringing to light the possible costs and benefits of the projected troop increases. Johnson demanded that his assembled counselors explain "what has happened in [the] recent past that requires this decision on my part? What are the alternatives? Also, I want more discussion on what we expect to flow from this decision."[64] While he cautioned that "we must make no snap judgments," and demanded of the gathering that "we must consider carefully all our options," the very language used to preface his questioning reveals an obsession with masculine "toughness" and "honor." Framing the debate in operational terms, Johnson instinctively led the discussion toward the issue of "prestige" and the appearance of "strength" and away from the assessment of economic, or directly strategic, costs and benefits. "Have we wrung every single soldier out of every country we can? Who else can help? Are we the only defenders of freedom in the world? . . . The negotiations, the pause [in the bombing campaign], all the other approaches have all been explored. It makes us look weak—with cap in hand. We have tried."[65] The president framed the issues to place the United States, under his leadership, at the center of a heroic narrative of moral and physical strength: would the assembled men act as strong men should? Would they shoulder the painful burden that others refused to defend, the central cultural value of freedom, or would they recommend that the United States crawl abjectly to face humiliation at the bargaining table? Unstated, but understood, was the assumption that such a humiliation would not only have dire international consequences, but would also undermine domestic political power and legitimacy.

George Ball, who understood the unspoken rules of loyalty and deference as the price of power, expressed his doubts about the course to be embarked upon—but first he reassured the assembled fraternity of his reliability: "I can foresee a perilous voyage—very dangerous—great apprehensions that we can win under these conditions. But, let me be clear, if the decision is to go ahead, I'm committed." He reassured his colleagues that his objections were strictly questions of pragmatism. He did not raise them because he thought escalation represented "a bad moral position." Ball did not challenge the propriety or wisdom of conducting an interventionist policy abroad to serve American interests. The question was simply whether or not the costs of intervention outweighed the benefits. Ball argued that a massive intervention did not serve to improve U.S. power in the world. He did not broach the issue of the legitimacy of the South Vietnamese state: he merely argued that it was moribund.

Henry Cabot Lodge agreed that the South Vietnamese State was moribund; his assessment reveals the imperial impulse that animated Vietnam policymaking under the rhetorical cover of defending democratic freedoms: "There is no tradition of a national government in Saigon. There are no roots in the country. Not until there is tranquillity can you have any stability. I don't think we ought to take this government seriously. There is no one who can do anything. We have to do what we think we ought to do regardless of what the Saigon government does. As we move ahead on a new phase—it gives us the right and duty to do certain things with or without the government's approval." Lodge argued, in essence, that it had proved impossible to arrange a suitable proxy to promote the "traditions and ideals" of American neo-stoic republicanism. The only politically organized subset of South Vietnamese society capable of creating and maintaining a state was the National Liberation Front, which was by definition outside the boundaries of inclusion in the "free world." Thus the "traditions and ideals" of the imperial brotherhood must hold sway; their "right" and "duty" was to discipline the unruly and chaotic imperial periphery by force of U.S. arms. None of the assembled apostles of freedom rose to defend the right of the South Vietnamese to democratic self-determination.

Ball, however, suggested that there were several operational flaws in the McNamara plan. The mission of the new troops "would be to seek out the VC in large scale units," McNamara and the generals asserted, and by "constantly harassing them, they will have to fight somewhere." The group conceded the likelihood that if the United States "put in 100,000 men, Ho Chi Minh" would "put in another 100,000," matching escalation with escalation. This prospect seemed to cheer General Wheeler, chief of an army possessing a fearsome industrialized technology of death. He blithely predicted that "this means greater bodies of men—which will allow us to cream them." Undersecretary Ball brought up the troubling possibility that "the VC will do what they did against the French—stay away from confrontation and not accommodate us." Ball predicted a quagmire: as American losses mounted the pressure to "create a larger war would be irresistible." Johnson asked Ball: "What other road can I go?" Ball's recommendation, to "take losses—let their government fall apart—negotiate—probable takeover by Communists," was, he conceded, "disagreeable." The president, who had read and discussed Ball's proposals for several months, found such a suggestion literally unthinkable; whatever the long-term dangers of intervention, negotiated withdrawal fell outside the boundaries of conceivable outcomes. Nonetheless, the ritual deliberations continued: "You have pointed out the danger, but you haven't proposed an alternative. We haven't always been right. We have no mortgage on victory. . . . I think it is desirable to hear you out—and determine if your suggestions are sound and ready to be followed."

Later that afternoon, the meeting reconvened. Ball listed reasons to avoid large-scale military entanglement in Vietnam: the possibility of intervention by China, as in the Korean War; the likelihood of losing public support as American casualties increased; world opinion turning against the United States with a protracted war. Ball expressed doubts that an "army of westerners can fight Orientals in Asian jungles and succeed." The undersecretary also attacked the notion that a war in Vietnam would buttress U.S. "prestige" and "credibility" with allies. Ball conveyed the opinion of the ambassador to Tokyo that "Japan thinks we are propping up a lifeless government and are on a sticky wicket. Between [a] long war and cutting our losses, the Japanese would go for the latter." Ball argued that Western European allies, too, believed that Vietnam was "not relevant to their situation." They were "concerned about their own security—troops in Berlin [had] real meaning, none in VN."[66]

Johnson quizzed Ball on the costs of abandoning South Vietnam to its fate: "Wouldn't all these countries say Uncle Sam is a paper tiger—wouldn't we lose credibility breaking the word of three presidents—if we get it up as you proposed. It would seem to be an irreparable blow. . . . You are not basically troubled by what the world would say about pulling out?" Ball replied that the damaging blow would come when "the mightiest power in the world can't defeat guerrillas." His face-saving prescription was to force the South Vietnamese government to invite the United States out, by stipulating conditions for involvement that the South Vietnamese would refuse to meet. Ball asked the president and his advisers to accept "a course that is costly, but can be limited to short-term costs."[67]

Ball's proposal was unthinkable to the conclave of national security managers. McGeorge Bundy complained that such a move threatened the legacy of U.S. imperial leadership: it "would be a radical switch without evidence that it should be done. It goes in the face of all we have said and done." Henry Cabot Lodge foresaw apocalyptic consequences if the United States failed to make war when challenged: "There is a greater threat [of] World War III if we don't go in." Appeasement, he argued, was the real danger, because of the "similarity to our indolence at Munich." Dean Rusk agreed with his virile patrician colleagues in their demand for unwavering defense of boundaries everywhere: "If the Communist world finds out we will not pursue our commitment to the end, I don't know where they will stay their hand."

During the next week, the president met several more times with civilian advisers, military leaders, and senior statesmen of the Cold War (the "wise men"). Paul Nitze, secretary of the navy, another distinguished patrician cold warrior (Hotchkiss School, Harvard, and the Porcellian club), counseled a deeper investment of men to prosecute the war, even though he estimated the chances of success at "about 60/40." Such poor odds were justified by the risks to U.S. power that would follow if the president avoided war: "to acknowledge that we couldn't beat the VC, the shape of the world will change."[68] Significantly, Nitze did not bother to explain the mechanics of the transformation, or even what the new shape might be. No one demanded that he explain. His "analysis," like that of the other imperial managers, was a merely ritual invocation of the need to exert U.S. power to keep rivals from presuming to challenge its preeminence. It was the reflex of a lifetime of immersion in the world of elite male power, sanctioned by the rewards of success in that world and reinforced by the history of the countersubversive struggles of the preceding fifteen years.

Robert McNamara did make predictions about the consequences of withdrawal, trotting out the image of toppling dominoes. The effect, he predicted, would be global, threatening even the eastern NATO territory and U.S. leadership of the Atlantic community: "Laos, Cambodia, Thailand, Burma, surely affect Malaysia. In 2–3 years Communist domination would stop there, but ripple effect would be great—Japan, India. We would have to give up some bases. Ayub [in Pakistan] would move closer to China. Greece, Turkey would move to neutralist position. Communist agitation would increase in Africa."[69] He provided no details about the mechanisms involved in the alarming transformation he foresaw, and no one asked for further explication.

The military brass, too, identified grave consequences to follow from withdrawal. While "the results of bombing actions" had not "been as fruitful and productive as we anticipated," persistence was the key, they argued. National security was at stake in Vietnam, General Greene asserted: "Matter of time before we go in some place else." The United States could not simply back out. "Pledge we made. Prestige before the rest of the world." Two courses of action were possible: "get out" or "stay in and win." The general did not address the first alternative. In the course of the colloquy Johnson expressed doubt about the necessity to honor a "commitment to jump off a building" after discovering "how high it is." He asked for reassurance: "I judge though that the big problem is one of national security. Is that right?" The assembled group unanimously assented to his proposition.[70]

Johnson had McGeorge Bundy read from a prepared memo to inoculate the assembled brotherhood against criticism they would face upon the announcement of escalation. Bundy's memo outlined the arguments against intervention: "For 10 years every step we have taken has been based on a previous failure. All we have done has failed and caused us to take another step which has failed . . . we have made excessive claims we haven't been able to realize. . . . We are about to fight a war we can't fight and win, and the country we are trying to help is quitting . . . aren't we talking about a military solution when the solution is political?"[71]

In meetings with the "wise men" only Clark Clifford recommended avoiding escalation, seeing nothing in store "but catastrophe for my country." "If we lose 50,000 +," Clifford warned, "it will ruin us." John J. McCloy disagreed: "The country is looking to getting on with the war."[72] Despite the objections of Ball and Clifford, the overwhelming weight of the "establishment" advised large-scale intervention. Johnson finalized the decision to escalate by July 28, 1965, setting the United States on precisely the course predicted by Mansfield, Ball, and Clifford: a spiraling expenditure of blood and money to achieve a higher level of stalemate. For another three years Johnson and his national security bureaucrats struggled to manage a "limited" war amid growing domestic unrest, in the process devastating large areas of Southeast Asia with napalm, high-explosives, and defoliants. Their decisions led to the deaths of millions. In the end, Johnson handed the problem to his successor, as Kennedy had done to him.

Lyndon Johnson and his advisers—Bundy, McNamara, Rusk, and others—did not, as Ball asserts, "turn logic on its head." They used a different and incommensurable logic, the political logic of neo-stoic warrior manhood. The president and his advisers had the information and the cost-benefit calculations at their disposal that would have dictated a prudent tactical withdrawal from one hardly crucial salient in the great game of empire, had they employed the "logic" that Ball preferred.

The identity narrative of the imperial brotherhood demanded relentless defense of boundaries and an utter rejection of appeasement. The president and the men of the Johnson national security bureaucracy identified manhood with militant imperial anticommunism. They obsessively managed the conduct of the war, endlessly meeting to pick bombing targets, to fine-tune the "messages" of pain and pleasure (i.e., bombing pauses) they believed they were sending the North Vietnamese.

Lyndon Johnson especially, while mobilizing other men's bodies to do the fighting, metaphorically cast himself and his advisers as combatants: "It's like a prizefight. Our right is our military power, but our left must be our peace proposals."[73] Johnson cast himself as a "prizefighter up against Jack Dempsey"—and the United States as a barroom brawler locked in a struggle with the North Vietnamese, hoping to find a way to "get our feet on their neck."[74] Johnson had a predilection for sexual metaphors that identified his body with imperial struggle; a tactical setback resulting from attempts to arrange "negotiations" might be equated with homosexual penetration: "Oh yes, a bombing halt, I'll tell you what happens when there is a bombing halt. I halt and then Ho Chi Minh shoves his trucks right up my ass. That's your bombing halt."[75] Conversely, aggressive military action against the enemy carried connotations of sexual conquest. During the spring of 1965 he reassured congressional critics that his bombing would not spark a Chinese intervention: "I'm going up her leg an inch at a time. . . . I'll get the snatch before they know what's happening, you see." To Johnson, the Gulf of Tonkin bombing symbolized a violent, sexualized male prowess: "I didn't just screw Ho Chi Minh. I cut his pecker off."[76]

The failure of ever increasing levels of U.S. military force to accomplish any of the hoped-for goals of the intervention became apparent as early as late 1965. Domestic criticism challenging the morality and rationality of the intervention grew too, just as Bundy had predicted. Many of the national security warrior-bureaucrats suffered physically from the contradictions between a mandatory unwavering resolve to continue the war until the other side backed down and the palpable failure and destructiveness of that policy. The failure of "air mobility" and aerial bombing, so central to the war strategy of the establishment, perhaps also took a toll on the self-conception of bureaucrats as active powerful agents in the prosecution of the war. Despite the pain inflicted on both American and Vietnamese people, and despite the self-inflicted pain suffered by the stoic bureaucrats, they pressed on with the war.

Some began to manifest stress symptoms, milder, but at least analogous to those of soldiers forced to be "passive" in dangerous circumstances. Dean Rusk's son recounts finding his father writhing in pain on the living room floor, convulsed with chronic stomach pains that "were never diagnosed despite dozens of physical exams and the best medical advice" obtainable. Rusk's pain began "in the months prior to the American build-up in Vietnam in 1965." William Bundy, assistant secretary of Far Eastern affairs, developed ulcers; nonetheless, unlike his brother McGeorge, he stayed on at his post until President Johnson left office. Robert McNamara, who began to realize the futility of the bombing campaign by late 1965 or early 1966, developed "bruxism," grinding his teeth in his sleep. He stoically managed the war for Johnson for the next two and a half years, but by 1967 he developed a propensity to break into tears at public appearances and in war planning meetings. Lyndon Johnson feared that McNamara would become "another Forrestal," referring to the first secretary of defense, a suicide who suffered a breakdown and leapt from a window at Bethesda Naval Hospital. President Johnson refused to heed his defense secretary's advice in late 1967 to stop the bombing and begin to extricate the United States from war in Southeast Asia. It took the Tet Offensive of February 1968 and the advice of McNamara's replacement, Clark Clifford, to push the president in that direction.[77]

Chapter 10

The War in America

THE VIETNAM WAR WAS NOT THE FIRST American conflict to inspire domestic protest, but by the late 1960s it had almost certainly become the most unpopular war in the nation's history. (The slight qualification is needed because there were no public opinion polls at the time of the War of 1812 or the Civil War.) Americans opposed the Vietnam War for a variety of reasons. Some people thought that the United States was immorally engaged in imperialism in Vietnam. Others continued to have faith in the rectitude of American foreign policy overall, but felt that the intervention in Vietnam was a mistake—a departure from the necessary (or generally benign) foreign involvements of the past. And surely some marched in antiwar demonstrations out of fear that if the war dragged on, they or someone they loved would be sent off to fight.

The readings in this chapter address these and other concerns. Christian Appy underscores the importance of social class in determining who went to war and who did not; Vietnam, as he puts it, was a "working-class war." The genesis of organized opposition to the war is the focus of Tom Wells's piece. He examines the tensions created when a group with a multifaceted reform agenda leaps onto a bandwagon playing just one song, and he describes the onset of large-scale protest, and the Johnson administration's response to it, in early 1965. The chapter concludes with a look at women who resisted the war: an excerpt from Myra MacPherson's book *Long Time Passing*. Implicit in this selection is the question of whether gender conditioned an individual's reaction to the war.

34

Working-Class War

Christian G. Appy

"We all ended up going into the service about the same time—the whole crowd." I had asked Dan Shaw about himself, why *he* had joined the Marine Corps; but Dan ignored the personal thrust of the question. Military service seemed less an individual choice than a collective rite of passage, a natural phase of life for "the whole crowd" of boys in his neighborhood, so his response encompassed a circle of over twenty childhood friends who lived near the corner of Train and King Streets in Dorchester, Massachusetts—a white, working-class section of Boston.

Thinking back to 1968 and his street-corner buddies, Dan sorted them into groups, wanting to get the facts straight about each one. It did not take him long to come up with some figures. "Four of the guys didn't go into the military at all. Four got drafted by the army. Fourteen or fifteen of us went in the Marine Corps. Out of them fourteen or fifteen"—here he paused to count by naming—"Eddie, Brian, Tommy, Dennis, Steve: six of us went to Nam." They were all still teenagers. Three of the six were wounded in combat, including Dan.

His tone was calm, almost dismissive. The fact that nearly all his friends entered the military and half a dozen fought in Vietnam did not strike Dan as unusual or remarkable. In working-class neighborhoods like his, military service after high school was as commonplace among young men as college was for the youth of upper-middle-class suburbs—not welcomed by everyone but rarely questioned or avoided. In fact, when Dan thinks of the losses suffered in other parts of Dorchester, he regards his own streetcorner as relatively lucky. "Jeez, it wasn't bad. I mean some corners around here really got wiped out. Over off Norfolk Street ten guys got blown away the same year."

Focusing on the world of working-class Boston, Dan has a quiet, low-key manner with few traces of bitterness. But when he speaks of the disparities in military service throughout American society, his voice fills with anger, scorn, and hurt. He compares the sacrifices of poor and working-class neighborhoods with the rarity of wartime casualties in the "fancy suburbs" beyond the city limits, in places such as Milton, Lexington, and Wellesley. If three wounded veterans "wasn't bad" for a streetcorner in Dorchester, such concentrated pain was, Dan insists, unimaginable in a wealthy subdivision. "You'd be lucky to find three Vietnam veterans in one of those rich neighborhoods, never mind three who got wounded."

Dan's point is indisputable: those who fought and died in Vietnam were overwhelmingly drawn from the bottom half of the American social structure. The comparison he suggests bears out the claim. The three affluent towns of Milton, Lexington, and Wellesley had a combined wartime population of about 100,000, roughly equal to that of Dorchester. However, while those suburbs suffered a total of eleven war deaths, Dorchester lost forty-two. There was almost exactly the same disparity in casualties between Dorchester and another sample of prosperous Massachusetts towns—Andover, Lincoln, Sudbury, Weston, Dover, Amherst, and Longmeadow.

These towns lost ten men from a combined population of 100,000. In other words, boys who grew up in Dorchester were four times more likely to die in Vietnam than those raised in the fancy suburbs. An extensive study of wartime casualties from Illinois reached a similar conclusion. In that state, men from neighborhoods with median family incomes under $5,000 (about $15,000 in 1990 dollars) were four times more likely to die in Vietnam than men from places with median family incomes above $15,000 ($45,000 in 1990 dollars).

Dorchester, East Los Angeles, the South Side of Chicago—major urban centers such as these sent thousands of men to Vietnam. So, too, did lesser known, midsize industrial cities with large working-class populations, such as Saginaw, Michigan; Fort Wayne, Indiana; Stockton, California; Chattanooga, Tennessee; Youngstown, Ohio; Bethlehem, Pennsylvania; and Utica, New York. There was also an enormous rise in working-class suburbanization in the 1950s and 1960s. The post-World War II boom in modestly priced, uniformly designed tract housing, along with the vast construction of new highways, allowed many workers their first opportunity to purchase homes and to live a considerable distance from their jobs. As a result, many new suburbs became predominantly working class.

Long Island, New York, became the site of numerous working-class suburbs, including the original Levittown, the first mass-produced town in American history. Built by the Levitt and Sons construction firm in the late 1940s, it was initially a middle-class town. By 1960, however, as in many other postwar suburbs, the first owners had moved on, often to larger homes in wealthier suburbs, and a majority of the newcomers were working class. Ron Kovic, author of one of the best-known Vietnam memoirs and films, *Born on the Fourth of July*, grew up near Levittown in Massapequa. His parents, like so many others in both towns, were working people willing to make great sacrifices to own a small home with a little land and to live in a town they regarded as a safe and decent place to raise their families, in hope that their children would enjoy greater opportunity. Many commentators viewed the suburbanization of blue-collar workers as a sign that the working class was vanishing and that almost everyone was becoming middle class. In fact, however, though many workers owned more than ever before, their relative social position remained largely unchanged. The Kovics, for example, lived in the suburbs but had to raise five children on the wages of a supermarket checker and clearly did not match middle-class levels in terms of economic security, education, or social status.

Ron Kovic volunteered for the marines after graduating from high school. He was paralyzed from the chest down in a 1968 firefight during his second tour of duty in Vietnam. Upon returning home, after treatment in a decrepit, rat-infested VA [Veterans Administration] hospital, Kovic was asked to be grand marshal in Massapequa's Memorial Day parade. His drivers were American Legion veterans of World War II who tried unsuccessfully to engage him in a conversation about the many local boys who had died in Vietnam:

> "Remember Clasternack? . . . They got a street over in the park named after him . . . he was the first of you kids to get it. . . . There was the Peters family too . . . both brothers. . . . Both of them killed in the same week. And Alan Grady . . . did you know Alan Grady? . . .
>
> "We've lost a lot of good boys. . . . We've been hit pretty bad. The whole town's changed."

A community of only 27,000, Massapequa lost 14 men in Vietnam. In 1969, *Newsday* traced the family backgrounds of 400 men from Long Island who had been killed in Vietnam. "As a group," the newspaper concluded, "Long Island's war dead have been overwhelmingly white, working-class men. Their parents were typically blue collar or clerical workers, mailmen, factory workers, building tradesmen, and so on."

Rural and small-town America may have lost more men in Vietnam, proportionately, than did even central cities and working-class suburbs. You get a hint of this simply by flipping through the pages of the Vietnam Memorial directory. As thick as a big-city phone book, the directory lists the names and hometowns of Americans who died in Vietnam. An average page contains the names of five or six men from towns such as Alma, West Virginia (pop. 296), Lost Hills, California (pop. 200), Bryant Pond, Maine (pop. 350), Tonalea, Arizona (pop. 125), Storden, Minnesota (pop. 364), Pioneer, Louisiana (pop. 188), Wartburg, Tennessee (pop. 541), Hillisburg, Indiana (pop. 225), Boring, Oregon (pop. 150), Racine, Missouri (pop. 274), Hygiene, Colorado (pop. 400), Clayton, Kansas (pop. 127), and Almond, Wisconsin (pop. 440). In the 1960s only about 2 percent of Americans lived in towns with fewer than 1,000 people. Among those who died in Vietnam, however, roughly four times that portion, 8 percent, came from American hamlets of that size. It is not hard to find small towns that lost more than one man in Vietnam. Empire, Alabama, for example, had four men out of a population of only 400 die in Vietnam—four men from a town in which only a few dozen boys came of draft age during the entire war.

There were also soldiers who came from neither cities, suburbs, nor small towns but from the hundreds of places in between, average towns of 15,000 to 30,000 people whose economic life, however precarious, had local roots. Some of these towns paid a high cost in Vietnam. In the foothills of eastern Alabama, for example, is the town of Talladega, with a population of approximately 17,500 (about one-quarter black), a town of small farmers and textile workers. Only one-third of Talladega's men had completed high school. Fifteen of their children died in Vietnam, a death rate three times the national average. Compare Talladega to Mountain Brook, a rich suburb outside Birmingham. Mountain Brook's population was somewhat higher than Talladega's, about 19,500 (with no black residents of draft age). More than 90 percent of its men were high school graduates. No one from Mountain Brook is listed among the Vietnam War dead.

I have described a social map of American war casualties to suggest not simply the geographic origins of U.S. soldiers but their class origins—not simply where they came from but the kinds of places as well. Class, not geography, was the crucial factor in determining which Americans fought in Vietnam. Geography reveals discrepancies in military service primarily because it often reflects class distinctions. Many men went to Vietnam from places such as Dorchester, Massapequa, Empire, and Talledega because those were the sorts of places where most poor and working-class people lived. The wealthiest youth in those towns, like those in richer communities, were far less likely either to enlist or to be drafted.

Mike Clodfelter, for example, grew up in Plainville, Kansas. In 1964 he enlisted in the army, and the following year he was sent to Vietnam. In his 1976 memoir, Clodfelter recalled, "From my own small home town . . . all but two of a dozen high school buddies would eventually serve in Vietnam and all were of working class families, while I knew of not a single middle class son of the town's businessmen, lawyers, doctors, or ranchers from my high school graduating class who experienced the Armageddon of our generation."

However, even a sketchy map of American casualties must go farther afield, beyond the conventional boundaries of the United States. Although this fact is not well known, the military took draftees and volunteers from the American territories: Puerto Rico, Guam, the U.S. Virgin Islands, American Samoa, and the Canal Zone. These territories lost a total of 436 men in Vietnam, several dozen more than the state of Nebraska. Some 48,000 Puerto Ricans served in Vietnam, many of whom could speak only a smattering of English. Of these, 345 died. This figure does not include men who were born in Puerto Rico and emigrated to the United States (or whose parents were born in Puerto Rico). We do not know these numbers because the military did not make a separate count of Hispanic-American casualties either as an inclusive category or by country of origin.

Guam drew little attention on the American mainland during the war. It was only heard of at all because American B-52s took off from there to make bombing runs over Vietnam (a twelve-hour round-trip flight requiring midair refueling) or because a conference between President Johnson and some of his top military leaders was held there in 1967. Yet the United States sent several thousand Guamanians to fight with American forces in Vietnam. Seventy of them died. Drawn from a population of only 111,000, Guam's death rate was considerably higher even than that of Dorchester, Massachusetts.

This still does not exhaust the range of places we might look for "American" casualties. There were, of course, the "Free World forces" recruited by and, in most cases, financed by the United States. These "third country forces" from South Korea, Australia, New Zealand, Thailand, and the Philippines reached a peak of about 60,000 troops (U.S. forces rose to 550,000). The U.S. government pointed to them as evidence of a united, multinational, free-world effort to resist communist aggression. But only Australia and New Zealand paid to send their troops to Vietnam. They had a force of 7,000 men and lost 469 in combat. The other nations received so much money in return for their military intervention that their forces were essentially mercenary. The Philippine government of Ferdinand Marcos, for example, received the equivalent of $26,000 for each of the 2,000 men it sent to Vietnam to carry out noncombat, civic action programs. South Korea's participation was by far the largest among the U.S. sponsored third countries. It deployed a force of 50,000 men. In return, the Korean government enjoyed substantial increases in aid, and its soldiers were paid roughly 20 times what they earned at home. More than 4,000 of them lost their lives.

The South Vietnamese military was also essentially the product of American intervention. For twenty-one years the United States committed billions of dollars to the creation of an anti-communist government in southern Vietnam and to the recruitment, training, and arming of a military to support it. Throughout the long war against southern guerrillas and North Vietnamese regulars, about 250,000 South Vietnamese government forces were killed. The United States bears responsibility for these lives and for those of third country forces because their military participation was almost wholly dependent on American initiatives.

In this sense, perhaps we need to take another step. Perhaps all Vietnamese deaths, enemy and ally, civilian and combatant, should be considered American as well as Vietnamese casualties. To do so is simply to acknowledge that their fates were largely determined by American intervention. After all, without American intervention (according to almost all intelligence reports at the time and historians since), Vietnamese unification under Ho Chi Minh would have occurred with little resistance.

However one measures American responsibility for Indochinese casualties, every effort should be made to grasp the enormity of those losses. From 1961 to 1975, 1.5 to 2 million Vietnamese were killed. Estimates of Cambodian and Laotian deaths are even less precise, but certainly the figure is in the hundreds of thousands. Imagine a memorial to the Indochinese who died in what they call the American, not the Vietnam, War. If similar to the Vietnam Memorial, with every name etched in granite, it would have to be forty times larger than the wall in Washington. Even such an enormous list of names would not put into perspective the scale of loss in Indochina. These are small countries with a combined wartime population of about 50 million people. Had the United States lost the same portion of its population, the Vietnam Memorial would list the names of 8 million Americans.

To insist that we recognize the disparity in casualties between the Unite States and Indochina is not to diminish the tragedy or significance of American losses, nor does it deflect attention from our effort to understand American soldiers. Without some awareness of the war's full destructiveness we cannot begin to understand their experience. As one veteran put it: "That's what I can't get out of my head—the bodies . . . all those bodies. Back then we didn't give a shit about the dead Vietnamese. It was like: 'Hey, they're just gooks, don't mean nothin.' You got so cold you didn't even blink. You could even joke about it, mess around with the bodies like they was rag dolls. And after awhile we could even stack up our own KIAs [killed in action] without feeling much of anything. It's not like that now. You can't just put it out of your mind. Now I carry those bodies around every fucking day. It's a heavy load, man, a heavy fucking load."

Presidents Kennedy, Johnson, and Nixon sent 3 million American soldiers to South Vietnam, a country of 17 million. In the early 1960s they went by the hundreds—helicopter units, Green Beret teams, counterinsurgency hotshots, ambitious young officers, and ordinary infantrymen—all of them labeled military advisers by the American command. They fought a distant, "rushfire war" on the edge of American consciousness. Beyond the secret inner circles of government, few predicted that hundreds of thousands would follow in a massive buildup that took the American presence in Vietnam from 15,000 troops in 1964 to 550,000 in 1968. In late 1969 the gradual withdrawal of ground forces began, inching its way to the final U.S. pullout in January 1973. The bell curve of escalation and withdrawal spread the commitment of men into a decade-long chain of one-year tours of duty.

In the years of escalation, as draft calls mounted to 30,000 and 40,000 a month, many young people believed the entire generation might be mobilized for war. There were, of course, many ways to avoid the draft, and millions of men did just that. Very few, however, felt completely confident that they would never be ordered to fight. Perhaps the war would escalate to such a degree or go on so long that all exemptions and deferments would be eliminated. No one could be sure what would happen. Only in retrospect is it clear that the odds of serving in Vietnam were, for many people, really quite small. The forces that fought in Vietnam were drawn from the largest generation of young people in the nation's history. During the years 1964 to 1973, from the Gulf of Tonkin Resolution to the final withdrawal of American troops from Vietnam, 27 million men came of draft age. The 2.5 million men of that generation who went to Vietnam represent less than 10 percent of America's male baby boomers.

The parents of the Vietnam generation had an utterly different experience of war. During World War II virtually all young, able-bodied men entered the service—some 12 million. Personal connections to the military permeated society regardless of class, race, or gender. Almost every family had a close relative overseas—a husband fighting in France, a son in the South Pacific, or at least an uncle with the Seabees, a niece in the WAVES, or a cousin in the Air Corps. These connections continued well into the 1950s. Throughout the Korean War years and for several years after, roughly 70 percent of the draft-age population of men served in the military; but from the 1950s to the 1960s, military service became less and less universal. During the Vietnam years, the portion had dropped to 40 percent: 10 percent were in Vietnam, and 30 percent served in Germany, South Korea, and the dozens of other duty stations in the United States and abroad. What had been, in the 1940s, an experience shared by the vast majority gradually became the experience of a distinct minority.

What kind of minority was it? In modern American culture, *minority* usually serves as a code word for nonwhite races, especially African Americans. To speak of American forces in Vietnam as a minority invites the assumption that blacks, Hispanics, Asian Americans, and Native

Americans fought and died in numbers grossly disproportionate to their percentage of the total U.S. population. It is a common assumption, but not one that has been sufficiently examined. For that matter, the whole experience of racial minorities in Vietnam has been woefully ignored by the media and academics. For Hispanics, Asian Americans, and Native Americans, even the most basic statistical information about their role in Vietnam remains either unknown or inadequately examined.

We know how many black soldiers served and died in Vietnam, but the more important task is to interpret those figures in historical context. Without that context, racial disproportions can be either exaggerated or denied. To simplify: At the beginning of the war blacks comprised more than 20 percent of American combat deaths, about twice their portion of the U.S. population. However, the portion of black casualties declined over time so that, for the war as a whole, black casualties were only slightly disproportionate (12.5 percent from a civilian population of 11 percent). The total percentage of blacks who served in Vietnam was roughly 10 percent throughout the war.

African Americans clearly faced more than their fair share of the risks in Vietnam from 1965 to 1967. That fact might well have failed to gain any public notice had the civil rights and antiwar movements not called attention to it. Martin Luther King was probably the most effective in generating concern about the number of black casualties in Vietnam. King had refrained from frequent public criticism of the war until 1967, persuaded by moderates that outspoken opposition to the war might divert energy from the cause of civil rights and alienate prowar politicians whose support the movement sought (President Johnson, for example). By early 1967, however, King believed the time had come to break his silence. As for diverting energy and resources from domestic social reform, King argued, the war itself had already done as much. More importantly, he could not in good conscience remain silent in the face of a war he believed unjust.

King's critique of the war was wide ranging, based on a historical understanding of the long struggle in Vietnam for national independence, on a commitment to nonviolence, and on outrage over the violence the United States was inflicting on the land and people of Indochina. Always central in King's criticism of the war, however, was its effect on America's poor, both black and white. "The promises of the Great Society," he said, "have been shot down on the battlefield of Vietnam." The expense of the war was taking money and support that could be spent to solve problems at home. The war on poverty was being supplanted by the war on Vietnam. Beyond that, King stressed, the poor themselves were doing much of the fighting overseas. As he put it in his famous speech at Riverside Church in New York City (April 1967), the war was not only "devastating the hopes of the poor at home," it was also "sending their sons and their brothers and their husbands to fight and to die in extraordinarily high proportions relative to the rest of the population."

While King focused attention on the economic condition of white and black soldiers, he emphasized the additional burden on blacks of fighting overseas in disproportionate numbers while being denied full citizenship at home: "We have been repeatedly faced with the cruel irony of watching Negro and white boys on TV screens as they kill and die together for a nation that has been unable to seat them together in the same schools. So we watch them in brutal solidarity burning the huts of a poor village, but we realize that they would never live on the same block in Detroit." In another speech he added, "We are willing to make the Negro 100 percent of a citizen in warfare, but reduce him to 50 percent of a citizen on American soil. Half of all Negroes live in substandard housing and he has half the income of white[s]. There is twice as much unemployment and infant mortality among Negroes. [Yet] at the beginning of 1967 twice as many died in action—20.6 percent—in proportion to their numbers in the population as a whole."

In his postwar apologia for U.S. intervention, *America in Vietnam*, Guenter Lewy accused King of heightening racial tension by making false allegations about black casualties in Vietnam. After all, Lewy argued, black casualties for the whole war were 12.5 percent, no higher than the portion of draft-age black males in the total U.S. population. Lewy's charge falls apart, however, as soon as one points out that black casualties did not drop to the overall figure of 12.5 until well after King was assassinated. During the period King and others were articulating their criticisms of the war, the disproportions were quite significant. To attack the antiwar movement for failing to use postwar statistics is not only unfair, it is ahistorical. Moreover, King was by no means the first prominent black to criticize the war or the disproportionate loss of black soldiers. Malcolm X, Muhammad Ali, Adam Clayton Powell, Dick Gregory, John Lewis, and Julian Bond were among those who spoke out repeatedly well before 1967. In fact, had the civil rights movement not brought attention to racial disproportions in Vietnam casualties, those disproportions almost certainly would have continued. According to Commander George L. Jackson, "In response to this criticism the Department of Defense took steps to readjust force levels in order to achieve an equitable proportion and employment of Negroes in Vietnam." A detailed analysis of exactly what steps were taken has yet to be written. It is clear, however, that by late 1967, black casualties had fallen to 13 percent and then to below 10 percent in 1970–72.

Blacks were by no means united in opposition to the war or the military. For generations blacks had been struggling for equal participation in all American institutions, the military included. In World War II the struggle had focused on integration and the "right to fight." Aside from some all-black combat units, most blacks were assigned to segregated, rear-area duty. The military was officially desegregated in 1948, and most blacks served in integrated units in the Korean War. It was the Vietnam War, though, that was hailed in the mass media as America's first truly integrated war. In 1967 and 1968 several magazines and newspapers ran major stories on "the Negro in Vietnam." While disproportionate casualties were mentioned, they were not the target of criticism. Instead, these articles—including a cover story in *Ebony* (August 1968)—emphasized the contributions of black soldiers, their courageous service, and the new opportunities ostensibly provided by wartime duty in an integrated army. The point was often made that blacks had more civil rights in the military than at home. In *Harper's* magazine (June 1967), Whitney Young of the Urban League wrote, "In this war there is a degree of integration among black and white Americans far exceeding that of any other war in our history as well as any other time or place in our domestic life." As Thomas Johnson put it in *Ebony* giving the point an ironic turn, "The Negro has found in his nation's most totalitarian society—the military—the greatest degree of functional democracy that this nation has granted to black people."

Whitney Young justified disproportionate black casualties as the result not of discrimination but of "the simple fact that a higher proportion of Negroes volunteer for hazardous duty." There was some truth to this. In airborne units—the training for which is voluntary—blacks were reported to comprise as much as 30 percent of the combat troops. Moreover, blacks had a reenlistment rate three times higher than whites. It fell dramatically as the war went on, but it was always much higher than that of white soldiers. These points surely suggest that many blacks were highly motivated, enthusiastic troops.

That enthusiasm itself does not prove that the military had equal opportunities for blacks or an absence of discrimination. After all, presumably the same blacks who volunteered for airborne (for which they received additional pay) might just as eagerly have volunteered for officer candidate school had they been offered the chance. Only 2 percent of the officers in Vietnam were black. Blacks might have taken advantage of opportunities to fill higher-paying noncombat positions, had they been offered. The military's response was that blacks were disproportionately enlisted combat soldiers because they were simply not qualified to fill other jobs. Of course, qualifications are determined by the crudest measurement—standardized tests—and black soldiers scored significantly lower than whites. In 1965, for example, 41 percent of black soldiers scored in the lowest levels of the Armed Forces Qualification Test (categories IV and V), compared to 10 percent of the white soldiers.

These scores account for much of the disproportion. To that extent they reflect the relationship of race and class in civilian society. Poor and working-class soldiers, whether black or white, were more likely to be trained for combat than were soldiers economically and educationally more advantaged. While enlisted men of both races were primarily from the bottom half of the social structure, blacks were considerably poorer. One study found that 90 percent of black soldiers in Vietnam were from working-class and poor backgrounds. This is a large part of the reason why more blacks reenlisted. Men who reenlisted were given bonuses of $900 to $1,400, equivalent to one-third of the median family income for black families in the mid-1960s. However, the military's assignment of blacks to low-ranking positions was not simply a reflection of the economic and racial inequalities of civilian society. The military contributed its own discrimination. In the first years of American escalation, even those blacks who scored in the highest test category were placed in combat units at a level 75 percent higher than that of whites in the same category.

Though racial discrimination and racist attitudes surely persisted in the military, class was far more important than race in determining the overall social composition of American forces. Precisely when the enlisted ranks were becoming increasingly integrated by race, they were becoming ever more segregated by class. The military may never have been truly representative of the general male population, but in the 1960s it was overwhelmingly the domain of the working class.

No thorough statistical study has yet been conducted on the class origins of the men who served in Vietnam. Though the military made endless, mind-numbing efforts to quantify virtually every aspect of its venture in Vietnam, it did not make (so far as anyone has discovered) a single study of the social backgrounds of its fighting men. Quantitative evidence must be gathered from a variety of disparate studies. Probably the most ambitious effort to gather statistical information about the backgrounds of Vietnam-era soldiers was conducted just prior to the large-scale American escalation. In 1964 the National Opinion Research Center (NORC) surveyed 5 percent of all active-duty enlisted men.

According to NORC's occupational survey (Table 1) roughly 20 percent of American enlisted men had fathers with white-collar jobs. Among the male population as a whole more than twice that portion, 44 percent, were white-collar workers. Of course, not all white-collar jobs are necessarily middle class in the income, power, and status they confer. Many low-paying clerical and sales jobs—typically listed as white collar—are more accurately understood as working-class occupations. While the white-collar label exaggerates the size of the middle class, it nonetheless encompasses almost all privileged Americans in the labor force. Thus, the fact that only 20 percent of U.S. soldiers came from white-collar families represents a striking class difference between the military and the general population.

The high portion of farmers in the sample is a further indication of the disproportionate number of soldiers from rural small towns. In the 1960s only about 5 percent of the American labor force was engaged in agriculture. In the NORC survey, more than twice as many, 12 percent, came from farm families. Though the survey does not reveal the economic standing of this group, we

Table 1 Occupations of Fathers of Enlisted Men, by Service, 1964 (Percent)

Father's Occupation	*Army*	*Navy*	*Air Force*	*Marines*
White-collar	17.0	19.8	20.9	20.4
Blue-collar	52.8	54.5	52.0	57.2
Farmer	14.8	10.7	13.3	9.11
Military	1.8	2.1	1.8	2.0
Father absent	13.6	12.9	12.0	11.3
(Approx. N)	(28,000)	(17,500)	28,000)	(5,000)

Source: 1964 NORC survey, in Moskos, *American Enlisted Man*, p. 195.

should avoid an American tendency to picture all farmers as independent proprietors. At the time of the survey about two-thirds of the workers engaged in agricultural labor were wage earners (farm laborers or migrant farmworkers) with family incomes less than $1,000 per year.

There is also a good reason to believe that most of the men with absent fathers grew up in hard-pressed circumstances. In 1965, almost two-thirds of the children in female-headed families lived below the census bureau's low-income level. All told, the NORC survey suggests that on the brink of the Vietnam escalation at least three-quarters of American enlisted men were working class or poor. . . .

The inclusion of officers would not dramatically raise the overall class backgrounds of the Vietnam military. Officers comprised 11 percent of the total number of men in Vietnam, so even if many of them were from privileged families, the statistical impact would be limited. Furthermore, though we need further studies of the social backgrounds of the Vietnam-era officer corps, it may well have been the least privileged officer corps of the twentieth century. For example, in his study of the West Point class of 1966, Rick Atkinson found a striking historical decline in the class backgrounds of cadets. "Before World War I, the academy had drawn nearly a third of the corps from the families of doctors, lawyers, and other professionals. But by the mid 1950s, sons of professionals made up only 10 percent of the cadets, and links to the upper class had been almost severed. West Point increasingly attracted military brats and sons of the working class." Also, as the war dragged on, the officer corps was depleted of service school and ROTC [Reserve Officers' Training Corps] graduates and had to rely increasingly on enlisted men who were given temporary field commissions or sent to officer candidate school. These officers, too, probably lowered the class background of the officer corps.

Class inequality is also strikingly revealed in the most important post-war statistical study of Vietnam veterans, *Legacies of Vietnam*. Commissioned by the Veterans Administration in 1978, about two-thirds of the *Legacies* sample of Vietnam veterans was working class or below. That figure is remarkable because the survey used sampling techniques designed to produce the widest possible class spectrum; that is, in choosing people for the study it sought a "maximum variation in socioeconomic context." Even so, the sample of Vietnam veterans was well below the general population in its class composition. When measured against backgrounds of nonveterans of the same generation, Vietnam veterans came out on the bottom in income, occupation, and education.

The key here is disproportion. The point is not that *all* working-class men went to Vietnam while everyone better off stayed home. Given the enormous size of the generation, millions of working-class men simply were not needed by the military. Many were exempted because they failed to meet the minimum physical or mental standards of the armed forces. However, the odds of working-class men going into the military and on to Vietnam were far higher than they were for the middle class and the privileged.

The *Legacies* study also suggests an important distinction between black and white soldiers. The black veterans, at least in this sample, were significantly more representative of the entire black population than white veterans were of the white population. This reflects the fact that whites and blacks have different class distributions, with blacks having a much larger portion of poor and working people and a much smaller middle class and elite. In the *Legacies* sample, 82 percent of black nonveterans were working class and below, compared with 47 percent of the white nonveterans. In other words, while black soldiers were still, as a group, poorer than white soldiers, in relationship to the class structure of their respective races, blacks were not as disproportionately poor and working class as whites. This is, I think, one reason why black veterans seem to have less class-based resentment than white veterans toward the men of their race who did not serve in Vietnam.

Education, along with occupation and income, is a key measure of class position. Eighty percent of the men who went to Vietnam had no more than a high school education (Table 2). This figure would compare well to statistics of some previous wars. After all, at the time of the Civil War and well into the twentieth century, only a small minority of Americans had high school educations. However, if considered in historical context, the low portion of college educated among American soldiers is yet another indication of the disproportionately working-class composition of the military. The 1960s was a boomtime for American education, a time when opportunities for higher education were more widespread than ever before. By 1965, 45 percent of Americans between eighteen and twenty-one had some college education. By 1970 that figure was more than 50 percent. Compared with national standards, American forces were well below average in formal education. Studies matching school enrollments to age and class show that the educational levels of American soldiers in Vietnam correspond roughly to those of draft-age, blue-collar males in the general population (Table 3). Of course, many veterans took college courses after their military service. However, the

Table 2 Educational Attainment of Vietnam Veterans at Time of Separation from the Armed Forces, 1966–1971 (Percent)

Fiscal year	*Less than 12 Years of School*	*12 Years of School*	*1 to 3 Years of College*	*4 or More Years of College*
1966	22.9	62.5	8.3	6.3
1967	23.6	61.8	90	5.6
1968	19.6	65.5	9.7	6.2
1969	18.3	60.0	15.9	5.8
1970	17.5	56.9	17.0	8.6
1971	14.7	55.4	19.4	10.5
Total, 1966–71	19.4	60.3	13.2	7.2

Source: Reports and Statistics Service, Office of Controller, Veterans' Administration, 11 April 1972, in Helmer, *Bringing the War Home*, p. 303.

Table 3 Percentage of Males Enrolled in School, 1965–1970

Age	*Blue-Collar*	*White-Collar*
16–17	80	92
18–19	49	73
20–24	20	43

Source: Levison, *Working-Class Majority*, p. 121.

Legacies study found that by 1981 only 22 percent of veterans had completed college compared with 46 percent of nonveterans.

The portion of soldiers with at least some college education increased significantly in the late 1960s as draft calls increased and most graduate school deferments ended. By 1970 roughly 25 percent of American forces in Vietnam had some college education. Impressive as this increase was, it still fell well below the 50 percent for the age group as a whole, and it came as American troop levels in Vietnam were beginning to drop. Moreover, college education per se was no longer so clear a mark of privilege as it had been prior to World War II. Higher education in the post-World War II era expanded enormously, especially among junior and state colleges, the kinds of schools that enrolled the greatest number of working-class students. Between 1962 and 1972, enrollments in two-year colleges tripled. College students who went to Vietnam were far more likely to come from these institutions than from elite, four-year, private colleges. A survey of Harvard's class of 1970, for example, found only two men who served in Vietnam. College students who did go to Vietnam usually secured noncombat assignments. Among soldiers in Vietnam, high school dropouts were three times more likely to experience heavy combat than were college graduates.

Young men have fought in all wars, but U.S. forces in Vietnam were probably, on average, the youngest in our history. In previous wars many men in their twenties were drafted for military service, and men of that age and older often volunteered. During the Vietnam War most of the volunteers and draftees were teenagers; the average age was nineteen. In World War II, by contrast, the average American soldier was twenty-six years old. At age eighteen young men could join or be drafted into the army. At seventeen, with the consent of a guardian, boys could enlist in the Marine Corps. Early in the war, hundreds of seventeen-year-old marines served in Vietnam. In November 1965 the Pentagon ordered that all American troops must be eighteen before being deployed in the war zone. Even so, the average age remained low. Twenty-two-year-old soldiers were often kidded about their advanced age ("hey, old man") by the younger men in their units. Most American troops were not even old enough to vote. The voting age did not drop from twenty-one to eighteen until 1971. Thus, most of the Americans who fought in Vietnam were powerless, working-class teenagers sent to fight an undeclared war by presidents for whom they were not even eligible to vote.

No statistical profile can do justice to the complexity of individual experience, but without these broad outlines our understanding would be hopelessly fragmented. A class breakdown of American forces cannot be absolutely precise, but I believe the following is a reasonable estimate: enlisted ranks in Vietnam were comprised of about 25 percent poor, 55 percent working class, and 20 percent middle class, with a statistically negligible number of wealthy. Most Americans in Vietnam were nineteen-year-old high school graduates. They grew up in the white, working-class enclaves of South Boston and Cleveland's West Side; in the black ghettos of Detroit and Birmingham; in the small rural towns of Oklahoma and Iowa; and in the housing developments of working-class suburbs. They came by the thousands from every state and every U.S. territory, but few were from places of wealth and privilege.

« 35 »

Seeds of a Movement

Tom Wells

IN LATE DECEMBER [1964] MEMBERS of the Young Socialist Alliance (YSA), youth group of the Socialist Workers Party, met in Chicago for their national convention. The YSA and SWP would come to play major roles in the anti-Vietnam War movement in the years ahead. At this time, however, the YSA "paid no special attention to Vietnam." It would continue to emphasize "general socialist education" focused on, as the YSA leader Lew Jones later remembered, "whatever issue we could get our hands on." Many of the conventioneers knew little about the war in any event. Some may not even have known where Vietnam was.

Simultaneously, the National Council (NC) of the Students for a Democratic Society, a politically diverse left-leaning organization, was gathered in the venerable meeting hall of the Cloakmakers' Union in New York. Before getting to the tasks at hand, the SDSers seized a large portrait of Lyndon Johnson gawking at them from a wall and turned it around. It was late afternoon by the time Todd Gitlin, SDS's co-point man on international issues with Paul Booth, proposed that the organization write and circulate a "We Won't Go" antidraft statement to protest the growing U.S. intervention in Vietnam. The war was not the main political issue on Gitlin's mind at this time (he was more concerned with U.S. funding of South African apartheid), but he felt *something* had to be done about it, and he and Booth had even invited the progressive journalist I. F. Stone to speak to the NC the evening before to rouse indignation over the issue.

Gitlin's proposal failed to take hold, as did another to send medical supplies to the National Liberation Front (NLF) in South Vietnam. They seemed a bit too radical to some, even procommunist. Jim Brook, a liberal SDSer, weighed in with a proposal to hold an April march against the war in Washington. The objections came fast and steady. Despite the fact that they were licking their wounds from a sobering summer in the ghettos, the many SDSers then bent on building "community unions" of the urban poor argued vehemently that antiwar protest was too centered on a single issue and not where the radical action was. Furthermore, it might alienate their constituents, more than a few of whom seemed hawkish on Vietnam. SDSers also opposed Brook's proposal on tactical grounds. Impressed by the grass-roots organizing in the South of the Student Nonviolent Coordinating Committee (SNCC), many felt large marches tended to stall local political motion, usurp inordinate amounts of time, energy, and resources, leave no lasting impact on their participants, and bring paltry political returns. "The past few years . . . have shown the government to be increasingly unresponsive to public mass protest," wrote two SDSers. "Even when concessions in legislation or public policy are granted, the concessions are generally sufficient to make the marcher, but not the grievances or problems, go away." The result, often enough, was "demoralization." SDSers also maintained that national marches tended to target specific government policies without challenging the "undemocratic" manner in which those policies were made. As Clark Kissinger, who was then SDS's national secretary, would recall, "There was a tendency to write national marches off on the basis of just the nature of the tactic alone without coming to grips with the political content of them and the role that they can play if they're done right." The 1963 March on Washington for Jobs and Freedom led by the Reverend Martin Luther King, Jr., was responsible for much of the antimarch sentiment inside SDS. It seemed to many activists to have been little more than an Establishment-led legislative exercise that had derailed local civil rights activity. "There was a real bad taste coming off the 1963 march," Kissinger said.

Come late evening, during a lull in the NC debate—and when a number of community organizers were out of the room—Brook's proposal squeaked by. The march's public appeal, the NC decided, would be gut-level: "SDS advocates that the U.S. get out of Vietnam for the following reasons: (a) the war hurts the Vietnamese people, (b) the war hurts the American people, (c) SDS is concerned about the Vietnamese and American people." SDS would be the event's sole organizational sponsor, but any group was welcome to participate. The first national action against the war was now in the works.

Carl Oglesby was a newcomer to SDS at the time of the group's meeting. When I met him years later, he was a freelance writer in Cambridge, Massachusetts. A slender, bespectacled man with gray-brown hair, a rough complexion, and a short beard, he looked younger than his fifty-one years. He spoke eloquently and effusively. In the fall of 1964, Oglesby was running the technical publications department of a major military contractor in Ann Arbor, Michigan. He commanded a sizable army of workers and was leading "a very high-powered bourgeois life-style." "I had a little red car, and my wife had a little blue car, and we jollied around town," Oglesby recalled. That November, an open letter he had written beseeching a newly elected local congressman to denounce the war was published in the University of Michigan's literary magazine. It quickly caught the alert eyes of local SDSers. Wondering why they had never heard of this guy Oglesby before, this articulate critic of the war living smack dab in their own backyard (surely they knew all the radicals around), they called him up. Two SDSers then "came out on a motorcycle in a couple of minutes and we wound up rapping the whole evening about SDS and change and politics and the country," Oglesby remembered. "I right away felt a real kinship with SDS people."

Oglesby was turned on by these "whippersnapper middle-class white kids" and decided to go to an SDS meeting. He was impressed by what he observed there:

> That was the best debate I ever heard. . . . That was an amazing meeting. I had never been around a bunch of people who were so smart and who were so sincere, in the sense that they listened to each other and they actually tried to meet one another's points. You could even see people have their minds changed because somebody showed them a reason or a fact that they hadn't known about. . . . And I was personally persuaded at that meeting, by that debate, that instead of coming into SDS as a director of research or some such thing, I should come into SDS as a community organizer and come with my wife and kids to live in Boston, in Roxbury, where we had a project.

Why community organizing? The "analysis," as Oglesby reconstructed it, was relatively simple. Since the path to change was through the Democratic Party, argued Tom Hayden and other SDSers, student activists had to build a base inside the party by organizing a new constituency. The urban poor were a logical target group for radicals inspired by SNCC's work among the downtrodden, particularly those convinced that economic trends would soon bloat the ranks of the poor. If impoverished whites and blacks could be mobilized together, the theory went, they would overcome the racial anxieties and hostilities then restraining the growth of a powerful "interracial movement of the poor." Many SDSers contended that such a movement was the only vehicle capable of wielding the political clout necessary to stop the war. SDS would halt "the seventh war from now," one offered.

Ghetto organizing also had romantic appeal. Many SDSers sentimentalized poverty. Whenever a community organizer would rise from his indigent element and drift into a meeting—soiled t-shirt, jeans, work boots, Marlboros, and all—"there would always be 'ooohhs' and 'aaahhs' and great deference, as though we were being visited by royalty," Oglesby recalled. " 'Hey, a real person is coming in.' . . . You could tell he was real, he pinched all the girls' asses, and the girls would put up with it from the working-class guy because they knew he didn't know any better, right, whereas from their true class brothers they would never tolerate this kind of behavior." SDS's "cult of the ghetto" was "slightly sick," one SDSer deduced.

According to the community organizers, then, SDS had to leave the campuses behind. Oglesby:

> The Tom Hayden program . . . meant students are not really that important. Students are debaters and debate is not important. Tom always is an anti-intellectual. He is now and he was then. He never had respect for the academic situation as such. To him it was in certain respects a necessary way station—you had to go there, you had to pass through it—but if you were going to grow as a person and mature as a political figure you had to put it behind you. You couldn't play around in the sandbox. . . . [Hayden] wanted to get students to drop out of school and go off to some ghetto in a big city far from home, live with cockroaches and racial torment and the agonies of poverty, and in that way try to blend into the community—in which they would, in fact, stand out like so many sore thumbs.

Although poised to mingle with cockroaches, Oglesby was a bit skeptical about the returns. The poor's "alienation" from the American political process struck him as more of an "obstacle" than a spur to political action. "They weren't people who tended to think of themselves as involved anyway," he said. "It wasn't their city, it wasn't their state, it wasn't their America—it was somebody else's." But middle-class people, Oglesby thought, "identified with the state or the government, they saw it as theirs, they felt like it should be responsive to them." Their expectations seemed to him "a powerful source of resistance to an administration that lied and deceived."

SDS's veteran community organizers were by then pessimistic themselves. During gloomy meetings in early January, they conceded that no interracial movement of the poor was going to arise soon. By late summer SDS's community organizing venture had proven "a failure."

Preparations for the spring peace march began immediately after the December NC meeting. Most SDSers were not expecting an earthshaking event. [Clark] Kissinger remembered that when he took the liberty of chartering a train to transport people to Washington "everybody else on the national committee almost had a fit, because they thought we'd be paying it off for the rest of our lives." Two to three thousand might show up if things went well. Todd Gitlin was feeling "doomed." Given the government's "enormous commitment to the war" and "so little opposition to it," he brooded, the fighting in Vietnam would probably drag on "for a very long time." "It felt to me simply a matter of existential ethics to do what you could [to stop the war], but without any great expectations," he recalled.

SDS sent out letters inviting all progressive political organizations to join the march. Most hedged. America's prominent peace groups—SANE [Committee for a Sane Nuclear Policy], Student Peace Union, Women's International League for Peace and Freedom, Turn Toward Peace, Committee for Nonviolent Action, War Resisters League, Fellowship of Reconciliation—simply ignored this bid to protest their government's violence in Vietnam. They were irritated that SDS had assumed sole sponsorship and failed to offer alternative U.S. policies in

Vietnam. Most disturbing, its nonexclusionary policy meant that communists would be on the scene (including the Communist Party's youth group, the Du Bois Clubs, whose name sounded so much like the Boys Club that the vigilant Richard Nixon called it "an almost classic example of communist deception and duplicity"); amid continuing Cold War fever at home, the antiwar groups perceived, cavorting with communists would be the peace movement's "kiss of death." The Du Bois Clubs and May 2nd Movement immediately expressed interest in the march, however. So did the Socialist Workers Party—in more ways than one.

Peter Camejo was then a major SWP leader. In 1986, when I met him, he was the president of Progressive Asset Management, a broker-dealership in Oakland, California, specializing in "socially responsible" investments. He had remained a radical and was still active in various political causes. Camejo left the SWP in 1981 after a nearly thirty-year association because of growing "sectarian" and "dogmatic" behavior by the organization. "I began to have doubts about our ability to work with anybody," he told me, likening his SWP days to living in a religious sect. "I *totally* believed that the SWP had all the answers to all questions. I was a *cultist* of the SWP." Camejo said SDS's call for the April peace march was the "decisive turning point" in the SWP's political trajectory during the war. The SWP promptly began flooding existing local antiwar committees and organizing new ones. "Our position was to go into the antiwar committees . . . and propose that they declare against both the Democrats and Republicans," Camejo remembered. "This was very sectarian, because that wasn't the issue—the issue was to unite people who opposed the war."

The SWP sensed that a national movement might take hold and wanted to build it not only for the purpose of stopping the war but also to radicalize the American people as a steppingstone on the path to socialist revolution, its ultimate goal. Since the Democratic and Republic parties were both "parties of the ruling class" that sold the capitalist system to the public according to the SWP, they had to be attacked. A national movement would also be fertile ground for recruiting new SWP members. "You know, we can build an organization of eight hundred to a thousand people off of this," Camejo told himself, gazing out a window in the SWP's national office in New York and licking his chops over the march's enlistment possibilities. ("That's how small we were thinking at the time," he would exclaim years later.) In Clark Kissinger's words, the SWP "perceived immediately when we said we were willing to do [the march] on a nonexclusionary basis that this was their big opportunity."

The SWPers' naked recruitment goals would soon anger large segments of the peace movement and fuel internal tensions. "They clearly put the recruiting of members above the issue of ending the war," the War Resister League Leader David McReynolds recalled.

Several months later, the SWP dropped its insistence that local antiwar committees denounce America's two bourgeois parties. Instead, they should simply demand "U.S. Out of Vietnam Now!" More significant, the SWP decided that by far the most effective antiwar activity was organizing large, legal demonstrations. Since most Americans were more likely to join a legal demonstration than more militant forms of protest, the SWP reasoned, that tactic would maximize the movement's size. "Our whole approach was focused on trying to find forms of activity that could be understood by the average working person and would seem possible for them to participate in when they reached the point of beginning to question the war," the later YSA leader Don Gurewitz remembered.

The SWP also believed that large demonstrations would be most likely to convince silent skeptics about the war that they were not alone; many would then voice their concerns. "Most people hear the media and think, 'I'm the only one who's doubting,' or, 'There's very few of us,'" Camejo explained. "And people in governmental power, from Johnson all the way to Nixon, continuously tried to emphasize that the opposition was a tiny minority. Our theory was that if a million people went into the streets that you would break that." The SWP also felt the government was more likely to respond to large protests than small ones. They demonstrated broader public opposition and threatened widespread upheaval. With small protests, officials "don't feel the pressure," Camejo said.

The SWP's robotlike promotion of mass demonstrations was to become its main badge of identity in the peace movement. Inside the SWP, the position assumed divine truth. Camejo remembered:

> It became like fundamental religious dogma that you were for single-issue, peaceful, legal demonstrations. And there were very few questioning it. We would pound away at this inside the SWP. Because, you see, it was the cutting edge. When new people came around to be in the Vietnam War movement in general, SWPers would explain why this is the key, and on that basis they would recruit. . . . So that was *a, b, c, d.* I mean, that was pounded away over and over and over again. . . . You wouldn't join the SWP unless you agreed with that. It was sort of like a definition of membership.

It was a definition other activists would come to know all too well. . . .

Three weeks before the Marines were turned loose [in March 1965 to engage in offensive operations rather than merely guard base areas], thirty faculty members at the University of Michigan gathered to plan an expression of opposition to the war. Present were many familiar faces, "veterans of a string of advertisements for the test ban, for a fair housing ordinance, for the election of Lyndon B. Johnson." They felt "betrayed." Their peace candidate, the man who had promised no wider war, had blood all over his hands. And they felt desperate. Despite preparing countless newspaper advertisements and letters to government officials protesting the bombings, the horror in Vietnam had only mounted. The State Department had had the gall to treat them like children: it answered their letters with pamphlets explaining the diabolical nature of communism illustrated by a leering [Nikita] Krushchev.

The sociology professor William Gamson rose to speak. The situation in Vietnam was too grave to continue treading the old tired ground, he said. Ads and letters just wouldn't do anymore. Gamson proposed that the group organize a one-day faculty moratorium on teaching-as-usual and transform the university into a massive classroom on the war. Nearly fifty faculty members signed a petition supporting the plan.

On March 16, a group of nervous signers met to reconsider. Michigan's faculty senate was discussing censure, deans were up in arms, the governor and legislators were hollering for disciplinary action. The anthropologist Marshall Sahlins suggested that, instead of holding a strike, teachers conduct their classes during the day and hold sessions on the war at night—all night. The Michigan organizers ultimately agreed on the all-night format, although some believed "that we were making a very bad mistake." The detractors felt that the time for polite academic give-and-take was gone; to them the move reeked of retreat. Worse, they thought few would show up for a nocturnal educational experience. "We thought, 'Sure, a few hundred, that would be good,'" Carl Oglesby recalled. With the switch to the evening design, however, university administrators, relieved that the brouhaha was over, virtually began promoting the event. "They fell all over themselves trying to cooperate with us," Oglesby remembered. Faculty and student interest skyrocketed.

On the evening of March 24, over three thousand people showed up on the Ann Arbor campus for the nation's first "teach-in" on the war. Lectures and debates ran until 8 A.M., despite a midnight bomb threat that temporarily forced people outside into 20°F weather (where they held a rally). Exchanges were both reasoned and passionate. "Facts were demanded and assumptions were exposed," one participant wrote. "On that night, people who really cared talked of things that really mattered." Hierarchical relations between faculty and students received a stiff jolt; students locked horns with professors whose classes they had hardly spoken in. Opponents of the war gained valuable social support, inciting many to plan future protests. Prowar participants were asked to explain their positions; some began questioning their allegiances. "It was such a powerful event," Oglesby fervently recalled. The campus was now alive with debate on Vietnam. It was impossible to avoid the controversy whether one wanted to or not.

During the rest of the spring, teach-ins spread like wildfire across America's campuses. Over a hundred took place. The "stroke of genius out there in Michigan . . . put the debate on the map for the whole academic community," Oglesby said. "And you could not be an intellectual after those teach-ins and not think a lot and express yourself and defend your ideas about Vietnam." With the surprising success of the Michigan teach-in, his own "faith in students and the academic situation and the importance of directly organizing on Vietnam was switched back, it came alive again, and from that time on there was never any real thought of my . . . coming to Boston to do community organizing."

The grandest of the teach-ins took place at the University of California in Berkeley. Two graduate students, Jerry Rubin and Barbara Gullahorn, had initially proposed the event to Stephen Smale, a mathematics professor and teachers' union activist. "The idea was to do something really big and exciting and very exceptional," Smale would recall. "To make it a very memorable kind of event." More than thirty thousand people participated in the 36-hour marathon, perhaps twelve thousand at one time. Some barely missed a beat. "I arrived there at the beginning and didn't leave until it was over," Marilyn Milligan recounted. "I was just totally taken by that teach-in, totally engaged. . . . I just didn't want to leave at all. We were there and that was it." Before wearily trudging home, Milligan signed up to work with the teach-in's sponsor, the Vietnam Day committee. She would shortly assume a leadership role in that organization.

The escalation of the war also fueled interest in the April SDS march. Besieged with requests for information on it, SDS organizers shifted into high gear. "We just rolled over the whole antiwar movement," Paul Booth said afterward—"they had never seen anything like this." Even activists with the old peace groups expressed interest. Estimates of attendance surged toward fifteen thousand.

The White House was less enthusiastic about the protest. Thousands of peaceniks parading around Washington would hardly keep the war out of the public spotlight, officials knew. The march might also give the North Vietnamese the wrong impression about the American public's enthusiasm for the war, thereby encouraging them. On April 14, McGeorge Bundy mentioned the upcoming "left-wing student protest" to Johnson and counseled, "A strong peaceloving statement tomorrow or Friday might help cool them off head of time." No statement was forthcoming.

April 17 was a gorgeous spring day. By early afternoon, twenty thousand people were gathered at the Washington Monument. Most were students. There were also many adults, including Communist Party members marching under their own banner for the first time since the birth of McCarthyism. The highlight of the afternoon was a moving closing speech by SDS's 25-year-old president, Paul Potter. The war, Potter declared, "has provided the razor, the terrifying sharp cutting edge that has finally severed the last vestige of illusion that morality and democracy are the guiding principles of American foreign policy." "What kind of system" allowed "good men" to work such evil? he asked. "We must name that system. We must name it, describe it, analyze it, understand it and change it." Despite pleas from the crowed to go ahead and name that system, Potter abstained. SDS's leaders feared that using the word *capitalism* would provoke more red-baiting and had earlier decided "to leave it as a mystery as to whether or not there was a capitalist system in the United States," Booth wryly recalled.

Not everyone in the crowd was enraptured by Potter's testimony. In fact, not everyone was there to protest the war. The sun was shining, the cherry trees were blossoming—love was in the air. Daniel Ellsberg, a Defense Department official, arrived on the scene with his attention focused on one Patricia Marx. Ellsberg had been admiring Marx for some time now and several days earlier had gathered the fortitude to call her up to ask for a date. He was thinking about Saturday, he had said, the first Saturday he would have off since staring work at the Pentagon the previous August. Unfortunately, Marx responded, she already had plans to go to the SDS demonstration, partly because she opposed the war, but also to conduct interviews for her public radio program in New York. She had plans to interview I. F. Stone, for instance. But she would be pleased if he would accompany her. Ellsberg suddenly felt a little dizzy. He *supported* America's "commitment" in Vietnam and had even helped produce the White Paper that Stone had so mercilessly demolished. "You *can't* ask me to take my first day off from the Pentagon to go to an antiwar rally!" he stammered, incredulous. Yes, she could. Ellsberg donned marching shoes. He even lugged Marx's bulky tape recorder around for the day. Ellsberg later made no bones that he "never would have gone" to the demonstration had it not been for the lure of romance. He married Marx in 1970.

Following Potter's speech, the crowd swept down the mall toward the Capitol. Youths wearing gas masks led the charge. Despite SDS's dislike of marches as a pressure tactic, the protesters planned to deliver to Congress a petition demanding an end to the war. Along the way, their exuberant mood began to hint of "something darker." Reaching a wall of police near the Capitol steps, a barrier through which only a few were ticketed to pass, a chorus of voices rang out, "Let's all go. LET'S ALL GO." According to one marcher, "it seemed that the great mass of people would simply flow on through and over the marble buildings, that our forward motion was irresistibly strong, and that even had some been shot or arrested, nothing could have stopped that crowd from taking possession of its government."

But it was not to be. No more than several hundred demonstrators proceeded up the Capitol steps. Many went home frustrated. The war makers would not heed legal demonstrations, they believed; militant civil disobedience was required to move murderers.

The feeling would grow.

Lyndon Johnson avoided the protest by spending the weekend at his ranch in Texas. In the face of a 400-strong picket led by SDSers at the front gate, he undoubtedly took solace from an earlier note from an aide, Marvin Watson, that twenty-two Secret Service agents would be on hand to protect him from the "so-called demonstrators."

The sudden outpouring of antiwar protest in the spring of 1965 struck a nerve in the American Establishment. James Reston, that titan of U.S. journalism, complained that many teach-ins had rejected "serious intellectual inquiry" for "propaganda of the most vicious nature. . . . This is no longer a casual form of campus spring fever." C. L. Sulzberger, a foreign affairs columnist for the *New York Times*, detected "a strange lemming instinct" among the protesters; they "refuse," he lamented, "to see the struggle in its true meaning as advertised quite openly by the Communists themselves: a showdown with global implications." In the early fall, Senator Thomas Dodd (D-Conn.) apprised the nation that the peace movement was under the control of "pseudo-Americans," soldiers in a "massive psychological warfare attack" on the war by the global "Communist apparatus." Dodd expressed the hope that his revelations would "assist loyal critics of Administration policy to purge their ranks of the Communists and crypto-Communists" so that debate on Vietnam could be restricted to "honest men."

Administration officials were the most agitated. On April 23, Dean Rusk abruptly departed from a prepared speech to take a shot at the war's opponents. "I continue to hear and see nonsense about the nature of the struggle" in Vietnam, commented the secretary of state. "I sometimes wonder at the gullibility of educated men and the stubborn disregard of plain facts by men who are supposed to be helping our young to learn." When a group of religious demonstrators publicly voiced their dissatisfaction with a meeting they'd held with Robert McNamara, Assistant Secretary Arthur Sylvester muttered angrily, "Only church people would do what you are doing." Johnson hit the roof when the poet Robert Lowell announced in early June that he was boycotting the White House Festival of the Arts to protest the war. "The roar in the Oval Office could be heard all the way into the East Wing," one White House staffer recorded. After other prominent American writers and artists declared their support for Lowell's stand, the president ranted about the "sonsofbitches" who had turned his perfectly decent cultural celebration into a goddamn platform on Vietnam. "None of us realized . . . the tawdry lengths that some people would go to in impoliteness and incivility," Jack Valenti, a White House aide, remarked later. Valenti exclaimed that he'd "never met a man with less civility, with less sense of good judgment about how you handle yourself when you're a guest in somebody's house" than the writer Dwight MacDonald, who circulated an antiwar petition at the festival. MacDonald, he gibed, "needed to gargle with Lavoris." Following the festival, Johnson determined that all future White House guests would have to receive FBI clearances. This type of thing led the presidential aides Richard Goodwin and Bill Moyers to conclude in alarm that Johnson was literally suffering from "paranoid disintegration." The war, public opposition to it and other developments seemingly out of Johnson's control were triggering frequent "irrational outbursts" and "unacceptable orders," Goodwin recalled. Listening to one bizarre tirade from the president, Moyers "felt weird, almost felt as if he wasn't really talking to a human being at all."

McGeorge Bundy, a former Harvard dean, exhibited an icy disdain for antiwar academics. "I cannot honestly tell you that I think your letter reflects great credit on its authors, either as a piece of propaganda or as a serious effort to engage in discussion," he told one correspondent from the teach-in movement. "If your letter came to me for grading as a professor of government, I would not be able to give it high marks." To a critic from the *Harvard Crimson*, Bundy acidly commented, "No useful purpose is served by assuming that Dr. Strangelove is in charge here."

Years later, Bundy was a professor of history at New York University, having received his professorship in 1979 over the objection of two dozen professors there that he had helped prosecute a war of "genocide" against the Vietnamese people. He subsequently said "I wish we had quit" the war before he left the government in 1966. A haughty man of privileged lineage, with a flint-sharp mind, caustic tongue, and little patience for lesser beings, Bundy could be particularly frosty on the subject of Vietnam, often refusing even to discuss the issue (although one journalist who interviewed him on the arms race, forewarned that he wouldn't touch Vietnam, got him talking about it after "a couple of tall Scotches"). When I interviewed him, Bundy was visibly defensive about the war, answering many queries with curt statements of little substantive content. He also exhibited remarkably persistent memory lapses. When asked about his expectations in early 1965 about future domestic opposition to the war, however, Bundy acted like a man eager to make an admission. He acknowledged that the spring upsurge in antiwar sentiment caught the administration off guard:

> I think that we were not paying a great deal of attention to what one thinks of now, looking back on it, as the "protest," or the people who were against the war from the beginning, largely out of their own perceptions of who were the good guys and who were the bad guys. And I think we underestimated the degree to which there had been a revival of what called itself the "New Left." So I think we weren't thinking very much about that. And I remember myself being somewhat surprised by the level of student and academic protest in the spring and summer of 1965. . . .
>
> My own encounter with direct opposition to the war came in [two teach-ins in June]. . . . It was all very sober and careful and well-behaved on both sides, but it did represent a kind of opposition that, even then was, I think, stronger than I would have predicted six months earlier. And in that sense . . . I think we were not fully alert to the way the country was going to see the matter.

William Bundy emphasized that administration officials were "very definitely . . . concerned about" the spring antiwar protests. Sitting in a barren room at the Council on Foreign Relations' New York office, the tall, drawn, proud Bundy recalled, "What the arguments of that period revealed—and we should have acted on it much sooner than we did—was how much of the past history was understood in . . . a misleading fashion." For example, teach-in speakers were claiming that the United States had reneged on the 1954 Geneva Peace Accords on the war by refusing to implement their provision for democratic elections in South Vietnam in 1956; Bundy and other officials knew the United States had only *pledged* to uphold the Accords, however, not actually signed them. The protesters were also arguing that the revolution in South Vietnam was home-grown, but Bundy and his colleagues were persuaded by intelligence reports that Hanoi was pulling the strings. And the protesters were alleging that Ngo Dinh Diem, the mystic whom the United States installed as president of South Vietnam in 1954 after it assumed France's colonial role in Vietnam and who died in a U.S.-backed coup in 1963, was "a terrible character," Bundy derisively recalled, who had tortured and killed his political opponents; yet officials had no doubt worse nastiness would be in store if the communists took over. "A great deal of arguments that we had long known existed and discarded and never thought needed to be reargued suddenly came to the surface," Bundy said. The White Paper and other administration propaganda just "hadn't made the case" for the war, he lamented. "We discovered tremendous weaknesses in the way the thing was understood. People really hadn't focused on it before we started the bombing. An awful lot of people hadn't been paying any attention and hadn't seen how critical the situation was becoming. This was true of somebody like Arthur Schlesinger, for example, who spent 1964 and 1965 writing his book on Kennedy and, as it were, came out of the cave and looked around and said, 'Gee whiz, look what happened'—and turned into an opponent of the war."

Feeble or not, however, realized officials, the protesters' arguments were influencing others. "Articulate critics" of the war from the universities and churches "have stimulated extensive worry and inquiry in the nation as a whole," McGeorge Bundy apprised Johnson in June. Dean Rusk was concerned the protests might be affecting Congress. Something had to be done to stem the onslaught. "We simply aren't doing our propaganda job right in this country," Jack Valenti told the president in April.

In early May, the government dispatched a four-person "truth team" to six midwestern universities to discuss "the facts of life in Vietnam" (as one official put it). The team included "young, articulate" representatives of the State Department, Agency for International Development, and U.S. Army, all "just back from Vietnam," Valenti informed Johnson. Although the officials evoked much sympathy from their audiences, they typically ended up on the defensive, with some forums turning into "hooting sessions" when students felt their intelligence had been insulted.

The University of Wisconsin in Madison was the scene of a particularly trying encounter for the administration's propagandists. Students laughed at the truth-team leader Thomas Conlon's assertion that the United States was fighting to defend South Vietnam's freedom. When he denied the United States "runs the show" there, shouts erupted from all over the room, "Aw, c'mon. Let's be honest." Conlon's angry directives to students to "Sit down!" and mail their questions to Washington did nothing to boost his popularity. As the official was leaving the wreckage, Arnold Lochlin, a biochemistry student, blocked his path. "Get this straight, sweetie," Lochlin taunted. "We're not going to fight your filthy fascist war. Go fight it yourself."

Other government spokesmen tried a different tack. Daniel Ellsberg was among the "bright young men" (as Valenti called them) that the administration sent out to campuses to explain the facts of life in Vietnam when requests for speakers came in. He used a "soft-sell" approach when talking to teach-in audiences:

> I conceded a great deal of the opponent's position. For instance, if they started telling me about Diem, I would say "I'm not here to talk about Diem. Diem is everything you say. Diem is dead. That was two years ago." And that was totally disarming, see, because they were all there prepared to talk about the GVN. . . . They were so amazed to hear a government official knock Diem that they didn't know what to say next. And my general case was not unlike that: "The GVN has its faults, but let's look at the VC. . . . Are we sure to win? No. But should we quit without trying?" . . . And I really talked about negotiations right then.

Ellsberg's teach-in career was not a long one, however. He was privy to the "inside story" of the U.S. invasion of the Dominican Republic in late April and wasn't eager to face opponents of the action in a public forum. "We were 100 percent lying about what we were doing in the Dominican Republic," he recalled. Although Johnson claimed the invasion was necessary to fend off another spate of communist aggression, Ellsberg knew the Dominican Republic was "one of the few communist-free environments in the whole world. And so the explanation of why you were sending twenty thousand Marines was a little difficult." Ellsberg called the government office responsible for scheduling officials' appearances on campuses and demanded, "Take me off the list *now*. I ain't going out there to face questions about the Dominican Republic. You can screw that."

As the government's truth teams were taking to the road, the Inter-University Committee for a Public Hearing on Vietnam (IUCPHV), a national antiwar body, was planning a national teach-in in Washington, D.C., on May 15–16. Many IUCPHV organizers lusted for a "confrontation" with a senior government official. They felt it would discredit the administration's justifications for the war in front of a wide audience. Other organizers argued that supporters of the war should not be part of the program; officials already had ready access to podiums for expressing their nonsense, they asserted, and the teach-ins' value lay in surfacing antiwar sentiment. The IUCPHV eventually decided on a confrontation. It solicited McGeorge Bundy's participation.

Bundy agreed to do battle—but only under certain conditions. He vetoed the IUCPHV's choice of Hans Morgenthau, a famous political scientist, as his main debating foe, citing "personal reasons." Bundy found Senator Wayne Morse unsuitable for that role as well. The national security adviser and his aides also required that the moderator of the teach-in establish a "high tone of discussion . . . ruling out of order any heckling, rudeness, or other unseemly conduct"; he would have to field questions alternately from pro- and antiwar audience members "to inhibit a stream of hostile questioning," and questioners could not make "speeches." In short, Bundy's presence required that the teach-in be conducted on a "non-emotional level." In addition, neither Bundy nor other officials would participate in a closing session on alternative policies in Vietnam. As the White House aide Chester Cooper warned Bundy, the IUCPHV organizers planned to issue "a climactic call for a Congressional investigation" of the war at the session, which might facilitate a "psychological victory" by the peace movement.

Bundy got his way on these points and signed on the dotted line. The administration's advance men then swung into action. State Department researchers prepared detailed analyses of the views the obviously feared Morgenthau (accepted as one of three antiwar panelists) had held on the war from 1962 on (he had been "essentially consistent," they reported), William Bundy and other officials briefed pro-administration participants in, according to Cooper, a "thorough and effective" manner. "There are excellent possibilities that our speakers, who have been doing their homework, will prevail in rational debate" with the "highly emotional" antiwar panelists, Cooper wrote Bundy. The White House snatched up a thousand tickets to the event (out of an audience capacity of five thousand) and made "a careful distribution" of them to ensure that "knowledgeable" questioners would be present. One hundred tickets were channeled to the Young Democrats, "who," Cooper knew, were "quite interested in supporting the President." The administration rented a nearby hotel room to house researchers in case the need for rapid-fire responses to troubling disclosures arose. Cooper advised Bundy that he had "underplayed the nature and extent of our advance preparations" in discussions with the media.

Based on his contacts with "alienated and semi-alienated" academics, James Thomson, a national Security Council staffer, counseled Bundy on appropriate behavior. The "growing and potentially dangerous chasm" between many ("often naïve") professors and government could "be bridged," analyzed Thomson, if Bundy demonstrated "reasonableness, good humor, patience, warmth," and "concern" for his critics at the teach-in. This would help "discredit" protesters' "caricature" of officials as "computerized, hard-nosed monsters," a chief reason for the chasm between them. Although "silliness and ignorance and fraud" should not "go unchallenged," Thomson recommended, "the education of our critics" was best considered "a secondary objective" at the event; it was a "less promising" one anyway. "In sum, if you do nothing more on Saturday than convey a clear image of the humaneness, reasonableness, and intelligence of top policymakers—whatever the provocation—you will do much to begin to bridge the chasm."

As curtain time approached, the government's star performer abruptly pulled out of the production. Tight-lipped officials initially refused to explain Bundy's absence. They later stated that Johnson had whisked him off to deal with the crisis in the Dominican Republic. Bundy subsequently explained that he "had a lot of differences with the president" over whether he should participate in the teach-in. "He felt I shouldn't go and there shouldn't be any such encounter between the administration and [its critics]. He may well have been right. But I had undertaken to have a debate—and then I got sent to the Dominican Republic." Johnson evidently threatened to fire him for "disloyalty." Bundy released a written apology to the teach-in that reflected his contempt for protesters. When it was read, many in the audience of several thousand groaned.

A speech by Arthur Schlesinger, Jr., whom Bundy had asked to serve as his replacement, also irked many at the teach-in. Schlesinger advocated sending more troops to Vietnam, cutting back on [Operation] Rolling Thunder, and negotiating. He also maintained that the United States was fighting partly to preserve Americans' right to free speech. When Schlesinger finished his remarks, audience members, "bursting with impatience," queued up to give him a piece of their minds. By the time he had stepped down from the stage, Schlesinger was badly shaken. "What kind of audience is this?" he murmured. Two decades later, Schlesinger called his recommendation of additional troops "a mistake I regret" and said that he was "quite rightly" attacked at the teach-in.

As a holding action, Walt Rostow wrote Dean Rusk afterward, the administration's participation in the event was "a good idea. . . . On a one-shot basis it defused quite a lot of tension on our flank." Rostow opined that "the only truly objectionable feature of the occasion was the sanctimonious assumption of higher virtue among the critics"—a curious statement coming from a man known among his colleagues for an unhealthy attachment to his own ideas. Rostow was not eager to set up additional encounters with the IUCPHV, though. "We should not encourage a regular relation between this group and the U.S. government," he advised.

Nagged by his hasty trip to the Dominican Republic, however, Bundy arranged to participate in two public "debates" on the war in June. He and his staff again secured favorable formats. With CBS, they planned a televised "dialogue" on June 21 moderated by their "preferred choice," Eric Sevareid. Believing the "rigid procedures of a debate . . . in which participants are primarily interested in attacking, defending, or scoring debaters' points" a "poor" arrangement for gaining "acceptance and support of present policies," Bundy and his aides insisted the event have an "informal" and "reasoning together" tone. Sevareid should concentrate on "keeping the discussion moving and pertinent" rather than mediating between sides. The administration knew the IUCPHV would be "less than pleased" with this format; "as a sop," it agreed to accept Morgenthau as Bundy's opponent.

During the CBS dialogue, Sevareid posed four questions central to the government's case on Vietnam. The questions allowed a scholarly looking Bundy, dipping heavily into classified material, to lay out the administration's arguments with studied precision (nonetheless, many viewers found his performance arrogant and shallow). Morgenthau weakly advocated peace "with honor." When Bundy attacked Morgenthau's "pessimism" on the war by noting mistaken political forecasts he had made in the past, the political scientist responded. "I admire the efficiency of Mr. Bundy's office." "I do my own [research]," Bundy lied. For teach-in activists, it was an agonizingly placid affair.

Over that spring and summer, the Johnson administration took other measures to counteract the growing peace movement. Following a talk with the president, who had "no doubt" that communists were behind the dissent, J. Edgar Hoover directed the FBI to prepare a memorandum linking SDS with communism. FBI agents infiltrated SDS chapters. Administration officials drafted speeches with the protesters' criticisms "in mind" and provided propaganda "kits" to friendly nongovernmental speakers. They recruited supportive students to tour the country and flew thirty such students to Vietnam to advance their expertise on the war. The administration suggested prowar youth come to Washington ("at their own expense") to meet officials, thereby receiving a few stimulative strokes ("it wouldn't take too much massaging to do the trick," predicted Cooper in advocating the visits). Compliant South Vietnamese intellectuals were flown to the United States to further educate Americans. The administration moved to get the Young Democrats "into the picture" too. And it shot a film entitled *Why Vietnam?* That was later distributed to the Army. Vietnam veteran David Cortright recalled that the film began with a southern Army officer wailing. "Whhhyy Veeetnam?" followed by "five minutes of bullshit," followed by another "Whhhyyy Veeetnam?" then five more minutes of bullshit, and so on. "This was at basic training, and people were hooting and hollering," Cortright amusedly recounted. The film evoked "mixed feelings" inside the administration.

« 36 »

Women at the Barricades, Then and Now

Myra MacPherson

WOMEN IN THE ANTIWAR MOVEMENT became media stars—from singer Joan Baez and actress Jane Fonda to extreme radicals and anarchists who advocated violent revolution, like Weathermen Bernardine Dohrn and Kathy Boudin. Others, less visible among the bomb throwers, like Jane Alpert, blew up their buildings, then became wanted fugitives who traveled underground and surfaced in the eighties to write about their experiences. Yet all along there were other women—nameless and faceless to the press—who threw themselves into the antiwar movement with dedicated passion. They were the reasonable, the caring, who did not make headlines. Like many veterans, some feel they were war casualties who lost time. They got off the track, but the train kept going. Curiously, while veterans feel they were discriminated against for having gone to war, many of these women feel they were also discriminated against because of their far-left credentials—especially as the country moved more to the right.

For most involved in antiwar work, writing a résumé in the mid-seventies became a game of artful dodging. "Only the top leaders landed jobs with the Carter administration. On the West Coast, the welcome mat was not out," recalls a former activist who wants to remain anonymous. "Frankly, I'm not at all anxious to portray myself as the agitator I was." She is in her late thirties and has been "trying to get legitimate for three years." Friends told her to rewrite her résumé when she came to Washington. She played up her skills—she was a superb editor of a sizable magazine—but deemphasized that they were acquired on a left-wing publication. She told her prospective bosses, "You might not agree with the content, but you have to admit I have the skills and experience." She attended both Harvard and Berkeley graduate schools but never acquired a master's, dropping out for antiwar work. She is now overqualified for her current researcher's job. "I'm doing the kind of work I used to *assign*," she says ruefully.

In many ways, she epitomizes the best of the women of her generation. Intelligent, gentle, thoughtful, she pursued antiwar activism with passionate and sincere intensity. She uses the constant phrase of many who sided with the NLF: "We were naïve. We idealized the 'noble Vietnamese.'" She sighs. "'If America was wrong, then they *must* be right.' There was no in-between. There was a real lack of ambiguity. Still, even if we had known it would turn out *exactly* as it did, our job was to get the U.S. *out*."

Some of her friends still work with causes. One female friend slogged through years of postwar schooling to catch up and become a doctor. Others, like herself, had not reckoned with either the shifting tides of conservatism or the heavy psychological toll of being an outsider all those years. "A lot have never left. The more their vision of the world isn't validated, the more they are convinced they are right. Getting an establishment job is still viewed as anathema to them."

During the war there had been a wrenching separation from parents and a brother in the Army. If her brother went to Vietnam and she continued to march in the streets, her mother warned she would not be welcome at home. She told her daughter, "I will never speak to you again." There was intense conflict; *she* could not understand how her mother could let a son go to Vietnam. Her brother did not go, but it took years to reunite the family.

For her, a demonstration was no Saturday-night revelry. "I took it terribly seriously." There is a touch of envy for those younger, less committed, who went on with their lives. "Even now, in their early thirties, they are young enough to start careers and families." She is approaching forty and knows that she will never have children. A marriage she has had, though not a documented one. She lived for a decade with an antiwar activist. When they parted it was, for her, like a divorce.

For women like her, Vietnam put her personal life on hold. "It didn't just interrupt your career, it could screw it up." During the early part of the seventies, she continued to speak out against the war—for a leftist radio network, newsletters, magazines—and became a foreign-policy analyst. By the late seventies, leftist views were out of fashion; few places would give her the benefit of believing she could separate her expertise from her beliefs. "Dropping out and spending ten years of your life very *actively* against the war doesn't seem the best resume for a job."

She lacks both a strident self-promotion and the arrogance of some in her age group. "You talk about people who thought we acted superior. I'm sure we *acted* that way—but I felt I was the 'enemy.'"

They were the outsiders—the hunted, the chased, the beaten. The women would dress for demonstrations; would wear heavy work boots and jackets to catch the blows, wetted handkerchiefs to cover the face and eyes when the tear gas came. It was an experience women in the generation before and those in college now, with their designer labels and sorority pins, could never know.

Polls consistently show that demonstrators had little backing in the country. Middle America eventually tired of the war, but they disliked student demonstrators even more. Those who viewed them as troublemakers seldom saw the confrontation through the eyes of students. Some drove police to a frenzy, true, but many of the dedicated rank and file were victims of nonprovoked attacks—chased into corners of alleys or buildings and then beaten. Many still recall the terror of being trapped by police swinging wildly with their clubs.

"I remember a demonstration when Dean Rusk was speaking at the Mark Hopkins [Hotel, in San Francisco]. It was the first time the police used *attack* techniques to stop us. They just started chasing us. *Anyone caught was beaten*." The concept of free speech and assembly was gone. "They chased us into a little chapel. I knew they could get in and beat the crap out of us, and we couldn't get out. A priest came out and talked to the police, and they let us out. They shot a demonstrator in People's Park. At Berkeley, they had to rotate the National Guard constantly. They were our age, and they didn't want them fraternizing with us." The police on attack were fearsome to this woman, barely 5'2". "They wore masks, helmets, and came down fiercely."

Mollie Ivins recalls the same reaction, the unleashed rage. "I had great admiration for good cops and great loathing for bad cops. There was that whole class thing, that generational hostility. Older cops would eye these long-haired kids, certain they were 'getting a lot of pussy.' I saw some ugly stuff—cops deliberately going after women. It happened to me in a couple of demonstrations."

Being an "enemy" of the establishment provoked a sense of lawlessness in the California activist who was clubbed and chased into the chapel. "Why was I bothering to stop at a red light? Why do I obey the law when they would beat the crap out of me if they could? We were outlaws in America. We assumed our phones were tapped, assumed half our friends were agents. It affected me for a long, long time."

Reentry into the establishment world was frightening. A wariness remains. It is vastly ironic that veterans and some women who fought so hard against the war would turn up in the eighties as survivors. They lived through a searing period as unwanted outsiders.

"I'm not saying it is anything as bad as veterans who can't find jobs, but believe me it has been hard. For a lot of people, taking up your life again was not easy. *Almost no one talks about it!* Imagine what we believed! For a long time we thought and were told, 'You're all privileged. You can do this and pop back in, whenever you want.' It just wasn't true. You had to be almost irresponsible—turn away from your personal goals."

After the war, she staked everything on a nonestablishment magazine that might have remained rewarding if it had ever become solvent.

She realizes now that she "never thought through what I was going to do with the rest of my life. The movement was an all-absorbing thing. I didn't stop to think ever what plans I should have. *Thinking personally wasn't highly regarded.* Living in a commune, working on the war. . . . There wasn't much time for yourself." Her voice gets a bit firmer. "I feel I gave a whole bunch of the best years of my life to that. Now I do not think of myself as an activist or an organizer. Now I have to put my own life together."

Jane Fonda remains the point-woman for the wrath of many veterans. The right, incorrectly, blame the whole antiwar movement for her actions. In any gathering of veterans there will always be an expletive for her. Even some who turned antiwar cannot forgive her for embracing Hanoi, for posing on one of their tanks. Dean Phillips, a much-decorated antiwar veteran, explodes, "Fonda did irreparable damage to the antiwar movement. She pissed off 80 percent of Americans not on the fringes. People needed to hear it from the guy who fought it—not those assholes at Yale whose biggest decision was getting Daddy's Mercedes and Fonda, who was not in danger of starving to death. There she was criticizing the capitalistic system—which is the hallmark of hypocrisy."

In the late seventies, Fonda further created discord by refusing to join Joan Baez and other antiwar activists in lending her name to an ad decrying the fate of Vietnam's boat people and those oppressed in Vietnam.

Today Fonda has moved on to making more millions as she deflabs the overweight women of America with her "Work-Out" books, records, and video cassettes. Most of the women who went through her regimen in 1982 have no idea that they were in fact subsidizing the political career of former SDS leader Tom Hayden. Fonda contributed handsomely to her husband's 1982 million-dollar-plus campaign for an insignificant state assemblyman seat.

When Hayden was deriving fame and power through antiwar leadership, women were discovering a cruel truth. Lip service to equality did not mean they joined the council of decision makers. Often excluded from meaningful roles at the top, many turned to the feminist movement. The civil rights and antiwar movements emphasized a heightened sense of injustice and—at least in rhetoric—created a more receptive climate for the women's movement. The rebirth of feminism was a welcome niche for those who had been burned by chauvinism in male antiwar ranks.

Margery Tabankin was a University of Wisconsin activist from 1965 to 1969 and later visited Hanoi. The first woman president of the National Student Association since 1947, she was elected on an antiwar platform. She recalls that "Hayden was my hero. We revered these guys. It was like 'what could we do for them?' When Hayden got off the plane to make a speech in Wisconsin, the first thing he handed me was his dirty laundry and asked if I would do it for him. I said, 'I'll have it for you by tonight.' "

Tabankin became one of the few women organizers, joined SDS, and helped coordinate the 1969 Moratorium. "Part of being a woman was this psychology of proving I was such a good radical, 'better than the men.' We felt we were motivated by something higher because we didn't have to go to war ourselves. Most guys didn't take women seriously, however. They were things to fuck. We once did a questionnaire to check reasons why students were drawn to antiwar rallies and demonstrations. One reason frequently checked was 'to make social contacts.' You went through this intense experience, and you went back and had sex." People forget that the women's movement was fledgling at the time. "It [sex] was much more on men's terms."

Despite such aspects of second-class citizenship, the antiwar movement gave Tabankin a sense of heightened consciousness: "You had the right to have opinions about anything—including your government.

"I got beaten up badly covering one of my first civil disobedience rallies for the University of Wisconsin paper. Seventy people were hospitalized," says Tabankin. "We were protesting Dow Chemical on campus. Kids were sitting in a building, refusing to move, and the cops walked in and shouted, 'Everybody out—we'll give you three seconds.'

"They started busting heads, and everyone just totally freaked out, running to get out, clustering in panic at two doors. I got hit in the stomach with a club. Because I was injured, I was the only reporter to get into the emergency room. I ended up being the person the *New York Times* was calling in the hospital to tell them what was going on, how many were injured." Her eyes still shine, recalling the moment. "I was, like, ecstatic—but on the other hand, my friends were hurt." The experience radicalized her. "I remember saying, 'I've had it with writing about things. I'm going to do it.'"

Tabankin abandoned everything for antiwar work. There are great gaps in her education. "For two semesters I literally never went to classes. Borrowed notes and took the tests. We were really self-righteous. We knew a better world, and we were going to make it. That wasn't even negotiable. Our demands were to stop the war, to guarantee the poor an annual income and racial equality. We really created in our minds what the world should be like. It was my *whole* reason to live. I found a passion in my life I never knew was there. Realistically, there were about 100 major activists out of 40,000 on campus. The rest were like soldiers who marched."

Like some other women who threw themselves totally into the movement, she is somewhat envious of those who did not. "They had a much more integrated life. They still came to the demonstrations, but they were graduating and going on. The guy I was in love with—I really think one reason he would not marry me was because of my Vietnam politics—went on to law school and is with a very establishment firm. He really changed."

Tabankin recognized the less committed for what they were. "People get emotional when self-interest is at stake. Young people didn't care enough when their lives weren't on the line. I'd say 5 percent felt intensely passionate about the issue."

She recognizes the deep schisms between some antiwar leaders and the radical left. She agrees with those who view Sam Brown and Tom Hayden as pragmatic manipulators thrust into prominence by the movement. "Some were only for stopping the war, but one faction of SDS got so caught up in being against the system and for economic and racial change. They saw this as totally interrelated. Then you had crazies splitting off, anarchists, and terrorists. I was between the SDS and the student government type. Although a little more to the left of student government, I wasn't totally an SDS person. Many in the Mobe viewed Sam Brown and Al Lowenstein as sell-out pigs. We just didn't see it, the polarization, then. We were so caught up, we didn't see how destructive it was."

Tabankin was arrested seven times and finally became a burned-out casualty. She dropped out of activism and went home. "The greatest luxury was having my mother's housekeeper do my laundry." She became a community organizer for youth projects, raised money for foundations, worked on two union-reform efforts for miners, and became head of VISTA when Sam Brown became Carter's director of the Action agency. She defends the activists of the sixties and sees ongoing commitment. "The same 5 percent *then* are the same 5 percent of our generation still working for causes—toxic waste, nuclear freeze, trying to get progressives elected. Much of it is grassroots."

The attempt of some in the media to lump "the generation" as idealistic causists was a mistake. "There never was a 'generation' that really meant it. Many didn't give a shit, then and now. Most got caught up in the time period—but it wasn't based on ideology, it was based on events. They weren't socialized then and they aren't now."

Today Tabankin, in her mid-thirties, is herself opting for profits while working for causes on the side. In 1981 Tabankin and Bill Danoff, author of the song "Country Roads," formed Danoff Music Company. They represent twenty-four Washington-area songwriters, plugging them to Los Angeles and Nashville producers and singers. They also manage a few bands. Tabankin's biggest coup was selling a song by Jon Carroll, Washington rock musician and songwriter, to Linda Ronstadt. Carroll's "Get Closer" became the title track of an album that went gold in 1982. The single made the Top Twenty. Tabankin tries to make a vague connection between yesteryear's activism and today's entrepreneurship. You need "commonsense networking skills" in both fields, she says—whom to contact and how, what will be effective. One difference, however, is the "profit motive."

Tabankin feels she acquired strength and self-confidence during the sixties and has been able to transfer organizing skills into business. The negatives? "It became my whole life, and I lost out on normal, lasting personal relationships."

The negatives for the generation? "People want to make it more than it was. Civil rights didn't change the fact that blacks still have problems, the women's movement doesn't mean women have equal rights, the antiwar movement doesn't mean our foreign policy isn't going to go totally crazy in the near future."

As women activists recall that era, it is striking how negatively they regarded American soldiers. "As we turned against the government, we turned against them as symbols," said Tabankin. "That was our biggest mistake. That was stupid tactically. The compassion wasn't there; the expressed view was that 'I don't want to get killed, and I don't think *they* should go do that.' Instead of the government, we blamed the foot soldier. If I have any regret, it's the way we treated them." At the time, reviling soldiers was part of the tactic—such as war-crime tribunals—to heighten the perception that the war had to be stopped. "You had to be for the North if you wanted the people to win."

Tabankin looks back with some chagrin at her naïveté. In 1972, as part of a delegation to Hanoi, she was imbued with the concept that the war was nationalistic in origin and had remained so. "I was witnessing destruction of civilian life. I saw their hospital forty-five minutes after it had been totally demolished. The ambulance was taking out the dead and living. That was in May 1972—the scariest time of my life. There were bombing attacks at all times of day and night. We brought the first footage out of North Vietnam and sold it to '60 Minutes.'"

"The North Vietnamese didn't want us to meet with POWs. We pushed and pushed and made ourselves obnoxious, and we saw ten of them," recalls Tabankin. "They looked pale but healthy. One black had heard that [George] Wallace had been shot and was interested in that. Another asked me to go back and tell his wife he was all right."

The prisoners said little about their treatment; it did not even occur to Tabankin at the time that they would have major difficulty expressing themselves with North Vietnamese officials in the room. The accounts of torture that emerged after POWs' return demolished reports of those who had seen them under such carefully controlled conditions. We talked of Susan

Sontag's ecstatic descriptions of the "gentle captors" of the North. Tabankin winces slightly, then reiterates, "It was so easy to be naïve."

The range of opinions among those twenty-seven million women who came of age during the Vietnam Generation was clearly vast.

Some dropped the sixties with a vengeance, like those who populate Jerry Rubin's Manhattan mix-and-mingle salons. Rubin, yesteryear's Yippie trying to make it in the eighties as an example of the "Me" Decade Meets Wall Street phenomenon, is a "networking" party giver. He talks about money, power, and "leveraged" women. "Leverage in financial terms is when a small amount of money controls a larger amount of money. Leverage is therefore power. I'm into leverage. Now Barbara Walters is leveraged. She speaks, you know, and people listen. Right? Huh? You get it? The leveraged woman."

Those serious in the movement always viewed Rubin as a member of the comic fringe, much overplayed by the media. They are not surprised that he shed his antiwar activism like an old worn overcoat and speaks without a scintilla of idealism about past motivation. "I get very nervous talking about the sixties. Who wants to live in the past?" More than anyone from the sixties antiwar, antiauthoritarian movement, Rubin epitomizes the view of one cynical observer: "Money is the long hair of the eighties." One evening incipient leveraged men and women—eager imitations of high-fashion gloss—moved around at one of his "networking" salons, handing out business cards as they used to pass around joints. Pat FYazer, who said she is a "commercial actress," spoke in a super-modulated voice and seemed to epitomize the women present. What was she doing? "Anything I can."

In the sixties, "Jerry was my ideal. At college I was involved. Now I'm involved in the eighties. You're on your own—and all of a sudden it's 'getting for yourself.' I'm interested in taxes." She had no quarrel with cutting social programs for the poor and disadvantaged. "That's okay. My priorities are now in defense and space." And in the sixties? "Then I was anti-American." Because it was chic? "Partly."

Of course there are other sixties women who wouldn't spend a minute at Rubin's mixers or embrace his values. They may be involved in careers or motherhood rather than issues—but they do not negate their past. Others remain active in causes. For some, a need for personal peace followed radical commitment. In 1983 a bright college graduate in Washington summed up the feeling of many taking time off to be a full-time mother. "I gave my *all* to the movement, but now it is time for myself. . . ."

The class division of the war created friction between some in the emerging women's movement and resuming veterans. Leaders in the women's movement had little or no firsthand experience with anyone who went to Vietnam. For them it was simple to cavalierly dismiss veterans' preference in civil service as discriminatory. In the early seventies, when returning veterans needed all the help they could get, various women's groups, particularly NOW [National Organization for Women], opposed laws which gave extra points to wartime veterans applying for civil service jobs. For example, the Federal Women's Program Committee of the Denver Federal Executive Board questioned whether the law was consistent with equal-employment rulings—acknowledging that those who were drafted "may have suffered disruptions in their normal lifestyles." That understatement enraged combat veterans since draftees comprised 60 percent of U.S. Army dead from 1967 through 1970.

Dean Phillips, special assistant to the VA director (1977–81), said, "Women were not beating down doors to demand entrance into the armed services during Vietnam." Phillips noted that women who served did not make up the 2 percent quota then established for females. They too would have been entitled to veterans' preference if they had entered the service. "Treatises on sex discrimination often ignore perhaps the most blatantly sexist policy in our country's history," said Phillips, "the limitation of the drafting of those who will die and be crippled in combat exclusively to the male sex. At no time during the war did any women's organization file any lawsuit claiming that restrictive draft or enlistment laws injured female employment opportunities by making it more difficult for women to serve in the armed forces. After virtually ignoring the issue of the male-only draft during the veterans' preference debate in the late seventies, NOW president Ellie Smeal made a fool out of herself in 1981 by claiming that past exclusion from the draft had discriminated *against* women. Feminists, who *avoided* service during Vietnam, were now saying that their younger sisters are discriminated against by not being included in draft registration—something *they* wanted no part of during Korea or Vietnam."

Phillips, an ex-paratrooper who went on long-range patrols in enemy-controlled areas with the 101st Airbome Division in 1967–78, won numerous decorations, including the Silver Star, Purple Heart, and two Bronze Stars. During law school in Denver in the early seventies, he had a compatible relationship with NOW. He even received letters of appreciation from them for his active support of the ERA [Equal Rights Amendment]. That union was shattered when NOW refused to alter its 1971 position of opposing *any* and *all* government laws or programs giving special preference to veterans, even those badly maimed in combat. Phillips points to a letter from NOW's national headquarters confirming in 1979 that the 1971 resolution—with no modifications—was still their official position. Phillips assisted in the defense of the constitutionality of veterans' preference, which was ultimately upheld by the Supreme Court in June of 1979.

Phillips contends that NOW's opposition to all forms of veterans' preference was a tactical error that helped defeat the ERA in several crucial states. "The two-million-member VFW [Veterans of Foreign Wars] passed a resolution opposing the ERA in *direct* response to the NOW resolution opposing all forms of veterans' preference. Then VFW people worked effectively against the ERA through their contacts with state legislators. Sure, they would not have been *for* the ERA in any case—but they wouldn't have even gotten involved to oppose it if it hadn't been for NOW's position."

Other veterans, less active than Phillips, also felt that the women's movement should have left veterans' preference alone. "In one way I felt the government was back to pitting all of us minorities against one another in a fight for jobs," said one combat veteran, "but we felt the women didn't understand what we had been through."

Today, in urban centers like Boston, New York, and Washington, there are curious permutations of friendships from the Vietnam Generation. Ann Zill, who helps spend millions in liberal causes for Stewart Mott, had a brother who was injured in Vietnam. One of her closet friends is a Marine combat veteran who argues vehemently that the United States should have been in Vietnam and could have won. Zill herself was an antiwar activist.

Ann Broderick Zill, the oldest of four children, grew up in a small town in Maine. Her father was a "corporate mogul" who worked for Chevrolet. At Barnard College in New York, she was among the early war protesters. Zill had violent arguments with her brother, Peter Broderick, five and a half years younger, about the war, and was devastated when he joined the Army in 1968 and became an officer. Two months into Vietnam, he was "literally blown up" and spent nearly fifteen months recuperating. "He lost a whole lot of his intestines and had a colostomy for a while and has 60 percent permanent disability, and he basically does nothing with his life," Zill said in 1981. "He's a town janitor and plays a lot of tennis." For a man loaded still with shrapnel, she says, "He's in very good shape."

The wounded brother and the "knee-jerk peacenik" sister were forced to confront each other's views. There was a night in 1981 when their mother died. The Irish Catholic family had always been able to drink and fight and laugh together. The drinks came heavily that night. "Peter was sobbing and reliving the Vietnam War, and this is 1981." Did he come to a political point of view? "He views it through a very small slit of consciousness. He does not deal with the larger moral questions. Yet I suspect that if pressed to the wall now he would be able to say some things were fundamentally wrong with the war—but he's never been able to in the past. He's scarred by the war.

"We don't fight now, but we used to back then. He was a young kid, and I could not believe that he believed in this war. I argued that it was stupid and wrong for us to be involved."

All the time her brother was in Vietnam, all the time he lay in the hospital, Zill marched and worked for peace. "I felt very conflicted. I watched this man of six feet two, who now weighs 190, go to something just over 100 pounds. Skin and bones and could barely walk. He kept getting pneumonia." His agony reinforced her feeling that the war was wrong. "But I couldn't talk about that with Peter. He didn't want to hear that. He liked to tell war stories and make us laugh, and I had to laugh at the damn fucking war stories whether I wanted to or not. I will *always* believe that war was senseless."

Her brother tells a story of a marine whose injuries were so overwhelming that he was encased in a plaster cast. For nights he kept begging for a knife. Broderick was convinced the man wanted to commit suicide. Then one night the marine, whose face was bandaged except for his [nose] and mouth, yelled, "I can't see, I'm caught in a net and can't get out." Broderick felt "deep elation. He *didn't* want to kill himself." He was trying to see. "I sensed a great pride in that marine; he hadn't given up. He didn't let my faith down. He was a fighter . . . never quitting the struggle or relenting an inch. . . . I never saw him again, although he remains with me forever."

It is this emphasis on personal bravery and courage that fills the memory of many veterans, not the ideological rights and wrongs of the war. Ann Zill, unlike many women in the movement, was able to broaden her perspective through her brother, to understand the motivation of some who went. "He was a very good antidote for my overall sense that if you were for the war, you were crazy. He forced me to realize that a lot of perfectly reasonable people had been trained to believe it was your patriotic duty to defend your country—and that they believed this war was about protecting Vietnam from the Communists."

Zill is now divorced from the husband who "used to joke that he made love, not war, because that's how he got out. By having babies." As a father he was deferred. In 1981 she was dating a Mexican American who was too young for Vietnam and now organizes against the draft, arguing that blue-collar and lower-class youths would still be the ones to go. "The inequities would still be there."

Zill loved growing up in the sixties. "The spirit of liberation and of questioning authority. Vietnam shaped my life. One of my closet friend's lifework grew out of war protest. She now does analytical think-pieces about Indochina and Southeast Asia. And I haven't changed my basic view—although I like to think I'm more effective now. I work for a man who gives away about a million a year, and his first interest is to prevent nuclear annihilation. Trying to prevent another going-to-war exercise is a very sobering, humbling exercise. The peace movement today is *meshuggina.* It's a terrible failure, completely inadequate. The selling of the Pentagon was brilliant. They played to the psychological needs of this country to be strong and protected after Vietnam—even as life is crumbling all around." Zill was talking in 1981, before public sentiment had shifted to some degree against the government's excessive defense budget.

She is asked to assess the sixties movement.

"I'm somewhat critical by nature. There were a lot of arrogant kids. Sam Brown so fumed me off that I have never been able to like him to this day, and I used to run into him at the same parties when he ran Action." Like many dedicated antiwar activists, she tried to overlook personalities. "My allegiance remained with the people who were trying to stop the war. And my efforts in that regard got more sensible as time went on. It never occurred to me to side with the North, but I can't blame those who did. Still, that is part of my brother's story. He was really rejected when he showed up on campus in his Army outfit one day because he had to wear it to get some discount on the cost of something—I've forgotten what. But how vilified he was!" She points up an important psychological reaction of many veterans in similar situations. "That made him cling to the *need* to defend that war longer, I think, than he would otherwise have done. And so that's an example of one of those great ironies about how much campus condemnation exacerbated and helped polarize an already tough situation. Yet I understand those people who did it."

Zill is not too optimistic about generational reconciliation. "You need to bring the extremes together, and I'm not sure that can happen. I doubt that I would ever to able to say that my sympathies are with my brother, who believed in it as he did. On the other hand, I will defend to the death his right to think that way. Maybe if more people can understand someone like I can my brother, there *will* be a coming together."

One of the problems of the Vietnam Generation was a tendency to stereotype, to divide into monolithic clumps of "them" and "us." Vestiges of that thinking remain. One female antiwar activist enjoys a close friendship with a veteran—but irreconcilable differences cloud it.

"We all viewed each other back then as some faceless mass. To the veterans, we were a faceless mass who treated them like shit. Just as I criticize people for not seeing us as individuals, we didn't see *soldiers* as people. We just wanted to stop the war. We felt so defensive, a minority of college kids clustered together. I remember being angry at the soldiers. It was good to say, 'Fuck you,' to let them know people didn't like it—that there were people who passionately *did not want this war*. We had a real macro view—do anything to stop it. We were more oblivious than arrogant about the crassness."

She pauses to reflect. "We were lucky to live in a time when there was a social movement. As a generation it set us apart in an irreconcilable way—even as it caused huge divisions within the generation. Maybe as time goes by, and people don't know where Vietnam is once again, maybe it will bring us together. The fact that we lived through it, on one hand, is all of our touchstone with reality. For us it will always be—and for the veterans it will always be. And yet on another level, we are on opposite sides."

She sighs. "I'm still emotional about it, and so are they. One friend thinks he's better because he faced death and we haven't. I think there is something more important to life than being on a battlefield—I don't see it as the highest value of life, and yet I appreciate his feeling.

"People who fought and people who fought against the war were at loggerheads—but it changed our lives forever." She sighs. "Still, there is no settling of accounts.

"No one can lay it to rest."

Chapter 11

The Legacy of War

THIS CHAPTER OFFERS A NECESSARILY BROAD overview of a huge subject: the impact of the Vietnam War on Vietnam and the United States. It begins with the Communist conquest of Saigon and the departure of the last Americans (and a few of their Vietnamese allies) in late April 1975. The author of this piece, Duong Van Mai Elliott, came from a large Vietnamese family that was split apart by war. She chronicles here the melancholy fate of several family members as the victors consolidated their control over the south. (Mai Elliott herself, who worked for the RAND Corporation in Saigon during the war, moved to the United States with her American husband.)

In the United States, the war was for many years considered an embarrassment, and thus little discussed or psychologically processed. U.S. veterans of the war, women and men, were generally ignored or reviled, as Arnold Isaacs's account here reveals. For most, social permission to talk about the experience of war came only well after it had ended. In the third excerpt, Thomas Bass reports on a group that still has not been fully acknowledged by governments or people on any side of the war: the children of American soldiers or officials and Vietnamese women. Bass finds a group of Amerasians in chilly Utica, New York, struggling to get their balance in limbo between two cultures. Their story is a sad but fitting coda to the war's narrative.

« 37 »

Saigon: The End and the Beginning

Duong Van Mai Elliott

After waiting in vain for the helicopters to return, Nam [the author's nephew] gave up and left to find his family. But most of those on the rooftop doggedly kept vigil, searching the sky for the dark speck and straining to hear the sound of rotor blades signaling that deliverance was on the way. Nam had never set foot in an American building before, let alone one occupied by the CIA whose hand Vietnamese thought they saw everywhere, pulling strings from behind the scenes to manipulate the generals and politicians. Curious about how they had lived, Nam wandered through the floors on his way out to take a look. The amenities astounded him. Every apartment was well appointed with fine furniture, fancy lights, a refrigerator, and air conditioning—average American creature comforts but unaffordable luxuries for most of the locals. Even while panic-stricken people on the roof were battling each other to get on the helicopters, poor families living nearby had pushed their way in and occupied the apartments. Through open doorways, Nam saw them relaxing in the air-conditioned living rooms, drinking beer and eating ham, chocolate, and other goodies they had found in the refrigerators. Men in undershirts and shorts that had turned dingy with wear wandered among the apartments, every one of which had been occupied.

Then the horde of looters arrived. They stormed into the building, overwhelming the squatters, and stripped the rooms of everything they could carry off, such as furniture, light fixtures, pictures, and fans. Some tried to haul away a couple of refrigerators, but—discovering that they were too heavy and too big for the narrow flights of stairs—pushed them to the window and heaved them into the street. Others tossed foam mattresses into the courtyard. It took them only a few minutes to turn the building into a shambles. Those that were mechanically adept dismantled air conditioners and carried them off. Outside the building, others gutted the cars that had belonged to the CIA, removing the tires, spare parts, and the seats, which they took back to their houses to use as furniture. Nam saw a family of seven straining to push an enormous Ford automobile home. They did not have the key to it, but could not pass up such a find. On the sidewalk, people were scurrying away from the building with their arms full of booty. He stayed and watched, riveted. He knew that this was a part of history that he would never witness again in his lifetime, and he did not want to miss anything.

Later that night, Nam returned to the building and climbed to the rooftop, now deserted. He looked out toward the outskirts of town. Fires were burning eerily miles away where some units of Saigon's army were battling in vain to stop the advancing communist columns, and he could hear the sound of gunfire and the echoes of helicopter gunships attacking Viet Cong positions. At intervals, American helicopters broke the silence over the city, making their last flights to the embassy. The death throes of Saigon and of South Vietnam, Nam thought. Feeling sad but also resigned to the inevitable communist victory and his being stuck in Saigon, he made his way down the stairs. Walking past the apartments taken over by squatter families, he could hear now and then the hum of an air conditioner. Several apartments had been stripped of their doors. In some of these, the occupants had pushed refrigerators into the doorway to block intruders.

At eleven o'clock that night, communist shelling began. Nam's house was located near the airport and the paratrooper barracks, the main targets of attack. The shells landed and burst with a terrifying din—a noise familiar to peasants, but jarring to Nam and most people in Saigon. The war that had been fought mostly in the countryside had arrived virtually at his doorstep. The shelling lasted for about half an hour, halted, and then resumed. Nam's family huddled in the lower floor of their house. Devout Catholic refugees from North Vietnam, they began to mumble prayers. Their lives had never seemed so precarious. In the morning, during a lull in the shelling, they decided to move in with a friend in the neighborhood. This house had four stories and was sturdy enough to protect them against artillery shells and rockets. Nam made several trips, taking his family members over one by one on the back seat of his motorcycle. As he was getting ready to make one last trip with his mother, they heard small arms fire and loud explosions. She said, "Let's not go right now. Let's wait for a while." After about fifteen minutes, the firing stopped, and they rushed out. A short distance away, they saw corpses lying in the street. Most of the victims were soldiers, but there was also one civilian whose head had been cleanly sliced off by a piece of shrapnel. Nam shuddered at the sight. If he and his mother had left earlier, they would have been caught in the same carnage.

That same morning, in downtown Saigon, my sister Yen was returning home when an airplane started to strafe near the dock area. People scurried for cover. Yen broke out in a run, thinking, "The attack's begun, and my four children are at home by themselves." People were shouting at her, 'Are you crazy? Do you want to get killed? Take shelter!" But she kept running. She did not feel afraid. The one thought on her mind was to get home to protect her children. When she arrived, she rushed up three flights of stairs and shouted out their names. She found the apartment empty. Wild with worry, she ran downstairs, and found them huddled for cover under the staircase with her husband and some neighbors. She squeezed in. From their shelter, they could hear thunderous explosions. As they waited for the artillery shells and rockets that would soon be raining destruction and death on Saigon, they told each other that they and the city were doomed. So when they heard that General Duong Van Minh had surrendered at 10:20 that morning, they were limp with relief. They felt like they had been taken from the guillotine just as the blade was about to come down.

By capitulating and averting a fiery attack, General Minh earned the gratitude of many people in Saigon. Many of Yen's neighbors said that he had saved their lives. Others, however, felt bitter. To them, the general had presented Saigon on a platter to the communists. Some believed that Minh, whose brother was a Viet Cong general, had conspired with Hanoi. In the house of their acquaintance, Nam and his family also caught Minh's speech on the radio. As the general ordered the Saigon army to lay down its arms and to give up without a fight, they listened in shock. With that, the guns fell silent. So Nam's family took their leave and started for home. Suddenly, down the street, there was a big commotion: "The Viet Cong are coming!" From the direction of the barracks, they saw soldiers running pell-mell. The paratroopers stopped only long enough to throw down their weapons and take off their uniforms, stripping down to their underwear. In front of Nam's house, the ground was strewn with discarded uniforms, boots, grenades, and firearms. The scene that Nam witnessed in his neighborhood was also unfolding all over town. At the order to surrender, panic had struck the entire army, which simply disintegrated. Discarded weapons littered the streets, yet no one bothered to pick them up.

As if by magic, many of Nam's neighbors produced Viet Cong flags and hung them from their houses to welcome the victors. He realized they must have made these flags in secret, to be ready for this eventuality. Some rushed into the street to sing and dance with joy. Most of the residents, however, hid inside their houses, feeling apprehensive and uncertain. Those who had worked for the Saigon regime in important positions set about feverishly to erase the traces of their pasts. Nam's father pulled out documents, medals, uniforms, and other incriminating items and burned them in a bonfire in the backyard. He took out his pistol, removed the firing pin, and gave the gun to Nam, telling him to throw it away. Then, for good measure, he grabbed Nam, pinned him to the floor, and cut off the long hair that his son had grown to copy the American rock stars whose songs he adored. Nam cried, not so much over the loss of his hair, but over what he believed was the end of a freedom he cherished. He knew that the austere communists would not allow him to listen to what they considered decadent music or to follow a way of life that they thought was dissolute.

At this point, Nam could not sort out his emotions. On the one hand, he feared and disliked communism and mourned the passing of a society and a system that he knew and found tolerable—and in many ways even pleasant—although at times terribly corrupt. On the other hand, he also admired the victors out of nationalistic pride. These were Vietnamese, like him, who had managed to defeat the most powerful nation on earth. He took personal satisfaction in their victory. It was as if, by winning, they had washed away his own hurt. He remembered the blue eyes of the American staring at him through the door of the helicopter; he had made no effort to pull him onboard and save him. Maybe the American was paralyzed by the horrifying sight, or perhaps he was afraid that he would be pulled to his own death. But Nam believed that the American was simply indifferent to his plight. He felt betrayed. The United States had let down not only South Vietnam but also him personally. He was bitter, angry, and resentful. Through the communist victory, he felt that he had somehow exacted a measure of revenge.

In the grip of these conflicting emotions, Nam went out to watch the arrival of troops from North Vietnam. They looked like they were in their mid-teens, with the sallow complexion of people who had spent months in the jungle. They did not storm in like belligerent conquerors, but marched like they were in a military parade. Perhaps the communist leaders had ordered this disciplined entry to reassure the population of their peaceful intentions. Still, the takeover was not entirely smooth. In some neighborhoods, remnants of the Saigon army had fired on the soldiers. There had been scattered casualties. Perhaps that was why Nam thought he saw fear in the eyes of the young troops: They may have been wondering whether they would become meaningless casualties in the first hours of peace. Looking at this long column of children, Nam's neighbors could not believe their eyes. Some said, "They're so young, and yet they've managed to defeat the South." Nam, too, stared in disbelief. The sight of armed children marching as victors into Saigon would remain stamped in his memory.

At the news of the surrender, people in the North and those in the South that had fought and supported the revolution exploded in celebration, overjoyed that the peace for which they had yearned and the victory for which they had fought had finally arrived. To my sister Thang and her family in Hanoi, the capitulation marked a happy beginning. But to middle-class Saigon residents, it was a calamity. From the balcony of her apartment, Yen could see some of her neighbors rushing around, trying to escape the communists. A man she knew raced by on his scooter with his wife and children. One of her neighbors came up and whispered, "Do you want to leave? It's still possible. All you have to do is go to the dock and get on a barge." Yen thought of the refugees who had fallen off these barges and drowned during the evacuation in Danang, and said, "No, that's too risky. Besides, I've decided to stay with my husband." In the first weeks after the communists' arrival, many people were still attempting to leave the country. Subordinates of Nam's father, confused and frightened, came to his house to discuss escape plans. They told him, "The Viet Cong haven't taken complete control of the Mekong Delta. Let's go there. We can find a boat and sail to the American Seventh Fleet." However, by this time Nam's father had lost heart and could not even contemplate such a dangerous move. My brother Giu also toyed with the idea of going to the delta to find a way out, but dropped it in the end, afraid of the anarchy that he might encounter along the way and of the possibility of getting captured by communist guerrillas. Others took the chance and managed to flee before communist control tightened.

On the morning of April 30, the North Vietnamese columns entered Saigon as if sauntering into an empty house. The victors' arrival was spearheaded by three tanks that raced toward the presidential palace to take it over. The crews, newly arrived from the North, did not know their way around town. With only a map to guide them, they got lost and had to ask for directions from two startled South Vietnamese. After a few false turns, they managed to get to the palace. They found it undefended, its grounds deserted, and its wrought-iron gate closed. The first tank knocked down the gate, and the other two followed close behind. The leader of the first tank leapt out and rushed inside with the Viet Cong flag. He saw General Minh, his aides, and members of his cabinet waiting for the arrival of the "other side" to hand over the reins of government. The officer asked how he could get to the roof, and one of the aides showed him the way. Reaching the top of the building, he ran to the flagpoles and hoisted the banner from the highest one to proclaim victory. The time was fifteen minutes past noon. Then more camouflaged tanks and trucks full of soldiers began pouring in, accompanied by youths on motorcycles who showed them the way, cheering and shouting, "Liberation, liberation!"

With the old police and army falling apart, social order started to break down. To control the city, all the communists had were their advance columns. Profiting from this power vacuum, prisoners broke out of jail. Armed soldiers robbed people at gunpoint. Looters ransacked businesses, empty homes, and American buildings. Yen saw a soldier hold up a man riding a motorcycle at gunpoint, stripping him of his money and other valuables. Afterward, she lived in fear that rogue soldiers would rob her family. From her balcony, she had a front row view of the looting that went on downtown. In the morning, she saw crowds converge on the Brinks building that had housed apartments for American officers. It took them until late afternoon to empty it of every item it had. The pillage was good-natured, like a street festival. Even ordinarily law-abiding people joined the action. Somehow, the usual stigma of taking other people's possessions did not seem to apply to things that no longer belonged to anyone. The teenager living next door to Yen hauled back a swivel chair and an armload of canned food. Neighbors were urging one another to go and take part in the fun. One woman told Yen, "Come on, what are you waiting for? Go and get things before they're all gone." Another called up to her, saying that crowds had broken into the Khanh Hoi warehouse to loot, and urged her to get her share. Yen just laughed at these cheerful invitations. To her stealing was wrong, no matter what the circumstances were.

For a while, to safeguard my parents' modest house in the alley off Cong Ly Street, Yen would go back every day to check on things. The first time she returned, the deserted house looked desolate and depressing. She went through the drawers and found family photos that my parents had left behind in their haste to flee. Looking at faces she thought she would never see again, she felt very alone. She bundled up the pictures to take back to her apartment as souvenirs. My parents had told her to let cousin Bieu and his family move in if they needed to, and to stay there as long as they could, so she did not remove anything else.

Amid chaotic scenes of looting, prison breakouts, and frightened residents rushing around looking for a way to flee, more and more communist troops rolled in. At first, people felt apprehensive. But then crowds started to converge toward the boulevard in front of the old presidential palace to welcome the victors, mingle with them, or just to take a look, out of curiosity, at the troops that had vanquished a regime backed by American power. In a wild swing of emotion, many people, elated over the peaceful takeover, now hailed the newcomers as saviors coming in to usher in a new era, washing away the garbage of the past. The middle-class people were not as rhapsodic. Most were simply relieved that a final bloody assault had not occurred and that at least the war was over. Those living in working-class neighborhoods, their hopes and expectations raised, were the most excited. At last, they thought, their lot would improve. The new regime, the champion of the poor and downtrodden, would see to that. They hung the new flag from their houses and poured into the street to sing and dance. But the rejoicing was marred by ugly incidents. In practically every quarter of town, tough characters rushed into the homes of people against whom they harbored grudges and abused them. Others tried to bully their neighbors by masquerading as Viet Cong cadres, firing their weapons in the air. Still others acted as "hunting dogs," denouncing their friends, acquaintances, and colleagues to the new government to curry favor. Saigon residents would refer to all those who took advantage of the confusion as the "April 30 gang" or simply as "the opportunists," and would come to despise, loathe, and fear them with a passion.

The Viet Cong soldiers, meanwhile, became the toast of the town. People had expected the worst from them, but instead of the brutal troops painted by Saigon's propaganda, residents found them disciplined and polite. In their relief, many people felt buoyed by hope and filled with affection, and would stop the soldiers in the street to talk to them, curious and anxious to get to know them better. Many, like Nam, felt a nationalistic pride in their victory. Looking at the troops' spartan lifestyle and naive honesty, they also came to view the soldiers as selfless revolutionaries with unquestionable integrity. Right after they took over the city, soldiers fanned out in groups of two or three to visit families and earn the goodwill of the population. The residents received them warmly. Many invited them to stay and share meals. Once again, residents of working-class neighborhoods were the most hospitable, and went to great lengths to show their appreciation, killing chickens and ducks to regale their liberators.

The students at the Buddhist university in particular—many of whom had been jailed by President Thieu for their opposition to the war and to him personally—felt energized by the arrival of peace and eager to help usher in a new and better order. Nevertheless, for the middle class, the appearance of victorious peasants was a bitter pill to swallow. As if to rub salt into a raw wound, their foes turned out to be not a sophisticated army, all spit and polish, but a force of undernourished peasant youths wearing ill-fitting uniforms, pith helmets, and rubber sandals, goggling at Saigon's tall buildings, large villas, and wide boulevards. In other words, country bumpkins with little education. For their part, the soldiers could not believe that their enemy had given up the fight so easily. Whenever people came up to them to talk, the soldiers would ask with wonder in their voices, "You've got so much here, such marvelous things, such riches. Why didn't you fight harder to keep all this?"

Of the two groups, the soldiers handled the culture clash with a lot more ease than their middle-class opponents. They were unselfconscious about their lack of sophistication, and carried on as if they were still living in their jungle bivouacs or in their villages in the Red River Delta. When they first got to the old presidential palace, the soldiers quartered there immediately removed their sandals and waded into the fountain to wash the dust off their faces, hands, and feet. They did not know that the fountain was for decoration only; to them, it was just a good source of fresh water. Instead of using the toilets, they dug latrines in the garden. They built fires in the yard to cook their meals, and they hung their wash on the wrought-iron fence to dry. Others billeted in American buildings took down windows and chopped them up into firewood. In the following months, middle-class Saigonese would regale one another with outrageous tales about the country ways of the troops from the North, like the story of the soldier who put a fishing line down a toilet because he thought that it was a small pond, or the one who got scared and ran away when the door to an elevator suddenly opened. Although the Saigon middle class made fun of their conquerors, deep down they felt ashamed that they had been defeated by such yokels. They could not understand that, in the end, commitment to a cause and willingness to accept sacrifices in order to achieve victory meant more than all the sophistication of Saigon's army and its American weaponry.

With the victory, the small number of cadres and guerrillas that had operated underground appeared to take over government offices and city quarters. When they emerged, they turned out to be the people one least suspected of working for the communists. The woman who ran one of the shops on Yen's street was a secret agent, married to a high-ranking Viet Cong cadre operating in War Zone D near Saigon. Later, this woman would become one of the leaders in the neighborhood. She told Yen about her husband, and how she used to make repeated trips into the war zone to bring supplies and information. Getting to know people like this underground cadre opened Yen's eyes. For the first time, those she used to call Viet Cong (but now had to refer to as revolutionaries or liberators) ceased to be caricatures in Saigon government propaganda and appeared in flesh and blood. They turned out to be normal human beings, with strengths and foibles like everyone else. The cadres rarely boasted about their pasts; they were simply too preoccupied with the present to think about what they had done. But once in a while, they would reminisce about the war. Two of the women cadres in Yen's Workers' Union had been guerrillas operating near Saigon, planting mines and booby traps of grenades. Many times, they were attacked by American helicopter gunships. "There was nothing I hated worse than the helicopters," one of them said to Yen. "They'd circle around and around right over my head, and then they'd point their guns down and keep firing and firing at me."

With the end of the war, the tangled web of relationships between the communist and noncommunist sides was revealed to its full complexity. People found out that practically everyone in their circle of acquaintances had relatives in the communist ranks. My family was not the only one with siblings, uncles, aunts, cousins, nieces, and nephews on the opposite side of the fence. Our situation was the rule, rather than an exception. Even generals in the former Saigon regime had communist relatives, including Prime Minister Tran Thien Khiem and General Duong Van Minh. My brother Giu found out that two of his wife's aunts with mysterious whereabouts were married to important Viet Cong cadres. But the relatives who arrived with the communists paid little attention to family ties: None of my relatives on the winning side did anything to help those on the losing side who now came under scrutiny. There was nothing they could have done to change the situation anyway. Trying to help would only have exposed them and their own families needlessly to suspicion and perhaps even punishment. Besides, at the beginning at least, they themselves believed that a short stint at *hoc tap*—indoctrination—would not only be harmless but allow their southern relatives, who had been so steeped in the Saigon regime's political culture, to rectify their thinking and become better citizens. After all, they themselves had regularly gone through many *hoc tap* sessions to learn about this and that policy, and had not found them oppressive. So, despite their connection to influential cadres, most of my family members who had worked for the Saigon regime could not escape from being sent away for indoctrination.

With the country at peace and no longer divided into two enemy states, travel to the north and south became possible for the first time in decades. This free flow had a tremendous psychological impact. For people who during French colonial days had to have a passport to go from one region to another, and who were kept apart by the demilitarized zone during the Vietnam War, it was exhilarating to be able to circulate freely from one end of the country to another. Reunification made the population feel as one again. Families could be reunited, and ties that had been severed were re-established. With roads safe from war, each year, relatives from Ha Tinh, the province from which my ancestors fled over a century ago, now travel to Van Dinh, my family's native village, to worship at an ancestral temple built for all five branches of my clan. They are joined by other relatives who come in from Hanoi. When I go back to Vietnam now, I can visit relatives stretching from near the Chinese border to Hanoi, Ha Tinh, and Saigon.

The communists, focusing on their drive to victory, had not worked out a blueprint on what to do once they won, but they moved quickly to cement their control. The first leaders to arrive in Saigon to install a temporary government were men who had directed the final campaign. One of them was Le Duc Tho, the negotiator at the Paris peace talks who had shared the Nobel peace prize with Henry Kissinger and a member of the Politburo. On May 1, they set up a military committee to govern Saigon until complete security could be restored. To Saigon residents, the first signs were encouraging. The new leaders proclaimed a policy of reconciliation with former foes. No retaliation took place, even against the former Saigon army. The widely predicted bloodbath failed to materialize. The only crackdown was against criminals. Those caught in the act were swiftly brought to public trial, condemned to death, and executed on the spot. In my parents' old neighborhood, my nephew Minh witnessed the trial and execution of two criminals. After the cadre read out the sentence, he asked whether anyone in the audience had any objection. No one breathed a word, and the culprits were shot right then and there. This draconian justice worked, and crime immediately dropped. The tough approach, combined with the initial goodwill of Saigon residents, allowed the government to restore order quickly. Also, people were tired of the turmoil and wanted nothing more than to see life return to normal. In this atmosphere, no one tried to challenge the new authority. Everyone did as they were told.

But normalcy was not what it used to be. Things had begun to change right after liberation. First, Saigon got a new name: Ho Chi Minh City, which even the most sympathetic residents hated. New flags flew over the buildings. New plaques appeared on government ministries and offices. Newspapers, movies, and music all changed as the government stepped up its efforts to destroy the old culture and impose a new one—the same purposeful, but restricted and politicized culture that had stifled creativity in the North. New ways of organizing and controlling the population took effect. Saigon residents were taken aback by the level of government intrusion. First, the cadres visited every family in the city to take a political census, largely to ferret out the people most likely to oppose the government. At this early stage, the communists were paranoid about sabotage, and in particular about secret agents planted by the Americans to overthrow their regime. In this, they shared a belief with the middle class: that the Americans would not give up the South so easily and would scheme to get it back. Another purpose of the census was to find out who among the residents could be used to help the cadres carry out government orders and policies.

Like everyone else in her neighborhood, Yen had to give detailed information not only on herself, her husband, and her children, but also on her close relatives. Yen's family report did not look good. Most of her family were living abroad, and, worse still, many had fled with the Americans. To be safe, she did not list me, afraid that my marriage to an American would make her situation difficult. The report for Do, her husband, looked a lot better, with many relatives in the revolution, including his oldest brother, who had joined the Viet Minh in 1945. After they finished confessing about their families, Yen and Do had to submit detailed accounts about themselves. From these, the cadres would decide how to group them. Do had been in charge of technical operations in the sugar mill, which earned him the classification of technician—a neutral one, because it implied that he had not been involved in the management and exploitation of workers. Yen had labored as a seamstress to supplement their income; now, this job, taken up in desperation, gave her an advantage. It prompted the cadres to list her as a worker—a trustworthy and respected figure in the eyes of the government. In spite of her family ties, these classifications earned her and her husband peace. Do did not have to report for political indoctrination, and Yen escaped harassment. [...]

The currency conversion happened suddenly, to catch everyone off guard and prevent people from subverting it. Its purpose was to wipe out the savings of the middle and upper middle class, and therefore reduce them to the level of the poor in order to achieve economic equality. Late one night, the cadre in charge of the neighborhood summoned Yen and other cell members and told them to visit each household and list the people living there, even those who were only temporary residents. He said this had to be done right away, although he did not tell them why. There were over ninety families for them to check. Most residents cooperated, but some would glare at Yen and refuse to give her a complete list. It took her until one o'clock in the morning to finish her rounds. She handed in the lists and went home, still puzzled by the whole thing. The next morning, like a thunderbolt, there was an announcement that the government would take the old currency out of circulation, and that each household was entitled to exchange a fixed sum of money based on the number of people living there. The ratio was 500 piasters of the old currency for one piaster of the new one. If a household had more money than it was allowed to exchange, the rest would be worthless.

In the neighborhood, people were in an uproar. But there was nothing they could do but line up at the exchange site to turn in their old money for the new. Several people carried large bags stuffed with bills, yet no one gave them a second look. Some got so mad that they started to toss their surplus money on the ground. Even criminals did not bother to show up to rob the long line of people. One of Yen's neighbors joked, "I've never seen Saigon so secure. Here we are, standing in line with tons of money, but no one's trying to grab it from us." In the end, each household could get at most 200 piasters in new money—actually a big sum considering how much each piaster could buy—even if the number of people living in it entitled them to more. Some residents, however, still managed to get more than the maximum allowed, through secret bargaining with the cadres in charge.

This conversion was only the first volley in the campaign to enforce economic equality. Subsequently, there were more exchanges—to the point that even if Yen could recover all of her husband's original savings from the bank now, they would be worth next to nothing. The conversions impoverished those foolish enough to keep their savings in local currency, but not those who had been clever enough to keep most of their assets in gold and dollars. Gold never lost its popularity, and remained the currency of choice for transactions like buying passage on a boat to flee the country. It became even more popular when galloping inflation eroded the value of paper money. Even now, with inflation tamed, people still prefer to buy and sell major assets like land and houses with gold, rather than with Ho Chi Minh banknotes. The dollar, too, remained attractive as the unofficial legal tender.

The next move for the government was to smash businessmen and entrepreneurs. This happened in two waves. At first, the big capitalists were targeted. The biggest of them all—Hoang Kim Quy, who had been known as the king of iron and steel—was arrested and sentenced to twenty years in jail, because he had produced the barbed wire used by the Saigon army. The second wave came in 1978 and focused on merchants. To prevent businessmen from dispersing their goods, the crackdown came like a bolt out of the blue. Cholon, the Chinese section of Saigon, was the hardest hit. Commerce had been its lifeblood, and practically every family there was engaged in it. Workers were mobilized as foot soldiers in this "anti-bourgeois" campaign, because they would not be inclined to feel sympathetic toward people more privileged than they. Young people were also recruited for this purpose, because they were most likely to carry out orders without hesitation.

As a dock worker, my nephew Minh got the tap on the shoulder to go into action. Accompanied by the cadres, he and his colleagues fanned out and invaded every shop and place of business to make an exhaustive inventory of the merchandise. Nothing escaped their vigilance. They would find everything—even valuables hidden inside pillows. Every item—soap, shoes, sunglasses, nuts, and bolts—went on the list. Nothing was too big or too small. Then all the items were seized and the businesses shut down. What the cadres had not counted on was the utter indifference of the workers and youths to both sides in this campaign. Their attitude was, "Pox on both your houses." The foot soldiers had no sympathy for the merchants, but neither did they have any sympathy for the state. When the cadres asked them to move the seized items to a collection point, they would casually drop things on the ground, damaging or destroying them in the process, or they would pile them up in the open under the monsoon rain. They would tell each other, "We're not getting anything out of this. Everything's going to the state anyway. So, who cares?"

Vietnamese merchants such as Mrs. An, a friend of Giu's wife and the owner of a large business, did not fare any better. In the sweep to convert the south to socialism, she became a target. One day, she received a notice asking her to attend a neighborhood meeting for business owners. At the meeting, a cadre got up and started to condemn the merchants, calling them exploiters, and threatening them. Then he passed out a form for each business owner to sign, voluntarily surrendering all his or her assets to the state. She signed. While she was at the meeting, a group of about thirty people led by a cadre arrived at her house. For two days, they systematically searched her residence. They did not miss anything that she might have used to hide her valuables. They overturned her potted plants and sifted through the dirt. They dumped out her bags of charcoal. They checked lamps and lamp shades. They opened up light switches. They slashed her mattresses. They checked the drain pipes and the garbage. They left her house in complete shambles, but found nothing. Before this happened, she had gotten rid of personal possessions she thought might get her into trouble, such as books and music tapes dating from pre-liberation days. In the end, she was allowed to stay in her house, but the government seized all her other assets.

In Yen's area, the campaign was not as harsh or intense. The merchants here were small shop owners, whose businesses could not compare in size and wealth to those of the Chinese or to that of Mrs. An. For this campaign, the cadres summoned all the cells in my sister's neighborhood. Yen and the other inventory takers had to go to every store and make an exhaustive list of the merchandise. They never went alone, but always in teams of three. Knowing the others might be watching, each one felt compelled to do a thorough job. For over a month, they visited all the shops and listed every single item of merchandise, down to each and every pair of costume earrings.

After they lost their businesses, the merchants had to face a second hurdle. Those classified as criminals who owed a blood debt to the people—for having aided the former Saigon regime in the war or for having ruthlessly exploited their workers—were kicked out of their homes and sent to a New Economic Zone, where they were given a piece of land, a hut with no walls, doors, or windows, a rice subsidy to tide them over until they could harvest their crop, mosquito nets, and blankets. Then the government seized their houses. This created panic among the merchants, many of whom started to flee the country, swelling the number of boat people taking to the sea. Others were able to bribe the cadres who had the power to decide who could stay in Saigon and who would have to resettle in a New Economic Zone. When I returned to Saigon in 1993, an acquaintance pointed out to me the house of one of the cadres involved in the campaign who had gotten very rich from bribes. This cadre and her husband later on became too grasping and corrupt for the government to ignore. In one of the periodic clean-up campaigns, usually window-dressing affairs that catch only the smaller fish, the government indicted them and took away their assets.

By the time it finished smashing the merchants, the government had taken over some of the choicest real estate in Saigon. These properties, along with those seized earlier from those that had fled the country, gave the government a huge holding of land and houses to parcel out to its cadres. This distribution would give rise to yet more corruption and lead to bitter squabbles over who got what. In other parts of the south, wholesale transfer of residential properties into the hands of the state and then to the cadres was also taking place. Although the new system was supposed to be egalitarian, with no one much better off than their neighbors, many cadres now seemed to live like kings, ensconced in the fine homes of businessmen who had been sent to the New Economic Zones or those of affluent residents who had fled.

With commerce killed off, downtown Saigon took on a sad and abandoned look. Shuttered stores lined the streets. Here and there, a few businesses continued to operate, such as hotels, cafes, and restaurants. But they were no longer privately owned. They were state enterprises run by bureaucrats. Their clients came from the small community of foreigners, the ranks of cadres who had gotten fat from bribes, or those middle-class residents who still had plenty of gold. No one else had the money to patronize them. Besides commerce and industry, the state also took over food production. It pressed peasants to join cooperatives in April 1978 and to deliver their surplus crops to the government at official prices. This was the biggest economic blunder of the postwar period. Unlike farmers in the north whose villages had known a more communal tradition, the peasants in the south, descendants of pioneering settlers in what had once been Cambodian land, were much more independent and individualistic. Also, life in the Mekong Delta was not harsh like that in the Red River Delta, and the safety net that the cooperatives offered did not appeal to southern peasants, who could be self-sufficient. The southern farmers, resentful at being forced into cooperatives and angry at having to deliver their crops to the government at an artificial, low price, caused food supplies to plummet. To control food distribution, the government set up checkpoints to curb private trade in commodities. As in the north, rationing and coupon books were introduced, and how much in basic staples each family could buy depended on the number and age of people officially registered with the police as part of their household. This householding system had a security purpose as well: It allowed the police to keep track of who belonged where and who was doing what in the neighborhood.

The heavy-handed state control that clamped down over the economy brought disastrous results. With peace, the standard of living declined, rather than rose. Shortages became serious. Part of the problem was due to the embargo that the United States had imposed—out of resentment against a former foe, but mostly out of anger at Hanoi's stubborn refusal to help clarify the status of those Americans listed as missing in action. When all of America's friends followed its lead, Vietnam became isolated. The embargo restricted Vietnam's foreign trade and denied the country access to Western aid and investments and international credit. Even with international help, it would have been difficult to get the country back on its feet. Without it, the task became herculean. The economy shriveled. The embargo caused a lot of damage, cutting off materials and spare parts to factories that had been built with American know-how and forcing them to shut down. It also choked off mundane supplies like flour, and bakeries that used to churn out the wonderful French baguettes had to close their doors. In 1993, during my first visit back home, the embargo was still in force, although Hanoi had been cooperating in the search for American MIAs. Vietnamese were puzzled by its long duration and harshness. They would say, "Why are we being singled out for punishment for so long? There were thousands of Americans missing in action in Germany and Korea after those wars, but the United States did not take revenge against them. Why us?"

38

Homecoming USA

Arnold Isaacs

"You don't go to war, come home, and not talk about it," Bobby Muller said from his wheelchair. But America's soldiers returning from Vietnam came back to a silence that, for years, silenced them as well.

"We lost the war in Vietnam, and that's why we don't talk about it," said a man in the audience the night Bobby Muller spoke. It was early 1979, nearly four years before the Vietnam Veterans Memorial dedication, almost ten years after Muller took a bullet in the spine near a place called Con Thien in the Republic of Vietnam.

He had wept with pride at the Marine Corps hymn after he enlisted, Muller recalled that night in Baltimore; had gone willingly to the war that crippled him, and then discovered that in his own country, nobody seemed to care. "Goddamn it, no one feels responsible," he said. "Everyone thinks, hey, it wasn't my war! I didn't do it. It all got delegated to a couple of schmucks out there in that country, and when they come back—hey, man, it's your bad luck."

In the discussion that evening, people tried, with evident difficulty, to grapple with the troubled silence that seemed to surround Vietnam and its veterans. One man, of an age to have been in World War II or maybe in Korea, put his finger on one cause: No one knew what to say about this more recent war; not the people at home, not the soldiers themselves. The national experience in Vietnam never rested on any foundation of understanding, and so the men who fought there "were not standing on anything," he said. "There was no solid ground under them. Those of us in previous wars had solid ground, we knew where we came from, knew who we were and why we were there."

A woman wanted to know "how does all this relate to the violence that sort of has come out of Vietnam?" She didn't mean the war itself; she meant riots and snipers and shootings and store holdups in Baltimore and elsewhere in America. Others pointed out that American society and moral codes changed for many more reasons than just the Vietnam war, but she shook her head, unconvinced. Somehow she knew the war did it, and nothing anyone said could change her mind.

People spoke of the My Lai massacre and Lt. William Calley, of the destruction of Dresden, the firebombing of Japan, the Germans. "The horrible thing is that we were the ones," said a young woman, in obvious confusion and with many long pauses. "Maybe we weren't exactly like Hitler, we can't compare ourselves to that—but I don't think we can compare this war to World War II at all. . . ." No one was suggesting—quite—that American soldiers in general were murderers or war criminals. But the words were spoken: "Calley," "Dresden," "Nazis," "body count." And they had an evil sound. It was painful to imagine how they might sound to Bobby Muller in his wheelchair on the stage or to the other veterans sitting with him or in the audience. Yet in its very incoherence and fragmented quality, the discussion that evening in a way explained the moral fog Vietnam had left in American minds: a confusion so deep that for many years, Americans found no way to speak about it to themselves and, consequently, no way to speak to their own returning soldiers, either.

The folklore that grew up around that homecoming, telling of soldiers routinely being cursed or spit on, was almost certainly exaggerated. But the sense of being silenced, which *felt* a good deal like being shunned, was part of almost every soldier's experience. And the hurt was deep. "I want to go back to Vietnam and make it different," wrote a former Army nurse named Kathy Gunson some years after her return. "I want to come home to a marching band and a red carpet. I want to hear a 'thank you.' I want to hear 'I'm sorry.'" Another veteran, Jamie Bryant, remembered: "It was the spookiest thing. . . . In over ten years, there has really never been anybody who has asked me: 'What happened to you over there? What was it like?' It's like having a whole year of your life that didn't exist. When you first get back, you don't think about it much. Then you begin to wonder why no one asks the questions. Then you begin to feel like maybe it really isn't something you should talk about."

Many never did. Not infrequently, veterans reentered civilian life and told nobody, not even wives or girlfriends, that they had served in Vietnam. The absence of words meant more than an absence of gratitude or sympathy or respect. Unable to speak about the war, many veterans also had no way to find a reason or purpose in what they had lived through, no way to complete their experience by telling about it and thus coming to understand it.

The great majority were able to find some pride in their own conduct. If you asked, they would tell you they went, did their job, conquered their fear, didn't let down their friends. Like soldiers in any war, they had learned something about endurance and comradeship and about their own inner resources. But if their discoveries gave some purely personal meaning to their experience, it was not the same as finding an explanation, a worthwhile *reason.* Thus the war remained "like a piece of buried shrapnel," as one of them wrote, in a hidden and tender place within them. And like bearers of some terrible secret that could never be told, the returning soldiers felt themselves strangers in their own society. When he came home, the writer Larry Heinemann recalled years afterward, "I had the distinct feeling (common among returning veterans, I think) that this was not my country, not my time."

It was that sense of alienation that separated the Vietnam veterans from those of earlier conflicts. The difference was not so much in the wars themselves, since the tension and boredom and petty restrictions and stupidities of military life and the terrors and exhaustion of combat don't vary much from one war to another. ("When somebody is shooting at you and you are shooting back," the veteran and novelist Jack Fuller once wrote, "all wars are pretty much the same.") What made Vietnam and America's other wars so different was how they were assimilated afterward into the veterans' and the nation's experience.

Men who fought in World War II or Korea might be just as haunted by what they had personally seen and done in combat. But they did not come home, as the Vietnam vets did, to a country torn and full of doubt about why those wars were fought and whether they had been worthwhile. Nor did they return as symbols of a great national failure. Whatever troubling private memories they brought back with them, those earlier veterans did not have to grope for an explanation of what their experience had meant and what its purpose was. Their country—its political and intellectual leaders, its journalists and educators, its movies and popular novels—gave them the answer. They had been heroes in a necessary cause, they were told, and eventually most of them came to believe it was true. But those who fought in Vietnam were told . . . nothing. Even several decades later, Americans reached no common understanding, no comforting myth that could give sense or logic to that war, or absolve soldiers who had trouble coming to terms with the violence they had participated in.

"In past wars," Jack Smith, a psychologist and Marine Corps veteran, told the author Myra MacPherson, "through cleansing acts, society *shared* the blame and responsibility" with those who had done the fighting. "Victory banners, medals, and parades were ways of recognizing the tasks they did in the country's name," Smith added, but the country refused to give its name to Vietnam. "The responsibility and blame was left on the heads of the guys who fought it. They were left to sort out who was responsible for what." Another psychologist, John Wilson, explained to a *Los Angeles Times* reporter: "All cultures recognize that when we send someone to battle, it's difficult psychologically. . . . After the battle, most cultures also have a ritualized way of welcoming back the warrior and giving him a new identity and a new status in society. But we didn't do it for Vietnam veterans. . . . Many men felt isolated after Vietnam. They had to create meaning and make sense of what they did in Vietnam—and they had to do it alone."

If parades and medals were rituals of reconciliation, perhaps it was inevitable that an unreconciled war like Vietnam sometimes turned those rituals inside out, as on an April afternoon in Washington in 1971 when hundreds of veterans marched past the U.S. Capitol and, instead of receiving medals from a grateful government, threw away their decorations to protest the war. The reverse imagery was complete, down to the eight-foot-high temporary security fence below the Capitol's west front physically keeping apart the veterans and the government whose uniform they had worn.

At the head of the procession were parents of three men who had died. Gail Olson, a high-school band teacher from Russell, Pennsylvania, wore his son's fatigue jacket and carried a bugle. After blowing taps, he stepped to a microphone that had been set up next to the barricade so the demonstrators could stop, if they wanted to, and say something. Olson said into the mike: "My son's name was Sergeant William Olson. We're playing taps for all the dead—Vietnamese, Laotian, Cambodian, all our wonderful sons. Let us pray there will be no more, no more." Next was Evelyn Carrasquillo of Miami, who carried a U.S. flag and her son's medals mounted in a frame. "I will not turn my back on this country . . . but we've done our best for the Vietnamese, "she said. "It's time to get out. Let's stop the war now." Unlike the veterans, she kept the medals—"all I have left of Alberto." The third Gold Star parent was Anna Pine, of Trenton, New Jersey, who carried her son's medals up to the microphone and then stepped away, weeping, with the medals still in her hand. Later she returned and threw them over the fence with the others.

Then, for two hours, the veterans filed by and tossed away their medals. Some simply dropped them over the fence. Others hurled them as hard as they could, as if aiming at the Capitol dome far overhead. Some men walked on crutches; a few were pushed in wheelchairs. Some of those who stopped to speak into the microphone sounded angry, some just sounded sad. "I'm turning in all the shit that wasn't issued and I had to buy it," one man said. Another said: "This is for all the dudes in Third Battalion, Charlie Company, Ninth Marines, who didn't make it." Another said: "Here's a Vietnamese Cross of Gallantry, which God knows I didn't earn until just now."

One of the men who marched that day was a tall, lean former Air Cavalry trooper with lank black hair named Ron Ferrizzi, who threw away a Purple Heart and a Silver Star he'd been awarded for pulling another soldier out of a burning helicopter. "My wife wanted me to keep these medals so my son would be proud of me," Ferrizzi told me. "But I'm not proud of them. It's all garbage. It doesn't mean a thing." He turned and walked away into the crowd. I watched him go, thinking with a pang that if Ron Ferrizzi had joined the fire department, say, instead of the Army, and if he'd been decorated for saving someone from a fire in his hometown in Pennsylvania instead of in Vietnam, he'd have kept that decoration, no doubt, and his son would be proud of him when he got old enough to understand, and he would be right to be proud. I thought about going after Ferrizzi to tell him that. But I didn't.

The next time I saw Ron Ferrizzi, twenty-three years later in the framing shop he and his wife Kathy owned in North Philadelphia, I mentioned that long-ago impulse. Ferrizzi shook his head. Nobody could take away what he'd done to earn those medals, he said, and throwing away the actual decorations was a necessary part of rejecting a war he passionately believed was wrong. "I was so relieved. It was like the seas parted for me. It was like physically striking back," he said. And there was another powerful reason: his two sons. "I never wanted my kids to come up to me and say, when am I going to get a chance to get my medals?"

Kathy Ferrizzi didn't disagree. But she still sounded a little sad when she remembered her own feelings at the time: "I was brought up, if you had medals you were proud of them, your children were proud of them, and they were handed down. And here he was throwing them all over the wall. I wasn't that thrilled. I didn't think that was the right thing to do.

"I never thought he was wrong" about the war, she added. "I just asked him not to give back his medals."

The veterans' march in 1971 was one of the last major antiwar protests, but it was not the last time Vietnam veterans would discard their medals. Nearly six years later, furious at President Jimmy Carter's amnesty for draft evaders, a former marine sergeant in North Carolina named Dale Wilson called on other outraged veterans to turn in their decorations to protest Carter's action. Wilson, whose grievous wounds in Vietnam had cost him both legs and his right arm, had not been bitter when he returned home, he wrote in a letter to his local newspaper, the *Statesville Record & Landmark*. He had enlisted in the Marine Corps "feeling that it was my patriotic duty to serve my country," he wrote, and even after being wounded, only days before he was due to rotate home, felt lucky that he had survived to see his country again.

But Carter's amnesty, Wilson felt, defiled his sacrifice and the service of every soldier who had fought in the war: "Now I am faced with the fact that those who ran when our country called can come back and take the jobs and positions in the community of those who deserve them: the United States veteran." Like Ron Ferrizzi, Wilson had a young son, and like Ferrizzi he felt his decorations were too tarnished to pass on. He would have kept them for his son, he wrote, "but as the war has been recognized as a mistake, I feel there is no honor in medals obtained through dishonorable conflict." A week after his letter was published, Wilson and other angry veterans, some from as far away as Pennsylvania and Ohio, gathered on a parking lot next to a Statesville grocery store. There, they nailed their decorations, and for good measure, an artificial limb, to the wall of an outhouse they had brought to the site — "a symbol," Wilson declared, "of the universal political platform which promises relief and ends up with —." When all the decorations had been hung on the wall, Doris Miller, whose son had been killed in Vietnam, touched a match to the outhouse, which had been soaked in kerosene, and with Wilson and the others, watched it burn to ashes.

The fact that men with such different opinions on the war as Dale Wilson and Ron Ferrizzi both ended up making the identical gesture of rage spoke volumes about how deeply Vietnam had torn the national spirit. Whether they were flung away by veterans at the Capitol protesting the war or by veterans on a North Carolina parking lot protesting the amnesty program, those discarded medals represented personal courage and sacrifice that deserved to be honored whether the war was justified or not. Tainting that honor for so many veterans might not have been the worst thing Americans did to themselves in Vietnam. But it was no small crime, either.

[. . .]

Among all the veterans of Vietnam, those who waited longest for recognition and respect were the women. Even long after the memorial and the emergence of the "new," sympathetic

Vietnam vet, the women were still virtually invisible. "Vietnam was on TV, and there were all the Vietnam movies," said Diane Carlson Evans, the former Army nurse who spent nearly ten years campaigning for a women's statue at the memorial, "but it was all about the men. . . . I didn't see anything to remind me that women were in Vietnam. . . . And the strangest thing. I started thinking, 'Maybe I *wasn't* really there. Maybe I am imagining it.'"

Women veterans were so invisible, indeed, that even twenty years later, no one seemed sure how many there were. The most exhaustive postwar study of the veterans' experience reported 7,166 women served "in or around Vietnam" during the war, though other estimates were several thousand higher. The great majority were nurses, most of them recently out of nursing school and only a few years older than the teenaged soldiers they treated. Eight women were killed in combat. However many women there were, it became clear—but only very gradually—that in many ways their memories of Vietnam may have been just as troubled as the men's. The combination of new medical techniques and quick helicopter evacuation from the battlefield meant that nurses regularly saw men so terribly wounded or burned that in any previous war, they would never have lived to reach a hospital. The fact that the Vietnam GIs were younger than soldiers in earlier wars carried a special pain, too.* "I thought of soldiers as grizzled John Wayne types," mourned Lynda Van Devanter many years after the war. "They weren't supposed to look like John-Boy. And they were supposed to get better."

Nurses went to war to heal, not to fight, and for many that was justification enough. "You knew what you were doing was right," said Jane Hodge, a nurse at the Ninety-fifth Evacuation Hospital in Da Nang in 1969–70. "The fact that we were in Vietnam might not have been right, but the guys who were being shot up weren't the ones that had that choice to make. That's why I think I was able to work and live under the conditions that we did for a year. It's because the kids—not all of them were kids, but a lot of them were—didn't have a choice about being there, and the least I could do was take care of them." Kathie Swazuk, who joined the Army at twenty-one right out of nursing school and was sent to Vietnam eight months later, told an interviewer: "Whether I believed in why we should be there or not had nothing to do with it. . . . What I did there helped save lives and helped get some of these guys back in one piece. I feel like the medicine that I saw practiced over there was phenomenal for the conditions and for the flow of patients. I felt more needed, or more useful, there than I ever felt in my whole life. Really I did."

Like Swazuk, many nurses found their Vietnam service professionally rewarding. But the experience often carried a price. A high percentage showed symptoms of post-traumatic stress disorder (PTSD): anxiety, depression, insomnia, nightmares, flashbacks, numbness, thoughts of suicide. More than one-quarter of the former nurses surveyed in the National Vietnam Veterans Readjustment Study were reported to have had "full-blown PTSD at some time in their lives." But even those vet center counselors and other therapists who pioneered the diagnosis and treatment of PTSD for male vets were slow to recognize the same disorder in women. So, for that matter, were the women themselves. Technically, they weren't "in combat"—so how could they have the same problems that were usually identified with combat experience?

Besides, these women were nurses; their training and instincts were to help others in need, not to look for help themselves. And their culture—not just American culture but the religiously and politically conservative Middle American–Roman Catholic background that so

---

* The average age of an American infantryman in World War II was twenty-six; in Vietnam, it was nineteen. "I was twenty-one years old at the time. I was one of the oldest people around," Ronald Ridenhour, the Americal Division veteran who brought the My Lai massacre to light, once told an interviewer.

many nurses shared—led them to stifle many of the emotions that sprang from their experience. Doubts about U.S. policy, for example. Or anger: "Girls don't get angry. When they do, they're called crazy, hysterical, and out of control." The sight of teenaged soldiers shredded by shrapnel or burned to blackened lumps left many nurses full of rage but with no place to let it out. Instead, typically, they buried that anger within themselves, in a place so deep and dark it could be seen only in the lurid light of their nightmares.

Even more than the men, women came home from Vietnam and found no way to speak about it, either about the things they were proud of or about the things that haunted them. "I guess some people did ask me about Vietnam, and I would say things like 'It was okay.' Or 'Actually it was the pits.' That's all I said for ten years," a former Army nurse named Anne Simon Auger told interviewer Keith Walker for his collection of women veterans' oral histories. (At the beginning of the interview, Walker noted, Auger "put one hand over her eyes, and it stayed there during the entire ninety minutes the tape recorder ran.") Kathie Swazuk remembered: "It was strange. There was no one to talk to. So basically I never talked to anyone about Vietnam for years and years and years. . . . It's something that you kind of locked up, at least that's what I did. I don't know if that's normal, but I didn't talk about it much, . . . I don't think I've ever not thought about Vietnam. I just know I never expressed it."

« 39 »

Amerasians: A People in Between

Thomas A. Bass

Looking for the Mohawk Valley Resource Center for Refugees, I drive into downtown Utica, New York, in the summer of 1990. I park my car and am standing in front of the Florentine Pastry Shop, when I stop someone to ask for directions.

He is a tall young man with red hair. He wears blue jeans and walks with a streetwise prowl. His exposed teeth are all I get by way of an answer. I look into his broad beaming face and realize the young man doesn't speak a word of English.

I meet a whole crowd of Amerasians across the street. They are milling beside a storefront window that bears a hand-lettered sign announcing the location of the refugee center. The former Brescia's Furniture Store is an eighteen-thousand-square-foot windowless cave that functions as Utica's Ellis Island. Played out here is what it means to migrate from the old world to the new. In some ways the passage is quicker than it used to be. In others, slower. Instead of sailing into New York Harbor, refugees now touch down at night into Oneida County Airport. As soon as they step off the plane they become supplicants placed in the hands of social workers who dress and feed them.

The famous "six-second medical" at Ellis Island lasted only long enough for doctors to chalk on one's sleeve an *E* for suspected eye diseases, *H* for heart problems, *Pg* for pregnancy, *X* for mental retardation, or *X* with a circle around it for insanity—all disqualifying conditions. The process today is longer, but no less intimidating. Arriving refugees submit to blood tests, TB tine tests, fecal exams, X-rays. They get three months of "services"—welfare, food stamps, clothing, counseling, a furnished apartment, "survival" English classes—and then they get a job.

About forty refugees a month arrive in Utica. These include Amerasians, their mothers and other family members, former Vietnamese reeducation camp prisoners, Byelorussian Pentecostals, and the odd Libyan, Eritrean, or Croatian Muslim. Founded by a Jew and staffed predominantly by Catholics, the Utica refugee center is affiliated with Lutheran Immigration and Refugee Services. LIRS is one of the dozen voluntary agencies, or "volags," that resettle displaced persons in the United States under State Department contracts.

The Mohawk Valley Resource Center for Refugees had twenty-one employees and a half-million-dollar budget when I first began visiting it. A special residential program for Amerasians called Welcome Home House, originally scheduled to open in the fall of 1990, would have a separate budget of $800,000 and a staff of twenty-five. Welcome Home House was the brainchild of Rose Marie Battisti, director of the MVRCR. It would take Amerasian kids fresh off the plane from Vietnam and house them in a building of their own. It would immerse them in American culture and offer a real welcome home. When hundreds of Amerasians started flying into Utica to join the two hundred already resettled there, this malled-over relic of an old mill town in upstate New York would suddenly become the Amerasian capital of the United States.

Into the refugee center walks a wobbly figure in a light blue polyester suit, white shirt, and striped tie. The suit is two sizes too big for him. His rubbery face is covered with sweat. His hands shake as he stubs out a cigarette. "The malaria is back," says Charlie. Out of his suit pocket he pulls a brown paper bag. He empties the bag onto the picnic table in front of the snack machines. A sea of Amerasian faces stares up at us. Carefully pencilled on the back of each passport photo is the subject's name, age, and last-known address. "These are some of the kids I took care of in Amerasian Park," he says. "I made them get their pictures taken in triplicate. Two for ODP [Orderly Departure Program]. One for the brown bag. I have two thousand of these pictures."

Charlie was born in Da Nang in 1959. His father was an American adviser to the Diem regime. "I never knew him or my mother," he says. "She threw me away." He lived in an orphan asylum until he was six. Then there was a big typhoon in Da Nang, and the dikes along the river broke. The First Marine Division, Seventeenth Corps of Engineers came to build a new bridge. "I ran away and started living in their camp," he says. "They gave me a Snoopy dog and called me Charlie Brown. Everybody loves Charlie Brown. I needed a name in this world, so I became Charlie Brown."

He takes a piece of paper out of his pocket and begins drawing a map of Da Nang, starting with Monkey Mountain to the north and Marble Mountain to the south. "Here's Red Beach Two where the Marines landed in 1965 to start the ground war. And here's Alpha Battery, 5/4 Artillery, Fifth Division, Fourth Battalion, where I lived next." Soon Charlie's map is a maze of airfields and military encampments lining the South China Sea.

Charlie moved to Chu Lai, where a captain in MAG 11 gave him helicopter rides and sent him to school. Then in 1971 he went to Laos. "I followed the Twenty-First Marine Battalion and a company of Vietnamese rangers through the mountains and jungles. I was the camp mascot. They dressed me in a cut-off GI uniform. When the men got drunk, they tossed me through the air like a football."

After his travels through Laos, Charlie joined Alpha Battery, 5/4 Artillery, 1/5 (Mechanized) at Ai Tu Fire Base in Quang Tri. "They taught me to shoot 155mm tank cannons. There were six guns in Alpha Battery. I lived with Gun Five. On this gun were Gary Sharp from Kentucky, Danny Lawson from Tennessee, William 'Tiny' Compton from Indiana, William Allred from North Carolina, and Smitty, our black soldier. At Khe Sanh we fired all day and night for twenty days. I saw a lot of GIs wounded and killed. We fired many, many rounds before falling back."

In December 1971 Charlie's battery got the order to stand down. William Allred cried and said he wanted to take Charlie home with him. "All I could do was write down their names and say I would remember them. They gave me money, cameras, electric guitars, radios. I couldn't take it all. I had no family to give these things to."

Charlie returned to Da Nang. It was 1972.

"I'm different from Vietnamese people," he says. "I can't eat rice, only bread or noodles. Because I grew up on American food, when I was twelve I looked like I was eighteen." He worked as a money changer on the black market. He sold newspapers and ice cream. He slept in the streets and markets. "I kept moving, so the military police, who threw kids like me in the army, wouldn't catch me. I was broke again, but I didn't want to live with Vietnamese. I have no relations with Vietnamese."

A half-dozen Amerasians have crowded around the table, listening to Charlie's story. "After 1975, when the Communists came in, I was afraid because of my past," he continues. "I changed my name and fled. All my life in Vietnam after that was just moving around the country, with worries and fear."

Charlie hid in the jungle with army veterans who foraged for food. Then he traveled to Cambodia and Laos, looking for ways to escape from Vietnam. "Amerasians are second-generation GIs," he says. "The first generation fought the Communists with guns. We fought them in our heads. The number of Amerasians equals the number of GIs killed in the war. We are their souls come back to carry on the battle."

Charlie was selling cigarettes aboard the Saigon-to-Hanoi train when he had the bad luck in 1982 to be caught by the police. Accusing him of being an American spy, they threw him in Hoa Lo Prison—the old Hanoi Hilton. Then they took him to Saigon and put him in a military prison called the Jack Tree Hotel.

"I was alone in a room like a coffin. There was no light. I had one bowl of rice a day and spoke to no one for six months. Later I was moved to a room with two generals and other top leaders from the South Vietnamese government. I had no bed or blanket. I stayed one year in that room."

Charlie was transferred to a prison camp in the jungle. For three months he planned his escape. He gathered food. He dried rice in the sun. He hid a knife and cigarettes in a tree trunk. Finally he made his move. The guards followed him for three days, until they caught him in an open field and blew off the top of his head with an M79 grenade launcher. Charlie pulls back his hair to show us the long red scar on his forehead.

"They locked me in leg irons and tied me to a tree. There was no medicine for my head wound. The other prisoners dropped leaves at my feet. When night came, I wet the leaves and put them on my head. I ate another jungle leaf like a taro that is Asian medicine against infection."

After two months tied to a tree, Charlie was moved to a jail near the Laos border. Again he escaped, this time heading for the Mekong River crossing into Thailand. "I got lost in the jungle. Ten days later the Laotian army caught me. They beat me unconscious. They tied my leg to a wire and pulled me behind a horse to the Vietnam border. From there they walked me twenty days through the jungle to another prison. My hands were tied behind my back. I had no coat against the monsoon rains. I was ready to die. I don't know why I didn't die."

Charlie spent the next year in a prison camp near Pleiku. Many of his fellow inmates, former collaborators with the French, had been incarcerated since 1945. This time when he escaped, Charlie zigzagged for eight days through the jungle, before reaching Pleiku. "An old woman working in the fields hid me and fed me. If she hadn't helped me, I would have died in that hell. The woman had an Amerasian daughter. I loved her when I saw her. I asked her to marry me. 'Wait until she finishes school,' said her mother."

Charlie tells us that the girl and her family will be arriving in Utica next month. "I sponsored them," he says. "I am getting them a house, beds, TV, everything. They saved my life."

It was too dangerous for him to stay in Pleiku. Charlie hid under a lumber truck and rode to Saigon, where he lived in the train station with several hundred other homeless people, until he was arrested again and sent to another jungle prison. A failed escape attempt ended in Charlie's being shot down with a CKC, a Russian weapon. He rolls up his trousers to show us the scars on his legs.

"They gave me a stick and walked me for two days to another prison camp. I was there five months before I escaped again. My guard had been drinking. He fell asleep against a tree. I hit him on the head with a stick. I tried to kill him, but it's not easy to kill someone. I took his shoes and ID card. I sold his watch and necklace and used the money to buy a bus ticket to Saigon. I didn't want to be a robber, but that's life. The fish eats the ant; sometimes the ant eats the fish."

Back in Saigon Charlie added Phuong to his name. He grew a Fu Manchu mustache and a wispy beard and shaved his hair to look like a Buddhist. He kept moving around the city, before finally settling in Cholon. A million Chinese used to live here before many of them fled Vietnam as boat people. "I survived like a rat in those narrow streets," says Charlie. "I got fat from eating Chinese food." He smiles, remembering his foraged meals.

Eight months later Charlie was arrested again. The police were rounding up the homeless in Saigon and sending them to New Life camps. Inmates in these camps gave the government eighty percent of the food they grew and kept the rest for themselves. After toiling for a year they got a piece of paper saying, "So-and-so has been a good worker. Help this person have a new life." This is why they were called New Life camps.

Following his year working as a buffalo boy in the rice fields, Charlie was called to headquarters and asked where he wanted to go. "Saigon," he said. "When I get there, I will apply to the Orderly Departure Program and go to America." They demanded money to write him a letter of introduction.

Charlie pulls out of his suit pocket a yellowed piece of paper, which he carefully unfolds to show us his New Life ID. It lists his birth date as 1964. "They didn't believe an Amerasian could be born before then," he says. The document describes how Charlie Brown Phuong, *con lai long thang,* wandering homeless Amerasian, has proved himself ready for a new life. It also mentions that the government expects this person will leave Vietnam and go to the United States.

Back in Saigon, Charlie let his hair grow and got a new girlfriend. "I look like an old man, but I act young," he says. "I like to joke and have fun." He started sleeping in the park in front of the former Presidential Palace. It is called Thong Nhat—Reunification—Park, but after Charlie and other Amerasians began living there, everybody started calling it Amerasian Park. Two hundred people slept there at night, lined up side by side on mats.

"You have to realize this park is very important," says Charlie. "It faces the Ministry of Foreign Affairs and many big government buildings." The police wanted to throw the Amerasians out of the park, but Charlie paid money to have stories about them run in the Saigon newspapers. He buttonholed foreign journalists and tourists. He began filling out ODP emigration forms for everybody living in the park and started getting them interviews.

American war veterans were just starting to return to Vietnam in 1988. Their eyes flew open when they saw hundreds of Amerasians living on the streets of Saigon. "Some of them started crying," says Charlie. "They gave us fifty or a hundred dollars, which in Vietnam is a lot of money. I counted the money in the park, so everyone would see how much there was."

He removes from his pocket a notebook with a drawing of Charlie Brown and his dog, Snoopy, on the cover. The notebook is filled with the names and addresses of vets he met in Vietnam. "They promised me apartments, jobs, everything when I got to America."

In March 1989, six months after applying to the Orderly Departure Program, Charlie was interviewed by Jonathan Cohen, a former officer in the First Marine Division. "I remember you," Cohen said. "You used to hang around our camp. Back then you were a little kid wearing an Army T-shirt down to your ankles. Now you look old."

Charlie was flown to a Philippines refugee camp in August 1989 and arrived in the United States the following March.

At noon the refugee center fills with the smell of steamed vegetables and fish sauce. Lunch is being served by the mothers who have accompanied their Amerasian children to Utica. These are work-hardened women, although, judging from the photos they carry, they were once slender girls in *ao dais,* the traditional Vietnamese dress of flowing trousers covered by a tight-fitting tunic slit to the waist. The women all tell similar tales of betrayal. The war drove them out of the countryside to seek jobs at American military bases as cashiers, waitresses, maids. There they met the soldiers who fathered their children and then abandoned them, sometimes willingly, sometimes regretfully, as evidenced by money sent from America or letters signed "Love." What little the women remember from those days is scribbled on the backs of photographs showing Vietnamese girls wrapped in the big-shouldered embrace of GI John.

When the South Vietnamese government collapsed in 1975, these women feared their Amerasian children would be killed or taken away from them. Many families living in Saigon were expelled to labor camps in the countryside. Their property was seized by north Vietnamese carpetbaggers moving south. The next important date in these women's lives was their application to the Orderly Departure Program, which began airlifting refugees out of Vietnam in 1980. The women mailed their life stories and other scraps of evidence to ODP officials in Bangkok. They paid the required bribes to Vietnamese officials, passed interviews and health tests, and then waited years to leave the country. In the meantime, they were fired from their jobs. Their children were thrown out of school.

When their airplane finally took off for America, it followed a circuitous route that began with ten days' incarceration in a Bangkok prison. This stop was later replaced by six months' internment in a Philippine refugee camp. Then comes another date everyone remembers. They can tell you down to the minute when they first set foot on American soil. I initially thought they were describing a second birthday—the hopeful start to a new life. Then I learned Vietnamese do not celebrate birthdays. They celebrate death days. Souls in the afterlife apparently need all the help they can get.

The former leader of the Amerasians is now working for a small company in Utica that makes paper towel holders. His boss has bought him a bicycle to ride to work. Not trusting the neighborhood, Charlie locks his bicycle inside the refugee center before we head to lunch at a nearby Chinese restaurant.

Charlie is telling me about the kids who lived with him in Amerasian Park in Saigon and how he tried to keep them from joining a gang led by a rival Amerasian named Chau Van Raymond.

Charlie divided his encampment into work details. One group cleaned the park. Other groups took care of bedding and shopping for food. Twice a day they ate together, cooking over charcoal stoves. They got water from a government building and paid money to use the toilets in a nearby movie theater. Charlie forbade panhandling or stealing in the park, and he posted guards to beat up the Vietnamese who came to buy Amerasians, hoping to use them as tickets to America.

A black man at the neighboring table interrupts and asks if Charlie is from Vietnam.

"Yeah," he says. "I was there."

The man tells us he was drafted the day after he graduated from high school. He spent his eighteenth birthday leading a night patrol of green recruits into the jungle. "It never leaves me. I think about it every day," he says. Then he starts crying, tears streaming down his cheeks.

"It's tough, it's really tough," says Charlie, turning back to his lunch.

[. . .]

The first thing one notices about Nguyen Anh Dung, or Clarence Taylor III, is how fast he moves. He hustles into the refugee center, greeting everybody by name, and looks at his watch before sitting down at one of the picnic tables in front of the snack machines, The skinny little Afro-Amerasian child whose mother filled a dish towel full of tears when they landed in Utica has grown into a barrel-chested young man. Anh Dung was the first Amerasian in Utica to finish high school, the first to go to college. He works part-time for the phone company. He runs a video rental operation and auto driving school. He coaches the Amerasian soccer team. He tutors refugees in English and leads the volunteer work crew getting Welcome Home House ready for its first Amerasian occupants.

Graced with a marriage certificate issued by the local police station, Anh Dung's mother, Bang, and his father, "Bill," (which is the only name she remembers, or chooses to remember, for this black soldier from Oklahoma) lived together in Vung Tau for two years. He was an Air Force radar technician. Bang got pregnant. Bill reenlisted for a second tour of duty, but his son was stubborn. He stayed in the womb two months past his due date.

Anh Dung (the "D" in his name is pronounced like a "Y") was born on a Navy medical ship off Vung Tau in 1968. Forty-five days later his father was discharged back to the United States. Bill wrote letters to his Vietnamese family, begging them to join him in Oklahoma, but Bang refused to leave her parents.

"Before, I wanted nothing to do with him," Anh Dung says of his father. "Now I want to tell him he has a son in America. I want to meet him once to know this man is my father. I don't need anything from him, but if he doesn't accept me, I can only feel worse. I have this emotional wound, and it can't be healed.

"It's bad enough not to know your father," he adds, "but it's worse to know he doesn't want you. This is why many Amerasians don't look for their fathers. We came here searching for a home and don't want to be abandoned again."

With increasing urgency, from 1968, when he left Vietnam, until 1975, when it was too late, Bill wrote to Bang, begging her to join him in the United States, where he remained unmarried and childless. In 1973, when Anh Dung was five years old and the war was nearly over, his uncle, a staff sergeant in the Air Force, came to Vung Tau with airplane tickets for the boy and his mother. He gave them twenty-four hours to think about it. When he returned, Bang said, "I'm not leaving. I have a family to support, and Vietnam is my land."

"Then give me the baby," he said. "I'll take him to America." Again she refused.

Anh Dung and his mother moved to Saigon, where she worked as a housekeeper for an American Air Force colonel and former B-52 pilot nicknamed Ong Diec, "the Deaf Man." "He paid my school fees," says Anh Dung. "We'd go shopping and I'd point to things and he'd buy them for me. I even had my own cyclo driver who'd wait for me when I went to the movies. One day the Deaf Man took me to the officers' club and got me a membership card. But the Communists came too fast. I never got to use it."

Two days before the collapse of the South Vietnamese government, the colonel handed Anh Dung and his mother airplane tickets to the United States. They drove to Tan Son Nhut airport and boarded a helicopter evacuating military personnel to ships in the South China Sea. The rotors had begun to turn when Anh Dung's mother started yelling, "Let me out! I'm going home!"

Grabbing her son, she jumped out of the helicopter. The colonel yelled to her, "When the Communists take over, you won't even have shit to eat!" Then he threw his wallet after her.

Anh Dung's mother opened a food stall on the street and began hawking the family furniture. She used the money to educate her son. He was forced to stay after school to clean the classrooms and got in lots of fights. In seventh grade, when they ran out of furniture, he left school and went to work. He sold rice in the market. He sang Vietnamese opera. He painted houses. He worked as a handyman, plumber, electrician—anything to make money.

"You take the pain and forget it," Anh Dung says about the special burden of being a black Amerasian. "Life is meant to have problems. If you are a good human being, you try to solve these problems quietly," he says, restating the Four Noble Truths of Buddhism, which begin by asserting that "existence is suffering."

"We are the war kids," he says. "Our fathers destroyed Vietnam. The Vietnamese know enough about racism in America to know that my father was 'lower class.' But the Vietnamese are also racist. They don't like the Chinese, Cambodians, Japanese. The Vietnamese are even racist among themselves. They look down on farmers whose skin is dark from working in the rice paddies."

In 1978 Anh Dung's mother changed her mind about going to America. This was a year before the Orderly Departure Program officially came into existence, and two years before the first refugee flights left the country. There was a rumor on the streets that the United States was taking back its kids. She went to the Fifth District police station in Saigon and demanded that she and her son be registered for ODP. "We have never heard of this program," they said. She kept shoving documents at them. "Take these papers. Even if nothing happens, I want my son registered." Later she would pay bribes to get the paperwork advanced.

"She was taking a big risk," says Anh Dung. "She was fifty-four, no longer a young woman. The Communists punished people who tried to leave the country. They seized your house and belongings. By the time we were finally allowed to leave, my mother was sick. She couldn't take care of her business, and I thought I was going to be dumped in an asylum. We were saved in the nick of time."

In 1983, after a five-year wait, they were called for an ODP interview. Termites had eaten holes in their papers, which had to be retyped. After being accepted by ODP, Anh Dung and Bang faced another wait. People advised them not to go. "They will kill you in the middle of the ocean and dump your body out of the airplane," they said.

Anh Dung was one of the first Amerasians allowed to leave Vietnam with his family. The police at the airport seized everyone's money and jewelry. But when people saw they were flying Air France to Bangkok, they knew it was going to be OK. They don't kill people on Air France, they thought.

There were seventy-one Amerasians on board, 291 people altogether. "Look out the window," said the pilot when they took off. "This may be the last time you see your native land. I wish you a happy future."

They spent nine days in Thailand's Phanat Nhikom refugee camp filling out paperwork and getting shots. This was a closed camp for boat people.

"It was a dangerous place," Anh Dung says. "You had to depend on others to survive. There were no beds or water. We slept on a cement floor, a dozen people to a room. This is where a lot of young girls got pregnant."

They spent another night sleeping in the Bangkok airport. When their plane took off, Anh Dung watched *Fistful of Dollars* and *Superman* and filled himself with American food. They stayed two days in a motel in San Francisco and then flew to New York. This time he watched a John Wayne movie. After a night in New York they started flying again on a little twenty-seater airplane. They had been traveling so many days that Bang was afraid they were going to end up back in Vietnam.

Three Amerasian families, nine people in all, landed in Utica on May 10, 1983. Rose Marie Battisti met them at the airport. She was waving an American flag. The ground was covered with snow. The trees were dead. "Is this where we are going to live?" asked Anh Dung's mother. "Yes, Mom," he told her. "We are going to be cowboys." She broke down crying. She thought they were going to die here.

The three families lived in the same apartment for a month. Anh Dung rode in a car for the first time when Rose Marie took him to the hospital for a checkup. "She asked me, 'What do you eat?' and tried to serve me milk and hamburgers." He was sent to ninth grade on the school bus. He was fifteen years old.

The teachers couldn't pronounce his name. "They gave me a huge pile of schoolbooks. When I tried to read them, the letters looked like ants shaken up in a jar." The school had no course in English as a second language. It didn't even have a Vietnamese dictionary. "I learned my English from Lucille Ball and Fonzie on *Happy Days*," he says. "I speak English like the Smurfs, not Hamlet."

On finishing tenth grade, Anh Dung became a tutor at the refugee center. By then another fifty Amerasians had been resettled in Utica. They were becoming a common sight, but people still called them names in the street, and once Anh Dung got arrested for fighting in the mall.

He graduated from high school in 1987. Rose Marie came to the ceremony. She was so proud she cried. He began studying computer science at Mohawk Valley Community College, until he noticed he was the only boy in a class of forty-nine girls. He switched to electrical tech, graduated, and began studying for an electrical engineering degree at the SUNY College of Technology in Utica.

"I'm going to be an air traffic controller," he says. This is the first of many career paths Anh Dung will mention, including joining the Air Force and opening a restaurant. "If I had money, I'd have America in my hands," he says. Ambition aside, there is one constant in Anh Dung's life—his mother. "I'll always take care of her like she took care of me."

The second mother in his life is Rose Marie Battisti. Anh Dung describes himself as "Rose Marie's sidekick. I do the outside work. I keep an eye on problems in the community. Without me, Rose wouldn't know what was going on." He and Battisti have appeared together at numerous conferences and congressional hearings. "My second year here, she had me give a speech in New York City in front of four thousand people and three congressmen. She makes them cry. I make them laugh."

On June 29, 1989, Anh Dung became a naturalized American citizen and legally changed his name to Clarence Taylor III. Soon after arriving in Utica, at the refugee center's annual Thanksgiving dinner at St. John' s Church, he had met Clarence Taylor, Jr., who would later adopt him as his godson. A retired Army officer and Korean war veteran, Taylor has a Korean wife named Star. "He is a black man," says Anh Dung. "His story is just like my mother and father's, only he doesn't have any children."

Anh Dung changed his name, he says, so he'd "have an easier time fitting into American society. There's discrimination here against foreigners. I didn't want to swim alone."

He describes how it feels to be a triple minority in America: black, Amerasian, and foreign-born. "I feel more accepted by the Vietnamese than the blacks. The blacks don't know who I am. First, they called me *wetback*. When they figured out that wasn't right, they started calling me *chink*. Anyone with 'flat' eyes, a flat nose, and yellow skin is called *chink*. Chinks eat dogs and worms. There are lots of fights in town between Asians and blacks. Blacks used to dominate, but now the chinks have formed their own gangs. We take advantage of the fact that the blacks can't tell one Asian from another. We single them out and beat them up one at a time, just like the Vietnamese used to do to the Americans in Vietnam.

"The grownups don't accept me either. The first few times I went to Thanksgiving dinner with Clarence Taylor's family, I could tell they didn't like having me there. When I'm with Vietnamese, I'm Vietnamese. When I'm with Americans, I'm American. I am more Vietnamese than black, but the longer I live in America, the less Vietnamese I become. Amerasians don't really fit in anywhere," he concludes. "We don't know who our people are. We don't belong."

Chapter 12

Afterword

The final selection comes from the memoir of a Vietnamese woman named Le Ly Hayslip. Born into conflict in 1949, Le Ly left Vietnam with an American husband in 1969. The memoir is intercut with a description of Le Ly's return to Vietnam in 1986, her attempt to come to terms with her tormented past. She had a harrowing life: she joined the NLF when she was twelve, was jailed and tortured several times by representatives of the South Vietnamese government, and then was falsely accused of treachery and raped by two of her Viet Cong comrades. She fled her village for Saigon and Danang, had a child out of wedlock, and became thickly involved with the urban black market, selling "souvenirs," including marijuana, to Americans. Her father committed suicide. Determined to leave Vietnam for a better life in the United States, Le Ly fell into a series of misbegotten relationships with Americans, who feigned tenderness but exploited her mercilessly. Finally, she met Ed Munro, a lonely old man who asked no hard questions about the past and just wanted "a good Oriental wife who knows how to take care of her man." Practicality overcomes romance in this melancholy passage.

◂ 40 ▸

Letting Go

Le Ly Hayslip

I found it very hard to concentrate at work after Ed made his proposal. He said that in return for marrying him and coming to America and taking care of him as his wife, he would see to it that I would never have to work again; that my little boy, Jimmy, would be raised in a nice neighborhood and go to an American school; and that neither of us would have to face the dangers and travails of war again. It was the dream of most Vietnamese women and the answer to my prayers—except—

I was still a young woman. The proper time to care for a sixty-year-old husband is at the end of a long and happy marriage, not the beginning. I knew I was attractive to young men and wanted a husband my own age—as my mother and Ba Xuan and Sister Hai all had. On the other hand, I did not especially want to wind up like my sister Lan, who had many lovers, both Vietnamese and American (and now a child by one of them) and no prospects for marriage and a better life at all. Those friends in whom I confided about this problem weren't much help. Some were jealous of my golden opportunity to flee the war, or at least to enjoy the easy life of an American housewife. Others only ridiculed me for even considering a union with someone old enough to be my father. It seemed an unsolvable dilemma.

Of course, Ed was as persistent as he was kind. Because I did not want to be disrespectful, I kept putting him off by saying, "It's too far away," meaning the idea was "so distant" that I didn't even want to think about it, although he took it to mean that I thought America was too far away, so he redoubled his efforts to assure me that it was a wonderful place to live. At the core of my problem, I knew, was the Vietnamese distinction between duyen and no—the components of marriage that every child learns when he or she becomes engaged. Duyen no together denotes a married couple's karma—the destiny they share and what they owe to each other to achieve it. Duyen means love—physical attraction and affection; no means "debt"—the duty that goes with the office of husband or wife. In a marriage without no, the flames of emotion run too high and the couple risks burning up in too much passion or despair. In a marriage without duyen, which is the union I would face with Ed, there would be no passion at all—no affection beyond good manners—and nothing to look forward to but the slow chill of a contract played out through all its clauses. Worse, marriages of no—quite common in Vietman—often led to the abuse of one spouse by the other, through extramarital affairs, wife-beating, and the thousand other games perfected by cheated souls.

It took me many months to come to grips with this problem and learn my own mind. Young men, I decided, were for marriageable young women—not unwed mothers, black marketeers, and Viet Cong fugitives. By trying to do my duty to everyone in my life—parents, Communist cadremen, rich employers, corrupt officials—I had wound up failing in my duty to myself and the child of my breast, who depended on me. I decided to read the handwriting on the wall. Younger men valued me as a companion, an ornament, and a plaything—that was true enough;

but not as a partner for their lives. And why should they? For any American to want me for a wife, he would have to have an extraordinary need—not for a party girl or bedmate or crutch to support his weaknesses, or for someone to help him pretend the times were normal when they were not—but as a companion for the completion of his own life's circle. For me to trust myself again to an American, that man must be such an extraordinary person. In Ed Munro, who was completely unlike the other men I had met in my life, perhaps I—and my fatherless son—had discovered such a man.

In August 1969, when Ed's contract in Vietnam was into its final year, I agreed to become his wife. It was a decision that turned out to be filled with many unexpected costs.

For example, instead of rejoicing wholeheartedly with me, my friends began to warn me about the many legal and practical roadblocks established to discourage Vietnamese-American marriages and emigration to the United States. To make matters worse, the detailed investigations that went into certifying every applicant for a visa made it almost inevitable that my previous arrests (for everything from aiding the Viet Cong to selling illegal drugs) would be discovered and I would quickly be branded an "undesirable alien." What such revelations might mean to my fiancé, I couldn't even think about.

Fortunately, Ed was a man of the world as well as a man of his word. He didn't ask about my past and said that as far as he was concerned, our new life began on the day we met and I could make of it anything I chose; that nothing in my past should stand between us and our future happiness. He said he would be willing to pay whatever was necessary to ensure that our paperwork was approved. Because he had never before dealt with the corrupt Republican machinery, he had no inkling of how costly this blank check might be. Because I had never tried to pull off anything this big either, I was in no position to tell him.

My first step, then, was to return to the landowner—the "dragon lady," Sister Hoa—who had helped me before. Our first meeting was not too productive because she only wanted to talk about the niceties of marriage and how wonderful life was in America; how happy she was that I had found a nice, mature American and how lucky I would be to live in Southern California. When we finally got around to talking turkey, I discovered this particular goose would take a lot of stuffing!

"What you want is very, very expensive!" she admonished me, as if she found the profit she was going to make distasteful. "You'll need permission from government agencies at the city, district, provincial, and national levels. You'll need a marriage certificate and favorable reports from both the Vietnamese and American counselors you'll have to visit. Do you plan to take your little boy with you?"

"Of course! He's my son!"

"That's too bad," she said, smiling pleasantly. "You'll need a birth certificate stating he's *con hoan*—a child without father—and we'll have to get an exit visa for him as well. Tsk!" She shook her head. "The best way to approach it is to tell me how much you and your man are prepared to spend, and I'll try to negotiate the best deal I can at each step, taking my fee from what's left over. That way, you'll know I'm not trying to cheat you."

"How much do you think all this will cost?" I asked.

"It's hard to say without knowing the problems I'll run into. When the war's going well, everything gets cheaper. When there's bad news from the front, everyone gets worried and wants more money for everything. I'd say the basic package should run about a hundred and fifty thousand *dong*—"

"I'll go to America with the caskets!" I start to get up. She was talking almost *double* the amount Ed and I had discussed. Even with my own savings, it would be impossible to pay what she asked.

"Hold on, take it easy!" She put her long-nailed fingers on my arm. "I said that's how much it *should* cost, not how much you will actually have to pay! Remember, you'll have me as your adviser. Now, let's talk things over like businesswomen, shall we? Would you care for some tea?"

By the end of the interview, we had agreed upon thirty to fifty thousand *dong* as a reasonable price—but this was for "guarantees" only, and did not include the official fees or gratuities (such as whiskey and cigarettes) that customarily went to decision makers at each level. Despite my earlier remark, I was glad I did not have to buy my way into the illegal transportation network out of the country, such as the occasional Vietnamese who, as rumors had it, rode empty American caskets to Guam or to the Philippines or Honolulu. Even an American's resources would be hard-pressed to fund such desperate and costly schemes.

While we waited for Sister Hoa to grease the proper wheels, I began to live with Ed—to become the kind of wife that he desired. At first, our jobs kept us apart a good deal of the time, which was okay with me. My shift at the Navy EM club ended about eleven, which was when Ed's night shift at the outlying camps was beginning. Although this didn't bother me at all (the idea of ministering to an old, fatherly man as a husband was still too queer to appeal to me), it was not what Ed had in mind for our relationship, so, shortly after we moved in together, he told me to quit my job. Ed's conception of a wife was not someone who worked shoulder to shoulder with her man "in the fields," which was the Vietnamese way, but a queen on a pedestal who spent her days at the beauty shop or overseeing the full-time maid he hired to do all the housework and so kept her long, red fingernails from getting broken. It was a curious role for Phung Thi women, who, for a thousand years, had never been without a day's work before them. Although I tried to please him and play the role he had in mind (idleness was infectious, I discovered—as though every day was New Year's!), I felt more guilt than pleasure. It was as if I had become Lien—an icy princess who seemed to have nothing better to do than read magazines and lord over her servants. Nevertheless, the gift of time was one I could now pass on to my son, and Jimmy began to rediscover his mother just as I began to rediscover what families were all about. Shortly after I accepted Ed's proposal, in fact, I was told by the doctor that my family was about to get a little bigger.

One Sunday, after my clothes began getting tight again at the belly, Sister Hoa came with the one-eyed policeman, an armful of papers—including a marriage certificate and a birth certificate for little Jimmy—and a justice of the peace, to the nice house Ed had rented. While we filled out the forms, Ed sent for his friends, who had agreed to be our witnesses, and told our maid to prepare for a little party to celebrate our marriage. To mark the occasion, I had borrowed one of Lan's fancy cocktail dresses, which (with a few pins and a short veil cut from a sun hat), I quickly turned into a makeshift, Western-style bridal gown.

Within an hour Ed and I were married in a civil ceremony. I had invited my sisters Ba and Lan to come, but they refused; so Hoa cried on behalf of my absent relatives. Although Lan's objections to my marriage seemed more to do with envy than principle (her American boyfriend, Robert, was a friend of Ed's and I think it nettled her that I received a marriage proposal first), Ba's complaints were more traditional. Custom demanded that a bride wait three years after the death of her father before she gives herself to a man, and even in wartime many people thought I was acting too rashly.

"*Phan boi*," Ba Xuan said one day after a particularly heated discussion of my situation. "You betray your ancestors!" She then sang a little song for my benefit, which I remembered singing myself with other girls in derision of a woman who left the village to marry a man in the city:

Da Da birds live only in Da Da trees,
They sing: Why do you marry and go far away,
Instead of loving a man nearby?
Your father gets weak;
Your mother gets old;
Who will be around
To bring them a bowl of rice,
Or serve them tea?

"Do you see now what you're doing?" Ba asked, genuinely concerned for my soul. "Americans are *thu vo thuy vo chung*—they have no beginning and no end. They don't care about their ancestors. Because they don't know what reincarnation is, they think they're free to do any cruel thing they want in this life—no matter how much it hurts others."

"Can't I be married to Ed without becoming an American myself?" I replied sincerely. "Can't I keep an altar in my house and pray to our father and to Sau Ban and to Grandma and Grandpa Phung, even if Ed doesn't believe in it himself?"

"Sure you can—of course you can—" Ba was really angry. "But secretly, he'll scorn you—and that scorn will come out later in cruelty and disrespect. I'm older than you, Bay Ly. I've been married a long time and know how men act. Why do you think all those little Amerasian bastards are shunned by our people, eh? Not because we don't think they're cute or need help, but because they're tainted with the invader's karma. You don't have to be Viet Cong to know that and hate them for it. Now you want your next child to become one of them! Honestly, Bay Ly—what gets into your head sometimes? And what will our mother think?"

That, of course, is what I regretted most: that my mother could not be with me anymore, even in spirit. Although I did not have the courage to speak to her directly about my plans, I believed the simple fact that I was marrying outside my race, let alone to an American invader, was enough to threaten her motherly love. Sadly, Lan kept me well apprised of my mother's black moods:

"*Dua con hy*, she calls you, Bay Ly," Lan told me shortly before the wedding. "A spoiled rotten child! She says you're acting ungrateful toward your parents and soiling the family name. She says that even though our father's dead, you have made him sad with your decision. It's not too late to call things off, you know."

I felt like challenging Lan—for her years of ignoring our customs herself and her own easy ways with Americans—but I knew it would be fruitless. Our mother usually sided with Lan because Lan had money and was a mature woman and was not the "baby of the family," which is how I gradually realized I would always be viewed, no matter what I did in life. Although Vietnamese are raised to respect their ancestors and love their nation, they are not above civil war. In the triangle formed by our family's sad situation—Lan's contest with me for our mother's affection, our struggle against the tide of a changing society, and our different feelings about Americans—I could almost see a fishpond version of the "Viet Cong war itself. If I could not make peace with my family in such matters, how could the real fighters on both sides expect to resolve their differences?

When the short ceremony was over, Ed shook the officials' well-greased palms and complimented them on their sense of duty—working on a Sunday just to help an American get married! Their attitudes, he said innocently, were what Vietnamese-American cooperation was all about. We then had a fine party with Ed's friends, but they, too, left quickly, as if embarrassed by their old friend's child bride. Later, my little niece Tinh, Hai's daughter, came over with sweet rice to wish me good luck and tell me that she loved me. We hugged and cried and I told her I would never forget her.

Unfortunately, our quest, which had begun so hopefully, soon bogged down in obstacles thrown up by destiny or luck—or the government.

First, there was the problem of marriage counseling, a requirement mandated by the American consulate in Danang. Now that his own child was on the way, Ed said he wanted to adopt Jimmy, which was fine with the Americans; but the Vietnamese counselor—a short, fat, greedy woman about Ed's age—raised a long list of objections. While Ed was at work, I attended sessions with this woman and negotiated a price for each objection. Unfortunately, the more I paid, the more she wanted, and each dispensation cost more than the last. After several of these "conferences," I was running out of money Ed allotted for our paperwork. (He gave me two hundred dollars a month to run our household, fifty of which went to pay rent. The rest was to buy food and wrap up our affairs with the government.) Because Ed didn't want me to work after we were married, I had nothing to draw on for the difference but my savings—most of which I had already given to my mother. For several weeks, the officials at the chief district headquarters dined well while my mother and Jimmy and I practically starved. Still, I made sure my husband never suspected our situation. His plate was always full and our refrigerator was always stocked with cold beer. I didn't want my American savior to know the depth of corruption into which my homeland had sunk.

Finally, just when the counselor was getting ready to sign our release, she paused, and said, "Oh, yes, about my bonus—"

"What bonus are you talking about?" I asked, amazed. "I've already paid you almost every dollar to my name—including every cent my husband gives me to run our house. What more could you possibly want?"

"Oh, it's not for me," she said, as if she were asking for church donations. "It's for our 'coffee fund' here at the office. You know, we have lots of volunteers who come in and help us with our cases. We can't afford to pay them, so we offer them coffee and tea and meals when they work overtime—the way they had to work for your application. And you know how long *that's* taken us!"

I couldn't believe what I was hearing. "So—how much coffee are we talking about?" I asked guardedly.

"Well, to tell you the truth," she gazed pensively out the window, tapping her yellow teeth with the end of the pencil, "cash loses its value quickly these days, have you noticed? Even American greenbacks. I was thinking more in terms of merchandise—something that holds its value. You know, like diamonds—"

"*Diamonds*!"

"Now, don't get excited." She opened her desk drawer and produced a page torn from a Sears catalogue. "I don't mean raw gemstones or anything like that. Just something nice that will keep its value better than paper money. Like this nice diamond watch, for example"—she pointed to a pretty lady's watch on a much-handled page—"or maybe a nice dinner ring—like this!" While she shopped from the catalogue, I wondered how many other poor applicants had spent their life savings just to furnish this greedy lady's home, wardrobe, or office on the eve of their departure. We finally decided that a genuine pearl necklace would be just what the volunteers needed for breakfast, so I used up my last favors from old black market partners and obtained one for half-price. I had now completely exhausted my reserves and prayed there would be no more surprises. In the world's shortest adoption ceremony, I slid the black velvet jewelry case across her desk, received Jimmy's papers in return, and was out of the office before the price could go up again.

Unfortunately, like a frog trying to jump from a table by leaping half the distance remaining on each try, my victories always fell just short of my goal. When I brought the signed papers back to Hoa, she informed me that my plans had hit another snag.

"Of course," she said, as if it were nothing, "we'll need your mother's signature. You're still under age, and even if you're married, you'll need your parents' consent before leaving the country."

Up to this point, I had been able to avoid the whole issue of what to do about my mother. As far as she was concerned, Ed was just another American "boyfriend" (marriage to an outsider was not valid in her eyes) and my life and future, whatever they would be—as well as the life and future of my son—would always be in Vietnam. Although I knew my mother must eventually learn what was going to happen to me, I was not so sure that I had to be the one to tell her; or that she should even know before I left. Now, my procrastination had caught up to me. I would have to be either an exceptionally brave and honest daughter or a very skillful liar. Like many young girls that age, I decided to be the latter.

"Here, Mama *Du*," I said casually, shoving a form and a pen at her one day after lunch. "You have to sign this."

"What is it?" I knew she couldn't read or write, although, like many peasants, she had been taught to make her mark when it was required on legal papers.

"It's nothing; just an application for a bank account. You've probably wondered where all our savings went, right? Well, I deposited them in a safe place. What if the house burned down? All our money would go up in smoke! With my second baby on the way, I have to be more responsible."

She looked at the mysterious form a long moment, and for a guilty instant, I thought that maybe she had learned to read and would discover what I was up to. As independent as I had become over the last few years, I knew I could never stand up against my mother if she made a really big fuss over things. If the choice came down to leaving the country or destroying my mother's love for me, I knew I would have no options—even if it meant raising a hated Amerasian baby as an outcast among our people. Fortunately, I had a lifetime of peasant's habits on my side.

"Okay, if you really think it's wise." She made her mark and gave me the form. "I still wouldn't trust anyone outside the family with my money, though. Why don't you just give it to Uncle Nhu's son? He's helped us before—"

I gave her a long, tight hug and kissed the top of her graying head. "Thanks, Mama *Du*. You won't regret it!"

On February 11, 1970, my second son was born in a clean hospital run by Americans for U.S. dependents. Although Ed already had two grown sons he greeted the arrival of this new spirit like a brand-new father. He passed out cigars to his friends and told them how proud he was of "Thomas"—a good Christian name for a strong and spirited little boy. Alone in the hospital room, I sang a song of welcome to the little soul I called "Chau"—one who was destined to wander—who lay nursing at my breast:

Go out every day and you will learn,
Each step that you take will make you wiser.
Go here, go there, go eveywhere—
How can you be smart by staying home?
In the world you will find many nations
And many people all over the land;
You'll cross deep oceans and tall mountains,
And roads that crisscross the sand.
You'll find people that come in four races:
Yellow, white, red, and black;

You'll float through the sky in four directions:
East, west, north, and south.
But you will never know all these things, my son,
Unless you get out of your house.

When I got out of the hospital, my mother came to stay with us at Ed's house and help me through my period of *buon de.* Although Ed always tried to treat her kindly, she was content to behave like a servant when he was around—grunting only when spoken to and showing indifference to his favors. She was mostly concerned about how little Tommy (she always called him Chau) would get by when the war was over. If the Communists won, she knew his invader's blood—*con lai*—would put all of us in danger. If the Republicans won, she knew that same foreign blood—his light skin and American features—would cause him to be shunned in the village as soon as the Americans withdrew. As a result, she spent hours pressing his nose against his face, hoping to flatten it like a Vietnamese. She fed him dark juice and rubbed the juice on his body and kept him outdoors in hopes that his skin would darken like ours. I didn't know if these things would work or not, but I could see in them the desperation that was rising inside my mother; desperation that made it harder for me even to think about telling her the truth: that Ed and I and my two fine boys would one day step on an airliner and, very likely, never be seen by her again.

A few months after Tommy was born, Ed's overseas contract expired and it was time for him to return to the States. The plan was for Ed to go to San Diego first and prepare his home and local relatives for our arrival. After seeimg him off at the airport, I moved my things to Lan's apartment where I would live until my own departure, now less than a week away.

During my last few weeks in Danang, when word of my marriage spread through the neighborhood and I dealt with people as "Mrs. Ed Munro" rather than Phung Thi Le Ly, the world around me began to change. Certainly, I was the same person I had always been, but now I was labeled in a different way. I was no longer completely Vietnamese, but I was not quite American either. Apparently, I was something much worse. Even people I had expected to understand me, to be sympathetic to my dreams, looked down on me and called me names—not always to my back: *Di lay My! Theo de quoc Ve My! Fai choi boi!* Bitch! Traitor! American whore! During many endless hours spent standing in line or sitting in waiting rooms or by desks of minor officials, I found myself on the receiving end of dirty glances from Vietnamese clerks, secretaries, errand boys, and janitors. No citizen of Danang was so poor or humble that he or she was not superior to Le Ly *Munro*—turncoat to her country. Teenagers and a few Republican soldiers who lived in our neighborhood gave me cat-calls and sang derisive songs when I passed and, on two occasions, threw stones at me when I appeared on the street alone. In one instance our home was broken into, burglarized (which was understandable), and vandalized (which was not).

Even people who forgave me my new American name could not excuse me for accepting an older man as my savior. On many occasions Ed and I were openly cheated—charged two or three times more than even the black market price for food or supplies—just so people could show us their indignation. It seemed as though the more we accepted their wrath, the more contempt they showed us. In private conversations, I was often pleasantly (and sometimes not so pleasantly) reminded that in America, people hated anyone—even other Americans—who came from Vietnam, and quoted the war protectors' slogans. They were a gallery of sullen, unforgiving faces that I often saw in my sleep: tattered victims on Vietnam's foundering ship of state watching jealously as I abandoned them for the lifeboat of America. I was experiencing, I discovered, not only what foreigners had faced in my own land for generations; but the ultimate price of my own independence. It made Sister Hoa's demands seems paltry by comparison.

In any event, after paying more bribes to obtain my passport, I was finally ready to depart Danang for Saigon; to get a visa at the American embassy—the last hurdle standing between my sons and me and our flight to a better life.

On March 20, 1970, Jimmy, Tommy, our maid, and I boarded the shuttle flight for Tan Son Nhut. All through the flight, I thought about my mother and how she would react when my maid (she drew the short straw—none of my sisters would do it!) returned to Danang and broke the news of our departure to my mother. Part of me wanted to believe she already knew the truth—learning it, perhaps, from a neighbor or by that intuition through which every mother knows her daughter—and that the truth had been in her eyes the last time I looked into her face: a benediction for my new life. Of course, unless I was to come back someday, I would probably never know.

During the two-month stay before our overseas flight, I had no trouble saying farewell to Saigon. As the capital of our country as well as Anh's home, it had become the symbol of everything I wanted to leave behind—to let go of and cut loose from my life. In the three years since I had been here, Saigon had become even bigger and noisier and dirtier and more wealthy and more wealth-driven and more cosmopolitan than it had ever been before. Rather than being less Vietnamese, which is how the Viet Cong described it, Saigon now seemed to be more and more what the Vietnamese people themselves were becoming: vicious, grasping, estranged, desperate, and dangerous—mostly to themselves. Still, I had one last piece of business to attend to before these chains were broken.

The great U.S. embassy was busy as a marketplace—full of staff and visitors. After a long wait, a junior American clerk received me only to tell me that Vietnamese citizens seeking visas were supposed to report to a different building, where such requests were processed by the Vietnamese Immigration and Naturalization Department. This distressed me greatly—not just for the extra step—but because dealing with Vietnamese bureaucrats always meant more cost and trouble.

The emigration office was located in a two-story white apartment building that was near the main post office and the Nha Tho Duc Ba Catholic Church. I was not encouraged when I walked through the door. Instead of a businesslike offfice, the apartment was the residence of a well-heeled Republican woman who had refined the art of administrative extortion to a science.

"How badly do you want to go to America?" she asked, cutting right to the heart of the matter. "You'll need documentation from the Vietnamese embassy in Washington. It's going to be expensive. How much do you have to spend?" Perhaps she phrased it this way so that if anybody ever challenged her, she could say she was simply separating the charity cases from those who could pay the government's fee.

I replied with a good, cheap guess.

"That's not enough," she said flatly. "Come into my house. We'll have to discuss your case."

After brief negotiations, accelerated by my early admission that my American husband was no longer around to pay my bills and that I could only raise more cash by selling my airline ticket, which would defeat the purpose of a visa, we agreed upon a price.

"Okay," she said, ushering me back outside. "You'll have to wait out here while I prepare your letter. My house isn't a bus station, you know. And by the way, there'll be a small surcharge for our tea fund—"

I spend the next few hours hoping that tea was cheaper than coffee— even at Saigon's inflated prices. By the end of the day, though, I went home with the all-important letter.

On May 27, 1970, my sons and I stood in line to board the big American jetliner to Honolulu. As the passengers shuffled forward, juggling their carry-on bags and jackets, they showed their tickets to one last Republican official. The Americans passed quickly. The Vietnamese, however, usually had to stop and delay the line while they fumbled through their purses or pockets. When my turn came, the official did not ask for passports or visas or certificates of any kind. He asked only a single question—the last phrase I would hear in my native tongue on the soil which held my father's bones:

"Are you carrying Vietnamese money? If so, please drop it in the basket before you go."

Notes

2. Lawrence: The United States, Its Allies, and the Bao Dai Experiment

1. NSC–51, "A Report to the National Security Council by the Secretary of State on U.S. Policy toward Southeast Asia," 1 July 1949, RG273, NSC papers, box 7, NA [National Archives of the United States].

2. Ibid.

3. Ibid.

4. Ibid.

5. Ibid.

6. ORE report, "Prospects for the Defense of Indochina against a Chinese Communist Invasion," 7 Sept. 1949, RG263, box 4, NA; Acheson to Abbott, 29 June 1949, *FRUS 1949,* 7:64. On the question of ministries, see, for example, Bruce to State Department, 13 Oct. 1949, RG59, 851G.00/10–1349, NA.

7. NSC–51, "A Report to the National Security Council by the Secretary of State on U.S. Policy toward Southeast Asia," 1 July 1949, RG273, NSC papers, box 7, NA; Bruce to Acheson, 29 June 1949, *FRUS 1949,* 7:65–66; Abbott to Acheson, 6 July 1949, RG59, 851G.01/7–549, NA.

8. Webb to Paris, 18 June 1949, RG59, 851G.00/6–1849, NA; Bruce to Acheson, 29 June 1949, *FRUS 1949,* 7:65–66.

9. Report by the Permanent Under-Secretary's Committee, "United Kingdom in South-East Asia and the Far East," 28 July 1949, FO 371, file 76030, PRO [Public Record Office, Great Britain]; brief for Bevin's talks with Nehru, 10 Nov. 1949, FO 371, file 76005, PRO; Foreign Office brief for Bevin, 11 Sept. 1949, FO 371, file 75969, PRO; Gibbs to Foreign Office, 9 April 1949, FO 371, file 75962, PRO.

10. Paper for Permanent Under-Secretary's Committee, "Regional Cooperation in South-East Asia and the Far East," 20 Aug. 1949, FO 371, file 76030, PRO.

11. Washington to Foreign Office, 6 Sept. 1949, FO 371, file 76033, PRO; memo by Ford (Washington), 8 Sept. 1949, FO 371, file 76005, PRO; Reed to Butterworth, 8 Sept. 1949, RG59, PSA, reel 7, NA.

12. Paper for Permanent Under-Secretary's Committee, "Regional Cooperation in South-East Asia and the Far East," 20 Aug. 1949, FO 371, file 76030, PRO.

13. Dening to MacDonald, 1 Oct. 1949, FO 371, file 76031, PRO; Franks to Foreign Office, 10 Nov. 1949, FO 371, file 75970, PRO; Scott to Hood (Paris), 9 Nov. 1949, FO 371, file 75969, PRO.

14. MacDonald to Foreign Office, 20 Dec. 1949, FO 371, file 61675983, PRO.

15. Memo by Ford, 8 Sept. 1949, FO 371, file 76005, PRO; 62nd Cabinet Conclusions, 27 Oct. 1949, CAB 128, vol. 16, PRO.

16. MacDonald to Dening, 2 Sept. 1949, FO 371, file 75967, PRO. For MacDonald's trip, see Massigli to Foreign Ministry, 21 Nov. 1949, Asie/Malaysie, file 15, MAE [Ministère Affaires External].

17. Foreign Office memo, 12 Nov. 1949, FO 371, file 75973, PRO; Bevin (Paris) to Foreign Office, 12 Nov. 1949, FO 371, file 75970, PRO.

18. Hopson to Scott, 24 May 1949, FO 371, file 75963, PRO; memo by Bevin, "South East Asia and the Far East—Conference of H.M. Representatives and Colonial Governors," 26 Nov. 1949, CAB 129, vol. 37, PRO.

19. High Commission to Commonwealth Relations Office, 13 June 1949, FO 371, file 75964, PRO; New Delhi to Dening, 1 Aug. 1949, FO 371, file 75966, PRO; Paris to Foreign Office, 15 Aug. 1949, FO 371, file 75966, PRO.

20. Acheson to New Delhi, 30 June 1949, RG59, 851G.01/6–3049, NA; Acheson to New Delhi, 5 July 1949, RG59, 85iG.01/7–549, NA; Abbott to State Department, 23 Sept. 1949, RG59, 851G.01/9–2349, NA; memcon, Acheson and Nehru, 12 Oct. 1949, Acheson papers, memoranda of conversations, box 65, HSTL; memcon, Bajpai with Noel-Baker, 11 Dec. 1949, FO 371, file 76016, PRO.

21. UK high commissioner in Ceylon to Foreign Office, 13 Oct. 1949, FO 371, file 75969, PRO; State Department memo, "Problem: To determine U.S. policy in regard to proposals for an association of non-Communist Asian states," 12 Sept. 1949, RG59, PSA, reel 6, NA; memcon, Reed and Landon with Prince Wan, 21 Dec. 1949, RG59, 751G.00/12–2149, NA.

22. Reed to Jessup, 22 Aug. 1949, RG59, 851G.00/8–2249, NA; Reed to Hickman, Oct. 1945, RG59, PSA, reel 9, NA.

23. Memo for Carpentier, 30 Nov. 1949, Archives de l'Indochine/10H, box 1583, CV [Chateau de Vincennes]; "Procès-verbal de la Conférence Militaire du 15 Juin 1949," 15 June 1949, Archives de l'Indochine/10H, box 170, CV; Pignon to Letourneau, Dec. 1949, F60, box 3036, AN; Pignon to Bidault, 3 Dec. 1949, ibid; Letourneau to Pignon, Nov. 1949, ibid; Pignon to Ministry of Overseas France, 15 Dec. 1949, Etats-Associés, file 135, MAE; memo by Far Eastern Command, "Besoins des Forces Terrestres en Extrême-Orient en matériel américain," 21 Jan. 1950, Archives de l'Indochine/10H, box 1586, CV; "Fiche: Matériels Britanniques qui seraient necéssaires aux Forces Terrestres en Extrême-Orient," 21 Nov. 1949, Archives de l'Indochine/10H, box 144, CV.

24. "Indo-China Policy of Paris Assailed," *New York Times* (19 July 1949).

25. Foreign Ministry to multiple posts, 1 Aug. 1949, Asie/Indochine, file 209, MAE.

26. Du Gardier to Foreign Ministry, 24 Oct. 1949, Asie/Indochine, file 256, MAE; memo for Bidault, "Avis du Comité Juridique relatif au statut du Viet-Nam selon les Accords du 8 Mars 1949," 2 Nov. 1949, ibid.; Du Gardier to Baeyens, 28 July 1949, Asie/Indochine, file 209, MAE; "Reunion Interministerielle sur la Situation du Viet Nam par Rapport aux Organizations et Conventions Internationales," 26 Aug. 1949, Nations Unies et Organizations Internationales, file 110, MAE; Saigon to Foreign Ministry, 16 Nov. 1949, Asie/Indochine, file 156, MAE.

27. Pignon to Foreign Ministry, 2 July 1949, Asie/Indochine, file 377, MAE; Abbott to State Department, 5 July 1949, *FRUS 1949,* 7:67–68; Washington to Foreign Office, 19 Sept. 1949, FO 371, file 75968, PRO; Schuman to Bevin, 21 Dec. 1949, FO 371, file 83626, PRO.

28. Bevin (Paris) to Foreign Office, 12 Nov. 1949, FO 371, file 75970, PRO.

29. Bangkok to Foreign Office, 9 Sept. 1949, FO 371, file 75968, PRO.

30. "Note de M. Pignon au sujet de l'aspet politique du problème indochinoise," Dec. 1949, Asie/Dossiers Généraux, file 179, MAE; memcon, Dening and Butterworth, 14 Sept. 1949, FO 371, file 75976, PRO; State Department memo, "Indochina," 28 Sept. 1949, RG59, 851G.00/9–2849, NA.

31. Pignon to Ministry of Overseas France, 26 Nov. 1949, F60, box 3036, AN; Pignon to Ministry of Overseas France, 7 Nov. 1949, ibid; Ashley-Clarke to Dening, 14 Oct. 1949, FO 371, file 75969, PRO.

32. Pignon to Ministry of Overseas France, 18 Oct. 1949, Asie/Indochine, file 213, MAE. Emphasis in original.

33. Pignon to Foreign Ministry, 27 Oct. 1949, Asie/Indochine, file 256, MAE; Hopson to Scott, 14 Nov. 1949, FO 959, file 33, PRO.

34. Washington to Foreign Ministry, 16 Sept. 1949, Asie/Indochine, file 256, MAE; Paris to Foreign Office, 12 Nov. 1949, FO 371, file 75970, PRO; "Note pour le Ministre," 16 Nov. 1949, Asie/Indochine, file 277, MAE; London to State Department, RG59, 851G.00/11–3049, NA; Pignon to Ministry of Overseas France, 27 Jan. 1950, Etats-Associés, file 138, MAE.

35. Pignon to Foreign Ministry, 26 Nov. 1949, Asie/Malaisie, file 15, MAE; Ashley-Clarke to Dening, 20 Oct. 1949, FO 371, file 75969, PRO.

36. Saigon to State Department, 5 Dec. 1949, RG59, 851G.00/12–549, NA; Bruce to State Department, 17 Jan. 1950, RG59, 751G.00/1–1750, NA; Foreign Office to Paris, 23 Nov. 1949, FO 371, file 75977, PRO.

37. Reuters dispatch, "Dock Halt Voted at Dunkerque," *New York Times* (21 Aug. 1949); AP dispatch "French to Strike Arms Ships," *New York Times* (30 Oct. 1949); UPI dispatch, "Marseilles Dockers Strike," *New York Times* (8 Dec. 1949); "Marseilles Strikers Clash with Police," New *York Times* (11 Jan. 1950); "French Leftists Ask Indo-China Plebiscite," *New York Times* (27 Dec. 1950).

38. MacDonald to Foreign Office, 28 Nov. 1949, FO 371, file 75977, PRO; Holmes to State Department, 5 Dec. 1949, RG59, 851G.01/12–549, NA.

39. Foreign Office to Paris, 16 Dec. 1949, PREM 8, file 1221, PRO; Massigli to McNeil, 2 Jan. 1950, PREM 8, file 1221, PRO.

40. On December 31, for example, the *New York Times* reported that London would recognize Bao Dai and Mao "concurrently." "Accord with French Gives Viet Nam Virtual Freedom," *New York Times* (31 Dec. 1949).

41. "Extracts from minutes of China and South-East Asia Committee of Cabinet," 16 Dec. 1949, PREM 8, file 1221, PRO; "Aide-mémoire," 26 Nov. 1949, Archives de l'Indochine/10H, box 144, CV; Ministry of Overseas France to Foreign Ministry, 27 Dec. 1949, Asie/Indochine, file 129, MAE.

42. Far Eastern Command to Chiefs of Staff (London), 13 Jan. 1950, FO 371, file 83648, PRO; minute by Scott, 22 Dec. 1949, FO 371, file 75990, PRO,

43. London to State Department, 9 Nov. 1949, PP (DoD), 8:223–224.

44. For Acheson's views, see, for example, Acheson testimony before Congress, 12 Oct. 1949, RG59, PSA, reel 11, NA.

45. Memcon, Reed with Graves, 28 Nov. 1949, RG59, 851G.01/11–2849, NA.

46. Bruce to State Department, 11 Dec. 1949, RG59, 851G.00/12–1149, NA.

47. Butterworth to Fosdick, 17 Nov. 1949, RG59, 751G.00/11–1749, NA; Acheson to Bangkok, 23 Dec. 1949, RG59, 851G.01/12–2349, NA.

48. Gibson to State Department, 19 Nov. 1949, 851G.00B/11–1949, NA; PPS memo, "East and South Asia," 6 June 1950, RG59, lot 64D563, Records of the Policy Planning Staff, box *26,* NA.

49. Kennan to Robert G. Hooker, 17 Oct. 1949, RG59, lot file 1, Acheson Undersecretary file, box 9, NA; Abbott to Folsom, 17 Dec. 1949, RG59, 751G.00/12–1749, NA.

50. Bruce to State Department, 22 Dec. 1949, RG59, 851G.00/12–2249, NA.

51. NSC-48/1, "A Report to the President by the National Security Council on the Position of the United States with Respect to Asia," 30 Dec. 1949, PP (DoD), 8:265–272.

52. Abbott to State Department, 27 Dec. 1949, RG59, 851G.01/12–2749, NA.

53. Paris to Foreign Office, 2 Feb. 1950, FO 371, file 83599, PRO.

54. Foreign Ministry to Ministry of Overseas France, 25 Jan. 1950, Asie/Indochine, file 209, MAE; Paris to Foreign Office, 25 Jan. 1950, FO 371, file 83599, PRO.

55. "Note by Division d'Asie-Océanie, "Attitude des principales puissances vis-à-vis du gouvernement vietnamien," 14 Jan. 1950, Asie/Indochine, file 205, MAE; note for Bao Dai, 27 Jan. 1950, FO 371, file 83559, PRO; Gibbs to Foreign Office, 3 Feb. 1950, FO 371, file 83599, PRO.

56. Zhai, *China and the Vietnam Wars*, 13–16; Chen Jian, *Mao's China and the Cold War*, 120–121.

57. Zhai, *China and the Vietnam Wars*, 15; Acheson press statement, 1 Feb. 1950, FO 371, file 83604, PRO; "U.S. Recognizes Viet Nam, Two Other Indo-China States," *New York Times* (8 Feb. 1950).

3. Anderson: Dwight D. Eisenhower and Wholehearted Support of Ngo Dinh Diem

1. *Public Papers of the Presidents of the United States: Dwight D. Eisenhower, 1959* (Washington, D.C.: GPO, 1960), 311–13.

2. *Public Papers: Eisenhower, 1954* (Washington, D.C.: GPO, 1958), 382–84.

3. Dwight D. Eisenhower, *Crusade in Europe* (Garden City, N.Y.: Doubleday, 1948), 476.

4. *Public Papers: Eisenhower, 1953* (Washington, D.C.: GPO, 1958), 16.

5. *Public Papers: Eisenhower, 1960* (Washington, D.C.: GPO, 1961), 1035–40. See also Clark Clifford memorandum to Lyndon Johnson, September 29, 1967, U.S. Department of Defense, *The Pentagon Papers: The Defense Department History of United States Decision Making on Vietnam*, Senator Gravel edition, 4 vols. (Boston: Beacon Press, 1971), 2:635–37.

6. John L. Gaddis, *Strategies of Containment: A Critical Appraisal of Postwar American National Security Policy* (New York: Oxford University Press, 1982), 145–61.

7. U.S. Senate, *Executive Sessions of the Senate Foreign Relations Committee (Historical Series)*, vol. 5, 83d Cong., 1st sess., 1953 (Washington, D.C.: GPO, 1977), 385–88.

8. George McT. Kahin, *Intervention: How America Became Involved in Vietnam* (New York: Knopf, 1986), 42; George C. Herring, *America's Longest War: The United States and Vietnam, 1950–1975*, 2d ed. (New York: Knopf, 1986), 25–29.

9. Arthur W. Radford, *From Pearl Harbor to Vietnam: The Memoirs of Admiral Arthur W. Radford*, ed. Stephen Jurika, Jr. (Stanford, Calif.: Hoover Institution Press, 1980), 391–95; Ronald H. Spector, *The United States Army and Vietnam: Advice and Support: The Early Years, 1941–60* (Washington, D.C.: GPO, 1983), 199–202; John Prados, *The Sky Would Fall: Operation Vulture: The Secret U.S. Bombing Mission to Vietnam, 1954* (New York: Dial Press, 1983), 152–56.

10. For examples of this Eisenhower revisionism, see Fred I. Greenstein, *The Hidden-Hand Presidency: Eisenhower as Leader* (New York: Basic Books, 1982); John P. Burke and Fred I. Greenstein, *How Presidents Test Reality: Decisions on Vietnam, 1954 and 1965* (New York: Russell Sage Foundation, 1989); Stephen E. Ambrose, *Eisenhower*, 2 vols. (New York: Simon & Schuster, 1983–84); and Robert A. Divine, *Eisenhower and the Cold War* (New York: Oxford University Press, 1981). For an appraisal of this revisionism, see Chester J. Pach, Jr., and Elmo Richardson, *The Presidency of Dwight D. Eisenhower*, rev. ed. (Lawrence: University Press of Kansas, 1991), 237–39.

11. Fred I. Greenstein, "Dwight D. Eisenhower: Leadership Theorist in the White House," in Fred I. Greenstein, ed., *Leadership in the Modern Presidency* (Cambridge, Mass.: Harvard University Press, 1988), 76–107.

12. Arthur Minnich memorandum of conversation, no date, U.S. Department of State, *Foreign Relations of the United States, 1952–1954*, vol. 13, *Indochina* (Washington, D.C.: GPO, 1982), 1413 (hereafter cited as *FRUS*).

13. Melanie Billings-Yun, *Decision against War: Eisenhower and Dien Bien Phu, 1954* (New York: Columbia University Press, 1988); Richard E. Neustadt, *Presidential Power and the Modern Presidents: The Politics of Leadership from Roosevelt to Reagan* (New York: Free Press, 1990), 295–302; Richard H. Immerman, "Between the Unattainable and the Unacceptable: Eisenhower and Dienbienphu," in Richard A. Melanson and David Myers, eds., *Reevaluating Eisenhower: American Foreign Policy in the Fifties* (Urbana: University of Illinois Press, 1987), 120–21, 142–44.

14. Quoted in Harvard Sitkoff, *The Struggle for Black Equality, 1954–1980* (New York: Hill & Wang, 1981), 25. See also Robert Burk, *The Eisenhower Administration and Black Civil Rights* (Knoxville: University of Tennessee Press, 1984); George C. Herring and Richard H. Immerman, "Eisenhower, Dulles, and Dienbienphu: 'The Day We Didn't Go to War' Revisited" *Journal of American History* 71 (September 1984): 343–63; and Robert J. McMahon, "Eisenhower and Third World Nationalism: A Critique of the Revisionists," *Political Science Quarterly* 101 (Fall 1986): 453–73.

15. Herring, *America's Longest War*, 37–40; Lloyd C. Gardner, *Approaching Vietnam: From World War II through Dienbienphu, 1941–1954* (New York: Norton, 1988), 248–56, 281–84.

16. Memorandum of conversation, June 29, 1954, *FRUS, 1952–54*, vol. 12, *East Asia and the Pacific* (Washington, D.C.: GPO, 1984), 588. See also U.S. Department of State, *Bulletin* (September 20, 1954): 394–96; and Immerman, "Between the Unattainable and the Unacceptable," 145–46.

17. Burke and Greenstein, *How Presidents Test Reality*, 269–70; David L. Anderson, "China Policy and Presidential Politics, 1952," *Presidential Studies Quarterly* 10 (Winter 1980): 79–90.

18. Eisenhower to Alfred M. Gruenther, June 8, 1954, *FRUS, 1952–54*, 13: 1667–69.

19. Discussion at the 218th NSC meeting, October 22, 1954, ibid., 2157.

20. For various interpretations of Diem's appointment, see Herring, *America's Longest War*, 49; Kahin, *Intervention*, 78; Chester L. Cooper, *The Lost Crusade: America in Vietnam* (New York: Dodd, Mead, 1970), 20–21; Bui Diem and David Chanoff, *In the Jaws of History* (Boston: Houghton Mifflin, 1987), 71–72, 86; William C. Gibbons, *The U.S. Government and the Vietnam War: Executive and Legislative Roles and Relationships*, part 1, *1945–1960* (Princeton, NJ.: Princeton University Press, 1986), 266–67; and Robert Scheer, *How the United States Got Involved in Vietnam* (Santa Barbara, Calif.: Center for the Study of Democratic Institutions, 1965), 13–15.

21. Edward G. Lansdale, *In the Midst of Wars: An American's Mission to Southeast Asia* (New York: Harper & Row, 1972).

22. Eisenhower to Collins, November 3, 1954, *FRUS, 1952–54*, 13:2207; Andrew J. Goodpaster memorandum of conference with the president, November 3, 1954, box 3, Diary series, Ann Whitman File, Dwight D. Eisenhower Papers, Dwight D. Eisenhower Library, Abilene, Kans.

23. Dulles to Collins, April 20, 1955, *FRUS, 1955–57*, vol. 1, *Vietnam* (Washington, D.C.: GPO, 1985), 270–72 (Dulles's italics). See also Collins to Dulles, March 31, 1955, and April 7, 1955, ibid., 168–71, 218–21.

24. J. Lawton Collins, *Lightning Joe: An Autobiography* (Baton Rouge: Louisiana State University Press, 1979), 405–7.

25. John Foster Dulles, "An Historic Week—Report to the President," May 17, 1955, pp. 4–5, box 91, John Foster Dulles Papers, Princeton University Library.

26. Pach and Richardson, *Eisenhower*, 113–14, 203–4.

27. For a good description of Diem's Vietnam, see Robert Scigliano, *South Vietnam: Nation under Stress* (Boston: Houghton Mifflin, 1963).

28. William J. Sebald memorandum to Dulles, May 10, 1956, *FRUS, 1955–57*, 1:680–82; Kahin, *Intervention*, 88–92; Gibbons, *U.S. Government and the Vietnam War*, 1:299–300.

29. Kenneth T. Young memorandum to Walter S. Robertson, October 5, 1955, Young to G. Frederick Reinhardt, October 5, 1955, *FRUS, 1955–57*, 1:550–54.

30. Reinhardt to Dept. of State, November 29, 1955, ibid., 589–92; Reinhardt to Dulles, March 3, 1956, file 751G.00/3–356, and Reinhardt to Dulles, March 8, 1956, file 751G.00/3–856, U. S. Department of State General Records, Record Group 59, National Archives, Washington, D.C. (hereafter cited as RG 59).

31. Reinhardt to Dulles, December 6, 1955, file 751G.00/12–655, RG 59; G. Frederick Reinhardt interview by Philip A. Crowl, October 30, 1965, John Foster Dulles Oral History Project, Princeton University Library; Bernard B. Fall, *The Two Viet-Nams: A Political and Military Analysis*, rev. ed. (New York: Praeger, 1964), 246–68.

32. Arthur Z. Gardiner to Dept. of State, August 2, 1956, file 751G.5–MSP/8–256, and C. E. Lilien memorandum of conversation, December 10, 1957, file 751G.131/12–1057, RG 59; Kahin, *Intervention*, 84–88.

33. Scigliano, *South Vietnam*, 193; Fall, *Two Viet-Nams*, 289–306.

34. Program for Ngo Dinh Diem Visit, May 3, 1957, box 73, Subject series, White House Central Files (Confidential File), Eisenhower Library; Burton I. Kaufman, *Trade and Aid: Eisenhower's Foreign Economic Policy* (Baltimore: Johns Hopkins University Press, 1982), 99–110.

35. United States Department of State, *Bulletin* (May 27, 1957): 851; *Public Papers: Eisenhower, 1957* (Washington, D.C.: GPO, 1958), 417.

36. Elbridge Durbrow memorandum of conversation, May 9, 1957, *FRUS, 1955–57*, 1:794–99; Ambrose, *Eisenhower*, 2:376–81.

37. Gibbons, *U.S. Government and the Vietnam War*, 1:301–5, 320–27; John D. Montgomery, *The Politics of Foreign Aid: American Experience in Southeast Asia* (New York: Praeger, 1967), 221–35; Eisenhower, *Crusade in Europe*, 347; Dulles memorandum for the file, April 5, 1954, *FRUS, 1952–54*, 13:1224–25.

38. Kahin, *Intervention*, 109–15; Jeffrey Race, *War Comes to Long An: Revolutionary Conflict in a Vietnamese Province* (Berkeley: University of California Press, 1972), 105–22; William J. Duiker, *The Communist Road to Power in Vietnam* (Boulder, Colo.: Westview, 1981), 187–99.

39. Dulles to Durbrow, November 19, 1957, *FRUS, 1955–57*, 1:863–64.

40. Durbrow to Christian Herter, May 3, 1960, Durbrow to Daniel V. Anderson, July 18, 1960, *FRUS, 1958–60*, vol. 1, *Vietnam* (Washington, D.C.: GPO, 1986), 433–37, 514–15.

41. Lansdale to Edward J. O'Donnell, September 20, 1960, ibid., 580. See also memorandum prepared in Dept. of Defense, May 4, 1960, ibid, 439–41; and Samuel T. Williams to R. E. Lawless, May 15, 1962, box 8, Samuel T. Williams Papers, Hoover Institution Archives, Stanford, Calif.

42. Durbrow to Richard E. Usher, April 18, 1960, *FRUS, 1958–60*, 1:394.

43. Lansdale to Williams, January 17, 1961, box 8, Williams Papers. See also Lansdale to secretary of defense and deputy secretary of defense, January 17, 1961, box 49, Edward G. Lansdale Papers, Hoover Institution Archives.

44. Clifford to Johnson, September 29, 1967, *Pentagon Papers*, 2:635–37.

45. See James David Barber, *The Presidential Character: Predicting Performance in the White House*, 3d ed. (Englewood Cliffs, NJ.: Prentice-Hall, 1985), 134, 148, for a description of Eisenhower as a "passive-negative" president. For a favorable view of Eisenhower's negative achievements, see Divine, *Eisenhower*, 154–55.

46. Billings-Yun, *Decision against War*; Burke and Greenstein, *How Presidents Test Reality*, 268; Ambrose, *Eisenhower*, 2:185.

47. Burke and Greenstein, *How Presidents Test Reality*, 263–64; Ambrose, *Eisenhower*, 1:104–18.

48. Neustadt, *Presidential Power*, 133–34, 301.

4. Hammer: Geneva, 1954: The Precarious Peace

1. In deference to popular usage, the less accurate term, "the Viet Minh," has been and will continue to be used here to designate the Ho Chi Minh regime, even though, technically, the Viet Minh as a national front movement has been absorbed into the Lien Viet.

2. According to a report of Colonel (now General) de Brebisson, who negotiated military questions with the Viet Minh at Geneva, the Viet Minh took the initiative to propose a private discussion at which, on June 10, the French were told that "for the Viet Minh, Tonkin was the essential and vital region, and that it was necessary to concentrate on two large regroupment zones, one in the north, for the Viet Minh, the other in the south, where the forces of the French Union would be regrouped. The dividing line between the two zones should be established somewhere near Hué." *Journal Officiel*, Assemblée Nationale, December 17, 1954, p. 6517.

3. M. Mendès-France reported to the National Assembly that the Viet Minh had first asked for the thirteenth parallel. (*Journal Officiel*, Assemblée Nationale, July 23, 1954, p. 3580.) Yet the line mentioned above, in the previous footnote, proposed by the Viet Minh some six weeks before the conclusion of the conference, was actually the seventeenth, the one finally agreed upon. It can be seen that the Viet Minh altered its strategy between June 10, when it offered concessions, and the following period when it found it more profitable to make demands.

4. For British and French texts of these accords, see British White Paper, Cmd. 9239, *Further Documents Relating to the Discussion of Indochina at the Geneva Conference June 16–July 21, 1954*. And *Notes et Etudes Documentaires* No. 1901, *Documents relatifs à la Conférence de Genève sur l'Indochine (21 juillet 1954)*; and *ibid.*, No. 1909, *Accords sur la cessation des hostilités en Indochine (Genève, 20 juillet 1954)*.

5. The independence of Viet Nam had been formally recognized by France on June 4. . . . And in December 1954 the three Associated States signed agreemeets with France giving them full financial and economic independence. (See *Notes et Etudes Documentaires* No. 1973, *Accords et Conventions signés lors de la conférence quadripartite entre le Cambodge, la France, le Laos, et le Viet-Nam, Paris 29 et 30 décembre 1954*.

6. Parmet: No "Non-Essential Areas": Kennedy and Vietnam

1. O'Donnell and Powers, *"Johnny,"* p. 378; cf. Travell, *Office Hours*, p. 421; Lincoln, *Twelve Years*, pp. 349–354; Gallagher, *My Life*, pp. 283–289.
2. Herring, *America's Longest War*, p. 92.
3. Walt W Rostow, JFK Symposium Remarks, Los Angeles, Califomia, November 14, 1980.
4. Gravel, *Pentagon Papers*, v. 2, pp. 690–691.
5. Ibid., p. 691.
6. Herring, *America's Longest War*, p. 90.
7. Memorandum, Chalmers Roberts, August 30, 1961, Roberts Personal Papers.
8. Kennedy, *Public Papers, 1963*, p. 659.
9. Michael Forrestal, interview, February 17, 1981; Roger Hilsman, JFKL-OH (Dennis J. O'Brien interview).
10. Gravel, *Pentagon Papers*, v. 2, pp. 717–725.
11. Herring, *America's Longest War*, p. 94.
12. O'Donnell and Powers, *"Johnny,"* p. 16.
13. Herring, *America's Longest War*, p. 96.
14. Cohen, *Rusk*, p. 189.
15. Robert F. Kennedy, JFKL-OH (John Bartlow Martin interview).
16. Geoffrey Warner, "The United States and the Fall of Diem," *Australian Outlook*, 28 (December 1974), p. 247.
17. Henry Cabot Lodge, Jr., JFKL-OH (Charles Bartlett interview).

18. Herring, *America's Longest War*, p. 97.
19. Ibid., p. 103; Robert E. Kennedy, JFKL-OH (John Bartlow Martin interview).
20. Warner, "Fall of Diem," pp. 249–250.
21. Gravel, *Pentagon Papers*, v. 2, pp. 734–735.
22. Roswell Gilpatric, JFKL-OH (Dennis J. O'Brien interview).
23. Taylor, *Swords*, p. 293.
24. Michael Forrestal, interview, February 17, 1981.
25. Hilsman, *To Move a Nation*, p. 489.
26. Warner, "Fall of Diem," p. 252.
27. Robert E. Kennedy, JFKL-OH (John Bartlow Martin interview).
28. Taylor, *Swords*, p. 293.
29. David Halberstam, *The Best and the Brightest* (New York: Random House, 1972), p. 264; Gravel, *Pentagon Papers*, v. 2, pp. 728–739.
30. Wamer, "Fall of Diem," p. 255.
31. Kennedy, *Public Papers . . . 1963*, p. 652.
32. Hilsman, *To Move a Nation*, p. 500.
33. Gravel, *Pentagon Papers*, v. 2, pp. 245–246.
34. *Washington Post*, September 18, 1963.
35. Gravel, *Pentagon Papers*, v. 2, pp. 750–751, 752–753.
36. Roswell Gilpatric, JFKL-OH (Dennis J. O'Brien interview); Sorensen, *Kennedy*, p. 659.
37. Geoffrey Warner, "The Death of Diem," *Australian Outlook* (April 1975), pp. 12–13; Roger Hilsman, JFKL-OH (Dennis J. O'Brien interview).
38. CIA Chronological Report, October 23, 1963, DDRS (78) 142A.
39. Henry Cabot Lodge, Jr., JFKL-OH (Charles Bartlett interview).
40. Warner, "Death of Diem," p. 14.
41. Gravel, *Pentagon Papers*, v. 2, p. 789.
42. Warner, "Death of Diem," pp. 15–16.
43. Taylor, *Swords*, p. 301.
44. George Smathers, JFKL-OH (Don Wilson interview).
45. Michael Forrestal, interview, February 17, 1981.
46. Blair Clark, interview, July 20, 1977.
47. Michael Forrestal, interview, February 15, 1981.
48. Torbert Macdonald, Jr., interview, August 6, 1979.
49. Phyllis Macdonald, interview, August 9, 1979.
50. Confidential interview, July 25, 1977.
51. Ibid.
52. O'Donnell and Powers, *"Johnny,"* p. 382.
53. Chester V. Clifion, interview, October 1, 1981.
54. Theodore C. Sorensen, JFKL-OH (Carl Kaysen interview).
55. Kennedy, *Public Papers . . . 1963*, p. 892.
56. Dean Rusk, interview, April 27, 1981.
57. Kenneth P. O'Donnell, interview, December 4, 1976.
58. Robert E. Kennedy, JFKL-OH (John Bartlow Martin interview).

7. McNamara: The Tonkin Gulf Resolution

1. See Edward J. Marolda and Oscar P. Fitzgerald, *The United States Navy and the Vietnam Conflict*, vol. 2, *From Military Assistance to Combat, 1959–1965* (Washington: Naval Historical Center, 1986), pp. 396 and 411.
2. See Socialist Republic of Vietnam, *Vietnam: The Anti-U.S. Resistance War*, p. 60; and Marolda and Fitzgerald, *U.S. Navy and the Vietnam Conflict*, p. 415.
3. See William Conrad Gibbons, *The U.S. Government and the Vietnam War: Executive and Legislative Roles and Relationships*, pt. 3, January–July 1965 (Princeton: Princeton University Press, 1989), p. 10.
4. Embtel 282, Taylor to Rusk, August 3, 1964, *FRUS, 1964–1968*, vol. 1, pp. 593–594.
5. 041727Z, Department of State, Central Files, POL 27 VIET S., cited in ibid., p. 609.
6. A Recording—Admiral Sharp to General Burchinal at 2:08 P.M. EDT, August 4, Transcript of Telephone Conversations, August 4–5, p. 31; and 041848Z, both in "Gulf of Tonkin (Miscellaneous)," Country File, Vietnam, Box 228, NSF, LBJL.

7. 4:08 P.M. Telephone Conversation between Secretary McNamara and Admiral Sharp, ibid.

8. A Recording—Admiral Sharp to General Burchinal at 5:23 P.M. EDT, August 4, ibid.

9. See Summary Notes of the 538th Meeting of the National Security Council, August 4, 1964, *FRUS, 1964–1968*, vol. 1, pp. 611–612.

10. See Notes of the Leadership Meeting, August 4, 1964, ibid., pp. 615–621.

11. See *U.S. News & World Report*, July 23, 1984, pp. 63–64; and James Bond Stockdale and Sybil B. Stockdale, *In Love and War* (New York: Harper & Row, 1984), pp. 21, 23.

12. *Joint Hearing on Southeast Asia Resolution before the Senate Foreign Relations and Armed Services Committees*, 88th Cong., 2d sess., August 6, 1964 (Washington: U.S. Government Printing Office, 1966); and *Executive Sessions of the Senate Foreign Relations and Armed Services Committees (Historical Series)*, 88th Cong., 2d sess., 1964 (Washington: U.S. Government Printing Office, 1988), pp. 291–299.

13. Senate debate is in Congressional Record, vol. 110, pp. 18399–471.

14. Michael Charlton and Anthony Moncrieff, *Many Reasons Why: The American Involvement in Vietnam* (New York: Hill & Wang, 1978), p. 108.

15. Ibid., p. 117; and William Bundy, Vietnam Manuscript (hereafter cited as WB, VNMS), p. 14A-36.

16. WB, VNMS, pp. 14A–38, 14A-40.

17. Senate Report 90-797 (1967), pp. 21–22.

18. Senate Foreign Relations Committee, *The Gulf of Tonkin, The 1964 Incidents*, Hearing on February 20, 1968, 90th Cong., 2d sess. (Washington: U.S. Government Printing Office, 1968), pp. 82–87 and 106.

8. Logevall: Lyndon Johnson Chooses War

1. For example, *Christian Science Monitor*, 6 January 1965; *Baltimore Sun*, 31 December 1964; *Philadelphia Inquirer*, 12 and 22 December 1964; *San Francisco Chronicle*, 24 December 1964; *Wall Street Journal*, 30 December 1964; *Oregonian*, 8 January 1965,

2. Bundy MS, chapter 18, page 20. See here also Barone, *Our Country*, 399; Thomson Jr., "How Could Vietnam Happen?" 52.

3. Thomson/Cooper to MB, 31 December 1964, box 13, Thomson Papers, JFKL [John F. Kennedy Library, Boston].

4. For one version of Rusk's comment on de Gaulle, see Geyelin, *Lyndon B. Johnson and the World*, 122. For the view that Rusk was correct in this assertion, see Ninkovich, *Modernity and Power*, 296.

5. Ball memo, 5 October 1964; *NYT*, 1 January 1965. See also Marquis Childs, "Scant Sympathy for U.S. in Asia," *WP*, 9 December 1964.

6. Memcon, 9 December 1964, *FRUS*, 1964–1968,1:502. On Soviet policy in the period, see Gaiduk, *Soviet Union*, 86–88.

7. Washington to FO, 8 January 1965, FO 371/180539, PRO [British Public Record Office].

8. Forrestal to WPB, 4 November 1964, box 10, NSF VN, LBJL [Lyndon Baines Johnson Library, Austin]; Thomson to MB, 30 October 1964, box 13, Thomson Papers, JFKL. For Ball's position, see his 5 October 1964 memo, as discussed in chapter 8.

9. Summary of Working Group Report, 21 November 1964, box 11, NSF VN, LBJL.

10. LBJ to Taylor, 3 December 1964, box 12, NSF VN, LBJL.

11. Taylor to State, 9, 11, and 16 December 1964; Taylor to LBJ, 16 December 1964, all in box 12, NSF VN, LBJL.

12. *Le Monde*, 21 December 1964; NYT, 21 and 22 December 1964; *PP* (DoD), vol. 4, part C, chapter 3, page 70.

13. Taylor to State, 20, 21, 22, and 23 December 1964, box 12, NSF VN, LBJL. For the Taylor-Khanh crisis, see also the reporting in *NYT*, 20–27 December 1964; and Lacouture, *Vietnam*, 146, 163–164.

14. State to Saigon, 25 and 26 December 1964, box 12, NSF VN, LBJL. For a different interpretation of Johnson's decision, see Gardner, *Pay Any Price*, 161. On the circumstances of the Brinks bombing, see Karnow, *Vietnam*, 423–425.

15. *NYT*, 24 December 1964; WP, 22 December 1964; USIA Daily Reaction Report, 24 December 1964, box 73, NSF Agency File, LBJL; *Le Monde*, 23 December 1964; London *Times*, 23 December 1964; *Manchester Guardian*, 29 December 1964.

16. William C. Westmoreland, *A Soldier Reports* (New York: Dell, 1980), 225. See also U. A. Johnson, *Right Hand of Power*, 415. The argument that Johnson had freedom to maneuver is made briefly but well in Burke and Greenstein, *How Presidents Test Reality*, 148.

17. Ball-LBJ telcon, 16 November 1965, box 7, Ball Papers, LBJL; Ball-Yost telcon, 17 November 1965, box 7, NSF VN, LBJL; Editorial Note, *FRUS, 1964–1968*, I:957–958. Walter Johnson, ed,, *The Papers of Adlai Stevenson*, 8 vols. (Boston: Little, Brown, 1972–1979), 8:661–666; Yost (UN) to State, 25 February 1965, box 1, Gibbons Papers, LBJL.

18. Saigon (Seaborn) to Ottawa, 19 November 1964, 29-39-1-2-A, NAC [National Archives of Canada] Washington to Ottawa, 3 December 1964, 20-22-VIETS-2-1, NAC; Ottawa to Seaborn, 4 December 1964, 20-22-VIETS-2-1, NAC. This 4 December cable read, in part, "[W]e are concerned about lack of substance in position you are being asked to adopt in

forthcoming visit to Hanoi." On 23 December, the Canadian embassy in Washington reported to Ottawa that the State Department's Michael Forrestal doubted that the United States would have anything to communicate to the DRV in the near future. Washington to Ottawa, 23 December 1964, 20-22-VIETS-2-1, NAC. For the curious argument that Johnson in this period made "continuing efforts to negotiate a settlement," see Dallek, *Flawed Giant,* 226.

19. Memcon, Mao Zedong and Pham Van Dong, Beijing, 5 October 1964, Westad et al., "77 Conversations," 83–84.

20. Washington to Ottawa, 3 December 1964, 20-22-VIETS-2-1, NAC; Saigon to FO, 28 December 1964, FO 371/180555, PRO. See also Bundy's comments to Australian official Alan Renouf in January 1965, as recorded in Washington to FO, 8 January 1965, FO 371/180539, PRO.

21. See Hanoi to FO, 13 February 1965, FO 371/180511, PRO; Bettelheim-PhamVan Dong Meeting Notes, 10 November 1964, SG, EM, #47, MAE.

22. Ball-Goldberg telcon, 17 November 1965, box 7, Ball Papers, LBJL; Ball-Rusk telcon, 17 November 1965, box 7, Ball Papers, LBJL.

23. On forcing the people to decide, see Powers, *War at Home,* 9. See also the perceptive analysis in Ronald A. Heifetz, *Leadership without Easy Answers* (Cambridge, Mass.: Harvard University Press, 1994).

24. Reedy, *Lyndon B. Johnson,* 5–7, 42, 156. See also Reston, *Deadline,* 310–311; Chafe, *Unfinished Journey,* 223–226, 244.

25. LBJ to Bundy, 29 December 1964, box 12, NSF VN, LBJL; LBJ to Taylor, 30 December 1964, *FRUS, 1964–1968,* I:1057. This cable was likely drafted by Bundy. For more on the Austin meeting, see Washington to FO, 31 December 1964, FO 371/175503, PRO.

9. Herring: The Tet Offensive, 1968

1. Quoted in Don Oberdorfer, *Tet!* (Garden City, N.Y., 1973), p. 34. For a more recent analysis, see Marc Jason Gilbert and William Head (eds.), *The Tet Offensive* (Westport, Conn., 1996).

2. Bernard Brodie, "The Tet Offensive," in Noble Frankland and Christopher Dowling (eds.), *Decisive Battles of the Twentieth Century* (London, 1976), p. 321.

3. This inference is confirmed in North Vietnamese sources. Ministry of Defense, Vietnam Institute of Military History, "Saigon-Gia Dinh Offensive Sector (1968)" (Hanoi, 1988), trans. by Robert J. Destatte, concludes among other observations that although a great victory was won at Tet the major goals were not achieved because they were unrealistic and because enemy strength was underestimated. My thanks to Dr. John Carland of the U.S. Army's Center of Military History for sharing this document with me.

4. Quoted in A. J. Langguth, *Our Vietnam: The War 1954-1975* (New York, 2000), p, 468. The fullest account of the decisions is Ang Chen Guan, "Decision-Making Leading to the Tet Offensive (1968)—The Vietnamese Perspective," *Journal of Contempomry History* 33 (July 1998): 341–353.

5. Quoted in William C. Westmoreland, *A Soldier Reports* (Garden City, N.Y., 1976), p. 321. For a full analysis of the U.S. intelligence failure at Tet, see James J. Wirtz, *The Tet Offensive: Intelligence Failure in War* (Ithaca, N.Y., 1991).

6. Quoted in Oberdorfer, *Tet!* p. 158.

7. *Washington Post,* February 6, 1968.

8. Townsend Hoopes, *The Limits of Intervention* (New York, 1970), p. 145.

9. Earle Wheeler oral history interview, Johnson Papers, Lyndon Baines Johnson Library, Austin, Texas.

10. Herbert Schandler, *The Unmaking of a President: Lyndon Johnson and Vietnam* (Princeton, N.J., 1977), p. 91; "March 31 Speech," Johnson Papers, National Security File, National Security Council Histories: March 31, 1968, Speech, Box 47.

11. John B. Henry, "February 1968, *Foreign Policy* 4 (Fall 1971), 17.

12. Ibid., 21.

13. Wheeler Report, February 27, 1968, excerpted in Neil Sheehan et al., *The Pentagon Papers as Published by the New York Times* (*New York, 1971*), pp. 615–621.

14. Lyndon B. Johnson, *The Vantage Point* (New York, 1971), pp. 392–393.

15. Quoted in U.S. Congress, Senate Subcommittee on Public Buildings and Grounds, *The Pentagon Papers (The Senator Gravel Edition)* (4 vols.; Boston, 1971), 4: 558. Hereafter cited as *Pentagon Papers (Gravel).*

16. Ibid., 563–564.

17. Ibid., 564–568.

18. Ibid., 568.

19. Sharp is quoted in Schandler, *Johnson and Vietnam,* pp. 166–167. For the views of the Joint Chiefs, see Clifford notes on meeting, March 18, 1968, Clark Clifford Papers, Lyndon Baines Johnson Library, Austin, Tex.

20. Notes on meeting, March 4, 1968, Johnson Papers, Tom Johnson Notes on Meetings, Box 1.

21. Draft presidential memorandum, March 4, 1968, in *Pentagon Papers (Gravel),* 4:575–576.

22. Schandler, *Johnson and Vietnam,* p. 179.

23. Ibid., pp. 181–193.

24. Of Rusk, Johnson once said: "He has the compassion of a preacher and the courage of a Georgia cracker. When you're going in with the marines, he's the kind you want at your side." Max Frankel notes of conversation with Johnson, July 8, 1965, Arthur Krock Papers, Seeley G. Mudd Manuscript Library, Princeton, N.J., Box 1.

25. For a critical analysis of press and television coverage of Tet, see Peter Braestrup, *Big Story* (New York, 1978).

26. Oberdorfer, *Tet!* pp. 251, 275; Braestrup, *Big Story*, p. 137.

27. Schandler, *Johnson and Vietnam*, pp. 200–205.

28. Oberdorfer, *Tet!* p. 273.

29. Schandler, *Johnson and Vietnam*, pp. 207–217.

30. Approval and disapproval of the war were measured by the question "Do you think the United States made a mistake sending troops to Vietnam?"—at best an imperfect way of judging a complex issue.

31. Louis Harris, *The Anguish of Change* (New York, 1973), pp. 63–64, and Burns W. Roper, "What Public Opinion Polls Said," in Braestrup, *Big Story*, 1:674–704.

32. James Rowe to Johnson, March 19, 1968, Johnson Papers, Marvin Watson File, Box 32.

33. Westmoreland, *A Soldier Reports*, p. 410; also Robert Elegant, "How to Lose a War," *Encounter* 57 (August 1981): 73–90.

34. Excellent analyses that challenge the view of the media as critic and minimize the media's impact on public opinion are Daniel Hallin, *The "Uncensored War": The Media and Vietnam* (Berkeley, 1986); William M. Hammond, *Public Affairs: The Military and the Media, 1962–1968* (Washington, D.C., 1988); and Clarence R. Wyatt, *Paper Soldiers: The American Press and the Vietnam War* (New York, 1993).

35. Chester J. Pach, Jr. "Tet on TV," in Carole Fink et al., eds., *1968: The World Transformed* (Washington, D.C., 1998), pp. 55–81; Michael J. Arlen, *The Living Room War* (New York, 1969).

36. Robert Buzzanco, *Masters of War: Military Dissent and Politics in the Vietnam Era* (Cambridge, U.K., 1996), 316–328.

37. Robert M. Collins, "The Economic Crisis of 1968 and the Waning of the 'American Century,'" *American Historical Review* 101 (April 1996): 396–422.

38. Acheson to John Cowles, March 14, 1968, Dean G. Acheson Papers, Yale University Library, New Haven, Conn., Box 7. The gold crisis is discussed at length in Paul Joseph, *Cracks in the Empire: State Politics in the Vietnam War* (Boston, 1981), pp. 262–266; Gabriel Kolko, *Anatomy of a War* (New York, 1986), pp. 313–320; and Diane B. Kunz, "The American Economic Consequence of 1968," in Fink, 1968, pp. 83–110.

39. Quoted in Walter Isaacson and Evan Thomas, *The Wise Men: Six Friends and the World They Made* (New York, 1986), pp. 684, 689.

40. Acheson to Johnson, March 26, 1968, Acheson Papers.

41. Clark Clifford, "A Viet Nam Reappraisal," *Foreign Affairs 47* July 1969): 613; memorandum of conversation with Clifford, March 20, 1968, Krock Papers; Harry McPherson oral history interview, Johnson Papers.

42. Schandler, *Johnson and Vietnam*, p. 248. Tom Johnson notes on meeting, March 26, 1968, Johnson Papers, Tom Johnson Notes on Meetings, Box 2.

43. Summary of notes, March 26, 1968, Johnson Papers, Meeting Notes File, Box 2. The Wise Men were Dean Acheson, George Ball, McGeorge Bundy, Douglas Dillon, Cyrus Vance, Arthur Dean, John McCloy, Omar Bradley, Matthew Ridgway, Maxwell Taylor, Robert Murphy, Henry Cabot Lodge, Abe Fortas, and Arthur Goldberg.

44. Quoted in Roger Morris, *An Uncertain Greatness: Henry Kissinger and American Foreign Policy* (New York, 1977), p. 44. Johnson was furious with the negative tone of the March 26 briefings. The "first thing I do when you all leave is to get those briefers," he told one of the Wise Men. Notes, March 26, 1968, Johnson Papers, Diary Backup File, Box 95. See also Depuy oral history interview, William Depuy Papers, U.S. Army Military History Institute, Carlisle Barracks, Pa.

45. *Public Papers of Lyndon B. Johnson, 1968–1969* (2 vols.; Washington, D.C., 1970), 1:469–476. On Johnson's decision not to run, see also George Christian memorandum, March 31, 1968, Johnson Papers, Diary Backup File, Box 96.

46. "March 31 Speech," Johnson Papers, National Security File, National Security Council Histories: March 31,1968, Speech, Box 47.

47. Johnson, *Vantage Point*, p. 422.

10. Ball: A Dissenter in the Administration

1. Based on Jack Valenti, *A Very Human President* (New York: W. W. Norton, 1975), pp. 319–40, supplemented and modified by the information from my own notes and recollections.

2. Though in the light of subsequent knowledge, I may have overstated the dangers of a possible Chinese intervention, we then knew almost nothing about what was going on in Chinese foreign policy. Governmental and party announcements repeatedly emphasized that an historic moment had arrived for the world revolution under Communist leadership, and the United States was ritualistically denounced as the major impediment. In September 1965, Marshall Lin Piao, Minister of Defense and the Deputy Premier, was to startle the Administration—and particularly upset Secretary of Defense McNa-

mara—by publishing a long harangue announcing China's support for "wars of national liberation." That emphasized the people's struggle against United States imperialism in Vietnam and elsewhere, including areas of Asia, Africa, and Latin America. In that climate, it was normal to feel concerned at the prospects of such a move. After all, my memorandum was written only fourteen years after we had precipitated a Chinese intervention in Korea by getting too near the Chinese border, and no American could say with assurance that we might not bring down Chinese mass armies on our troops.

3. *The Pentagon Papers*, as published by the *New York Times* (New York: Bantam Books, Inc., 1971), p. 470.

4. *The Pentagon Papers*, the Senator Gravel Edition, *The Defense Department History of the United States Decisionmaking on Vietnam* (Boston: Beacon Press, n.d.), vol. 4, p. 623.

5. Betraying his prime interest in influencing American opinion, President Johnson told me with some pride: "That's the right touch. Send a Jew to see the Pope."

6. Janos Radvanyi, *Delusion and Reality: Gambits, Hoaxes & Diplomatic One-Upmanship in Vietnam* (South Bend, Indiana: Gateway Editions, Ltd., 1978).

7. *The Pentagon Papers, New York Times, op. cit.*, pp. 579–80.

8. Before his appointment to the Pentagon, Clifford had, as chairman of the President's Foreign Intelligence Advisory Board, toured the Pacific with General Maxwell Taylor to solicit Asian governments to send troops to assist in Vietnam. He was, he told me later, profoundly shaken by the refusal of Asian nations to offer anything more than advice and encouragement. If Vietnam's neighbors did not take the war seriously enough to help the United States, why should we carry on alone at such great cost?

9. He was later sufficiently generous to observe in my presence and that of a number of other people that "George Ball was the only one who was right all along and we made a great mistake not to follow him."

11. Kimball: Nixon, Kissinger, and a Pax Americana

1. *NYT*, October 8, 1968.

2. *Public Papers of the Presidents of the United States, Richard Nixon: 1969* (Washington, D.C.: GPO, 1971), 1.

3. *RN*, 348. Nixon enumerated additional noble goals in his public statements and postwar books, e.g., obtaining the release of American POWs; see *No More Vietnams*, 100. Other administration officials spoke in principled terms as well. Concerning the protection of the South Vietnamese, self-determination, opposition to aggression, and commitment, President Johnson's defense of U.S. policies presaged Nixon's. In *Vantage Point*, Johnson wrote: "We had kept our word to Southeast Asia. We had opposed and defeated aggression, as we promised we would. We had given 17 million South Vietnamese a chance to build their own country and their own institutions. And we had seen them move well down that road" (529).

4. Quoted in *Time*, July 29, 1985, 49.

5. *No More Vietnams*, 100.

6. The McNaughton memoranda are revealing of how national security advisers and policy makers weigh multiple goals. Nixon's goals and the way he combined them were not very different. McNaughton wrote at least two memoranda in which he ranked America's aims in Vietnam: "Action for South Vietnam," November 6, 1964, and "Annex— Plan for Action for South Vietnam," [appended to memorandum from McNaughton to McNamara], March 24, 1965, *Pentagon Papers*, Senator Gravel edition, vol. 3: 601 and 695.

7. Ibid., 216–217.

8. Briefing, n.d, folder: Vietnam-Rostow, box 16, WHSF: PPF, 1969–74, NPM [Nixon Presidential Materials]. Nixon often lectured to his staff about the "whys" of Vietnam; see, e.g., *HRHD* [The Haldeman Diaries], May 15, 1969.

9. *RN*, 348–349.

10. *HRHD*, July 21, 1969. See also September 5, 1969, regarding the "need to show [the] reestablishment of American leadership around the world."

11. *WHY*, 70, 228–230.

12. Henry A. Kissinger, *Diplomacy* (New York: Simon and Schuster, 1994), 675.

13. Nguyen Tien Hung, Thieu's special assistant, quoted in Hung and Schecter, *Palace File*, 21.

14. Chennault, *Education of Anna*, 197–198. In her conversations with Dirksen, Chennault assured him that she was no longer angry, but said, "I'm going to tell the story some day." Her attitude about the 1968 intrigue was that there had been nothing wrong with it, so convinced was she of its moral correctness. The Nixon camp apparently thought otherwise, and so did the Democrats and the press; ibid., 195.

15. Kissinger, "The Viet Nam Negotiations," 233.

16. On the phrase "game plan," see *HRHD*, October 3, 1969. Nixon used it on this day in the sense of game-planning the alternatives for Vietnam.

17. Haldeman paraphrasing Kissinger; ibid., March 9, 1969.

18. Options Paper, December 27, 1968 (provided to the author by Daniel Ellsberg), [p. 2]. (This document, dubbed "options paper" by the Library of Congress archivist who received it from Ellsberg in 1992, can be found in the March

1998 release by the National Archives of previously classified NSC files in the folder labeled Vietnam—RAND, box 3, NSC: HAKOF, HAKASF, NPM. There it is titled Vietnam Policy Alternatives and is filed with two related documents: The Situation in Vietnam and Sample Questions. In the following notes of this book, the main document, Vietnam Policy Alternatives, is referred to as Ellsberg Options Paper.) Henry Rowen, president of RAND was also present at the first meeting; Isaacson, *Kissinger,* 162. This definition of victory was also reflected in National Security Study Memorandum I, which represented the Nixon government's understanding. See Revised Summary of Responses to National Security Study Memorandum 1, March 22, 1969, *Documents of the National Security Council: Second Supplement* (Frederick. Md.: University Publications of America, 1983), microfilm, reel 3 pp. 2, 24, 27, 28.

19. Ellsberg Options Paper, December 27, 1968. n.p. [page following table of contents].

20. Ibid., [p. 1].

21. Ibid., [p. 6].

22. Kissinger quoted in *HRHD,* July 7, 1969.

23. Ellsberg Options Paper, [p. 15].

24. Ibid., [p. 19].

25. Ibid., [p. 18].

26. Quoted in Isaacson, *Kissinger,* 164.

27. NSSM 1, January 21, 1969. Twenty-eight questions were asked of the Department of State and the CIA, twenty-nine of the DOD and JCS.

28. Revised Summary, NSSM 1. March 22, 1969, 1.

29. Ibid., 2.

30. Ibid., 2–3.

31. Jeffrey J. Clarke. *United States Army in Vietnam: Advice and Support: The Final Years. The US Army in Vietnam* (Washington, D.C.: Center of Military History, 1988), 344.

32. Revised Summary, NSSM 1, 15.

33. *WHY,* 238–239. See also Revised Summary, NSSM 1. March 22, 4 ff.

34. Revised Summary, NSSM 1, 16, 26.

35. Ibid., 16, 27.

36. Ibid., 27.

37. Ibid., 27–28.

38. NSSM 1 Directive, January 21, 1969, 5.

39. Clarke, *Advice and Support,* 362.

40. See, e.g., Revised Summary, NSSM 1, 27.

41. Ibid., 30–32.

42. Kissinger claimed in *WHY,* 238, that the summary was prepared by his staff. Isaacson, *Kissinger,* 164, said that Ellsberg, still working as a consultant, collated the responses from February to March.

43. *RN, 293.*

44. *No More Vietnam,* 103–107.

45. *HRHD.* April 23, 1970.

46. See also, *NYT,* May 9, 1969: "The decision to demonstrate to Hanoi that the Nixon administration is different and 'tougher' than the previous administration was reached in January, well-placed sources say, as part of a strategy for ending the war." Joan Hoff argued that "Nixon had no clear idea in 1969 of how to end the war quickly" but pursued those options available to him—secret negotiations and the expansion of the war in Cambodia and Laos; *Nixon Reconsidered,* 210. It is true that these were Nixon's only options, given his commitment to victory (aka ending the war), but to his mind at the beginning of 1969, it was reasonably clear that these options would work, especially when combined with other options.

47. Memorandum of Conversation with H. Kissinger, Dobrynin to A. Gromyko. July 12, 1969, Communist Party of the Soviet Union Central Committee Archive, reprinted in *Cold War International History Project Bulletin,* Issue 3 (Fall 1993): 65.

48. *HRHD,* April 15, 1969.

49. Memo, Kissinger to Nixon, September 10, 1969, sub: Our Present Course on Vietnam, folder Tony Lake Chron File (Jun. 1969–May 1970) (5 of 6), box 1048, NSC: SF—LCF, NPM. The memo is reprinted in *WHY,* 1480 n. II.

50. One part of his domestic plan of action was to effect reforms in the Selective Service system, in which the public had lost confidence, and to engage in more vigorous prosecution of draft resistors and evaders. On March 27, 1969, Nixon announced the formation of a commission to look into the creation of an all-volunteer force, and on May 19 he asked Congress to make changes in the Selective Service system that would have the effect of reducing draft calls of men who were twenty years old and older while increasing those for eighteen- and nineteen-year-olds, with the result, presumably, of muting the former's opposition to the war. Nixon's reforms, namely, the lottery (1971) and the all-volunteer system (1973), came at a time when draft calls were declining because troops were being withdrawn from Vietnam, or after the Paris cease-fire agreement, too late to have much effect on protest but early enough to influence the 1972 election,

51. *HRHD,* March 20, 1969.

52. *WHY*, 266–267.
53. Morris, *Uncertain Greatness*, chap. 4 passim.
54. *HRHD*, October 17, 1969, and May 26, 1971.
55. Ibid., passim.
56. Ellsberg quoted in Strober and Strober, *Nixon: An Oral History of His Presidency*, 172.
57. *WHY*, 258.
58. *HRHD*, January 23 and 31, 1969.
59. Ibid., boxed comment, October 8, 1969. Haldeman recalled that on taking office, "there was an absolute conviction on Nixon's part that, by the fall of 1969, he would have Vietnam settled"; quoted in Strober and Strober, *Nixon: An Oral History of His Presidency*, 183. See also, Haldeman, *Ends of Power*, 82; and *NYT*, April 6, 1969,
60. *HRHD*, March 20, 1969.
61. *RN*, 349.
62. Quoted in Marvin Kalb and Bernard Kalb, *Kissinger* (Boston; Little, Brown. 1974), 120. According to the Kalbs, these words were spoken in the "first six months." Hersh, in *Price of Power*, 119, quotes Kissinger as having said "three months" to the Quakers.
63. Quoted in Isaacson, *Kissinger*, 165. In April 1969, however, Lake described the administration's strategy as one of "settlement or 'Vietnamizing' the conflict by 1971/72," which suggested that it was considering a decent-interval solution and an extended timetable for ending American intervention; Lake to Richard Sneider, April 17, 1969, folder: W. A. K. Lake File (Apr. 1969), box 1048, NSC: SF—LCF, NPM. But the reference is obscure, and he may have meant that the administration expected to achieve a mutual withdrawal of North Vietnamese and American forces in 1969 or 1970, which would be followed by a struggle between the South Vietnamese belligerents (with Saigon receiving indirect American assistance) that would be settled in Saigon's favor by 1971/72. Or it could have been the case that Lake was not privy to the real Nixinger strategy.
64. *WHY*, 262.
65. Quoted in Haldeman, *Ends of Power*. 81.
66. *HMD*, October 8, 1969.
67. Memo, Rita Hauser to Nixon, April 29, 1965. folder; Ex 6-1, Paris Peace Talks (sub: Vietnam) [1969-70), WHCF: SF, FO. NPM. Hauser was the American UN representative. See also Memo for the record, Daniel P. Moynihan, March 8, 1969, ibid. For more on Harriman, see Sieg, "W. Averell Harriman, Henry Cabot Lodge," 237, 249.
68. *WHY*, 261.
69. Ibid., 284.

14. Jacobs: Ngo Dinh Diem, the Impossible Ally

1. Frances FitzGerald, *Fire in the Lake: The* Vietnamese *and the Americans in Vietnam* (New York: Vintage, 1972), 5–8.
2. The Secretary of State to the Special Representative in Saigon, 4 April 1955, *FRUS, 1955-1957* (Washington, D.C.: Government Printing Office, 1985), 1:196–197.
3. Mendès-France cited in Collins Papers: Dulles to Collins/Dillon, 24 November 1954: Box 25, EL [Eisenhower Library].
4. The Ambassador in Saigon to the State Department, 4 July 1954, *FRUS, 1952–1954* (Washington, D.C.: Government Printing Office, 1982), 13:1460; Colby cited in Cecil B. Currey, *Edward Lansdale: The Unquiet American* (Boston: Houghton Mifflin, 1988), 152.
5. Hinh cited in Edward G. Lansdale, *In the Midst of Wars: An American's Mission to Southeast Asia* (New York: Harper & Row, 1972), 183.
6. Dulles and Southeast Asia Treaty Organization (SEATO) terms cited in David L. Anderson, *Trapped by Success: The Eisenhower Administration and Vietnam, 1953–1961* (New York: Columbia University Press, 1991), 71.
7. Dulles cited in George Kahin, *Intervention: How America Became Involved in Vietnam* (New York: Anchor Books, 1986), 71.
8. Collins Papers: Report on Indochina: A Report by Senator Mike Mansfield on a Study Mission to Vietnam, Laos, and Cambodia, 15 October 1954: Box 25, EL.
9. Dulles Papers, White House Memoranda Series: Memorandum of Conversation with the President, 30 October 1954: Box 1, EL.
10. Dulles cited in J. Lawton Collins, *Lightning Joe: An Autobiography* (Baton Rouge: Louisiana State University Press, 1979), 378.
11. Collins cited in Ellen J. Hammer, *A Death in November: America in Vietnam, 1963* (New York: Dutton, 1987), 71.
12. Collins Papers: Collins to Dulles, 13 November 1954: Box 25, EL.
13. Ely cited in Collins Papers: Collins to Dulles, 10 November 1954: Box 25, EL; Diem cited in the Ambassador in Vietnam to the Department of State, 10 November 1954, *FRUS, 1952–1954*, 13:2229–2230.

14. Collins Papers: Collins to Dulles, 13 November 1954: Box 31, EL.

15. Collins Papers: Staff Meeting, 1 January 1955: Box 25, EL.

16. Collins Papers: Collins to Dulles, 23 November 1954: Box 25, EL.

17. Collins Papers: Collins to Dulles, 13 December 1954: Box 25, EL; Collins to Dulles, 16 December 1954: Box 25, EL.

18. Collins Papers: Dulles to Collins, 24 December 1954: Box 25, EL.

19. White House Office, NSC Staff Papers, 1948–1961, OCB Central File Series: Draft Progress Report, 19 January 1955: Box 38, EL; the Special Representative in Saigon to the Department of State, 15 January 1955, *FRUS*, 1955–1957, 1:37–40.

20. The Secretary of State to the Department of State, 1 March 1955, *FRUS*, 1955–1957, 1:101–102; Transcript Dulles Non-attributable Conference, 1 March 1955, John Foster Dulles Papers, Seeley Mudd Library, Princeton University, Princeton, New Jersey [hereafter Dulles Papers], Box 98.

21. Collins Papers: Proclamation of the Binh Xuyen, Cao Dai, and Hoa Hao Sects at the Press Conference of Pope Pham Cong Tac, 4 March 1955: Box 30, EL.

22. Ely cited in the Special Representative in Saigon to the Department of State, 10 March 1955, *FRUS*, 1955–1957, 1:116–119; Collins Papers: Voice of the Unified Front of All the Nationalist Forces in Vietnam, 21 March 1955: Box 30, EL.

23. Collins Papers: Collins to Dulles, 24 March 1955: Box 31, EL; Broadcast Statement of Premier Ngo Dinh Diem on 24 March 1955, file 751G.00/3-2455, RG 59.

24. Collins Papers: Collins to Dulles, 29 March 1955: Box 31, EL.

25. Collins Papers: Collins to Dulles, 7 April 1955: Box 26, EL.

26. Eisenhower cited in Dulles Papers, Telephone Calls Series: John Foster Dulles to Allen Dulles, 1 April 1955: Box 3, EL.

27. Mansfield cited in Young to Dulles, 8 April 1955, file 751G.00/4-855, RG 59; Collins Papers: Collins to Dulles, 10 April 1955: Box 26, EL.

28. Sebald to Dulles, 23 April 1955, file 751G.00/4-2355, RG 59.

29. White House Office, Office of the Special Assistant for National Security Affairs, Records, 1952–1961, Special Assistant Series, Chronological Subseries: Memorandum for the Record: South Vietnam—General Joe Collins's Comments, 22 April 1955: Box 1, EL.

30. Mansfield cited in Gregory Alan Olson, *Mansfield and Vietnam: A Study in Rhetorical Adaptation* (East Lansing: Michigan State University Press, 1995), 59.

31. Young to Robertson, 30 April 1955, *United States–Vietnam Relations, 1945–1971* (Washington, D.C: Government Printing Office, 1971) [hereafter *U.S.-VN Relations*], 10:945–947.

32. Collins Papers: Dulles to Kidder/Dillon, 27 April 1955: Box 25, EL.

33. Dulles Papers, Telephone Calls Series: Dulles to Collins, 28 April 1955: Box 3, EL; Dwight D. Eisenhower, Papers as President of the United States, 1953–1961, Ann Whitman File, NSC Series: Memorandum of Discussion at the 246th Meeting of the National Security Council, Thursday, 28 April 1955: Box 6, EL.

34. Humphrey cited in "Conditions in South Vietnam," *Congressional Record* 101 (2 May 1955); 5288–5291; Dodd cited in "Collins's Removal as Aide Urged by Dodd," *Washington Post*, 2 May 1955.

35. "U.S. in Middle of Gang War," *U.S. News and World Report*, 13 May 1955, 39–41; Henry Luce, "Revolution in Vietnam," *Life*, 16 May 1955, 3; "Trouble in Vietnam," *New York Times*, 6 April 1955.

36. The Secretary of State to the Embassy in Vietnam, 1 May 1955, *FRUS, 1955–1957,* 1:344–345.

37. Faure cited in the Secretary of State to the Department of State, 8 May 1955, *FRUS, 1955–1957,* 1:375; the Secretary of State to the Department of State, 7 May 1955, *FRUS*, 1955–1957, 1:377.

38. Bonesteel memorandum, 9 May 1955, *U.S.-VN Relations*, 10:975.

15. Catton: Ngo Dinh Diem, Modernizer

1. B. B. Fall, *The Two Viet-Nams: A Political and Military Analysis,* 2nd rev. ed. (New York, 1967), p. 235.

2. For Vietnamese hagiographies, see Phan-Thanh-Nghi, *Dao-Duc Cach-Mang Cua Chi-Si Ngo-Dinh-Diem* (Saigon [?], 1956); *Than-The va Su-Nghiep Tong-Thong Ngo-Dinh-Diem* (Saigon [?], 1956); Phan Thanh, Nguyen-Huu-Tiep, *Ngo-Dinh-Diem: Salazar Viet-Nam.* (Saigon [?], 1957); and Presidency (RVN), *Ngo Dinh Diem of Viet-Nam* (Saigon, 1957). For quotations from the US media, see R. Scheer, *How the United States Got Involved in Vietnam* (Santa Barbara, 1965), pp. 38-44.

3. See many of the articles collected in *Cach Mang Mien Nam Nhat Dinh Thang Loi Nhung Phuc Tap, Lau Dai* (Hanoi, 1963); and Tran Van Giau, *Mien Nam Giu Vung Thanh Dong: Luoc Su Dong Bao Mien Nam Dau Tranh Chong My Va Tay Sai* (Hanoi, 1964), i. 35-8.

4. F. FitzGerald, *Fire in the Lake: The Vietnamese and the Americans in Vietnam* (New York, 1973), pp. 138-5.

5. The term is taken from A. Trawick Bouscaren, *The Last of the Mandarins: Diem of Vietnam* (Pittsburgh, 1965). Despite its title, this is an uncritical biography of Diem.

6. See, e.g., R. Buzzanco, *Masters of War: Military Dissent and Politics in the Vietnam Era* (Cambridge, 1996), p. 65; G. C. Herring, *America's Longest War: The United States and Vietnam, 1950-75,* 2nd ed. (New York, 1986), pp. 48-9, 64; G. Kolko,

Anatomy of a War: Vietnam, the United States, and the Modern Historical Experience (New York, 1985), pp. 83-4, 91; D. M. Shafer, *Deadly Paradigms: The Failure of US Counterinsurgency Policy* (Princeton, 1988), pp. 254-8; W. S. Turley, *The Second Indochina War: A Short Political and Military History, 1954-75* (New York, 1987), p. 13; F. X. Winters, *The Year of the Hare: America in Vietnam. January 25, 1963-February 15, 1964* (Athens, Ga., 1997), pp. 148, 156-60; and M. B. Young, *The Vietnam Wars, 1945-90* (New York, 1991), pp. 37–104.

7. Diem's interview with the North American Newspaper Alliance, 14 Aug. 1959, in Presidency (RVN), *Interviews of Ngo Dinh Diem* (Saigon, 1960). The best discussion of this topic is J. C. Donnell, 'Personalism in Vietnam', in *Problems of Freedom: South Vietnam since Independence*, ed. W. R. Fishel (New York, 1961), pp. 29–67.

8. Diem's address, 26 Oct. 1956, in Presidency (RVN), *Major Policy Speeches by President Ngo Dinh Diem*, 3rd ed. (Saigon, 1957), pp. 18-20; 'President Ngo Dinh Diem Addresses the Opening Session of the Second National Assembly', *News from Viet-Nam* (Embassy of Vietnam), 16 Oct. 1959, p. 4.

9. Commissariat General for Land Development (RVN), *The Work of Land Development in Viet Nam Up to June 30, 1959* (Saigon [?], n.d.), pp. 3-7.

10. For strategic considerations, see memo of con., 9 May 1957, *F[oreign] R[elations of the] U[nited] S[tates]*, 1955-7, i [Vietnam], 799-801. Saigon to state, 30 Aug. 1957, ibid., pp. 841-3; and memo of con., 20 Dec. 1957, ibid., pp. 888-94. For economic benefits, see *Work of Land Development*, pp. 4-6, 17-18. For psychological benefits, see Ngo Dinh Diem, 'Democratic Development in Vietnam', *Free China Review*, v (1955), 33-4; and Diem's 1957 address in Melbourne, in Presidency (RVN). *Toward Better Mutual Understanding*, 2nd ed. (Saigon, 1958), i. 30-1.

11. *Work of Land Development*, pp. 27-9 and attached maps and diagrams.

12. *Khu Tru Mat (Agrovilles)* (Saigon, 1960) [Ho Chi Minh City, Cuc Luu Tru II], [Van-Phong] B[o]-T[ruong tai Phu Tong-Thong], 517/1; Nguyen Khac Nhan, 'Policy of Key Rural Agrovilles', *Asian Culture*, iii (1961), 29-49.

13. For a case study, see J. J. Zasloff, *Rural Resettlement in Vietnam: An Agroville in Development* (Saigon [?], 1963).

14. Draft notes on the 1st mtg. of the presidential task force on Vietnam, 24 April 1961, *FRUS, 1961-3*, i.78.

15. Dai-Bieu Chanh-Phu tai Mien-Dong Nam-Phan to Quy Ong Tinh-Truong [TT], 20 Nov. 1959, [Ho Chi Minh City, Cuc Luu Tru II], [Tai Lieu Do] S[o] [Luu Tru Va] C[ong Bao Phu Thu Tuong Viet Nam Cong Hoa] 08 15266; Burns to chief, CATO, 22 March 1960 [Stanford, Hoover Institution], Lansdale Papers, folder 1182, correspondence, box 42; Dai-Bieu Chanh-Phu tai Mien-Dong Nam-Phan to Ong Tinh-Truong, 31 May 1960, SC 02 4308/2; Dai-Bieu Chanh-Phu tai Mien-Dong Nam-Phan to Ong Dong-Ly Van-Phong, Phu Tong-Thong, 1 Aug. 1960, SC 02 4308/2; Saigon to state, tel. 866, 20 Oct. 1960 [College Park, United States National Archives, Record Group 59], S[tate] D[epartment] D[ecimal] F[ile] 60-3, 751K.00/10-2060.

16. Saigon to state, air. G-505, 10 June 1961, SDDF 60-3, 751K.11/6-1061. For the punishment of corrupt officials, see Saigon to state, air. G-383, 18 March 1961, SDDF 60-3, 751K.00/3-1861; and Saigon to state, tel. 1887, 15 June 1961, SDDF 60-3, 751K.5-MSP/6-1561. For local elections, see 'Project for Important Structural Reform in Government Announced', *News from Viet-Nam*, Feb. 1961, p. 6 and Diem's comments in Ban Tom Tat Phien Hop Hoi-Dong Noi-Cac, 30 May 1961, SC 05 10.001.

17. W. Colby, with J. McCargar, *Lost Victory: A Firsthand Account of America's Sixteen-Year Involvement in Vietnam* (Chicago, 1989), pp. 32-3, 85-6, 99; Lansdale to Taylor, 21 Oct. 1961, *FRUS, 1961-3*, i. 412-15; CIA information report, 28 Nov. 1961, ibid., pp. 690-1. For the general influence of Marxist-Leninist concepts on the regime's thinking, see J. C. Donnell, 'Politics in South Vietnam: Doctrines of Authority in Conflict' (Ph.D. dissertation, Berkeley, 1964), pp. 224-8.

18. Saigon to state, des. 316, 24 Jan. 1961, SDDF 60-3, 751K.00/1-2461 (the observer was probably William Colby of the CIA); same to same, des. 422, 23 March 1961, SDDF 60-3, 751K.5/3-2361.

19. Ban Tom Tat Phien Hop Hoi-Dong Noi-Cac, 19 June 1961, SC 05 10.001; Tinh-Truong An giang to Bo-Truong Dac-Nhiem Phoi-Hop An-Ninh, 31 July 1961, SC 06 10618 (mentions instructions of 10 July regarding pacification plans); Saigon to state, tel. 181, 4 Aug. 1961, SDDF 60-3, 751K.00/8-461.

20. Bo-Truong Noi-Vu to TT, 5 Oct. 1961, BT 576.

21. TT Vinh Long to Ong Bo-Truong tai Phu Tong-Thong, 8 Sept. 1961, BT 577; TT Vinh Long, Phieu-Trinh Kinh De Tong-Thong Viet-Nam Cong-Hoa, 21 Oct. 1961, SC 03 5571/23.

22. McGarr to Felt, 1 Sept. 1961 [USNA], RG 334, MAAG Vietnam, adjutant general division 1961, 268 Training – Viet Nam Armed Forces, box 26, p. 8; Colby, *Lost Victory*, pp. 31-3, 85-92, 99-100

23. Colby, *Lost Victory*, p. 101. US plans included the 'Counterinsurgency Plan' of 1960-1; MAAG's 'Geographically Phased, National Level Operation Plan for Counterinsurgency' of Sept. 1961; and the US country team's 'Outline Plan for Counterinsurgency Operations', completed in Jan, 1962.

24. For the disagreements over the land development programme, see J. D. Montgomery, *The. Politics of Foreign Aid: American Experience in Southeast Asia* (New York, 1962), pp. 73-9 and W. Henderson, 'Opening New Lands and Villages: The Republic of Vietnam Land Development Program', *Problems of Freedom*, ed. Fishel, pp. 127-30, 134-5. For the planning of the agroville programme, see C. L. Cooper et al., *The American Experience with Pacification in Vietnam* (Arlington, 1972), iii. 139.

25. For Thompson's 1960 visit, see embassy, Saigon, to F[oreign] O[ffice], 5 Aug. 1960 [Public Record Office], F[oreign] O[ffice Records] 371/152790, DV1631/4. His recommendations to the palace in Nov. 1961 are in Department of Defense, *United States-Vietnam Relations, 1945-67*, xi (1971), 345–58.

26. Embassy Saigon, to FO, 28 Feb. 1962, FO 371/166701, DV1015/64; same to same, 12 June 1962, FO 371/166748, DV 1201/30; Lee to Jones, 26 July 1962, FO 371/166749, DV 1201/47; W. B. Rosson's comments, Carlisle Barracks, Pa., US Army Military History Institute, Rosson Papers, Senior Officers Oral History Program, iii. 135; D. J. Duncanson, *Government and Revolution in Vietnam* (New York, 1968), p. 314.

27. Bo-Truong Noi-Vu to Quy Ong Bo-Truong tai Phu Tong-Thong [et al.], 8 Jan. 1962, BT 576; Tom Trinh ve Ap chien luoc, SC 04 8676; Tong-Thong, Viet-Nam Cong-Hoa, Sac-Lenh so 11/TTP, 3 Feb. 1962, SC 14 1073.

28. *Press Interviews with President Ngo Dinh Diem, Political Counselor Ngo Dinh Nhu* (Saigon[?], 1963), p. 69.

29. Bo Truong Noi-Vu to Bo-Truong tai Phu Tong-Thong, 15 Dec. 1961, SG 03 5571/23. See also Nhu's address of 17 March 1962, *Ban Ghi Chep: [Nhung Buoi Noi Chuyen Than Mat Cua Ong Co Van Chinh Tri Ve Ap Chien Luoc*], i, SC 04 8676.

30. *Press Interviews,* p. 72.

31. Nhu's speech in Directorate General of Information (DGI) (RVN), *Viet Nam's Strategic Hamlets,* 2nd rev. ed. (Saigon, 1963), pp. 26-8; 'The Strategic Hamlet—In the Perspective of Vietnamese History', *Times of Viet Nam Magazine,* 28 Oct. 1962, pp. 34-7; Dinh Ro Vi-Tri Chinh-Sach Ap Chien-Luoc, 25 Sept. 1962, SC 25 956.

32. DGI (RVN), *Viet Nam's Strategic Hamlets,* 2nd rev. ed., p. 26; 'SH, The Quintessence Of Vietnamese Traditions—President Ngo', *Times of Viet Nam Magazine,* 21 April 1963, p. 2.

33. Nhu's talk in DGI (RVN), *Viet Nam's Strategic Hamlets*, 2nd rev. ed., pp. 25-38; 'SH, The Quintessence of Vietnamese Traditions—President Ngo', *Times of Viet Nam Magazine,* 21 April 1963, p. 2. The Vietnamese Communists' emphasis on struggle is discussed in D. Pike, *Viet Cong: The Organization and Techniques of the National Liberation Front of South Vietnam* (Cambridge, Mass., 1967), pp. 85-99.

34. Nguyen Van Chau, *Giong Lich-Su* (Saigon, 1961), pp. 7–9.

35. 'Muc-Dich: Xay-Dung Ap Chien-Luoc', *Chien Si,* Jan., Feb. 1962, p. 14; 'Ap Chien-Luoc', *Chien Si,* March 1962, p. 7; Nhu's speech, 19 March 1962, *Ban Ghi Chep,* ii, SC 03 5570.

36. Nhu's formulation was *Tam-tuc* (self-sufficiency) + *Tam-giac* (self-consciousness) = *Tam-Nhan* (Personalism); see Bien-Ban so 23 [Phien hop] U[y]-B[an] L[ien]-B[o] D[ac]-T[rach] A[p] C[hien]-L[uoc], 5 Oct. 1962 [Lubbock, TX, Indo-China Archive), GVN S[trat] H[ams], pp. 20-2.

37. Hoang Khanh, *Tim Hieu Quoc Sach Ap Chien Luoc* (Saigon, 1962), pp. 103-4; DGI (RVN), *Viet Nam's Strategic Hamlets,* 2nd rev. ed., p. 16.

38. Bien-Ban so 16 UBLBDTACL, 13 July 1962, GVN SH, pp. 10-13; *Press Interviews,* p. 63 (for the quotation). Nhu likened this dependency to a child's reliance on its parents (see his comments in a palace meeting on 2 Feb. 1962, *Ban Ghi Chep,* i, SC 04 8676).

39. Bien-Ban so 16 UBLBDTACL, 13 July 1962, GVN SH, pp. 18-19.

40. N. Sheehan, *A Bright Shining Lie: John Paul Vann and America in Vietnam* (New York, 1988), p. 50.

41. Nhu's address, 19 March 1962, *Ban Ghi Chep,* ii, SC 03 5570; DGI (RVN), *Viet Nam's Strategic Hamlets* (Saigon, 1963), p. 19.

42. DGI (RVN), *Viet Nam's Strategic Hamlets,* 2nd rev. ed., pp. 7-9, 17; Khanh, *Ap Chien Luce,* pp. 73-98. For Nhu's thoughts on NLF defections, see talk, Oct. 1961, *Ban Ghi Chep,* i, SC 04 8676. For the Diem quotation, see 'How to Beat the Reds in Southeast Asia: Interview With President Diem of South Vietnam', *US News & World Report,* 18 Feb. 1963, p. 71.

43. Nhu's address, Oct. 1962, to the national assembly, *Ban Ghi Chep,* ii, SC 03 5570; talk to cadres, July 1963, *Nhung Huan Thi* [*Cua Ong Co Van Chinh Tri Ve Quoc Sach Ap Chien Luoc tai Suoi Lo O*], v, SC 04 8676; 'The Strategic Hamlet and Military Policy', *Times of Viet Nam Magazine,* 28 Oct. 1962, pp. 38-9; embassy, Saigon, to external affairs, Canberra, sav. 34, 35, 9 April 1963, FO 371/170090, DV1015/24.

44. Bien-Ban so 6 UBLBDTACL, 23 March 1962, GVN SH, pp. 34-5.

45. Bien-Ban so 26 UBLBDTACL, 1 Nov. 1962, GVN SH, p. 26; Bo Cong Dan Vu, Tai-Lieu Hoc-Tap: Ap Chien Luoc, SC 03 5570/8; Khanh, *Ap Chien Luoc,* pp. 19-23, 87, 102-4; 'Worth Repeating', *Times of Viet Nam Magazine,* 28 Oct. 1962, p.3,

46. Bien-Ban so 6 UBLBDTACL, 23 March 1962, GVN SH, pp. 31-41.

47. Bien-Ban UBLBDTACL, 20 Jan. 1962, BT 491; Bien-Ban so 5 UBLBDTACL, 16 March 1962, GVN SH, p. 12.

48. S. Labin, *Vietnam: An Eye-Witness Account* (Springfield, Va., 1964), p. 55.

49. DGI (RVN), *Viet Nam's Strategic Hamlets,* 2nd rev. ed., pp. 14-15; Khanh, *Ap Chien Luoc,* pp. 136-61.

50. Bien-Ban so 9 UBLBDTACL, 13 April 1962, GVN SH, pp. 31-2; editorial, *Chi-Dao,* April 1962, pp. 1-3; 'Xay-Dung Mot Nen Kinh-Te Moi Cho Cac Ap Chien-Luoc', *Chan-Hung Kinh-Te,* 20 Dec. 1962, p. 25; 'Nam Qui-Mao La Nam Xay-Dung kinh-te nong-thon tren can-ban nhan-vi', *Chan-Hung Kinh-Te,* 17 Jan. 1963, pp. 10-11; DGI (RVN), *Viet Nam's Strategic Hamlets,* p. 19.

51. Nhu's comments at Thi Nghe, *Ban Ghi Chep,* ii, SC 03 5570; Pham Chung, *An Analysis of the Long-Range Military, Economic. Political, and Social Effects of the Strategic Hamlet Program in Viet Nam* (Washington, 1965), p. 241.

52. 'Strategic Hamlets to Keep the Roots in the Ground', *Times of Viet Nam Magazine,* 27 May 1962, p. 17.

53. For a summary of the relevant RVN decree that finalized these electoral guidelines, see Saigon to state, air. A-812, 20 June 1963 [USNA, RG 59], S[tate] D[epartment] S[ubject]-N[umeric] F[ile], POL 26-1 S VIET.

54. Bien-Ban so 9 UBLBDTACL, 13 April 1962, GVN SH, pp. 5-6.

55. Bien-Ban so 4 UBLBDTACL, 9 March 1962, GVN SH, pp. 10, 19; Bien-Ban so 6 UBLBDTACL, 23 March 1962, GVN SH, p. 37; Bien-Ban so 24 UBLBDTACL, 12 Oct. 1962, GVN SH, pp. 31-2; Nhu's address, 17 March 1962, *Ban Ghi Chep*, i, SC 04 8676; and that of 19 March 1962, *Ban Ghi Chep*, ii, SC 03 5570. For a foreign observer's view of the government's role in elections, see R. Scigliano, *South Vietnam: Nation under Stress* (Boston, 1964), p. 186.

56. For the official explanation and model set of communal rules, see *Huong Uoc* (Saigon, n.d.); and an example of a locally adapted set of rules in Saigon to state, air. A-318, 13 Dec. 1962, SDDF 60-3, 751K.5/12-1362.

57. For the issue of local misrule, see the comments by Tran Ngoc Chau in *The American Syndrome: An Interview with the BBC* (1991), Washington, Library of Congress Manuscripts Division, Vann-Sheehan Vietnam War Collection, folder 1, box 62, pp. 9-10. For the palace's thinking, see DGI (RVN), *Viet Nam's Strategic Hamlets*, p. 19; Nhu's talk, March 1962, *Ban Ghi Chep*, ii, SC 03 5570; and Bien-Ban so 9 UBLBDTACL, 13 April 1962, GVN SH, p. 21.

58. *Press Interviews*, p. 4; embassy, Saigon, to FO, 17 Jan. 1962, FO 371/166699, DV1015/26; Colby, *Lost Victory*, p. 86.

59. Excerpts from the inter-ministerial committee meeting, 1 March 1963, SDSNF, POL 26-1 S VIET; DGI (RVN), *Viet Nam's Strategic Hamlets*, 2nd rev. ed., p. 22.

60. 'Strategic Hamlets to Keep the Roots in the Ground', p. 4.

61. Bien-Ban so 7 UBLBDTACL, 30 March 1962, GVN SH, p. 31; Nhu's speech, March 1962, *Ban Ghi Chep*, ii, SC 03 5570; embassy, Saigon, to FO, 17 Jan. 1962, FO 371/166699, DV 1015/26.

62. Memo for the record, 14 Sept. 1962, *FRUS, 1961-3*, ii. 637.

63. Quoted in W.J. Rust and the editors of US News Books, *Kennedy in Vietnam* (New York, 1985), pp. 66-7.

64. See the plans drafted by the civic action official, Vo Qui Hy, esp. Ap Kien Thiet: Mot Chinh Sach Cach Mang Doi Song Nong Dan Va Phat Trien Kinh Te Nong Thon, 15 March 1962, SC 25 956.

65. Nhu's talk, Feb. 1962, *Ban Ghi Chep*, i, SC 04 8676; Bien-Ban so 3 UBLBDTACL, 2 March 1962, GVN SH, pp. 4-5; Bien-Ban so 16 UBLBDTACL, 13 July 1962, GVN SH, pp. 21-2.

66. Bien-Ban so 26 UBLBDTACL, 1 Nov. 1962, GVN SH, p. 23; Tong Thu-Ky Ban Thuong-Vu, UBLBDTACL, to Ong Co-Van Chanh-Tri, 15 Dec. 1962, BT 576.

67. Nhu's talk to a graduating class of the national institute of administration, *Chan-Hung Kink-Te*, 9 May 1963, pp. 3-6; and to officials at Suoi Lo-O, *Chan-Hung Kinh-Te*, 30 May 1963, pp. 3-9.

68. Pike, *Viet Cong*, pp. 66-7.

69. Bien-Ban so 5 UBLBDTACL, 16 March 1962, GVN SH, pp. 11-12; Bien-Ban so 16 UBLBDTACL, 13 July 1962, GVN SH, pp. 10-13; 'Vai-tro Kinh-te Cua Ap Chien-Luoc', *Chan-Hung Kinh-Te*, 17 April 1963, p. 22; Tong Thu-Ky Ban Thuong-Vu, UBLBDTACL, to Ong Co-Van Chanh-Tri, 15 Dec. 1962, BT 576.

70. DGI (RVN), *Viet Nam's Strategic Hamlets*, pp. 11-12; 'Vai-tro Kinh-te Cua Ap Chien-Luoc', *Chan-Hung Kinh-Te*, 17 April 1963, p. 22; Truong Tieu-Ban Thuong-Vu, UBLBDTACL, to Ong Dong-Ly Van-Phong Bo-Truong tai Phu Tong-Thong, 30 May 1963, BT 576.

71. Nguyen Dang Thuc, *Democracy in Traditional Vietnamese Society* (Saigon[?], 1961), pp. 5-6. See also DGI (RVN), *Viet Nam's Strategic Hamlets*, pp. 3-4.

72. For references by the Ngos to this goal, see Thompson to McGhie, 27 Nov. 1961, FO 371/160119, DV 1015/258; embassy, Saigon, to FO, 1 Aug. 1962, FO 371/166706, DV 1015/166; and M. Higgins, *Our Vietnam Nightmare* (New York, 1965), pp. 166-7, 173.

73. Ngo Dinh Diem, 'Democratic Development in Vietnam', pp. 25-36.

74. Higgins, *Vietnam Nightmare*, p. 166.

75. Saigon to state, tel. 313, 18 Sept. 1962, SDDF 60-3, 751 K.00/9-1862; M. Maneli, *War of the Vanquished* (New York, 1971), p. 145.

76. Nhu's talk to cadres, 20 July 1963, *Nhung Huan Thi*, v, SC 04 8676. Diem's comments are in Saigon to state, air. A-574, 1 April 1963, SDSNF, POL 15-1 S VIET; and in 'How to Beat the Reds in Southeast Asia', p. 72.

77. 'Strategic Hamlets for Democracy and Development', *Times of Viet Nam Magazine, 28* Oct. 1962, pp. 30-2; DGI (RVN), *Viet Nam's Strategic Hamlets*, p. 21; Bien-Ban so 20 UBLBDTACL, 7 Sept. 1962, GVN SH, pp. 5-7.

78. Ho Quy Ba, *Quoc Sach Ap Chien Luoc cua My-Diem* (Hanoi, 1962), pp. 31-40; Liberation Editions, *Outlines of 'Strategic Hamlets'* (n.p., 1963).

79. Tran Van Giau, *Mien Nam Giu Vung Thanh Dong* (Hanoi, 1966), ii. 157-65.

80. For a more detailed analysis, see P. E. Catton, 'Parallel Agendas: The Ngo Dinh Diem Regime, the United States, and the Strategic Hamlet Program, 1961-1963" (Ph.D. dissertation, Ohio, 1998).

81. For settlements in the Mekong Delta, see J. B. Hendry, *The Small World of Khanh Hau* (Chicago, 1964), esp. pp. 6-7, 248-62; G. C. Hickey, *Village in Vietnam* (New Haven, 1964), esp. pp. 276-85; and P. Brocheux, *The Mekong Delta: Ecology, Economy, and Revolution, 1860-1960* (Madison, 1995). Contrast with evidence of the corporate identity of a northern Vietnamese village in Hy V. Luong, *Revolution in the Village: Tradition and Transformation in North Vietnam, 1925-88* (Honolulu, 1992).

82. J. Breman, *The Shattered Image: Construction and Deconstruction of the Village in Colonial Asia* (Dordrecht and Providence, 1988), p. 38.

16. Duiker: The Foreign Policy of North Vietnam

1. For a brief discussion of the traditional Sino-Vietnamese relationship, see King C. Chen's classic study, *Vietnam and China, 1938–1954* (Princeton NJ: Princeton University Press, 1969).

2. For an overview of this period, see Huynh Kim Khanh, *Vietnamese Communism, 1925–1945* (Ithaca, NY: Cornell University Press, 1982).

3. Details of the establishment of this arrangement between the Vietminh Front and U.S. military intelligence units in South China are provided in Archimedes L. A. Patti, *Why Viet Nam? Prelude to America's Albatross* (Berkeley: University of California Press, 1980).

4. Ho Chi Minh's efforts at the close of World War II to deny his past experience as an agent of the Comintern are well known. Only in the late 1950s, when the DRV had become a loyal member of the socialist camp, did he disclose his real identity. See my *Ho Chi Minh: A Life* (New York: Hyperion Press, 2000), especially chapters 9, 10, and 14.

5. Ho's speech, which was presented to the ICP Central Committee in mid-August, was eventually included in a resolution entitled "Nghi quyet cua Toan quoc Hoi nghi Dang Cong san Dong duong" (Resolution of the national conference of the Indochinese Communist Party) and printed in *Van kien Dang* (1930–1945) (Party Documents [1930–1945]), vol. 3 (Hanoi: Ban Nghien cuu lich su Dang Truong uong, 1977), 412–417.

6. The letter was written in August 1945. See Charles Fenn, *Ho Chi Minh: A Biographical Introduction* (New York: Scribners, 1973), 8.

7. The DRV's abortive overtures to the United States are discussed in Mark Bradley's "An Improbable Opportunity: America and the Democratic Republic of Vietnam's 1947 Initiative," in Jayne S. Werner and Luu Doan Huynh eds., *The Vietnam War: Vietnamese and American Perceptions* (Armonk, NY: M.E. Sharpe, 1993), 3–23.

8. For his analysis, see Truong Chinh, *The Resistance Will Win*, translated in *Truong Chinh: Selected Writings* (Hanoi: Foreign Languages Press, 1977).

9. Moscow also agreed for the first time to grant diplomatic recognition to the DRV, but Stalin made it clear that China would be assigned primary responsibility for carrying out socialist bloc assistance to the DRV. For a discussion and references, see my *Ho Chi Minh*, 422.

10. Cited in ibid., 450.

11. The interview, which appeared in the journal *Expressen*, was summarized in U.S. Embassy (Stockholm) to Department of State, November 29, 1953, in Record Group (RG) 59, U.S. National Archives. For a Vietnamese-language version, see *Ho Chi Minh Toan Tap* (The complete writings of Ho Chi Minh), 1st ed., (Hanoi: Su that, 1980–1989), vol. 6, 494–496. (Hereafter cited as *Toan Tap*.)

12. For a discussion, see Qiang Zhai, *China and the Vietnam Wars, 1950–1975* (Chapel Hill: University of North Carolina Press, 2000), 60–62.

13. Report to the Sixth Plenum, in *Ho Chi Minh: Selected Writings* (Hanoi: Foreign Languages Press, 1977), 181–183.

14. Ho's speech is printed *in Toan Tap*, vol. 1, vol. 7, 286–289.

15. Cited in *Cuoc khang chien chong My cuu nuoc 1954–1975* (The Anti-U.S. War of National Salvation, 1954–1975) (Hanoi: Quan doi Nhan dan, 1980), 35.

16. Ibid., 49–50.

17. Ang Cheng Guan, *Vietnamese Communists Relations with China and the Second Indochina Conflict, 1956–1962* (Jefferson, NC: McFarland, 1997), 86–87.

18. Zhai, *China and the Vietnam Wars*, 88, 90–91.

19. Le Duan, *Thu Vao Nam* (Letters to the South) (Hanoi: Su That, 1986), 63–66.

20. Robert Brigham, *Guerrilla Diplomacy: The NLF's Foreign Relations and the Viet Nam War* (Ithaca, NY: Cornell University Press, 1999), 47–48.

21. For a discussion of the decision and its domestic and foreign policy consequences, with citations, see my *Ho Chi Minh: A Life*, 534–539.

22. Zhai, *China and the Vietnam Wars*, 132–133; Ilya Gaiduk, *The Soviet Union and the Vietnam War* (Chicago: Ivan R. Dee, 1996), 13–14.

23. During his visit to Hanoi in February 1965, Kosygin did warn his hosts not to provoke the United States. Although the warning had little immediate effect—the Viet Cong attack on Pleiku took place shortly afterward—Soviet leaders were generally confident that pragmatists within the DRV would contain the war to the South. Gaiduk, *Soviet Union*, 67.

24. For a discussion of this issue between Vietnamese and American representatives thirty years later, see Robert S. McNamara, James G. Blight, and Robert K. Brigham, *Argument Without End: In Search of Answers to the Vietnam Tragedy* (New York: Public Affairs, 1999), 224–232.

25. Duan, *Thu Vao Nam*, letter to Xuan, May 1965. Brigham, *Guerrilla Diplomacy*, 44–48.

26. Zhai, *China and the Vietnam Wars*, 168.

27. Gaiduk, *Soviet Union*, 17.

28. See the illuminating discussion in Qiang Zhai, *China and the Vietnam Wars, 1950–1975*, 134–139.

29. The "stab in the back" remark was by Vo Nguyen Giap. See Douglas Pike, *Vietnam and the Soviet Union: Anatomy of an Alliance* (Boulder, CO: Westview, 1987), 87.

30. Donald Zagoria, *Vietnam Triangle* (New York: Pegasus, 1967), 84.

31. Zhai, *China and the Vietnam Wars, 1950–1975,* 138–139.

32. As for the Red Guards, Mao Zedong told Pham Van Dong, "just hand them over to us." Odd Arne Westad et al., *77 Conversations Between Chinese and Foreign Leaders on the Wars in Indochina, 1964–1977* (Washington, DC: Woodrow Wilson Center, 1998), 96, 104.

33. For a discussion, see McNamara et al., *Argument Without End,* 292–301.

34. Duan's comment, which initially had been made on an earlier occasion, is from *Thu Vao Nam,* letter to Xuan [Nguyen Chi Thanh], February 1965.

35. Westad et al., *77 Conversations,* 125–129.

36. Ibid., 140, 143.

37. Ibid., 159.

38. Zhai, *China and the Vietnam Wars,* 194–197.

39. Westad et al., *77 Conversations,* 189–191. The meaning of this conversation is admittedly somewhat ambiguous, since both Zhou and his Vietnamese visitors insisted on the importance of party leadership over the government in the South, something that had certainly not been achieved in the Paris agreement. According to Duan, the current government in Saigon could exist for ten to fifteen years before being transformed into a socialist entity.

40. The most lengthy account of Hanoi's complaints against its northern neighbor appeared in Hanoi's White Paper entitled *The Truth About Vietnam-Chinese Relations over the Last Thirty Years* (Hanoi: Ministry of Foreign Affairs, 1979).

23. Gaiduk: The Soviet Union and American Escalation

1. *Pravda,* March 5, 1965.

2. L. V. Kotov and R. S. Yegorov, eds., *Militant Solidarity, Fraternal Assistance* (Moscow, 1970), p. 49; *Pravda,* March 13, 1965.

3. *Ibid.,* p. 50.

4. *Pravda,* March 21, 1965.

5. Parker, *Vietnam,* p. 83.

6. *Pravda,* March 24, 1965.

7. Telegram, Foy Kohler to Washington, March 23, 1965. Johnson Library, NSF, Country File, Vietnam, box 46.

8. Memorandum of Conversation, Shcherbakov-Hoang Van Loi, March 26, 1965. SCCD [Strategic Center for Contemporary Documentation, Moscow], f. 5, op. 50, d. 721, p. 117.

9. Memorandum of Conversation between Petrov, an interpreter at the Soviet embassy in the DRV, and a researcher at the Institute of Economy in Hanoi, June 6, 1965. *Ibid.,* p. 178.

10. *Soviet Union–Vietnam,* pp. 103–104, 105; *Pravda,* April 18, 1965.

11. *Pravda,* April 20, 1965.

12. Special Memorandum No. 11-65, "Future Soviet Moves in Vietnam," Office of National Estimates, April 27, 1965. Johnson Library, NSF, Country File, Vietnam, vol. 33, box 16.

13. Memorandum, "The Arrival of Soviet Military Aid to the DRV May Be Imminent," May 7, 1965. Johnson Library, NSF, Country File, Vietnam, Special Intelligence Material, vol. 6(B), box 50.

14. Intelligence Memorandum, "Asian Communist and Soviet Views on the War in Vietnam," May 25, 1965. *Ibid.*

15. Department of State to Moscow, May 26, 1965. NSA, V-16, Vietnam, Kahin Donation, box 4. State Department analysts suggested in this cable that by providing Hanoi with such sophisticated weaponry Moscow hoped to maintain its position in the DRV and to acquire new leverage there, although they were uncertain whether the Soviets would use this leverage to persuade Hanoi to negotiate.

16. Harold Wilson, *The Labour Government, 1964–1970: A Personal Record* (London, 1971), p. 85. Gromyko's position with regard to a Geneva-like international conference on Vietnam was not surprising if one takes into account Hanoi's refusal to agree to Soviet proposals made in February to assist in the convocation of such a conference. The standard North Vietnamese reply to the Soviet suggestion was that the time had not yet come for a conference.

17. Memorandum for the President, Personal and Sensitive, March 6, 1965. Johnson Library, NSF, Memos to the President, McGeorge Bundy, vol. 9, box 3.

18. NSA, V-16, Vietnam, Kahin Donation, box 4. They argued that U.S. acceptance of the idea of the conference on Cambodia "would be a 'victory' for the Soviets (who need such a victory, and *whose victory we need, if they are to [be] a useful counter-weight to the Chicoms* [Chinese Communists] *in Southeast Asia*). . . ." Emphasis added.

19. See, for example: Kahin, *Intervention;* Wallace J. Thies, *When Governments Collide: Coercion and Diplomacy in the Vietnam Conflict, 1964–1968* (Berkeley, 1980); Brian VanDeMark, *Into the Quagmire: Lyndon Johnson and the Escalation of*

the Vietnam War (New York, 1991).

20. VanDeMark, *Into the Quagmire,* p. 134.

21. Cable, Washington to Saigon, May 10, 1965. Johnson Library, NSF, NSC History, Deployment of Major U.S. Forces to Vietnam, vol. 4. See also Herring, *Secret Diplomacy of the Vietnam War,* p. 54.

22. *Ibid.,* p. 57.

23. *Ibid.,* p. 58. Emphasis added.

24. First Secretary of the USSR Embassy to the DRV G. Zverev to Moscow, July 8, 1965. SCCD, f. 5, op. 50, d. 721, p. 181.

25. Herring, *Secret Diplomacy of the Vietnam War,* p. 63.

26. Ibid., p. 63.

27. Ibid., p. 67.

28. Ibid., p. 69.

29. On the shift in Hanoi's negotiating stance in May, see VanDeMark, *Into the Quagmire,* pp. 137–138.

30. Gibbons, *US. Government and Vietnam War,* p. 255.

31. *Pravda,* June 5, 1965.

32. *Pravda,* July 13, 1965.

33. *Pravda,* July 24, 1965.

34. Moscow not only knew that its weaponry was being transferred to Viet Cong combat units, it also knew what routes Hanoi was using. On May 3, 1965, the Main Intelligence Directorate (GRU) of the Soviet General Staff informed the CC International Department that a supply of arms and ammunition for "regular troops and guerrilla detachments" under command of the NLFSV was found in depots located in Vinh and Dong Hoi provinces of the DRV. Weapons were being delivered by land through Laotian territory under control of the Pathet Lao; by air through a Cambodian airfield near the South Vietnamese border; and by sea. They were stored in jungle areas controlled by the Liberation Front. GRU to Central Committee, May 3, 1965. SCCD, f. 5, op. 50, d. 721, p. 120.

35. *Pravda,* June 4, 1965.

36. Report on the negotiations between German Chancellor Erhard and Foreign Minister Fanfani in the U.S.A. and on the latter's talks in France, June 1965. SCCD, f. 5, op. 50, d. 690, p. 93.

37. Still-classified report of August 20, 1965, no. 2806. SCCD, First Sector, "Special Dossier." One interesting fact laid a foundation for Soviet concerns. As General William Westmoreland, former head of the U.S. Military Assistance Command in Vietnam, noted during a Vietnam Symposium in 1991, when American marines came to Danang in March 1965 they brought eight-inch howitzers that were nuclear-capable, though they did not have nuclear warheads. Therefore it was easy for the United States, once it was decided, to change the character of the war to a nuclear one. See Ted Gittinger, ed., *The Johnson Years: A Vietnam Roundtable* (Austin, Tex., 1993), p. 64.

38. Foy Kohler to Washington, June 25, 1965. Johnson Library, NSF, Country File, Vietnam, vol. 36, box 19.

39. *Ibid.*

40. *Ibid.*

41. Memorandum, H. Sonnenfeldt to L. Thompson, June 26, 1965, "Personal and Confidential." Library of Congress, W. Averell Harriman Papers, Special Files: Public Service, Trips and Missions, box 546.

42. Memorandum of Conversation, Rusk-Dobrynin, July 3, 1965. Johnson Library, NSF, Memos to the President, McGeorge Bundy, vol. 12, box 4. Emphasis added.

43. Rudy Abramson, *Spanning the Century: The Life of W. Averell Harriman, 1891–1986* (New York, 1992), p. 628.

44. *Ibid.,* p. 638.

45. Telephone Conversation, Harriman-McCloy, October 19, 1964. Harriman Papers, Special Files: Public Service, Chronological File, box 583.

46. Memorandum of Telephone Conversation, Harriman-Dobrynin, June 29, 1965. *Ibid.*

47. *Ibid.*

48. Johnson Library, NSF, Memos to the President, McGeorge Bundy, vol. 12, box 4.

49. Memorandum, "Governor Harriman's Trip," from Special Assistant Monteagle Stearns to Assistant Secretary of State for Public Affairs James L. Greenfield, July 6, 1965. Harriman Papers, box 546.

50. Telegram, U.S. Embassy in France to State Department, July 8, 1965. *Ibid.,* Chronological File, box 575.

51. Abramson, *Spanning the Century,* p. 638.

52. *The Johnson Presidential Press Conferences,* Vol. 1 (Stanfordville, N.Y., 1978), p. 342.

53. *Pravda,* July 16, 22, 1965.

54. Telegram, Harriman to Washington, July 23, 1965. Harriman Papers, Trips and Missions, box 546. See also Harriman's memorandum for the president and the secretary of state with excised portions on China, Germany, and Vietnam, in Johnson Library, NSF, Country File, Vietnam, Harriman Talks on Vietnam (July and August 1965), box 193.

55. Harriman's report on his conversation with Yugoslavian Foreign Minister Marko Nikezic, July 27, 1965. Harriman Papers, Trips and Missions, box 546.

56. Harriman's report for Johnson and Rusk. *Ibid.*

57. *Ibid.*

58. McG. Bundy to the President, July 15, 1965. Johnson Library, NSF, Memos to the President, McG. Bundy, vol. 12, box 4.

59. Memorandum, Thomas L. Hughes to Secretary Rusk "Kosygin's Suggestion of an American Counter Proposal to the Four Points," July 24, 1965. Harriman Papers, Trips and Missions, box 546.

60. Memorandum of Conversation, Harriman-Tito, July 28, 1965. Harriman Papers, Trips and Missions, box 546.

61. Gibbons, *U.S. Government and Vietnam War*, pp. 399–407.

62. *Ibid.*, p. 438.

63. Telegram, Kohler to Washington, August 6, 1965. Harriman Papers, Trips and Missions, box 546.

24. Qiang: China and the American Escalation

1. Herring, *America's Longest War*, 131–33.

2. Sandra Taylor, "Laos," 73–90; Timothy Castle, *At War in the Shadow of Vietnam*, 70–72; Prados, *Hidden History of the Vietnam War*, 232.

3. *Zhou waijiao dashiji*, 410–11.

4. Zhou's talk with Ne Win, July 10,1964, *Zhou nianpu*, 2:655.

5. *Zhou waijiao dashiji*, 411. See also *Zhou nianpu*, 2:650.

6. Quoted in Li Danhui, "ZhongSu guanxi yu Zhongguo de yuanYue kangMei," 112.

7. Xue Mouhong and Pei Jianzhang, *Dangdai Zhongguo waijiao*, 159; Qu Aiguo, Bao Mingrong, and Xiao Zuyao, *YuanYue kangMei*, 9.

8. Present at the meetings were Zhou Enlai, Chen Yi, Wu Xiuquan, Yang Chengwu, and Tong Xiaopeng of the CCP; Ho Chi Minh, Le Duan, Truong Chinh, Pham Van Dong, Vo Nguyen Giap, Nguyen Chi Thanh, Hoang Van Hoan, and Van Tien Dung ofthe VWP; and Kaysone Phomvihane, Prince Souphanouvong, Nouhak Phoumsavan, and Phoumi Vongvichit of the LPP (*Zhou waijiao dashiji*, 413; Tong Xiaopeng, *Fengyu sishinian*, 2:220–21).

9. In July 1964, Mao, Liu Shaoqi, and Zhou Enlai instructed that China should increase the supply of military materials to the Pathet Lao and be ready to cover all the logistical needs of the Pathet Lao forces. See Han Huaizhi and Tan Jingqiao, *Dangdai Zhongguo jundui de junshi gongzuo*, 1:560.

10. Li Ke and Hao Shengzhang, *Wenhua dageming zhong de renmin jiefangjun*, 408; Qu Aiguo, Bao Mingrong, and Xiao Zuyao, *YuanYue kangMei*, 9.

11. "77 Conversations," 74.

12. Wang Dinglie and Lin Hu, *Dangdai Zhongguo longjun*, 384; Qu Aiguo, Bao Mingrong, and Xiao Zuyao, *YuanYue kangMei*, 10; Chen Jian, "China's Involvement in the Vietnam War," 364.

13. Whiting, "How We Almost Went to War with China," 76; Gurtov and Byong-Moo Hwang, *China under Threat*, 160–61.

14. Li Ke, "Zhongguo renmin yuanYue kangMei de yeji biaobing qingshi," 30.

15. Mao's talk with Pham Van Dong and Hoang Van Hoan, Oct. 5, 1964, in "77 Conversations," 74–77.

16. Gurtov and Byong-Moo Hwang, *China under Threat*, 162; Herring, *America's Longest War*, 143–45.

17. Han Huaizhi and Tan Jingqiao, *Dangdai Zhongguo jundui de junshi gongzuo*, 1:539–40; Li Ke and Hao Shengzhang, *Wenhua dageming zhong de renmin jiefangjun*, 415; Guo Ming, *ZhongYue guanxi yanbian sishinian*, 69–70; Li Ke, "Zhongguo renmin yuanYue kangMei de yeji biaobing qingshi," 31.

18. Han Huaizhi and Tan Jingqiao, *Dangdai Zhongguo jundui de junshi gongzuo*, 1:539–40; Wang Xiangen, *YuanYue kangMei shilu*, 44; Li Ke, "Zhongguo renmin yuanYue kangMei de yeji biaobing qingshi," 31.

19. Xue Mouhong and Pei Jianzhang, *Dangdai Zhongguo waijiao*, 161.

20. Wang Xiangen, *YuanYue kangMei shilu, 45.*

21. Ibid., 35, 44; Li Ke and Hao Shengzhang, *Wenhua dageming zhong de renmin jiefangjun*, 422. R. B. Smith dates the Ho-Mao meeting at May 16–17. His source is the diary of Ho's personal secretary. See R. B. Smith, *International History of the Vietnam War*, 3:139.

22. Wang Xiangen, *YuanYue kangMei shilu*, 46–48; the CCP Central Documentary Research Department and the PLA Military Science Academy, *Zhou Bnlai junshi wenxuan*, 4:527– 29.

23. Li Ke and Hao Shengzhang, *Wenhua dageming zhong de renmin jiefangjun*, 417.

24. *White Paper*, 33. According to Luu Doan Huynh, a senior research fellow at the International Relations Institute of the Ministry of Foreign Affairs of Vietnam, Beijing informed Hanoi in June 1965 that it would not be able to defend North Vietnam from U.S. air attacks. Quoted in Whiting, "China's Role in the Vietnam War," 71–76.

25. *Beijing Review*, Nov. 30, 1979, 14; Xue Mouhong and Pei Jianzhang, *Dangdai Zhongguo waijiao*, 161; Qu Aiguo, Bao Mingrong, and Xiao Zuyao, *YuanYue kangMei*, 12.

26. My interview with researchers at the PLA Military Science Academy, Beijing, July 2, 1996.

27. Guo Ming, *ZhongYue guanxi yanbian sishinian*, 71; Li Ke and Hao Shengzhang, *Wenhua dageming zhong de renmin*

jiefangjun, 427.

28. Li Ke and Hao Shengzhang, *Wenhua dageming zhong de renmin jiefangjun,* 410–11.

29. *Mao wengao,* 11:478.

30. Li Ke and Hao Shengzhang, *Wenhua dageming zhong de renmin jiefangjun,* 410.

31. Ibid., 412–14.

32. Li Ke, "Zhongguo renmin yuanYue kangMei de yeji biaobing qingshi," 31; Guo Ming, *ZhongYue guanxi yanbian sishinian,* 69.

33. According to the French scholar Marie Alexandrine Martin, on November 25, 1965, General Lon Nol, chief of staff of the Royal Khmer armed forces, visited Beijing on Sihanouk's orders and concluded with Luo Ruiqing a military treaty, which stipulated: "(1) Cambodia would permit the passage and the refuge of Vietnamese combatants in the border regions, granting them protection if necessary and permitting them to establish command posts; (2) Cambodia would permit the passage of material coming from China and intended for Vietnam." See Martin, *Cambodia,* 92–93. For a Chinese account of Beijing's use of Sihanoukville to send military supplies to the NLF between 1966 and 1967, see Kang Daisha, "Zai Jianpuzhai de rizi," 482–83. Kang Daisha is the wife of Chen Shuliang, who was China's ambassador to Cambodia between 1962 and 1967.

34. Gilks and Segal, *China and the Arms Trade,* 50.

35. Sihanouk worked out an arrangement with Beijing and Hanoi in 1964 to retain 10 percent of the Chinese weapons delivered to the Vietnamese through Sihanoukville. Additional fees were charged for transporting food and other goods to the Vietnamese border in Cambodian army trucks and private vehicles contracted for that purpose. Many officers who had profited by trading with the Vietnamese Communists later supported General Lon Nol's coup against Sihanouk in 1970. See Chanda, *Brother Enemy,* 420, and Chandler, *Tragedy of Cambodian History,* 140.

36. Li Ke and Hao Shengzhang, *Wenhua dageming zhong de renmin jiefangjun,* 416; Chen Jian, "China's Involvement in the Vietnam War," 378–79.

37. Whiting, *Chinese Calculus of Deterrence,* 186; Whiting, "Forecasting Chinese Foreign Policy," 506–23.

38. Quoted in Schulzinger, "Johnson Administration, China, and the Vietnam War," 149–50.

39. *Zhou waijiao dashiji,* 445; *Zhou nianpu,* 2:723; Xue Mouhong and Pei Jianzhang, *Dang-dai Zhongguo waijiao,* 160–61.

40. The strains in U.S.-Pakistani relations as a result of Karachi's deepening ties to Beijing between 1964 and 1965 are covered in detail in McMahon, *Cold War on the Periphery,* 309–24.

41. *Zhou nianpu,* 2:736.

42. Editorial note, *FRUS, 1964–1968,* 2:700–701.

43. Bundy to Rusk, June 5, 1965, ibid., 729. See also Schulzinger, "Johnson Administration, China, and the Vietnam War," 150. On William Bundy's role in the making of U.S. policy toward Vietnam, see Bird, *Color of Truth.*

44. Notes of meeting, July 22, 1965, in *FRUS, 1964–1968,* 3:215. See also Schulzinger, "Johnson Administration, China, and the Vietnam War," 151.

45. Garver, "Chinese Threat in the Vietnam War," 75.

46. Kenneth Young, *Negotiating with the Chinese Communists,* 270; Rogers, "Sino-American Relations and the Vietnam War," 298.

47. Schulzinger, "Johnson Administration, China, and the Vietnam War," 150; Rogers, "Sino-American Relations and the Vietnam War," 310–11. According to Anatoly Dobrynin, the Soviet ambassador to the United States, Walt Rostow, President Johnson's national security adviser, told him in June 1966 that a tacit understanding had been established between Washington and Beijing: "The United States would not attack or bomb mainland China, and China would at least not use its armed forces to interfere in the Vietnam War" (*In Confidence,* 142).

48. For Mao's view of the United States, see his January 12, 1964, statement in support of the struggle of the Panamanian people in *Mao wengao,* 11:6–7.

49. Quoted in Sun Dongsheng, "Woguo jingji jianshe zhanlue bujiu de dazhuanbian," 44.

50. Ma Qibin et al., *Zhongguo gongchandang zhizheng sishinian,* 248; *Mao wengao,* 11:103–4.

51. *Mao wengao,* 11:103–4.

52. Mao's talk with Pham Van Dong, Nov. 17, 1968, *Mao waijiao wenxuan,* 582.

53. Mao to Wang Dongxing, Aug. 6, 1964, *Mao wengao,* 11:120.

54. Yuan Dejin, "Lun xinZhongguo chengli hou Mao Zedong zhanzheng yu heping lilun de yanbian," 36.

55. On the origins, development, and consequences of the Third Front, see Naughton, "Third Front," 351–86.

56. For the text of the report, see *Dangde wenxian,* no. 3 (1995): 34–35.

57. Mao to Luo and Yang, Aug. 12,1964, ibid., 33. See also *Mao wengao,* 11:126–27.

58. For the text of the Special Committee report of August 19, 1964, see *Dangde wenxian,* no. 3 (1995): 33–34.

59. Mao's remarks are quoted in Sun Dongsheng, "Woguo jingji jianshe zhanlue bujiu de dazhuanbian," 45.

60. Ibid., 44.

61. Naughton, "Third Front," 368.

62. Mao's talk with He Long, Luo Ruiqing, and Yang Chengwu, Apr. 28, 1965, in *Mao junshi wenji,* 6:404.

63. For Snow's version of his talk with Mao, see Snow, *Long Revolution,* 215–16. For the Chinese version, see *Mao waijiao wenxuan,* 544–62.

64. Li Ke and Hao Shengzhang, *Wenhua dageming zhong de renmin jiefangjun,* 341.

65. Ibid., 341–42; *Mao junshi wenji,* 6:403.

66. Lin Hu, *Kunjun shi,* 188.

67. *Liu nianpu,* 2:618.

68. *Mao wengao,* 11:359–60.

69. Zhou's talk with Spiro Koleka, May 9, 1965, *Zhou waijiao dashiji,* 455.

70. Liu Shaoqi's speech at the war planning meeting of the Central Military Commission, May 19, 1965, in *Dangde wenxian,* no. 3 (1995): 40.

71. The CCP Central Documentary Research Department, *Zhu De nianpu,* 537–38.

72. Ra'anan, "Peking's Foreign Policy 'Debate,'" 23–71; Zagoria, "Strategic Debate in Peking," 237–68; Yahuda, "Kremlinology and the Chinese Strategic Debate," 32–75; Harding, "Making of Chinese Military Power," 361–85; Lieberthal, "Great Leap Forward and the Split in the Yan'an Leadership," 129–30.

73. Barry Naughton has made a similar criticism in "Third Front," 370–71.

74. Lin Biao, "Long Live the Victory of People's War," 9–30.

75. Xu Yan, *Junshijia Mao Zedong,* 149; Huang Yao, *Sanci danan busi de Luo Ruiqing Dajiang,* 263, 265, 270–71. This book is based on sources from the Central Archives, the PLA General Staff Archives, and the Ministry of Public Security Archives.

76. On the Luo-Lin dispute, see Huang Yao, *Sanci danan busi de Luo Ruiqing Dajiang,* chs. 24–34, and Huang Yao and Zhang Mingzhe, *Luo Ruiqing zhuan,* chs. 13–15. Roderick MacFarquhar also reports that he has found no evidence that views on Vietnam policy played any role in the purge of officials in 1965 (*Origins of the Cultural Revolution,* 3:377).

77. For a critique of the Western assumption that politics was about policy in China, see Teiwes and Sun, *Tragedy of Lin Biao,* 164–65.

78. Michael Hunt has also criticized the emphasis on factions to account for Chinese foreign policy formation. He poses this question: "Does the factional model transpose on China the competitive ethos of American politics and underestimate the restraining authoritarian and hierarchical qualities of China's political culture?" See Hunt, "CCP Foreign Policy," 170.

79. Mao to Yang Chengwu and Lei Yingfu, Jan. 30, 1965, *Mao junshi wenji,* 6:402.

80. Thomson, "On the Making of U.S. China Policy," 236; Tucker, "Threats, Opportunities, and Frustrations in East Asia," 103.

81. McNamara, *In Retrospect,* 215.

82. On the role of Mao's united front doctrine in China's foreign policy, see Armstrong, *Revolutionary Diplomacy.*

83. For Mao's Statements on the "Two Intermediate Zones," see *Mao waijiao wenxuan,* 506–9. See also Chi Aiping, "Mao Zedong guoji zhanlue sixiang de yanbian," 46–52, and Li Jie, "Mao Zedong guoji zhanlue sixiang yanjiu," 1–16.

84. Mao Zedong, "Talks with the American Correspondent Anna Louise Strong," in *Selected Works of Mao Tse-tung,* 4:99.

85. On China's policy toward Angola and Mozambique, see Jackson, "China's Third World Foreign Policy," 387–422. On Beijing's efforts to woo Sihanouk during the late 1950s and early 1960s, see Wang Youping, "Qu Jinbian zhixing teshu shiming," 66–82. Wang Youping was China's ambassador to Cambodia in 1958–62. On Chinese-Indonesian relations, see Mozingo, *Chinese Policy toward Indonesia.* On Beijing's economic and military aid to Cuba in the early 1960s, see Lin Ping and Ji Ni, "Bujuan de kaituo zhe," 150–51.

During his visit to Morocco in December 1963, Zhou Enlai heard a report from Chinese ambassador Yang Qiliang regarding China's contacts with African nationalist organizations based in that country. According to Yang, many African nationalist groups had offices and military training camps in Morocco and the Chinese embassy maintained close and friendly relations with them. Zhou commended Yang for his work. See Yang Qiliang, "Dui Zhou zongli liangci chufang de huiyi ji qita," 332.

86. On Beijing's attempt to divide the Soviet-led bloc, see Hoxha, *Reflections on China,* and Halliday, *Artful Albanian,* ch. 5. For an overview of Chinese-Albanian relations, see Fan Chengzuo, "ZhongA guanxi de 'chun xia jiu dong,' " 50–52. Fan Chengzuo is a former ambassador to Albania.

87. Mao's talk with the Chilean Journalist Delegation, June 23, 1964, *Mao waijiao wenxuan,* 529–33.

88. Mao's talk with delegates from Asia, Africa, and Oceania on July 9, 1964, ibid., 534–39.

89. On anti-imperialism in Chinese foreign policy, see Van Ness, *Revolution and Chinese Foreign Policy,* and Friedman, "Anti-Imperialism in Chinese Foreign Policy."

90. On the Chinese foreign policy setbacks in 1965 and their impact on China's internal development, see Garver, *Foreign Relations of the People's Republic of China,* 152–57.

91. McNamara, *In Retrospect,* 215.

92. The CCP delegation included about sixty members, an indication of the importance Beijing attached to the mission. See MacFarquhar, *Origins of the Cultural Revolution,* 3:364–65, and Gurtov and Byong-Moo Hwang, *China under Threat,* 161.

93. For a detailed, first-hand account of Zhou Enlai's visit to Moscow, see Yu Zhan, "Yici buxunchang de shiming." Yu Zhan was director of the Department of the Soviet Union and Eastern Europe of the Chinese Foreign Ministry in 1964. He accompanied Zhou to Moscow. See also Gu Yongzhong and Liu Yansheng, *He Long zhuan*, 530–33.

94. *Zhou waijiao dashiji*, 428.

95. Zhou's talk with Ho Chi Minh and Le Duan, Mar. 1, 1965, in ibid., 438.

96. R. B. Smith, *International History of the Vietnam War*, 3:54.

97. *White Paper*, 30. See also Chanda, "Secrets of Former Friends," 38–39. I have not seen any Chinese material that confirms the Vietnamese claim.

98. Xie Yixian, *Zhongguo waijiao shi*, 344. According to the Russian scholar Vladislav Zubok, Kosygin represented the "China Lobby" within the Soviet leadership, which wanted to restore Sino-Soviet unity and placed its hopes on Zhou Enlai. Other members of the lobby included Mikhail Suslov, a party secretary, and Alexander Shelepin, a former KGB chief. One of the purposes of Kosygin's Beijing trip was to "clarify misunderstandings" with the Chinese. After the failure of the visit, the China Lobby "calmed down." See Zubok, "Unwrapping the Enigma," 165–66. According to Georgi Arbatov, the debacle of the Kosygin mission made Soviet leaders realize that they could not easily mend fences with the Chinese without abandoning fundamental principles of domestic and international policies. See Arbatov, *System*, 113.

99. *Peking Review*, Mar. 11, 1966, 5.

100. Dittmer, *Sino-Soviet Normalization and Its International Implications*, 334.

101. Xie Yixian, *Zhongguo waijiao shi*, 345.

102. Ibid., 346–48; *Peking Review*, May 6, 1966, 25–26; Lawson, *Sino-Vietnamese Conflict*, 167.

103. For detailed coverage of the chaos in Guangxi between 1967 and 1968 and Zhou Enlai's efforts to restore order there, see Jiao Hongguang, "'Wenge' zhong Zhou Enlai chuli Guangxi wenti deng youguan qingkuang," 73–76. Jiao Hongguang was an air force officer in the Guangzhou Military District during the Cultural Revolution. He participated in Zhou Enlai's meetings with the Red Guards' representatives from Guangxi between 1967 and 1968. See also *Zhou nianpu*, 3:161, 166, 181–82, 189–90, 200, 207, 215, 220–22, 232.

104. Douglas Pike describes Hanoi's strategy to put the Sino-Soviet dispute to its own use in service of its war as "the alternating tilt gambit." See Pike, *Vietnam and the Soviet Union*, 54–55.

105. For Mao's reaction to Dulles's policy, see Bo Yibo, *Ruogan zhongda juece yu shijian de huigu*, 2:1137–57.

106. Lieberthal, "Great Leap Forward and the Split in the Yan'an Leadership," 143.

107. On Mao's attempt to use the escalation of the Indochina conflict to radicalize China's political and social life, see Chen Jian, "China's Involvement in the Vietnam War," 361–65.

108. Wang Xiangen, *YuanYue kangMei shilu*, 60–68.

109. Li Weixian, "YuanYue kangMei fangkong zuozhan 300 tian," 19–23. Li Weixian was a deputy commander of a Chinese antiaircraft artillery division, which was dispatched to North Vietnam in October 1966.

110. Zhao Xuemei, "Qinli jianwen," 25–30. Zhao Xuemei was a Chinese engineering soldier in North Vietnam between 1965 and 1968.

111. Wang Xiangen, *YuanYue kangMei shilu*, 74–75.

112. Guo Ming, *ZhongYue guanxi yanbian sishinian*, 102.

113. "77 Conversations," 94–98. The Le Duan delegation was making a stopover in Beijing after attending the Twenty-third Congress of the Soviet Communist Party.

114. Cong Jin, *Quzhe fazhan de suiyue*, 607.

115. *Mao wengao*, 11:394–95.

116. Kojima, *Record of the Talks between the Japanese Communist Party and the Communist Party of China.*

117. Quoted in Zagoria, *Vietnam Triangle*, 112. On Hanoi's delicate act of distancing itself from Beijing in Soviet eyes while simultaneously using the NLF's diplomats to placate China, see Brigham, *Guerrilla Diplomacy*, ch. 4.

118. Lawson, *Sino-Vietnamese Conflict*, 165.

119. Zagoria, *Vietnam Triangle*, 112; Sulzberger, *Age of Mediocrity*, 323–24.

25. Westad: The Vietnamese and Global Revolutions

1. Chin Peng, as told to Ian Ward and Norma Miraflor, *Alias Chin Peng: My Side of History* (Singapore: Media Masters, 2003), p. 354.

2. Record of conversation between Soviet ambassador Leonid Sokolov and Pham Van Dong, 3 May 1960, AVPRF [Arkhiv vneshnei politiki Rossiiskoi Federatsii], f. 079, op. 15, pa. 28, d. 6, pp. 101–104.

3. See Mari Olsen, "Changing Alliances: Moscow's Relations with Hanoi and the Role of China, 1949-1964," Ph.D. dissertation, University of Oslo, 2000.

4. Record of conversation between Zimyanin and Li Zhimin, 18 September 1957, AVPRF, f. 079, op. 12, pa. 17, d. 6, p. 69.

5. See Matthew Jones, *Conflict and Confrontation in Southeast Asia: Britain, the United States, Indonesia and the Creation of Malaysia* (Cambridge: Cambridge University Press, 2001).

6. Sukarno, as told to Cindy Williams, *Sukarno: An Autobiography* (Indianapolis, IN: Bobbs-Merrill, 1965).

7. Quoted in John Legge, *Sukarno: A Political Biography*, 3rd edn (Singapore: Archipelago Press, 2003), p. 396.

8. Record of conversation between Tito and Sukarno, Cairo, 5 October 1964. Arkhiv Srbije i Crne Gore (hereafter ASCG), A CK SKJ IX, 43/IV–30.

9. Hoover to Jenkins (White House), 7 April 1964, FBI report on January 1964 visit to Indonesia by Canadian and Bulgarian Communists, DDRS [Declassified Documents Reference Service].

10. Soviet Embassy, Jakarta, to Foreign Minister, "Report on comments in the PKI newspaper Harian Rakjat on Soviet domestic and foreign policy," April 1965, RGANI, f. 5, op. 55, d. 144, pp. 4–14; see also embassy report on Aidid, n.d. (spring 1965), AVPRF, f. 091, op. 16, pa. 22, d. 20, pp. 2–8. The archives of the International Departments of the former Communist Party of the Soviet Union, now part of the Russian State Archive of Contemporary History RGANI, in Moscow, is by far the most important source for the study of Soviet Third World policies in the late Cold War era. It consists of a very large collection of materials with differing provenances—among them embassy reports, documents created for the Politburo or the party Secretariat, intelligence summaries, and records of conversations with foreign leaders. A very large percentage of the files in RGANI are unfortunately still classified.

11. Soviet Embassy, Jakarta, to MO (n.d., early 1964), "On the position of the PKI leadership," RGANI, f. 5, op. 55, d. 116, p. 7. See also *ibid.*, pp. 10–14, on Soviet views of recent Chinese policy toward Southeast Asia.

12. Soviet ambassador to MO, 16 October 1965, "On the political situation in Indonesia in connection with the 30 September 1965 affair," RGANI, f. 5, op. 33, d. 218. I am grateful to Pål Johansen for alerting me to this key document. On Nasution's relations with the Soviets, see record of conversation between Soviet ambassador and General Nasution, 29 May 1964, RGANI, f. 5, op. 55, d. 116, pp. 18–22, and CIA intelligence information cable, "Sukarno's Actions and Plans to Balance the Power of Forces in Indonesia," 14 May 1965, DDRS.

13. US Embassy, Jakarta, to Department of State, 24 August 1964, in *FRUS, 1964–1968,* vol. XXVI.

14. Memorandum prepared in the Central Intelligence Agency, 9 November 1965, "Covert Assistance to the Indonesian Armed Forces Leaders," *ibid.*

15. For a discussion, see Theodore Friend, *Indonesian Destinies* (Cambridge, MA: Belknap, 2003).

16. Komer to Johnson, 12 March 1966, in *FRUS, 1964–1968,* vol. XXVI.

17. 557th Meeting of the National Security Council on 10 May 1966, in *FRUS, 1964–1968,* vol. IV.

18. Jose Maria Sison with Rainer Werning, *The Philippine Revolution: The Leader's View* (New York: Crane Russak, 1989), especially pp. 27–32.

19. Hans-Jürgen Krahl, speech in court, 1968, in Lutz Schulenburg, ed., *Das Leben ändern, die Welt verändern* (Hamburg: Nautilus, 1998), p. 391.

20. Günther Grass, *Denkzettel: Politische Reden und Aufsätze* (Darmstadt: Luchterhand, 1978), p. 85.

29. FitzGerald: A Clash of Cultures

1. Viet Hoai, "The Old Man in the Free Fire Zone," in *Between Two Fires: The Unheard Voices of Vietnam*, ed. Ly Qui Chung, pp. 102–105.

2. Léopold Cadière, *Croyances et pratiques religieuses des viêt-namiens*, vol. 2, p. 308.

3. Nghiem Dang, *Viet-Nam: Politics and Public Administration*, p. 53.

4. Confucius, *The Analects of Confucius*, p. 127.

5. Conversation with Paul Mus.

6. Confucius, *Analects*, p. 104. According to Waley, "The saying can be paraphrased as follows: If I and my followers are right in saying that countries can be governed solely by correct carrying out of ritual and its basic principle of 'giving way to others,' there is obviously no case to be made out for any other form of government. If on the other hand we are wrong, then ritual is useless. To say, as people often do, that ritual is all very well so long as it is not used as an instrument of government, is wholly to misunderstand the purpose of ritual."

7. Charles Gosselin, *L'Empire d'Annam*, p. 149.

8. Truong Buu Lam, *Patterns of Vietnamese Response to Foreign Intervention: 1858–1900*, p. 77. From an anonymous appeal to resist the French (1864).

9. Paul Mus, "Les Religions de l'Indochine," in *Indochine*, ed. Sylvain Lévi, p. 132.

10. There were also handicraft guilds and Buddhist and Taoist priesthoods, but these are details. The generalization is true enough for the purposes of contrast.

11. For the French, the emperor's persecution of French Catholic missionaries (though there were relatively few cases) served as a pretext for intervention in Vietnam. But to the French emperors conversion to Catholicism signified not just a religious apostasy but alienation from the state itself.

12. The Gia Long code, promulgated by the early nineteenth-century founder of the Nguyen dynasty was a much more exact copy of the Chinese codes than the Le code that governed Vietnam from the fifteenth to the nineteenth centuries.

13. Le Thanh Khoi, *Le Viêt-Nam.* According to the French historian, Henri Maspero, the land did not belong to the emperor, but to the people, whose will was expressed by the mouth of the sovereign. This reflexive relation between the people and the sovereign is typical of the Vietnamese political philosophy derived from Mencius.

14. Truong Chinh, *President Ho Chi Minh*, p. 68.

15. In the seventeenth century a French missionary, Alexandre de Rhodes, transcribed the Vietnamese language into the Roman alphabet, using diacritical marks to indicate the different tones. His aim was to render the Bible and other Christian texts into Vietnamese. The first people to use *quoç ngu*, as his system was called, were therefore the Vietnamese Catholics. The Latin alphabet came into general use only after the French conquest.

16. A hypothesis: the spoken language with its five tones may also be more concrete (more allusive, less abstract) than Western languages because of the element of music in it. In the way that people recall particular situations and particular people from the sound of a familiar tune, so the Vietnamese may associate words more directly with particular events than do Westerners. Cf. A. R. Luria, *The Mind of a Mnemonist* (New York: Basic Books, 1968).

17. Gosselin, *Empire*, p. 27.

18. Douglas Pike, *Viet Cong*, pp. 379, 383.

19. *New York Times*, 8 October, 1970.

20. Nguyen Truong To, "Memorials on Reform," in *Patterns of Response*, ed. Truong Buu Lam, p. 98.

21. If the Buddhists were, for instance, to be proved wrong in the end, then their statement would be both untrue and useless.

22. Phan Thi Dac, *Situation de la personne au Viet-Nam*, pp. 137–156.

23. Phan Thanh Giang, "Letter on His Surrender," in *Patterns of Response*, ed. Truong Buu Lam, pp. 87–88.

24. Ibid., p. 88. Phan Thanh Giang may have been wrong in his assessment of the military situation. Other mandarins had behaved differently, many of them resisting the French to the last. Given his assessment, however, there was little else for him to do.

25. Confucius, *Analects*, p. 168.

26. Paul Mus, "Cultural Backgrounds of Present Problems," p. 13. In the *Analects* the Master recounts this story about one of the divine sages of the past.

27. Ho Chi Minh, *Ho Chi Minh on Revolution*, p. 145.

30. Porter: An Opportunity for Power

1. Leslie Gelb and Richard K. Betts, *The Irony of Vietnam: The System Worked* (Washington, D.C.: Brookings Institution, 1978).

2. Quoted in Graham T. Allison, *Essence of Decision: Explaining the Cuban Missile Crisis* (Boston: Little, Brown, 1971), 148.

3. Roger Hilsman, *To Move a Nation: The Politics of Foreign Policy in the Administration of John F. Kennedy* (Garden City, N.Y.: Doubleday, 1967), 554–55, 561.

4. Gen. Matthew Ridgeway, memo, April 2, 1954, *FRUS, 1952–1954,* 13: 1220–21. For the views of the other service chiefs, see ibid., 1221–23.

5. Thomas J. Dodd, speech to the U.S. Senate, February 3, 1965, in Marcus G. Raskin and Bernard B. Fall, eds., *The Viet-Nam Reader,* rev. ed. (New York: Vintage Books, 1967), 35.

6. See Wohlforth, "The Stability of a Unipolar World," *International Security* 24, no. 1 (Summer 1999): 24–28; Michael Mastanduno, "Preserving the Unipolar Moment: Realist Theories and U.S. Grand Strategy," *International Security* 21, no. 4 (Spring 1997): 44–98.

7. See Christopher Layne, "The Unipolar Illusion: Why New Great Powers Will Rise," *International Security* 17, no. 4 (Spring 1993): 5–51; Kenneth N. Waltz, "The Emerging Structure of International Politics," *International Security* 18, no. 2 (Fall 1993): 44–79; id., "Structural Realism after the Cold War," *International Security* 25, no. 1 (Summer 2000): 27–28.

8. Kenneth N. Waltz, "International Structure, National Force and Balance of World Power," *Journal of International Affairs* 2 (1967): 228.

9. For discussion of this point in the realist literature, see Hans J. Morgenthau, *Politics among Nations*, 3d ed. (New York: Knopf, 1965), 33–35; Michael Mandelbaum, *The Fate of Nations: The Search for National Security in the Nineteenth and Twentieth Centuries* (Cambridge: Cambridge University Press, 1988), 134–42; William C. Wohlforth, "Realism and the End of the Cold War," *International Security* 19 (Winter 1994–95): 107–8; Robert Gilpin, *War and Change in World Politics* (Cambridge: Cambridge University Press, 1981), 146–48.

10. Waltz, "Structural Realism," 13.

31. Podhoretz: A Defense of Freedom

1. Jason Epstein, "The CIA and the Intellectuals," *New York Review of Books*, Apr. 20, 1967.
2. Robert L. Heilbroner, "Counterrevolutionary America," *Commentary*, Apr. 1967.
3. "Indochina and the American Conscience," *Commentary*, Feb. 1980.
4. Tom Wicker, *New York Times*, July 8, 1979. Quoted in Charles Horner, "America Five Years After Defeat," *Commentary*, Apr. 1980.
5. Carl Gershman, "After the Dominoes Fell," *Commentary*, May 1978.
6. Nguyen Cong Hoan, Hearings before the Subcommittee on International Organizations of the House Committee on International Relations, July 26, 1977, pp. 145–67.
7. Truong Nhu Tang, "Vietnam, the Myth of a Liberation," unpublished ms., 1981.
8. See note 6 above.
9. Doan Van Toai, "A Lament for Vietnam," *New York Times Magazine*, Mar. 29, 1981.
10. Jean Lacouture, interview with François Fejto, in *Il Giornale Nuovo* (Milan), quoted in Michael Ledeen, "Europe—The Good News and the Bad," *Commentary*, Apr. 1979.
11. Jean Lacouture, quoted in "After the Dominoes Fell," *Commentary*, May 1978.
12. "A Lament for Vietnam," *New York Times Magazine*, Mar. 29, 1981.
13. Ibid.
14. Quoted in "A Lament for Vietnam," *New York Times Magazine*, Mar. 29, 1981.
15. "A Lament for Vietnam," New York Times Magazine, Mar. 29, 1981; "After the Dominoes Fell," *Commentary*, May 1978.
16. Truong Nhu Tang, "Vietnam, the Myth of a Liberation," unpublished ms., 1981.
17. *Foreign Report*, July 16, 1981.
18. To Huu, quoted in "A Lament for Vietnam," *New York Times Magazine*, Mar. 29, 1981.
19. "A Lament for Vietnam," *New York Times Magazine*, Mar. 29, 1981.
20. "After the Dominoes Fell," *Commentary*, May 1978.
21. Quoted in "After the Dominoes Fell," *Commentary*, May 1978.
22. "After the Dominoes Fell," *Commentary*, May 1978.
23. Truong Nhu Tang, "Vietnam, the Myth of a Liberation," unpublished ms., 1981.
24. Quoted in "After the Dominoes Fell," *Commentary*, May 1978.
25. "After the Dominoes Fell," *Commentary*, May 1978.
26. "Indochina and the American Conscience," *Commentary*, Feb. 1980.
27. Quoted in "After the Dominoes Fell," *Commentary*, May 1978.
28. "Indochina and the American Conscience," *Commentary*, Feb. 1980.
29. Irving Howe and Michael Walzer, "Were We Wrong about Vietnam?," *New Republic*, Aug. 18, 1979.
30. Stanley Hoffmann, "The Crime of Cambodia," *New York Review of Books*, June 28, 1979.
31. Peter W. Rodman, "Sideswipe," *American Spectator*, Mar. 1981.
32. William Shawcross, "Shawcross Swipes Again," *American Spectator*, July 1981.
33. François Ponchaud, *Cambodia: Year Zero*. New York: Holt, Rinehart & Winston, 1978, p. 21. Quoted in "Sideswipe," *American Spectator*, Mar. 1981.
34. "Shawcross Swipes Again," *American Spectator*, July, 1981.
35. William Shawcross, *Sideshow*, New York: Pocket Books, 1979, p. 243.
36. Kenneth Quinn, quoted in "Shawcross Swipes Again," *American Spectator*, July 1981.
37. *Cambodia: Year Zero*, pp. xvi, 192. Quoted in "Sideswipe," *American Spectator*, Mar. 1981.
38. "Sideswipe," *American Spectator*, Mar. 1981.
39. "The Crime of Cambodia," *New York Review of Books*, June 28, 1979.
40. Anthony Lewis, *New York Times*, Mar. 17, 1975. Quoted in "Sideswipe," *American Spectator*, Mar. 1981.
41. *New York Times*, Apr. 13, 1975. Quoted in "Sideswipe," *American Spectator*, Mar. 1981.

32. Chomsky: An Act of Imperialism

1. *Far Eastern Economic Review*, May 23, 1975.
2. Truong Buu Lam, *Patterns of Vietnamese Response to Foreign Intervention: 1858–1900*, Monograph Series No. 11, Southeast Asia Studies, Yale University, 1967.
3. Helen B. Lamb, *Vietnam's Will to Live*, New York, *Monthly Review Press*, 1972.
4. Cited by Ngo Vinh Long, *Before the Revolution*, Cambridge, MIT Press, 1973; emphasis in original.

5. *Viet Nam: A Historical Sketch*, Foreign Languages Publishing House, Hanoi, 1974.

6. Paulin Vial, cited by Lam, *op. cit.*

7. Léopold Pallu, cited by Lamb, *op. cit.*

8. French resident minister Muselier, 1897, cited in *Vietnam: Fundamental Problems*, Vietnamese Studies no. 12, Foreign Languages Publishing House, Hanoi, 1966.

9. Lam, *op. cit.*

10. Cited in *Viet Nam: A Historical Sketch*.

11. Major F. M. Small, memorandum of Strategic Services Unit, War Department, 25 October 1945, cited in Frank M. White, *Causes, Origins, and Lessons of the Vietnam War*, Hearings before the Committee on Foreign Relations, U.S. Senate, 92nd Congress, 2nd session, May 1972, U.S. Government Printing Office, 1973. The intelligence reports cited below are from the same source.

12. Congressional testimony, May 11, 1972. In *Causes*.

13. Cited from the Government edition of the *Pentagon Papers* in my *For Reasons of State*, New York, Pantheon, 1973, p. 128. Unless otherwise indicated, citations from the *Pentagon Papers* are given with precise sources here.

14. For a review of the intelligence record as presented in the *Pentagon Papers*, see *For Reasons of State*, pp. 51f.

15. Arthur M. Schlesinger, Jr., *A Thousand Days*, 1965; Fawcett Crest Book, New York, p. 695.

16. See note 48 below.

17. For some discussion, see my article in *Ramparts*, July 1975.

18. Ithiel de Sola Pool, formerly chairman of the Council on Vietnamese Studies of SEADAG and chairman of the Political Science department at MIT, cited, with some discussion, in my *American Power and the New Mandarins*, Pantheon, New York, 1969, p. 36. For further discussion of his contributions and those of his colleague, Samuel Huntington, also past chairman of the Council on Vietnamese Studies and chairman of the Department of Government at Harvard, see my *At War with Asia*, Pantheon, New York, 1970, pp. 54–63, and *For Reasons of State*. It was Huntington who first explained how "In an absent-minded way the United States in Vietnam may well have stumbled upon the answer to 'wars of national liberation,' " namely, "forced-draft urbanization and modernization" by application of military power "on such a massive scale as to produce a massive migration from countryside to city."

19. George K. Tanham and Dennis J. Duncanson, "Some dilemmas of counterinsurgency," *Foreign Affairs*, vol. 48, no. 1, 1969.

20. For evidence on this matter, cf. Jeffrey Race, *War Comes to Long An*, University of California Press, Berkeley, 1971; Robert L. Sansom, *The Economics of Insurgency in the Mekong Delta*, MIT Press, Cambridge, 1970; Georges Chaffard, *Les Deux Guerres du Vietnam*, La Table Ronde, Paris, 1969; David Hunt, *Organizing for Revolution in Vietnam, Radical America*, vol. 8, nos. 1 & 2, 1974. Race and Sansom were associated with the U.S. military; Hunt's study is based on material released from the RAND Corporation's "Viet Cong Motivation and Morale" project; Chaffard was a French journalist with many years experience in Vietnam. There are many other sources. For the "Mansfield Reports," cited below, see *Two Reports on Vietnam and Southeast Asia*, Dec. 18, 1962 and Dec. 17, 1965, U.S. Government Printing Office, April 1973. For a despairing assessment of the success of the guerrillas and the popularity of the Hanoi government, see Konrad Kellen, "1971 and beyond: the view from Hanoi," June 1971; paper delivered at SEADAG meeting, May 8, 1971. Kellen is a RAND analyst.

21. Alex Carey, "Clockwork Vietnam: psychology of pacification (i)," mimeographed, 1972. See *Meanjin Quarterly*, Australia, 1973 for parts of this and subsequent sections of his "Clockwork Vietnam." Carey is lecturer in Psychology of International Relations at the University of New South Wales. His investigations are based in part on several months research in South Vietnam in 1970.

22. See, for example, Charles Wolf, *United States Policy and the Third World*, Boston, Little Brown and Co., 1967. For discussion of this and other similar contributions, see *American Power and the New Mandarins*, chapter 1, my *Problems of Knowledge and Freedom*, Pantheon, New York, 1972, chapter 2, and *For Reasons of State*, pp. 98f.

23. Hearings before the Subcommittee on Health of the Committee on Labor and Public Welfare, U.S. Senate, 93rd Congress, First Session. February 21 and 22, 1973, Part 1, U.S. Government Printing Office, 1973, p. 268. For the original study, see Dr. Lloyd Cotter, *American Journal of Psychiatry*, July 1967.

24. See the obituary in *Newsweek*, June 19, 1972.

25. Carey, "Clockwork Vietnam: the social engineers take over (2)," *Meanjin Quarterly*.

26. Quotes in Carey, "Clockwork Vietnam: psychology of pacification (i). "From Colonel Reuben Nathan, "Psychological warfare: key to success in Vietnam," *Orbis*, Spring 1967. Nathan was director of U.S. psychological warfare in Vietnam.

27. On the collapse of the military forces, see David Cortright, *Soldiers in Revolt*, New York, Doubleday, 1975.

28. Ithiel de Sola Pool, Introduction to his privately printed "Reprints of publications on Vietnam: 1966–1970," May 1971.

29. David G. Marr, "The rise and fall of 'counterinsurgency,' " in Chomsky and Zinn, eds. *op. cit.*, p. 208. Marr was a U.S. Marine Corps intelligence officer, the only Vietnamese-speaking American in the first marine helicopter squadron sent to Vietnam by President Kennedy.

30. For a review of such programs, see *For Reasons of State*, chapter 4.

31. "Max Austerlitz," pseudonym of a journalist who remained in Danang after its "fall." "After the Fall of Danang," *New Republic*, May 17, 1973.

32. NSC Memorandum 5612/1, 5 September 1956. Volume 10 of *United States–Vietnam Relations 1945–67*. U. S. Government Printing Office, 1971: the government edition of the *Pentagon Papers*.

33. On this period in Cambodia, see D. R. SarDesai, *Indian Foreign Policy in Cambodia, Laos, and Vietnam, 1947–1964*, Berkeley, University of California Press, 1968. Also Malcolm Caldwell and Lek Tan, *Cambodia in the Southeast Asian War*, New York, Monthly Review Press, 1973. See also references cited in *For Reasons of State*, chapter 2.

34. Philip Jones Griffiths, *Vietnam Inc.*, New York, Macmillan, 1971, p. 137. Griffiths is a British journalist-photographer who was in Hué at the time. For more on the massacres at Hué, both the actual and fabricated ones, see *For Reasons of State*, pp. 230f; N. Chomsky and E. S. Herman, *Counterrevolutionary Violence*, Warner Modular Inc., 1973; and references cited in these sources. For a recent summary, see E. S. Herman and D. G. Porter, "The myth of the Hué massacre," *Ramparts*, May–June 1975.

35. Interview with Vann in Carey. "Clockwork Vietnam: psychology of pacification (i)." On the great progress allegedly being made on all fronts by the Saigon government, as revealed by "applied social science," cf. Pool. *op. cit.* His final conclusion: "Not that South Viet Nam will fall after American combat troops are withdrawn: it seems too strong for that."

36. Cable from Buckley and Shimkin to *Newsweek* U.S. offices, January 18, 1972.

37. Cf. interview in the *Ottawa Citizen*, January 12, 1970; cited in *For Reasons of State*, p. 222.

38. See references in *For Reasons of State*, p. xx; also the two studies by Seymour Hersh: *My Lai Four*, Random House, New York, 1970; *Cover-up*, Random House, 1972.

39. Ithiel de Sola Pool, letter, *New York Review of Books*. February 13, 1969. For news reports on the exploits of the 9th Division in early 1969, cf. *At War with Asia*, pp. 99f.

40. For references and further details, see *At War with Asia*, p. 104; *For Reasons of State*, p. 225. For additional comment on this military operation ("Bold Mariner," reportedly the largest American amphibious operation since World War II), which coincided with "Speedy Express," see the statement by Martin Teitel of the American Friends Service Committee, Hearing before the Subcommittee to Investigate Problems Connected with Refugees and Escapees (Kennedy Subcommittee) of the Committee on the Judiciary, U.S. Senate, 92nd Congress, Second Session, May 8, 1972, U.S. Government Printing Office, 1972. Teitel also describes the U.S.-GVN atrocities of April 1972 in the same area subsequent to the bloodless liberation by the NLF-NVA.

41. Cf. note 20.

42. On the relative U.S.-DRV troop levels, as revealed by the *Pentagon Papers*, see my article "The Pentagon Papers as propaganda and as history," in Chomsky and Zinn, eds., *op. cit.*: also *For Reasons of State*, pp. 82 (and note 147), 239f.

43. General Maxwell D. Taylor, *Swords and Plowshares*, New York, Norton, 1972.

44. Speaking in Paris, January 26, 1965, Khanh released correspondence with Huynh Tan Phat, then Vice-President of the Central Committee of the NLF, from late January 1965, indicating that agreement was close. Cf. my article in *Ramparts*, July 1975, for further details. There is, incidentally, also evidence that the Diem regime may have been approaching a negotiated settlement just prior to the U.S.-backed coup in which Diem was murdered. Cf. Chaffard, *op. cit.*, chapter 8 and Mieczyslaw Maneli, *War of the Vanquished*, New York, Harper and Row, 1971. John P. Roche, an unreconstructed hawk, claims that he had furnished evidence to the Pentagon historians, which they ignored, that the Kennedy Administration had decided not to permit a deal between Diem and Ho Chi Minh. Cf. His "Pentagon Papers," *Political Science Quarterly*, vol. 87, no. 2, 1972.

45. For details on this important document misrepresented beyond recognition in the *Pentagon Papers* history, see *For Reasons of State*, pp. 100f.

46. For details on these matters see my "Endgame: the tactics of peace in Vietnam," *Ramparts*, April 1973; and "Reporting Indochina: the news media and the legitimization of lies," *Social Policy*, September/October 1973.

47. On United States intervention in Laos, see the articles by Haney and Chomsky in Chomsky and Zinn, eds., *op. cit.*; *At War with Asia*, chapter 4, and For *Reasons of State*, chapter 2, and the references cited there.

48. See the comment by the editors in *Dissent*, Spring 1975, in response to a letter of mine correcting a wholly fabricated version of my criticisms of their earlier editorial position. As indicated in their response, they prefer to restrict attention to the fabrication rather than attending to the entirely different original, which suggests that they perhaps do have some reservations about their long-held position. For further details, see the interchange in the *New Republic* referred to in this exchange.

49. *Op. cit.*, pp. 104–106.

50. Koji Nakamura, "Japan: a new face for Asia." *Far Eastern Economic Review*, May 23, 1975.

51. Correspondent, "Putting Washington before ASEAN," *ibid.* The text gives the date 1968 instead of 1972, presumably, an error.

52. Cf. *At War with Asia*, chapter 1; *For Reasons of State*, chapter 1, section V; the articles by John W. Dower, Richard B. Du Boff and Gabriel Kolko in Chomsky and Zinn, eds., *op. cit.*

53. For discussion of some misunderstandings of this critique by Richard Tucker, Charles Kindelberger and others, cf. *For Reasons of State*, pp. 42–46, 56–58.

54. John K. Fairbank, "Our Vietnam tragedy," *Newsletter*, Harvard Graduate Society for Advanced Study and Research,

June 1975. Fairbank also remarks that our "greatly accelerating the urbanization of Vietnam" after 1965 was "not necessarily to our credit or to the benefit of the South Vietnam." Scholarly caution, perhaps appropriate in an issue of the *Newsletter* that announced a new professorship of Vietnamese Studies named for Kenneth T. Young, formerly Chairman of SEADAG and Director of Southeast Asian Affairs in the State Department in 1954–58, when the United States took over direct responsibility for repression and massacre in South Vietnam. Young was one of those to urge publicly that the United States and its local subordinates "should deliberately increase urbanized markets and the town groupings coupled with fewer remote villages and fewer dispersed hamlets outside the modernizing environment" to "outmatch and outclass the Viet Cong where they are weak" (cf. note 18), thus making "a virtue out of necessity," *Asian Survey*, August 1967. At that time, no rational person could be deceived as to how "urban realignment," as Young called it, was being and must be effected by the American Expeditionary Force.

Perhaps some day the University of Berlin will institute an Eichmann chair of Jewish Studies.

55. William Y. Elliott, ed., *The Political Economy of American Foreign Policy*, New York, Holt, 1955, p. 42.

56. Quoted in Akire Iriye, *Across the Pacific*, New York, Harcourt, Brace and World, 1967, p. 77.

57. Cited by Frank Freidel, in *Dissent in Three American Wars*, Cambridge, Harvard University Press, 1970.

33. Dean: An Assertion of Manhood

1. Conversation with McGeorge Bundy, May 2, 1964, transcribed in Beschloss, *Taking Charge*, 341; Goodwin, *Remembering America*, 258.

2. Memorandum for the record, subject: South Vietnam situation, 25 November, 1963, box 1, Meeting Notes File, Lyndon B. Johnson Library.

3. Transcript of telephone conversation, LBJ and McGeorge Bundy, Monday, March 2, 1964, in Beschloss, *Taking Charge*.

4. Memorandum, president's special assistant for national security affairs (Bundy) to the president, January 7, 1964; memorandum, Joint Chiefs of Staff to the secretary of defense (McNamara), May 19, 1964, *Foreign Relations of the United States, 1964–1968: Vietnam 1964* (hereafter *FRUS: Vietnam 1964*).

5. Transcript of telephone conversation, LBJ and John S. Knight, Monday Feb. 3, 1964, in Beschloss, *Taking Charge*, 213.

6. Memorandum, Michael V. Forrestal to the president's special assistant for national security affairs (Bundy), March 18, 1964; memorandum, secretary of defense (McNamara) to the president, March 16, 1964, *FRUS: Vietnam 1964*.

7. Memorandum, McGeorge Bundy to the president, May 22, 1964, Memos to the President, box 1, National Security Files, Lyndon B. Johnson Library (LBJL); see also draft memorandum for the president prepared by the Department of Defense, subject: scenario for strikes on North Vietnam, May 24, 1964, *FRUS: Vietnam 1964*.

8. Message from the ambassador in France (Bohlen) to the president, April 2, 1964, *FRUS: Vietnam 1964*. Also see Logevall, *Choosing War*, on de Gaulle and his recognition of the nationalist roots of the conflict in Vietnam.

9. See chapter 4 above.

10. Memorandum, Senator Mike Mansfield to President Johnson, January 6, 1964; memorandum, McGeorge Bundy to the president, January 9, 1964, Memos to the President, McGeorge Bundy, box 1, folder vol. 1, National Security Files, LBJL; draft memorandum to the president, comment on memoranda by Senator Mansfield, July 1, 1964, Memos to the President, folder vol. 2, National Security Files, LBJL; Thomas Hughes statement in Gittinger, *Johnson Years*, 12–13.

11. Transcripts of telephone conversations, LBJ and McGeorge Bundy, March 2, May 15, 1964, in Beschloss, *Taking Charge*, 262, 356.

12. Joseph Alsop, "President Johnson's Choice," *Washington Post*, May 22, 1964.

13. See this chapter's epigraph in which Johnson expresses fear of being seen as "a coward, an unmanly man, a man without a spine" (quoted in Kearns, *Lyndon Johnson and the American Dream*, 253). Halberstam, *Best and Brightest*, 605–6; Merry, *Taking on the World*, 414–16; Joseph Alsop, "Harsh Test for Johnson," *Washington Post*, September 2, 1964; Alsop, "Johnson's Cuba II," *Washington Post*, December 30, 1964; Alsop, "The World He Never Made," *Washington Post*, November 30, 1964.

14. Transcript of telephone conversation, LBJ and Senator Richard Russell, May 27, 1964, in Beschloss, *Taking Charge*, 367, 369.

15. Ibid.

16. Ibid., 369.

17. Ibid.

18. Ibid., 370–71.

19. Ibid., 371–72.

20. Transcript of telephone conversation, LBJ with Richard Russell, June 11, 1964, in Beschloss, *Taking Charge*, 401–3.

21. Ibid.

22. Ibid.

23. The destroyer attacked on August 2, 1964, was in proximity to a U.S.-supported commando assault on North Vietnamese coastal installations, part of the secret OPLAN 34-A, not revealed to Congress or the public. See Kahin, *Intervention,* 219–25; or, for a discussion of Tonkin Gulf by some of the principals involved, see Gittinger, *Johnson Years,* 17–38. For a thorough treatment of OPLAN 34-A operations, the Tonkin Gulf incidents, and the reprisal air attacks, see Moise, *Tonkin Gulf.*

24. LBJ phone call with Robert Anderson, August 3, 1964, Cit. 4631–32, audiotape WH6408.03; notes taken at leadership meeting on August 4, 1964 (McNamara's and Rusk's statements not included), box 1, Meeting Notes File.

25. Hughes statement, 45.

26. Hughes statement, 44–45; advertisements, California Goldwater for President Committee and Goldwater for President Committee, Santa Clara County [1964], in author's possession; Goldwater quotes in Logevall, *Choosing War,* 195.

27. McGeorge Bundy, memorandum for the record, meeting on South Vietnam, September 9, 1964, box 1, Meeting Notes File; summary notes of the 541st meeting of the National Security Council, August 25, 1964, *FRUS: Vietnam 1964;* memorandum from the president's special assistant for national security affairs (Bundy) to the president, August 31, 1964, *FRUS: Vietnam 1964.*

28. Gittinger, *Johnson Years,* 41; see chapter 3 above for a discussion of Johnson's use of cultural narratives of war heroism.

29. *Public Papers of the Presidents: Lyndon B. Johnson, 1387–1393.*

30. Ibid., 1126.

31. Ibid., 1390–91.

32. Morton Mintz, "Jenkins, Aide to LBJ, Resigns after Arrest," *Washington Post,* October 15, 1964; Max Frankel, "President's Aide Quits on Report of Morals Case," *New York Times,* October 15, 1964; Clifford, *Counsel,* 399–402; Kalman, *Abe Fortas,* 234–35. An analysis of 1960s counterperversion discourse centered on the Walter Jenkins episode can be found in Edelman, "Tearooms and Sympathy."

33. O'Donnell, interview, 79; Clifford, *Counsel,* 400–402.

34. Transcript of taped office conversation, February 20, 1964, in Beschloss, *Taking Charge,* 248.

35. Clifford, *Counsel,* 401–2; DeLoach, *Hoover's FBI,* 384–87.

36. Press release, Office of the White House Press Secretary, statement of the president, October 15, 1964, Jenkins, box 11, Aides Files.

37. "Lyndon Aid[e] Quits in Morals Case," *Chicago Tribune,* October 15, 1964; Mintz, "Jenkins"; Frankel, "President's Aide Quits."

38. "Lyndon Aid[e]"; Mintz, "Jenkins"; Frankel, "President's Aide Quits"; James Reston, "Setback for Johnson," *New York Times,* October 15, 1964; "The Jenkins Case," *New York Times,* October 16, 1964; "White House Morality," *Chicago Tribune,* October 16, 1964; editorial, "The Security Sieve," *New York Times,* October 18, 1964; Arthur Krock, "The Jenkins Case: The Issue of National Security Is Raising Some Vital Questions," *New York Times,* October 18, 1964.

39. See Hughes statement, 45. Senator Lyndon B. Johnson to the State Department, January 27, 1953; and Assistant Secretary of State Thruston B. Morton to Senator Johnson, February 18, 1953, both in RG 59, Department of State decimal file, 1950–54, box 479, National Archives, College Park, Md.; Gentry, *J. Edgar Hoover,* 579; Joseph Hearst, "Barry Reveals Early Morning Quiz by FBI," *Chicago Tribune,* October 20, 1964; E. W. Kenworthy, "Goldwater Asks F.B.I. to Explain Check on Jenkins," *New York Times,* October 20, 1964. Hughes (head of State Department Intelligence and Research in 1964) actually argues that the discovery of Goldwater's efficiency reports on Jenkins was a "stroke of luck" that "quashed" the issue. But an examination of the *Chicago Tribune, Washington Post,* and *New York Times* from October 15 to November 2, 1964, reveals that the issue was not "quashed"; it played a prominent role in coverage of the election, and continued to get front-page headlines despite the October 16 news that Nikita Khrushchev had been deposed in the USSR, and the October 17 revelation of the first successful atomic bomb test in communist China.

40. Richard L. Lyons, "Goldwater Bars Jenkins Issue but for Security," *Washington Post,* October 16, 1964; Charles Mohr, "Goldwater to Shun Jenkins Case but Not Its Aspects of Security," *New York Times,* October 16, 1964; Roland Evans and Robert Novak, "The Jenkins Affair," *Washington Post,* October 16, 1964; Robert E. Baker, "Barry Assails 'Curious Crew' in White House," *Washington Post,* October 25, 1964; "G.O.P. Aide Sees Strong Impact on Campaign in Jenkins Case," *New York Times,* October 15, 1964; "Jenkins Report Sought by Nixon," *New York Times,* October 16, 1964; "White House Cloud Darker, Miller Holds," *Chicago Tribune,* October 22, 1964; "Miller Urges: Demand Full Jenkins Story," *Chicago Tribune,* October 24, 1964: Laurence Stern, "FBI Finds No Security Breach: Blackmail Indications Missing," *Washington Post,* October 23, 1964; "Finds Jenkins Report Vague," *Chicago Tribune,* October 24, 1964.

41. "Miller Urges"; Philip Warden, "Calls for Tightened Security Screening," *Chicago Tribune,* October 20, 1964.

42. Tom Wicker, "Secret Service Had Jenkins File," *New York Times,* October 17, 1964; Walter Trohan, "Fought to Get Pervert Reinstated," *Chicago Tribune,* October 24, 1964; "FBI Files Jenkins Report," *Chicago Tribune,* October 23, 1964.

43. John D. Morris, "Democrats Calm on Jenkins Case," *New York Times,* October 17, 1964; Austin C. Wehrwein, "Global Events Seen Overshadowing Jenkins Case in Midwest," *New York Times,* October 19, 1964; Charles Mohr, "Campaign Issues— V," October 29, 1964; "Johnson Up 2% in Poll Taken after Jenkins Case, Red Crisis," *Washington Post,* October 23,

1964; Walter Lippmann, "His Last Ploy," October 29, 1964; Fendall W. Yerxa, "Johnson Finds 'Smearlash' Costing Goldwater Votes," *New York Times,* October 22, 1964; "Ike Also Faced a 'Jenkins Case' Johnson Says," *Washington Post,* October 29, 1964; "Ike Doesn't Recall 'Jenkins Problem' during His Terms," *Washington Post,* October 29, 1964; "Nixon Says Johnson Smeared Ike's Aides," *Washington Post,* October 31, 1964. It is clear from a sanitized FBI memorandum that the Eisenhower White House was directly touched by the homosexual purges, although details are still classified. When Hoover reported the attempted Soviet sexual blackmail of journalist Joseph Alsop to presidential aide Sherman Adams, he justified deploying the sexual secrets because "one of the employees in the White House who was involved in homosexual acts admitted he had seen a report in the Executive Office referring to [one or more words deleted] being in the same category. [2 lines deleted] In view of this I told Mr. Rogers I felt the Governor should be aware of the Alsop matter." John Edgar Hoover, memorandum for Mr. Tolson, Mr. Boardman, Mr. Belmont, Mr. Nichols, April 17, 1957, JEH O&C#26, FBI Freedom of Information Act request.

44. Memorandum to the president, January 9, 1964, Memos to President, box 1, National Security Files, LBJL.

45. Ellsberg, "Quagmire Myth," 90–91. James C. Thomson, too, testified to White House strictures against producing a paper trail connected to deliberations on negotiated withdrawal: "the very concept of negotiation was, for a while, so anathema that any concept of turning down an escalatory track and turning away from it was considered so subversive that Mac Bundy would tell Chet Cooper under no circumstances to put anything on possible peace negotiations in a typewriter, but instead to put it in handwriting, so that there would be no copy." This was "because such issues were regarded as so potentially explosive both upward and outward." Thomson, interview, 24.

46. See for example, paper prepared by the National Security Council Working Group: Summary, Courses of Action in Southeast Asia, November 21, 1964; telegram from the commander in chief, Pacific (Sharp) to the chairman of the joint Chiefs of Staff (Wheeler), November 22, 1964; memorandum from the Joint Chiefs of Staff to the secretary of defense (McNamara), November 23, 1964; memorandum of the meeting of the Executive Committee, Washington, November 24, 1964; paper prepared by the Executive Committee: Position Paper on Southeast Asia, December 2, 1964; all in *FRUS: Vietnam 1964.*

47. [Handwritten] meeting notes, Cabinet Room—ExCom (SVN), December 1, 1964, box 1, Meeting Notes File.

48. McGeorge Bundy, memorandum for the president, re: basic policy in Vietnam, January 27, 1965; telegram, Department of State, for Ambassador Taylor from the president, February 8, 1965, Bundy, box 2, Aides Files.

49. Bundy's report to the president, February 7, 1965, quoted in Bird, *Color of Truth,* 307. The best account of the complexities of U.S.-South Vietnamese politics surrounding the bombing is Kahin, *Intervention,* 286–305.

50. Meeting notes, March 10, 1965, box 1, Bundy Papers.

51. Logevall, *Choosing War,* 136–39; Mike Mansfield to the president, February 1, 1964; Mike Mansfield to the president, January 6, 1964; see also Mike Mansfield to the president, December 7, 1963, Memos to the President, box 1, National Security Files, LBJL; O'Donnell, interview, 109.

52. Hubert Humphrey, memorandum to President Johnson, February 15, 1965, reprinted in Gittinger, *Johnson Years,* 156–58.

53. DiLeo, *George Ball,* 11–12; George Ball, *The Past Has Another Pattern.*

54. DiLeo, *George Ball,* 72, 73; Ball, quoted in Stein, *American Journey,* 208; on Ball's position on the "margins of power" in the Kennedy administration because of his "second tier" educational background, his skepticism about Third World development schemes and counterinsurgency, and his "Eurocentrism," see DiLeo, *George Ball,* 38–43.

55. Ball, *Past Has Another Pattern,* 153.

56. Ibid., 380–84.

57. William Bundy, memorandum for Secretary Rusk, Secretary McNamara, Mr. Ball, Mr. McGeorge Bundy, "Attached Think-Piece on Our Choices in Southeast Asia," October 19, 1964, quoted in Bird, *Color of Truth,* 291–92.

58. Bird, *Color of Truth,* 294–96.

59. Joseph Alsop, "The Deceptive Calm," *Washington Post,* November 23, 1964; William Bundy to Joseph Alsop, November 23, 1964; Alsop to Wm. Bundy, n.d. [late November 1964]; McGeorge Bundy to Alsop, Saturday [probably November 28, 1964]; Alsop to McGeorge Bundy, n.d. [end of November 1964]; all in box 69, Alsop Papers.

60. Ball, *Past Has Another Pattern,* 395–98.

61. McGeorge Bundy, memorandum for the president, subject: meeting Friday morning on Vietnam, July 1, 1965, Memos to the President box 4, National Security Files, LBJL.

62. Extensive accounts of the July 1965 meetings and decisions can be found in Ball, *Past Has Another Pattern;* Berman, *Planning a Tragedy;* Kahin, *Intervention;* VanDeMark, *Into the Quagmire;* Barrett, *Uncertain Warriors.*

63. Ball, *Past Has Another Pattern,* 383, 389.

64. Notes, Cabinet Room, Wednesday, July 21, 1965, subject: Vietnam, box 1, Meeting Notes File. Present at this meeting were: McNamara, Rusk, [Cyrus] Vance, [McGeorge] Bundy, General Wheeler, George Ball, Bill Bundy, Len Unger, [Richard] Helms, Admiral Raborn, [Henry Cabot] Lodge, [Carl] Rowan, [John] McNaughton, [Bill] Moyers, [Jack] Valenti.

65. Notes of meeting, July 21, 1965, 10:40 A.M., Meeting Notes File. Quotations in the paragraphs that follow are from this source.

66. Meeting notes, July 21, 1965, resume same meeting at 2:45 P.M., box 1, National Security Files, LBJL. Throughout 1964 U.S. allies, with the exception of Australia, had expressed profound doubts or outright opposition to U.S. escalation of the war. See Logevall, *Choosing War,* esp. 130–33, 222–28.

67. Notes of meeting, July 21, 1965, Meeting Notes File.

68. Notes of meeting, Cabinet Room, July 22, 1965, box 1, Meeting Notes File. Present were: the president, McNamara, Vance, General Wheeler, General Johnson, Secretary Resor, General McConnell, General Greene, Admiral McDonald, [Clark] Clifford, Nitze, Secretary Zuchert, Secretary Brown, [McGeorge] Bundy.

69. Notes of meeting, July 22, 1965, 12 noon, Meeting Notes File.

70. Ibid.

71. Ibid.

72. Notes of meeting, Camp David, Aspen Lodge, July 25, 1965, 5:00 P.M.; Cabinet Room, July 22, 1965, 3:00 P.M.; both in box 1, Meeting Notes File.

73. Notes of meeting, July 22, 1965, 3:00 P.M.

74. Notes of meetings, July 28 and April 1, 1965, box 1, Bundy Papers.

75. Johnson, quoted in DiLeo, *George Ball,* 132.

76. Johnson, quoted in Emerson, *Winners and Losers,* 377; Johnson, quoted in Halberstam, *Best and Brightest,* 414.

77. Rusk, *As I Saw It,* 418; Isaacson and Thomas, *Wise Men, 657;* Shapley, *Promise and Power,* 426, 434–35; Clifford, *Counsel,* 456–57.

Sources

Grateful acknowledgment is made to the publishers and authors for their permission to reprint their works in whole or in part.

1. Robert Shaplen, *The Lost Revolution: The U.S. in Vietnam, 1946–1966,* rev. ed. (New York: HarperCollins, 1966), 27–54. © 1955, 1962, 1963, 1964, 1965, 1966 by Robert Shaplen. Reprinted by permission of HarperCollins.
2. Mark Atwood Lawrence, *Assuming the Burden: Europe and the American Commitment to War in Vietnam* (Berkeley and Los Angeles: University of California Press, 2005), 235–61 (notes 324–28). © 2005 by the Regents of the University of California. Reprinted by permission of the University of California Press.
3. David L. Anderson, ed., *Shadow on the White House: Presidents and the Vietnam War, 1945–1975* (Lawrence: University Press of Kansas, 1993), 43–62. Reprinted by permission of the University Press of Kansas.
4. From Ellen J. Hammer, *The Struggle for Indochina, 1940–1955* (Stanford, CA: Stanford University Press, 1966), 326–37. © 1961 by the Institute of Pacific Relations. All rights reserved. Used with the permission of Stanford University Press, www.sup.org.
5. Edward Geary Lansdale, *In the Midst of Wars: An American's Mission to Southeast Asia*, 2d ed. (New York: Fordham University Press, 1991), 215–27. © 1991 by Fordham University Press. Reprinted by permission of Fordham University Press.
6. Herbert S. Parmet, *JFK, The Presidency of John Kennedy* (New York: Doubleday, 1983), 325–37, 389–91. © 1983 by Herbert S. Parmet. Used by permission of Doubleday a division of Bantam, Doubleday, Dell Publishing Group.
7. Robert S. McNamara, *In Retrospect* (New York: Random House, 1995), 127–43, 471–72. © 1995 by Robert S. McNamara. Used by permission of Times Books, a division of Random House.
8. Fredrik Logevall, *Choosing War: The Last Chance for Peace and the Escalation of War in Vietnam* (Berkeley: University of California Press, 1999), 288–99 (notes 481–83). © 1999 by the Regents of the University of California. Reprinted by permission of University of California Press.
9. George C. Herring, *America's Longest War: The United States and Vietnam, 1950–1975,* 4th ed. (New York: McGraw-Hill, 2002), 225–29, 231–52. Reprinted by permission of McGraw-Hill.
10. George W. Ball, *The Past Has Another Pattern* (New York: W.W. Norton, 1982), 399–409, 505–6. © 1982 by George W. Ball. Used by permission of W.W. Norton.
11. Jeffrey Kimball, *Nixon's Vietnam War* (Lawrence: University Press of Kansas, 1998), 87-102. Reprinted by permission of the University Press of Kansas.
12. Stephen E. Ambrose, *Nixon: The Triumph of a Politician*, vol. 2 (New York: Simon and Schuster, 1989), 1962–1972, 525–41. Copyright © 1989 by Stephen E. Ambrose. Reprinted with the permission of Simon & Schuster.
13. William Colby, *Lost Victory: A Firsthand Account of America's 16-Year Involvement in Vietnam by the Former Director of the CIA* (McGraw Hill Contemporary, 1980), 325–42. Reprinted by permission of McGraw-Hill Companies.
14. Seth Jacobs, *Cold War Mandarin: Ngo Dinh Diem and the Origins of America's War in Vietnam, 1950-1963* (Lanham, MD: Rowman & Littlefield, 2006), 59–82. Reprinted by permission of Rowman & Littlefield.
15. Philip E. Catton, "Counter-Insurgency and Nation Building. The Strategic Hamlet Programme in South Vietnam, 1961–1963," *International History Review* 21, no. 4 (December 1999), 918–40. Reprinted by permission of the International History Review.
16. William J. Duiker, "Victory by Other Means: The Foreign Policy of the Democratic Republic of Vietnam," in *Why the North Won the Vietnam War*, ed. Marc Jason Gilbert, 47–75 (New York: Palgrave, 2002). Reproduced with permission of Palgrave Macmillan.
17. Tom Mangold and John Penycate, *The Tunnels of Cu Chi* (New York: Random House, 1985), 17, 19–24. © 1985 by Tom Mangold and John Penycate. Used by permission of Random House.
18. Philip Caputo, *A Rumor of War 2d ed.* (New York: Holt, Rinehart, and Winston, 1996), 276–85 © 1977 and 1996 by Philip Caputo. Reprinted by permission of Henry Holt.

19. Wallace Terry, *Bloods: An Oral History of the Vietnam War by Black Veterans* (New York: Random House, 1984), 113–19. © 1984 by Wallace Terry. Used by permission of Random House.
20. Lynda Van Devanter, with Christopher Morgan, *Home before Morning: The Story of an Army Nurse in Vietnam* (New York: Beaufort Books, 1983), 79–85, 134–37, 209–12.
21. Tim O'Brien, *Going after Cacciato* (New York: Dell Publishing, Random House, 1978), 262–73. (c) 1975, 1976, 1977, 1978 by Tim O'Brien. Used by permission of Dell Publishing, a Division of Random House.
22. Michael Bilton and Kevin Sim, "My Lai, March 16, 1968: AM" in *Four Hours in My Lai* (New York: Penguin Books, 1992), 102–23. © 1992 by Michael Bilton and Kevin Sim. Used by permission of Viking Penguin, a division of Penguin Group.
23. Ilya V. Gaiduk, *The Soviet Union and the Vietnam War* (Chicago: Ivan R. Dee, 1996), 35–56 (notes 261–63). © 1996 by Ilya V. Gaiduk, reprinted by permission of Ivan R. Dee, Publisher.
24. Qiang Zhai, *China and the Vietnam Wars, 1950–1975* (Chapel Hill: University of North Carolina Press, 2000), 130–35, 137–55 (notes 247–53). © 2000 by the University of North Carolina Press. Used by permission of the publisher.
25. Odd Arne Westad, *The Global Cold War* (New York: Cambridge University Press, 2005), 180–94 (notes 429–31). © 2005 by Odd Arne Westad. Reprinted with the permission of Cambridge University Press.
26. Timothy N. Castle, *At War in the Shadow of Vietnam* (New York: Columbia University Press, 1993), 128–37. © 1993 Columbia University Press. Reprinted with permission of the publisher.
27. William Shawcross, *Sideshow: Kissinger, Nixon and the Destruction of Cambodia* (New York: Simon and Schuster, 1979), 19–26, 28–35. Reprinted by permission of William Shawcross.
28. Henry A. Kissinger, *White House Years* (Boston: Little, Brown, 1979), 239–47, 249–54. © 1979 by Henry A. Kissinger. Reprinted courtesy of Henry A. Kissinger.
29. Frances FitzGerald, *Fire in the Lake: The Vietnamese and the Americans in Vietnam* (Boston: Little, Brown and Co., 1972), 4–27, 445–46. © 1972 by Frances FitzGerald. Reprinted by permission of Little, Brown.
30. Gareth Porter, *Perils of Dominance: Imbalance of Power and the Road to War in Vietnam* (Berkeley: University of California Press, 2005), 259–76 (notes 359). © 2005 by the Regents of the University of California. Reprinted by permission of University of California Press.
31. Norman Podhoretz, *Why We Were in Vietnam* (New York: Simon and Schuster, 1983), 195–210, 239–40. © 1982 by Norman Podhoretz. Reprinted by permission of Norman Podhoretz.
32. Noam Chomsky, "U.S. Involvement in Vietnam," *Bridge: An Asian American Perspective* 4, no. 1 (October–November 1975): 4–9, 11–16, 18, 20–21. Reprinted by permission of Noam Chomsky.
33. Robert D. Dean, *Imperial Brotherhood: Gender and the Making of Cold War Foreign Policy* (Amherst: University of Massachusetts Press, 2001), 210–32, 234–40 (notes 300–305). © 2001 by University of Massachusetts Press and published by University of Massachusetts Press.
34. Christian G. Appy, *Working-Class War: American Combat Soldiers and Vietnam* (Chapel Hill: University of North Carolina Press, 1993), 11–28. © 1993 by the University of North Carolina Press. Used by permission of the publisher.
35. Tom Wells, *The War Within: America's Battle over Vietnam* (New York: Henry Holt, 1996), 13–18, 23–33. Notes omitted. © 1996 by Tom Wells. Reprinted by permission of Henry Holt.
36. Myra MacPherson, *Long Time Passing* (Garden City, NY: Doubleday, 1984), 463–77. © 1984 by Myra MacPherson.
37. Duong Van Mai Elliott, *Sacred Willow* (New York: Oxford University Press, 1999), 405–16, 424–29. © 1999 by Duong Van Mai Elliott. Reprinted by permission of Oxford University Press.
38. Arnold Isaacs, *Vietnam Shadows: The War, Its Ghosts, and Its Legacy* (Baltimore: Johns Hopkins University Press, 1997), 9–15, 25–28. © 1997, Arnold R. Issacs. Reprinted with permission of the Johns Hopkins University Press.
39. Thomas A. Bass, *Vietnamerica: The War Comes Home* (New York: Soho Press, 1997), 7–16, 152–58. Reprinted by permission of Soho Press.
40. Le Ly Hayslip, with Jay Wurts, *When Heaven and Earth Changed Places: A Vietnamese Woman's Journey from War to Peace* (New York: Doubleday, 1989), 343–55. © 1989 by Le Ly Hayslip and Charles Jay Wurts. Used by permission of Doubleday, a division of Random House.